Exploring Globalization

Robert Gardner
Teacher of Social Studies and History
Harry Ainlay High School
Edmonton Public School Board

Wayne Lavold
Teacher of Social Studies and History
Harry Ainlay High School
Edmonton Public School Board

 McGraw-Hill Ryerson

Toronto Montréal Boston Burr Ridge, IL Dubuque, IA Madison, WI New York
San Francisco St. Louis Bangkok Bogotá Caracas Kuala Lumpur Lisbon London
Madrid Mexico City Milan New Delhi Santiago Seoul Singapore Sydney Taipei

McGraw-Hill Ryerson

COPIES OF THIS BOOK
MAY BE OBTAINED BY
CONTACTING

McGraw-Hill Ryerson Ltd.

WEB SITE

http://www.mcgrawhill.ca

E-MAIL

orders@mcgrawhill.ca

TOLL-FREE FAX

1-800-463-5885

TOLL-FREE, CALL

1-800-565-5758

OR BY MAILING YOUR
ORDER TO

McGraw-Hill Ryerson
Order Department
300 Water Street
Whitby, ON L1N 9B6

Please quote the ISBN and
title when placing your order.

Student text ISBN

978-0-07-078084-2

Exploring Globalization

ISBN-13: 978-0-07-078084-2
ISBN-10: 0-07-078084-6

http://www.mcgrawhill.ca

2 3 4 5 6 7 8 9 10 TCP 6 5 4 3 2 1 0 9 8 7

Printed and bound in Canada

PROJECT MANAGER: Joseph Gladstone
PROJECT EDITOR: Dyanne Rivers
DEVELOPMENTAL EDITOR: Maryrose O'Neill
ASSOCIATE DEVELOPMENTAL EDITORS: Ellen Munro, Jocelyn Wilson
ADDITIONAL WRITING: Graham Draper, Joseph Gladstone, Usha James, Denyse O'Leary, Maryrose O'Neill, Dyanne Rivers, and Jocelyn Wilson
MANAGER, EDITORIAL SERVICES: Crystal Shortt
SUBMISSION DEVELOPMENT: Patty Pappas
SUPERVISING EDITOR: Janie Deneau
COPY EDITOR: Sheila Wawanash
PHOTO RESEARCH / PERMISSIONS: Linda Tanaka
EDITORIAL ASSISTANT: Erin Hartley
REVIEW CO-ORDINATOR: Jennifer Keay
MANAGER, PRODUCTION SERVICES: Yolanda Pigden
PRODUCTION CO-ORDINATOR: Zonia Strynatka
INTERIOR DESIGN: First Image
ELECTRONIC PAGE MAKE-UP: First Image
MAP DESIGNER: Gary Birchall
COVER DESIGN: Cathie Ellis / Liz Harasymczuk
COVER IMAGE: Courtesy of First Light

Reviewers

Acknowledgements

To my parents, Ron and Eve Gardner, who encouraged this and many other projects over the years.

Robert Gardner

Special thanks to Dorothy Vreeswyk-Kidd and Linda-Rae Carson for all their ideas and help with this book, as well as to my wife, Anita, and son, Joshua, who were without their husband and daddy all too often during this project.

Wayne Lavold

Table of Contents

Related Issue 1
To what extent should globalization shape identity?

Chapter 7   Legacies of Historical Globalization in Canada

Chapter 8   Living with the Legacies of Historical Globalization

Related Issue 3
To what extent does globalization contribute to sustainable prosperity for all people?

Chapter 9   Foundations of Economic Globalization

Related Issue 4
To what extent should I, as a citizen, respond to globalization?

Chapter 13   Human Rights, Democracy, and Globalization

TOUR OF THE TEXTBOOK

Welcome to *Exploring Globalization*. Take some time to go over these pages and understand how this textbook is set up to help you complete this course successfully.

By the time you finish *Exploring Globalization,* you will be in a better position to answer the key question for this course: To what extent should we embrace globalization? As you work your way through the book, keep this key question in mind as you think about the various ideas, points of view, perspectives, and insights you encounter. They will help you formulate a response to this question.

Cover

The photograph on the front cover of *Exploring Globalization* shows a group of people silhouetted against a stylized globe. Around the globe are bright, orbit lines — but no space ship. This image symbolizes the concepts behind this textbook and course: people, global connections, and global communication and transportation. Look carefully at the globe. Why do you suppose the artist showed Europe and Asia rather than North and South America?

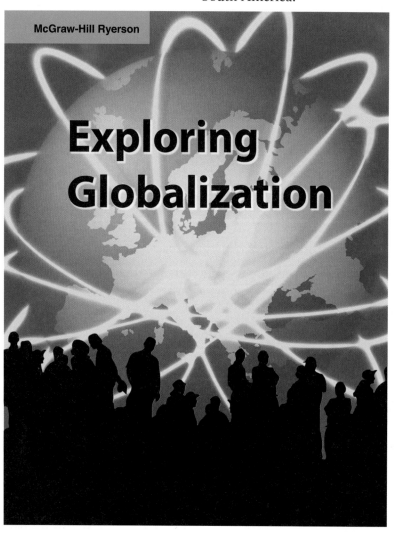

Globalization, as you will discover, is not something happening to other people in other places. As the cover illustration suggests, it is happening to you, here and now. As with any human endeavour, globalization is made by everyone, every day. Your decisions, actions, and involvement change the face of globalization and its many effects on people everywhere. Every action, every decision, no matter how small, changes globalization. You shape the future, just as those who came before you shaped the past.

How This Book Is Organized

Review the table of contents to get a feel for how *Exploring Globalization* is organized. The book is divided into four related issues. Each related issue includes four chapters. Each chapter includes three or four inquiry questions to help guide your exploration, analysis, and evaluation of the chapter issue.

The **prologue** introduces key ideas as you begin the course.

The **related-issue question** provides a focus as you explore, analyze, and evaluate the material.

Each related issue opens with an overview titled **The Big Picture**.

Your Challenge is a guide to the assignment you will complete as you progress through the related issue.

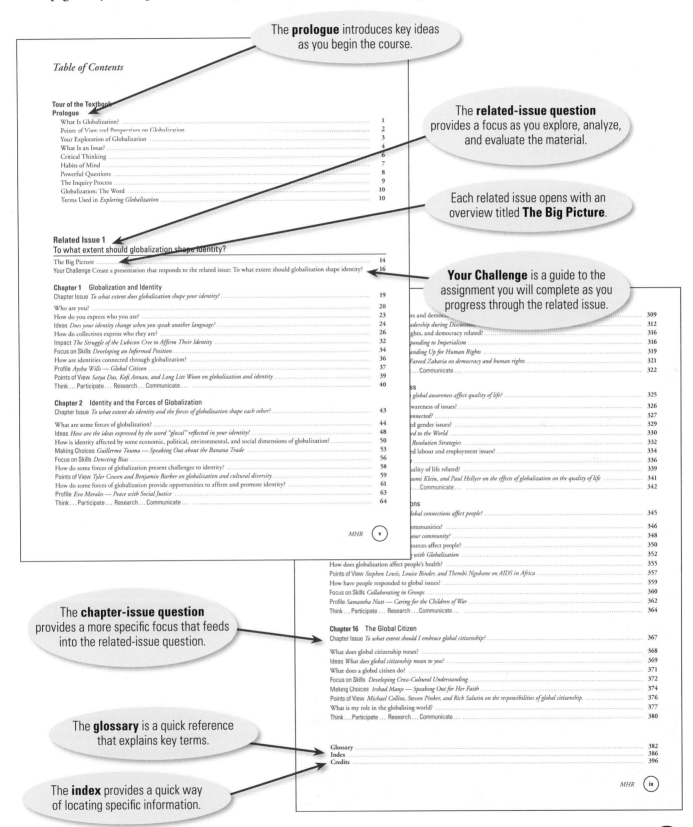

The **chapter-issue question** provides a more specific focus that feeds into the related-issue question.

The **glossary** is a quick reference that explains key terms.

The **index** provides a quick way of locating specific information.

The Big Picture

The Big Picture provides a general overview of what will be explored in the related issue. Like a trailer for a movie, this opening two-page spread touches on the highlights of the related issue and prepares you for the "feature presentation."

The **related-issue number** appears at the top of the page.

The **related issue** provides the focus for the following four chapters.

The **colour bar** identifies the related issue throughout the four chapters of the section. It is a different colour in each of the four related issues.

RELATED ISSUE 2
To what extent should contemporary society respond to the legacies of historical globalization?

Key Issue
To what extent should we embrace globalization?

Related Issue 1
To what extent should globalization shape identity?

Related Issue 2
To what extent should contemporary society respond to the legacies of historical globalization?

Related Issue 3
To what extent does globalization contribute to sustainable prosperity for all people?

Related Issue 4
To what extent should I, as a citizen, respond to globalization?

Chapter 5
FOUNDATIONS OF GLOBALIZATION
To what extent did early globalization affect peoples of the world?

Why and how did globalization begin?
How did the foundations of historical globalization affect people?
How did the consequences of historical globalization affect people?

Chapter 6
LEGACIES OF HISTORICAL GLOBALIZATION
To what extent do the legacies of historical globalization affect peoples of the world?

What are some legacies of historical globalization?
How has cultural contact affected people?
How has the exchange of goods and technologies affected people?
How are the legacies of historical globalization continuing to affect people?

Chapter 7
LEGACIES OF HISTORICAL GLOBALIZATION IN CANADA
To what extent have the legacies of historical globalization affected Canada?

How did historical globalization affect Canada?
What are some legacies of historical globalization in Canada?
How has historical globalization affected Indigenous peoples in Canada?
How do some legacies of historical globalization continue to affect Canada?

Chapter 8
LIVING WITH THE LEGACIES OF HISTORICAL GLOBALIZATION
To what extent have attempts to respond to the legacies of historical globalization been effective?

How effectively have people responded to the legacies of historical globalization?
How effectively have governments responded to the legacies of historical globalization?
How effectively have organizations responded to the legacies of historical globalization?
How does historical globalization continue to affect the world?

THE BIG PICTURE

Events that happened in the past often affect people's lives today. In some ways, it is as if the past were still alive. Past events can affect the choices that are available to you now — but other choices are not yours to make.

Your birth, for example, was not a choice. You were born in a specific country, in a specific community, and to a specific family, and you had no choice in this. But you do have a choice in deciding how to respond to the forces that have shaped — and been shaped by — your country, your community, and your family.

These forces are legacies — things that have been passed on by those who lived in the past. These legacies of the past can colour the present — but the ability to analyze these legacies, to understand how they evolved, to recognize their effects on the present, and to respond thoughtfully is essential to becoming an informed participant in today's society.

In Related Issue 1, you explored some of the relationships between identity and the globalizing process, and you analyzed and evaluated how globalization affects aspects of your life — and the lives of others. In this related issue, you will discover that globalization is an evolving phenomenon with roots that stretch far back in time. As you explore the legacies of historical globalization, you will encounter actions, ideas, values, and forces that promoted globalization in the past. You will also analyze and evaluate how historical globalization continues to affect societies today.

One of the ideas you will encounter in this related issue is that historians and economists do not agree on exactly what historical globalization is or when it took place. But some argue that no matter when this phenomenon started and ended, people today continue to struggle with its repercussions.

Descendants of Aboriginal peoples around the world, for example, continue to struggle with the effects of historical globalization on many aspects of their daily lives and their identity. The specifics may differ, but in some respects, this common struggle has united Indigenous peoples in various countries. Understanding historical globalization and its effects will help you develop an appreciation of contemporary, cross-cultural perspectives.

The chart on the previous page shows how you will progress through Related Issue 2. As you explore this related issue, you will come to appreciate

- how decisions made and actions taken in the past are legacies of historical globalization
- how struggles between peoples with differing points of view and perspectives continue to affect the world today
- how governments, groups, and individuals are attempting to respond to the effects of historical globalization
- how you can develop a deeper understanding of the relationship between historical globalization and your own life
- how you can respond to the effects of historical globalization

111

The **key issue** is the overarching issue for the course.

This **organization chart** clearly maps how you will proceed through each related issue.

Visuals provide clues about what will be covered in the four chapters of the related issue.

Your Challenge

Each related issue presents one challenge. The challenge is presented at the beginning so you know ahead of time what assignment you may be required to complete. This helps you think about, develop, and prepare the ideas and materials you will need to successfully complete the challenge as you progress through the related issue

Specific instructions explain what the challenge involves.

An **example** of parts of the challenge or of a finished product helps you envision what you need to do to be successful. Your finished challenge need not look like the example. It is meant to provide ideas only.

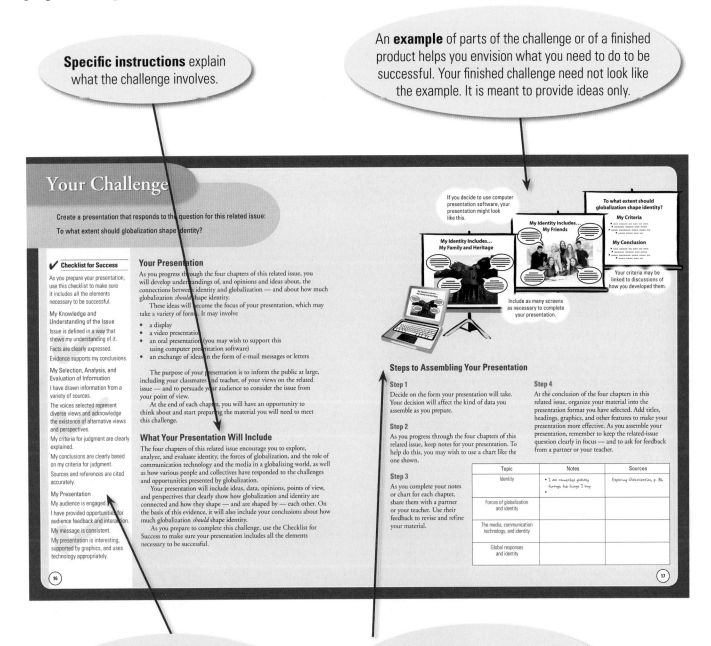

The **Checklist for Success** is a quick review of how various elements of your challenge may be evaluated. This checklist can also be used as a self-assessment tool to help you complete the challenge successfully.

Steps provide specific instructions for organizing, developing, and completing your challenge.

Chapter Openers

Every chapter opens with a two-page spread. On the left page is a visual or set of visuals designed to provide insight into the related and chapter issues, as well as to spark thought and discussion. The issue is introduced on the right page.

The **course issue** is always identified at the top of the page.

The **chapter number and title** appear below the colour bar.

The **large visual** provides a point of view or perspective on the related and chapter issues.

TO WHAT EXTENT SHOULD WE EMBRACE GLOBALIZATION?

Chapter 1   Globalization and Identity

CHAPTER ISSUE
To what extent does globalization shape your identity?

THE WORK OF ART shown on the previous page is a self-portrait — a portrait of the artist by the artist herself. But Joane Cardinal-Schubert's self-portrait is different. Rather than portraying herself at a particular moment, Cardinal-Schubert uses words and images to create a collage that shows the people and events, ideas and beliefs, that played an important role in her developing sense of herself. *Before and After* shows her becoming who she is and indicates that her identity is a work in progress. It is not yet complete. In the portrait, Cardinal-Schubert portrays herself as she shapes — and is shaped by — others. Even the frame that surrounds the piece expresses an important aspect of her identity.

Examine *Before and After* carefully. Find and make note of elements, objects, words, and people that show or symbolize

- Cardinal-Schubert's roots, heritage, and history
- her connection to the land
- her family
- at least three different stages in her life
- who she was when she completed the work
- what the title she chose — *Before and After* — expresses about her sense of identity

Examine the images that make up the frame of the painting. Cardinal-Schubert created this frame to give her audience a message. What do you think this message is? How does this message further your understanding of Cardinal-Schubert's identity?

Figure 1-1 Kainai artist Joane Cardinal-Schubert created the work of art, titled *Before and After*, on the previous page.

KEY TERMS

context

role model

collective

LOOKING AHEAD

In this chapter, you will explore answers to the following questions:

- Who are you?
- How do you express who you are?
- How do collectives express who they are?
- How are identities connected through globalization?

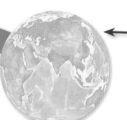

My Point of View on Globalization

Based on your current understanding, use words or images — or both — to express your current point of view on globalization. Date your ideas and keep them in a notebook, learning log, portfolio, or computer file so that you can return to them as you progress through this course.

Special Features

The special features present information, data, ideas, and issues in different ways.

Voices
A quotation that substantiates an idea or provides an alternative point of view or perspective.

The costs and benefits of trade have been unevenly distributed across and within countries, perpetuating a pattern of globalization that builds prosperity for some amid mass poverty and deepening inequality for others.

— United Nations, Human Development Report 2005

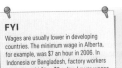

FYI
Wages are usually lower in developing countries. The minimum wage in Alberta, for example, was $7 an hour in 2006. In Indonesia or Bangladesh, factory workers might be paid $1 or $2 a day. Lower wages help transnational corporations remain competitive and meet profit targets.

FYI
These are interesting facts and ideas that enhance your understanding of the issues. This feature often provides a broader context for exploring the issues.

Web Connection
To find out more about how the Francophonie jeunesse de l'Alberta affirms and promotes the identity of French-speaking youth, go to this web site and follow the links.

www.ExploringGlobalization.ca

Web Connection
The web address in this feature takes you to a central site that provides connections that will expand your research and exploration of an issue.

Activity Icon
These quick activities are designed to help you think about and explore the issues you are reading about.

REFLECT AND RESPOND
Recall what you learned in Chapter 9 about the ideas of economists John Maynard Keynes, Friedrich Hayek, and Milton Friedman. Then think about what you have learned about trade liberalization. Whose ideas do you believe have been most influential in shaping contemporary economic globalization? Explain the reasons for your judgment.

Create a cartoon or poster to illustrate your judgment. You may use words or images — or both.

Reflect and Respond
These activities conclude each inquiry section by encouraging you to reflect on aspects of the related issue, the chapter issue, and the inquiry question. They provide you with an opportunity to assess your understanding and review ideas from various points of view and perspectives.

CHECKBACK
You learned about the digital divide in Chapter 3.

CHECKFORWARD
Chapter 4 will explore more connections between language and identity and how these connections shape — and are shaped by — globalization.

CheckForward and CheckBack
These icons appear at various points in the textbook. They direct you to chapters where the ideas you are reading about are explored further.

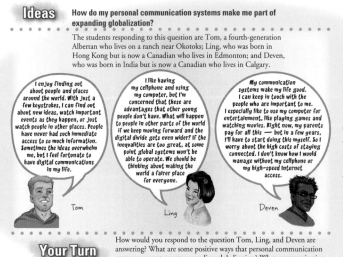

Ideas How do my personal communication systems make me part of expanding globalization?

The students responding to this question are Tom, a fourth-generation Albertan who lives on a ranch near Okotoks; Ling, who was born in Hong Kong but is now a Canadian who lives in Edmonton; and Deven, who was born in India but is now a Canadian who lives in Calgary.

I enjoy finding out about people and places around the world. With just a few keystrokes, I can find out about new ideas, watch important events as they happen, or just watch people in other places. People have never had such immediate access to so much information. Sometimes the ideas overwhelm me, but I feel fortunate to have digital communications in my life.

I like having my cellphone and using my computer, but I'm concerned that these are advantages that other young people don't have. What will happen to people in other parts of the world if we keep moving forward and the digital divide gets even wider? If the inequalities are too great, at some point global systems won't be able to operate. We should be thinking about making the world a fairer place for everyone.

My communication systems make my life good. I can keep in touch with the people who are important to me. I especially like to use my computer for entertainment, like playing games and watching movies. Right now, my parents pay for all this — but in a few years, I'll have to start doing this myself. So I worry about the high costs of staying connected. I don't know how I would manage without my cellphone or my high-speed Internet access.

Tom   Ling   Deven

Ideas
In every chapter, three students respond to a question suggested by the focus of the chapter. You are asked to add your point of view by responding to the same question.

Your Turn How would you respond to the question Tom, Ling, and Deven are answering? What are some positive ways that personal communication systems connect you to expanding globalization? What communication challenges might you face over the next few years as a result of expanding globalization? Explain the reasons for your answers.

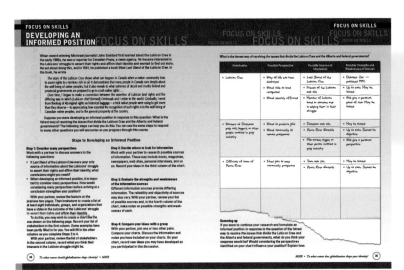

Focus on Skills helps you develop a specific social studies skill in every chapter. Each skill relates to the chapter content.

Photographs, **charts**, **graphs**, and **other visuals** support your learning and provide context for the material being studied. The photo captions often include challenging questions designed to stimulate thought and reflection.

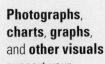

Country	GDP per Person (U.S. Dollars)
United States	$39 676
Norway	$38 454
Canada	$31 263
South Africa	$11 192
China	$5896
Ecuador	$3963
India	$3139
Honduras	$2876
Kenya	$1140

Sub-Saharan Africa 44.6 / 44.0

Southern Asia 39.4 / 31.2

Eastern Asia 33.0 / 14.1

Southeastern Asia and Oceania 19.6 / 7.3

South America and the Caribbean 11.3 / 8.9

Southern Africa and Western Asia 2.2 / 2.4

Transition countries of Southeastern Europe 0.4 / 1.8

Russia and former Soviet States 0.4 / 2.5

Developing regions 27.9 / 19.4

1990
2002
2015 target

0   10   20   30   40   50
Percentage

Legend
European Overseas Empires
- British
- French
- Spanish
- Portuguese
- Dutch

Trade Networks
- British
- French
- Spanish
- Portuguese
- Dutch
- Baltic
- Mediterranean

Maps show you where events happened, provide information in a graphic format, and expand the meaning and context of the ideas and issues you are exploring.

Making Choices presents the issue-related choices made by an individual or organization. Exploring, analyzing, and evaluating these actions will provide you with opportunities to consider the range of choices open to you.

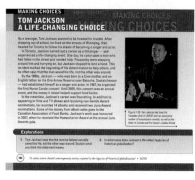

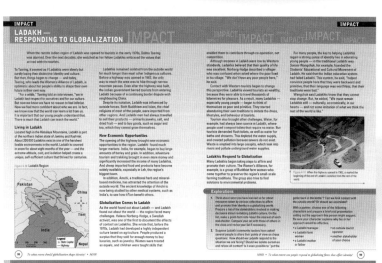

Impact focuses on a specific aspect of an issue. These features highlight how a group, place, person, or event has shaped — and been shaped by — the issue.

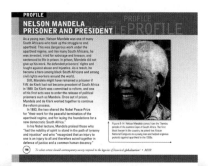

Profile presents a brief, highly focused examination of an individual or organization. These features show how people act and react in different ways and illustrate the power and effectiveness of actions taken to initiate change.

Points of View is a one-page feature that examines an issue through the words of people who are directly involved. The writers' or speakers' differing ideas provide you with an opportunity to deepen your understanding of an issue by exploring, analyzing, and evaluating various points of view.

At the end of each chapter, two pages titled **Think … Participate … Research … Communicate …** include activities designed to help you reinforce your skills, enhance your understanding of issues, and explore, analyze, and evaluate ideas and issues developed in the chapter.

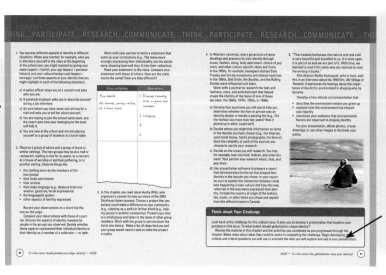

Think about Your Challenge is a reminder of the challenge you are preparing to complete as you progress through the related issue. It also provides tips to help you consider approaches that will help you achieve success.

EXPLORING GLOBALIZATION

Exploring Globalization is built around a single key issue: To what extent should we embrace globalization?

You do not need to answer this question today. But as you progress through this course, you will come to understand the relationships and recognize the forces that shape — and are shaped by — globalization. By the time you finish the course, you will be equipped to make a reasoned judgment on this issue.

What Is Globalization?

As you explore, analyze, and evaluate various aspects of globalization in response to the issue and inquiry questions that comprise the framework of *Exploring Globalization*, you will discover that people have differing understandings of what "globalization" means.

To understand the range of points of view and perspectives on how this word could be defined, scan the definitions in the margin of this page. How are they similar? How are they different? Why do you suppose the range of points of view and perspectives is so broad? If you were required, right now, to choose one of these definitions to defend, which would you select? Explain the reasons for your judgment.

Your point of view

As this course unfolds and you learn more about globalization, you are likely to find that your views on this phenomenon — and how the word could be defined — will change. To help you keep track of these changes, a brief activity titled "My Point of View on Globalization" begins every chapter and asks you to note your current understandings of globalization.

At the end of the course, you can use this record to look back and trace the evolution of your thinking about globalization. This process will help you respond to the key issue question, which is also a focus of the challenge for Related Issue 4: To what extent should we embrace globalization?

RESEARCH TIP

Just as people disagree over how to define globalization, they also disagree over how to spell this word. In Britain, it is often spelled with an *s*: globalisation. In the United States, it is usually spelled with a *z*: globalization. Most Canadian publications, including this textbook, use the *z* spelling.

This difference in spelling may become important when you are carrying out Internet searches. The spelling you enter into a search engine can affect results, so it is a good idea to conduct separate searches using each spelling. This will ensure that your search results are as complete as possible.

Definitions of Globalization

The Canadian Oxford Dictionary
The act of making or becoming global.

Horst Köhler, managing director, International Monetary Fund
A process of increasing international division of labor and the accompanying integration of national economies through trade in goods and services, cross-border corporate investments and financial flows. This integration is boosted by technological progress, in particular in transport and communications.

Forum on Globalization
The present worldwide drive toward a globalized economic system dominated by supranational corporate trade and banking institutions that are not accountable to democratic processes or national governments.

Pascal Lamy, director general, World Trade Organization
A historical stage of accelerated expansion of market capitalism, like the one experienced in the 19th century with the Industrial Revolution. It is a fundamental transformation of societies because of the recent technological revolution which has led to a recombining of the economic and social forces on a new territorial dimension.

Alberta Social Studies Kindergarten to Grade 12 Program of Studies
The process by which the world's citizens are becoming increasingly connected and interdependent.

Points of View and Perspectives on Globalization

As the definitions on the previous page suggest, the phenomenon of globalization arouses strong feelings in many people. They may agree that globalization is changing the world, but they have radically differing points of view and perspectives on the value of these changes and how people should respond to them.

But no matter how people define globalization and no matter what they think about it, most agree that it is happening. And many people would also agree with J. Michael Adams and Angelo Carfagna, who wrote in *Coming of Age in a Globalized World* that the extraordinary changes this phenomenon is bringing about are nothing short of revolutionary.

> We see sweeping changes in all dimensions of human existence. The driving forces of globalization are technological changes that begin with the power of digital computing. We are living in the age of the Internet, the laptop, mobile phones, iPods, dramatic advances in genetic science, and a longer list of trivial and significant programs and gadgets. These advances enable us to extend our reach faster and further than ever before.

For Adams and Carfagna, a global education that leads to an understanding of global citizenship is the key to responding effectively to the revolutionary forces of globalization. They believe that this will help people to understand the links that unite the people of the world and to develop the global outlook necessary to adapt to the changes that are happening now and that will continue to happen in the future.

As you progress through this course and learn more about how you, your community, your country, and the world are affected by the forces of globalization, you will encounter a variety of points of view and perspectives — and you will develop the skills necessary to draw your own conclusions about this phenomenon and to make your own judgments about how you should respond to the forces that are driving it.

Figure P-1 These protesters belong to a group called Global Call to Action against Poverty. In September 2006, they gathered in Singapore, where officials of the World Trade Organization and the International Monetary Fund were meeting. Both these organizations support globalization. Which definition on the previous page do you think the people in the photograph would support? Explain the reasons for your judgment.

Your Exploration of Globalization

Exploring Globalization is designed to provide you with many opportunities to explore, analyze, and evaluate points of view and perspectives on globalization. Your goal as you progress through the course is to develop a response to the overarching issue question: To what extent should we embrace globalization?

To help guide your exploration and analysis of possible responses to this question, four related issues are identified. Each evolves from — and feeds into — the overarching question.

Within each related issue, each of the four chapters focuses on a chapter issue that evolves from — and feeds into — the related-issue question. And within each chapter, inquiry questions are designed to guide your exploration, analysis, and evaluation of topics raised by the chapter-issue question, the related-issue question, and the overarching issue question.

The following chart shows the relationship between the issue and inquiry questions. To examine these questions in greater detail, turn to the table of contents.

CHECKFORWARD

Charts on the opening page of each related issue show how these elements are interconnected.

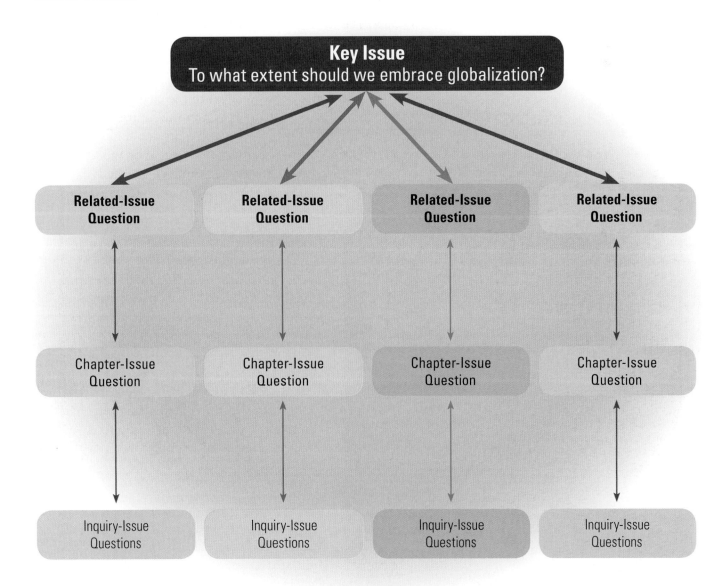

What Is an Issue?

Exploring Globalization is built around a key overarching issue question, as well as a series of related-issue questions. But what is an issue?

An issue is a question or situation that involves thoughtful, well-informed, and well-meaning people in honest and sincere dialogue that may lead to different conclusions about how to respond. An issue can also be a dilemma that requires you to make a choice or decision that involves responsible action. An issue question has no easy — or even correct — answer, but an answer or decision is required nonetheless.

An issue is more than simply a disagreement. People can disagree over the quality of a TV show, but this not an issue because no decision, action, or change in policy is expected as a result.

The crime rate, for example, is *not* an issue, though there may be disagreement over how serious it is or how the rate is calculated. What to do about the crime rate *is* an issue, because thoughtful people might arrive at different decisions and propose radically different solutions.

As a result, clarifying the issue question is very important — because the term "issue" may be used carelessly.

Dealing with an issue requires you to gather information, analyze various points of view and perspectives, and develop criteria for making your own judgment. This process requires you to consider values, beliefs, worldviews, past experiences, and expected outcomes.

Elements of issues

Identifying and distinguishing elements of issues can help you understand the debate over issues and develop a process for arriving at an informed judgment about how they might be resolved. Many issues involve a combination of the following elements.

Policy — What should governments or organizations do? These questions involve taking action or making a change. They require you to think about solutions that are in the best interests of the community or society. Here is an example:

> *Should the government lower the legal drinking age?*

If the answer is yes, the government would make the change that is in the best interests of the broader community and pass a law to bring about the change.

Figure P-2 When Québec's Parti Québécois decided in 1995 to hold a referendum on the issue of whether Québec should become a nation, people on both sides of the issue held rallies. This photograph shows yes supporters waving flags and posters at a rally.

Values — What is good or bad, right or wrong, more or less important or desirable? These questions involve ethical and moral conduct or beliefs. They require you to think about value systems and ask yourself, Why do I believe certain things? Here is an example:

Should violent TV shows be banned?

Answers to these questions provide a basis for improving the quality of life. Governments or groups would act in accordance with some general goals of society.

Definition — What is the meaning of a word or term? These questions explore how language is used and how concepts are understood. They require you to think about how to classify or categorize ideas. Here is an example:

Is Hezbollah a terrorist organization?

The way terms are defined often dictates the action that is taken — or whether action is taken at all.

Fact — What is true or correct? These questions concern the truth of a matter. They require you to examine and weigh evidence. Is the information correct? Here is an example:

Is climate change part of the natural cycle of Earth?

These are difficult issues because they involve "facts." There may be legitimate disagreement over how to weigh evidence and what evidence to accept or reject.

History — Was an action justified? Did an event have a positive outcome? These questions examine the merits of past actions or events to inform future choices. They require you to judge — in context — decisions made in the past. Here is an example:

Should U.S. president Harry Truman have authorized dropping an atomic bomb on Japan?

The way past events are interpreted often influences contemporary decisions.

Figure P-3 Québec voters were divided nearly equally on the referendum question: Do you agree that Québec should become sovereign after having made a formal offer to Canada for a new economic and political partnership within the scope of the bill respecting the future of Québec and of the agreement signed on June 12, 1995? What elements of issues does this question involve?

PRACTISE IDENTIFYING AND ASKING ISSUE QUESTIONS

With a partner, examine the following questions and identify the issue elements involved in each. Discuss whether any of the questions involve more than one element. Then, for each category, work together to create an issue question of your own.

1. To what extent is globalization creating a single homogenized world culture?

2. Is imperialism an acceptable outcome of historical globalization?

3. Should Canada develop free-trade agreements with other countries?

4. Is it a good idea for all cultures to be assimilated into a single global culture?

5. Is globalization simply "Americanization" by another name?

Critical Thinking

The process of making decisions about issues involves critical thinking. Critical thinking requires you to make reasoned judgments about issues by considering evidence and using clear criteria to guide your decisions. An effective critical thinker

- considers all relevant evidence
- makes reasoned judgments
- bases judgments on clear criteria
- works on developing the character traits, or habits of mind, that promote effective decision making

The benefits of using criteria to make reasoned judgments go well beyond the social studies classroom. You make decisions every day — in your other courses, at home, with friends, and at work. You may need to decide whether to take a part-time job, whether to participate in a club excursion, or what courses to take next year. Using criteria to guide these decisions will help you succeed in school and ensure that you make the best possible choices when faced with challenges in all aspects of your life.

Choosing criteria

When selecting criteria to guide your judgments

- keep the number of criteria manageable: a minimum of two and a maximum of four
- be sure the criteria reflect only the most important or relevant considerations

---

WHAT CRITERIA WOULD YOU USE?

The two following cases are imaginary, but they will help you practise choosing criteria to make reasoned judgments. In the first case, two criteria are already filled in. You should choose at least one more criterion. In the second case, only one criterion is filled in. You should choose at least two more criteria. In each case, turn your criteria into questions.

Case 1

Your school is searching for a new name for its sports teams. The name should

- match your school's values and character (Does the name match our values and character?)

- not offend any person or group (Is the name inoffensive to everyone?)

-
-
-

Case 2

The school cafeteria is changing its menu. You are one of the students who have been asked to help staff decide what to keep on the menu, what to drop, and what to add. The food on the menu should

- include fresh local produce (Is the produce fresh and local?)

-
-
-

Habits of Mind

Effective critical thinking requires — and fosters — certain habits of mind. Whether you are completing a social studies assignment or dealing with other challenges, these habits of mind can help you achieve success at school and in life.

I'm flexible.

I'm willing to change my tactics or approach.

I allow my beliefs to change until I have enough evidence to support a definite point of view.

I'm ready to compromise and take my thinking in new directions.

I'm an active thinker.

I explore alternatives and consider their strengths and weaknesses.

I persevere. The first — or most obvious — solution is not always the best.

I resist pressure to adopt opinions just because they are popular.

I'm respectful.

I listen carefully to others.

I'm aware of the limits of my knowledge and avoid claiming to know more than I do.

I judge ideas based on their strengths and weaknesses.

I'm curious.

I do not take everything at face value.

I take time to think about things and explore unanswered questions.

I look for various sources of information and expert opinions.

I'm open-minded.

I'm open to the views of others, especially when their views are different from my own.

I judge ideas on the basis of their strengths and weaknesses.

I explore options beyond my personal interests and biases.

I'm thoughtful.

I think before I act. I consider the consequences of various alternatives.

I think about my own thinking and examine my biases.

I set goals and understand what I'm trying to achieve. I try to visualize what success will look like.

I'm collaborative.

I'm willing to work with others to brainstorm and combine ideas.

I'm prepared to give — and take — constructive feedback.

I make sure everyone has opportunities to contribute and share ideas.

I'm empathetic.

I listen to and try to understand others' points of view.

I don't pass judgment until I've gathered enough information.

I'm aware of the effects of my actions on others.

Powerful Questions

The renowned scientist Albert Einstein said, "The important thing is to never stop asking questions." Asking powerful questions is a key element of learning. A powerful question helps you think critically and provides a focus for all research and inquiry. A powerful question is one that requires a decision or judgment in response — and this decision or judgment should be based on clearly established criteria and evidence.

Exploring Globalization is built around powerful questions. These are the issue questions that provide the structure for this textbook and set out

- the key course issue
- each of the four related issues
- each of the chapter issues

Characteristics of powerful questions

Powerful questions

- generate curiosity and encourage creativity
- are open-ended — they do not have one correct answer
- are thought-provoking, requiring you to make choices, decisions, and judgments
- lead to more questions

makes reasoned judgments

considers all relevant evidence

bases judgments on clear criteria

An effective critical thinker

works on developing the habits of mind that help generate powerful questions

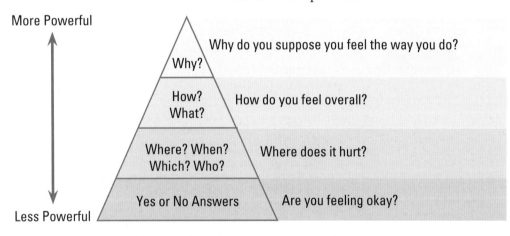

More Powerful

Why? — Why do you suppose you feel the way you do?

How? What? — How do you feel overall?

Where? When? Which? Who? — Where does it hurt?

Yes or No Answers — Are you feeling okay?

Less Powerful

Economist Eric E. Vogt developed a pyramid like the one shown here to illustrate the difference between more powerful and less powerful questions.

PRACTISE IDENTIFYING AND ASKING POWERFUL QUESTIONS

As you progress through *Exploring Globalization*, you will be asked to respond to powerful questions — and to develop powerful questions of your own. With a partner, discuss the following questions about free trade and decide which are powerful and which are not.

1. When did the Canadian government sign the first free-trade agreement?

2. In what ways will free trade stimulate economic growth?

3. Why do you think some groups supported — or opposed — free trade?

4. What is the most important benefit or drawback of free trade for Canadians?

5. Should Canada enter into more free-trade agreements?

Now, choose a topic (e.g., recycling in your community, a school rule). Imagine that a speaker will visit your school to discuss this topic. Create three powerful questions to ask your guest.

The Inquiry Process

To gather the information necessary to respond thoughtfully to powerful questions, you may need to begin by asking inquiry questions. Inquiry questions are designed to elicit information that you will use to support your judgments in response to a powerful question.

The key overarching course question — To what extent should we embrace globalization? — is a powerful question that presents an issue. To respond thoughtfully to this question, you may need to ask a series of inquiry questions, such as

- How have various people defined globalization?
- What are the most important benefits of globalization?
- What are the most serious drawbacks of globalization?
- Where do people think globalization will take the world in the future?

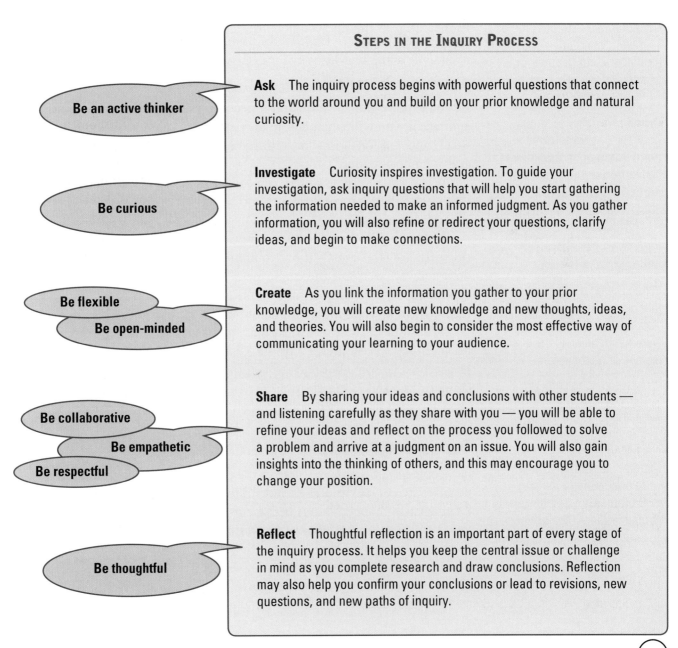

STEPS IN THE INQUIRY PROCESS

Be an active thinker

Ask   The inquiry process begins with powerful questions that connect to the world around you and build on your prior knowledge and natural curiosity.

Be curious

Investigate   Curiosity inspires investigation. To guide your investigation, ask inquiry questions that will help you start gathering the information needed to make an informed judgment. As you gather information, you will also refine or redirect your questions, clarify ideas, and begin to make connections.

Be flexible

Be open-minded

Create   As you link the information you gather to your prior knowledge, you will create new knowledge and new thoughts, ideas, and theories. You will also begin to consider the most effective way of communicating your learning to your audience.

Be collaborative

Be empathetic

Be respectful

Share   By sharing your ideas and conclusions with other students — and listening carefully as they share with you — you will be able to refine your ideas and reflect on the process you followed to solve a problem and arrive at a judgment on an issue. You will also gain insights into the thinking of others, and this may encourage you to change your position.

Be thoughtful

Reflect   Thoughtful reflection is an important part of every stage of the inquiry process. It helps you keep the central issue or challenge in mind as you complete research and draw conclusions. Reflection may also help you confirm your conclusions or lead to revisions, new questions, and new paths of inquiry.

global

global + *ize* = globalize
(a verb meaning " to
become or make global")

globalize + *ation* = globalization
(a noun meaning "the act
of becoming or making
global")

-ize

A suffix that transforms a
noun or adjective into a verb
meaning "to make or become."

fertilize — to make fertile
civilize — to make civil
Canadianize — to become or
make Canadian
globalize — to become or
make global

-ation

A suffix that transforms a
word into a noun that means
"an action or the result or
product of an action."

starvation — the result of
starving
donation — the result of
donating

When *–ation* is added to words
that already include the suffix
–ize, it turns this verb form into
a noun that means "the act of
making or becoming."

fertilization — the act of
becoming or making fertile
civilization — the act of
becoming or making
civilized
Canadianization — the act
of becoming or making
Canadian
globalization — the act of
becoming or making global

Globalization: The Word

The word "globalization" is the focus of this social studies course. This word appears in the title of this course — "Perspectives on Globalization"— and in the title of this textbook — *Exploring Globalization*. It is the focus of the key course issue, as well as of the four related issues.

"Globalization" is now a common word. But if you had lived in the first half of the 20th century, it would not have been part of your vocabulary. No one is sure when this word was coined or who coined it, but language experts agree that it did not appear until the 1940s or 1950s. And even then, it was rarely used. It did not come into widespread use until the 1980s, when American economist Theodore Levitt made it popular by using it to describe changes in technology and social behaviour that allow huge corporations such as Coca-Cola and McDonald's to sell the same products around the world.

The person who coined this word was following a common pattern in English: taking a root word and adding suffixes that change or expand its meaning. In the case of "globalization," the root word is "global." The suffixes added are "-ize" and "-ation."

About -ize and -ation

As you explore globalization and reflect on the extent to which you should embrace it, you will encounter many words that include both the suffixes "–ize" and "–ation" (e.g., "revitalization," "hybridization," "universalization," and "democratization").

When you see these words, you can easily dissect their meaning by identifying the root word, then thinking about how the suffixes change or expand this meaning.

Although new words can be — and sometimes are — created by adding the suffixes "–ize" and "–ation" to nouns and adjectives, English speakers do not always welcome these coinages. Thoughtful writers and speakers are cautious about adopting terms that have been formed this way and often regard them as ungainly examples of bureaucratic jargon.

Still, some of these terms, such as "globalization," do gain acceptance because they serve a useful purpose. Other terms, such as "prioritize," may be accepted by some but rejected by others. And terms like "couponize," "minoritize," and "securitization" are examples of coinages that have never been accepted or are used only in small, specialized circles of interest.

Terms Used in *Exploring Globalization*

As people have become sensitive to the power of language to reinforce negative stereotypes and to exclude individuals and groups, the English language has changed. It has become more inclusive as people have come to recognize the importance of respecting diversity — and of showing this respect through their choice of words.

Developed or developing, North or South

After World War II, much of the world was divided into countries that supported either the United States or the Soviet Union. But some countries supported neither — and these countries became known as the "Third World." Because many Third-World countries were less economically developed than Western countries such as the United States, Britain, and Canada, the term "Third World" gradually came to mean poor countries. Today, "Third World" is considered derogatory and out of date.

Economists and others now prefer terms such as "developing country" to describe countries whose economies are not as strong as those of the wealthy North American and European democracies, which are called developed countries.

The term "global North" is also used to describe developed countries, while "global South" describes developing countries. These terms are often shortened to simply "the North" and "the South."

Although both "developed" and "developing" and "North" and "South" are commonly used, they are also somewhat vague, because no firm guidelines exist for classifying a country as developed or developing, North or South. The map in Figure P-4, for example, shows the approximate division of the world into North and South countries. Although Australia and New Zealand are located in the southern hemisphere, they are considered part of the global North. And many countries in the northern hemisphere are actually part of the global South.

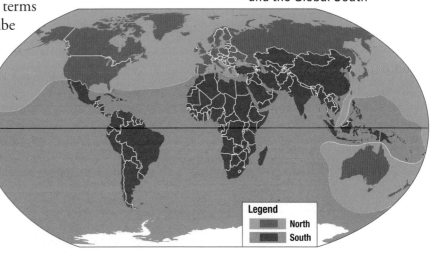

Figure P-4 The Global North and the Global South

Legend
North
South

Francophone references

Exploring Globalization includes many references to Francophones — people whose first language is French. Canada is an officially bilingual country, as Francophone colonists were one of Canada's founding people. Though Québec is home to most Canadian Francophones, Canada's other provinces and territories also have Francophone populations. Francophones may also have immigrated to Canada from other French-speaking countries, such as France, Haiti, Rwanda, Lebanon, and Senegal.

Aboriginal references

When Europeans arrived in Canada, they often imposed their own names on the First Peoples they met. In Eastern Canada, for example, the French gave the name "Huron," an old French term for "boar's head," to the Ouendat. The term referred to the bristly hairstyles worn by Ouendat men.

In recent years, many First Nations, Métis, and Inuit have reclaimed names derived from their own language and prefer to be known by these names. These are the names used in *Exploring Globalization*. Though considerable variation in spelling and usage continues to occur, the chart on the following pages provides a guide to many of these names.

> **RESEARCH TIP**
>
> When conducting research into Aboriginal peoples, be prepared to encounter various names and to check both alternative names and alternative spellings.

First Nations, Métis, and Inuit Names

Contemporary Name	Alternative Names
A'aninin	Gros Ventre, White Clay People, Aaninen
Aamskaapipikani	South Peigan, South Piikani, Blackfeet
Anishinabé or Saulteaux	Ojibway, Ojibwa, Anishinaabe, Anishnabe, Anishnabeg, Bungee
Apsaroke	Crow
Asakiwaki	Sauk
Baffinland Inuit	Eskimo
Cayuga	Cayuga
Cree or Nehiyaw	Cris
Dakota	Sioux
Dene Sułiné	Chipewyan, Dene Souline, Denesuline
Dené Tha'	Dene Dháa, Slavey
Dunne-za	Beaver, South Slave
Gitxsan	Tsimshian, Gitksan
Haida	Haida
Haisla	Kitimat
Heiltsuk	Bella Bella
Innu	Montahfais, Montagnais-Naskapi
Inuit	Eskimo
Inuvialuit	Western Inuit, Eskimo
Haudenosaunee	Iroquois
Kainai	Blood
Kaska Dena	Kaska
Kichesiprini	Algonquin
Kitlinermiut	Copper Inuit, Eskimo
Ktunaxa	Kutenai, Kootenay
Kwakwaka'wakw	Kwakiutl, Kwagiud, Kwagiulth, Kwakwawaw
Labrador Inuit	Sikumiut, Eskimo
Lakota	Sioux
Loucheaux, Kutchin, Tukudh	Gwich'in
Meshwahkihaki	Fox
Métis	Half-breed, Country-born, Mixed-blood
Mi'kmaw (s.) Mi'kmaq (pl.)	Micmac, Mi'maq, Micmaw
Mohawk	Mohawk

Contemporary Name	Alternative Names
Nakoda	Stoney, Assiniboine, Nakota
Nakota	Assiniboine
Nisga'a	Nishga, Nisga
Netsilingmiut	Netsulik Inuit, Eskimo
Nlaka'pamux	Thompson, Couteau
Nuu-chah-nulth	Nootka
Nuxaulk	Bella Coola
Odawa	Ottawa
Okanagan	Okanagan
Oneida, Six Nations Confederacy	Oneida
Onondaga, Six Nations Confederacy	Onondaga
Ouendat	Huron
Oweekeno	Kwakiutl, Kwagiud, Kwakwawaw, Kwagiulth
Piikani	Peigan, Pikuni, North Peigan
Qairnirmiut	Caribou Inuit, Eskimo
Secwepemc	Shuswap
Sekani	Sekani
Seneca, Six Nations Confederacy	Seneca
Siksika, Blackfoot Confederacy	Blackfoot
Stl'atl'imx	Lilloet
Sylix	Lake Okanagan
Tagish	Tagish
Tahltan	Tahltan
Thcho	Dogrib
Tlingit	Tlingit
Tsilhqot'in	Chilcotin
Tsimshian	Tsimshian
Tsuu T'ina	Sarsi, Sarcee
Tuscarora, Six Nations Confederacy	Tuscarora
Tutchone	Tuchone
Ulliniwek	Illinois
Wet'suwet'en	Babine Carrier
Woods Cree	Wood Cree, Woodland Cree

To what extent should globalization shape identity?

Key Issue
To what extent should we embrace globalization?

Related Issue 1
To what extent should globalization shape identity?

Related Issue 2
To what extent should contemporary society respond to the legacies of historical globalization?

Related Issue 3
To what extent does globalization contribute to sustainable prosperity for all people?

Related Issue 4
To what extent should I, as a citizen, respond to globalization?

Chapter 1
GLOBALIZATION AND IDENTITY
To what extent does globalization shape your identity?

Who are you?

How do you express who you are?

How do collectives express who they are?

How are identities connected through globalization?

Chapter 2
IDENTITY AND THE FORCES OF GLOBALIZATION
To what extent do identity and the forces of globalization shape each other?

What are some forces of globalization?

How is identity affected by some economic, political, environmental, and social dimensions of globalization?

How do some forces of globalization present challenges to identity?

How do some forces of globalization provide opportunities to affirm and promote identity?

Chapter 3
IDENTITY, THE MEDIA, AND COMMUNICATION TECHNOLOGY
To what extent is identity affected by communication technology and the media in a globalizing world?

How is identity affected by opportunities to communicate with people around the world?

How is diversity influenced by the media and communication technologies?

How is identity affected by media coverage of world events?

How is diversity affected by the dominance of American media?

Chapter 4
AFFIRMING IDENTITY, LANGUAGE, AND CULTURE
To what extent can people respond to globalizing forces that affect identity?

How do people affirm and promote their language in a globalizing world?

How do people affirm and promote their culture in a globalizing world?

How do governments affirm and promote languages and cultures in a globalizing world?

How do international organizations affirm and promote languages and cultures in a globalizing world?

THE BIG PICTURE

Who you are — your identity and how you express it — is not always easy to define, explain, or describe. You change; you grow; you adapt your beliefs, values, and ideas. Around and within you, things happen to reshape your thinking. You are constantly influenced by many forces: your family, your heritage and language, your peers, the mass media, your religious spiritual beliefs, your school, your physical environment, and your own changing body.

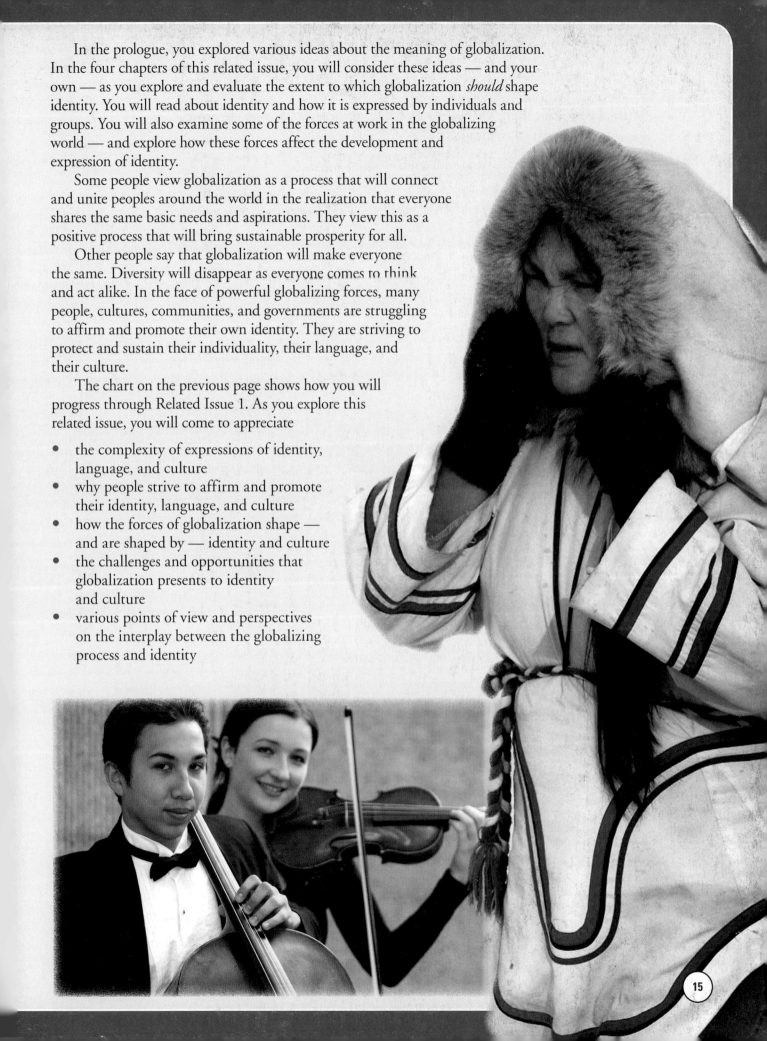

In the prologue, you explored various ideas about the meaning of globalization. In the four chapters of this related issue, you will consider these ideas — and your own — as you explore and evaluate the extent to which globalization *should* shape identity. You will read about identity and how it is expressed by individuals and groups. You will also examine some of the forces at work in the globalizing world — and explore how these forces affect the development and expression of identity.

Some people view globalization as a process that will connect and unite peoples around the world in the realization that everyone shares the same basic needs and aspirations. They view this as a positive process that will bring sustainable prosperity for all.

Other people say that globalization will make everyone the same. Diversity will disappear as everyone comes to think and act alike. In the face of powerful globalizing forces, many people, cultures, communities, and governments are struggling to affirm and promote their own identity. They are striving to protect and sustain their individuality, their language, and their culture.

The chart on the previous page shows how you will progress through Related Issue 1. As you explore this related issue, you will come to appreciate

- the complexity of expressions of identity, language, and culture
- why people strive to affirm and promote their identity, language, and culture
- how the forces of globalization shape — and are shaped by — identity and culture
- the challenges and opportunities that globalization presents to identity and culture
- various points of view and perspectives on the interplay between the globalizing process and identity

Your Challenge

Create a presentation that responds to the question for this related issue:

To what extent should globalization shape identity?

Your Presentation

As you progress through the four chapters of this related issue, you will develop understandings of, and opinions and ideas about, the connections between identity and globalization — and about how much globalization *should* shape identity.

These ideas will become the focus of your presentation, which may take a variety of forms. It may involve

- a display
- a video presentation
- an oral presentation (you may wish to support this using computer presentation software)
- an exchange of ideas in the form of e-mail messages or letters

The purpose of your presentation is to inform the public at large, including your classmates and teacher, of your views on the related issue — and to persuade your audience to consider the issue from your point of view.

At the end of each chapter, you will have an opportunity to think about and start preparing the material you will need to meet this challenge.

What Your Presentation Will Include

The four chapters of this related issue encourage you to explore, analyze, and evaluate identity, the forces of globalization, and the role of communication technology and the media in a globalizing world, as well as how various people and collectives have responded to the challenges and opportunities presented by globalization.

Your presentation will include ideas, data, opinions, points of view, and perspectives that clearly show how globalization and identity are connected and how they shape — and are shaped by — each other. On the basis of this evidence, it will also include your conclusions about how much globalization *should* shape identity.

As you prepare to complete this challenge, use the Checklist for Success to make sure your presentation includes all the elements necessary to be successful.

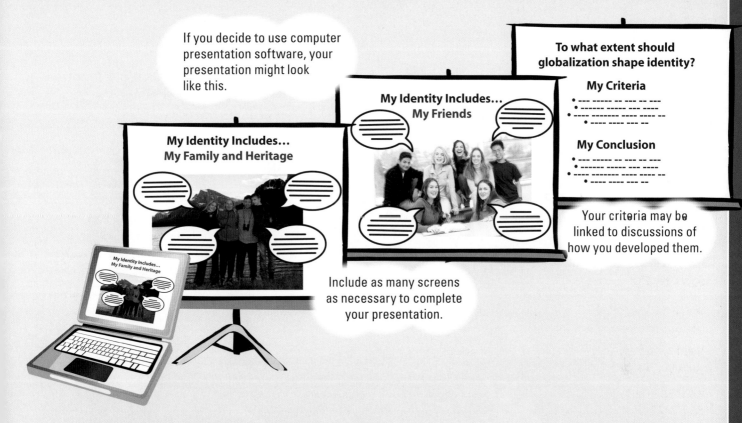

If you decide to use computer presentation software, your presentation might look like this.

Include as many screens as necessary to complete your presentation.

Your criteria may be linked to discussions of how you developed them.

Steps to Assembling Your Presentation

Step 1

Decide on the form your presentation will take. Your decision will affect the kind of data you assemble as you prepare.

Step 2

As you progress through the four chapters of this related issue, keep notes for your presentation. To help do this, you may wish to use a chart like the one shown.

Step 3

As you complete your notes or chart for each chapter, share them with a partner or your teacher. Use their feedback to revise and refine your material.

Step 4

At the conclusion of the four chapters in this related issue, organize your material into the presentation format you have selected. Add titles, headings, graphics, and other features to make your presentation more effective. As you assemble your presentation, remember to keep the related-issue question clearly in focus — and to ask for feedback from a partner or your teacher.

Topic	Notes	Sources
Identity	• I am connected globally through the things I buy. •	Exploring Globalization, p. 36.
Forces of globalization and identity		
The media, communication technology, and identity		
Global responses and identity		

Chapter 1   Globalization and Identity

THE WORK OF ART shown on the previous page is a self-portrait — a portrait of the artist by the artist herself. But Joane Cardinal-Schubert's self-portrait is different. Rather than portraying herself at a particular moment, Cardinal-Schubert uses words and images to create a collage that shows the people and events, ideas and beliefs, that played an important role in her developing sense of herself. *Before and After* shows her becoming who she is and indicates that her identity is a work in progress. It is not yet complete. In the portrait, Cardinal-Schubert portrays herself as she shapes — and is shaped by — others. Even the frame that surrounds the piece expresses an important aspect of her identity.

Examine *Before and After* carefully. Find and make note of elements, objects, words, and people that show or symbolize

- Cardinal-Schubert's roots, heritage, and history
- her connection to the land
- her family
- at least three different stages in her life
- who she was when she completed the work
- what the title she chose — *Before and After* — expresses about her sense of identity

Examine the images that make up the frame of the painting. Cardinal-Schubert created this frame to give her audience a message. What do you think this message is? How does this message further your understanding of Cardinal-Schubert's identity?

Figure 1-1 Kainai artist Joane Cardinal-Schubert created the work of art, titled *Before and After*, on the previous page.

KEY TERMS

context

role model

collective

LOOKING AHEAD

In this chapter, you will explore answers to the following questions:

- Who are you?
- How do you express who you are?
- How do collectives express who they are?
- How are identities connected through globalization?

My Point of View on Globalization

Based on your current understanding, use words or images — or both — to express your current point of view on globalization. Date your ideas and keep them in a notebook, learning log, portfolio, or computer file so that you can return to them as you progress through this course.

WHO ARE YOU?

Do you carry a document — such as a birth certificate, passport, or student card — that identifies you in some way? Your birth certificate, for example, shows your name, who your parents are, and when and where you were born. Your passport shows some of the same information. It also identifies you as a citizen of Canada or another country. Your student card identifies you as a member of your high school community. You may be a student at St. Mary's School in Taber, or Lester B. Pearson High School in Calgary, or Bear Creek School in Grande Prairie, or another school.

Documents like these give some information about your identity, but this information tells only a small part of the story of who you are. Like the story Joane Cardinal-Schubert told in her artwork, your personal story includes much more than the information contained in official documents. Many factors will play a role in shaping your identity, just as they have shaped — and will continue to shape — Cardinal-Schubert's identity.

Figure 1-2 Your religious and spiritual beliefs help shape who you are. Are you, for example, a Christian? A Muslim? A Jew? An atheist? A Buddhist? A Confucian? A humanist? Do you hold other religious or spiritual beliefs that shape your identity?

Figure 1-3 The role you play in your family is one factor that shapes who you are. Are you, for example, a brother or sister? A daughter or son? An uncle or aunt? A niece or nephew? A stepson or stepdaughter? An only child? A first-born child? A middle child? A youngest child? Do you play another family role that shapes your identity?

Figure 1-4 Your interests and talents are other factors that shape who you are. Are you, for example, a hockey player? A soccer player? A baseball fan? A musician? A video gamer? A photographer? Do you have other interests or talents that shape your identity?

Some Factors That Shape Who You Are

Your family relationships, your interests and talents, and your religious and spiritual beliefs are only some of the factors that shape who you are. Think about other factors that have shaped — and continue to shape — your identity. What language(s) do you speak? Do you speak a different language at home and at school? How does language affect your identity? What traditions do you follow? How do these affect your identity? What is your heritage and history, and how do you view this history? What other factors have been important in shaping your identity?

Your family, your heritage, your history, your language(s), your traditions, and many other factors that affect identity are all part of the **context** — the circumstances or surroundings — in which your identity developed. But context is also important in other ways. It may dictate how you respond in various circumstances. In some contexts, for example, you may be a **role model** for others who look up to you. Perhaps you are an older brother or sister whom younger siblings rely on for help in making decisions. Or perhaps you are the captain of a sports team, and your teammates look to you for leadership. How might being a role model affect your identity?

In different contexts, you may have your own role models to whom you look for guidance. These people may be family members, friends, or public figures whom you admire. What people do you think of as role models for yourself? How might these role models affect your identity?

Figure 1-5 On Canada Day in 2002, these young people gathered in Ottawa at the Tomb of the Unknown Soldier. The tomb contains the remains of an unidentified Canadian soldier who died in World War I. What symbols of identity do you see? What aspect of their identity were these young people highlighting on July 1, 2002? How does the context — where they are and what they are doing — affect the aspect of their identity they chose to highlight?

When you take on different roles in different contexts, you are highlighting different aspects of your identity. Sometimes, these roles may be dictated by other people's expectations of you. Think about the aspects of your identity you highlight at school. How much do the expectations of others affect the way you act? Are the aspects of identity you highlight at school different from those you highlight at home? When you are with friends at the mall? When you are at a concert or playing a sport? When you are taking music lessons or at an after-school club?

Time and who you are

The passage of time also plays a role in shaping identity. Recall who you were when you were six years old. Then think about who you were last year — and who you are today. Are you the same as, or different from, the person you were when you were six? Have you changed since last year? How would you describe yourself as a six-year-old? Last year? Today? Are your descriptions different? If so, in what ways? What factors contributed to the changes?

In *Before and After*, the work of art on the opening page of this chapter, Joane Cardinal-Schubert used words and images to make statements about her identity. Create a mind map showing the words and images you would choose if you were asked to create a similar collage to describe your identity. Explain the importance of the words and images you would choose. Do you think your choices will change as you grow older? Why or why not? What frame might you choose to enclose your collage? Why? Keep this mind map for reference as you progress through this chapter.

Web Connection

As a Kainai who struggled to achieve recognition as an artist and to express her identity through art, Joane Cardinal-Schubert has become a role model for young Aboriginal artists. To find out more about Cardinal-Schubert's point of view on her identity and the factors that shaped it, go to this web site and follow the links.

www.ExploringGlobalization.ca

REFLECT AND RESPOND

If you were asked to choose the five aspects of your identity that are the most important to you, which would you select? What influences (e.g., language, family, heritage, physical location) helped shape each of the aspects you chose? List your choices on a chart like the one shown. An example is entered for you.

One way to answer this question is to imagine what you would miss most if you were required to give it up. If you moved, for example, what would you miss more: your school or the skateboarding park?

Share your ideas with a partner or a small group. When you finish this discussion, decide whether you wish to change your choices.

MOST IMPORTANT ASPECTS OF MY IDENTITY RIGHT NOW	MAJOR INFLUENCE ON THIS ASPECT OF MY IDENTITY
Environmentalist	Parents. My parents are environmentalists who like camping and hiking. My beliefs about the importance of the environment come from them.

HOW DO YOU EXPRESS WHO YOU ARE?

Every day, you tell the world about yourself in many different ways. The language(s) you speak, the friends you choose, the clothes you wear, the food you eat, the things you buy, the music you listen to, the leisure activities you choose — and many other actions you take — all express aspects of your identity. They make statements about who you are.

One important way Joane Cardinal-Schubert, the Kainai artist whose work appears on the first page of this chapter, expresses her identity is by creating works of art that reflect her Aboriginal heritage. Other people choose different ways of expressing aspects of their identity. Hindus, for example, express part of their identity that is rooted in their heritage by not eating beef. Other people choose not to eat meat because they believe that animals should not be killed to provide food for human beings. This choice expresses a belief that is an important aspect of their identity.

Return to the mind map you created earlier. It contains words and images you would include in a collage that describes your identity. With a partner, discuss how you express the aspects of identity you described. If you described yourself as a skateboarder, for example, you might say that you express this aspect of your identity by dressing in skater gear and using skater slang. Record notes about your discussion on your mind map.

Expressing Individual Identity: Traditions

Many people of Iranian heritage continue to celebrate Chahar Shanbeh Suri, or Last Wednesday. This is an ancient festival that celebrates the coming of a new year and coincides with the spring equinox. On the last Tuesday of the year, Iranians build — and jump over — a bonfire to symbolize purification. They believe that jumping over the fire will banish illness and bad luck.

This festival is one example of a tradition that expresses an aspect of identity. Other people follow different traditions. For many people of Finnish heritage, for example, a sauna — a kind of sweat bath — is an important tradition that expresses an aspect of their identity. They believe that a sauna not only cleans and heals the body, but also purifies the mind.

Other people may say special prayers, eat certain foods, wear specific clothing, gather to perform certain rituals, or follow other traditions. Individuals, families, and groups may also create their own traditions. What traditions do you follow? How does each express an aspect of your identity?

Expressing Individual Identity: Language

Suppose it is snowing outside. What words might you use to describe this? Perhaps you would say that light snow is falling or that it is snowing heavily. You might also say that the snow is wet, powdery, or drifting. No matter how you put the words together, if you are speaking English, you would nearly always use a form of the word "snow" in your description. This is because English has relatively few words for snow.

Figure 1-6 The young people in these pictures are expressing aspects of their identity through the way they dress and their body decorations. What aspect of her or his identity do you think each young person is expressing?

FYI

Here are some other Inuit words that describe specific kinds of snow.

akkilokipok   soft snow
aput   snow on the ground
aput masannartuq   slush on the ground
mangiggal or *mangikaajaaq*   hard snow
nittaalaq   air that is thick with snow
nittaalaaqqat   hard grains of snow
pukak   fine snow (like salt) or snow crust
qaniit   falling snow or snow in the air
putsinniq or *puvvinniq*   wet snow on top of ice
tipvigut   snowdrift

Language and worldview

Compare this with the many different words that describe snowy conditions in Inuktitut, the language spoken by the Inuit who live in Canada's North. An Inuk might say "*mauja*" to describe soft, deep snow or "*apirlaat*" to describe new-fallen snow. The Inuit also use many other words to describe specific kinds of snow or snow conditions. What factors might explain the difference in the way the idea "snow" is expressed in English and Inuktitut? How does this aspect of identity reflect a sense of place?

Many language experts and anthropologists — people who study people, societies, and customs — believe that language expresses the way people view and understand the world around them. As a result, they say, language is an important aspect of people's identity.

Think about how, where, and why you learned the language or languages you speak. What aspect(s) of your identity are you expressing when you speak English? Do you speak another language? If so, what aspect(s) of your identity are you expressing when you speak this language?

Ideas

Does your identity change when you speak a different language?

The students responding to this question are Deven, who was born in India but is now a Canadian who lives in Calgary; Gord, a member of the Beaver First Nation near High Level; and Marie, a Francophone student from Medicine Hat.

I learned English when I came to Canada, and I speak it at school and with my friends. But when I talk to my parents at home, we usually speak Hindi. I'm so used to switching back and forth that I don't even notice. It's no big deal. I'm me — no matter which language I'm speaking. My identity doesn't change. The things I believe stay the same. Like, I'm still a soccer player whether I'm talking about a game in Hindi or in English.

Deven

My parents speak only English and I grew up speaking only English, but now I'm taking classes to learn Cree, my people's language. So are some of my friends. The better I learn to communicate in my own language, the more I feel as if I'm taking back part of my identity that was missing. This is really important to me. So, yes, I think my identity is changing as I learn my own language.

Gord

I grew up in a French-speaking family, I go to a Francophone school, and most of my friends speak French. Still, I'm part of a minority in Canada. I've learned English, but I don't feel like me when I speak English. I am my language — and my language is French. When I speak English to someone who speaks French, I don't feel like the real me.

Marie

Your Turn

How would you respond to the question Deven, Gord, and Marie are answering? If you speak only English, how do you think this affects your response? If you speak English and at least one other language, how do you think this affects your response? Explain the reasons for your answer.

Expressing Individual Identity: Clothing and Body Adornment

Think about what you're wearing today. Do your clothing choices express aspects of your identity? Are you dressed in a way that reflects your interests, heritage, traditions, or beliefs?

Wearing a jacket, jersey, or cap that sports a team logo may make a statement about one of your interests. Wearing a T-shirt splashed with a slogan may make a statement about a cause you believe in. Wearing a yarmulke, turban, hijab, or crucifix may make a statement about your religious beliefs. Dressing in the latest style may make a statement about the role of fashion in your sense of identity. Wearing items purchased in a vintage or used-clothing shop may make a statement about other beliefs you hold.

Even the clothes you choose not to wear may express aspects of your identity. People who choose not to wear clothing that displays trendy brand names may be expressing a belief that is important to them. The same may be true of people who choose not to wear leather or fur. What might these beliefs be?

Tattoos and piercing

Just as clothing is often an expression of identity, so is body adornment. People have been adorning their bodies for thousands of years. Women in Iran, for example, have been wearing earrings in their pierced ears for more than 4000 years. Body piercing was also popular in India and Pakistan, as well as in other ancient cultures, such as the Aztecs and Maya of Mexico.

Tattoos are another ancient form of body adornment. At various times, peoples such as Egyptians, Polynesians, Maoris, Maya, Incas, Celts, Danes, Japanese, Samoans, Saxons, and Scots wore tattoos to make statements about themselves. Their tattoos might have shown their marital status or membership in a clan or other group. They might also have commemorated important battles, journeys, or visions.

In many Western societies, piercing and tattooing were frowned on for a long time. Even today, some cultures, such as Jews and Rastafarians, prohibit marking the skin. Among other groups, however, body decoration has become a popular way of making a statement about individual identity.

Figure 1-7 In India and Pakistan, women traditionally decorate their hands and feet with mehendi to celebrate festive occasions. Henna paste is used to create the ornate designs. How does this expression of identity compare with the way some North American women decorate their hands and feet?

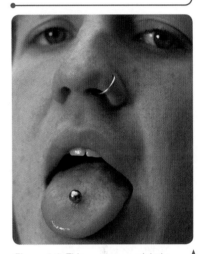

Figure 1-8 This young man might be surprised to learn that body piercing has a long tradition in many cultures. What statement might he be making about his identity?

REFLECT AND RESPOND

Choose a holiday, ceremony, or tradition that you participate in. It might be religious (e.g., Christmas or Ramadan), family (e.g., a birthday or reunion), school-based (e.g., graduation or a field trip), or spiritual (e.g., a solitary retreat).

Create a word web with the holiday, ceremony, or tradition at the centre. Around it, group words and phrases that describe the event (e.g., special clothing or adornments, special language used or prayers said). To each of these words or phrases, link words and phrases that describe how each connects you to the celebration or your feelings about each. An example is shown.

HOW DO COLLECTIVES EXPRESS WHO THEY ARE?

When you follow a particular tradition, speak a particular language, wear specific clothing, or adorn your body with particular decorations, you may be expressing aspects of your individual identity. But at the same time, you may also be expressing your identity as a member of a group, or **collective**.

You may belong to many collectives. There are many understandings of what it means to be a member of a collective. Some people are born into and maintain their affiliation with a particular collective because they develop deep-seated values and beliefs associated with the ideas, language, traditions, religion, and spirituality of others in the collective.

Collectives and Identity

When you were younger, your family was probably the most important collective in your life. Your family helped shape aspects of your identity and probably defined the collectives you belonged to. Your family, for example, would have defined the first language you spoke and the cultural traditions you followed. If your parents or guardians belonged to a collective such as a church, synagogue, mosque, or temple, you probably did, too. You would have learned the beliefs, traditions, and rituals followed by members of this collective, and these would have played an important role in shaping your individual identity and your identity as a member of the collective.

As you grew older, however, other collectives may have begun to play a role in shaping aspects of your identity. When you were a young child, for example, you may have worn the clothes your parents or guardians chose for you. Their choices may have been influenced by a number of factors, including their beliefs about appropriate dress for young children. As you grew older, however, you may have begun making your own clothing choices. And these choices may have been influenced more by what others in your collective of friends were wearing than by what your parents or guardians wanted you to wear.

Return to the mind map you created earlier. It contains words and images you would include in a collage that describes your identity. With a partner, discuss which words and images reflect your membership in a collective. If being a skateboarder is one aspect of your identity, for example, you might belong to a collective of skaters who practise tricks after school. You might also belong to an organized skateboarding club.

Figure 1-9 How are the people in these photographs expressing their collective identity? To what extent do you think their choices were influenced by where they live? What other factors may have influenced their choices? To what extent do you think their choices are influenced by their individual identity? By their collective identity?

Expressing Collective Identity: Language

What is the purpose of language? Why do people learn the sounds and symbols that make up a language?

From earliest infancy, babies hear the sounds used by older children and adults. And when babies imitate these sounds, they are praised and rewarded. Think, for example, about how a father responds when a baby says "dada" for the first time. The father's delight is a powerful motivator for the baby to continue saying "dada."

As babies begin to distinguish the sounds they hear, they learn that different sounds have different meanings and that they can manipulate these sounds to express their needs. They learn to communicate — in the language they hear spoken around them. This language is an important shaper of their identity. Anthropologists such as Edward Sapir and Benjamin Lee believe that language shapes and determines how people perceive and understand the world. People who speak different languages view the world differently. How might this be so?

Some links between language and identity

Just as language is an important aspect of individual identity, it is also an important aspect of collective identity. Leroy Little Bear, a Kainai writer and professor of Native studies, has described how people's individual and collective identity are linked through language. "Language embodies the way a society thinks," Little Bear wrote. "Through learning and speaking a particular language, an individual absorbs the collective thought processes of a people."

Language can help unite people. In Québec, for example, speaking French helps unite people of various backgrounds. Many Francophones are native-born Québecers, and many native-born Québecers are the descendants of French settlers who arrived in Canada centuries ago. But other Québecers are more recent immigrants from countries, such as Haiti, Lebanon, and Egypt, where French is spoken. Speaking the same language — French — gives people from various cultural backgrounds something in common. They belong to the same official-language collective.

Examine Figure 1-10. It is possible for Francophones to live and work in French in any of the cities shown on the pie charts. But if you were a Francophone who planned to immigrate to Canada, would the information shown on the charts influence your decision about which city to settle in? Explain why or why not. How might your identity affect your decision — and vice versa?

Web Connection

Some children are born deaf or become deaf at an early age. This means that they cannot hear the language spoken around them. How does this affect the development of their identity? To find out more about the language and personal development of children who are deaf, go to this web site and follow the links.

www.ExploringGlobalization.ca

Figure 1-10   People Who Use Only English or Only French as Their Language of Work in Selected Canadian Cities

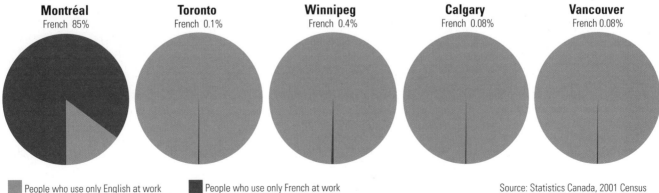

Montréal	Toronto	Winnipeg	Calgary	Vancouver
French 85%	French 0.1%	French 0.4%	French 0.08%	French 0.08%

■ People who use only English at work   ■ People who use only French at work

Source: Statistics Canada, 2001 Census

CHECKFORWARD

Chapter 4 will explore more connections between language and identity and how these connections shape — and are shaped by — globalization.

Web Connection

To find out more about how la Francophonie jeunesse de l'Alberta affirms and promotes the identity of French-speaking youth, go to this web site and follow the links.

www.ExploringGlobalization.ca

Affirming collective identity

In Québec, Francophones form a majority of the population, but in other provinces, they form a minority — sometimes a small minority. In Alberta, for example, Francophones make up a little more than two per cent of the population. What challenges might their small number present to Franco-Albertans who wish to affirm their identity as Francophones?

One way Francophone Albertans affirm their identity is by founding associations and institutions to protect and affirm their rights and to affirm their collective identity. Founded in 1926, l'Association canadienne-française de l'Alberta is an example of an association for this purpose. Similarly, la Francophonie jeunesse de l'Alberta is an association for young people between the ages of 14 and 25. It was formed in the 1970s to encourage Alberta's Francophone youth to promote their identity, and its aims are like those of l'Association canadienne-française de l'Alberta. Francophone schools are examples of institutions the community has founded to provide French first-language education and to affirm the identity of students. Why would it be especially important for young people to be part of associations and institutions that affirm their language and identity?

Other groups also form organizations to ensure that their voices are heard and to affirm and promote their rights, language, culture, and heritage. Some Canadians of Chinese heritage, for example, formed the Chinese Canadian National Council, which has chapters in many cities across the country. In Alberta, many Métis have united under the banner of the Métis Nation of Alberta. How might creating organizations like these help members of various collectives affirm their identity?

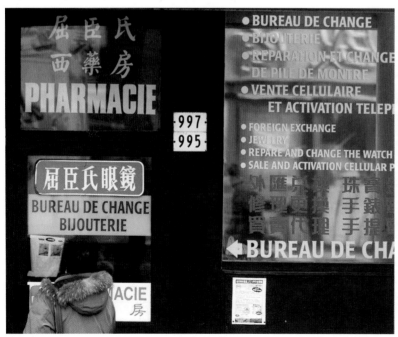

Figure 1-11 In the photograph on the left, a Montréal shop displays signs in three languages. What are the languages? The photograph at the top right shows the sign at a McDonald's restaurant in China, and the photo at the bottom right shows how Coca-Cola products are presented for sale in Saudi Arabia. In all three instances, what aspects of customers' identity are these commercial enterprises appealing to? What challenges might businesses face when selling products in global markets?

Slang, Jargon, and Collective Identity

Are you sagging? Chilling? Flamboasting? As a teenager, you probably understand what these slang terms mean. But do your teachers? Or your parents? What is some other up-to-date slang you and your friends use? Why do you use these terms?

Slang is often defined as a collection of terms used by the members of a social collective, such as teenagers. Jargon is similar to slang. It, too, is a collection of terms, but it is often used by members of professional collectives, such as computer technicians, teachers, doctors, and musicians. Language experts believe that people use slang and jargon

- to avoid long descriptions and explanations
- to convey precise meaning to other members of the collective
- to affirm their identity as a member of a particular collective

Using slang and jargon maintains group solidarity because everyone in the collective understands the same "language," while those outside the group do not. People feel a sense of belonging to the collective when they share this special language with one another, and this sense of belonging helps affirm their identity as a member of the collective.

Gender-neutral language and identity

For centuries, English used the masculine form of many words to apply to both men and women. "Mankind," for example was the word used for all human beings. Someone who chaired a group was usually called a "chairman," and "policemen" and "firemen" helped keep people safe.

In the 20th century, more women began to enter positions and occupations that had traditionally been dominated by men. As this happened, the words commonly used to describe these positions and occupations changed to gender-neutral terms that could describe both women and men. Someone who chaired a meeting came to be called the "chairperson" or "chair." "Policemen" came to be called "police officers," and "firemen" changed to "firefighters." And people began replacing "mankind" with words like "humanity" and "humankind." English became more inclusive.

What difference do you think these changes in the way people use English would make to the identity of young men? Of young women?

Figure 1-12 All the people in this cartoon speak English, yet they do not speak the same "language." How does this cartoon show the misunderstandings that can occur when people do not speak the same "language"?

Such a friendly new neighbour, Cecil— we've been invited to something called a rave up to-night!

FYI

Communicating between cultures is sometimes difficult, even when people know each other's language. The following are examples of how large companies ran into problems when they tried to translate advertising messages directly from English to another language. In each case, the message was definitely lost in translation.

- When Braniff Airways translated a slogan promoting the leather upholstery on its seats, "Fly in leather" came out in Spanish as "Fly naked."
- When Chevrolet introduced a model called the Nova to Spanish-speaking countries, it did not sell well. In Spanish, "No va" means "It doesn't go."
- When Pepsi started marketing its products in China, the company translated its slogan — "Pepsi brings you back to life" — literally. But in Chinese, it came out as "Pepsi brings your ancestors back from the grave."
- When Clairol introduced its "Mist Stick" curling iron to Germany, the company found that "mist" is slang for "manure." Not many people had use for a manure stick.

Collective Identity and Context

Think about the various contexts in which you interact with others. Your list might include the following:

- at home with family members
- at school in classes
- after school with a sports team or club
- at a house of worship with other worshippers
- at the mall with friends

In each of these contexts, you may be expressing an aspect of your collective identity — and each collective probably has ground rules that its members accept without question. These "rules" may be written or unwritten, and they may be expressed in the form of customs, traditions, and rituals that affirm the beliefs and identity of members of the collective.

If you are a Muslim attending mosque, for example, you probably remove your footwear before entering. If you are a member of a hockey team, you may wear a uniform for games. If you are eating lunch in the school cafeteria with friends, you may sit in a specific area and pepper your conversation with particular slang. These formal and informal customs, traditions, and rituals affirm your identity as a member of a particular collective.

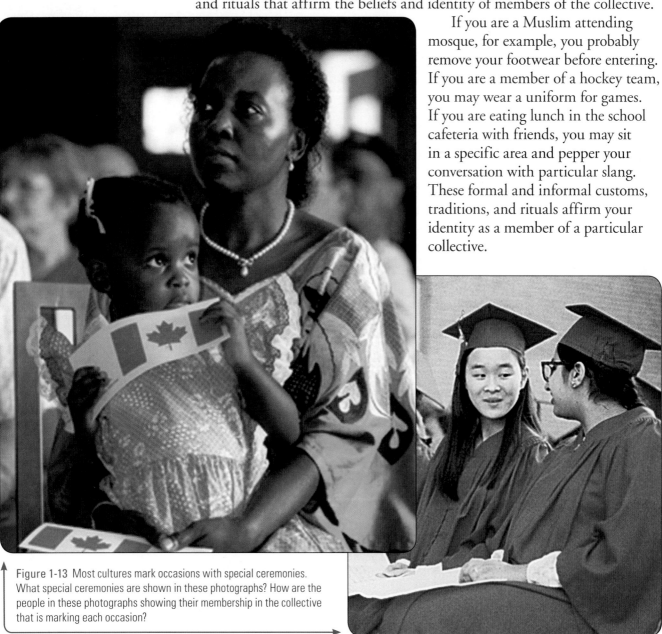

Figure 1-13 Most cultures mark occasions with special ceremonies. What special ceremonies are shown in these photographs? How are the people in these photographs showing their membership in the collective that is marking each occasion?

The context in which you interact with others may be as specific as your own backyard or school, but it may also be much broader. Context may refer to the broader community or landscape in which your identity develops. If you live in a city, you will be accustomed to seeing and dealing with various things in your urban surroundings. If you live in a rural area, the things you see and deal with may be quite different. What might some of these urban and rural things be? How might they affect your identity?

REFLECT AND RESPOND

List five collectives you belong to (e.g., your class at school). Identify at least one purpose for each collective — and at least one custom, tradition, or ritual followed by the members of each collective.

Compare your list with that of a partner. In what ways are they the same? In what ways are they different? Discuss reasons for the similarities and differences. How do the similarities and differences reflect similarities and differences in your identity and that of your partner?

COLLECTIVE	PURPOSE	TRADITION
My class	To learn together	Taking attendance at beginning of class

THE STRUGGLE OF THE LUBICON CREE TO AFFIRM THEIR IDENTITY

IMPACT

In 1973, war broke out half a world away from the Lubicon Cree of northern Alberta — but it changed their lives forever. Israel and a group of Arab nations led by Egypt and Syria were fighting what came to be known as the Yom Kippur War. The United States and many European countries supported Israel, while Saudi Arabia and many of the oil-rich countries of the Middle East supported Egypt and Syria.

Many of the Middle Eastern countries belonged to the Organization of Petroleum Exporting Countries. OPEC members decided to stop shipping oil to the United States and other countries that supported Israel. This helped create an energy shortage, and the price of oil quadrupled.

In 1952, oil had been discovered in the territory where the Lubicon Cree traditionally hunted, trapped, and fished. When OPEC stopped shipping oil to the U.S., Americans began to look to Canada to supply more of their oil — and the oil and gas in Lubicon territory became very valuable. To help resource companies gain access to it, the Alberta government started building roads into the area.

The roads enabled oil and gas companies to set up and service oil wells on land where the Lubicon hunted and trapped. The roads also opened up the area to other development. In the years that followed, a sour gas plant was built, and the Daishowa Paper Manufacturing Co., an international corporation based in Japan, opened a pulp mill nearby in Peace River. The Alberta government granted Daishowa logging rights to a huge area that included nearly all the Lubicon territory. To feed the mill, up to 11 000 trees a day are cut.

Effects on the Lubicon Cree Way of Life

When resource companies started moving into the territory where the Lubicon Cree hunted, fished, and trapped, the forests began to disappear. As the forests disappeared, so did the animals that lived there. This destroyed the Lubicon way of life.

Figure 1-15 Lubicon Cree and Global Connections

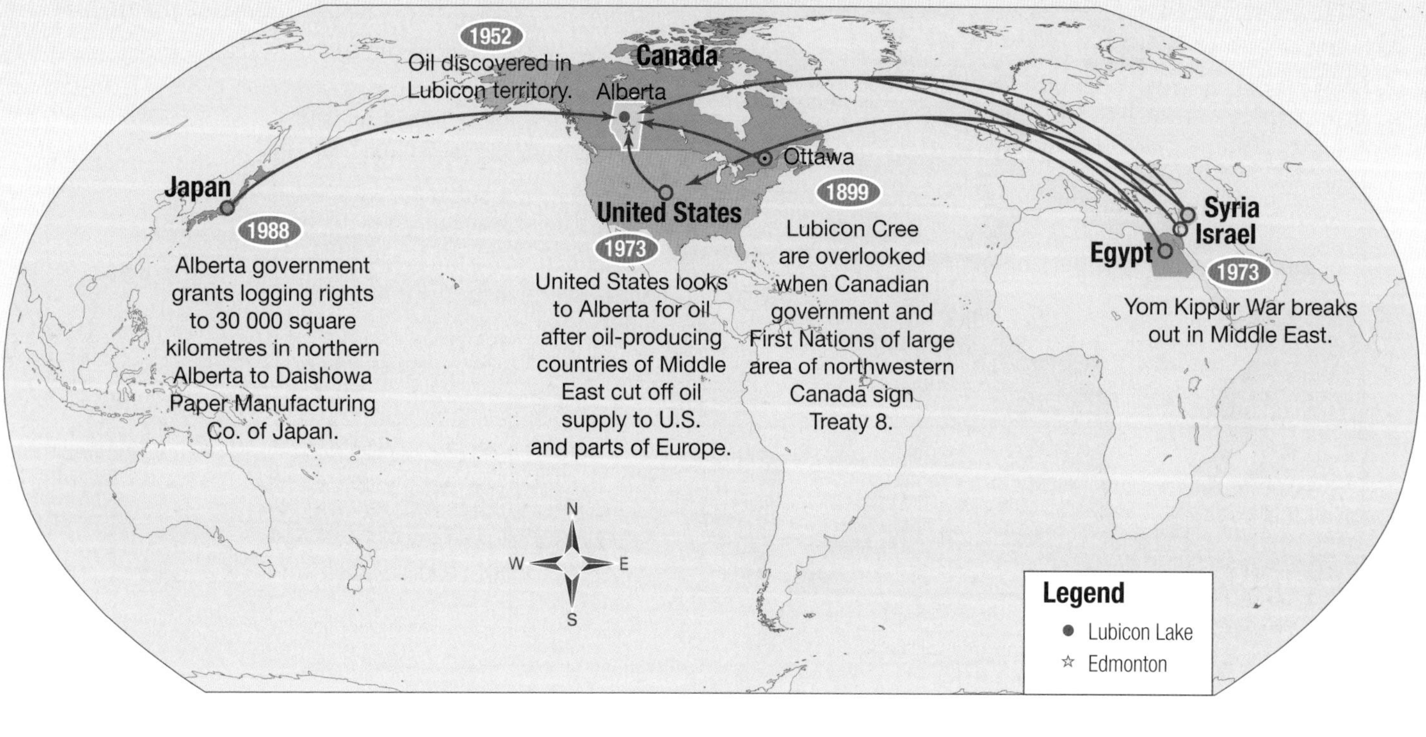

1952 Oil discovered in Lubicon territory.

Canada
Alberta
Ottawa

1899 Lubicon Cree are overlooked when Canadian government and First Nations of large area of northwestern Canada sign Treaty 8.

Japan

1988 Alberta government grants logging rights to 30 000 square kilometres in northern Alberta to Daishowa Paper Manufacturing Co. of Japan.

United States

1973 United States looks to Alberta for oil after oil-producing countries of Middle East cut off oil supply to U.S. and parts of Europe.

Syria
Israel
Egypt

1973 Yom Kippur War breaks out in Middle East.

N W E S

Legend
● Lubicon Lake
☆ Edmonton

Effects of Resource Development on the Lubicon Way of Life

Indicator	1979	1983
Annual moose harvest	219	19
Annual trapping income per family	$5000	$400
Welfare rate	Less than 10%	More than 90%

Source: Friends of the Lubicon

The Roots of the Conflict

The roots of the conflict over title to Lubicon territory go back to 1899, when Treaty 8 was signed by the federal government and many of the First Nations who live in present-day northern Alberta. But some bands who lived in remote areas were missed. The Lubicon were one of them. They did not sign Treaty 8.

Because of this, their territory is considered crown land — land that is owned and controlled by the government. The government collects the oil and gas royalties and other fees related to the development of crown land.

For more than 100 years, the Lubicon have been trying to correct the Treaty 8 oversight and negotiate a treaty that affirms their right to control their territory. They also say that they are entitled to a share of the royalties and fees from the developments that have destroyed their way of life. So far, their efforts have been unsuccessful.

Estimated Receipts from Oil and Gas Revenues and Royalties in Lubicon Territory

To Resource Companies	To Alberta Government in Royalties	To Lubicon
$13 billion	$2.6 billion	$0

Source: Friends of the Lubicon

The Lubicon Affirm Their Identity

One tactic governments used to avoid signing a treaty with the Lubicon Cree was to deny their identity as a separate Aboriginal nation. In 1942, for example, a federal official decided that some band members were not Aboriginal people and deleted their names from the band list. Similar tactics have been used in later decades.

But Chief Bernard Ominayak and many Lubicon have refused to give up their identity. In the 1980s, they launched a campaign to win support for their cause and to press the Alberta and federal governments to recognize their claim, compensate them for what they have lost, and grant them a reserve on the shore of Lubicon Lake.

To gain support for their struggle, the Lubicon have appealed to international organizations, such as the World Council of Churches, Amnesty International, and the United Nations Human Rights Committee. All these organizations have supported their claim. The Lubicon are also supported by many other Aboriginal people, as well as groups such as Friends of the Lubicon.

Explorations

1. Create a timeline showing the events that have affected the identity of the Lubicon Cree. For each event, write a phrase or sentence that identifies its connection to the Lubicon Cree.

2. Think about your understandings of globalization so far. Name at least two aspects of globalization that have affected the Lubicon. Would you rate these effects as positive or negative? Explain why.

3. Name at least two ways the identity of the Lubicon Cree has been challenged. Think about the aspects of your own identity you described earlier in this chapter. How would you respond if someone told you that you are wrong about one or more aspects of your identity — that you are not who you say you are?

DEVELOPING AN INFORMED POSITION

When award-winning Montréal journalist John Goddard first learned about the Lubicon Cree in the early 1980s, he was a reporter for Canadian Press, a news agency. He became interested in the Lubicons' struggle to assert their rights and affirm their identity and wanted to find out more. He set about doing this, and in 1991, he published a book titled *Last Stand of the Lubicon Cree.* In the book, he wrote

> The story of the Lubicon Cree shows what can happen in Canada when a native community tries to assert rights to a territory rich in oil. It demonstrates that many people in Canada care deeply about the well-being of native peoples; but it also reveals to what extremes of deceit and cruelty federal and provincial governments are prepared to go to crush native rights …
>
> Over time, I began to make a connection between the assertion of Lubicon land rights and the differing way in which [Lubicon chief Bernard] Ominayak and I relate to the world. Gradually, I went from thinking of Aboriginal rights as historical baggage — a trick native people were using to get more than they deserve — to appreciating how essential the recognition of such rights is to the well-being of Canadian native peoples, and to the general prosperity of the country.

Suppose you were developing an informed position in response to this question: What is the fairest way of resolving the issues that divide the Lubicon Cree and the Alberta and federal governments? The following steps can help you do this. You can use the same steps to respond to many other questions you will encounter as you progress through this course.

Steps to Developing an Informed Position

Step 1: Consider many perspectives
Work with a partner to discuss answers to the following questions:

- If *Last Stand of the Lubicon Cree* were your only source of information about the Lubicons' struggle to assert their rights and affirm their identity, what conclusions might you reach?
- When developing an informed position, it is important to consider many perspectives. How would considering many perspectives before arriving at a conclusion strengthen your position?

With your partner, review the feature on the previous two pages. Then brainstorm to create a list of at least eight individuals, groups, and organizations that have a stake in the outcome of the Lubicons' struggle to assert their rights and affirm their identity.

To do this, you may wish to create a chart like the one shown on the following page. Record your list of stakeholders in the first column. Some examples have been partly filled in for you. You will fill in the other columns as you complete Steps 2 to 4.

With your partner, review the list of stakeholders. In the second column, record what you think their interests in the Lubicon struggle might be.

Step 2: Decide where to look for information
Work with your partner to research possible sources of information. These may include books, magazines, newspapers, web sites, personal interviews, and so on. Record your ideas in the third column of the chart.

Step 3: Evaluate the strengths and weaknesses of the information sources
Different information sources provide differing information. The reliability and objectivity of sources may also vary. With your partner, review your list of possible sources and, in the fourth column of the chart, make notes on possible strengths and weaknesses of each.

Step 4: Compare your ideas with a group
With your partner, join one or two other pairs. Compare your charts. Discuss the information and notes you have included on your charts. On your chart, record new ideas you may have developed as you participated in this discussion.

FOCUS ON SKILLS

FOCUS ON SKILLS   FOCUS ON SKILLS
FOCUS ON SKILLS
FOCUS ON SKILLS   FOCUS ON SKILLS

What is the fairest way of resolving the issues that divide the Lubicon Cree and the Alberta and federal governments?

Stakeholder	Possible Perspective	Possible Sources of Information	Possible Strengths and Weaknesses of Sources
• Lubicon Cree	• Way of life has been destroyed • Want title to land recognized • Want identity affirmed	• *Last Stand of the Lubicon Cree* • Friends of the Lubicon web site • Member of Lubicon band or someone who is helping them in their struggle	• Detailed. Old — published 1991. • Up to date. May be biased in favour of the Lubicon. • Will give a personal point of view. May be biased in favour of the Lubicon.
• Workers at Daishowa pulp mill, loggers, or other people involved in pulp industry	• Want to preserve jobs • Want community to remain prosperous	• Daishowa web site • *Peace River Gazette* • Mill worker, logger, or other person involved in pulp industry	• May be biased in favour of the company. • Up to date. Should be objective. • Will give a personal perspective.
• Officials of town of Peace River	• Need jobs to keep community prosperous	• Town web site • *Peace River Gazette*	• May be biased to the extent that conclusions are suspect. • Up to date. Should be objective.

Summing up

If you were to continue your research and formulate an informed position in response to the question of the fairest way to resolve the issues that divide the Lubicon Cree and the Alberta and federal governments, what do you think your response would be? Would considering the perspectives identified on your chart influence your position? Explain how.

Figure 1-16

Symbolic white string bracelet is worn by some Buddhists

Made in Canada

Made in Japan

Made in USA

Made in Indonesia

Made in Korea

Made in Thailand

HOW ARE IDENTITIES CONNECTED THROUGH GLOBALIZATION?

One perspective on globalization suggests that it is a process by which the world's citizens are becoming more connected and interdependent. The connections that link people to one another take many forms and are expanding faster than ever before. These connections make everyone more interdependent — and affect everyone's identity.

Think about the wide range of connections in your life. You may not actually travel to China, India, or the United States, but international trade connects you directly to people in these countries. Where, for example, was the shirt or top you are wearing manufactured? Where was the TV program you watched last night produced? What about the banana you ate for breakfast? Where did it come from?

Trade is not the only link between people. You may, for example, share a connection with people in other parts of the world through your religious or spiritual beliefs. Or you may share an enthusiasm for a sport or a particular kind of music.

Coltan and Connected Identities

About half of Canadians — more than 15 million people — owned a cellphone in 2005. One of the components of cellphones is a metal called coltan, which is short for columbite-tantalite. Coltan helps control the flow of electricity in a cellphone's miniature circuits. It serves the same purpose in other electronic equipment, such as laptop computers and MP3 players.

Much of the world's coltan is mined in the eastern region of the Democratic Republic of Congo. This means that when you use a cellphone, boot up your laptop computer, or listen to music you have downloaded, you may be linking your identity with the identity of a Congolese coltan miner.

The rising demand for coltan has increased the value of this metal — and this has sparked conflict in the Democratic Republic of Congo, a country that was already torn by brutal civil wars. To survive, some people turned to coltan mining. But this is dangerous work. Because this metal is so valuable, groups of armed thieves try to steal it. This often places miners' lives in danger.

Figure 1-17 **Democratic Republic of Congo**

Impact of Civil Wars

Number of People Who Have Died: 4 million

Number of Refugees Created: 3 million

Mountain gorillas threatened

Coltan mining also presents another challenge. Much of the DRC's coltan is mined in the Kahuzi-Biega National Park, home of the mountain gorilla. To make mining easier, the land in the area was cleared. This reduced the gorillas' food supply. It also destroyed the way of life of people who lived in the area. Desperate for money, some people have killed gorillas and sold the meat to coltan miners. As a result, the mountain gorilla population has dropped by half.

Coltan mining has also affected gorillas in the DRC's eight other national parks, where the number of eastern lowland gorillas has declined by 90 per cent to about 3000.

Create a flow chart to show how your identity is connected to the identity of coltan miners in the Democratic Republic of Congo. Explain your chart to a partner and be prepared to answer questions about it.

Figure 1-18 Coltan is mined by digging holes in streams. As the miners slosh the water around the hole, the coltan ore settles to the bottom, where it is collected. A team of miners can collect a kilogram of coltan a day. How might the livelihood of miners in the Democratic Republic of Congo be affected if companies stop buying their coltan?

PROFILE

AYSHA WILLS
GLOBAL CITIZEN

PROFILE PROFILE PROFILE PROFILE PROFILE

When a tsunami crashed ashore in Southeast Asia on December 26, 2004, governments, aid organizations, and individuals rushed to help the survivors. By February 2005, however, people had started to forget about the tsunami. But Aysha Wills, who was 10 years old at the time, could not forget. She wanted to help.

Aysha, a musician, asked her teachers at Edmonton's Tempo School to help her organize a benefit concert for the tsunami survivors. Members of the Edmonton Symphony Orchestra, Senator Tommy Banks, and other artists joined her — and raised more than $600 000.

Aysha later explained some of the influences that helped shape her identity.

> I was born in Canada into a family with a Vietnamese-Chinese mom and a New Zealander dad, who had met in Turkey and were living in Hong Kong . . . Luckily, my parents were both very proud of their own cultures and at the same time fascinated by the cultures they had encountered in their many years of travelling. They managed to pass this fascination on to me, and my first five years growing up in Hong Kong gave me opportunities to travel to many countries, to meet people from all over the world and most importantly . . . to eat their food! In fact, food and music are my two favourite things in life, and I love having the chance to hear something new or taste something different.

Figure 1-19 Aysha Wills is the first youth heritage ambassador of the Heritage Community Foundation in Edmonton.

Globalization: Beyond Individual and Collective Identities

In the summer of 2006, people around the world connected with one another through a sporting event. Soccer teams from 32 countries, including Germany, Italy, France, Japan, Ghana, Brazil, and Saudi Arabia, went to Germany to play in the finals of the World Cup. Team supporters, in their home country or in the country to which they had immigrated, identified with their teams and celebrated their participation.

Thanks to global communication systems, a shared interest connected soccer fans around the world. For a couple of weeks, these fans formed a global collective. The World Cup is just one example of the vast and growing network of interconnections that shape — and are shaped by — the lives and identities of people everywhere.

The identities of people around the world are also connected through membership in other collectives. These collectives may be created as a result of shared interests or goals. People who are interested in the environment can connect through organizations such as the Sierra Club or Greenpeace, and people who are interested in humanitarian causes can connect through groups such as Amnesty International, Médecins sans frontières, and World Vision.

Collectives may also be created to celebrate and promote a shared language or culture. La Francophonie, for example, is a group of countries and governments that are connected through their shared French language or culture. Canada is a member of la Francophonie, as are the provinces of Québec and New Brunswick, where French is widely spoken.

No matter what their purpose, however, global collectives like these help countries and individuals affirm and promote aspects of their identity and share their perspectives with others.

Figure 1-20 On July 9, 2006, these soccer fans in Québec City were among an estimated 1.2 billion people, or 17 per cent of the world's population, who watched the final game of the World Cup of Soccer. The game between France and Italy took place in Berlin, Germany, but was watched on TV by people around the world. What technology helped link these fans?

Opportunities and Challenges of Making Global Connections

Many people believe that these growing connections and interdependence enable people from diverse backgrounds and cultures to connect and communicate in a way that expands their individual identity and promotes understanding and co-operation.

But do global connections and interdependence always lead to positive results? Many people worry that they do not. They believe that globalization is reducing diversity — that people's distinct identities, both individual and collective, are disappearing. They say that globalization will erase the differences between peoples.

For some, balancing the pressures of globalization presents one of the great challenges of the 21st century.

How does globalization shape — and how is it shaped by — the culture and identity of people around the world? Here is how three people have tried to grapple with this question.

Satya Das is an Edmonton journalist who was born in India and immigrated to Canada as a young boy. The following excerpt is from his book *Dispatches from a Borderless World*.

Who are you? The answer to this question takes many forms in a borderless world. Do we define ourselves as individuals or as part of a collective identity? Do we define ourselves by ethnicity, citizenship and racial origin?

In Canada … the fundamental question of identity has many answers. In accommodating the diversity of the world, Canada has bound itself to a momentous human experiment, a constructive exercise in living together. A Canadian identity, both individual and collective, offers a fascinating foundation for explorations and encounters in a borderless world …

Kofi Annan, who is from Ghana, was secretary-general of the United Nations when he made the following remarks in a speech that opened the 1999 Francophonie Summit in Moncton, New Brunswick.

It is often said nowadays that although globalization brings us closer to one another, there is a danger that it may also turn our world into a place of dreary uniformity. Moreover, although globalization promises increased prosperity, it at the same time continues to widen existing gaps. These paradoxical trends have, understandably, led to considerable confusion. The general feeling is that globalization carries with it tremendous potential, but that some of its aspects require careful management …

Long Litt Woon was born in Malaysia but now lives in Norway and has been active in a variety of organizations that deal with international migration and gender issues.

I am originally from Malaysia, but I obtained my degree in social anthropology at the university in Oslo. I have work experience from both the Norwegian central administration and from the private sector. I have been the Norwegian representative to the Council of Europe's steering committee for migration for several years. Until recently I was the director of the Norwegian Centre for Gender Equality. Currently, I am the co-founder and director of a consulting firm specializing in organisational development and diversity management …

I am often asked how long I have lived [in Norway]. "Twenty years," I say. The next remark often is, "Oh, you are almost Norwegian!"

The assumption here is that I have become less Malaysian because it is common to think about identity as a zero-sum game; if you have more of one identity, you have less of another. Identity is somehow imagined to be like a square box with a fixed size.

Explorations

1. With a partner, examine the words of these three speakers. What evidence do the word choices of each speaker offer about his or her point of view on how globalization shapes cultural identity — and vice versa?

2. In small groups, use the three excerpts as the starting point of a brainstorming session to develop answers to this question: To what extent should we embrace globalization?

1. You express different aspects of identity in different situations. When your teacher, for example, asks you to introduce yourself to the class at the beginning of the school year, you might respond by giving your name (aspect = family), your age (aspect = personal history), and your cultural background (aspect = heritage). List three aspects of your identity that you might highlight in each of the following situations:

a) A police officer stops you at a concert and asks who you are.

b) A potential employer asks you to describe yourself during a job interview.

c) An aunt whom you have never met arrives for a visit and asks you to tell her about yourself.

d) You are hoping to join the school swim team, and the coach asks how your belonging to the team will help it.

e) You are new at the school and are introducing yourself to a group of students at a lunch table.

2. Observe a group of adults and a group of teens in similar settings. The two groups may be at a mall or restaurant, waiting in line for an event, at a concert, at a house of worship or spiritual gathering, or in another setting. Observe things like

- the clothing worn by the members of the two groups
- their body adornments
- their actions
- their body language (e.g., distance from one another, gestures, facial expressions)
- the language(s) spoken
- other aspects of identity expressed

Record your observations on a chart like the one on this page.

Compare your observations with those of a partner. Discuss the aspects of identity revealed by people in the groups you observed. Decide whether these aspects represented their individual identity or their identity as a member of a collective — or both.

Work with your partner to write a statement that sums up your conclusions (e.g., The teens were strongly expressing their individuality, but the adults were showing how well they fit into their collective).

Read your statement to the class. Compare your statement with those of others. How are the statements the same? How are they different?

Group and Setting	Observations
Five adults All female, having coffee at a food court	1. Dressed casually: most in jeans and sneakers 2. Laughing 3. 4.

3. In this chapter, you read about Aysha Wills, who organized a concert to help survivors of the 2004 Southeast Asian tsunami. Choose a project that you believe could make a difference to your community (e.g., cleaning up a park) or farther afield (e.g., helping people in another community). Present your idea to a small group and listen to the ideas of other group members. Work with the group to narrow down the list to one choice. Make a list of steps that you and your group would need to take to make the project a reality.

4. In Western countries, every generation of teens develops and presents its own identity through music, fashion, slang, body adornment, choice of pop stars, and other culture-specific ideas and items. In the 1950s, for example, teenagers idolized Elvis Presley and his hip movements and slicked-back hair. In the 1960s, Bob Dylan, the Beatles, and the Rolling Stones were influential rock stars.

Work with a partner to research the fads and fashions, stars, and entertainment that helped shape the identity of the teens of one of these decades: the 1960s, 1970s, 1980s, or 1990s.

a) Develop four questions you will use to help you determine whether the item or person was an identity shaper or merely a passing fad (e.g., Did the fashion last more than two years? Was it picked up in other countries?).

b) Decide where you might find information on teens in the decade you have chosen (e.g., the Internet, used-book stores, family photographs, the library). Note the reliability of each of the sources you choose to use for your research.

c) Decide on the areas you will research. You may, for example, look into food, fashion, and entertainment. Your partner may research music, fads, and pop stars.

d) Use presentation software to prepare a report that demonstrates the forces that shaped teen identity in the decade you chose. In your report, be sure to explain the connection between what was happening in teen culture and how this was reflected in the way teens expressed their identity. Include the country of origin of the fashion, fad, music, or other items you chose and explain how this affected teens in Canada

5. "This treeless landscape that seems arid and cold is very beautiful and bountiful to us. It is wide open. It is part of us and we are part of it. With time, we learned to read it the same way you learned to read the writing in books."

Film director Bobby Kenuajuak, who is Inuit, said this in an interview about his 1999 film, *My Village in Nunavik.* It expresses his feelings about the importance of the Arctic environment in shaping who he became.

Develop a two-minute oral presentation that

- describes the environment where you grew up
- explains how this environment has shaped your identity
- convinces your audience that environmental factors are important in shaping identity

For your presentation, obtain photos, create drawings, or use other images to illustrate your points.

Think about Your Challenge

Look back at the challenge for this related issue. It asks you to develop a presentation that explains your position on this issue: To what extent should globalization shape identity?

Review the material in this chapter and the activities you completed as you progressed through the chapter. Make notes about ideas that could be useful in completing the challenge. Begin developing the criteria and critical questions you will use to evaluate the data you will explore and use in your presentation.

Chapter 2 Identity and the Forces of Globalization

Figure 2-1   Forces like trade, transportation, communication technology, and international media have increased the pace of globalization and changed what you buy, watch, and read, how you communicate, where you go, and how you get there. These changes have shaped — and been shaped by — people's individual and collective identity.

CHAPTER ISSUE

To what extent do identity and the forces of globalization shape each other?

YOU WON'T FIND the word "glocal" in dictionaries. At least, not yet. But enter this word in an Internet search engine, and you will get hundreds of thousands of hits.

What might this one example of a word that is widely used but does not yet appear in dictionaries tell you about the pace of change sparked by the forces of globalization? "Glocal" combines the words "global" and "local" to create a new word that expresses how the global and the local are related. It sums up the idea that things that happen at a global level, such as international trade, affect things that happen at a local level, such as what you buy in local stores — and vice versa. In other words, the globalizing world shapes your everyday life and your everyday life shapes the globalizing world.

Examine the photographs on the previous page. Each shows a force that links the global and the local.

- What forces do you think the photographs show?
- How do you think each connects the global and the local?
- How do these connections affect your everyday life, your relationships with family and friends, and your views on global and local events — your identity?

KEY TERMS

transnational corporation

media concentration

media convergence

economies of scale

biodiversity

homogenization

acculturation

accommodation

assimilation

cultural revitalization

LOOKING AHEAD

In this chapter, you will explore answers to the following questions:

- What are some forces of globalization?
- How is identity affected by some economic, political, environmental, and social dimensions of globalization?
- How do some forces of globalization present challenges to identity?
- How do some forces of globalization provide opportunities to affirm and promote identity?

My Point of View on Globalization

Look back at the notes you recorded at the beginning of Chapter 1. Have your understandings of globalization changed since then? Use words or images — or both — to explain how. Date your ideas and add them to the notebook, learning log, portfolio, or computer file you are keeping as you progress through this course.

WHAT ARE SOME FORCES OF GLOBALIZATION?

Did you eat a banana or an orange for breakfast today? Did you season your eggs with pepper? Spread peanut butter on your toast? If you did any of these things, you were taking part in the same exchange of goods that has connected people around the world for thousands of years.

Bananas, oranges, and pepper do not grow in Canada. And though a small number of farmers in southern Ontario grow peanuts, they do not produce nearly enough to supply the demand across the country. Yet Canadians can enjoy these foods — and many others — because of international trade.

International trade is a major globalizing force — a power that promotes change. But trade is not the only globalizing force at work in the world. Transportation, communication technology, and the media have all speeded up the pace at which the world's people are becoming interconnected and interdependent. How do you think this growing interconnectedness and interdependence affects your individual and collective identity?

Trade as a Globalizing Force

People have always reached out to others to obtain things they cannot grow or make themselves. In North America, for example, some areas of the Eastern Arctic are rich in soapstone, a soft rock that can be easily carved. At the same time, wood is scarce. So the Inuit of the Eastern Arctic reached out to other Aboriginal groups, such as the James Bay Cree, who lived farther south, where wood was more plentiful. The Inuit traded their soapstone for wood.

In the same way as the Inuit connected with nearby peoples through the exchange of goods, people who live in different parts of the world have connected with one another through trade for thousands of years. People trade with one another to obtain goods and services that are

- not available in their own region
- better quality or less expensive
- different from goods produced at home

Trade goods may be anything from natural resources, such as lumber and oil, to clothing, car parts, agricultural products, and stocks and bonds. Goods may be imported into a country from other countries — or exported out of a country to other countries.

Except in a small area of southern Ontario, for example, the Canadian climate is unsuitable for growing peanuts. So Canadian supermarkets import peanuts grown in the United States and other countries, such as China. At the same time, Canada is rich in oil, which is exported to the United States and other countries.

Figure 2-2 Creating soapstone sculptures is a traditional Inuit art. This carving, titled *Bird Creature*, was created in 1990 by Inuit artist Kiawak Ashoona, who lives near Cape Dorset, Nunavut. How do carvings like this link the identity of today's Inuit with their heritage?

Figure 2-3 During summer, when the weather is warmer, many Inuit once lived in tents like this, photographed in 1915. This photograph also shows one way the Inuit used wood. What other uses might the Inuit have had for wood? Why would they have prized wood so highly? Does this reflect Inuit lives today?

Transnational corporations and international trade

You probably recognize the logos on this page. All three are symbols that represent familiar "Canadian" companies — but none is now owned by Canadians.

The Hudson's Bay Company, North America's oldest corporation, was sold to American billionaire Jerry Zucker in 2006. Zellers, which was founded during the Great Depression of the 1930s and later bought by the Bay, went to Zucker in the same sale. Tim Hortons was founded by and named for Tim Horton, a Stanley Cup–winning Toronto Maple Leaf defenceman in the 1960s. This company was sold to the American fast-food chain Wendy's International in 1995. Where do you think the decisions about running these companies are now made?

A business like Wendy's is a **transnational corporation** — also called a multinational corporation. A transnational corporation is a company that is based in one country while developing and manufacturing its products, or delivering its goods and services, in more than one country. Transnationals such as Wendy's, Wal-Mart, Nike, Coca-Cola, McDonald's, Microsoft, Dole, Del Monte, and Daishowa provide goods and services to Canadians and other people around the world every day.

This means that when you buy a donut at Tim Hortons or a banana at your neighbourhood supermarket, you are participating in the global economy. How is this so?

Transnationals and globalization

Transnational corporations play an important role in the globalization process. Companies like McDonald's, Coca-Cola, and Nike sell fast food, soft drinks, and shoes around the world. In many countries, they provide training and jobs for people who might not otherwise have work.

But critics of transnationals say that the jobs are often "McJobs": low-level positions that require little skill and provide few opportunities to advance. Critics also argue that the profits earned by transnationals, such as Daishowa Paper Manufacturing of Japan and Coca-Cola of the United States, go to the country where the company has its headquarters. The profits do not benefit the people of the country where the goods are actually made or sold.

If you ran a transnational corporation, what do you think your three most important goals would be? Rate these goals in order of importance. With a partner or group, discuss the goals you identified. Are your lists and ratings the same or different? What might account for the similarities and differences?

Figure 2-4 These commercial logos are probably familiar to most Canadians, and all three companies were Canadian-owned at one time. They are now owned by American companies. Does it matter that so many "Canadian" businesses are owned by American corporations?

CHECKBACK

You read about the Japanese company Daishowa Paper Manufacturing in Chapter 1 when you learned about the struggle of the Lubicon Cree to affirm their identity.

FYI

Of the world's top 500 transnational corporations based on total revenues, 170 are in the United States, 70 in Japan, 38 in Britain, 38 in France, 35 in Germany, and 14 in Canada.

FYI

Although Canadian author Douglas Coupland did not coin the word "McJob," he made it popular in his 1991 book, *Generation X: Tales for an Accelerated Culture.* A play on the McDonald's brand name, this bit of slang pokes fun at the company's habit of adding the prefix "Mc" to its products (e.g., McMuffin). "McJob" is defined in *Merriam-Webster's Collegiate Dictionary* as "a low-paying job that requires little skill and provides little opportunity for advancement."

Transportation as a Globalizing Force

Transportation is essential for trade. Over the millennia, various forms of transportation — people, camels, draft horses, carts, ships, trains, trucks, and planes — have been used to move products to market, the place where they are sold.

Today, products can be moved farther and faster than ever before. About 40 per cent of the world's trade goods are shipped in containers: large metal shipping boxes built in standard sizes so they can be sealed, then transferred easily from one form of transport, such as a ship, to another, such as a truck or train. At any time, about 18 million containers are moving across the world's seas and oceans.

Containers revolutionized the shipping industry when they were introduced in the late 1950s. Until then, stevedores — people who load and unload ships — usually moved crates and cartons piece by piece onto ships. Twenty stevedores could load about 20 tonnes in an hour.

Goods are now loaded into containers. Cranes then hoist the containers on and off specially designed ships such as the *Emma Maersk*, shown in the photograph. In a few minutes, a crew of 10 can load 40 tonnes of goods onto a container ship.

Containers made it much cheaper and faster to ship goods over long distances. It also made shipping more reliable because it is easier to keep track of one large container than many smaller crates and cartons. It is also harder to steal goods from a sealed container. How do you think cheaper, faster, and more reliable transportation affects the price of goods? How might this affect your identity as a consumer?

The container revolution of the last half of the 20th century speeded up the globalizing process. "Low transport costs help make it economically sensible for a factory in China to produce Barbie dolls with Japanese hair, Taiwanese plastics and American colorants, and ship them off to eager girls all over the world," wrote Marc Levinson in *The Box: How the Shipping Container Made the World Smaller and the World Economy Bigger*. As a result, containers are sometimes called the building blocks of the global village.

Other transportation changes, such as the development of passenger jets after World War II, also meant that people could move around the world much more quickly and easily. This development also increased the pace of globalization. How do you think travel might have done this?

Figure 2-5 When the *Emma Maersk* was launched, it was the biggest container ship ever built. Nearly as long as four Canadian football fields and wider than the Panama Canal, this floating giant can carry up to 11 000 20-foot (6.1 m) containers. The containers are transferred to trucks, trains, and even planes, which carry them to local markets. How might the availability of larger volumes of imported goods affect your buying decisions — and your individual and collective identity?

How does the subtitle of Marc Levinson's book capture the importance of containers to the globalizing process? On a two-column chart, list people who might have benefited — and those who might have suffered — because of the container revolution. Discuss your ideas with a partner, then revise your chart to reflect changes that resulted from this discussion.

MAERSK LINE

Communication Technology as a Globalizing Force

Just as containers revolutionized the way goods are transported, so the computer revolutionized the way information flows. The development of computers took a big leap forward during World War II, but these early machines were huge, complex, and very expensive to build. They could be operated only by highly trained experts, and only businesses, governments, and the military could afford to run them. This began to change when the first personal computers — computers that were simple enough for individuals to buy and use — appeared in the late 1970s.

Since then, advances in digital technology, which involves changing data into numerical digits that can be processed by a computer, have allowed these machines to become cheaper, smaller, more powerful, and even easier to operate. The digital technologies that sparked advances in computers also paved the way for the development of other devices, such as cellphones, MP3 players, and digital cameras.

The Internet and the World Wide Web

The Internet is a network that connects millions of personal computers around the world. But when the Internet was first created, it was slow and awkward to use. This changed when the World Wide Web developed in the 1990s.

The Web is a system of Internet servers that support specially formatted documents that can be linked to other documents — and to graphic, audio, and video files. This new tool made accessing the Internet much easier, and more and more people started going online.

Because of the World Wide Web, a business can now go online to seek out a supplier, who might be anywhere in the world. The business can then remain online to view pictures of the product, request and compare prices, place an order, and receive notice of when to expect delivery. And the growing popularity of portable wireless devices, such as cellphones, laptop computers, and personal digital assistants, or PDAs, means that the people involved in the transaction could be sitting in an office — or they could be at home, in a coffee shop, or in a park kilometres away from the office.

Examine the bar graphs on this page. What trends do the statistics reveal? Do you think the trends shown on the graphs will change in the future? Check the Internet to see whether changes have already occurred. Does access to the Internet and the World Wide Web affect your understanding of the world today? How? How do you think the changes you predicted might affect your individual and collective identity in the future? Explain the reasons for your predictions.

CHECKFORWARD

You will read more about communication technology and globalization in Chapter 3.

FYI

Canadian James Gosling played an important role in the development of the World Wide Web. As a teenager in Calgary, Gosling was fascinated by computers and even wrote software for the University of Calgary's physics department. As an adult, he went to work for Sun Microsystems, a California company. There, he invented the Java programming language, which is used on the World Wide Web.

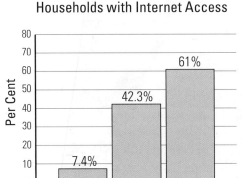

Figure 2-6   **Percentage of Canadian Households with Internet Access**

- 1996: 7.4%
- 2000: 42.3%
- 2005: 61%

Source: Statistics Canada

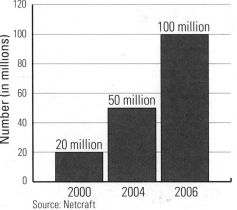

Figure 2-7   **Growth in Number of Web Sites on the Internet**

- 2000: 20 million
- 2004: 50 million
- 2006: 100 million

Source: Netcraft

MHR • To what extent do identity and the forces of globalization shape each other?

CheckForward

You will learn more about the media as a globalizing force that affects identity in Chapter 3.

The Media as a Globalizing Force

When the World Wide Web developed, individuals, businesses, governments, and organizations began to understand its potential as an interactive communication tool that could be used to broadcast — and gather — information. People now go online to do things like banking, shopping, taking courses, conducting research, playing games, blogging, communicating with friends and online acquaintances, listening to music, and watching videos.

Newspapers, for example, began to publish online editions that people could read on their home computers. If you want to read about the Chinese government's response to a world event, for example, you can check the online edition of the *People's Daily*, which publishes versions in Chinese, English, French, Arabic, and other languages. Readers can even e-mail comments that are published on the paper's web site. How might the ability to read about events in a newspaper from another country, as well as the comments of other readers, affect your understanding of an issue?

Ideas

How are the ideas expressed by the word "glocal" reflected in your identity?

The students responding to this question are Marie, a Francophone student from Medicine Hat; Deven, who was born in India but is now a Canadian who lives in Calgary; and Gord, a member of the Beaver First Nation near High Level.

My parents are always talking about how things were different when they were growing up — no French-language TV stations, and no Internet. Now, we have a satellite dish, so I can watch loads of things in French, and a lot of web sites are in French. I can do things in French that my parents never could. So I'd say that the "glocalizing" force of technology has made it easier for me, here in Medicine Hat, to be a Francophone.

Marie

I live "glocally" every day. In Calgary, immigrants like me and my parents have created a demand for Indian products that used to be quite hard to get — and stores have opened to meet this demand. So we can buy imported CDs of Indian music, DVDs of Indian movies, and the ingredients for just about any Indian food we want to make, plus lots of other stuff. This makes it much easier to maintain our identity.

Deven

Yeah, globalization shapes me — but I also try to shape globalization. I get this from my parents. They make a point of buying things from local stores, and so do I. Right now, this is pretty easy because not many transnationals operate on our reserve or in High Level. If they did, buying locally might be a harder choice. But I think we'd stick to our principles, because they're an important part of our identity.

Gord

Your Turn

How would you respond to the question Marie, Deven, and Gord are answering? Do you think globalization shapes you more — or less — than you shape globalization? Explain the reasons for your judgment.

Digital technology also allows signals to be sent to communication satellites in space, then bounced back to receivers on Earth. This is the technology that enabled people around the world to gather at the same time in front of TV sets to watch live satellite transmissions of the 2006 World Cup soccer games. It also enables news organizations such as the BBC, CNN, Al-Jazeera, and the CBC to broadcast their programs around the world. What news programs do you watch or listen to? Do these choices help shape an aspect of your identity? If so, how?

CHECKBACK

You read about satellite transmissions of World Cup games in Chapter 1.

Media concentration and convergence

Since the 1980s, two trends — **media concentration** and **media convergence** — have changed the way newspapers, television, and cable services operate. "Concentration" refers to a trend that concentrates ownership of newspapers and other media in the hands of a few large corporations. "Convergence" refers to the use of electronic technology to integrate media such as newspapers, books, TV, and the Internet. It enables print and broadcast media to work together to develop stories and create content for their web sites. These two trends, concentration and convergence, have become stronger since the Web became a force in communications.

In Canada, for example, CTVglobemedia now owns *The Globe and Mail*, Canada's biggest national newspaper, as well as CTV, the country's biggest privately owned TV network. Through these properties, CTVglobemedia also owns Report on Business Television, TSN, radio stations, and other media.

CanWest Global Communications, which owns the Global Television Network, also owns a chain of newspapers that include the *Edmonton Journal* and the *Calgary Herald*, as well as a controlling interest in Alliance Atlantis Communications, Canada's biggest entertainment company. And Quebecor, a huge Québec-based printing company, added to its holdings by buying another newspaper chain that includes the *Edmonton Sun* and the *Calgary Sun*.

Critics of media concentration and convergence believe that these trends encourage the news media to reduce the number of reporters and other staff they employ. They also believe that concentration and convergence reduce the diversity of voices in Canada and around the world. How might a reduction in the diversity of media voices affect your identity? Would these effects be positive or negative? Why?

VOICES

Thirty years ago, when I started working [in the media], 40 per cent of English and 50 per cent of French-language daily newspapers in Canada were independently owned. Today, 96 per cent of those papers are in chains; that means they are owned by corporations. CanWest Global owns 50 per cent [of those]. Only three daily newspapers in Canada — the *Winnipeg Free Press*, the *White Horse Star*, and Montréal's *Le Devoir* — are privately owned.

— *Dave McLauchlin, CBC Radio journalist, in 2003.*

REFLECT AND RESPOND

Create a T-chart like the one shown. In the first column, identify three globalizing forces and how they shape your identity. In the second column, briefly explain how your identity shapes each force. An example is filled in for you. When you finish, compare your chart with that of a partner. Work together to add two more items to your charts.

| GLOBALIZING FORCES AND MY IDENTITY | |
Shape My Identity	Are Shaped by My Identity
International trade means there is a wider selection of goods in local stores for me to choose from — and what I choose to buy is part of my identity.	What I buy in local stores affects demand for products, and this influences the products that are traded internationally.

How is identity affected by some economic, political, environmental, and social dimensions of globalization?

If you have peeled and eaten a banana this week, you are like many other Canadians. Canadians eat about three billion bananas a year — about 100 bananas a person. After apples, bananas are the most popular fruit in Canada. What factors do you think contribute to this popularity?

Unlike apples, bananas do not grow in Canada. Most bananas sold in Europe and North America are imported from developing countries in Central and South America, where they are a source of controversy for many reasons. Banana production is one example of the forces of globalization at work — and of how the economic, political, environmental, and social dimensions of these forces affect, and are affected by, people's identity.

Figure 2-8 These bananas were marketed by Chiquita Brands, an American transnational corporation that is one of the biggest players in the international banana trade. Three American-based transnationals — Chiquita, Dole, and Del Monte — control most of the world's banana exports. How might this concentration of control in the hands of a few companies help or hurt Canadian consumers?

Identity and Some Economic Dimensions of Globalization

For many Canadians, price is an important factor in buying decisions — and low prices help explain the popularity of bananas in Canada. Bananas are the cheapest fruit sold in Canadian supermarkets. A kilogram of apples, for example, can cost more than $3, while a kilo of bananas can usually be purchased for less than $1.50.

Many economic factors contribute to the price difference between apples, which are grown in Canada, and bananas, which grow in the tropics and must be shipped at least 5000 kilometres before they can be sold in Canadian supermarkets. The following factors help keep banana prices low for Canadian consumers:

- Most bananas sold in Canada are grown on huge plantations owned or controlled by transnational corporations. This enables the transnationals to take advantage of **economies of scale** — savings that come from producing, using, and buying things in large quantities.
- On plantations, banana yields are often high because of heavy use of chemical fertilizers and pesticides. This means that the supply — the number of bananas grown — is often greater than the demand — the number of bananas customers order. This leads to reduced prices.
- The transnationals also reduce their costs by controlling many of the ships, containers, and warehouses that are part of the banana distribution network. Transnationals can give themselves a deal and keep the profits in the company. Labour in Central and South America is cheap, and few workers are protected by union agreements This keeps wages low.

Figure 2-9 **From Ecuador to Canada**

Banana plantation
Grown for 9 months
Picked, sorted,
and transported to packing house

⌄

Packing house
Cleaned, packaged, and transported to port

⌄

Export port
Placed in sealed container and loaded
onto container ship

⌄

Import port
Still in containers, are transferred to trucks for
distribution to supermarket warehouses

⌄

Supermarket warehouse
Ripened for 8 to 10 days and shipped
to individual stores

Ecuador, bananas, and the economics of globalization

Ecuador exports more bananas than any other country — and is the leading exporter of the bananas that are sold in North American supermarkets. If you ate a banana today, chances are that it grew in Ecuador. This is because bananas from Ecuador are cheap.

Ecuadorean bananas are cheap because the cost of producing them is low. One reason costs are low is that Ecuadorean banana workers are the lowest-paid in Latin America. In 2002, male banana-plantation workers earned about $6.40 Cdn a day. Women were paid even less, and children were sometimes not paid at all. There was no overtime pay, and few workers received benefits, such as paid vacations and sick leave.

Figure 2-10 **Ecuador**

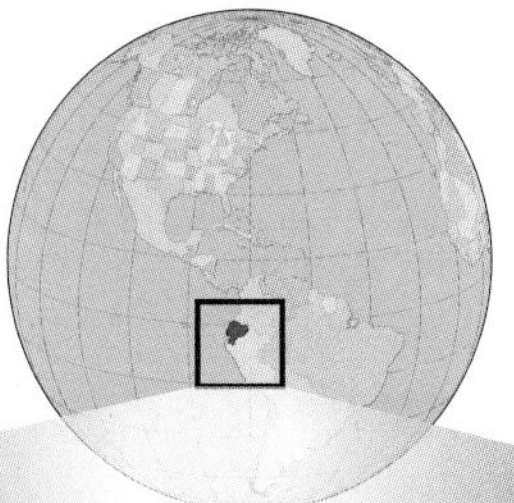

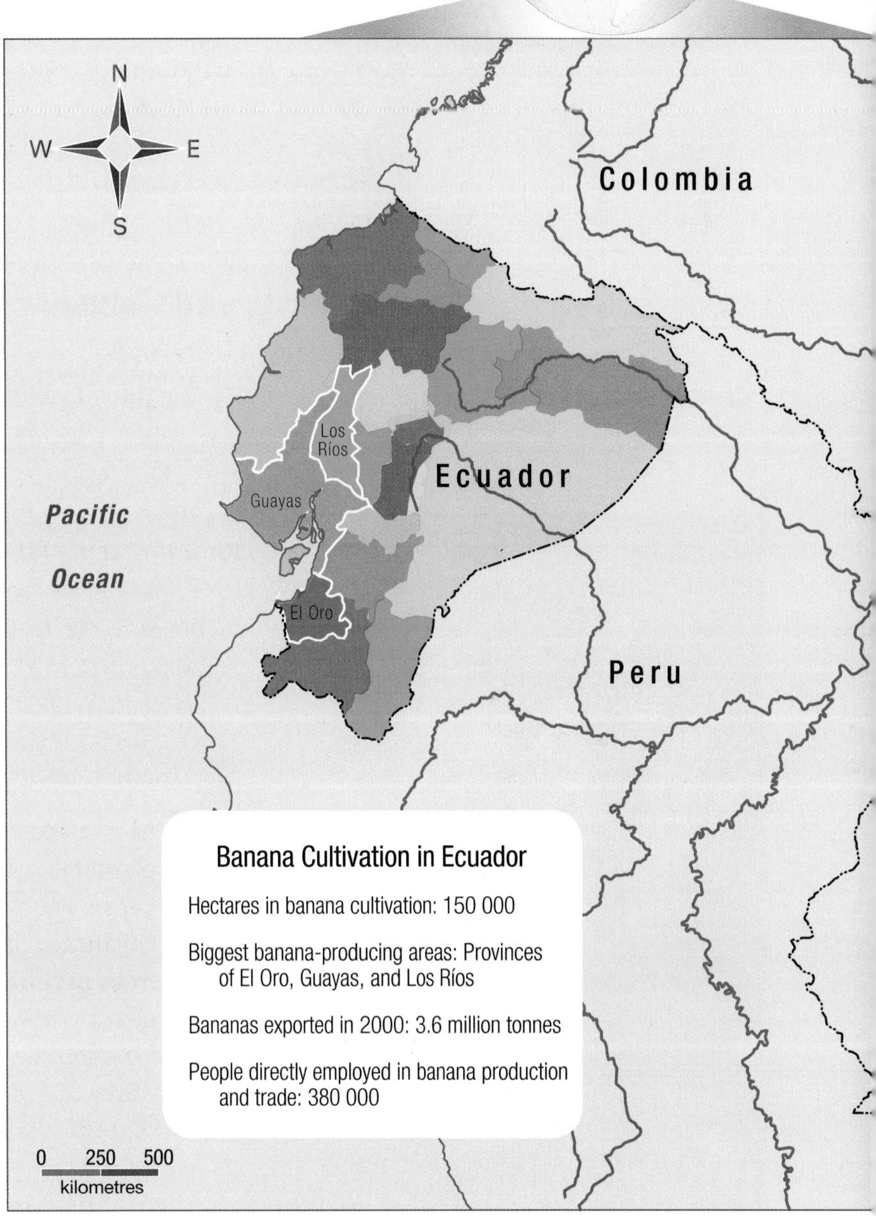
N
S
W
E
Colombia
Ecuador
Peru
Pacific
Ocean
Los Ríos
Guayas
El Oro
Banana Cultivation in Ecuador
Hectares in banana cultivation: 150 000
Biggest banana-producing areas: Provinces of El Oro, Guayas, and Los Ríos
Bananas exported in 2000: 3.6 million tonnes
People directly employed in banana production and trade: 380 000
0 250 500
kilometres

Calculate how much a male Ecuadorean banana-plantation worker who spent six days a week on the job would make in a month. (Multiply his weekly earnings by 4.3, the number of weeks in a month.) The Ecuadorean government estimated that a family of four needed at least $220 (Cdn.) a month to meet basic needs. How did the worker's monthly earnings compare with this minimum?

Although Ecuadorean laws are supposed to protect workers, these laws are often ignored. Workers who try to form a union to fight for better conditions are often fired, and their names are put on a blacklist. No one else in the banana industry will hire blacklisted workers, so they have an even harder time earning a living.

In the past few years, the situation has improved somewhat, but working conditions are still poor. To survive, many Ecuadorean families must put their children to work in the banana fields. As a result, children are either often absent from school or do not go to school at all. In 2002, Human Rights Watch, a non-profit organization that monitors human rights around the world, interviewed a group of 45 child banana workers. The children worked an average of 12 hours a day, and most had started working when they were between the ages of 8 and 13. Less than 40 per cent were still in school.

Does education help people define who they are as individuals and collectives? Does education help define aspects of your identity? How might a lack of schooling create a cycle that affects the individual and collective identity of child banana workers in Ecuador?

CheckForward

You will read more about child labour and globilization in Chapters 5 and 14.

Identity and Some Political Dimensions of Globalization

A continuing dispute over bananas shows how economic concerns often affect political decisions — and vice versa.

In many Central and South American countries, banana production is largely controlled by the big three American transnationals: Chiquita, Dole, and Del Monte. But bananas are also grown in Caribbean countries, such as Jamaica and St. Lucia. In these countries, farms are smaller and are often run as family businesses. These small farms cannot achieve the same economies of scale as huge banana plantations. As a result, their costs are higher. To make money, they must sell their bananas at higher prices than the transnationals.

The "banana wars"

During the 1990s, European governments agreed to continue extending an economic helping hand to former colonies, such as Jamaica and St. Lucia, by giving preferred treatment to bananas imported from these countries. No tariffs — taxes or duties — were placed on these bananas. At the same time, bananas from other countries were taxed and subjected to other strict import rules.

Few of the banana plantations controlled by the leading transnationals were in countries that received preferred treatment. As a result, most of the bananas produced by the transnationals were taxed when they entered Europe. They also had to abide by other strict rules. How would the European policy have helped small banana farmers compete against cheaper bananas controlled by transnational corporations?

This situation sparked a trade conflict that has been called the "banana wars." The transnationals protested the European policy, saying that it was unfair. An American company, Chiquita, persuaded the United States government to take the case to the World Trade Organization, or WTO — even though no bananas are grown in the continental United States.

About 150 countries, including Canada, the United States, Britain, and France, belong to the WTO, which governs how its members trade with one another. WTO rules say that member countries must treat one another equally. A country cannot, for example, impose a tariff on goods from one member country but not on those of another.

Web Connection

The "banana wars" were an international trade conflict that pitted governments against one another. To learn more about the economic and political dimensions of this conflict, go to this web site and follow the links.

www.ExploringGlobalization.ca

Figure 2-11 This worker is preparing for the harvest on a banana plantation in Costa Rica. What might his interest in the "banana wars" have been?

The WTO and the banana wars

In 1997, the WTO ruled that European countries must change some of the trade rules that helped banana farmers in their former colonies. But these changes did not go far enough to satisfy the American transnationals. To try to force even more changes, the American government imposed tariffs on many European exports to the United States. How might these tariffs have become weapons in the banana wars? Who would be hurt by these weapons? Why? How might these economic measures influence the political decisions made by European governments?

In response, European countries changed their banana-importing system again to make it easier to import bananas from all countries. Though these changes eased the conflict, they did not end the dispute.

CHECK FORWARD

You will read more about the WTO and its role in globalization in Chapter 9.

MAKING CHOICES

MAKING CHOICES MAKING CHOICES MAKING CHOICES

GUILLERMO TOUMA
SPEAKING OUT ABOUT THE BANANA TRADE

When Ecuadorean Guillermo Touma was 14, he started working on a banana plantation during his summer holidays. By the time he was 18, he was a full-time banana worker. For the next 17 years, he worked long hours for low pay on a banana plantation.

This experience transformed Touma. He became convinced that banana workers must unite to seek better conditions, and he now leads Ecuador's very small banana workers' union. One of his strategies is to work with other unions and non-profit groups such as Banana Link, which is dedicated to raising global awareness of conditions in the banana trade.

"Sadly, everyone profits so much from bananas except the people who work in the fields," Touma told *The Guardian*, a British newspaper. "We suffer, yet the supermarkets and the companies are very rich. Consumers in Europe and elsewhere must find a way to help. We need a fairer system, one which benefits the employees. We are paying the price in Ecuador to bring you good fruit."

Figure 2-12 Guillermo Touma is general secretary of the Equadorean Confederation of Free Trade Union Organizations. A former banana plantation worker, Touma is trying to improve conditions for Ecuadoreans who help grow and harvest bananas. "Seeing all the exploitation there, I became convinced that only the setting up of a trade union could help improve the quality of life," he has said. "That is why I became a union leader in the 1970s."

Explorations

1. If you wished to take action to help banana workers, what might the most appropriate action be? What criteria might you use to decide this?

   Some groups believe that boycotting — refusing to buy — bananas produced by transnationals with poor labour records will bring about change by reducing the profits of these corporations.

   In a small group, plan steps you could take to lead a successful boycott in your community. Think about how you will identify the product and the transnational you wish to target, and how you might persuade consumers to join the boycott.

   How would you measure the success of your boycott?

2. What might be some unintended consequences of a boycott like this? Do you believe that a boycott is the best way of achieving the goal of improving conditions for workers?

Identity and Some Environmental Dimensions of Globalization

In 1992, a historic meeting took place in Rio de Janeiro, Brazil. Its full name was the United Nations Conference on Environment and Development, but it was also known as the Earth Summit. At this meeting, representatives of governments and other organizations talked about how they could encourage economic development — while protecting the environment.

The Earth Summit marked a turning point in awareness of environmental issues. One area people began to focus on was large-scale agriculture, which is sometimes called agribusiness. Banana production controlled by transnationals is an example of agribusiness.

Banana production and the environment

To create large areas for growing bananas, tropical forests must be cut down. The loss of forests leads to soil erosion and flooding. It also destroys the natural habitat of plants and animals, reducing **biodiversity** — variety in plant and animal species. In Costa Rica, for example, about 60 per cent of the country's rainforests have been cut down to clear land for banana plantations and other agricultural uses. Some environmentalists estimate that, as a result, nearly 18 per cent of tree species in that country may disappear.

In addition, the large plantations controlled by transnationals produce just one variety of banana: the Cavendish. This variety is the most popular with North American and European consumers because of its taste and texture. But focusing on growing just one variety of banana means that pests and diseases can spread quickly and wipe out the crop.

Like many other agricultural producers, many banana plantations use synthetic fertilizers to keep crops healthy, maintain high production levels, and ensure that the bananas shipped to North American and European supermarkets appeal to consumers because they are similar in size and free of blemishes. Many banana plantations also apply large volumes of synthetic pesticides — chemicals that kill insects and other pests — and synthetic herbicides — chemicals that kill plants that can interfere with the growth of the bananas.

Many of these chemicals are considered hazardous to human health — and applying them puts the health of workers at risk. In addition, the fertilizers, pesticides, and herbicides run off into rivers, lakes, and oceans, poisoning fish, birds, and other wildlife.

Some banana growers, especially those in Caribbean countries, have always grown their crops organically — without using synthetic chemicals. And some transnational corporations have taken steps to improve their environmental record. Dole, for example, has switched to producing organic bananas on some of its plantations.

Organic bananas are more environmentally friendly, but they are expensive to produce. As a result, they usually cost at least twice as much. Would you pay twice as much to buy organic bananas? What criteria would you use to help you make this decision? How would this decision affect your identity? The identity of banana workers?

FYI

Cavendish bananas, the most popular variety in North America and Europe, are sterile: they produce no seeds. New plants are created by planting shoots cut from plants that are already growing. This means that farmers have no seeds if the crop is destroyed by pests, disease, fungus, or a natural disaster such as flooding. Some biologists have warned that bananas could disappear from stores around the world as a result.

Web Connection

Various organizations are trying to improve conditions on banana plantations. To learn more, go to this website and follow the links.

www.ExploringGlobalization.ca

Identity and Some Social Dimensions of Globalization

Just as large-scale banana production illustrates some of the economic, political, and environmental dimensions of globalization, it also shows some of the social dimensions — and how all these dimensions are related.

Cheap bananas that are tasty, nutritious, uniform in size, and free of blemishes appeal to Canadian consumers. But to keep prices low, banana workers in many countries face challenges. Among them are low wages and unsafe working conditions.

For example, workers are rarely trained in how to safely handle the synthetic chemicals used to protect crops. In some cases, workers have been required to continue working while planes flew overhead spraying chemicals on the plants — and the workers. As a result, many workers have suffered long-term health problems. In addition, toilet facilities are rarely provided for workers. They must relieve themselves among the plants.

In countries such as Ecuador and Colombia, workers who try to do something about conditions often face firing and blacklisting. On occasion, they have even been attacked by armed thugs.

Displacing Indigenous peoples

The need for large tracts of land to create banana plantations has also meant that Indigenous peoples were often displaced — forced off their land. Unable to carry on their traditional way of life, some went to work on the plantations, while others were forced to move to cities, where they often live in poverty.

Even when Indigenous peoples managed to remain on their land, the environmental destruction caused by the widespread use of chemicals sometimes affected their way of life. People who relied on fishing, for example, found that the chemical-laced runoff from the plantations killed fish in rivers and lakes. When the fish disappeared, so did these people's ability to feed themselves and earn a living.

VOICES

I got a fever . . . I told my boss that I felt sick, and he didn't believe me [but] told me to go home. I went home, and my mother took me to the doctor . . . [The second time,] I became covered with red things. They itched. I had a cough. My bones hurt.

— Fabiola Cardozo, Ecuadorean child worker, describing what happened when chemicals were sprayed on a banana plantation where she worked

Figure 2-13 In 2002, the 14-year-old boy in the photograph, was living with his mother in this shanty outside San José, Costa Rica. About 18 per cent of Costa Ricans live in poverty — but this situation is improving as the country's economy grows. How might a strong economy affect the number of people living in poverty? How might poverty affect people's identity?

REFLECT AND RESPOND

Create a diagram (e.g., a flow chart or mind map) to show how conditions on banana plantations and the expectations of European and North American consumers are related economically, politically, environmentally, and socially.

Explain your diagram to a partner or a small group and discuss how it shows the effects of globalization on your identity — and vice versa.

When you read or hear about globalization or any other issue, it is important to decide whether the point of view or perspective presented is valid. One test of validity is to decide whether the writer's or speaker's view is biased. The following steps can help you do this.

Steps to Detecting Bias

Step 1: Ask important questions

To detect bias, it is important to ask questions like those on the chart on this page. With a partner, examine the questions on the chart and discuss how each might help you identify bias.

Step 2: Consider one source of information

Read "Maude Barlow's View." With your partner, discuss the answer to this question:

- If Barlow's words were your only source of information, what conclusion might you reach about globalization?

Step 3: Consider other sources of information

Read "Pascal Lamy's View." With your partner, discuss the answer to this question: Does reading this excerpt cause you to question the conclusion you reached after reading the excerpt from Barlow's speech? If so, why? If not, why not?

How much are your conclusions influenced by your own biases?

Note: To achieve a balanced understanding of an issue, you should use four or five sources that represent various points of view.

Step 4: Practise detecting bias

Create a chart like the one shown on this page. With your partner, examine both excerpts and record your answers on the chart. To help you get started, sample responses are shown. When you finish, talk about whether answering the questions caused you to change the conclusions you reached earlier.

Detecting Bias		
Question	One Point of View or Perspective	Another Point of View or Perspective
Who is the writer or speaker?	Maude Barlow, chair, Council of Canadians, and a director of the International Forum on Globalization	
What is the writer's or speaker's purpose?	To convince people that globalization has negative results	
Who is the intended audience?		
Does the writer or speaker support statements with evidence?		
Does the writer or speaker seem to favour one person, group, or point of view? Is any relevant person or group ignored or presented negatively?		
Does the writer or speaker use propaganda techniques, such as name calling, stereotyping, overgeneralizing, or appealing to fear or other emotions?		
How does the information fit with what you already know? Are there any contradictions? What other sources might you use to verify the account?		

VOCABULARY TIP

When thinking about bias, it helps to know two key words: **stereotyping** and **overgeneralizing**.

- **Stereotyping** — Placing people into categories according to preconceived beliefs about how members of a particular group think or behave. Saying that Canadians are polite is an example of stereotyping.

- **Overgeneralizing** — Drawing a conclusion based on too little information. Meeting a polite Canadian and concluding that all Canadians are polite is an example of overgeneralizing.

Maude Barlow's View

 Maude Barlow is national chairperson of the Council of Canadians, a citizens' group, and a director of the International Forum on Globalization, an organization that monitors the effects of globalization. She made the following remarks in a 2004 speech to delegates at a conference on alternative economics.

[Globalization] was created by the few for the many. [It] was designed carefully and deliberately by powerful forces within business and politics to counter what one of them called the "excess of democracy" that had grown out of the great social movements in the 1960s. They form powerful business lobbies and "think tanks" to influence the political culture everywhere. They put themselves on the boards of universities to influence the next generation of thinkers. They bought the newspapers and the television studios and they created powerful global institutions like the World Bank and the World Trade Organization to bring a binding regulatory framework to cement their revolution. They knew it would take years to achieve and they knew they could not succeed if they directly challenged the rights that had been gained by women, minorities and workers in the industrialized North. However, they didn't need to worry, as they knew that the unregulated market capitalism that they were bringing to the world would do that for them.

The proof of their failure is everywhere for us to see. It's in the deepening rift between rich and poor, both between the Global South and the Global North, but also within countries. There is a Third World in the First World . . . Their failure is found in the startling decline of natural resources – fish, forests, fossil fuels, freshwater supplies – all of them are in crisis.

. . . And we see its failure in the startling rise in national violence: Yugoslavia, Bosnia, Rwanda, the Congo, Afghanistan, and Iraq. Was this new system not supposed to replace politics and war with the discipline and stability of the market?

Pascal Lamy's View

Pascal Lamy, director general of the World Trade Organization, made the following remarks in a speech to Chilean politicians and business leaders on January 30, 2006.

Globalization has enabled individuals, corporations and nation-states to influence actions and events around the world – faster, deeper and cheaper than ever before – and equally to derive benefits for them. Globalization has led to the opening, the vanishing of many barriers and walls, and has the potential for expanding freedom, democracy, innovation, social and cultural exchanges while offering outstanding opportunities for dialogue and understanding.

But the global nature of an increasing number of some worrisome phenomena – the scarcity of energy resources, the deterioration of the environment and natural disasters (including, recently, hurricane Katrina and the Asian tsunami), the spread of pandemics (AIDS, bird flu), the growing interdependence of economies and financial markets and the ensuing complexity of analysis, forecasts and predictability (financial crisis), and the migratory movements provoked by insecurity, poverty or political instability are also a product of globalization.

Indeed it can be argued that in some instances, globalization has reinforced the strong ones and weakened those that were already weak.

It is this double face of globalization that we must seek ways of addressing if we want to "humanize globalization." To do this, we need to "reform globalization" with a clear view to enhancing the development of social, economic and ecological aspects of humanity.

Summing up

As you progress through this course, you will encounter many opinions about globalization. Returning to the questions on the chart will help you detect bias and assess the validity of the information.

Figure 2-14 Medina Mohammed sings on *Ethiopian Idols*. The Idol franchise, which started in Britain, has been picked up in 35 countries including the United States, Canada, Israel, and Ethiopia. Is the popularity of this TV program an example of a challenge to people's identity — or is it an opportunity to promote identity? Or is it both?

CHECKFORWARD

You will read more about globalization and challenges to identity in Chapters 3 and 4.

HOW DO SOME FORCES OF GLOBALIZATION PRESENT CHALLENGES TO IDENTITY?

Many people believe that the connections and interdependence created by globalization will help individuals expand their individual and collective identity and promote understanding and co-operation. Others believe that globalization is reducing diversity — and leading to cultural **homogenization**. Homogenization erases the differences among peoples, and as a result, they become more and more similar.

When people from different cultures come into contact, **acculturation** often occurs. "Acculturation" refers to the cultural changes that occur when two cultures accommodate, or adapt to, each other's worldview — the way they see the world. This **accommodation** involves accepting and creating space for one another. Accommodation may affect the customs, traditions, technologies, values, beliefs, and languages of both cultures.

Both acculturation and accommodation may lead to **assimilation**, which occurs when the culture of a minority group is absorbed by another culture. In this process, the cultural identity of the minority group disappears as its members take on the identity of the other culture.

Creation of a Nation: The Métis People

As the fur trade developed in Canada in the 17th, 18th, and 19th centuries, some First Nations women married European fur traders. Their children were of mixed ancestry — and they laid the foundation for the creation of a distinct Aboriginal people: the Métis. "Métis" is the French word for "mixed." According to the Métis National Council, the organization that represents Métis people in Canada, "Métis means a person who self-identifies as Métis, is of historic Métis Nation Ancestry, is distinct from other Aboriginal Peoples and is accepted by the Métis Nation."

Métis people blended the cultures and spiritual values of their various origins. They also share music, other art forms, technologies, knowledge, and sometimes language. Michif — a mixed language made up of Cree and French words and grammatical structures — is spoken by some Métis people in northern Alberta, Saskatchewan, Manitoba, and the Northwest Territories.

Think about your own heritage and cite examples that show how your identity has been affected by acculturation, accommodation, or assimilation.

Figure 2-15 During the opening ceremonies of the 2002 North American Indigenous Games, young people carried a huge Métis sash. The sash is a powerful symbol of unity. Its strands, patterns, and colours represent the various peoples who have come together to form the Métis Nation. Think of a symbol that is important to your individual or collective identity. If you were describing the significance of this symbol to someone who knew nothing about it, what would you say?

Economist and author Tyler Cowen believes that globalization supports cultural diversity and freedom of choice, while political theorist Benjamin Barber believes that globalization threatens cultural diversity. In March 2003, these two American thinkers met to debate the impact of globalization on world cultures. Here is some of what they said.

TYLER COWEN

Trade gives artists a greater opportunity to express their creative inspiration . . . When two cultures trade with each other they tend to expand the opportunities available to individual artists . . . Trade played an important role in . . . artistic revolutions [in developing countries].

So if we look, for instance, at Cuban music or reggae music, we find that Cuban music was produced largely for American tourists who went to nightclubs in Cuba in the 1950s. Persian carpets started being produced in large numbers again in the 19th century, largely to sell to European buyers who sold to North American buyers. The blossoming of world literature — writers from Mahfouz to Marquez — the bookstore, the printing press, the advent of cinema around the globe are all cases in which trade has made different countries, different regions, more creative, given us more diversity.

Countries do look more alike, but they look more alike in the sense of offering some commonly diverse choices. So today you can buy sushi [a Japanese delicacy] in either France or Germany. This makes France and Germany more alike, yet in my view this is closer to being an increase in diversity than a decline in diversity.

BENJAMIN BARBER

One of the problems of globalization and cultural borrowing and cultural mimicry is that they depend, not on isolated cultures, but on authentic cultures. And I quite agree that the "authentic culture" is itself a cultural product of earlier cultural interactions . . . We all know the difference between getting crêpes in Dijon and getting them in a New York place called Les Halles. Even though you do get something like the original product, there's a real difference between those crêpes . . .

EuroDisney, outside Paris, now gets more visitors than Paris does every year. I'm sure that, among other things, people go to the French theme park at EuroDisney to sample French culture along with Danish and German and other cultures that are there. Some might think they'd do better to travel the 17 kilometres into Paris.

In effect, the "theme-parking" of culture, which is part of globalization and part of the theme-parking of our world, is, yes, a kind of diversity, but it is the diversity of the theme park. It is increasingly synthetic; it's increasingly distanced from the authentic origin. Increasingly, it takes a toll on that authentic origin, as when an American crêpe maker ends up back in Paris selling the American version of crêpes to people in Paris who don't make them anymore because there's a much cheaper global product they can get in place of what they've had. Globalization has a tendency to move that process forward at alarmingly dispiriting rates.

Explorations

1. Think about what you learned earlier about detecting bias. Do you detect bias in the remarks of either Benjamin Barber or Tyler Cowen? Explain your response. Does your response affect your assessment of the validity of the arguments of either speaker? Why or why not?

2. Is bias always a negative thing? Explain your answer.

3. In one or two sentences, describe what you think Barber means by the "theme-parking" of culture. Create a drawing or collage that represents how your own culture or community might look in the world he envisions.

Language, Acculturation, and Accommodation

Just as Michif, the language spoken by some Métis, is an example of acculturation and accommodation, other languages also show what happens when acculturation occurs. Written Japanese, for example, is adapted from characters borrowed from Chinese. One of the earliest Japanese written works, *Kojiki*, dates from about 700 CE. It uses Chinese characters with small phonetic signs to help Japanese readers with pronunciation. When this borrowing occurred, the Chinese form of writing was already very old and was widely admired in Japan.

Inuktitut is the language of the Inuit. Although Inuktitut has a long history, it was an oral language until the mid-1800s. In some parts of Nunavut, the language is written using the English alphabet; in other parts, it is written in syllabics, symbols that represent entire syllables rather than individual letters. These symbols were developed by missionaries. Today, the Inuit people have created new Inuktitut words — both written and spoken — to represent certain legal, political, and scientific concepts like "representation by population" and "global climate change."

Inuktitut in danger

Although Inuktitut is one of the official languages of Nunavut, some people, such as teachers Alexina Kublu and Mick Mallon, fear that it is in danger of disappearing. In an article titled "Our Language, Our Selves," Kublu and Mallon highlighted "the overwhelming power of English" in today's world. They noted that few children in western Nunavut now speak, or even understand, Inuktitut.

"And it is the children who count," wrote Kublu and Mallon. "Visit a community and listen to the children playing. It doesn't matter how much Inuktitut is spoken in the store by adults shopping, or in the kitchens among elders visiting. What language are the children using? The first sign of decay is when the children play in English. The second is when the parents speak in Inuktitut and the children reply in English. The third is when the language of the home is English, except for the elders in the corner, a generation cut off from their grandchildren."

Figure 2-16 Susan Aglukark is an award-winning Inuk performer who composes and sings her songs in both Inuktitut and English. Do you think Aglukark's choice to express her artistic vision in these two languages supports diversity and intercultural understanding or increases the risk that Inuktitut will disappear? Why?

CHECK FORWARD

You will read more about language and globalization in Chapter 4.

Figure 2-17 The *Nunatsiaq News* is a newspaper published in Iqaluit, Nunavut. Its masthead — the part of the front page that shows a newspaper's title — displays its name in both English letters and Inuktitut syllabics.

REFLECT AND RESPOND

In *The Wall Street Journal*, American political commentator John J. Miller wrote: "The most important reason some languages are disappearing is that their native speakers don't regard them as . . . precious. They view linguistic adaptation — especially for their kids — as a key to getting ahead. This is understandable when about half the world's population speaks one of only 10 languages and when speaking English in particular is a profitable skill."

Why might people consider learning English a "profitable skill"? Write a short paragraph explaining how this view reflects the forces of globalization at work — and how this might affect people's identity. In your paragraph, use at least two of the following words:

acculturation   accommodation

assimilation   homogenization

How do some forces of globalization provide opportunities to affirm and promote identity?

The forces of globalization could be called a double-edged sword. Cutting one way, they can lead to assimilation and the homogenization of cultures; cutting the other way, they can also provide minority groups with opportunities to affirm and promote their cultural identity. The Métis people of Canada and the Indigenous people of Bolivia are examples of how globalization has provided tools that people can use to revitalize — breathe new life into — their culture.

Throughout much of the 20th century, Métis culture was threatened. The traditional Métis way of life had changed, and some Métis people suffered discrimination. In addition, Métis communities were scattered, and the number of people who spoke Michif was shrinking. The first language of most Métis people was English, French, Cree, or Ojibway — or a combination of an Aboriginal language and English or French. Some current estimates place the number of Michif speakers in Canada at between 500 and 1000 — out of a total Métis population of more than 290 000.

What is more, for most of the 20th century, no one knew for sure how many Métis people there were in Canada. Until 1996, Canadian census forms did not include a category that allowed people to identify themselves as Métis — which is one reason Métis sometimes call themselves "Canada's forgotten people."

Figure 2-18 In 2005, Métis people staged a journey to celebrate the settlement of Métis Crossing, one of the first permanent Métis communities in Alberta. This celebration is just one of many events Métis people organize to affirm and promote their identity. Have you ever attended a Métis celebration or a similar cultural event? How did the experience affect your identity?

The Métis and Cultural Revitalization

As Métis people and others became aware that the distinct Métis culture was in danger of disappearing, individuals and groups began to take steps to ensure that this did not happen.

The Métis Nation of Alberta, for example, was formed in the 1920s to affirm and promote the collective identity of Métis people. But the MNA remained a relatively small group for decades. Then a number of factors, including federal government policies that promoted multiculturalism and diversity, combined to change not only the way minority groups were viewed, but also the way they viewed themselves.

During the 1990s and into this century, more and more Métis people became interested in **cultural revitalization** — the process of affirming and promoting individual and collective cultural identity. As a result, membership in the MNA rose by 300 per cent. Today, more than 35 000 Métis people belong to this organization.

Affirming the Métis heritage

To promote interest in the Métis heritage, Métis groups began to stage events and celebrations that fostered a sense of community and encouraged Métis people — and others — to celebrate and find out more about Métis history and culture.

The World Wide Web was one of the tools that helped the Métis achieve these goals. Many Métis organizations set up web sites that included pages on Métis history, customs, and traditions, as well as discussions of issues that concern Métis people today. Online forums enabled Métis people in various parts of Canada to conduct research and communicate with one another. Magazines and newspapers geared to Métis audiences also became available online.

Figure 2-19 Métis organizations such as the Métis National Council and the Métis Nation of Alberta created web sites that people can access to find out more about Métis history and cultural traditions, as well as current issues.

Web Connection

To hear the Michif language and learn some phrases, go to this web site and follow the links.

www.ExploringGlobalization.ca

Keeping Michif vibrant

The Michif language is an important part of Métis identity, and many Métis believe that ensuring that this language survives will ensure that their culture remains vibrant. "The revitalization of the Michif language is a key element to a thriving culture and the well-being of Métis people," wrote Norman E. Fleury, director of the Manitoba Métis Federation Michif Language Program and national co-chair of the Métis National Council's Michif Language Revitalization Program. "Language is fused with our way of life, as it holds the stories of our people and the essence of our identity. My grandmother called Michif, now the official and historical language of the Métis, a God-given spiritual language born with the Michif people."

The Web has played an important role in the revitalization of Michif. People who wish to learn Michif can go online to access lessons and hear the language spoken. Courses for teaching Michif have been developed, teachers have been trained, and Michif dictionaries have been published as books and online.

Have you ever gone online to find out more about your heritage? How did access to this information affect your identity?

Figure 2-20 How would publishing a dictionary like *The Canadian Michif Language Dictionary* help ensure the vitality of the Michif language?

Cultural Revitalization in Bolivia

The South American country of Bolivia has a turbulent history. In the 1500s, it was colonized by the Spanish, who were attracted by its rich silver mines. Many of Bolivia's Indigenous people — the Quechua and Aymara — were forced to work in these mines.

Although Bolivia gained independence in 1825, this did little to help the Quechua and Aymara. Spanish settlers continued to take over their land, and the country's Indigenous people continued to live in poverty. On many occasions, this sparked violence and revolutions.

Besides silver, Bolivia is rich in other natural resources, such as natural gas. Bolivia has some of the largest natural gas reserves in South America — and transnational corporations are very interested in these reserves. But many Bolivians do not want transnationals to be the only ones that benefit from the country's natural resources. They believe that all Bolivians should benefit from the international trade in natural gas and other resources.

Figure 2-21 Bolivia

PROFILE

EVO MORALES
PEACE WITH SOCIAL JUSTICE

In early 2006, Evo Morales became president of Bolivia — the first Indigenous person to hold this office. During his election campaign, Morales promised Indigenous people, who make up about 55 per cent of the population, a greater say in governing and more control over the country's natural resources. Morales wants the wealth from Bolivia's resources to benefit Bolivians rather than transnational corporations.

At the same time, Bolivia is in debt and needs foreign money to become prosperous. For example, to sell its natural gas to other countries, Bolivia must build long, expensive pipelines. Doing this requires foreign investment, so Morales must balance the needs of Bolivians and those of foreign investors who want to be sure that their investments in projects like pipelines are safe — and profitable.

Before he was sworn in, Morales tried to build partnerships by visiting countries such as Cuba, Venezuela, Brazil, Spain, France, China, and South Africa. He said his visit to South Africa was the most important trip of his life.

"It was a meeting of the struggle of two people, of two continents, and a symbol of the courage of the rebellion against discrimination, inequality and against oppression . . ." he told reporters. "Together we look for peace with social justice. I am much more convinced after seeing the struggle of the South African people, our black brothers, in the power of the people."

Morales must find a way to attract investment to Bolivia while ensuring that the people benefit from the country's resources.

Figure 2-22 When Evo Morales (left) was elected president of Bolivia, he took part in a special ceremony at Tiahuanaco, site of an ancient civilization and a sacred place for Bolivia's Indigenous people. How might this ceremony have helped revitalize the culture of Indigenous people?

1. This page includes a short news report about the swearing in of Evo Morales as president of Bolivia. Rewrite this report from the point of view of someone who was passionately for — or against — his becoming president. You may add or delete sentences, or you may rewrite the story completely.

   Whichever route you choose, use verbs and descriptive words that show the writer's bias. Someone who was against Morales, for example, might describe him as "a communist rabble rouser" rather than an "Indigenous president," while a supporter might say that he is "a friend of the people."

   Share your news story with a partner. Compare the words you used to indicate the writer's bias.

2. Examine the map on page 63 and answer the following questions:
   - How might the fact that Bolivia is landlocked — enclosed entirely by land — affect its international trade prospects?
   - How might this geographic factor affect Evo Morales's decisions about his country's relations with the rest of the world?
   - Are any Alberta industries similarly affected by geographic factors? Explain your answer.

President Evo Morales Pledges to End Injustice

LA PAZ, BOLIVIA: Jan. 23, 2006 — When Evo Morales was sworn in today as Bolivia's first Indigenous president, he pledged to end 500 years of injustice against his people.

"Enough is enough," Morales told a cheering audience that included thousands of Bolivians, as well as foreign dignitaries. "We are taking over now for the next 500 years."

At the colourful ceremony, which took place at the Congress in La Paz, Bolivia's capital, Morales also pledged to take control of the country's natural resources out of the hands of private corporations and return it to the people.

The 46-year-old former llama herder and coca leaf farmer said that the free-market model has not worked in Bolivia, and that the privatization of basic services and natural resources should be reversed.

Morales, who is a fierce critic of the United States, also acknowledged that he faces a huge task during his five-year term. Bolivia is the poorest country in South America.

3. To help reduce pollution and ensure that workers are treated fairly, some international organizations, as well as the governments of some developed countries, have suggested inserting special clauses in international trade agreements. These clauses would require companies in exporting countries to meet specific environmental standards and to agree to fair labour practices before their goods can be imported into countries that have signed the agreement.

   In a small group, discuss the possible advantages and disadvantages of these special clauses.

   - Why do you think some organizations and governments would support this idea?

   - Why do you think others would oppose it? Try to achieve consensus — general agreement — on whether these clauses would help or hurt the stakeholders involved in international trade.

   - Choose one group member to summarize your discussion and present the conclusions to the class.

RESEARCH TIP

When conducting Internet research, you can narrow down your search by entering specific search terms. If you are searching for information on T-shirt production, for example, you might enter "T-shirt" and "labour practices." It sometimes helps to try alternative spellings, such as "tee-shirt" and "labor practices."

---

4. You read about coltan mining in Chapter 1 and banana production in this chapter. These two products show the links between globalization and identity, both personal and collective.

   With a partner, choose another important trade item (e.g., coffee, chocolate, jeans, T-shirts, an electronic device) and prepare a two-minute documentary in the form of a radio or video report, or a report using computer presentation software. Your purpose is to show how the item reflects the economic, political, environmental, and social dimensions of globalization.

   As you conduct your research, think "glocally" — locally and globally. In your presentation, set out the process involved in bringing the item you chose to market. Indicate the stakeholders — the individuals or groups with an interest in the product — at each major stage of this process (e.g., farmers, factory workers, shippers, salespeople, consumers).

   Your goal in preparing the documentary is twofold:

   - to educate your classmates about how the economic, political, environmental, and social dimensions of producing the item link various aspects of the identity of the stakeholders

   - to draw conclusions about whether the item shows positive or negative aspects of the forces of globalization

   To help your audience respond to your presentation, prepare three discussion questions that will help you decide whether your documentary was persuasive (e.g., Which group of stakeholders deserves people's support?).

Think about Your Challenge

Look back at the challenge for this related issue. It asks you to develop a presentation that explains your position on this issue: To what extent should globalization shape identity?

Review the material in this chapter and the activities you completed as you progressed through the chapter. Make notes about ideas that could be useful in completing the challenge. Begin developing the criteria and critical questions you will use to evaluate the data you will explore and use in your presentation.

Chapter 3 Identity, the Media, and Communication Technology

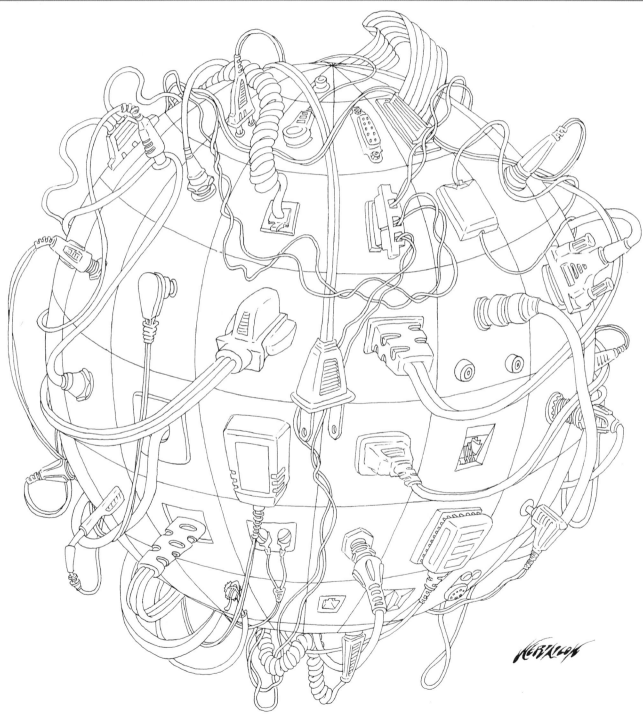

Figure 3-1 Advances in communication technology and media have affected global diversity, identity, and culture. This cartoon, titled "Globalization," was created by Mexican cartoonist Antonio Neri Licon, also known as Nerilicon.

CHAPTER ISSUE

To what extent is identity affected by communication technology and the media in a globalizing world?

THE CARTOON on the facing page first appeared in a daily newspaper published in Mexico City. It was then posted to a web site where it can be viewed by anyone with Web access.

In today's wired world, people in many different countries can communicate almost instantly to explore current events, discuss issues, carry on business, and find out media reactions to world events.

As you think about the message of the cartoon, consider the following questions:

- What communication technologies were used to bring this cartoon to you?
- What communication technologies are represented by the plugs and cords used in the cartoon? How do people use these technologies to connect to other people around the world?
- How are the technologies shown already becoming out of date?
- Why do you suppose the cartoonist left out geographic features, such as land masses and oceans?
- How do you think interconnected communication technologies are affecting cultural diversity and people's cultural identity?

Write a one-sentence caption that captures the message of this cartoon. This caption may be a statement or question. Compare your caption with that of a partner. Is the main idea of your captions similar?

If they are different, discuss the reasons for the differences. How does your caption express your thinking about the influence of communication technologies on your life?

KEY TERMS

digital divide

propaganda

pop culture

universalization

hybridization

LOOKING AHEAD

In this chapter, you will explore answers to the following questions:

- How is identity affected by opportunities to communicate with people around the world?
- How is diversity influenced by the media and communication technologies?
- How is identity affected by media coverage of world events?
- How is diversity affected by the dominance of American media?

My Point of View on Globalization

Use words or images — or both — to express your current point of view on globalization. Compare this with the points of view you have already recorded in your notebook, learning log, portfolio, or computer file. Is your point of view changing? If so, how? Date your ideas and record them so that you can continue to return to them as you progress through this course.

How is identity affected by opportunities to communicate with people around the world?

VOICES

The more we find our lives determined by global forces and confronted with difference, the more we find ourselves driven inward to affirm our roots in our local communities. The more we become members of a global community, the more we insist on our local identity, and cherish the ties that bind us to smaller groups — a shared language, shared traditions and culture, or a common history.

— Beverley McLachlin, chief justice of Canada, in a 2004 speech

When you want to communicate — share information — with someone, how do you do this? If the person you want to communicate with is a classmate, you might talk to each other in the hall between classes. If it's a grandparent in a different community, you might use the telephone or e-mail, or send a letter or greeting card. If it's a friend at another school, you might use instant messaging or send a text message on your cellphone.

Think about the methods you use for communicating with others and list the factors that influence the method you choose (e.g., it may depend on the reason for your message).

FYI

In 2006, the cellphone was the fastest-selling consumer electronic device in the world. In 2005, more than 700 million cellphones were sold around the world. More camera-equipped cellphones are sold every year than digital cameras alone. And more cellphones with MP3 players are sold than MP3 players alone. Rapid advances in technology are also leading to more multi-purpose mobile devices, such as Internet-enabled cellphones and personal data assistants, or PDAs.

Communication Technology and Choices

Contemporary digital communication technologies — telephones, cellphones, computers, and the World Wide Web — expand the communication choices available and help you stay closely connected to friends and family, as well as to others in your community and beyond.

At one time, distance was a huge barrier to communication, but today's digital technology has nearly eliminated this barrier. Scientists with the National Aeronautics and Space Administration in the United States, for example, run a program called NASA Quest. This program enables students around the world to participate with NASA scientists in live, interactive, real-time webcasts. Students can also share ideas about their own explorations, e-mail questions to the scientists, and receive answers.

Closer to home, you can establish an electronic network of people you can go to when you want to discuss or find out information about something. By chatting online with school friends, for example, you can develop a sense of belonging to your school community. By e-mailing an older sibling who is travelling in another country, you can stay in contact with family.

Figure 3-2 Many young people communicate with one another by cellphone. Why do you think cellphones are so popular among teenagers?

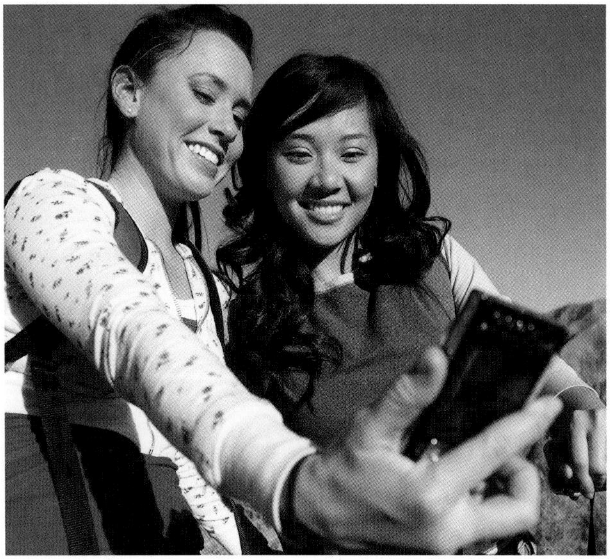

Digital technology also enables you to offer instant feedback on TV programs or the content of web sites. The CBC and other news broadcasters, for example, invite viewers to transmit digital photographs and even videos of newsworthy events. And web sites dedicated to specific issues may also ask for your response or support.

Connections like these help affirm people's membership in the world community. They provide opportunities for people to share their views with others beyond their local community.

Interview a parent, grandparent, or someone else from an earlier generation about how she or he communicated with others as a teenager. Discuss how the range of choices has expanded. Does the person you interviewed think these technological changes have made a difference to your identity as a teenager? Do you agree? Explain your reasons.

The Digital Divide

The first source of information many people choose is the Internet. But most of the world's people do not have Internet access. The gap that separates people who do — and do not — have access to up-to-date digital technology is often called the **digital divide**. Former U.S. president Jimmy Carter described the digital divide when he said, "Globalization, as defined by rich people like us, is a very nice thing . . . you are talking about the Internet, you are talking about cellphones, you are talking about computers. This doesn't affect two-thirds of the people of the world."

Even in countries like Canada, a digital divide exists. High-speed Internet access is not available in many rural areas. For some people, money is a barrier. They cannot afford Internet service. Language also presents a challenge. Few web sites, for example, are available in Aboriginal languages.

Examine the map on this page (Figure 3-3). Where is Internet use highest? Lowest? How might this affect people's identity?

Figure 3-3 **Internet Use, 2007 (Percentage of Population)**

North America 69.7%
Europe 38.9%
Middle East 10.0%
Asia 10.5%
Central and South America and Caribbean 17.3%
Africa 3.6%
Oceania 53.5%

Legend
▶ Users Non-Users
% Percentage of Population

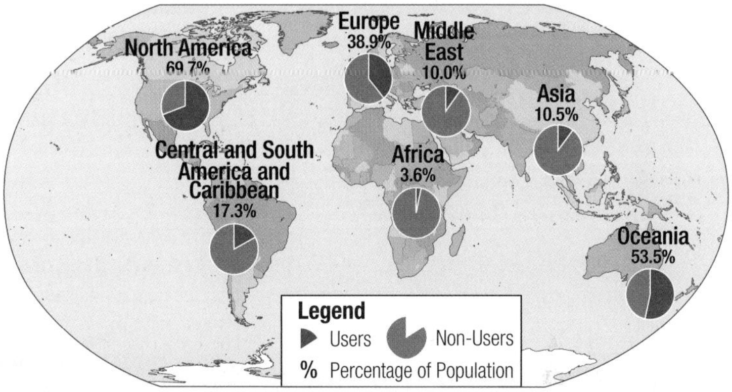

MAKING CHOICES

NICHOLAS NEGROPONTE — ONE LAPTOP PER CHILD

Nicholas Negroponte and a group of computer experts set themselves a goal: to help people in developing countries cross the digital divide — by putting cheap, easy-to-maintain and -use laptop computers into the hands of students.

This group formed One Laptop per Child, a non-profit organization, and set about finding ways to build and sell a laptop computer for less than $150.

By November 2006, they had created a prototype called the 2B1. The 2B1 can connect to the Internet through satellite links, cellular network connections, or long-range antennas. This will allow even many people in rural areas to connect to the Internet.

When the organization announced this development, five countries — Argentina, Brazil, Libya, Nigeria, and Thailand — expressed interest in equipping students with 2B1s. Special international loans will help with this. In addition, people in developed countries will be invited to donate to the project.

Figure 3-4 Because the display screen has fewer colour filters than normal, the 2B1 children's laptop uses just 2 watts of power compared with the 25 to 45 watts required to power a conventional laptop. Each 2B1 has its own antenna and video camera lens.

Explorations

1. Bill Gates, chair of Microsoft, criticized One Laptop per Child, saying it is "just taking what we do in the rich world and subsidizing its use in the developing world." What do you think he meant? Do you agree? Explain the reasons for your judgment.

2. Find out what has happened to One Laptop per Child. Write a short paragraph updating the information in this feature. Explain whether what you found out has changed the view you expressed in response to Question 1.

Technology at Work: The Aboriginal Peoples Television Network

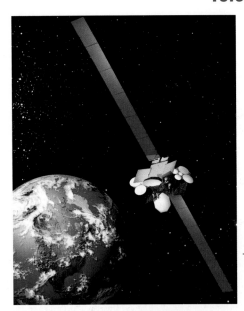

In 1972, Canada launched a satellite called the Anik A1 — and initiated a new era of communication in Canada's North and other remote areas. Over the following decades, satellite technology — which captures signals sent from transmitters on Earth and bounces them back to receivers in TV sets — improved greatly. In 1999, this technology helped the Aboriginal Peoples Television Network create a nationwide TV service for Aboriginal people.

Based in Winnipeg, Manitoba, APTN was the world's first national public Aboriginal television network. Its goal is to create programs "by, for and about Aboriginal peoples" — and to share these programs with all Canadians.

Figure 3-5 The Anik A1 was the world's first satellite designed for non-military uses. The Anik A1 and later generations of communication satellites, such as the one shown in this photograph, enabled people in Canada's North and other remote areas to receive telephone and TV signals.

PROFILE

MARSHALL MCLUHAN
LIVING IN THE GLOBAL VILLAGE

Edmonton-born Marshall McLuhan is respected around the world as one of the most influential thinkers of the 20th century. By the time he died in 1980, this media guru's works had been analyzed by millions who shared his belief that people can understand the world only if they also understand how they are affected by various media.

McLuhan's belief is reflected in his most famous saying: "The medium is the message." This means that a message, whether on an advertising billboard or TV program, in a newspaper, or on a web site, is shaped and influenced by the way it is delivered to its audience — and this can be as important as the message itself. Reading about a world event in a print copy of the *Edmonton Journal* is different from watching live coverage of the event on CBC Newsworld, and this is different from going online to read breaking news about the event on the web site of *The Irish Times*.

McLuhan is also often credited with coining the term "global village" to symbolize the growing connections among people around the world. He predicted that as people communicated more quickly and more often, geographic and cultural distances would stop mattering as much. In *Understanding Media*, he wrote: "Since the inception of the telegraph and radio, the globe has contracted, spatially, into a single large village."

In McLuhan's global village, people can know, affect, and be affected by people on the other side of the world in much the same way as they can know, affect, and be affected by their neighbours across the street. But McLuhan didn't think this knowledge would end all conflicts; rather, it would mean that people would no longer be citizens only of their local community, province, or country. They would also be citizens of the world.

Figure 3-6 Long before the creation of the Internet and the World Wide Web, Marshall McLuhan studied the impact of print and electronic media on culture and identity.

with Madeleine Allakariallak

Figure 3-7 Madeleine Allakariallak is the host and producer of *Contact*, a weekly live phone-in program that focuses on issues that are important to Aboriginal people in the 21st century. How might programs like this help Aboriginal people affirm their individual and collective identity? APTN also operates a web site where viewers can find out more about programs and check TV listings.

with Donna Smith

APTN produces about 70 per cent of its programming in Canada. The remaining 30 per cent is made up of programs and films from other countries. Many of these programs tell the stories of Indigenous people around the world. About 30 per cent of APTN programs are broadcast in Aboriginal languages such as Inuktitut, Cree, Inuinaqtuun, Ojibway, Mohawk, Dene, Gwich'in, Chipewyan, and Tlingit. About 55 per cent of the remaining programs are in English, and 15 per cent are in French.

APTN's entertainment and news programs focus on Aboriginal issues and current events. Series such as *Hank William's First Nation* and *Moccasin Flats* tell Aboriginal stories in Aboriginal voices and from Aboriginal points of view and perspectives. The network also broadcasts children's shows, documentaries, cooking shows, and educational programs.

Some programs feature traditional oral storytelling in a contemporary format. Community leaders and Elders speak in their own languages about environmental issues, land claims, and promoting their culture.

APTN's success has inspired Aboriginal peoples in other countries to launch their own television networks. In New Zealand, for example, Maori Television was launched in 2004.

REFLECT AND RESPOND

Based on what you have read so far, do you believe that the globalizing force of contemporary communication technologies is a positive or negative force in affirming and promoting people's individual and collective identity — or is it both?

Provide at least two examples to support your response. Conclude with a general statement summarizing how contemporary communication technologies affect your personal identity.

HOW IS DIVERSITY INFLUENCED BY THE MEDIA AND COMMUNICATION TECHNOLOGIES?

FYI

English has always borrowed words from other languages — and these words have sometimes taken a complicated route to make their way into English. Here are some examples:

caravan — Borrowed from French, which borrowed it from Persian

alarm — Borrowed from French, which borrowed it from Italian

veranda — Borrowed from Hindi, which borrowed it from Portuguese

tea — Borrowed from Dutch, which borrowed it from Chinese

CHECKBACK

You read about media concentration and convergence in Chapter 2.

Whenever people from different cultures met and exchanged goods, some acculturation and accommodation always occurred. Languages, for example, have always borrowed terms from other languages, and English is no exception. Some language experts estimate that as many as 66 per cent of English words may be borrowed from other languages.

What is new today is the speed and complexity of the exchanges that take place — and for many people, the challenge is to balance the positive and negative effects of acculturation and accommodation. On the one hand, as people learn about different cultures, they come to respect and appreciate differences. On the other hand, a minority culture may be assimilated by a dominant culture — and the customs, traditions, and beliefs of the minority culture may disappear.

Diversity and Global Media Concentration

Just as media concentration and convergence is occurring in Canada, so is it also occurring around the world. Shashi Tharoor, a former United Nations official, told an international conference how this point was driven home to him: "Nowhere is globalization more apparent than in the media . . . Any doubt I might have had about the reach and influence of global mass communications was dispelled when I [was at a conference in Russia] and was approached by a Tibetan Buddhist monk in his saffron robes, thumping a cymbal and chanting his mantras, who paused to say, 'I've seen you on BBC!'"

Like the Internet, mass media such as television and radio have the power to reach millions of people. These media can be forces that encourage cultural diversity — or forces that promote cultural homogenization.

Disney, for example, is an American transnational corporation that is tapping into the world market for children's entertainment. The company either has or plans to set up channels in Taiwan, France, Italy, Germany, and the Middle East. And ESPN International is the most popular global sports broadcaster. To appeal to local tastes, it emphasizes soccer in South America, table tennis in Asia, and cricket in India.

Disney is one of nine transnational media corporations, many of them based in the United States, that dominate the global media. Others include Time Warner, Sony, News Corporation, Viacom, and Bertelsmann. These transnationals control all but one of the major American television networks, as well as many in Europe and Asia. They also control 85 per cent of the world music market, most satellite broadcasting, a great deal of magazine and book publishing, and most global cable broadcasting, as well as other activities.

When transnational media corporations such as Disney and ESPN set up channels in other countries, they often recruit local production crews and on-air personalities. Why do you suppose they do this? Is this an effective strategy for promoting diversity?

Figure 3-8 ESPN adapts its local coverage to suit the interests of audiences around the world. Does this promote diversity or homogenization?

Diversity and the free flow of information

Critics of media concentration and convergence argue that it reduces competition and diversity of opinion. American author and columnist Jill Nelson, for example, has said that media convergence "may be good for business, but it's bad for people and the free flow of information. In our lust for profits, we have forgotten democratic principles. This can only increase the public's deep skepticism of the quality of the news."

In Canada, critics support their arguments by pointing to a controversy involving CanWest Global Communications, one of the largest Canadian media companies. In late 2001, the company's owners ordered most of their daily newspapers, including Montréal's *Gazette*, the *Ottawa Citizen*, the *Edmonton Journal*, the *Calgary Herald*, and the *Victoria Times-Colonist*, to take the same editorial position, regardless of local and regional differences. Journalists who resisted were fired. The publisher of the *Ottawa Citizen*, for example, lost his job after the paper published an editorial that had not been approved by the CanWest head office. The incident sparked a national outcry, and CanWest later changed the policy.

Several years later, Gordon Fisher, a CanWest official, told a conference on control of Canada's media: "The most odious ownership intentions would not change one facet of this great Western democratic society. There is just too much free information out there and our citizens are smart enough to go get it."

Do you agree with Gordon Fisher's statement? When you want more information about current events, what sources do you consult? Do these sources provide you with alternative points of view?

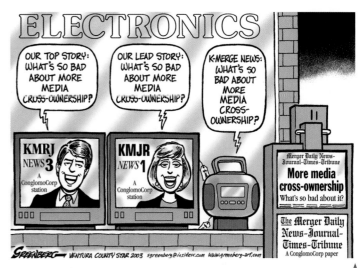

Figure 3-9 "Media cross-ownership" is another term for media convergence. What is the cartoonist's opinion of media convergence? How does the cartoonist make his opinion clear? Note the name of the newspaper. How does the cartoonist use humour to make a point?

Al-Jazeera in North America

In 1996, satellite technology, cable networks, and the Internet enabled Al-Jazeera, an Arabic TV station, to begin broadcasting internationally from Qatar, a country in the Arabian Peninsula. Some people believe that Al-Jazeera provides nothing but **propaganda** — ideas and information spread for the purpose of achieving a specific goal. But others disagree. They believe that being exposed to a wide range of views is important.

So far, North American TV viewers cannot watch Al-Jazeera. In 2004, the Canadian Radio-television and Telecommunications Commission, the agency that regulates broadcasting in Canada, ruled that Al-Jazeera could broadcast an English-language version of its programs in this country. But the CRTC also set strict conditions: cable operators who offered Al-Jazeera would, for example, be required to monitor its broadcasts and delete anything that broke Canada's hate laws. Doing this would be difficult — and so far, no Canadian cable company has agreed to these terms.

VOICES

At a time when issues in the Middle East, Iran, and Iraq are defining our world, why wouldn't Al-Jazeera English be available on our television sets in Canada and the United States?

— *Tony Burman, CBC's chief news editor, in an editorial on the CBC web site*

FYI

The conditions imposed on cable operators who might choose to broadcast Al-Jazeera are unusual. In all other cases, broadcast media are challenged only after someone believes they have broken the rules — not before.

Diversity and the Internet

Not everyone is in a position to benefit from global communication technologies. What are some reasons for this?

Indigenous peoples, for example, have had to struggle to make sure their many voices are heard on the World Wide Web. In 2003, representatives of governments, organizations, and Indigenous peoples from around the world met at the World Summit on the Information Society in Geneva, Switzerland. They agreed that information and communication technologies can be a powerful force in improving everyone's quality of life and promoting dialogue among people, nations, and civilizations. But they also said that this effort requires co-operation and attention to the special needs of marginalized and vulnerable groups, as well as the preservation of the heritage and cultural legacy of Indigenous peoples.

VOICES

Cultural diversity has a key role to play in this era of the new economy . . . We must listen to one another and take the time to appreciate our respective cultures . . . And that respect must become the cornerstone of our relationships.

— *Sheila Copps, former minister of Canadian Heritage, in a 2003 speech*

POINTS OF VIEW

IT stands for "information technology" — and the web site TakingITGlobal.org connects students around the world who are interested in getting involved in their community, both local and global. Tamoy, Richa, and Frederick are three of TIG's 137 000 members. Tamoy is from Jamaica, Richa from India, and Frederick from Britain. When TIG asked these three students whether the organization has helped them achieve some of their goals, this is what they said.

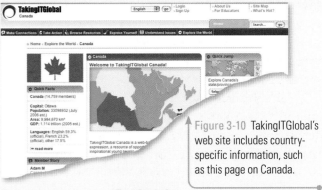

Figure 3-10 TakingITGlobal's web site includes country-specific information, such as this page on Canada.

Tamoy

Yes, TakingITGlobal can help me to achieve some of my goals; actually it has already. TIG has provided me with a forum to express my thoughts to young people . . . in over 100 countries worldwide. I am able to learn about other cultures, and I get to see what youth are doing in other countries. It has made me realize that young people everywhere are all the same: we share similar views, go through similar things. I learn about opportunities and I find old friends.

Richa

TakingITGlobal is a good place where people can interact and share their culture and inspirations. I always wanted to know people from different cultures and countries so that I could learn about them and share my views with them. TIG is helping me to accomplish my goal and to understand the world I live in.

Frederick

TIG helps achieve the major goal of spreading positive publicity about young people. In the "bad news" society we live in, where scandal rather than success hits the headlines, a tool like this is crucial to reversing the trend. Young people are continuously demonized by the media (at least where I live) and this can create low morale or confidence. Resources like TIG can help by going some way to restoring faith within the global youth population.

Explorations

1. On the TakingITGlobal web site, members were asked to describe an issue that matters to them — and to explain how they became aware and involved. How would you respond if you were asked to do the same thing?

   Discuss your response with a partner, then write a one- to three-paragraph summary of your response.

2. If you wish to read more responses by TIG members, go to this web site and follow the links.

   www.ExploringGlobalization.ca

In Canada, the commissioner of official languages produced a report stressing that, in a globalizing world, maintaining a strong French presence on the Internet requires continuous effort.

In Western Canada, media and services are overwhelmingly English, and Francophone communities are often widely separated. In Alberta, Francophone communities are taking steps to keep their culture strong. With the help of the Alberta government, they are, for example, digitizing their histories and posting them on the Internet. French-language services are also listed on web sites. What do you think is the most significant way measures like these help Alberta Francophones affirm and promote their identity?

Figure 3-11 Cartoonist Mike Keefe is making a comment on one possible result of contemporary communication technology. Make up a title for this cartoon. What view of technology does your title imply?

Techno-Isolation

Think about how current communication technologies can enable you to create your own world. Your MP3 player, for example, gives you a customized soundtrack and blocks out the rest of the world. You can go online to play games with people on the other side of the world. At lunch, you can talk or send text messages on your cellphone while sitting at a table surrounded by people you are not communicating with.

Though some people believe that technology increases connections among people, others argue that it actually promotes social isolation by encouraging people to become "high-tech hermits." Technology enables people to pursue their own interests, but doing this can reduce their sense of community, psychotherapist Tina Tessina told the *Edmonton Journal*. "People don't automatically have the same cultural events to talk about," she said. "We have so much choice that people at the water cooler haven't all seen the same thing, read the same book or heard the same news."

At the same time, those who deny that technology is isolating say it can result in interesting new ways of interacting. *Wired* magazine, for example, reported that in New York, owners of MP3 players listen to one another's music. Strangers meeting on the street listen to each other's selections, creating different kinds of social connections.

REFLECT AND RESPOND

In your notebook or on a sheet of paper, create a continuum like the following. Then assess the effects of technology on cultural diversity. If you think the effects are completely positive, place an X at the positive end of the continuum. If you think they are completely negative, place an X at the negative end. And if you think the effects are somewhere in between, place an X at the appropriate spot between positive and negative.

Compare your assessment with that of a partner and explain the reasons for your assessment. When you finish this discussion, decide whether you wish to change your assessment. If so, mark the change on your continuum and make a point-form note about the comment that was most effective in changing your mind.

Effects of Technology on Cultural Diversity

Negative   **Positive**

HOW IS IDENTITY AFFECTED BY MEDIA COVERAGE OF WORLD EVENTS?

Figure 3-12 Coverage of the 1963 assassination of John F. Kennedy in Dallas, Texas, changed the way the media covered world events. The photograph on the left shows Lee Harvey Oswald, the alleged assassin, just before he was murdered by Jack Ruby — as TV cameras rolled. The photo on the right shows Kennedy's young son saluting his father's coffin as the funeral procession passes.

On Friday, November 22, 1963, news of the assassination of American president John F. Kennedy flashed around the world. In many countries, including Canada, TV stations suspended regular programming to broadcast events as they unfolded. American TV networks issued a bulletin at 1:45 that afternoon and soon started coverage that continued without commercial interruption for the next three days. During that time, an estimated 96 per cent of all American TV sets were on for an average of 31 hours.

Millions of people in other countries also watched TV coverage of the story. Many people who were alive in 1963 remember exactly where they were when they heard the news — and many were riveted to the live coverage as it unfolded through the weekend. Why do you suppose so many people gathered in front of TV sets that weekend?

The Kennedy assassination was one of the first examples of the kind of TV coverage people in Western countries have come to expect when momentous events occur. Since then, people who have access to communication technologies have become accustomed to witnessing events — natural disasters, political unrest, sporting events, and cultural festivals — in real time as they happen all over the world.

September 11, 2001 — The World Watches

On September 11, 2001, four passenger airliners were hijacked in the United States. Two were flown into the World Trade Center in New York City, the third crashed into the Pentagon in Washington, D.C., and the fourth crashed in a field in Pennsylvania. More than 3000 people were killed in the attacks.

As a result of the attacks, U.S. president George W. Bush declared "war on terror." He vowed to track down Osama bin Laden and members of al-Qaeda, the extremist network that had been declared responsible for the attacks.

On the hijacked planes, some passengers and crew members made cellphone calls to report what was happening. After the planes crashed into the World Trade Center, many people in the buildings used their cellphones to call loved ones and some used them to send farewell messages to their families.

A few early spectators videotaped events on cellphones or videocams and transmitted the images to TV stations. News crews arrived at the same time as emergency medical crews, firefighters, and police. By the time the second plane flew into the south tower of the World Trade Center, CNN was already broadcasting live — and horrified viewers watched the plane hit the building.

Figure 3-13 On September 11, 2001, two hijacked airplanes flew into the World Trade Center in New York City, causing the towers to burn and collapse. Have you seen media coverage of this event? If so, how did watching this coverage affect your identity?

The world responds

After the attacks of September 11, 2001, many people around the world sympathized — and identified — with the United States and other countries whose citizens had died on that day. In Turkey and Israel, flags on government buildings were lowered to half-mast. In Bangladesh, people held a candlelight vigil. In Moscow, children left flowers outside the U.S. Embassy. In Gander, Newfoundland, people took in airline passengers who were stranded when all air traffic over the U.S. was halted after the attacks. Firefighters and police officers from Canadian cities went to New York to help with recovery efforts.

But not everyone responded this way. CNN reported that some people in some countries took to the streets to applaud the attacks. A year later, a survey of people in six European countries found that 55 per cent of those polled agreed that American foreign policy in the Middle East had contributed to the attacks.

Dealing with the backlash

In some Western countries, people of Middle Eastern heritage — or people who looked as if they might be from the Middle East — were harassed. Mosques were firebombed in the U.S, France, Australia, and Canada, and some Muslims were mistakenly arrested for engaging in "terrorist" activities.

The situation became so serious that, in 2005, the United Nations Commission on Human Rights adopted a resolution calling on Western countries to combat defamation campaigns against Islam and Muslims. Kofi Annan, who was secretary-general of the United Nations at the time, told delegates at a seminar titled Confronting Islamophobia: Education for Tolerance and Understanding: "Since the September 11 attacks on the United States, many Muslims, particularly in the West, have found themselves the objects of suspicion, harassment, and discrimination. Too many people see Islam as a monolith and as intrinsically opposed to the West. Caricature remains widespread and the gulf of ignorance is dangerously deep."

In the Western media, some news editors began to think carefully about how their choice of words influenced readers and viewers — and to examine how they used words such as "terrorist," "freedom fighter," "militant," and "insurgent."

In 2002, Maher Arar, a Syrian-born Canadian citizen, was unjustly arrested in the United States and deported to Syria, where he was held for a year and tortured before he was allowed to return to Canada. Here are the headlines that appeared when two different Canadian news sources reported Arar's deportation:

U.S. deports respected Canadian to Syria

United States deports suspected terrorist to Syria

The two headlines are almost the same. Which words are different? What bias do these words represent? How might these headlines have influenced readers' points of view on Arar's identity?

VOICES

On September 11th, great sorrow came to our country. And from that sorrow has come great resolve. Today, we are a nation awakened to the evil of terrorism, and determined to destroy it. That work began the moment we were attacked; and it will continue until justice is delivered.

— *U.S. president George W. Bush, in a speech on October 11, 2001*

VOICES

While I was looking at these destroyed towers in Lebanon, it sparked in my mind that the tyrant should be punished with the same and that we should destroy towers in America, so that it tastes what we taste and would be deterred from killing our children and women.

— *Osama bin Laden, head of al-Qaeda, explaining how U.S. support of the 1982 Israeli bombing of Lebanon inspired him to seek revenge.*

Web Connection

To find out more about the media debate over the use of words such as "terrorist," "freedom fighter," "militant," and "insurgent," go to this web site and follow the links.

www.ExploringGlobalization.ca

ASSESSING THE AUTHORITY AND VALIDITY OF INTERNET INFORMATION

The Internet provides greater access to information than ever before. But so much material is available that the challenge is often to decide which information is accurate and useful.

Suppose you are accessing the Internet to find a timeline of events that occurred on September 11, 2001. The following steps can help you assess the authority and validity of the information you find. Similar steps can help whenever you need to evaluate information on the Internet.

Steps to Assessing the Authority and Validity of Internet Information

Step 1: Decide on assessment criteria

With a partner, examine the questions on the Internet information checklist on this page. Discuss how each question can help you assess the authority and validity of Internet information.

Step 2: Practise responding to criteria

On a sheet of paper, in your notebook, or in a computer file, create a chart like the one on this page. A portion of a CNN web page that shows a timeline of events on 9/11 appears on the facing page. With your partner, examine this web page and use the information you find to fill in the answers on your chart. To get you started, some sample answers are provided.

When you finish, discuss your answers with a small group or the class. Are you missing any important answers? What is your overall assessment of the authority and validity of the information? You may wish to express your rating on a scale of 1 to 10 (1 = not authoritative at all; 10 = highly authoritative).

Step 3: Choose and assess information on another web site

Go online, choose another web site, and assess it in the same way. This web site may be one that you plan to use when you complete the challenge for this related issue — or it may be another web site that includes information on globalization.

Internet Information Checklist

Web Site	
Name and URL	CNN.com./U.S. — September 11: Chronology of terror http://archives.cnn.com/2001/US/09/11/chronology.attack/

Authority	
Is the source of the information identified?	Yes. CNN, or Cable News Network — at top and bottom of page.
Does the creator have knowledge of the subject?	Yes. CNN reporters were at the scene.
Are qualifications provided?	No qualifications provided.
Does the URL provide clues to help you assess the information?	

Objectivity	
Does the site state facts or opinion?	
Do you suspect bias? If so, why?	
Is the source of the information clearly stated?	
Does the site include advertising? If so, does this affect the reliability of the information?	

Comprehensiveness	
Does the content meet your research needs?	
Does the content cover a specific period or an aspect of the topic — or is it comprehensive?	
Do you need to find additional sources to add to the information provided?	

Currency	
If it matters to your topic, has the site been updated recently?	

Links	
Are links to other sources provided?	
Do the links work?	
Are they useful?	

RESEARCH TIP

When examining a web site, the URL (uniform resource locator, or web address) can provide clues that help you assess the authority of the information. The following suffixes, for example, provide information about the sponsor of the site. The country of origin — as well as other information — may also be included in the URL (e.g., the suffix .ca tells you that the web site is Canadian).

.edu — educational or research material

.gov — government resources

.com — commercial product or commercially sponsored site

.org — organization, either non-profit or for-profit

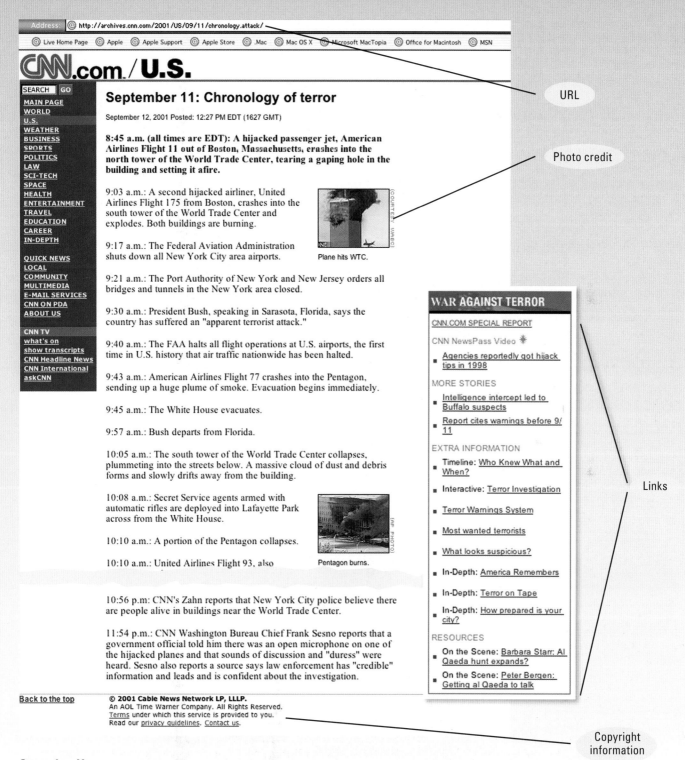

URL

Photo credit

Links

Copyright information

Summing Up

When you finish answering the questions about the web site you have chosen, decide whether you have enough information to assess the authority and validity of the information on the site. Rate the authority and validity of the information on a scale of 1 to 10, just as you did earlier. Be prepared to defend your rating.

Web Connection

Make Poverty History is a coalition of non-profit organizations around the world. To find out more about the coalition's campaigns and members, and to see video footage of the Live 8 concerts and of children in Africa, go to this web site and follow the links.

www.ExploringGlobalization.ca

Make Poverty History and Live 8

On July 2, 2005, a series of concerts organized by Make Poverty History occurred in cities around the world. Satellite links connected the concerts as they were happening in Tokyo; Johannesburg; Moscow; Berlin; Rome; Paris; London; the Eden Project in Cornwall, England; Philadelphia — and Barrie, Ontario. Hundreds of international artists performed at the concerts.

Make Poverty History, a coalition of non-profit organizations around the world, is dedicated to eradicating poverty. The concerts were held to increase awareness of global poverty and influence world leaders to take action to end poverty — to make it history.

The concerts took place in July because officials from the world's eight leading industrial countries — the Group of Eight, or G8 — were meeting in Edinburgh, Scotland, at the time. The concerts were called Live 8 as a play on "G8." Leaders of the G8 countries, which include Canada, meet every year to discuss international issues. The Live 8 organizers asked the G8 leaders to ensure justice in trade, cancel debt in the poorest countries of the world, and deliver more and better aid to people in those countries.

About three billion people around the world participated in the concerts through radio, television, and Internet communication links. During the concerts, more than 26.4 million people sent text messages to support the goal of making poverty history.

Figure 3-14 In London, England, more than 200 000 people attended a Live 8 concert that was broadcast live around the world. What contemporary communication technologies made this broadcast possible?

Missing voices

Nelson Mandela spoke to concert-goers in London, but only two African-born performers — Youssou N'Dour from Senegal and Dave Matthews from South Africa — were scheduled to appear at the main concerts.

Some critics wondered what this said about the organizers' attitude to Africans. British singer Damon Albarn, for example, said that failing to include black artists at the main concert venues undermined the whole project: "If you are holding a party on behalf of people, then surely you don't shut the door on them."

In response to the criticisms, African entertainers organized Africa Calling, a concert in Cornwall, England, though this event was not televised. Angélique Kidjo, a Beninese performer who appeared at Africa Calling, said that she was not concerned about who was performing and who was getting the biggest share of media coverage: "Why are we having this controversy? They are big rock and roll stars and without them we would not have the media interest. What is important is that we all work together against poverty."

Do you agree with Kidjo's point of view? Without the international celebrities, would Live 8 have captured international media interest? What does this say about media responses to world problems and about celebrity status in the media?

Figure 3-15 Angélique Kidjo is a singer and songwriter who was born in the West African country of Benin. In her view, music crosses international boundaries. She believes that music is "really the thread of the memory of mankind."

Stories That Are Told — and Those That Are Not

Though some disasters capture media attention and spark a generous response from people around the world, others do not.

On December 26, 2004, for example, an earthquake in the Indian Ocean created a tsunami that caught the attention of the media — and the world. By the end of that day, more than 150 000 people in 11 countries were dead or missing and millions more were homeless.

People around the world responded by offering money, supplies, and help of all kinds. The money donated to help people cope with this one disaster exceeded the money that some groups had raised during fundraising campaigns that had lasted for years.

In 2004, for example, Médecins sans frontières — Doctors without Borders — had campaigned in Canada to raise money for the crisis-torn Darfur region of Sudan. There, 50 000 people had been killed and 1.5 million had been driven from their homes. MSF's campaign raised $350 000, much less than expected. But in less than three weeks after the tsunami, MSF took in $5 million — without making any requests for aid.

Untold stories

According to the International Federation of Red Cross and Red Crescent Societies, the disasters that attract the most coverage are those that are unusual but can be explained. "Editors sort stories by death tolls," a Red Cross report said. Stories about continuing tragedies that don't have clear causes or solutions attract less media attention. Think about the disasters making news right now. Do you agree with this assessment?

The Red Cross analyzed 200 English-language newspapers worldwide and found that "the tsunami generated more column inches in six weeks than the world's top 10 'forgotten' emergencies combined over the previous year." They also found that by February 2005, people around the world had donated the equivalent of $500 U.S. for each person affected by the tsunami, compared with just 50 cents U.S. for each person affected by a war that had been raging in Uganda for 18 years.

Figure 3-16 This cartoon was created by Patrick Chappatte and appeared 14 days after the tsunami of December 26, 2004. What is the cartoonist saying about how media coverage affects aid to disaster victims? What does his comment say about the people receiving the media messages?

VOICES

Media coverage of the 26 December tsunami dominated headlines worldwide well into January — much longer than any other disaster in modern history. After the tsunami came a metaphorical tidal wave of donations. Aid workers worried that the tsunami would divert donor money and media attention away from the world's "hidden disasters."

— *International Federation of Red Cross and Red Crescent Societies*

REFLECT AND RESPOND

What is one world event that recently captured media attention? Why do you think the media selected this event as a focus of attention? Is this the kind of event that you think the media should focus on? Explain your response.

Decide on a world event that you think merits more media coverage. Then use authoritative and valid print or online sources to find out more about it.

Create a script for a one-minute radio or TV report that presents the story from a point of view that you think people should consider. Alternatively, you might create an editorial cartoon to convey this point of view and to convince people of its value.

Ask a classmate to respond to your message. Is the response the one you expected? Explain.

HOW IS DIVERSITY AFFECTED BY THE DOMINANCE OF AMERICAN MEDIA?

Though media coverage of world events can shape the way you view the events and the people involved, **pop culture** also shapes your point of view — and your identity. "Pop culture" is short for "popular culture" and means the culture of the people. This term often refers to current cultural trends that are spread by commercial mass media.

Many people equate "pop culture" with "American culture" because they believe the commercial mass media are controlled by American transnational corporations, such as Disney and Time Warner. Critics of globalization say the American media giants have the resources to dictate what becomes popular around the world. In the process, other voices and ideas may be lost.

Figure 3-17 lists the movies that made the most money from global ticket sales in 2006. Which companies made these movies? How many of these companies are among the largest transnational media corporations that you read about earlier in this chapter? What difference do you think it makes to global cultural diversity that these media companies — and their movies — are American?

Figure 3-17 **Top Movies of 2006 (Box-Office Receipts)**

Rating	Title	World Box Office Receipts (U.S. Dollars)	Company and Country
1	Pirates of the Caribbean: Dead Man's Chest	$1 065 396 812	Walt Disney Co. (U.S.)
2	Cars	$461 801 982	Walt Disney Co. (U.S.)
3	X-Men: The Last Stand	$458 751 448	20th Century Fox, owned by News Corporation (U.S.)
4	Superman Returns	$391 081 192	Warner Brothers, owned by Time Warner (U.S.)
5	Happy Feet	$180 594 614	Warner Brothers, owned by Time Warner (U.S.)

Pop Culture and Global Media

Pop culture has always been part of human cultural activities. Folktales and songs, for example, gave people a sense of collective identity and of belonging to the group that shared the stories and songs. But in the past, these groups were often relatively small.

Today, contemporary mass media and communication technologies mean that many more people can share in various aspects of pop culture, such as TV shows, trendy products, fashion, music, movies, and even information about celebrities.

When you take part in activities associated with pop culture — whether you are buying a particular brand of MP3 player or listening to the music of a particular individual or group — it influences your values and beliefs and helps define your identity. At the same time, your choices help define what becomes "pop culture." What TV shows or music, for example, do you and your friends share and enjoy? Where do these originate? How does this sharing affect your sense of collective identity? How does your sharing contribute to the creation of a global pop culture?

Global media and communication technologies enable the creators of pop culture to sell their products anywhere in the world, and this has led to the **universalization** of pop culture. Everyone with access to a TV or movie screen or a computer with an Internet connection can share in cultural events and trends. But some people warn that this universalization leads to cultural homogenization because so much of pop culture is produced in the United States and exported around the world.

Figure 3-18 Among the top pop-culture advertising symbols of the 20th century were the Energizer Bunny, Ronald McDonald, and Tony the Tiger. Which companies own these symbols? Where are the head offices of these companies located?

Sesame Street in the global village

Perhaps you watched the television program *Sesame Street* when you were young. This show was produced by the Children's Television Network — now the Sesame Workshop — for broadcast on the American TV network NBC.

From the beginning, one of *Sesame Street's* main themes has been respect for cultural diversity. Because of this emphasis and the show's multicultural cast, some U.S. television stations would not run *Sesame Street* when it was first produced in 1969. But in the years since, Big Bird and the other characters have become well-known elements of pop culture in North America and around the world. They appear not only on the TV show, but also in books, games, puzzles, and toys. How do you think this popular, long-running program has affected the identity of young people in the U.S. and Canada? How has it influenced acceptance of diversity?

Figure 3-19 *Sesame Street's* Big Bird is shown here with children in a kindergarten classroom in Shanghai. Since 1997, the popular American television show has been co-produced in Mandarin for a Chinese audience.

Sesame Street and hybridization

Over the years, *Sesame Street* has become a global enterprise. In 2005, it was seen by children in 120 countries. Sometimes the shows are dubbed into local languages; other times, new shows are co-produced by local media companies. The result is a **hybridization** that combines elements of American culture with those of the country where the show is co-produced.

Hybridization not only mixes elements of different cultures, but it can also create new cultural products that enable people to connect with one another in new ways. In China, for example, local experts in child development, education, and media helped co-producers re-present the program — called *Zhima Jie* in Mandarin — for the Chinese market. The original *Zhima Jie* series was sponsored by General Electric, one of the world's largest corporations and owner of NBC, Universal Pictures, and many U.S. TV stations.

When *Sesame Street* episodes are shown in countries outside the U.S., they are produced under licensing agreements that return money to Sesame Workshop's New York headquarters. Merchandising arrangements for *Sesame Street* books and toys bring in even more revenue.

In many countries, the response to *Sesame Street* has been positive. According to *China Daily*, a Beijing newspaper with a circulation of three million, "Exporting American culture often is greeted with skepticism or even hostility, yet *Sesame Street* seems to find a warm reception wherever it goes." This positive reception may be in part because local co-producers decide which social issues to highlight on their shows. In South Africa, for example, one out of nine children is infected with the AIDS virus — so the South African version of the show includes Kami, a muppet who is HIV-positive.

Figure 3-20 These illustrations show the *Sesame Street* sign as it appears in Kosovo, South Africa, and Bangladesh.

Figure 3-21 Anime characters are so much a part of the pop culture of Japan that fans adopt the costumes of their favourite characters.

Cultural Diversity beyond the American Media

Around the world, various countries have developed their own media industries — sometimes in response to the American influence on pop culture. Modern communication technologies have given creators of these cultural products the opportunity to promote their culture and identity at home and abroad.

Anime and manga

In the early 21st century, some of the most universally popular products of pop culture came from a form of cartooning and animation from Japan: manga, a bold, colourful cartoon style based on Japanese graphic novels; and anime, animated cartoons based on manga.

Manga books and anime films first became popular in Japan and throughout Asia, where some stores specialize in anime videos and manga books. Many of the books tell action stories that have been extended into series. On TV, anime series earn very high ratings and have become symbols of Japanese identity. One popular anime character — Doraemon — has been around since 1969 and has appeared on Japanese postage stamps and even as a cursor on Sony computer screens.

Anime characters such as Pokémon, Goku, and Sailor Moon have also become part of the global cultural landscape — so much so that one anime film won an Academy Award in 2002. In Canada, some book and video stores devote entire sections to manga novels and anime productions. Young people join anime clubs at local public libraries, where librarians can't keep up with the demand for manga graphic books.

Some critics have suggested that manga and anime are so popular because they reflect values that are held by many people, not only in Japan, but also around the world. These art forms started after World War II, when the Japanese people were struggling to overcome the losses suffered during the war. According to Joanne Bernardi, who teaches Japanese film and media at the University of Rochester, the physical, economic, and emotional devastation people experienced as a result of the war helped establish the themes of manga books and anime films: "good versus evil, the conflict between human-made technology and nature, even the basic questions of the meaning of humanity."

What do Bernardi's comments say about manga and anime culture and values? In what ways might these products influence diversity and shape identity? To what extent do they reflect diversity — and a collective identity — among fans of anime and manga?

Figure 3-22 In 2002, the anime film *Spirited Away* by Hayao Miyazaki won Hollywood's Academy Award for best animated feature. The version shown in North America, which was released by Disney, was dubbed into English.

Figure 3-23 Canadian teenagers are snapping up manga books at a rate that has surprised booksellers and librarians. Why do you think manga books appeal to teenage readers?

Korean pop culture

When the Korean film and television industries were overpowered by American media in the late 1980s, two events impressed Koreans with the need to promote their culture. First, the Korean film *Sopyonje,* about a family that performs traditional music, renewed interest in Korean folk culture. Then, a government report recommended renewing the country's cultural industries to improve the economy.

Korea introduced the most restrictive quota of any country that imports American entertainment. To protect Korean culture, 40 per cent — 146 days — of the country's screen time is reserved for Korean-made films. Koreans also imitated the American media system. Large conglomerates such as Samsung, Hyundai, and Daewoo expanded into the media sector. The result is that Korean TV shows have become popular not only in Korea but also in China, Singapore, Vietnam, and Indonesia.

In the late 1990s, a regional TV station, Channel V, began featuring Korean music videos, creating a strong K-pop fan base in Asia. Performers like Rain and BoA attracted large audiences. Some Korean stars — such as Danny Im, also known as Taebin, and Micky Yoochun, of the group TVXQ — grew up in the United States. Their music blends American and Korean traditions.

Figure 3-24 Korean pop musicians like BoA have a huge fan base. Like other pop fans around the world, their followers imitate the musician's hair and clothing styles, makeup, and jewelry. Why do fans do this?

 **Ideas**   **How does what you choose to watch on television affect your point of view on diversity?**

The students responding to this question are Katerina, who lives in St. Albert and whose grandparents emigrated from Ukraine in 1948; Deven, who was born in India but is now a Canadian who lives in Calgary; and Gord, a member of the Beaver First Nation near High Level.

> I watch Canadian newscasts, but sometimes I switch to CNN or BBC World just to compare. You can really see a difference in the things they choose to cover and the way they cover things . . . their approach. Quite often, things that are big issues in Canada are not even mentioned on American and British newscasts, and vice versa. So switching around gives me different views on what's important — and I think this is good.

Katerina

> I watch lots of American TV shows and movies, and I also watch sports — well, soccer, actually — on the sports channel. Canadian programs? Not so much, but sometimes. Some of the comedy stuff is pretty good. My parents like to watch Indian movies on DVD, and I sometimes watch with them. I suppose you could say that I'm influenced by three cultures — but this gives me more to enjoy.

 Deven

> I watch APTN sometimes, and I like shows like Hank William's First Nation. It's pretty good. But I also watch a lot of American shows, especially reality shows. But they hardly ever show Aboriginal people. Sometimes, I think I should write a letter. Where are the Aboriginal people? How come I only see them on APTN? Where's the diversity?

 Gord

Your Turn   How would you respond to the question Katerina, Deven, and Gord are answering? What choices do you make in your television viewing? Why do you make those choices? How does what you watch influence your views of people who are different from you? How do your choices shape your identity?

1. Everyone has a tendency to want what psychologists describe as personal space. This is the amount of physical space people feel comfortable about placing between themselves and others in various situations. When you are with friends or family, for example, you may feel quite comfortable if they are close to you and even touch you at times. But on an elevator, you may feel uncomfortable if people are squeezed in tightly.

   Your personal space includes audio space — the amount of sound that intrudes on you. Joshua Quittner, an information technology writer for *Time* magazine, wrote the following:

   > We don't need better cellphone technology from Finland, or Lapland, or anywhere else. What we need is anti-cellphone technology, to take back the streets (and passenger trains and restaurants and theaters and airplanes) from the cell-people before we all go crazy.

   Work with a partner to create a poster about the rights and responsibilities of cellphone use; for example, cellphone users have a right to use this communication tool, but they also have a responsibility to respect the personal space of others. Join four or five other pairs to create a display of your posters.

2. Whose news are you watching, reading, and listening to? The list of those who shape and deliver the news is long — and not always obvious. There is the editor who cuts and assembles the images for TV reports, and the photo editor who decides which photographs to print with a newspaper story. Then there are the reporters, who decide whose voices will be heard in stories. There are also advertisers, whom media owners must please. And in some countries, government policy can dictate the point of view a story must take.

   Watch a TV news report or read a news story in a newspaper or online. List at least five people who may have had a hand in shaping the report — and think about how each may have influenced what you saw or read. Was the photo editor, for example, sending a subtle message by choosing a flattering — or unflattering — picture of someone involved in the story?

   Then, rewrite the main idea of the news story from the point of view of one of the other people involved in shaping the story. How might this change the story?

   How does what's reported as news affect your view of global events and your identity? Explain your response.

3. According to Marshall McLuhan, all media affect people's identity in some way. Think about five messages you have recently received via the media: TV, radio, a magazine, a billboard, a movie, or another source. Consider how each message might be trying to influence or change you — to manage your worldview in some way — and how these influences might be affecting who you are: your identity.

   Create a chart like the one shown and use it to assess each of the five messages you selected. A sample response has been filled in for you.

Medium and Item	Main Message	Source Country	How does it try to influence me?	How is its message tied to culture and identity?
Movie shown on TV: How the Grinch Stole Christmas	Happiness comes not from having more "things" but from appreciating the value of what you do have.	USA	The Grinch's identity changes from evil to good when he learns that "things" aren't the basis of happiness. But at the same time, 30 commercials were shown during the show.	It shows that friendliness and respect are the basis of a positive view of oneself. But the commercials seemed to contradict this message by telling me that to be happy, I must buy the things advertised.

4. Zara Houshmand is an Iranian-born American writer who wrote the poem on this page soon after the September 11, 2001, attacks on the United States. At the time, the news was full of accusations against various Muslim groups — and "Another Day and Counting" expressed Houshmand's feelings about the media messages that were affecting her identity.

a) Select five words and phrases Houshmand uses to express her emotional state. Describe her emotional state in your own words.

b) After the twin towers of the World Trade Center collapsed, dust filled the air for days. In the second stanza, Houshmand uses the word "dust" five times. Explain the meaning contained in this word each time she uses it.

c) In the final stanza, Houshmand wrote: "The tiny paper stars and stripes seem far away." Explain what this sentence means. How does it reflect her mixed emotions about her identity as an Iranian and as an American?

d) Reread the final sentence of the poem. It starts, "The waitress smiles . . ." Explain how this sentence sums up Houshmand's mixed feelings about what has happened — and what is happening.

Another Day and Counting

by Zara Houshmand

It's routine now:
I drive my son to school,
the sun just breaking through Pacific mist.
Driving home, I listen to the news
and quietly cry.

My son won't listen anymore:
"All opinions, hot air. Call me when they
    find some facts."
Proud and fragile privilege of youth:
demand the truth.

The sky recedes, ashamed.
What passes now for truth on this cold ball?
The sky is pink with shame
beyond the concrete ribbons where commuters crawl.
What's in that microscopic dust
that bends our light to post-card pinks?
Dust of concrete hopes exploded,
dust of homes of sun-baked brick,
complex chains of human dust
and dust of promises to youth.

Tonight my cheeseburger arrives
with a flag poked proudly in the bun.
The tiny paper stars and stripes seem far away,
victory through the wrong end of the telescope,
moon-landing on the circle of my plate.
The waitress smiles broadly,
but the food tastes bad,
or maybe I've just lost my appetite.

Think about Your Challenge

Review the challenge for this related issue: a presentation that explains your position on the extent to which globalization should shape identity.

Think about the material in this chapter and the activities you completed as you progressed through it. Note ideas that could be useful as you prepare your presentation. After reading this chapter, do you wish to add to the list of criteria and critical questions you created to help evaluate the data you are putting together? Or do you wish to change any of the questions?

Chapter 4 Affirming Identity, Language, and Culture

Figure 4-1 Every summer, the people of Calgary celebrate their community and their cultural heritage at the Calgary Stampede. These photographs show highlights from the parade that opens the Stampede, as well as the chuckwagon races that are a crowd favourite.

CHAPTER ISSUE

To what extent can people respond to globalizing forces that affect identity?

THE PHOTOGRAPHS of the Calgary Stampede on the previous page show an event that Albertans — and hundreds of thousands of visitors — celebrate every summer. Individuals and collectives from Calgary, from other parts of Alberta, from Canada's other provinces and territories, and from countries around the world celebrate together by sharing, affirming, and promoting their traditions, languages, and cultures.

Examine the photographs on the previous page. Find and list elements that show

- people affirming their cultural identity
- the traditions that are part of Alberta's cultural heritage
- people sharing one another's culture
- ways that community celebrations help people share their culture
- the influences of global connections and interdependence

Think about the significance to cultural identity of community events like the Calgary Stampede. How do celebrations like this help bring communities together? How do these events reflect ways in which Albertans are responding to globalization?

KEY TERMS

cultural content laws

cultural diversity

LOOKING AHEAD

In this chapter, you will explore answers to the following questions:

- How do people affirm and promote their language in a globalizing world?
- How do people affirm and promote their culture in a globalizing world?
- How do governments affirm and promote languages and cultures in a globalizing world?
- How do international organizations affirm and promote languages and cultures in a globalizing world?

My Point of View on Globalization

Look back at the notes you recorded as you began each of the previous three chapters. How have your understandings of globalization changed? Use words or images — or both — to answer this question. Date your ideas and add them to the notebook, learning log, portfolio, or computer file you are keeping as you progress through this course.

HOW DO PEOPLE AFFIRM AND PROMOTE THEIR LANGUAGE IN A GLOBALIZING WORLD?

To some people, language *is* identity. Language is so important to cultural identity that peoples, governments, and organizations around the world use many different strategies to affirm their language in a globalizing world. How important is your language to you? How does it shape your identity?

People have always expressed their traditions, values, world views, and cultures through language. In *Empires of the Word: A Language History of the World*, language expert Nicholas Ostler wrote that written and oral languages do more than just help people communicate with one another: "Even when they are unwritten, languages are the most powerful tools we have to conserve our past knowledge, transmitting it, ever and anon, to the next generation. Any human language binds together a human community, by giving it a network of communication; but it also dramatizes [the community], providing the means to tell, and to remember, its stories."

Think about a typical day in your life. Up in the morning. Prepare for school. Go to classes. See friends. Homework. TV. Bed. Choose a day and list your activities. Beside each, indicate what role language played. Did you, for example, read the label on the juice box at breakfast? How many people did you speak to at school? What was the reason for each conversation? Keep this list for future reference.

The table on this page shows the percentage of Canadians whose first language was English, French, or a language other than Canada's two official languages in three different years. What changes do these statistics show? How do you think globalization has contributed to these changes? What changes do you think might show up in statistics for 2006? For 2011?

Figure 4-2 Language Groups in Canada, 1991–2001

Designation	1991	1996	2001
Anglophone	60.4%	59.8%	59.1%
Francophone	24.3%	23.5%	22.9%
Allophone (people whose first language is a non-official language)	15.3%	16.6%	18.0%

Source: Statistics Canada, "Population and growth rate of language groups, Canada, provinces, territories and Canada less Quebec, 1991, 1996, and 2001"

Differing Views

Some advocates of globalization believe that increased communication and interdependence will bring greater understanding among the peoples of the world. They say that if everyone speaks a common language, it could reduce the differences among peoples. Do you agree? If everyone spoke the same language, would fewer conflicts occur? What criteria might you use to make this prediction?

Other people believe that though globalization provides opportunities, it also presents challenges. They believe that globalization threatens cultural diversity. As proof, they sometimes point to the growing number of endangered languages. They believe that the challenge in a globalizing world is to find ways to affirm and promote all languages and cultures.

Figure 4-3 Inuit people have always handed down their culture and knowledge orally. This photograph shows Inuit teacher Rhoda Ungalaq telling students — in Inuktitut — about the *quilluliq*, the traditional lamp used for cooking and warmth.

Endangered Languages

The map on this page highlights two regions, the northwestern Caucasus and Vancouver Island, where languages have either disappeared or are endangered — at risk of disappearing.

The number of languages spoken in the world declines every year. On average, one language disappears every two weeks. Language experts believe that between 6000 and 7000 languages are spoken on Earth. Of these languages, 96 per cent are spoken by only four per cent of the world's people. More than half these languages are endangered.

Even linguists — people who study language — disagree over exactly how many languages exist and how many are in danger. How many languages can you name? You may be able to name the top three global languages in terms of number of speakers — Chinese, English, and Spanish — but it is much harder to know the total number of languages. There are many reasons for this. New languages are still being discovered in remote regions. Some countries don't keep track of the languages spoken by their citizens. And even if a country does keep track, people may disagree over what is a separate language and what is a dialect — one of a group of closely related languages.

Why languages disappear

Languages can disappear when few people can speak them. When Tevfik Esenç died in 1992, for example, the Ubykh language died with him. His people had come from the northwestern Caucasus region that is now part of Russia (see Figure 4-4). At one time, Ubykh was widely spoken in this area. But by the time Esenç died, even his three sons could not speak Ubykh. Before his death, Esenç wrote the inscription that he wanted placed on his tombstone: "This is the grave of Tevfik Esenç. He was the last person able to speak the language they called Ubykh."

Individuals and groups across Canada and around the world are working to keep endangered languages alive. Aboriginal Elder Carrie Little, for example, teaches the Nuuc'aańu, or Nootka, language to small groups of her people on Vancouver Island. This language has been in decline for more than 100 years — and today, only a few hundred people speak and understand Nuuc'aańu.

Why does the number of people who speak a language matter? Based on the stories of Tevfik Esenç and Carrie Little, what do you think are some of the challenges faced by language communities in a globalizing world? What do you think will happen to the Nuuc'aańu language in the future?

Figure 4-4 **Vancouver Island and the Caucasus**

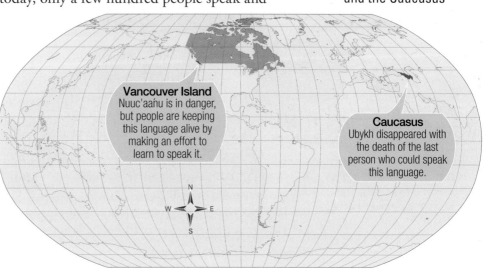

Vancouver Island
Nuuc'aańu is in danger, but people are keeping this language alive by making an effort to learn to speak it.

Caucasus
Ubykh disappeared with the death of the last person who could speak this language.

Dominance of English

Around the world, English has become the major language of business, scientific research, and popular culture. English is spoken by billions of people in dozens of countries. English is also the main language of the Internet and the World Wide Web. How would this affect you if you did not speak English? What challenges might you face in expressing your identity and your culture?

When computers first began to connect to the Internet, most users lived in English-speaking countries. Even in countries where English was not the first language, people who had access to the Internet were usually able to communicate in English. Accessing and understanding the Internet was not difficult for people whose first or second language was English.

The Internet was also designed to use the Roman alphabet (a, b, c, d, etc.), not characters like those in Arabic, Russian, Chinese, and Japanese. The result is that more than 90 per cent of the content on the Internet is now in only 21 languages. Most of the speakers of the world's more than 6000 languages do not benefit from — and often do not have access to — the Internet.

Christian Huitema, a wireless communications developer, believes that better translation tools are a possible answer to this problem. Translation cannot, however, carry the meaning of many ideas and feelings that are expressed in a language. Have you ever tried one of the translation tools available on the Web? If so, what was the result?

In addition, thousands of languages are just not represented on the Internet. Various international organizations warn that if nothing is done to correct this situation, it will lead to a loss of cultural diversity.

But some people are predicting that the dominance of English may not continue. Around the world, the number of people who grow up speaking English as their first language is declining. In the middle of the 20th century, nearly nine per cent of the world's population grew up speaking English. By 2050, this figure is expected to drop to five per cent.

CHAPPATTE
Int'l Herald Tribune

Figure 4-5 In 1998, a U.S.-based non-profit organization took over the control of the Internet. Why do you think cartoonist Patrick Chappatte, along with other commentators, is concerned about American control of the World Wide Web?

In 2006, the world's largest language group, in terms of first-language speakers, was Mandarin Chinese.

What difference will it make if the number of people who speak English as a first language declines? Consider the countries where English speakers are being born. Where, in general, do these countries rate as world powers? In a globalizing world, which is more influential: the number of speakers of a language or the dominance of a language group?

Magic Carpet

In this story, Mitali Perkins tells how her childhood need to assimilate into Western culture caused the loss of her first language, Bangla, and many of her family connections.

I had a magic carpet once. It used to soar to a world of monsoon storms, princesses with black braids, ferocious dragons, and talking birds.

"Ek deen chilo akta choto rajkumar," my father would begin, and the rich, round sounds of the Bangla language took me from our cramped New York City apartment to a marble palace in ancient India.

Americans made fun of my father's lilting accent and the strange grammatical twists his sentences took in English. What do they know? I thought, perching happily beside him.

In Bangla, he added his own creative flourishes to classic tales by Rabindranath Tagore or Sukumar Roy. He embellished folktales told by generations of ancestors, making me chuckle or catch my breath. "Tell another story, Dad," I'd beg.

But then I learned to read. Greedy for stories, I devoured books in the children's section of the library.

In those days, it was easy to conclude that any tale worth publishing originated in the so-called West, was written in English, and featured North American or European characters.

Slowly, insidiously, I began to judge my heritage through colonial eyes. I asked my mother not to wear a sari, her traditional dress, when she visited me at school.

I avoided the sun so that the chocolate hue of my skin couldn't darken. The nuances and cadences of my father's Bangla began to grate on my ears. "Not THAT story again, Dad," I'd say. "I'm reading right now."

My father didn't give up easily. He tried teaching me to read Bangla, but I wasn't interested. Soon, I no longer came to sit beside him, and he stopped telling stories altogether.

As an adult, I've struggled to learn to read Bangla. I repudiate [argue against] any definition of beauty linked to a certain skin color. I've even lived in Bangladesh to immerse myself in the culture.

These efforts help, but they can't restore what I've lost. Once a child relinquishes her magic carpet, she and her descendants lose it forever.

Figure 4-6 Mitali Perkins was born in Kolkata, which was formerly known as Calcutta. Her family lived in Cameroon, Ghana, Mexico, and New York before settling in San Francisco.

REFLECT AND RESPOND

"The loss of a language is more than the loss of the ability to communicate with others." Explain what this statement means. How does Mitali Perkins's story illustrate this statement?

In groups, brainstorm to create a list of reasons why languages have been lost. In your session, talk about the consequences for the identity of members of a language group when their language is lost. Then list four positive steps that members of a group might take to affirm their language and identity.

PREDICTING LIKELY OUTCOMES

Around the world, the number of people who speak Indigenous languages is dropping. An Indigenous language is one that originated in a specific place and was not brought from somewhere else. Various individuals, groups, and organizations are trying to stop this language decline.

Consider this question: How successful will efforts to save the world's endangered languages be?

No one can know the answer to this question. But to do something about the situation, people need to develop informed opinions. How would you develop a prediction that is informed and is based on reliable factual evidence?

The following steps can help you conduct research to develop an informed prediction in response to the question. As you progress through this course, you can use these steps to help you make predictions in response to other questions.

Steps to Predicting Likely Outcomes

Step 1: Review prior knowledge

When researching to predict what is likely to happen in the future, the present is a good place to start.

- Think about what you already know. You might start by making notes on the section of this chapter that talked about Indigenous languages.
- Think about your own experience. The language you speak at home, for example, may not be English. You may take language learning classes outside school, or you may have discussed the life of the language with Elders or teachers.
- What is your point of view as you start this inquiry? You may believe, for example, that Canada is not doing enough to save endangered languages. Or you may not have formed an opinion yet.

Step 2: Establish criteria for making judgments

Establish criteria for judging whether efforts to save endangered languages will be successful. You can express these criteria as questions (e.g., Is the number of speakers of endangered languages rising? What do people who have studied the issue say?).

You may wish to check the prologue to review strategies for developing criteria.

Step 3: Create a point-proof-comment organizer

A point-proof-comment organizer can help you prepare to make and back up a prediction.

On a sheet of paper or in a computer file, create an organizer like the one shown here. Repeat the point-proof-comment pattern several times. Use a full page so you will have plenty of room for writing and thinking through the evidence you gather. An example is provided below.

How successful will efforts to save the world's endangered languages be?	
Research Source 1: <u>Exploring Globalization</u> (page 91)	
Point	Many languages are endangered because few people speak them.
Proof	96% of endangered languages are spoken by only 4% of the world's people.
Comment	More people need to be encouraged to learn to speak endangered languages.
Research Source 2:	
Point	
Proof	
Comment	

RESEARCH TIP

Remember that your criteria — and question — can change. As you conduct your research, you may want to alter your criteria to reflect your changing point of view.

Step 4: Conduct research

Examine the sources on this page. As you review each, ask, What do I think? How does this information meet my criteria for judgment?

You will also need to conduct other research. Where could you locate a variety of relevant, useful, up-to-date resources? Consider the kind of data you need. For example, do you want numerical data? Then the Statistics Canada web site may be the place to go.

Record a point, a proof, and a comment on the evidence the source offers.

Summing up

Review your criteria. Do you need to change any of your questions? Review your notes and point-proof-comment organizer. Which arguments are most reliable and authoritative? Reflect on your findings and whether your position has changed since you started.

Write a paragraph that states your prediction, explains why you are making it, and supports it with reliable evidence. If you can't make a prediction, explain why not. Edit your paragraph until it clearly says exactly what you want it to say.

● ● ● ● ●

Source 1 According to the Worldwatch Institute, an international research organization, many of the world's Indigenous languages are endangered.

> More than half of the world's 7000 languages are endangered, and nearly 550 languages are spoken fluently by fewer than 100 people, increasing the likelihood that they will disappear quickly. Of these, 516 are considered nearly extinct. A language is classified as nearly extinct when the speaker population is fewer than 50 or when the number of speakers represents a very small fraction of an ethnic group.

Source 2 Statistics Canada reports that, in 1996, 29 per cent of Aboriginal peoples in Canada said they had enough knowledge of an Aboriginal language to carry on a conversation. By 2001, this figure had dropped to 24 per cent (see Figure 4-7).

Source 3 Mark Abley, a Canadian writer, studies languages. In his book *Spoken Here: Travels among Threatened Languages*, he talks about the Hebrew language, which is used in everyday life in Israel: in schools, in government, on television and radio, in songs and theatres. In the 1995 census, 4 510 000 people in Israel — or 63 per cent of the population — spoke Hebrew.

> In 1880 no child in the world spoke Hebrew as a first language. Although it had a rich vocabulary, Hebrew was a sacred language that was used mainly for prayer and recitation. Today, after many years of determined efforts by the Jewish people to revitalize and modernize the language, Hebrew is the official language of Israel.

Figure 4-7
Aboriginal Language Speakers in Canada

Aboriginal Language	Speakers in 1996	Speakers in 2001	Percentage Change
Cree	95 555	92 630	−3.1
Inuktitut	29 400	31 945	8.7
Ojibway	29 735	27 955	−6.0
Dene	9525	10 500	10.2
Montagnais-Naskapi	9335	10 285	10.2
Micmac	7975	8625	8.2
Oji-Cree	5480	5610	2.4
Attikamekw	4075	4935	21.1
Dakota/Sioux	4710	4875	3.5
Blackfoot	5530	4415	−20.2
Salish languages not included elsewhere	2285	2675	17.1
Algonquin	2555	2340	−8.4
Dogrib	2430	2265	−6.8
Carrier	2830	2000	−29.3

Source: Statistics Canada, "Aboriginal-identity population with knowledge of an Aboriginal language and with an Aboriginal language as mother tongue, for selected languages with 2,000 or more speakers, Canada, 1996 and 2001."

HOW DO PEOPLE AFFIRM AND PROMOTE THEIR CULTURE IN A GLOBALIZING WORLD?

When you affirm your identity, you strengthen your sense of self through your personal expressions. When the descendents of people who came to Alberta from Ukraine created a heritage village (see Figure 4-8), they strengthened their collective identity. Collectives affirm their identity when they speak their language or express their culture, nation, or gender. But how does globalization affect collective cultural identity? How can people affirm their culture and avoid being fed into what Gwynne Dyer calls "the industrial-strength blender" (see Voices on this page)?

Figure 4-8 The Ukrainian Heritage Village near Edmonton affirms the culture and heritage of people who came to Alberta from Ukraine. How do sites like this promote a community's culture in a globalizing world?

Some people affirm their cultural identity by reclaiming what has been lost. In 2006, for example, the Haisla people of British Columbia reclaimed a totem pole, called the G'psgolox pole, from the National Museum of Ethnography in Stockholm, Sweden. The totem pole had been taken from the Haisla in 1927.

The Na na kila Institute of the Haisla Nation explained what the return of the G'psgolox pole meant: "This totem represents so much more than just a monument; it is symbolic of our character, our integrity, our fortitude, and our identity as a nation. We are no longer frozen in time or put on display for others to see; this repatriation process reminds all that as a nation, we are present and active participants in our societies today."

Other people affirm their cultural identity by helping others promote their culture. The Krymsky Education Society of Edmonton, for example, is an organization of Albertans of Ukrainian descent and is helping Tartar people revitalize their culture and language.

The Tartar people live in the Crimean region of Ukraine, and UNESCO — the United Nations Educational, Scientific and Cultural Organization — lists their language as "seriously endangered." The language's status as endangered results partly from the fact that, after three centuries of Russian rule, the major language in the region is Russian. At the end of World War II, the Crimean Tartar language and culture were further weakened when Soviet dictator Joseph Stalin exiled about 200 000 Tartars to Central Asia. Because there are fewer Tartar speakers today than there once were, there are not many schoolbooks in the Tartar language.

On the other side of the world, the Krymsky Education Society of Edmonton is helping revitalize the Tartar culture by producing bilingual Ukrainian and Tartar textbooks for children in the Crimea.

VOICES

One culture after another, we are all being fed into an industrial-strength blender, and we all come out changed. What would a global culture mean? It would mean that the world goes on speaking 50 major languages and hundreds of little ones, but increasingly it talks about the same things from the same perspectives in all of them.

— *Gwynne Dyer, columnist and filmmaker, in* Millennium, *a series produced for CBC Radio*

Cultural Revitalization — Challenges and Opportunities

Cultural revitalization is one way for a nation or a people to keep their cultural identity from being absorbed into the "industrial-strength blender" of globalization.

Douglas Cardinal's design for the First Nations University of Canada (see Figure 4-9) preserves the past at the same time as the institution offers opportunities for future generations. The past is represented in the design of the building, which revitalizes aspects of traditional First Nations architecture.

The cultural treasures of many Aboriginal peoples have survived in museums in Canada and around the world. These objects, or artifacts, include clothing, tools, jewelry, historical documents, and photographs. Though some of these artifacts were obtained legally, others were not.

Many of the Aboriginal artifacts on display in these museums have spiritual significance to the Aboriginal people from whom they were acquired. Slowly, over the years, museums have started to return these treasures to their original owners: Aboriginal peoples.

Figure 4-9 Canadian Aboriginal architect Douglas Cardinal designed the First Nations University of Canada in Regina, Saskatchewan, in consultation with First Nations Elders. First Nations peoples run the university. How do you think this university represents both the challenges and the opportunities that First Nations young people face in a globalizing world?

Ideas

Should museums return Aboriginal artifacts to the people who originally created and used them?

The students responding to this question are Deven, who was born in India but is now a Canadian who lives in Calgary; Gord, a member of the Beaver First Nation near High Level; and Katerina, who lives in St. Albert and whose grandparents emigrated from Ukraine in 1948.

I love going to museums—you get to see the actual things that people created and used. The artifacts pull you back to the people who made them; they help you understand those people. And the artifacts in museums are well taken care of.

Deven

Of course the museums should give artifacts back. They aren't supposed to be looked at by themselves, away from the people who made them and the places that inspired them. How can you find out about a people from a museum display? If you want to know what artifacts mean, you have to listen to the people who made them.

Gord

My uncle belongs to the Krymsky Education Society. He says that when the Tartar people were expelled from the Crimea, they carried only basic necessities with them. They couldn't take their cultural treasures all the way to Central Asia. If it hadn't been for the museums, the treasures would have been lost forever.

Katerina

Your Turn

How would you respond to the question Deven, Gord, and Katerina are answering? Explain the reasons for your answer. What aspects of your own experience and your own background influence the way you respond to this question?

MHR • To what extent can people respond to globalizing forces that affect identity?

LADAKH — RESPONDING TO GLOBALIZATION IMPACT

When the remote Indian region of Ladakh was opened to tourists in the early 1970s, Dolma Tsering was alarmed. Over the next decades, she watched as her fellow Ladakhis embraced the values that arrived with the tourists.

To Tsering, it seemed as if Ladakhis were slowly but surely losing their distinctive identity and culture. But then, things began to change — and today, Tsering, who leads the Women's Alliance of Ladakh, is optimistic about her people's ability to shape their own future in their own way.

"For a while," Tsering told an interviewer, "we in Ladakh lost respect for ourselves and for our culture. But now we know we have no reason to feel inferior. Now we feel more confident about who we are. In fact, we know now that the world can learn a lot from us. It is important that our young people understand that. There is much that Ladakh can teach the world."

Living in Ladakh

Located high in the Himalaya Mountains, Ladakh is part of the northern Indian state of Jammu and Kashmir. About 200 000 Ladakhis exist in one of the harshest livable environments in the world. Ladakh is covered in snow for about eight months of the year — and the extreme altitude, cold, and isolation helped create a unique, self-sufficient culture that thrived for centuries.

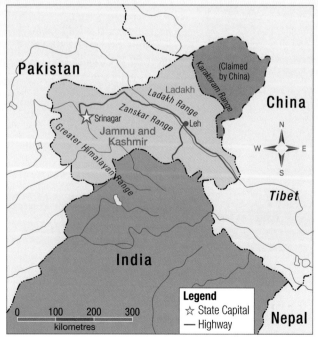

Figure 4-10 Ladakh Region

Ladakhis remained isolated from the outside world for much longer than most other Indigenous cultures. Before a highway was opened in 1962, the only way to reach the area was to hike through narrow mountain passes. Even after the highway was built, the Indian government barred tourists from entering Ladakh because of a continuing border dispute with neighbouring China.

Despite its isolation, Ladakh was influenced by outside forces. Both Buddhism and Islam, the chief religions of most of the people, were imported from other regions. And Ladakhi men had always travelled to sell their products — primarily jewelry, salt, and dried fruit — and to buy goods, such as sugar and tea, which they cannot grow themselves.

New Economic Opportunities

The opening of the highway brought new economic opportunities to the region. Ladakhis found much larger markets. India, for example, began to buy large amounts of barley and grain. In addition, adventure tourism and trekking brought in even more money and significantly increased the income of many Ladakhis. And cheap imported food and products have become widely available, especially in Leh, the region's biggest town.

In addition, Amchi, a traditonal herb- and mineral-based medicine, has attracted the attention of the outside world. The ancient knowledge of Amchi is now being studied by other medical systems, such as India's, to see how it can benefit others.

Globalization Comes to Ladakh

As the world found out about Ladakh — and Ladakh found out about the world — the region faced many challenges. Helena Norberg-Hodge, a Swedish activist, was one of the first to document the effects of contact on Ladakhis. She wrote that, before the 1970s, Ladakh had developed a highly independent culture based on agriculture. People produced a surplus that they sold for enough money to buy luxuries, such as jewelry. Women were treated as equals, and children were taught skills that enabled them to contribute through co-operation, not competition.

Although incomes in Ladakh were low by Western standards, Ladakhis believed that their quality of life was excellent. Norberg-Hodge described a villager who was confused when asked where the poor lived in his village. "We don't have any poor people here," he said.

Contact with Western tourists began to change this perspective. Ladakhis viewed tourists as wealthy, because they were able to travel thousands of kilometres for pleasure. As a result, many Ladakhis — especially young people — began to think of themselves as poor and primitive. They started abandoning their own traditions to imitate the dress, lifestyles, and behaviour of tourists.

Tourism also brought other challenges. Water, for example, had always been scarce in Ladakh, where people used compost toilets that require no water. But tourists demanded flush toilets, as well as water for baths and showers. This depleted the water supply, and created pollution because sewers do not exist. Waste is emptied into large cesspits, which leak into rivers and pollute underground water supplies.

Ladakhis Respond to Globalization

Many Ladakhis began taking steps to affirm and promote their culture. The Women's Alliance, for example, is a group of Buddhist farm women who came together to preserve the region's small-scale farming traditions. The group also tries to find solutions to environmental problems.

For many people, the key to helping Ladakhis regain a strong sense of identity lies in educating young people — in the traditional Ladakhi way. Sonam Wangchuk, for example, founded the Students' Educational and Cultural Movement of Ladakh. He said that the Indian education system had failed Ladakh. This system, he said, "helped convince people here that they were backward and primitive, that their language was worthless, that their traditions were bad."

Wangchuk said Ladakhis know that they cannot stop change. But, he added, "We must remain Ladakhis still — culturally, economically, in our hearts — and not some imitation of what we think the rest of the world is like."

Figure 4-11 When this highway opened in 1962, it marked the beginning of the end of Ladakh's isolation from the rest of the world.

Explorations

1. Think about what you have learned so far about measures taken by various collectives to affirm and promote their identity in a globalizing world. Prepare a list of the stakeholders involved in making decisions about revitalizing Ladakhi culture. On the list, make a point-form note about the interest of each stakeholder. Compare your list with those of others in the class and revise your list if necessary.

2. Suppose Ladakhi community leaders have asked several people to share their points of view on these questions: How should we Ladakhi respond to the situation we are facing? Should we isolate ourselves and refuse all contact? Is it even possible to "put the genie back in the bottle"? Can we limit contact with the outside world? Or should we assimilate?

With a partner, choose one of the following characters and prepare a brief oral presentation setting out the approach this person might suggest. Be sure your character explains why his or her approach would be effective.

- a Ladakhi teenager
- a Ladakhi farm woman
- a Ladakhi mother or father
- an outside tourist operator
- another stakeholder of your choice

Akaitapiiwa: Ancestors exhibit

In 2002, Loretta Sarah Todd, who is Métis and Cree, made a film — *Kainayssini Imanistaisiwa: The People Go On* — about the struggle of the Kainai people of Standoff, Alberta, to reclaim their ancestral treasures from museums in Canada and England. These treasures include medicine bundles made up of objects that are sacred to the Kainai people.

The film explains that during the late 19th and early 20th centuries, anthropologists expected Aboriginal languages and cultures to die. Some believed that if cultural artifacts were not taken away and put into museums, they would be lost forever.

But now, the Kainai people, who are part of the Blackfoot Nation, want their artifacts returned. They believe that restoring these artifacts to their territory in southern Alberta is an important step in revitalizing and affirming their cultural identity. The land on which they and their ancestors have lived is very important to Blackfoot people. Annabel Crop Eared Wolf explains in the film: "This is our home where our land and culture are one." The land holds the memory of the people.

In May 2002, the Kainai people created an exhibit of 250 artifacts — lent to them by the British Museum and museums in Canada — at the Sir Alexander Galt Museum in Lethbridge. How could this be viewed as a possible first step in bringing these artifacts home?

During the month before the exhibit opened, Kainai Elders selected regalia, clothing, tools, jewelry, historical documents, and photographs for the exhibit. The Elders also helped museum staff decide on the most appropriate way to display the artifacts. In some cases, the Elders identified artifacts that belonged to specific families. This identification helped the descendants of the original owners make a direct link to their ancestors. In what ways might these links affect how some young people of the Kainai Nation see themselves?

Figure 4-12 Myron Beebe puts together a teepee at the Sir Alexander Galt Museum in Lethbridge, Alberta, in 2002. The teepees were set up as part of an exhibit titled Akaitapiiwa:Ancestors, which featured more than 200 Kainai artifacts.

REFLECT AND RESPOND

If you were to contribute artifacts to a virtual museum promoting your culture, what items would you include? Select treasures that would help your classmates understand who your people were in the past, who they are today, and who they want to become in the future.

HOW DO GOVERNMENTS AFFIRM AND PROMOTE LANGUAGES AND CULTURES IN A GLOBALIZING WORLD?

In 1971, Canada became the first country in the world to adopt multiculturalism as official government policy. This policy, which encourages Canada's many cultural groups to preserve, enhance, and share their heritage, was adopted by Parliament and proclaimed by Prime Minister Pierre Elliott Trudeau.

At the time, Trudeau said that a policy of multiculturalism within a bilingual framework is "the most suitable means of assuring the cultural freedom of Canadians . . . National unity, if it is to mean anything in the deeply personal sense, must be founded on confidence in one's own individual identity; out of this can grow respect for that of others and a willingness to share ideas, attitudes, and assumptions."

Since 2003, Canadians have celebrated Multiculturalism Day on June 27. On Multiculturalism Day in 2006, Canada's governor general, Michaëlle Jean, reaffirmed the policy, saying, "Today's Canada contains the world. Rich in its demographic and cultural diversity, Canada is a model of openness and harmony in the concert of nations."

Jean continued: "Bringing together so many cultures and perspectives certainly enriches us all, but it is also a challenge that all of humanity must now face in this age of globalization . . . Together, let us build on the strengths of our diversity and on dialogue rather than become mired in the clash of cultures."

What do you think Jean's remarks meant? What role might your community or school play in helping citizens become stronger by affirming and promoting their various languages and cultures?

Figure 4-13 **Official Languages in Selected Jurisdictions**

Country or Territory	Languages
New Zealand	English and Maori
Belgium	Dutch, French, and German
India	Hindi, Bengali, Telugu, Marathi, Tamil, Urdu, Gujarati, Malayalam, Kannada, Oriya, Punjabi, Assamese, Kashmiri, Sindhi, and Sanskrit (English is not an official language of India)
Canada	English and French
Northwest Territories	English, French, and languages belonging to the Dene, Inuit, and Cree language families

Web Connection

For her coat of arms, Michaëlle Jean, Canada's governor general, carefully selected elements that symbolize her identity. To find out more about Jean's heritage and the meaning of these symbols to her and her heritage, go to this web site and follow the links.

www.ExploringGlobalization.ca

BRISER LES SOLITUDES

Figure 4-14 Michaëlle Jean, who was born in Haiti, became the governor general of Canada in 2006. Her personal coat of arms, shown here, includes words and symbols from Africa, Haiti, and Canada, the cultures that have helped shape her identity. If you were to create a personal coat of arms to affirm your language and culture, what symbols and words would you include?

Government Roles in Promoting Language and Culture

Around the world, various governments are developing programs, policies, and laws to protect and promote language and culture. In Canada, for example, the Official Languages Act of 1969 extended the idea of English and French as the country's official languages. And in 1982, the Charter of Rights and Freedoms helped strengthen minority English and French language rights across the country.

Some cultural and language policies are national; others are regional. The Canada Day Poster Challenge is an example of a national initiative. In 2004, the government of the Northwest Territories introduced a policy requiring school boards to provide 90 hours of instruction in Aboriginal languages every year. Considering that many homes in the Territories have satellite dishes that beam in TV programs from around the world — and that most of these programs are in English — do you think this instruction in Aboriginal languages will be effective?

Figure 4-15 Sofia Hou, a 14-year-old student from Ottawa, won the 2006 Canada Day Poster Challenge sponsored by the federal Department of Canadian Heritage. The theme for the challenge was "Images of Canada." Do you believe that government-sponsored competitions like this help Canadians affirm their cultures in a globalizing world?

Controlling content

Much of the television that Canadians watch is produced in the United States. Some Canadians believe that this puts Canadian stories, songs, myths, and dreams at risk. As a result, Canada has passed **cultural content laws** to protect artists, performers, songs, movies, and literature.

Since 1968, the Canadian Radio-television and Telecommunications Commission has enforced quotas for Canadian content on radio and TV. The goal of the CRTC rules is to protect and preserve Canada's cultural identity by ensuring that Canadians hear Canadian voices and see Canadian stories. Thirty per cent of music played by Canadian radio stations and 60 per cent of programming on Canadian TV stations must be Canadian. And in Québec, the Québec Cinema Act of 1988 requires filmmakers to create and produce their films in Québec.

Many other countries have also passed laws and regulations about media content to help protect their cultural identities. The following are some examples:

- In France, theatres must show French feature films for 20 weeks a year.
- In Australia, 55 per cent of Australian television programs must be made in Australia.
- The Chinese government has created a list of about 20 000 English words that must be translated into Chinese.
- In Mexico, films from other countries may be shown with Spanish subtitles, but dubbing — adding a sound track that replaces the foreign-language dialogue with Spanish — is not allowed.

REFLECT AND RESPOND

Develop three criteria you could use to judge the success of a government policy or law designed to affirm and promote minority languages and cultures. One of your criteria, for example, may require you to research historical data to answer this question: Has this law or policy really increased the promotion of minority language and culture in Canada?

BOBBY KENUAJUAK
TELLING HIS PEOPLE'S STORIES

PROFILE PROFILE
PROFILE
PROFILE
PROFILE

Bobby Kenuajuak, who is Inuit, was 23 years old when he received a National Film Board internship for Aboriginal filmmakers. The NFB is a federal cultural agency whose mandate is to produce and distribute films that tell Canadian stories. Kenuajuak studied at the NFB's Montréal headquarters, where he produced *My Village in Nunavik* in 1999.

Kenuajuak's film portrays life in and around his village of Puvirnituq, on Hudson Bay in northern Québec. In the film, Kenuajuak describes his heritage: "My village, Puvirnituq, is barely 60 years old, but my land is as old as time. When you hear about us in the South, it is often through stories of disaster and human suffering. While this does exist, there is far more, a kind of joy we take from being together."

The Inuit who speak in the film tell stories — in both Inuktitut and English — about who they were in the past and who they are today. They reflect on their village and their land and on issues that affect them. The film paints a vibrant picture of the strength and humour of Kenuajuak's people as he reflects on how his own cultural experiences shaped his identity.

Today, the people of Puvirnituq live in the village most of the time. But they still go out on the land and the sea to hunt and fish to sustain both their lives and their cultural identity. "It is impossible to describe the feeling of freedom you get at sea," Kenuajuak says. "We are between sky and water on our way to another world. Each of us searches the sky for birds, imagining a great hunt . . . We are always heavy-hearted when we have to return to the village."

Figure 4-16 Since 1999, Bobby Kenuajuak (top) has been a television producer with Taqramiut Nipingat Incorporated, or Voice of the North, which broadcasts radio in Inuktitut. It also produces Inuktitut TV programs, which are broadcast on the Aboriginal Peoples Television Network. The photograph at the bottom was taken during filming of Arpik Jam, a music festival that takes place every year in Kuujjuaq, Nunavik.

HOW DO INTERNATIONAL ORGANIZATIONS AFFIRM AND PROMOTE LANGUAGES AND CULTURES IN A GLOBALIZING WORLD?

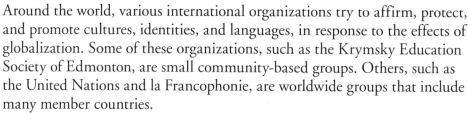

Web Connection

To find out more about the objectives, selection criteria, and action plans of UNESCO's Masterpieces of the Oral and Intangible Heritage of Humanity program, go to this web site and follow the links.

www.ExploringGlobalization.ca

Around the world, various international organizations try to affirm, protect, and promote cultures, identities, and languages, in response to the effects of globalization. Some of these organizations, such as the Krymsky Education Society of Edmonton, are small community-based groups. Others, such as the United Nations and la Francophonie, are worldwide groups that include many member countries.

UNESCO, which includes 191 member states, is one of the largest international organizations promoting **cultural diversity**. In November 2001, UNESCO adopted the Universal Declaration on Cultural Diversity, which includes this motto: The cultural wealth of the world is its diversity in dialogue. The September 11, 2001, attacks on the United States had taken place just two months earlier. UNESCO members wanted to affirm their belief that dialogue among peoples of different cultures was the best way to achieve peace around the world.

The International Network for Cultural Diversity

Some masterpieces of cultural heritage, such as buildings and monuments, are solid and permanent. But how do you promote and protect masterpieces of intangible heritage: the carnivals, songs, stories, theatre pieces, teachings, and celebrations that are part of a people's cultural identity?

In 2000, many people around the world decided that globalization was seriously threatening the intangible treasures of traditional cultures. By 2006, more than 50 countries had agreed to protect treasures like these through a UNESCO program called Masterpieces of the Oral and Intangible Heritage of Humanity. They wanted to make sure that these masterpieces would be preserved and passed on to future generations.

Intangible masterpieces include oral traditions. In the central Asian country of Kyrgyzstan, for example, storytellers have related epics — long poems about cultural heroes and events of the past — for centuries. These epics transmit the cultural knowledge and history of the Kyrgyz people. Though there are fewer storytellers today than in the past, some Kyrgyz young people are still willing to spend the years it takes to learn these epic poems.

The masterpieces on UNESCO's list also include dances that are sacred to various peoples. In the Drametse community of Bhutan, the mask dance, which honours a Buddhist teacher who lived centuries ago, has cultural and religious significance for the Drametse people. Today, the dance represents the cultural identity of not just the Drametse but of all the people of Bhutan.

Figure 4-17 This photographs shows the mask dance of the drums of the Drametse community in Bhutan. This dance is an example of what UNESCO has officially designated Masterpieces of the Oral and Intangible Heritage of Humanity. What does "intangible" mean? Why do you think UNESCO has created a special list for "masterpieces of oral and intangible heritage"?

La Francophonie

In July 2001, Canada hosted the 4th Games of la Francophonie, which involved 3000 participants from 51 countries. This event is one of the few international competitions in which people vie for both cultural and athletic awards.

In September 1999, Canada hosted the 8th Francophonie Summit in Moncton, New Brunswick. A major goal of the Moncton Summit was to respond to the needs of Francophone young people. Kofi Annan, the secretary general of the United Nations at the time, opened the summit. He said that la Francophonie wanted to encourage young people to build an international community "based not simply on a common language but on a common way of thinking and a common purpose, cemented by a set of shared values and ideals." Why do you think la Francophonie was so concerned about responding to issues that mattered to young people?

The youth delegates to the Moncton Summit had already met to discuss issues that mattered to them. In Canada, meetings had been held in Edmonton, Saint-Boniface, Sudbury, Chéticamp, Bouctouche, and Shawinigan. Finally, in Ottawa, they told ministers of the Canadian government that they were concerned about their future as Francophones in a globalizing world.

Youth delegates asked summit participants to address human rights and global citizenship issues. They said that they cared about issues that involved international co-operation and development. They were also concerned about the challenges that they and other young Francophones faced in integrating into a local or global workforce in which French was not most people's first language.

In response to the youth delegates' concerns about the challenges they faced when using new technologies, the Moncton Summit brought together web masters from all over the Francophone world. They discussed ways of protecting Francophone cultural identity on the Internet and helping keep globalization from turning the world into what Kofi Annan called "a place of dreary uniformity." At the end of the summit, la Francophonie created the Portail jeunesse, a web site that serves as a virtual meeting place for Francophone youth in countries around the world.

Figure 4-18 At the games of la Francophonie, both athletics and culture play important roles. Medals are awarded for the arts, as well as for sports. At the 2005 games in Niger, Africa, Canadian Kwaku Boateng (top) competed in the high jump, while François Lavallée and Normand Perron (bottom) competed in the storytelling category.

CHECKBACK
You read about la Francophonie in Chapter 1.

Figure 4-19 The Portail jeunesse web site was established after the Moncton Summit. Francophone youth from around the world use this portal to meet and discuss issues that concern them. How do you think this would help these young people affirm and promote their cultural identity?

MHR • To what extent can people respond to globalizing forces that affect identity?

The Assembly of First Nations and the Declaration on the Rights of Indigenous Peoples

In October 2006, Indigenous peoples from around the world met in New York to try to persuade the United Nations General Assembly to adopt the Declaration on the Rights of Indigenous Peoples. A month later, 87 countries, including many African countries as well as Canada and the United States, voted to delay passage of the declaration. As a result, it was not adopted by the UN in 2006.

The Conservative government of Prime Minister Stephen Harper issued a statement explaining the government's reasons for voting for the delay. The statement said that parts of the declaration were "vague and ambiguous" and subject to different "and possibly competing" interpretations. The statement also said that "parts of the current Declaration could be interpreted as being inconsistent with the Canadian Constitution Act, 1982, the Canadian Charter of Rights and Freedoms, and previous decisions of the Supreme Court of Canada."

Among the groups who support the declaration is the Assembly of First Nations, a Canadian group that is made up of representatives of the more than 600 First Nations across Canada. Under the umbrella of the AFN, these groups work together to achieve common goals: Aboriginal and treaty rights, self-determination, and rights over natural resources. Internationally, the AFN works with international organizations on issues such as Native culture, history, and education.

Phil Fontaine, an Anishinabé from Sagkeeng First Nation in Manitoba, was the national chief of the Assembly of First Nations in 2007. He said that the draft Declaration on the Rights of Indigenous Peoples "affirms diverse rights regarding lands, territories and resources that are essential to the cultural identities of Indigenous peoples and the fulfilment of their basic human rights."

Figure 4-20 Since 1977, Wilton Littlechild, a member of the Ermineskin Cree Nation and the former MP for Wetaskiwin, has worked for Indigenous peoples' rights at the United Nations. He is the regional chief for Alberta of the Assembly of First Nations, and in 2003, the Alberta-based Confederacy of Treaty 6 First Nations named him the international chief of Treaty 6.

Web Connection

To find out more about the current status of the Declaration on the Rights of Indigenous Peoples, go to this web site and follow the links.

www.ExploringGlobalization.ca

Figure 4-21 This is the logo of the Assembly of First Nations. How might this logo also represent the struggle for cultural revitalization of Indigenous peoples around the world?

In 2004, two international organizations — the Oxfam International Youth Parliament and UNESCO — asked young people in 10 countries to express their views on the Universal Declaration on Cultural Diversity. This declaration, which was adopted by the United Nations in 2001, affirms that all the peoples of the world have distinct cultural rights.

The young people were asked: How is cultural diversity a source of your identity? How does cultural diversity foster greater dialogue among peoples of different cultures? Some of their responses follow. Each response is paired with a summary of one of the 12 articles of the declaration. The young people are identified only by the countries they represent.

Figure 4-22 The foreword of *All Different, All Unique*, a report on how young people responded to the Universal Declaration on Cultural Diversity, said this: "All cultures are creative and dynamic, but they are also unique, fragile and irreplaceable. A culture neglected for a single generation can be lost forever. It is therefore crucial to create a safe environment in which all cultures can develop freely."

Colombia

Our country is rich in diversity. In Colombia, we speak Spanish. We have 65 Indigenous American languages and we also have languages spoken by people of African origin . . . Within this diversity, we young people constitute 24 per cent of the population. We have in our hands the dream to create a just country, more tolerant and respectful.

Article 1
Cultural diversity is part of our common history and is shared by all of us today. Its importance should be recognised by all people today and tomorrow.

Jordan

Although globalization may benefit the world through economic growth, communication and exposure, it can also cause confusion, loss of identity, loss of cultural heterogeneity (diversity), depletion of environmental resources, anarchy, war, and world domination.

Article 2
Respect for cultural diversity is the starting point for peaceful coexistence and the inclusion of all people. It should be the basis for life in a complex and multicultural world.

Australia

When cultural goods and services are treated as a commodity, there is a risk that they will be exploited. For example, the art of the Indigenous peoples of Australia is sometimes appropriated and sold for profit by non-Indigenous people whose sole objective is economic profit . . . The distribution of cultural goods and services must benefit the community from which they come.

Article 8
Cultures should be recognised as being valuable and unique. Thus, cultural goods and services must be treated with respect.

Explorations

1. Which of the issues raised by these young people matters most to you? Are you most concerned, for example, about Indigenous communities benefiting from the sale of their cultural goods?

2. Once you have made your choice, meet with a small group. Pool your issue selections and work together to choose one as a focus of research. Prepare a brief joint presentation that offers your informed opinion on this issue to the rest of the class.

1. Transnational corporations such as McDonald's, Coca-Cola, and Nike like to present the same "face," or identity, wherever they do business. Some people think this globalization of products and brand names threatens Indigenous and local cultures, languages, and identities. Prepare two charts like the ones shown to summarize your ideas about whether these corporate products and logos do, in fact, present a danger. One example has been filled in. Provide at least four others in each chart.

The Danger	Why a danger?
Not in the local language	This forces people to speak English words rather than their own language when they buy the product.

The Gain	Why a gain?
Same product everywhere	It makes me feel part of a large global community all enjoying the same thing.

2. At an Oxfam International Youth Parliament, an Australian young person said, "Increased awareness of cultural diversity will decrease ignorance and stereotyping. Everyone will have the opportunity to be who they are and to see their own culture in a positive way."

In a small group, prepare for a round-table discussion of the ideas expressed in this quotation — and how they relate to globalization and your identity. During the discussion, each group member should present a short statement, then be ready to respond to questions from other group members.

As a group, develop a consensus statement that reflects your group's perspective on the ideas.

3. Read the excerpt from the poem by Tom Wayman on this page.

a) In two or three sentences, sum up the main theme of the poem. How does this theme relate to the issues you have explored in this chapter? You may say, for example, that language — "these words" — has been handed down to you and connects you to other people like a "hall of global string." This connects to this chapter's exploration of responses to identity in a globalizing world.

b) Create a display that shows the central idea of the ball of global string connecting people all over the world. Your display may include quotations, newspaper headlines, data, and photographs from a variety of sources including this textbook, newspapers, the Internet, libraries, and expert opinions. Arrange these items around the central idea, and use different-coloured wool or markers to show the links and their meanings. Include a legend, such as the following, to explain the meaning of your links:

Green — People should be very cautious about their response to this aspect of globalization. It may present dangers to languages and cultures.

Red — This aspect of globalization offers genuine opportunities for people to affirm and promote their cultural identities.

Blue — This aspect of globalization offers both challenges and opportunities.

Yellow — I'm not sure what this aspect of globalization will mean.

c) When you present your display, explain where the items came from and why you chose to use them.

The Thread
by Tom Wayman

Moments after each of us is born
The umbilical cord is cut. But other fibres that tie us
   to our parents
commence at once to stretch
into bands that feed us and join us to the rest of the
   room
and beyond. We remain enmeshed our entire lives,
pulling the net this direction and that
as we travel and age, the web that holds us
flexible enough to let some of us journey to the
   moon.
Yet the anchor
of each of the million cords that wrap me,
that connect me to justice and injustice,
remains that closely-wound, pulsing ball
of global string.

Even these words
were handed to me
containing the grammars and syntaxes
others built and tore down
and constructed again, new verbs
forming, and nouns
appearing in my mouth or from under my pen:
airborne seeds from elsewhere
that find root in my days
— some destructive, some helpful,
each word trailing a resilient tendril,
another thread
that weaves me and all I do
into the warp of our world.

Think about Your Challenge

Look back at the challenge for this related issue. It asks you to develop a presentation that explains your position on this issue: To what extent should globalization shape identity?

   Review the material in this chapter and the activities you completed as you progressed through the chapter. Make notes about which of these could be useful in completing the challenge. Add to the list of criteria and critical questions you will use to evaluate the data you will explore and use in your presentation. Continue preparing your presentation.

RELATED ISSUE 2
To what extent should contemporary society respond to the legacies of historical globalization?

Key Issue
To what extent should we embrace globalization?

Related Issue 1
To what extent should globalization shape identity?

Related Issue 2
To what extent should contemporary society respond to the legacies of historical globalization?

Related Issue 3
To what extent does globalization contribute to sustainable prosperity for all people?

Related Issue 4
To what extent should I, as a citizen, respond to globalization?

Chapter 5
FOUNDATIONS OF GLOBALIZATION

To what extent did early globalization affect peoples of the world?

Why and how did globalization begin?

How did the foundations of historical globalization affect people?

How did the consequences of historical globalization affect people?

Chapter 6
LEGACIES OF HISTORICAL GLOBALIZATION

To what extent do the legacies of historical globalization affect peoples of the world?

What are some legacies of historical globalization?

How has cultural contact affected people?

How has the exchange of goods and technologies affected people?

How are the legacies of historical globalization continuing to affect people?

Chapter 7
LEGACIES OF HISTORICAL GLOBALIZATION IN CANADA

To what extent have the legacies of historical globalization affected Canada?

How did historical globalization affect Canada?

What are some legacies of historical globalization in Canada?

How has historical globalization affected Indigenous peoples in Canada?

How do some legacies of historical globalization continue to affect Canada?

Chapter 8
LIVING WITH THE LEGACIES OF HISTORICAL GLOBALIZATION

To what extent have attempts to respond to the legacies of historical globalization been effective?

How effectively have people responded to the legacies of historical globalization?

How effectively have governments responded to the legacies of historical globalization?

How effectively have organizations responded to the legacies of historical globalization?

How does historical globalization continue to affect the world?

THE BIG PICTURE

Events that happened in the past often affect people's lives today. In some ways, it is as if the past were still alive. Past events can affect the choices that are available to you now — but other choices are not yours to make.

Your birth, for example, was not a choice. You were born in a specific country, in a specific community, and to a specific family, and you had no choice in this. But you do have a choice in deciding how to respond to the forces that have shaped — and been shaped by — your country, your community, and your family.

These forces are legacies — things that have been passed on by those who lived in the past. These legacies of the past can colour the present — but the ability to analyze these legacies, to understand how they evolved, to recognize their effects on the present, and to respond thoughtfully is essential to becoming an informed participant in today's society.

In Related Issue 1, you explored some of the relationships between identity and the globalizing process, and you analyzed and evaluated how globalization affects aspects of your life — and the lives of others. In this related issue, you will discover that globalization is an evolving phenomenon with roots that stretch far back in time. As you explore the legacies of historical globalization, you will encounter actions, ideas, values, and forces that promoted globalization in the past. You will also analyze and evaluate how historical globalization continues to affect societies today.

One of the ideas you will encounter in this related issue is that historians and economists do not agree on exactly what historical globalization is or when it took place. But some argue that no matter when this phenomenon started and ended, people today continue to struggle with its repercussions.

Descendants of Aboriginal peoples around the world, for example, continue to struggle with the effects of historical globalization on many aspects of their daily lives and their identity. The specifics may differ, but in some respects, this common struggle has united Indigenous peoples in various countries. Understanding historical globalization and its effects will help you develop an appreciation of contemporary, cross-cultural perspectives.

The chart on the previous page shows how you will progress through Related Issue 2. As you explore this related issue, you will come to appreciate

- how decisions made and actions taken in the past are legacies of historical globalization
- how struggles between peoples with differing points of view and perspectives continue to affect the world today
- how governments, groups, and individuals are attempting to respond to the effects of historical globalization
- how you can develop a deeper understanding of the relationship between historical globalization and your own life
- how you can respond to the effects of historical globalization

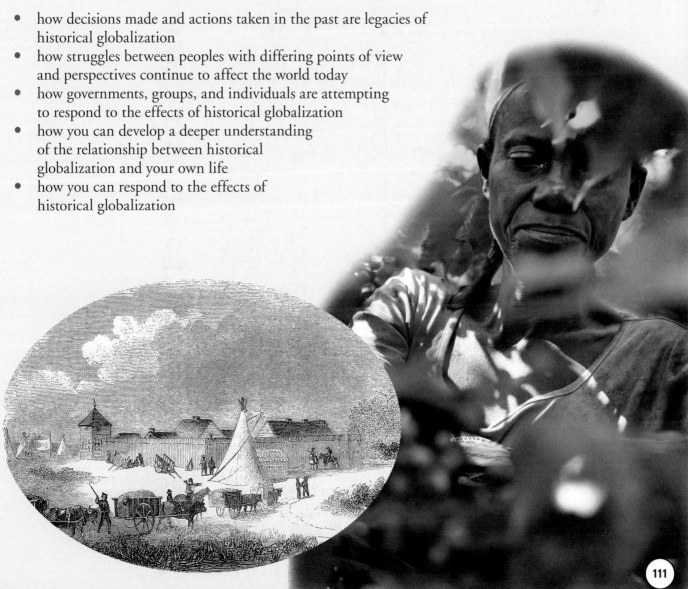

Your Challenge

Participate in a four-corners debate that discusses, analyzes, and evaluates responses to the question for this related issue:

To what extent should contemporary society respond to the legacies of historical globalization?

Your Participation in the Debate

As you progress through the four chapters of this related issue, you will develop understandings of, and opinions and ideas about, the legacies of historical globalization and how they continue to affect the world today.

These ideas will become the focus of a four-corners debate on this statement: Contemporary society has done enough to respond to the legacies of historical globalization. This statement stems directly from the question for this related issue.

When the debate begins, you will see four signs — Strongly Agree, Agree, Strongly Disagree, and Disagree — posted in the four corners of the classroom. These signs indicate levels of agreement, or disagreement, with the debate statement.

When the debate begins, you will take a position under the sign that best represents your views on the debate statement. During the debate, you will have an opportunity to present evidence explaining why you chose this position. You will also have an opportunity to listen to, consider, and ask questions about the views of others, as well as to decide whether their arguments are convincing enough to persuade you to change your position.

Your teacher will explain the debate procedure in more detail.

How You Will Prepare for the Debate

The four chapters of this related issue encourage you to explore the legacies of historical globalization, to analyze contemporary responses, and to evaluate whether these responses are appropriate. As you do this, you will be gathering the background and materials you need to participate effectively in the four-corners debate. At the end of each chapter, you will have an opportunity to think about and start preparing the material you will need to complete this challenge.

The key to a successful four-corners debate is the quality of the questions that are asked and answered. By asking and answering powerful questions, and listening thoughtfully and respectfully to the responses of others, you and your classmates will have many opportunities to evaluate and respond to informed positions on the debate statement.

Steps to a Four-Corners Debate

STRONGLY AGREE

STRONGLY DISAGREE

AGREE

DISAGREE

Step 1

To create powerful questions and prepare an informed position on an issue, it is important to analyze the issue — to break it down into its parts and try to understand the relationships among the parts and the whole.

Examine the parts of the debate statement. What, for example, does the term "contemporary society" mean? Is this the society you live in — or is it another society? Are these societies the same? If not, what are the differences and why are they important? When preparing for a debate, you must examine every aspect of the debate statement and decide on its meaning.

As you progress through this related issue, prepare questions that you want to find answers to before making an informed decision about your position on the issue. Make notes that will help you answer your own questions.

Step 2

Take a starting position. Do you strongly agree, agree, disagree, or strongly disagree with the debate statement? The ideas you encounter as you progress through this related issue will help you develop your position — and decide whether you need to carry out additional research before deciding what position to take.

When the debate begins, you will be asked to move to the area of the classroom with the sign that best represents your position on the issue. The number of students taking each position will be counted.

Step 3

Present your informed position — and be prepared to listen to others present theirs.

To add interest and depth of meaning to your presentation, consider including visuals such as maps, charts, and diagrams.

During the discussion, you will have an opportunity to change your position. After hearing several presentations, for example, you may decide that you want to change your position from "strongly agree" to "disagree." If you do this, you will move to a different area of the classroom. Be prepared to identify the arguments that persuaded you to make the change.

Step 4

When the debate ends, the number of students in each corner of the classroom will reflect the final views of the class as a whole. Take note of the number of students in each area. Sum up the debate, commenting on

- the process and main discussion points
- whether, how, and why your position or the position of your classmates changed
- the quality of the evidence presented
- the value of this kind of debate as a learning tool

Challenge Tip

To get the most out of a four-corners debate, consider these pointers.

Listening	Thinking	Participating
Try to hear other points of view and perspectives.	Resist pressure to go with the flow.	Listen respectfully to others.
Don't pass judgment until you've heard all the evidence.	Be open to compromise.	Accept that others may know more than you do.
Be open to the views of others.	Don't take things at face value.	Be prepared for others to persuade you.
Assess the information, not the person providing it.	Be open to changing your ideas.	Allow your ideas to go in directions you hadn't considered.
Be willing to consider challenges to your point of view.	Examine your own biases as you listen.	Share your ideas.

Chapter 5   Foundations of Globalization

The nine Indian figures are

9 8 7 6 5 4 3 2 1

With these nine figures, and with the sign 0 . . .
any number may be written.

— Leonardo Fibonacci (Leonardo of Pisa), Italian mathematician,
in his book *Liber Abaci* (*Book of Calculation*), 1202

Figure 5-1 For thousands of years, societies used their own number systems to complete mathematical calculations and to keep track of time, place, distance, and resources. Some of these systems are shown on this page. Because Rome ruled much of Europe for centuries, most Europeans used the Roman number system — Roman numerals — until the Italian mathematician Leonardo Fibonacci published *Liber Abaci* in 1202 and introduced the Indo-Arabic system to the continent.

CHAPTER ISSUE

To what extent did early globalization affect peoples of the world?

AT ONE TIME, the peoples of the world used a variety of number systems to count, measure, and calculate the value of trade goods.

But what happened when people wanted to trade with neighbours who used a different system? To understand what this was like, make up a counting system of your own. Then try to sell your pen or pencil to a partner who has made up a different system. What problems did you run into? Think about how hard it would be for societies that used different number systems to trade with each other.

Examine the collage of number systems on the previous page.

- How many different counting systems can you see? Which can you identify?
- What trade difficulties might have arisen when a buyer and seller used different number systems?
- What benefits do you think Leonardo Fibonacci might have seen in the Indo-Arabic numerals?
- Why do you think the Indo-Arabic number system came to be so widely used?
- How might the development of a uniform international numbering system affect merchants?
- How might the use of a single number system contribute to globalization?

KEY TERMS

imperialism

historical globalization

mercantilism

capitalism

grand exchange

Industrial Revolution

LOOKING AHEAD

In this chapter, you will explore answers to the following questions:

- Why and how did globalization begin?
- How did the foundations of historical globalization affect people?
- How did the consequences of historical globalization affect people?

My Point of View on Globalization

Look back at the notes you recorded as you progressed through Related Issue 1. What new ideas did you add to your understandings of globalization? Use words or images — or both — to answer this question. Date your ideas and add them to the notebook, learning log, portfolio, or computer file you are keeping as you progress through this course.

Web Connection

The First Peoples of the western hemisphere also developed complex trade routes, such as the grease trails of the Pacific Northwest. To find out more about the grease trails, go to this web site and follow the links.

www.ExploringGlobalization.ca

WHY AND HOW DID GLOBALIZATION BEGIN?

Experts disagree about exactly why and how globalization began. Some say globalization is as old as trade among peoples. Others say it began in about 325 BCE when the Buddhist leader Chandragupta Maurya combined religion, trade, and military might to create a vast protected trading area in much of present-day India. What advantages might a protected trading area provide?

Still others say that globalization started in the 1100s when Genghis Khan, the Mongolian warrior-ruler, introduced the idea of fighting from horseback. Using this new strategy, he created an empire that stretched from the Adriatic Sea to the Pacific coast of China — and he integrated trade routes linking Europe and Asia into one long, controlled pathway.

And many other experts date the rise of globalization to 1492, the year Christopher Columbus made his first trip to the Americas.

Is pinpointing a starting date important to understanding the effects of globalization on the peoples of the world? Think about the history you have studied in previous grades. What point would you identify as the start of globalization? Explain the reasons for your choice.

Early Trade Routes

As early as the third century BCE, a fragile network of caravan tracks linked Asia and Europe. Known as the Silk Road after the beautiful cloth made in China from thread harvested from silkworms, the various routes provided a way of distributing many prized goods, such as peppercorns.

But trade goods were not the only things that travelled the Silk Road. Ideas also moved along this trade route. The Indo-Arabic number system is one example. This system originated in India and was later adopted in the Middle East. In the 11th century, Europeans who traded with Middle Eastern merchants introduced the system to Italy, where the Roman system had been used. From Italy, this new system quickly spread throughout Europe — and today, it is used around the world.

Examine the map of the Silk Road. Trace the route of the Indo-Arabic number system from India to the Middle East and Italy. Why might Italian merchants have been the first in Europe to use this system?

Figure 5-2 **Empires of the Silk Road, 100 CE**

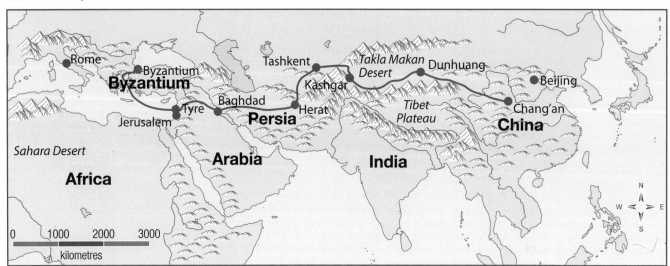

One Theory of the Evolution of Globalization

The Indian journalist, author, and technology consultant Ashutosh Sheshabalaya believes that globalization evolved in three distinct phases, or rounds:

- **First round** — Goods and ideas were exchanged along ancient trade routes. During this phase, writes Sheshabalaya, the Arab civilizations "were among the first ambassadors of the realm of ideas." They transferred knowledge of Indian science, medicine, literature, and mathematics to Europe.
- **Second round** — This phase grew out of the first round and began in the late 1400s. Building on new ideas, Europeans developed technologies that enabled them to sail much farther than ever before. The growth of globalization was related to European **imperialism**, a term that refers to one country's domination of another country's economic, political, and cultural institutions.
- **Third round** — The world is now in this phase, which evolved from the second round and began after World War II. It is a time of rapid growth of world markets and nearly instant communications and will be marked by the rapid rise of China and India as economic powers.

The Concept of Historical Globalization

Some economists and historians refer to Sheshabalaya's so-called second round as **historical globalization**. The beginning of this period is often identified as 1492, the year Christopher Columbus made his first voyage to the Caribbean. Some experts, such as Sheshabalaya, say that this period ended only when the United States and the Soviet Union emerged as superpowers after World War II. This post-World War II period is often called contemporary globalization.

But not everyone agrees with this view. Economists Kevin O'Rourke and Jeffrey Williamson, for example, point out that, until the 1800s, most trade goods were imported luxuries, such as fine sewing needles for First Peoples and beaver furs to make hats for fashionable Londoners. These luxury goods did not substantially change societies.

In O'Rourke and Williamson's view, globalization began in the 1800s, when low-cost goods from farms and factories poured into markets around the world — and access to these goods began to change the way masses of people lived.

Figure 5-3 These are just two of the many monuments erected in cities in Europe and the Americas to commemorate Christopher Columbus's voyages. What do these monuments say about some people's views on the importance of Columbus's voyages? Does the large number of monuments help convince you that globalization began with Columbus's first voyage in 1492?

REFLECT AND RESPOND

Each of the following statements represents a theory about when globalization began:

- Globalization has been around since the world began.
- Globalization began in 1492, when Christopher Columbus made his first voyage to the Americas.

- Globalization began in the 1800s, when access to cheap trade goods began to change societies.

Think about what you have learned so far about globalization and add two more statements to this list. List three criteria you would use to judge which of the five statements you agree with most strongly.

ANALYZING HISTORICAL AND CONTEMPORARY PERSPECTIVES WITHIN AND ACROSS CULTURES

In the early history of contact between the Americas and Europe, few names are better known or more controversial than that of Christopher Columbus.

When Columbus sailed from Spain in 1492, his goal was to find a new route to China. He never did reach China — but on October 12, 1492, his expedition landed on an island in the Caribbean Sea. He named the island Hispaniola and claimed it for Spain. Today, this island is divided into two countries: Haiti and the Dominican Republic.

Many Europeans regard Columbus as a hero who "discovered" the "New World" and started the era that is often called the Age of Discovery.

But not everyone views Columbus as a hero. When some American cities proposed celebrations to mark October 12, 1992 — the 500th anniversary of Columbus's landing on Hispaniola — protests erupted. Many

Indigenous people in particular preferred to celebrate "500 years of resistance." Why might some Indigenous peoples object to celebrating Columbus as a hero?

The controversy over celebrating this anniversary shows how historical figures continue to affect people today and how events can be viewed differently by different individuals and cultural collectives. The following steps can help you analyze and understand various points of view and perspectives. As you progress through this course, you can use the same steps to analyze and understand points of view and perspectives on other controversial people and events.

Steps to Analyzing Historical and Contemporary Perspectives within and across Cultures

Step 1: Prepare to analyze

Analyzing involves breaking down a topic or event into its parts and trying to understand the relationships among the parts — and the whole.

With a partner or small group, prepare five charts similar to the one shown on the following page. You will need one chart for each quotation.

Discuss how the questions in the first column of the chart help you analyze a point of view or perspective.

Step 2: Analyze the points of view and perspectives

With your partner or small group, read the quotations on the following page and work together to analyze each by answering the questions on one of the charts.

Step 3: Compare the points of view and perspectives

To compare the points of view and perspectives, you may choose to divide the charts into categories such as the following:

- historical and contemporary points of view and perspectives
- individual points of view and group perspectives
- European points of view and perspectives
- Aboriginal points of view and perspectives

What conclusions can you draw about the way Columbus is — and was — viewed by various groups at different times?

Step 4: Complete your analysis

Assess how these points of view and perspectives influenced your own thinking about the topic by answering the following questions:

- What were your opinions when you started this analysis?
- Which speaker or writer do you think provides the most balanced assessment? What criteria did you use to make this choice?
- Does the validity or importance of a point of view or perspective depend on who is expressing it? Why or why not?
- How did these various points of view and perspectives influence your understanding of the topic?

Summing up

If your community decided to hold an event to commemorate Columbus, what suggestions could you offer to ensure that all voices are heard? Would the points of view and perspectives you identified in this activity influence your suggestions? Explain the reasons for your response.

Inscription on the Columbus monument, erected in 1912 in Washington, D.C.

To the memory of Christopher Columbus, whose high faith and indomitable courage gave to mankind a new world.

British writer V.M. Hillyer in *A Child's History of the World*, first published in 1924

Of all the men of whom we have heard, whether kings or queens, princes or emperors, none can compare with Columbus. Alexander the Great, Julius Caesar, Charlemagne were all killers. They took away. But Columbus gave. He gave us a new world.

John Mohawk, Seneca author and educator, 1992

Christopher Columbus is a symbol, not of a man, but of imperialism . . . Imperialism and colonialism are not something that happened decades ago or generations ago, but they are still happening now with the exploitation of people . . . The kind of thing that took place long ago in which people were dispossessed from their land and forced out of subsistence economies and into market economies — those processes are still happening today.

Ronald Wright, Canadian historian and novelist, in his book *Stolen Continents*, published in 1993

When I interviewed people for the final chapters of this book, I was told by Dehatkadons, a traditional chief of the Onondaga Iroquois, "You cannot discover an inhabited land. Otherwise I could cross the Atlantic and 'discover' England." That such an obvious point has eluded European consciousness for five centuries reveals that the history we have been taught is really myth.

American Indian Movement of Colorado, 1994

Columbus' arrival was a disaster from the beginning. Although his own diaries reveal that he was greeted by the Tainos [the Indigenous people of Hispaniola] with the most generous hospitality he had ever known, he immediately began the enslavement and slaughter of the Indian peoples of the Caribbean.

Analyzing a Point of View or Perspective	
Topic _____	
Who is the speaker or writer?	
When did she or he speak or write?	
What is his or her background?	
How might this background influence his or her point of view or perspective? Do you think this perspective or point of view is biased? Why or why not?	
Do you think she or he is sharing a group perspective or an individual point of view?	
What is the message?	
What words emphasize this message?	
What questions about the topic does the message raise or leave unanswered?	
Whose perspective or point of view is not included?	

VOCABULARY TIP

When analyzing points of view and perspectives, it helps to understand the difference between **denotation** and **connotation**.

Denotation The dictionary meaning of a word or phrase.

Connotation The emotional associations people may attach to a word or phrase.

Think, for example, about the word "snake." A snake is a limbless reptile. But to many people, the word "snake" connotes evil, treachery, and fear.

HOW DID THE FOUNDATIONS OF HISTORICAL GLOBALIZATION AFFECT PEOPLE?

When Johannes Gutenberg, a German inventor, pioneered a printing method that used movable type, he set in motion changes that would have far-reaching effects on Europe — and the world. Gutenberg's method was so revolutionary that it has been called the most important invention of the second millennium.

Until Gutenberg's innovation in the mid-1400s, books in Europe had been painstakingly copied by hand. In the years after his printed books first appeared, the number of printing presses in Europe increased dramatically. As books were produced more quickly and cheaply, more people could afford to buy them, and this encouraged more people to learn to read. The printed word played an important role in spreading new ideas about science, religion, politics, and philosophy across Europe.

Figure 5-4 Johannes Gutenberg, in the dark cloak, examines a page printed on his flatbed press, which is in the background. By today's standards, these early presses were very slow — but they were much faster than copying manuscripts by hand. How might the availability of more and cheaper books have affected the worldviews of Europeans?

The Rise of a European Middle Class

In the centuries after the fall of Rome in 476 CE, European society was engulfed in wars. People often lived in isolated, self-sufficient communities. Social status was often determined by birth, and social power was defined by the amount of land a person owned. The economy was based on arrangements between the lords who owned large rural estates and the peasants or serfs who worked for them. In return for the lord's protection, peasants and serfs gave their loyalty and obedience.

At the same time, however, towns and cities were growing. They attracted traders, craftspeople, bankers, entrepreneurs, artists, and scholars. Townspeople and city dwellers were usually independent. Their survival depended on their knowledge of a craft or their skill as traders and entrepreneurs. This knowledge and skill gave them new ways of accumulating wealth — and wealth became a measure of social status.

Many historians believe these townspeople and city dwellers were the earliest middle class — people who earned money by practising a trade or craft. Their independence fostered a sense of individualism, a belief

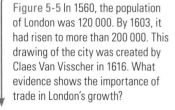

Figure 5-5 In 1560, the population of London was 120 000. By 1603, it had risen to more than 200 000. This drawing of the city was created by Claes Van Visscher in 1616. What evidence shows the importance of trade in London's growth?

that people should be able to act freely. As a result, they often valued education and welcomed innovations such as exploration, scientific discoveries, and new technologies. How might the growing availability of printed books be linked to European attitudes toward individualism and innovation? How might these attitudes have helped foster historical globalization?

As the middle class grew larger and more influential, trade became even more important — and Europeans began to look for ways to increase profits by expanding trade.

Embracing New Ideas

The growth of towns and cities and the increasing importance of trade provided fertile ground for the development of new ideas and technologies. The Indo-Arabic counting system that moved from India to the Middle East, and from there to Europe, is just one example of an idea that was embraced by Europeans because it helped improve trade.

These new ideas and new technologies, combined with a desire to profit through trade, helped lay the foundations of historical globalization.

New Ideas, New Technologies, and Historical Globalization

From about the 9th to the 13th century, Middle Eastern civilizations were centres of innovation and learning. Europeans drew on many of these innovations, especially in astronomy, to develop technologies that made travel, trade, exploration — and conquest — easier.

- The introduction of large, square sails and the lateen — a triangular, mobile stern sail that could be set at an angle to the wind — meant that larger ships could be built. These ships were also faster and more manoeuvrable.
- Improvements in navigational tools, such as the magnetic compass, the mariner's astrolabe, the sextant, and maps, meant that sailors could travel farther from land without losing their way.
- Gunpowder, which was invented in China, was first used in European warfare in 1324. Its introduction marked a dramatic change in the way wars were conducted. Muskets and cannons came to be widely used.

Think about the effects of each of these developments on trade and travel. Record one prediction about the significant role each development might play in the growth of globalization.

FYI

For many Indigenous peoples, keeping track of natural objects that differ in key ways is important. As a result, words might change to reflect the essential features of an object, such as its dimensions and whether it could be manipulated by humans. Psychologist J. Peter Denny reports, for example, that in Ojibwa, "two" as in "two blueberries" is *niizho-minag* because blueberries are perceived as three-dimensional (*minag*) and can be manipulated. But "two" as in "two bears" is simply *niizh*, because bears cannot be manipulated. Awareness of distinctions like these is a critical communication and survival skill.

Figure 5-6
Notice the square sails on these 18th-century English ships, painted by Francis Swaine. How might these large, square sails have helped ships travel faster? Why would speed be important?

Global Competition for Trade

In the centuries after Columbus's first expedition, many European countries — especially those with strong seafaring traditions — began competing to establish colonial empires in the Americas and on other continents. Why would countries with strong seafaring traditions have an advantage in the race to establish colonies?

This European imperialism — the policy of extending a country's power by acquiring new territories and establishing control over other countries and peoples — was motivated by trade. European monarchs believed that colonies would increase trade by providing both cheap raw materials and markets for goods produced in the home country. Trade brought economic prosperity, and economic prosperity brought power. But whose interests were ignored in the race to claim colonies?

Mercantilism

In the 16th, 17th, and 18th centuries, European governments strictly controlled trade. To ensure prosperity, they believed that the balance of trade must favour the home country: its exports must be higher than its imports. As a result, colonies were viewed as a source of cheap raw materials.

Laws often required a colony's raw materials to be shipped to the home country. Only there could they be used to make finished products. Colonial entrepreneurs were not allowed to set up factories and use the colony's raw materials to manufacture goods in the colony. The products made in the home country were then shipped back to the colony and sold.

And to keep their own colonial markets strong, governments often prohibited colonies from importing goods from other European countries. This eliminated competition and meant that people in colonies could buy only goods made in the home country.

This policy of strictly controlling trade was called **mercantilism**. Who do you think did — and did not — benefit from mercantilism? How might this have affected their opinions of mercantilism?

The decline of mercantilism

As the 18th century unfolded, many people began to resist mercantilism. What do you think might have inspired this resistance?

Dissatisfaction with mercantilism was especially strong in Britain's American colonies. In 1776, these colonists rebelled, and the American Revolution began. This war resulted in the creation of the United States as an independent country.

In that same year, the Scottish economist Adam Smith published a four-volume work titled *An Inquiry into the Nature and Causes of the Wealth of Nations*. This book, whose title is often shortened to *The Wealth of Nations*, challenged government economic control and advocated free trade, competition, and choice as routes to economic prosperity. In writing this book, Smith was laying the groundwork for an economic system that would later become known as **capitalism**.

FYI

The European mercantilists of the 16th, 17th, and 18th centuries did not call themselves "mercantilists" — because this word did not exist at the time. Like many historical terms, the word "mercantilism" was coined to describe a way of organizing a country's economy only after the mercantilist period was nearly over. The term "mercantilist" did not appear in English until 1838.

Web Connection

Many historians and economists view *The Wealth of Nations* as the first great work of political economy — and Adam Smith's theories continue to influence many thinkers today. To find out more about Smith and his theories, go to this web site and follow the links.

www.ExploringGlobalization.ca

Dividing up the world

As the map on the following page shows, the British, French, Dutch, Spanish, and Portuguese had established large colonial empires by 1770. On which continents did they focus their attention at that time?

When the European imperial powers set about staking their colonial claims, they believed that their own customs, culture, and beliefs were superior to those of the Indigenous peoples they met. As a result, European governments simply declared that Indigenous peoples were their subjects — and often displaced and even enslaved them. Naval power, as well as guns and cannons, gave early European colonizers a significant military advantage over those who tried to resist. The Europeans also represented large central governments that could send many ships and soldiers. Few peoples in the Americas, Africa, India, Australia, and South Asia had developed strong central governments. As a result, most could organize only limited resistance — and the Europeans were eventually able to overcome this.

In countries such as China and Japan, European colonization efforts were less successful because these countries had strong central governments.

VOICES

There is nothing but grief and suffering in Mexico and Tlatelolco [part of Mexico City], where once we saw beauty and valour. Have you grown weary of your servants? Are you angry with your servants, O giver of life?

— *An Aztec poet, writing just after the Spanish conquest in 1519*

Ideas

Is "cultural imperialism," which some people define as a non-violent form of imperialism in which one country imposes its values and beliefs on another, nothing but a different form of colonization?

The students responding to this question are Deven, who was born in India but is now a Canadian who lives in Calgary; Gord, a member of the Beaver First Nation near High Level; and Marie, a Francophone student from Medicine Hat.

> Sure, it is. Just think about the Canadian film industry. Canadian films win international awards, but I know lots of people who don't watch them. They go to Hollywood movies. The big studios have the money for top stars and great special effects ... prizes, promotions, you name it. No one forces Canadians to go to Hollywood movies. For most of us, it's just a choice we make — even if the choice is manipulated by Hollywood's huge advertising budgets.

Deven

> Yes, I think cultural imperialism is a form of colonization, but I think it can actually make people stronger. First Peoples have been resisting various forms of imperialism — including cultural imperialism — for more than 350 years. If people are aware of it, and talk about it, and think about it, then they can make decisions and take actions that affirm their own culture.

Gord

> English is pretty much the language of the Internet. Is this a form of imperialism? I'm not sure. Maybe it's just how things worked out. But it makes a big difference to surfers who speak French. French is an official language of Canada, but French speakers must safeguard our rights if we want equal opportunities on the Internet.

Marie

Your Turn

How would you respond to the question Deven, Gord, and Marie are answering? Do you think living next door to the U.S. affects your opinions on this issue? Should governments pass laws to resist cultural domination? What might these laws say? Why?

Effects of European colonial settlement

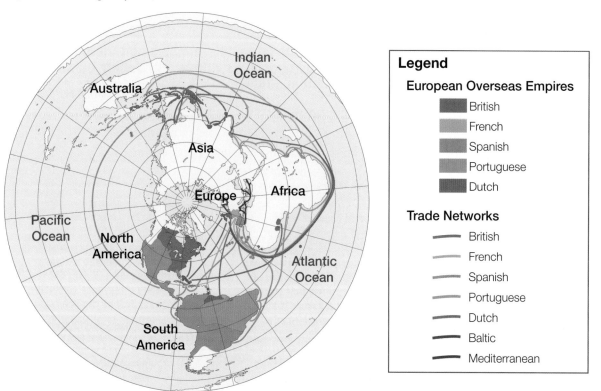

Once European countries established colonies, they encouraged settlers to emigrate from their home country to the newly acquired lands. This emigration served a number of purposes.

Settlers provided a pool of people to run the colony, supervise the gathering of resources, and protect the home country's trading interests.

Emigration also helped reduce conflict at home. Pressure to make European agriculture more efficient had created unrest as many peasants were driven off land their family had worked for generations. Encouraging these peasants to emigrate reduced the potential for conflict at home and helped establish European customs and culture in the colony.

As new settlers moved in, they usually displaced the Indigenous peoples who had lived on the land. This disrupted the way of life of Indigenous peoples and sometimes created conflict as one Indigenous group was forced to migrate to land that had traditionally been regarded as another group's territory.

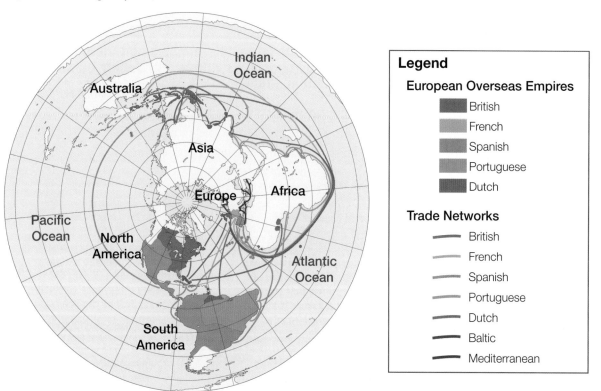

CHECK FORWARD

You will read more about the displacement of Indigenous peoples in Chapter 7.

Figure 5-7 **Trading Empires, 1770**

Legend

European Overseas Empires

- British
- French
- Spanish
- Portuguese
- Dutch

Trade Networks

- British
- French
- Spanish
- Portuguese
- Dutch
- Baltic
- Mediterranean

Indian Ocean
Australia
Asia
Europe
Africa
Pacific Ocean
North America
Atlantic Ocean
South America

REFLECT AND RESPOND

In 1776, colonists in many of Britain's American possessions rebelled and launched a war that resulted in independence for the United States. In Britain, this war is often called the American War of Independence. In the United States, it is generally called the American Revolution.

Many First Peoples were drawn into this conflict. Some sided with the British, while others sided with the colonists. What name might First Peoples have given to this war? Sum up the perspective of each group — the British, the rebellious American colonists, and First Nations — in a statement of one to four sentences. Explain how the perspective of each group might have been shaped by the effects of colonial policies.

HOW DID THE CONSEQUENCES OF HISTORICAL GLOBALIZATION AFFECT PEOPLE?

Suppose a swarm of heavily armed people arrived at your front door and announced that they were going to move in and live with you. Your family could continue to live in the basement or another room, but you would have access to the rest of your home only when it suited the newcomers. How would you respond? Would you give in, fight back, or try to negotiate a better deal? Or would you come up with a different solution?

Results of Contact

The Indigenous peoples of various continents faced difficult choices when the imperialist powers colonized their lands. And no matter where the contact occurred, the outcome was catastrophic for Indigenous peoples.

In Mexico, for example, Spanish soldiers led by Hernán Cortés had defeated the extensive Aztec Empire by 1521. In the aftermath, the Spanish imported plants and animals to the territory, set up gold and silver mines, and enslaved many Indigenous people to provide labour. The profits from these new industries flowed to Spain.

In North America, some First Peoples benefited from the fur trade and the introduction of European tools and technologies — but these benefits did not last. As Europeans built settlements and began farming, First Peoples were forced out of their traditional territories.

A more subtle issue was acculturation. Most colonists believed that the First Peoples they encountered should assimilate and try to be more like Europeans. And as First Peoples adopted new goods, technologies, and worldviews, their cultures began to change.

European diseases

Some historians believe that contagious diseases imported with European soldiers and settlers took the greatest toll on Indigenous peoples. In *Settling with the Indians*, for example, Karen Kuperman wrote: "European diseases did more than European technology to vanquish the American Indian in the early years of colonization."

Some estimates suggest that 75 to 90 per cent of the Indigenous people of the Americas — 8 to 10 million people — may have died as a result of contact. Most of these deaths were the result of diseases contracted by people who had no natural immunity against European illnesses and infections.

Examine the chart on this page (Figure 5-8). Does the evidence it provides support or refute estimates that as many as 10 million Indigenous people may have died as a result of contact? This chart appeared in a book published by New Internationalist Publications. Conduct an online search to find out more about this company. Does what you found out affect your view of the reliability of the evidence provided in the chart? Explain your response.

VOICES

Europe's encounter with and treatment of the world's tribal peoples is . . . a tale of extraordinary human achievement in adversity, conferring on the victors the possession of much of the world's physical resources, and a tragedy of staggering proportions, involving the deaths of many millions of victims and the complete extinction of numerous distinct peoples. When viewed as a single process, the European consumption of tribal society could be said to represent the greatest, most persistent act of human destructiveness ever recorded.

— *Mark Cocker, British journalist, in* Rivers of Blood, Rivers of Gold, *1998*

Figure 5-8 Estimated Indigenous Population of the Americas, 1492 and 1992

Region	Population, 1492 (millions)	Population, 1992 (millions)
North America	4.40	2.54
Mexico	21.40	8.0
Caribbean	5.85	0.001
Central America	5.65	5.07
Lowland South America	8.5	0.9
Andes	11.5	17.0
Total	57.3	33.51

Source: Ellwood, Wayne. *The No-Nonsense Guide to Globalization.* New Internationalist Publications, 2001.

Differing Approaches to the Indigenous Peoples of the Americas

When Europeans and the Indigenous peoples of the Americas first encountered each other, neither group had reliable information about the other. The early European explorers thought they had reached India, so they mistakenly called Indigenous peoples Indians. And the Indigenous peoples could not know that tens of millions of Europeans would soon leave their homelands to start over in the Americas, or that millions of Africans would also arrive — as slaves.

In many cases, the survival of both Indigenous peoples and Europeans depended on the relationships they were able to form with the newcomers. In northeastern North America, for example, the French and British were after furs, particularly beaver pelts. But they did not know their way around or how to survive in the forests that covered the region.

As a result, they relied on First Peoples to trap animals for them — and the two groups established a mutually beneficial trading relationship. The First Peoples delivered the furs to the Europeans. In return, they received trade goods, such as tools, cooking utensils, weapons, and decorative items.

Indigenous peoples who lived farther south encountered a different situation. The Aztecs of Mexico, for example, lived in an area where gold could be mined — and gold meant money, power, and status in Europe. When the Aztecs lost the battle for gold, the survivors were enslaved and put to work in mines and on plantations.

Figure 5-9 This drawing, which appeared on an early map of Canada, shows a European perspective on the fur trade. What does the title reveal about this perspective? If the drawing had been created by a First Nations artist, what do you think it might have shown? What title might it have been given?

Efforts to halt the destruction

Some Europeans, such as Bartolomé de Las Casas, were troubled by the destruction of Indigenous cultures. A Spanish priest and historian, Las Casas had taken part in the conquest of Cuba, but he had been disgusted by the terrible cruelty he had witnessed.

Afterwards, Las Casas devoted his life to securing justice for Indigenous peoples. Unlike many Europeans, he believed that the Indigenous peoples were the true owners of the land where they lived. He tried to persuade Spanish authorities to change their policies and create communities where Indigenous peoples and Spaniards could work together to create a new civilization. But Las Casas's efforts were undermined by powerful European interests. Why might his efforts have been unpopular among Europeans?

One idea Las Casas regretted was his suggestion that Africans be imported to work on the new plantations. He had hoped — mistakenly — that they would be treated fairly.

Today, Las Casas is honoured in Spain and some former Spanish colonies as one of the first Europeans to speak out in defence of Indigenous peoples.

Figure 5-10 The Spanish priest Bartolomé de Las Casas tries to persuade the Spanish king and his council to treat Indigenous peoples fairly. Las Casas's pleas fell on deaf ears.

Slavery

Slavery has existed in many civilizations. In the ancient Middle East and Africa, for example, slavery was often used as an alternative to imprisonment or execution for criminals and people who could not pay their debts. People captured during wars were sometimes also enslaved. But enslavement for unpaid debts lasted only for a specified period. And other slaves, especially those who were well educated, might become high-ranking civil servants or tutors to the children of aristocrats.

The growing demand for labour to work on colonial plantations brought about two changes in these ancient approaches to slavery:

- Chattel slavery became common. A chattel is a possession, and chattel slavery meant that the slaves and their descendants were the private property of their owner.
- Indigenous peoples and captured Africans were enslaved specifically because of their racial origins.

In traditional civilizations, where anyone might become a slave through bad luck, slaves were granted some rights. But chattel slaves had no legal standing as human beings. The Europeans who dominated the Americas could not be enslaved, and they had no incentive to grant rights to slaves.

PROFILE

OLAUDAH EQUIANO
FROM KIDNAPPED CHILD TO GLOBAL CITIZEN

When he was just 11 years old, Olaudah Equiano was kidnapped in Nigeria by slave traders. Renamed Gustavus Vassa by the British naval captain who bought him, Equiano saw action as a gunpowder carrier during the Seven Years' War between Britain and France. Between naval battles, he learned to read and write, and by 1766, he had succeeded in buying his freedom. He remained at sea and in 1773 took part in the search for a polar route to Asia. Later, he returned to England and joined the growing movement to abolish slavery.

Equiano was a gifted writer, and in 1789, he published his autobiography, *The Interesting Narrative of the Life of Olaudah Equiano, or Gustavus Vassa, the African.* Describing the day he bought his freedom, he wrote: "All within my breast was tumult, wildness, and delirium! My feet scarcely touched the ground, for they were winged with joy . . . Every one I met I told of my happiness . . . I who had been a slave in the morning, trembling at the will of another, now became my own master and compleatly free."

The abolitionist movement was gaining strength, and more than 100 books on slavery were published that year. But Equiano's book was the only one written by a former slave.

Figure 5-11 This portrait of Olaudah Equiano appeared in his autobiography. Although Equiano campaigned to end slavery, he died in 1797 — more than three decades before slavery was abolished in the British Empire.

CHEAP LABOUR — THE LIFEBLOOD OF HISTORICAL GLOBALIZATION

IMPACT

To maintain the steady flow of trade between colonies and home countries, the imperial powers needed an abundant, reliable supply of cheap labour. Workers in the colonies kept plantations operating while others churned out finished products in factories at home. But cheap labour was critical to achieving high profits — and to find it, employers turned to slaves, indentured labourers, and children.

Slave Labour

Portuguese traders first arrived in West Africa in the early 1400s, and African slaves became one of the "products" they traded. This trade required the co-operation of West African leaders, who helped round up people to trade with the Portuguese.

At the time, most of these slaves were sold in Europe as servants, and slavery was not an important part of the trading relationship between Portugal and West Africa. The Portuguese were more interested in other products, such as gold, pepper, ivory, gum, beeswax, leather, and timber.

This changed in the early 16th century when Spain needed large numbers of slaves to work on the large plantations that were being established in its colonies. As other European imperial powers, such as

Holland, France, and Britain, colonized the Caribbean and set up their own plantation economies, they, too, joined the slave trade. Later, the United States also became involved.

African slaves were considered ideal plantation workers because they were often skilled in agriculture. They were also used to working in tropical conditions and were able to resist the tropical diseases that often killed other workers.

Slavery continued in some parts of the world until well into the 20th century. Though estimates of the number of Africans transported as slaves vary, French historian Jean-Michel Deveau has suggested that between 11 and 15 million were forced to migrate in the 18th and 19th centuries, when the brutal trade was at its height.

Figure 5-12 The Slave Routes

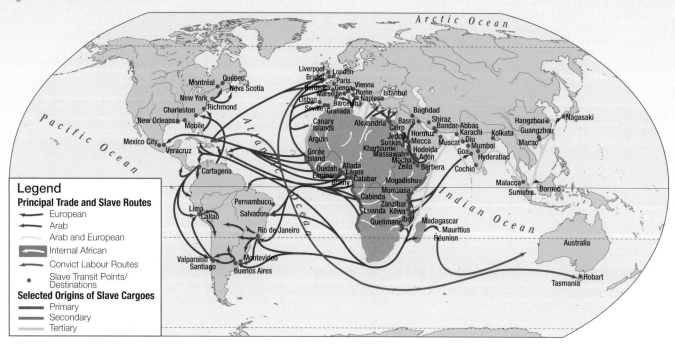

Indentured Labour

Slavery was legal and widely accepted in North America, where it was common in warmer southern areas that supported a plantation economy. It was less common in northern parts of the continent, where the climate would not allow year-round agriculture. Maintaining large numbers of slaves over long, cold northern winters was not practical.

In northern areas, a more common source of cheap labour was indentured workers. An indenture is a contract, and European workers — usually the poor — could sign a contract with a colonial employer who would pay to transport them to the colony. In return, an indentured labourer agreed to work for little or no pay. The indenture usually covered a period of four to seven years, but once this term ended, the worker was free.

In the 1600s, between half and two-thirds of all European immigrants to what is now the United States arrived as indentured workers. The indenture system was also common in South America. In the 1800s, for example, slavery was abolished in Guyana, and many slaves started farming for themselves. As a result, plantation owners turned to India as a source of cheap indentured labour.

Child Labour

The industrialists whose factories in home countries turned colonial raw materials into finished products rarely used slaves. They preferred to hire labourers who would work long hours for low wages — and who could be dismissed during slowdowns.

Children were an ideal source of cheap labour. The children of the poor had always been put to work as soon as possible to help their family. But working with other family members was quite different from working in a factory under an overseer. Children were especially valued for sweeping chimneys and dragging carts though mines because their small bodies could fit into tight spaces.

Starting in the 1830s, reformers tried to improve labour conditions, especially for children, but often without much success. In North America and many European countries, child labour continued until well into the 20th century. In some parts of the world, it continues today.

Figure 5-13 These children are carrying clay that will be used to make bricks. Child labour ended only when countries introduced compulsory education. Children who, by law, must be in school cannot also be at work.

Explorations

1. How did business owners benefit from slave labour, indentured labour, and child labour? Who else benefited? Why do you think it took so long to persuade governments to pass laws banning these practices? Whose interests would governments have had to take into account?

2. Create a slogan to rally people to protest slave labour, indentured labour, or child labour. Think about how companies use slogans to advertise their products today (e.g., McDonald's "I'm lovin' it!" and Nike's "Just do it"). Your slogan should be short and convey a powerful message. Adding a visual or logo would enhance the message.

Responses to Slavery

Slaves were rarely allowed to learn to read or write or to leave their plantations unsupervised. They worked in harsh — often brutal — conditions and had little control over their lives. But few people outside the plantations knew what was going on.

By the late 1700s, however, books like Olaudah Equiano's autobiography started to publicize the harsh treatment of slaves and many Europeans came to oppose the practice. The abolition movement began to grow.

At first, abolitionists experienced little success. The people who wanted to maintain slavery were often wealthy and powerful slave owners — and they lobbied governments to maintain slave laws. Gradually, however, public opinion turned against slavery, and by the 19th century, many countries were passing laws to make it illegal.

MAKING CHOICES

MAKING CHOICES MAKING CHOICES

WILLIAM WILBERFORCE
SPEARHEADING THE CAMPAIGN TO END SLAVERY

When William Wilberforce joined the British abolitionist movement, his stand was unpopular. Well-educated and cloquent, he had been elected to the House of Commons as a young man in 1780. Four years later, he converted to Methodism, a religious movement that encouraged social reform, including opposition to slavery. It was then that he started

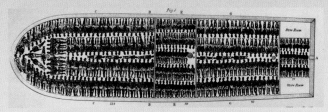

Figure 5-14 This drawing shows slaves crammed into the hold of a ship. During the month-long voyage across the ocean, people were fed little and had to lie in their own filth.

his lifelong campaign to end what he called the "wretched" business of slavery.

In 1807, Wilberforce scored an important victory when he persuaded Parliament to pass a law banning the trade in slaves, but his goal was to ban slavery completely. His dedication to this cause won him many powerful enemies, and his critics often accused him of being a fanatic. In a speech, he replied to critics, "They charge me with fanaticism. If to be feelingly alive to the sufferings of my fellow creatures is to be a fanatic, I am one of the most incurable fanatics ever permitted to be at large."

It took a long time, but Wilberforce and the abolitionists finally triumphed. The Emancipation Act, which abolished slavery in Britain and the British Empire, was passed by Parliament in 1833 — three days before he died. The law came into force in 1834.

Explorations

1. William Wilberforce was often called a fanatic. Is strongly supporting a cause always good (that is, constructive)? Always bad (that is, destructive)? Work with a partner to list five examples of constructive and destructive ways of expressing strong opinions. An example is provided.

Constructive	Destructive
Raise money for trip to the team finals to show strong support	Badmouth visiting fans

2. Was involvement in the slave trade morally better or worse than owning slaves — or did it amount to the same thing? Reflect on this question and summarize your view in writing. Share your summary with a partner and discuss the differences in your positions. Did your partner's view persuade you to change your position? Prepare a final position to share with the class and be prepared to defend it.

The Grand Exchange

When Columbus returned to the Americas in 1493, he had no way of knowing that his voyage would change the world. Aboard his ships were seeds, fruit trees, and livestock. This cargo would start a revolution that would change the diet of the world forever — and form the basis of a trading process that is sometimes called the **grand exchange**.

Changing the diet of the world's peoples

Sunflowers are an example of how the grand exchange worked. Sunflowers are native to the Great Plains of North America. Exported to Europe, they thrived in cold northern areas, such as Russia. When Russians started growing them, they provided people with a welcome new cooking oil. In return, wheat, barley, and oats arrived in North America from Europe and the Middle East, eventually making the Great Plains "the breadbasket of the world."

Coffee had been cultivated in Africa and, later, Arabia before it was imported to the Americas. There, it became an important new crop in the Caribbean and Brazil. Cacao, which originated in tropical America, was exported to Europe, where it was used to make cocoa and chocolate. Peanuts, vanilla, sweet and hot peppers, lima beans, pineapple, tobacco, tomatoes, and potatoes are some of the many other crops that arrived in Europe and Asia from the Americas. And cattle, poultry, and pigs were exported from Europe to the Americas, where they are staples in the diet of people today.

In many cases, these new crops started out as luxuries that only wealthy Europeans could afford. But they were grown in such large quantities that prices fell, and more and more people were able to afford them. This changed the diet of entire societies, both in Europe and elsewhere. Because of these widespread changes in the way people lived, many historians believe that the grand exchange was a key factor in historical globalization.

Figure 5-15 Coffee houses, such as Lloyd's Coffee House in London, England, became popular meeting places in 17th-century Europe. They were favourite places to exchange information, as well as drink coffee. How is this development echoed today?

Figure 5-16 **The Grand Exchange**

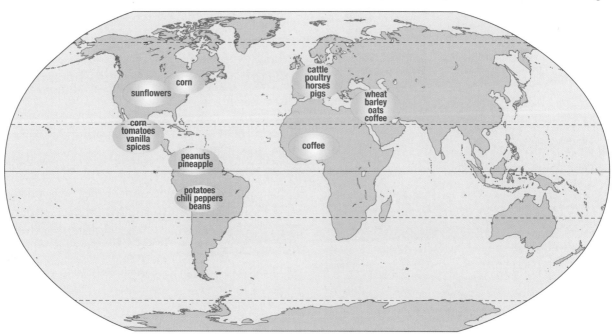

FYI

Industrialization was such a powerful force that it even changed the English language. At one time, "manufacture," a word formed by combining the Latin words *manus* (hand) and *facere* (to make), meant exactly what it says: to make by hand. With industrialization, the meaning of this word changed. It now means "to make by machine." And at one time, a place where goods were made was called a "manufactory" — but this was shortened to the word that is familiar today: factory.

CHECKFORWARD

You will learn more about how industrialization affected colonies in Chapter 6.

Industrialization and Social Change

The improved technology that enabled Europeans to travel far and wide had far-reaching economic, social, and cultural effects on the entire world. But these were not the only technological changes that would profoundly affect societies and cultures.

The Industrial Revolution

By 1750, European consumers were demanding more goods and industrial entrepreneurs were stepping forward to meet this demand by developing machines that could produce goods more quickly, more efficiently, and more cheaply than ever before. This process started in Britain when the steam-powered engine was invented. Other inventors used the steam engine to create new ways to mechanize the manufacturing process.

Until then, most manufacturing had occurred in people's homes. In the textile industry, for example, spinners would work at home to make thread from raw wool or cotton. This thread would then go to a weaver, who would work on a hand-operated loom.

Ten spinners were needed to make enough thread to supply one weaver. This changed in 1764, when the spinning jenny was invented in Britain. This mechanical spinning wheel enabled spinners to keep up with weavers. Later, the power loom was invented, enabling weavers to make more cloth even more quickly.

These new machines were large, expensive, and often required many workers to operate them. Only the rich could afford to buy them, to build factories to house them, and to hire the workers needed to operate them. As factories were built, cheap machine-made products gradually replaced handcrafted goods — and traditional craftspeople were driven out of work.

This new way of working — in factories — sparked dramatic economic, social, and cultural changes. As a result, the century between about 1750 and 1850, the era when industry became mechanized, has become known as the **Industrial Revolution**.

As the first country to industrialize, Britain had a head start on the world. By 1830, it had become the leading industrial power, producing two-thirds of the world's coal, half its iron, and half its cotton cloth.

Think about what might have happened if you were a home-based British weaver in 1800. What choices might you have faced when machines began doing your work? How do you think you would have responded to these choices? How might your children's lives have been different from yours?

Figure 5-17 Before industrialization, some families, like the one shown in this painting, worked together to both spin thread and weave cloth. What evidence about the family's lifestyle does this painting provide?

Figure 5-18 The workers in this cotton mill are doubling thread — making it into a thinner, more uniform strand. Compare this drawing to the painting in Figure 5-17. What differences do you see?

Points of view and perspectives on the consequences of historical globalization have changed over time. The following are examples of some of these points of view and perspectives.

JOHN STUART MILL was a 19th-century British philosopher and political economist. The following excerpt is from his book *Principles of Political Economy*.

The removal of population from the overcrowded to the unoccupied parts of the earth's surface is one of those works of eminent social usefulness . . . To appreciate the benefits of colonization, it should be considered in its relation, not to a single country, but to the collective economical interests of the human race . . .

• • • • •

TUNDE OBADINA is an author and director of Africa Business Information Services, an online source of information and analysis on African business and economics. The following excerpt is from an article published in 1999.

It is difficult to give an objective balance sheet on colonialism. Those who contend that it made no positive impact are as dogmatic as those who present it as the salvation of Africa. What is unequivocal is that it was an imposition of alien rule. Whatever may have been its pluses and minuses, colonialism was a dictatorial regime that denied people's right of self determination. It brought death, pain and humiliation to millions of its victims.

JIMMIE DURHAM is a Cherokee visual artist and activist in the American Indian Movement. The following are verses from a 1993 poem he wrote about Columbus Day, a holiday that is celebrated in the United States and other countries.

Columbus Day
by Jimmie Durham

In school I was taught the names
Columbus, Cortez, and Pizarro and
A dozen other filthy murderers.
A bloodline all the way to General Miles,
Daniel Boone and General Eisenhower.

No one mentioned the names
Of even a few of the victims.
But don't you remember Chaske, whose spine
Was crushed so quickly by Mr. Pizarro's boot?
What words did he cry into the dust?
. . .

In school I learned of heroic discoveries
Made by liars and crooks. The courage
Of millions of sweet and true people
Was not commemorated.

Let us then declare a holiday
For ourselves, and make a parade that begins
With Columbus' victims and continues
Even to our grandchildren who will be named
In their honor.

Explorations

1. Write a short summary of the message of each writer. Share your summary with a partner. Discuss the similarities and differences in your interpretations. Did your own responses change as a result of your discussion? Explain why or why not.

2. Explain how the excerpts illustrate differences in points of view and perspectives over time and across cultures.

1. Review the three rounds of globalization identified by Ashutosh Sheshabalaya on page 117 of this chapter. Predict what a fourth round might involve and when it might begin. Explain the reasoning behind your prediction (e.g., what is happening today to influence your prediction).

2. With a partner or small group, create a visual — on paper or in a computer program — that shows one point of view or perspective on one way historical globalization has affected the world today.

   Then ask your classmates to analyze the point of view or perspective you selected. To help them do this

   • provide a detailed description of the people — who could be you and your partner — or group whose point of view or perspective you have chosen
   • develop at least two powerful questions to help guide the analysis

3. Suppose a time machine has brought Christopher Columbus into the present. He spends a few days here before returning to his own time. While he is here, he studies up-to-date maps of the world and hears the news that flows in from everywhere.

   What message about each of the following do you think he would take back?

   a) colonization

   b) the treatment of Indigenous peoples

   c) the results of his voyages

   d) his place in history, from several points of view and perspectives

   Write a short speech — two or three paragraphs — that Columbus might make to the Spanish king and queen, who sponsored his voyages, when he returns to his own time.

4. Over the next three school days, keep a list of the basic foods that you eat (e.g., ketchup is not a basic food, but potatoes are).

   At the end of this period, conduct research to find out where these basic foods originated (e.g., potatoes are native to Peru in South America).

   Choose the food that you think had the greatest effect when it was introduced to new countries and cultures. Create a poster that shows the importance of this effect. On your poster, include the three or four criteria you used to help make your choice.

Basic Foods		
Day 1	Day 2	Day 3
puffed wheat		
milk		
sugar		

5. Read the following two quotations on this page and summarize the message of each. Then explain how each is linked to this chapter's issue: To what extent did early globalization affect peoples of the world?

Share your responses with a partner. Discuss the differences, and if necessary, edit your response.

• • • • •

J. Michael Adams and **Angelo Carfagna** retell this story in their book, *Coming of Age in a Globalized World*:

In the 1770s, [residents of the Virginia colony in the United States] invited a local Native American community to send six of their members to Williamsburg College. Here is the reply from the Native Americans:

We thank you heartily. But you, who are wise, must know that different nations have different conceptions of things, and you will therefore not take it amiss, if our ideas of education happen not to be the same as yours . . . Several of our young people were formerly brought up at your colleges: they were instructed in all your sciences; but when they came back to us, they were bad runners, ignorant of every means of living in the woods, unable to bear either cold or hunger, knew neither how to build a cabin, take a deer, or kill an enemy, spoke our language imperfectly, were therefore neither fit for hunters, warriors, nor counsellors, they were totally good for nothing.

. . . to show our grateful sense of [your offer], if the gentlemen of Virginia will send us a dozen of their sons, we will take care of their education; instruct them in all we know and make men of them.

In their book, *Indigenous Cultures in an Interconnected World*, **Claire Smith**, an Australian archeologist, and **Graeme Ward**, a senior research fellow at the Australian Institute of Aboriginal and Torres Strait Islander Studies, wrote:

The unchecked expansion of European nations since the sixteenth century has signaled over 400 years of significant change for the world's Indigenous peoples. This process of colonization did not end with the arrival of European people but persisted as European goods, European technology and European beliefs perpetuated the process of invasion. Globalization threatens to accelerate this process of colonization.

Think about Your Challenge

Review the material in this chapter and the activities you completed as you progressed through it. Make notes about ideas that could be useful in preparing for the four-corners debate. Start preparing the criteria and critical questions you will use to evaluate the material you are thinking of exploring as your contribution to the debate.

Chapter 6 Legacies of Historical Globalization

Figure 6-1 These illustrations show two symbols of the British Empire: the imperial lion and the British flag, known as the Union Jack. For hundreds of millions of people around the world, these symbols became rallying points — or hated signs of oppression. These two symbols were also included in Canada's coat of arms (right) when it was adopted in 1921.

CHAPTER ISSUE

To what extent do the legacies of historical globalization affect peoples of the world?

EARLY IN THE 20TH CENTURY, the British Empire, the largest in history, included more than 450 million people. About 25 per cent of the world's people, including Canadians, were British subjects — people who were ruled by the British monarch.

The British flag and the imperial lion shown in the illustrations on the previous page were symbols that were repeated in colonial monuments and popular media throughout the empire. Canada's coat of arms, for example, includes both symbols.

Examine the illustrations and Canada's coat of arms — and think about the messages the symbols of empire might have sent.

- What feelings might these symbols have inspired in Britain?
- Why do you think the lion symbol is so prominent on the Canadian coat of arms? What might this reveal about Canadian attitudes in 1921, when the coat of arms was created?
- Which other peoples are represented by the symbols on Canada's coat of arms?
- What feelings might these symbols have inspired among Indigenous — and non-Indigenous — people in British colonies around the world?
- What attitudes on the part of Britain do you think these symbols imply?
- How might these attitudes have contributed to the long-term effects of imperialism and historical globalization?

KEY TERMS

legacy

ethnocentrism

Eurocentrism

depopulation

deindustrialization

gross domestic product

LOOKING AHEAD

In this chapter, you will explore answers to the following questions:

- What are some legacies of historical globalization?
- How has cultural contact affected people?
- How has the exchange of goods and technologies affected people?
- How are the legacies of historical globalization continuing to affect people?

My Point of View on Globalization

Look back at the notes you recorded as you began each of the previous chapters. What aspects of globalization do you feel most strongly about? Use words or images — or both — to answer this question. Date your ideas and add them to the notebook, learning log, portfolio, or computer file you are keeping as you progress through this course.

VOICES

It is this consciousness of the inherent superiority of the European which has won for us India. However well educated and clever a native may be, and however brave he may prove himself, I believe that no [military] rank we can bestow on him would cause him to be considered an equal of the British officer.

— *Lord Kitchener, British commander-in-chief in India, 1902–1909, on Indian soldiers in the British army*

VOICES

They resemble us, but in appearance are the colour of pumpkin-porridge . . . They are rude of manners and without any graces or refinement. They carry a long stick of fire. With this they kill and loot from many nations.

— *Zulu epic poem "Emperor Shaka the Great," which drew on the memories of Zulu oral historians*

Figure 6-2 On Australia Day in 2006, Australians celebrated the landing of the first fleet from Britain more than 200 years earlier. In the centre of this photo is the Australian flag. In what ways does this celebration honour the legacies of historical globalization in this former British colony?

WHAT ARE SOME LEGACIES OF HISTORICAL GLOBALIZATION?

A **legacy** is something that has been passed on by those who lived in the past. Legacies can include political structures, such as parliamentary democracy; buildings and monuments, such as houses of worship and statues or plaques; and oral histories and stories, as well as tangible artifacts. They may also include cultural traditions and celebrations, such as the one shown in the photograph on this page. In some respects, a legacy is an effect caused by past events.

Much that has shaped your identity can be traced to the legacies that have been passed on to you. Your language, for example, is a legacy from your past. So are your traditions, and the symbols of those traditions, as well as many of your values and your attitudes toward other people.

Think about your own legacies. Create a mind map showing how the legacies you value have affected your identity. Place the word "legacies" in the centre. Around this, fill in important legacies you have received. Think in terms of your language(s), beliefs, family, friends, community, and country, as well as global connections. Keep this mind map handy so you can return to it later.

Ethnocentrism and Eurocentrism

Ethnocentrism — a word that combines "ethnic" and "centre" — refers to a way of thinking that centres on one's own race and culture. Ethnocentric people believe that the only valid worldview is their own, and they judge other people according to their own beliefs, customs, and traditions. In the early 20th century, for example, more than half of Canadians were of British heritage, and some of them looked down on people who had immigrated from non-British countries, such as Ukraine and China.

What values and attitudes do you use to judge people who are different from you? Where do these attitudes come from? Are these attitudes one of your legacies?

Eurocentrism is a form of ethnocentrism that uses European ethnic, national, religious, and linguistic criteria to judge other peoples and their cultures. In the late 19th and early 20th centuries, for example, some Canadians of European heritage looked down on immigrants from Asia. In 1907, for instance, R.B. Bennett — who later became prime minister — told British Columbians that their province "must remain a white man's country."

Lord Kitchener, who is quoted on this page, was a popular British military hero. He successfully led British forces in Africa and commanded British troops in India. How do Kitchener's words reflect his Eurocentric views? How would views like these have fostered a legacy of ethnocentric and Eurocentric attitudes in the British Empire?

Building Empires

Between 1876 and 1914, the imperial powers greatly expanded their global possessions. During that time, many Indigenous peoples — especially those in the South Pacific, Asia, and Africa — came under the control of one of the imperial powers.

Examine the data on the chart (Figure 6-3). Suggest what these empires might have looked like in 1924 if the trend that you see had continued. What event occurred in 1914 to interfere with empire building? How might the legacies of historical globalization be different today if the empire-building trend had continued?

Figure 6-3 Colonial Expansion, 1876–1914

Imperial Power		1876		1914	
		Area (Millions of sq. km)	People (Millions)	Area (Millions of sq. km)	People (Millions)
	Britain	22.5	251.9	33.5	393.5
	France	0.9	6.0	10.6	55.5
	Germany	0	0	2.9	12.3
	United States	0	0	0.3	97.0
	Japan	0	0	0.3	19.2
	Russia	17	15.9	17.4	33.2

Ideas

How ethnocentric are you?

The students responding to this question are Katerina, who lives in St. Albert and whose grandparents emigrated from Ukraine in 1948; Gord, a member of the Beaver First Nation near High Level; and Ling, who was born in Hong Kong but is now a Canadian who lives in Edmonton.

This question is tough. My grandparents have told me stories about how people made fun of them when they first came from Ukraine. So, yes, they were definitely targets of ethnocentrism. But I don't think much about whether I look down on other people. I don't think I do, but it's sometimes hard to balance pride in your heritage with respect for people who are different. I guess it's sort of easy to see ethnocentricity in others, but not in yourself.

Katerina

As a member of the Beaver First Nation, I'm aware of the downside of the legacy of Eurocentrism in Alberta — and Canada. And I've thought about prejudice, though I hadn't heard the word "ethnocentrism" before. I know how it feels when my traditions and culture aren't valued, so it's really important to me to try to value other people and honour their traditions. But I also know that sometimes you can be hurtful without even knowing it.

Gord

My family lived in China and then in Vietnam and New Zealand before we came to Canada. So I'm sort of used to being around people who are different from us. I really don't think I'm ethnocentric. But I was surprised to read that bigoted comment from a Canadian prime minister. Talk about Eurocentrism! I guess that's one of the uglier legacies from the past — and we could do without it.

Ling

Your Turn

How would you respond to the question Katerina, Gord, and Ling are answering? What is your own experience with ethnocentrism? Do you recognize when you are being ethnocentric? Do you live in a culturally diverse community? How do you think your experiences with diversity affect your attitudes?

The Scramble for Africa

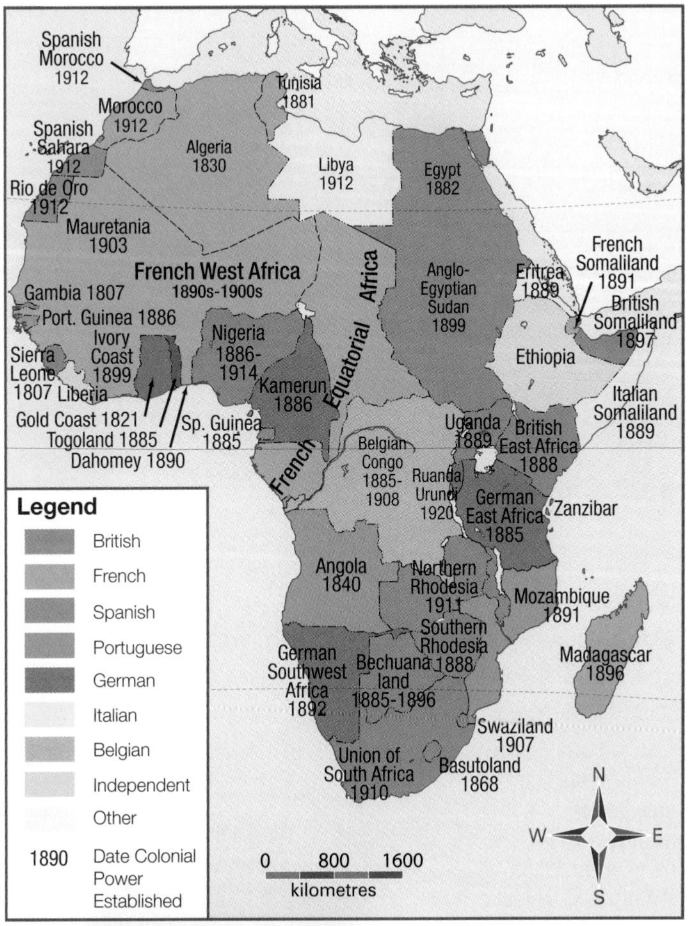

By the late 19th century, large parts of Africa remained independent of control by European empires. This changed in 1884, when representatives of the United States, Austria-Hungary, Belgium, Denmark, France, Germany, Britain, Italy, the Netherlands, the Ottoman Empire, Portugal, Russia, Spain, and Sweden-Norway met in Berlin, Germany, to divide Africa among themselves. They wanted to avoid conflicts with other imperial powers, protect existing trade routes, and gain control of the continent's natural resources, which included gold, diamonds, and rubber. Who was missing from this conference?

Once European political and military power bases were established in Africa, traders and settlers followed. No one consulted the Indigenous peoples whose lands and resources were taken over by Europe's imperial powers.

The arrival of Europeans — an oral history

Though few written records exist, oral histories tell of Indigenous peoples' responses to the European arrival. The following account dates from the 16th century, when Portuguese sailing ships first appeared at the mouth of the Congo River. When the Portuguese arrived, they were thought to be *vumbi* — ancestral ghosts — because the Indigenous people of the region believed that a person's skin turned white after death.

The account was related by Mukunzo Kioko, a 20th-century oral historian of the Pende people, who live today in the southwestern part of the Democratic Republic of Congo.

> Our fathers were living comfortably. They had cattle and crops; they had salt marshes and banana trees. Suddenly they saw a big boat rising out of the great ocean. This boat had wings all of white, sparkling like knives.
>
> White men came out of the water and spoke words which no one understood.
>
> Our ancestors took fright; they said these were vumbi, spirits returned from the dead.
>
> They pushed them back into the ocean with volleys of arrows.
>
> But the vumbi spat fire with a noise of thunder. Many men were killed. Our ancestors fled.
>
> The chiefs and wise men said that these vumbi were the former possessors of the land.
>
> From that time to our days now, the whites have brought us nothing but wars and miseries.

In your own words, tell Mukunzo Kioko's story to a partner — as if you are passing on the essential message of this story to the next generation.

Figure 6-4 European Imperial Rule in Africa, 1914

Spanish Morocco 1912
Morocco 1912
Spanish Sahara 1912
Rio de Oro 1912
Mauretania 1903
Gambia 1807
Port. Guinea 1886
Sierra Leone 1807
Ivory Coast 1899
Liberia
Gold Coast 1821
Togoland 1885
Dahomey 1890
Tunisia 1881
Algeria 1830
Libya 1912
Egypt 1882
French West Africa 1890s-1900s
Nigeria 1886-1914
Kamerun 1886
Sp. Guinea 1885
French Equatorial Africa
Anglo-Egyptian Sudan 1899
Eritrea 1889
French Somaliland 1891
British Somaliland 1897
Ethiopia
Italian Somaliland 1889
Belgian Congo 1885-1908
Ruanda Urundi 1920
Uganda 1889
British East Africa 1888
German East Africa 1885
Zanzibar
Angola 1840
Northern Rhodesia 1911
German Southwest Africa 1892
Southern Rhodesia 1888
Bechuanaland 1885-1896
Mozambique 1891
Madagascar 1896
Swaziland 1907
Union of South Africa 1910
Basutoland 1868

Legend
- British
- French
- Spanish
- Portuguese
- German
- Italian
- Belgian
- Independent
- Other
- 1890 Date Colonial Power Established

0   800   1600
kilometres

N W E S

Figure 6-5 Queen Elizabeth II holds the royal sceptre, which contains the world's largest polished diamond, the Great Star of Africa. This diamond, which is worth nearly $463 million (Cdn), was cut from a larger stone discovered in a South African mine in 1905. The Indigenous people who lived in the area received no benefit from this discovery. Should they be compensated today for this loss of resources?

King Léopold and the Congo

In the early 1880s, King Léopold II of Belgium sparked the scramble for Africa by claiming as his own personal property all the lands drained by the Congo River and its tributaries. Today, this vast area forms two countries: the Republic of Congo and the Democratic Republic of Congo.

Léopold ruled this land — and the Indigenous peoples who lived there — as his own personal colony. His sweeping claim to the region was one of the reasons the imperial powers gathered in Berlin in 1884. They recognized Léopold's claim to the Congo but wanted to be first to stake their own claims to other areas.

By 1885, Léopold had forced the Indigenous peoples of the Congo region to give up much of their land and to work harvesting natural rubber. Rubber became a source of great personal wealth to Léopold because, at the time, demand for this product was growing. Manufacturers in North America and Europe needed rubber to make tires for bicycles and the newly invented automobile.

Indigenous people who resisted were brutally punished. Some were beaten; others had their ears, hands, or feet cut off; and many were killed. In addition, many starved or died of diseases. Some experts estimate that as many as 10 million people — equivalent to the combined population of Manitoba, Saskatchewan, Alberta, and British Columbia — died during and immediately after Léopold's rule.

Léopold tried to prevent knowledge of these atrocities from reaching the outside world. His employees were forbidden to leave the Congo, and news reporters were forbidden to enter. Léopold also bribed publishers to write positive stories, and he accused critics of working for other colonial powers that wanted to grab some of the profits for themselves. Although some rumours did leak out, Léopold's strategy worked for more than a decade. Do you think a strategy like this could work today? Why or why not?

Léopold finally handed control of the Congo to the Belgian government in 1908. But this did not end the suffering of the Indigenous peoples. Many Indigenous leaders became representatives of the Belgian government. But many of these leaders were puppets who served as go-betweens linking the colonizers with Indigenous communities. In return for favours from the Belgian government, these leaders collected taxes and supplied labourers to the colonizers.

Figure 6-6 During his rule over the Congo region, King Léopold II of Belgium never visited the area that was the source of his great wealth. If he had visited the area, do you think things might have been different?

CHECKFORWARD

In Chapter 8, you will read more about the legacies of historical globalization in Africa.

REFLECT AND RESPOND

With a partner, create a two-column chart like the one shown. In the first column, list three pieces of evidence supporting the idea that the imperialism of the late 19th and early 20th centuries was grounded in ethnocentric and Eurocentric attitudes. In completing this activity, you may find it helpful to review material included in Chapter 5. Then think about the situation in the world today. In the second column, suggest a continuing legacy of these attitudes. An example has been filled in.

Legacies of Ethnocentric and Eurocentric Attitudes in Africa	
Evidence (Late 19th and Early 20th Centuries)	**Continuing Legacy** (Situation Today)
Imperial powers divided Africa without considering Indigenous peoples	Conflict in places like Democratic Republic of Congo and Somalia

Suppose you are carrying a stack of dishes from the dinner table. You trip on your dog's favourite toy and drop the dishes, which shatter. The immediate effect of this accident is clear — a mess of broken dishes. But what was the cause? Did you trip because your parents asked you to clear the table? Because no one moved the toy out of the way? Because you were in a hurry and tried to carry too many dishes at once?

And what about the long-term effects of this incident? What might they be?

An analysis of this incident shows that what appears to be a straightforward cause-and-effect relationship can raise complex issues.

Think about this question: To what extent did the causes of the imperial powers' division of Africa affect the future of the Indigenous peoples of that continent?

The following steps can help you respond to this question, which deals with causes and effects. As you progress through this course, you can use the same steps to help you understand the complex cause-and-effect relationships that link other events and outcomes.

Steps to Analyzing and Interpreting Cause-and-Effect Relationships

Step 1: Clarify your opening opinions and assumptions

Review the chart titled "Legacies of Ethnocentric and Eurocentric Attitudes in Africa," which you completed earlier. Then consider your assumptions about the legacies of the imperial powers' scramble for Africa. Discuss these with a partner. Think about the relationship between the causes of each piece of evidence listed on your chart and the legacies — or effects — you identified.

Step 2: Create a graphic organizer

A cause-and-effect organizer like the one shown on the following page can help you analyze an event that has many causes and effects. It can also help you interpret complex cause-and-effect patterns. Create an organizer like this and use it to record, organize, understand, and interpret information and opinions as you respond to the question. If necessary, you may add more boxes to show causes and effects.

Step 3: Analyze your initial findings

Work with your partner to respond to the following questions, which will help guide your analysis:

- Rank the factors that led to the imperial powers' scramble for Africa in order of importance. What criteria did you use to arrive at this ranking? How do these factors relate to the broader patterns of European imperialism, which had been going on for centuries?
- What were the most significant short-term effects of the scramble for Africa? What were the most significant long-term effects — legacies that have lasted to the present day? How might the short- and long-term effects be connected?
- What evidence do you need to complete your analysis and arrive at a reasonable interpretation of the causes and effects? How will you find this evidence?

VOCABULARY TIP

The words "effect" and "affect" are often confused because both can be nouns and verbs. Deciding when to use each depends on the meaning you want to convey.

Effect
- Assimilation was one *effect* of imperialism.
  A noun meaning "result."
- European imperial powers *effected* change in their colonies.
  A verb meaning "brought about" or "caused."

Affect
- My friend's lack of *affect* made it hard to figure out what she was thinking.
  A noun meaning "emotion."
- European imperialism *affected* people around the world.
  A verb meaning "influenced."

Step 4: Research multiple perspectives

Research sources of information (e.g., first-hand historical accounts, oral histories, maps and other visual evidence) that are likely to provide differing points of view and perspectives on the causes and effects of the division of Africa by the imperial powers.

To help evaluate these points of view and perspectives, you may use a bias chart similar to the one found in Chapter 2 (p. 56).

- What differing perspectives do various speakers or writers offer on the causes and effects that relate to the event?
- In each resource, who is the speaker or writer? What is her or his point of view? How does the speaker or writer interpret the causes of the event? The effects of the event?
- Does the speaker or writer represent a larger community or collective? What is its perspective?
- What connections does the speaker or writer make between causes and effects? Are these connections logical? Are they biased?

Step 5: Interpret your findings

When you conclude your research and analysis, revise your organizer so that it clearly shows your interpretation of the causes and effects.

Then create a brief summary of your position on the extent to which the causes of the imperial powers' division of Africa affected the future of the Indigenous peoples of that continent. Present this orally to your classmates. As you listen to other students' presentations, keep your graphic organizer handy so you can revise it when you hear convincing arguments.

RESEARCH TIP

To answer the question posed in this feature, you will need to interpret factual information and explore various points of view and perspectives on this information. As you do this, keep in mind that causes can be effects of previous events and effects can be causes of future events.

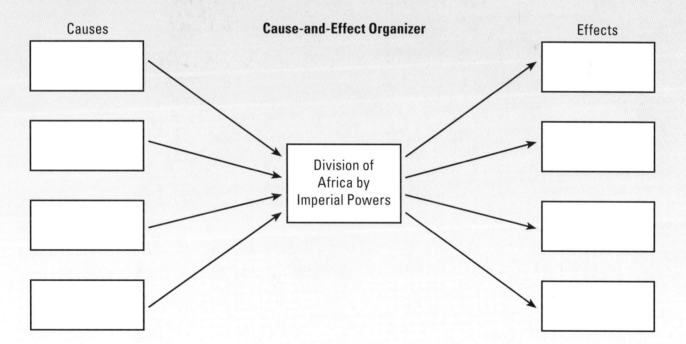

Cause-and-Effect Organizer

Causes   Division of Africa by Imperial Powers   Effects

Summing up

As you progress through the chapters of this related issue and the course, you will encounter many situations where analyzing causes and effects will help you explore the theme of continuity and change. Following the steps set out in this activity will help you analyze and interpret these issues. It will also help you successfully complete the challenge for this related issue.

HOW HAS CULTURAL CONTACT AFFECTED PEOPLE?

Web Connection

The Algerian War of Independence was a long, bitter, and brutal struggle. To find out more about it, go to this web site and follow the links

www.ExploringGlobalization.ca

Nineteenth-century Europeans were not the first to create powerful empires, to come into contact with peoples different from themselves, and to leave legacies among the people they conquered. In earlier times and in different places, the Ottoman — or Turkish — Empire ruled large parts of Asia and Europe. China once had a complex and powerful imperial system, and the Roman Empire conquered and imposed political institutions on much of northern Europe and North Africa.

In North Africa, for example, Algeria has served as a gateway between Europe and Africa for centuries. The region was conquered by Rome in the first century CE, then by the Umayyads, who started building a large Muslim empire in the seventh century. In the 15th century, the area came under Spanish control, but the Spanish were driven out by the Ottomans in the 16th century. In 1830, the region became a French colony. Each of these empires left legacies in the region. After a long struggle with the French, Algeria became independent in 1962.

By the early 20th century, the European empires had fundamentally changed the lives and cultures of the people under their rule. The map in Figure 6-7 illustrates that these changes were global in reach. Which regions of the world were under the control of European empires? How might this control have affected Indigenous people living in these regions? Think about world news today. What news stories reflect the legacies of the European empires?

Figure 6-7 **Colonial Possessions, 1914**

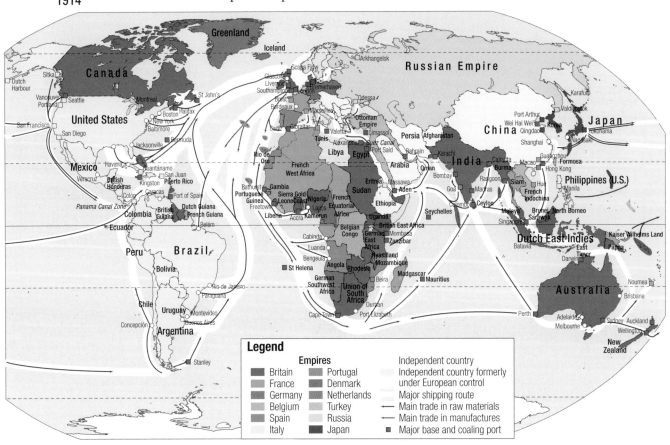

Legend

Empires

Britain	Portugal
France	Denmark
Germany	Netherlands
Belgium	Turkey
Spain	Russia
Italy	Japan

Independent country
Independent country formerly under European control
Major shipping route
⟶ Main trade in raw materials
⟶ Main trade in manufactures
■ Major base and coaling port

What legacies do imperial powers leave among the peoples they conquer? The following speakers, from different regions of the world and at different times, respond to this question.

DADABHAI NAOROJI, president of the Indian National Congress in 1886, 1893, and 1906, at the conclusion of a speech delivered in London in 1871.

The British rule has been: morally, a great blessing; politically, peace and order on one hand, blunders on the other; materially, impoverishment, relieved as far as the railway and other loans go. The natives call the British system "Sakar ki Churi," the knife of sugar. That is to say, there is no oppression, it is all smooth and sweet, but it is the knife, notwithstanding. I mention this that you should know these feelings. Our great misfortune is that you do not know our wants.

THE DALAI LAMA, in a statement to the Foreign Affairs Committee of the German Parliament on June 19, 1995.

In Tibet my people are being marginalized and discriminated against in the face of creeping Sinicization [assimilation into Chinese culture]. The destruction of cultural artefacts and traditions coupled with the mass influx of Chinese into Tibet amounts to cultural genocide. The very survival of the Tibetans as a distinct people is under constant threat . . . Fundamentally, the issue of Tibet is political. It is an issue of colonial rule: the oppression of Tibet by the People's Republic of China and resistance to that rule by the people of Tibet.

ATIKU ABUBAKAR, vice-president of Nigeria, in a speech at the University of California on March 25, 2004.

Colonial rule, in whatever form, did more than subjugate the sovereignty of African states and societies. It ensured that Africa's experience in the evolution of the modern international system was largely from a disillusioned perspective . . . The nature of colonial rule itself left devastating social and economic and psychological effects on African people. Overpowered and denied the opportunity to develop their potentials along the lines of their unique social, cultural peculiarities, African countries were forced to grow according to the whims and preferences of their colonial masters.

Explorations

1. In your own words, rewrite each speaker's statement to capture its main idea.

2. On the basis of what these three speakers have said, what do you think is the single most important legacy of colonial rule? Support your judgment by selecting words or phrases from the three quotations, as well as information you have learned so far.

Legacies and Patterns of Historical Change

Over time, the imperial powers changed the culture of the peoples in their colonies. In many cases, the patterns of change were similar. The official languages of a country and the makeup of the population, for example, may be legacies of imperial rule. Think about Canada today. What legacies of French and British imperial rule continue to exist in this country?

One way imperial powers altered the lives of the Indigenous peoples in their colonies was to change the languages they spoke. In all the European empires, the pattern of change was much the same: the language of the imperial power came to dominate. This is one of the reasons European languages are so common in former colonies, such as Canada.

Today, French is spoken in North Africa; Spanish and Portuguese are spoken in Central and South America; and English is spoken in Ireland. Although the official language of Vietnam, which was once part of French Indochina, is now Vietnamese, French is still spoken in that country. And though English is not an official language in India, it is still widely used in national, political, and commercial communications.

Figure 6-8 These photographs show symbols of continuing legacies of colonial influence in Argentina, which became a Spanish colony in the early 1500s. The street signs in Buenos Aires show that Spanish is now the official language of the country. The Argentine government palace — Casa Rosada — resembles in style many Spanish and European buildings. And the Argentinian flamenco dancer is carrying on a tradition that originated in the Andalusia region of Spain.

Figure 6-9 Origin of Immigrants to Canada, 1913

Origin	Number
Austrian	3232
British	158 398
Chinese	6298
Finnish	3508
German	5710
Jewish*	11 574
Italian	27 704
Polish	13 339
Russian	28 758
Ukrainian	18 907
American	97 712

Source: Statistics Section, Citizenship and Immigration Canada

Note: Does not include groups with fewer than 3000 immigrants.

*Discriminatory immigration policies listed Jews by religion, not nationality.

Legacies of migration

During the late 19th and early 20th centuries, millions of people were on the move, often from the home country of a European empire to one of its colonies and sometimes from one colony to another. These migrants were searching for a better life and, at times, fleeing famine or conflict in their home country. From 1871 to 1914, for example, 30 million people migrated from Europe to the United States, Canada, Australia, New Zealand, South America, Algeria, and South Africa.

In 1913 alone, more than 400 000 people immigrated to Canada — a record that still stands today. As the chart in Figure 6-9 shows, about 40 per cent of these immigrants came from Britain. Few were of African, Asian, or South Asian origin because rules limited immigration from Africa, Asia, and South Asia. How did this limit reflect a legacy of British imperial rule?

Migrants were leaving what they knew and setting off into the unknown. What legacies of historical globalization might have been powerful enough to persuade people to leave their country of birth? What factors might have attracted them to the countries to which they immigrated? How were these factors legacies of historical globalization?

Legacies of displacement

When European imperialists moved into a colony, they paid little attention to Indigenous peoples' relationship with the land where they lived. Indigenous peoples were displaced — forced off their land — when colonizers needed land for settlements, railways, mining and lumbering, and large plantations.

In addition, traditional forms of government and community boundaries were often ignored by European colonial empires. "National frontiers laid down by European colonizers largely ignored the boundaries of Indigenous peoples," said Julian Burger, a United Nations human rights advocate. "Consequently, many groups straddle frontiers, and are administered by more than one government."

The colonizers' disregard for Indigenous people's lives, beliefs, and traditions left legacies of civil war and starvation. It also destroyed cultures and communities.

Return to the mind map you created earlier. For each of the legacies you identified, add a word or phrase that describes how you would feel if you lost that legacy. If you identified language, for example, you might write "anger at loss of identity."

VOICES

The Earth is the foundation of Indigenous peoples, it is the seat of spirituality, the fountain from which our cultures and languages flourish. The Earth is our historian, the keeper of events and the bones of our forefathers. Earth provides us with food, medicine, shelter and clothing. It is the source of our independence, it is our Mother. We do not dominate her; we must harmonize with her.

— *Poka Laenui (Hayden Burgess), Hawaiian sovereignty activist and head of the Institute for the Advancement of Hawaiian Affairs*

PROFILE

CHINUA ACHEBE
THINGS FALL APART

PROFILE PROFILE PROFILE PROFILE PROFILE PROFILE

When Nigerian writer Chinua Achebe published *Things Fall Apart* in 1958, the book became a bestseller. More than eight million English copies of the book have been sold, and it has been translated into 50 languages.

Things Fall Apart tells the story of Okonkwo, a leader of the Igbo people of the Umuofia region of present-day Nigeria. Parts of Nigeria had been colonized by various European imperial powers, but in the late 19th century, the British took over. Okonkwo speaks of the loss of identity that his people suffered as a result of British colonialism and imposed Christianity.

Figure 6-10 Born in 1930 in Ogidi, Nigeria, Chinua Achebe was the son of Igbo parents who had converted to Christianity. Achebe went to university in Ibadan and worked as a broadcaster, publisher, teacher, and writer.

[The white man] says that our customs are bad; and our own brothers who have taken up his religion also say that our customs are bad. How do you think we can fight when our own brothers have turned against us? The white man is very clever. He came quietly and peaceably with his religion. We were amused at his foolishness and allowed him to stay. Now he has won our brothers, and our clan can no longer act like one. He has put a knife on the things that held us together and we have fallen apart.

In 2000, Achebe explained how Igbo society was completely disrupted by the coming of the European government and missionaries.

With the coming of the British, Igbo land as a whole was incorporated into a totally different polity, to be called Nigeria, with a whole lot of other people with whom the Igbo people had not had direct contact before. The result of that was not something from which you could recover, really. You had to learn a totally new reality, and accommodate yourself to the demands of this new reality, which is the state called Nigeria. Various nationalities, each of which had its own independent life, were forced by the British to live with people of different customs and habits and priorities and religions. And then at independence, fifty years later, they were suddenly on their own again. They began all over again to learn the rules of independence.

Legacies of depopulation

CHECKBACK
You read about slavery and indentured labour when you explored historical globalization in Chapter 5.

The forced migration of African slaves led to the **depopulation** of many parts of the continent — and the effects of this population loss were devastating. Families and communities were shattered. Those forced into slavery were often young and strong. In the future, they would have become leaders. Their skills and labour would have helped support their family and community. And unlike many of today's migrants, who send money and goods to help family members at home, slaves could do nothing for those left behind.

In 1834, the British abolitionist movement triumphed and slavery was abolished throughout the empire. As a result, colonies that had relied on slave labour looked elsewhere for cheap workers. One source was indentured labour — and India, which was then a British colony with many poor and desperate people, became a source of these workers.

From 1834 until the system was abolished in 1920, millions of Indians were recruited as indentured labourers. They were sent to work on plantations in other British colonies, such as Trinidad, Jamaica, Malaysia, Myanmar, and South Africa. When their indenture period ended, they often remained in their new land, forming large communities. What factors might have prevented their return home?

When the French and Dutch later abolished slavery, plantation owners in their colonies also turned to India for indentured labour. Just as slavery depopulated Africa, the indenture system depopulated India — with similar effects.

Famine and disease also played a role in depopulating India. From 1876 to 1879, for example, between 6 and 10 million Indians died of starvation. And from 1896 to 1902, as many as 19 million people may have died of starvation and disease. How might famine have influenced people's decision to sign on as indentured labourers?

Figure 6-11 This drawing shows African slaves working on a Barbados sugar plantation. The slaves cut the sugar cane, then processed it to produce molasses, which was distilled into rum. What are at least two ways in which this process contributed to globalization?

REFLECT AND RESPOND

Language changes, migration, displacement, and depopulation are legacies of historical globalization. What choices by Europe's imperial powers (the causes) led most directly to each of these legacies (the effects)? To respond to this question, use a cause-and-effect organizer similar to the one you completed earlier. Remember that a single cause may have many effects.

Consider the causes you identified. Which would you say had the greatest effect on colonized people? Explain the reasons for your judgment.

HOW HAS THE EXCHANGE OF GOODS AND TECHNOLOGIES AFFECTED PEOPLE?

Many of the foods and beverages you consume today — potatoes, tomatoes, tea, coffee, chocolate, and bananas — are available because of the worldwide exchange of goods, technologies, and ideas that started in the late 15th century. This exchange sparked chains of events that often led to dramatic changes in cultures around the world.

For thousands of years, for example, the First Nations of North America's Plains relied on the buffalo — or bison — for many of the necessities of life. As the illustration on this page shows, every part of this wild animal, which could weigh up to 900 kilograms, was used.

When the Spanish arrived in Mexico in the early 1500s, they brought horses with them. Indigenous peoples realized how useful this animal could be, and a lively trade in horses began. This trade gradually expanded northward, and by the mid-1700s, horses had become an important part of the culture of the First Nations who live today on the Canadian Prairies.

First Nations peoples quickly learned to ride, train, and breed horses. Horses helped Plains peoples travel and transport goods faster and farther than ever before, and these animals became important symbols of wealth and status. As the Plains peoples became expert riders, they were able to hunt buffalo much more efficiently.

At about the same time, Europeans were starting to move into the West, and guns became more and more common on buffalo hunts. By the mid-1800s, commercial hunters had come to view the buffalo as a money-making commodity. These hunters had begun killing buffalo to feed the European demand for buffalo hides, which were used as blankets and to make leather. In addition, the American government encouraged the slaughter of buffalo to make way for settlements and farming on the American Plains.

In 1800, an estimated 30 million buffalo roamed the North American Plains. A hundred years later, this number had dwindled to less than 1000. Buffalo were nearly extinct — and the way of life that relied on this animal had been destroyed.

CHECKBACK

You read about the grand exchange in Chapter 5.

FYI

A prehistoric horse had existed in North America, but this animal died out during the Ice Ages. By the time the Spanish brought European horses to the continent, the prehistoric horses had been unknown in North America for at least 10 000 years.

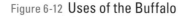

Figure 6-12 Uses of the Buffalo

Skin (hides): clothing, bags and cases for carrying and storing, horseshoes, knife sheaths, drums, saddles, bridles, bedding, tipi covers, saddlebags

Sinew: threads, strings for hunting bows, games

Hair: plaited into halters, stuffed into saddle pads

Tail: brush to kill flies and mosquitoes

Stomach: cooking pot, water bucket

Hoofs: boiled for glue, made into rattles

Bladder: food bag

Dung and chips: fuel

Bones: saddle horns, implements for dressing skins, needles, games

Meat: food (heart, liver, kidneys, and tongue were also eaten)

Ribs: arrow shafts

Shinbone: knives, tools for scraping hides

Shoulderblade: digging tool, hammer

Skull: painted and used in religious ceremonies

Bone marrow: fat, fuel for fires

Bone-ends: paint brushes

Hide from neck: warrior shields

Horn: spoons, drinking cups, ladles

Brains: for tanning skins

Teeth: necklaces

Beard: decorating a hunting bow

Source: Adapted from *Defining Canada: History, Identity, and Culture.* McGraw-Hill Ryerson, 2003.

Contact and Cultural Change in India

When Queen Elizabeth I of Britain granted the British East India Company a monopoly on trading in India and Asia in 1600, the company's chief interest was in making money through trade. From India, the company imported cotton cloth, tea, and spices, such as pepper, cardamom, ginger, and turmeric. From the company's perspective, the people of India were useful facilitators of this trade.

The British East India Company

As the British East India Company came to control trade with India, company officials in that country became more and more powerful. To protect their monopoly, company officials formed political alliances with traditional Indian rulers, whom they counted on to persuade their subjects to co-operate with the company and keep goods flowing smoothly.

Figure 6-13 Spices like these were originally traded along the Silk Road. In Europe, they were extremely expensive, so only the wealthy could afford to use them. Transporting them to Europe by ship reduced their cost and made them more affordable. As they became more widely used, they transformed European cooking.

The company also created its own army. Officers were usually British, but enlisted men, called *sepoys*, were Indians. This army not only supported the company's Indian allies, but also protected its monopoly by keeping out rival trading companies, such as the Dutch East India Company, which had been formed in Holland.

British East India Company officers such as Robert Clive, who became known as "Clive of India," sometimes became heroes in Britain as a result of their actions in India, where they used military might, bribery, and extortion to ensure that trade continued to flow smoothly — and in the company's favour.

Although the term "transnational corporation" did not exist at the time, some historians today have called the East India Company the world's first transnational. The company's vast and prosperous trading network, as well as its military might, made it one of the most powerful commercial organizations the world has ever seen.

Imagine that one of today's transnational corporations decided to create an army to protect its interests. What do you think the effects of this action would be? Explain the reasons for your judgment.

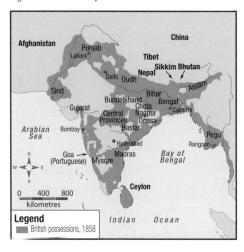

Figure 6-14 India, 1858

Legend
British possessions, 1858

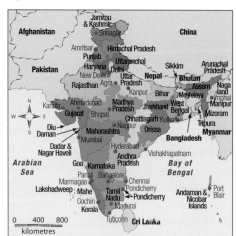

Figure 6-15 India, 2006

The Raj

The sometimes brutal business practices of the East India Company, the high taxes it imposed on Indian people, the corruption of many company officials, and numerous other factors sparked alarm in both India and Britain. Finally, in 1858, the British government took over direct rule of India and the period known as the Raj — a term taken from the Hindi word for "rule" — began.

Cotton and deindustrialization in India

As the Industrial Revolution took hold in Britain, British manufacturers needed raw materials to supply the factories that produced their products. They also needed markets where they could sell their surplus manufactured goods, such as cloth, iron, and pottery. Their solution was to sell these goods to people in British colonies. As a result, colonies took on added importance. They became not only a source of raw materials, but also an important market for British-made goods.

In Britain, technological developments such as the spinning jenny and the cotton gin enabled manufacturers to produce vast amounts of cotton cloth — and cotton became an important British export. But cotton cloth was also an important Indian export, and Indian cotton competed directly with the British-made fabric.

In 1700, the British government bowed to the demands of British weavers and banned the import of all dyed and printed cloth from India. Over the next 200 years, other laws also restricted trade in cotton. The goal of these laws was to protect the British textile industry against competition from cloth produced in other countries, such as India and the United States.

The British actions crushed the Indian cotton industry. Indians who had, for centuries, made a living growing, harvesting, spinning, and weaving cotton could no longer do so. The British laws, and similar laws that affected other industries, helped contribute to **deindustrialization** — the loss of industry — in India.

Think about the situation of an Indian cotton weaver whose family had been weavers for generations. How might British laws restricting cotton imports have affected his life and identity? His family's? His community's?

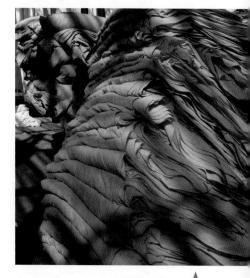

Figure 6-16 As early as 1000 BCE, people in India were growing and harvesting cotton, spinning it into thread, and weaving this thread into cloth. Long before the era of historical globalization, this fabric was transported to Europe along the Silk Road.

The cotton trade and Mohandas Gandhi

Known as Mahatma — Great Soul — Mohandas Gandhi successfully led India to independence in 1947. His strategy of peaceful non-co-operation with the British was based on the principle of *swadeshi*, a Hindi word that means "self-sufficiency."

Gandhi was born in 1869 in Porbandar, on the west coast of India. Educated in India, he became a lawyer in England and lived in South Africa for 20 years. There, he worked for the rights of Indians, many of whom were the descendants of indentured labourers. When Gandhi returned to India, he became a leader of the Indian National Congress Party, which was one of the earliest — and most influential — nationalist movements in European colonies.

Gandhi believed that every Indian should be self-sufficient — and he used cotton as a powerful symbol of both British oppression and Indians' desire for self-sufficiency and independence. He said that one way for people to become self-sufficient was to hand-spin cotton thread to make their own cloth. If Indians wore homespun cotton, he said, they would not only free themselves of the need to buy British-made cloth, but also help solve India's unemployment problem.

Gandhi extended this belief to other products. He believed that Indians should eat locally grown food and buy locally manufactured products. In 1924, he explained his beliefs this way:

With God as my witness, I solemnly declare that from today I shall confine myself, for my personal requirements, to the use of cloth manufactured in India from Indian cotton, silk, or wool, and I shall altogether abstain from using foreign cloth, and I shall destroy all foreign cloth in my possession.

— Mohandas Gandhi's pledge, which was sent to the governor of Bombay — now Mumbai — on April 30, 1919

Figure 6-17 This photograph of Mohandas Gandhi spinning cotton thread was taken in 1946 by the famous American photojournalist Margaret Bourke-White. What aspects of Gandhi's identity does her photograph capture?

What I object to is the craze for machinery, not machinery as such. The craze is for what they call labour-saving machinery. Men go on "saving labour" till thousands are without work and thrown on the streets to die of starvation. I want to save time and labour, not for a fraction of mankind, but for all. I want the concentration of wealth, not in the hands of a few, but in the hands of all. Today machinery helps a few to ride on the backs of millions. The impetus behind it is not philanthropy to save labour, but greed . . .

Swadeshi . . . is a call to the consumer to be aware of the violence he is causing by supporting those industries that result in poverty, harm to workers and to humans and other creatures.

REFLECT AND RESPOND

Are the effects of new technology always beneficial?

Explain your response to this question. Support your position by including historical and contemporary examples and by citing short- and long-term effects.

A contemporary example might be downloading music from the Internet. Who did — and did not — benefit immediately when it became possible to download music? Who might — and might not — benefit in the long term?

How are the legacies of historical globalization continuing to affect people?

No one knows what the world would have looked like today if European countries had not expanded their empires in the 19th century. The actions of imperialists often denied Indigenous and non-Indigenous peoples in colonies the ability to control their own destiny. And though the lives of some Indigenous and non-Indigenous people improved, many cultures disintegrated. Personal and collective identities, as well as economic and political systems, were destroyed, and many people suffered poverty and oppression.

Many Indigenous people were, for example, forced to abandon their traditional way of life. To survive, they had to work in faraway mines, plantations, and factories. There, they often laboured in appalling conditions for very low wages. The wealth produced by the colonies benefited rich people and rulers in the home countries, not the workers or the colony itself. Many people believe that this inequality laid the foundation for the inequalities that continue to exist in today's global economy.

Figure 6-18 The Chhatrapati Shivaji railway station in Mumbai was originally named after Queen Victoria. A statue of the queen still sits atop the dome of the station, which was built in 1888 and modelled after a station in London, England. Is this station a positive or negative legacy of historical globalization?

Cultural Change

Imperialism changed not only economic relations among countries, but also the cultures of people under European rule. European religious beliefs, for example, were often exported to the colonies. Christianity changed the lives of the peoples who adopted it, just as Islam and Buddhism had changed lives in earlier empires.

Even Indigenous art changed. Art that was created for export to Europe had to reflect European tastes and preferences — or it would not sell. At the same time, European architecture was exported to the colonies. Throughout India, for example, the British built huge buildings, such as the railway station shown on this page, in the European style.

Review the data in Figure 6-19. GDP is short for **gross domestic product**, which is a measure of the strength of a country's economy. It refers to the value of all the goods and services produced annually within a country's borders. What conclusions, if any, does this chart help you draw about today's legacies of historical globalization? What other factors might you need to consider when drawing conclusions about these legacies?

Figure 6-19 **GDP per Person in Britain and Some Former British Colonies, 2006**

Country	GDP per Person (U.S. Dollars)
Hong Kong	36 500
Canada	35 200
Australia	32 900
Britain	31 400
Sri Lanka	4600
Jamaica	4600
India	3700
Pakistan	2600
Myanmar (Burma)	1800
Kenya	1200
Tanzania	800

AUNG SAN SUU KYI AND DICTATORSHIP IN MYANMAR (BURMA)

For all but six years between 1989 and 2007, Aung San Suu Kyi was under house arrest in her homeland, Myanmar. Her crime? To work for democracy and human rights in this country, which was once a province of the British colonial empire in India.

Suu Kyi, who finds inspiration in the teachings of Mohandas Gandhi and American civil rights leader Martin Luther King, is a devout Buddhist who believes that non-violent resistance will one day bring peace and democracy to Myanmar. The country has been racked by turmoil since the British took over the kingdom in 1886.

Figure 6-20 Myanmar (Burma)

British Colonial Rule

After a series of devastating wars with Britain, the kingdom of Burma — now widely known as Myanmar — became a province of India in 1886. The country's king was exiled. Some people continued to resist, but they were harshly punished. British troops carried out mass executions, burned entire villages, and transported people suspected of working against British rule to other parts of the country.

Gradually, Britain integrated Burma into its vast colonial trading network. To achieve this, the British used tactics similar to those that had worked in India and other colonies.

Burma's traditional leaders were undermined, and the British paid little attention to the differences between the Burman, Shan, Karen, Rakhine, Chinese, Indian, and Mon peoples who lived in the country. The British created more unrest by ignoring the traditional close relationship between the dominant Buddhist religion and the country's leaders. In addition, the British favoured some of Burma's ethnic minorities, such as the Karen people, at the expense of others.

The British also encouraged Christian missionaries to open schools, which Burmese children were forced to attend. Teachers in these schools criticized Buddhism and encouraged children and their families to convert to Christianity.

In addition, British farmers and businesspeople were encouraged to hire Indian indentured labourers, a tactic that kept wages low and created high unemployment among the Indigenous peoples of Burma. Even those who were able to find jobs earned little money and often lived in poverty. Educated Indians were also imported to work in the province's civil service, though senior positions were usually filled by white Britons.

Independence

As in India, a strong independence movement took root in Burma. Suu Kyi's father, Aung San, helped spearhead this movement, but he was assassinated in 1947, a year before the country gained independence and established a form of parliamentary government.

Independence did not end the conflict among the peoples of Burma, however, and in 1962, military leaders seized control and set up a dictatorship. In the aftermath, Burma's economy declined. A country that had once grown more than enough rice to feed its own people began to suffer shortages.

For much of this time, Suu Kyi was out of the country. Only two years old when her father died, she was a teenager when her mother, Khin Kyi, was appointed ambassador to India in 1960. Suu Kyi went with her mother to India, then attended university in England and continued her education in New York, where she also worked for the United Nations.

Return to Myanmar

In 1988, Suu Kyi returned to Myanmar to care for her ailing mother. At the time, the country was in turmoil as people protested more than 25 years of military rule. Suu Kyi became involved and helped found a political party called the National League for Democracy. "I could not, as my father's daughter, remain indifferent to all that was going on," she said in a speech.

For her role in promoting democracy, Suu Kyi was placed under house arrest in 1989. Still, the strength of the protests persuaded the government to hold free elections in 1990 — and the NLD won 82 per cent of the vote.

But NLD leaders were either in exile or, like Suu Kyi, under arrest. They could do little when military leaders ignored the election results. The dictatorship — and Suu Kyi's house arrest — continued.

Although Suu Kyi was freed for about five years in the late 1990s, she continued her political activities and was rearrested in 2000. She was freed again in 2002 but was arrested again a year later.

Myanmar's military rulers have offered to allow Suu Kyi to go into exile, but she has refused. She prefers to remain under house arrest in Yangôn, the country's largest city. There, she is a symbol of resistance against the military dictatorship.

Economic and Humanitarian Legacies

According to Canadian Friends of Burma, more than 40 years of military rule have transformed Myanmar into "a severely impoverished and underdeveloped nation." The country's leaders rule with an iron fist, using fear and intimidation to stifle protest.

Figure 6-21 In 1991, Aung San Suu Kyi won the Nobel Peace Prize for her efforts to bring democracy to Myanmar. Members of the Nobel committee praised Suu Kyi's efforts to reconcile "the sharply divided regions and ethnic groups in her country."

Explorations

1. Identify examples of migration, depopulation, and displacement as legacies of historical globalization in Myanmar.

2. Create a cause-and-effect organizer that identifies Myanmar's 1990 elections as the central event.

3. Create a second cause-and-effect organizer that identifies a different central event, one you select yourself. Then compare the causes and effects of the two events. Comment on the comparison.

Legacies of Imperialism in India

When the first European traders arrived in India, they had little effect on Indian culture. The British Empire, however, left a powerful legacy that had lasting effects on India's economic, political, and social structures.

Under British rule, areas that had been controlled by local rulers were unified under a single political and economic system. The British controlled the country's civil administration, as well as the economics of the export and import trade. Land was transformed to imperial uses. In the province of Ceylon, for example, vast areas were taken over and transformed into tea plantations.

After gaining independence in 1947, India became a federal republic made up of 22 states. In 1950, the country's constitution made India a parliamentary democracy based on the British model.

In 2007, India boasted a wide range of manufacturing and service industries, especially in the technology sector. These industries were helping the Indian economy grow — but the country also had major problems with rapid population growth, poverty, sexual discrimination, high illiteracy rates, and continuing conflicts with neighbouring countries.

Figure 6-22 Under British rule in the 19th century, Sri Lanka was an Indian province called Ceylon. Thousands of hectares were taken from Indigenous farm families and turned into large tea plantations. Tea became a major export — and a source of great wealth for the Europeans who owned the plantations. Do you think these tea plantations benefited the people of Ceylon?

India and Pakistan

In the period leading up to independence, the Indian National Congress, Mohandas Gandhi's party, campaigned for one central Indian government. The Muslim League, however, wanted to divide India into two countries: one for Hindus and one for Muslims. At independence, the decision was for partition and two countries — India and Pakistan — were created.

Pakistan was made up of two widely separated areas, East and West Pakistan, divided by about 1600 kilometres of Indian territory. In 1971, East Pakistan became a separate country called Bangladesh.

When the borders between India and Pakistan were drawn, millions of Hindus found themselves living in East and West Pakistan, while many Muslims lived in India. During this time, emotions ran high. Riots were common, and people were attacked and killed because of their religious beliefs. In 1948, for example, Mohandas Gandhi was assassinated by a Hindu extremist who believed that Gandhi had weakened India.

Many Hindus in Pakistan and Muslims in India no longer felt comfortable in their homes and communities. They made the wrenching decision to move to the country where their religious beliefs and traditions dominated.

Continuing conflicts

Although the creation of India and Pakistan satisfied many Hindus and Muslims, some minorities believed that their interests had been ignored.

When the borders were drawn, the British province of Punjab, for example, was divided between India and Pakistan. Many Sikhs live in Punjab and believe that this state should become an independent country. Their campaign to separate from India has been marked by continuing violence and civil unrest.

Kashmir

Kashmir is located where the borders of India, Pakistan, and China meet. During the British Raj, the area was a province of India. When India gained independence, Kashmir's rulers decided to join India, but Pakistan believed that this region should be part of Pakistan.

Pakistan wanted residents of Kashmir to vote on whether to join India or Pakistan, but India claimed that Kashmir had already decided to remain part of India. The two countries went to war over this issue from 1947 to 1949 and again in 1965. These wars accomplished little, and Kashmir remained disputed territory.

In the years since 1965, both India and Pakistan have developed nuclear weapons — and some observers fear that another war over Kashmir could trigger a nuclear conflict. In 2006 and early 2007, India and Pakistan held talks in an attempt to find a peaceful resolution to the dispute, but Kashmir's fate remains unsettled.

Figure 6-23 In 1984, armed Sikhs who were fighting for independence barricaded themselves in the Golden Temple of Amritsar, considered their holiest shrine. The Indian government, led by Indira Gandhi, who was not related to Mohandas Gandhi, ordered troops to storm the temple. Hundreds were killed. In retaliation, Indira Gandhi was assassinated a few months later.

Examine a map of Alberta. Suppose the Canadian government decided to split the province in two. Where would you draw the new boundary line? Who would you consult when redrawing the borders? List those who would probably agree with your new boundary and those who would not. Give reasons for their opinions.

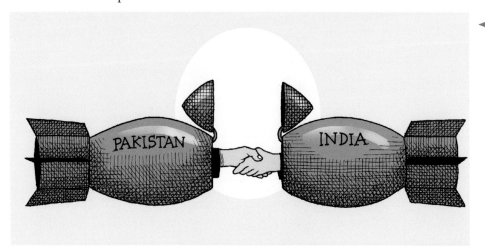

Figure 6-24 This editorial cartoon, created by Arcadio Esquivel of Panama, is called "India–Pakistan Pause." What is the cartoonist's view of the fact that both countries have nuclear weapons?

1. The map of Africa on this page shows the political divisions of the continent in 2006. Compare this with the map showing how Africa was divided in 1914 (Figure 6-4).

   a) In point form, describe some of the political changes that occurred over those 92 years.

   b) Choose a change that you think highlights the legacies of historical globalization. In making your choice, you may wish to conduct research into current conditions in the region. Explain the reasons for your choice.

   c) Of the legacies you highlighted, which do you think had the greatest effect on the peoples of the region? List three criteria you used in making your judgment.

   d) Write a short paragraph predicting how you think this legacy will continue to play out over the next 10 years. In the opening sentence, identify the legacy and where you think it will lead. In the next three or four sentences, explain your reasons for making the prediction. Restate your point of view in the concluding sentence.

Figure 6-25 Africa, 2006

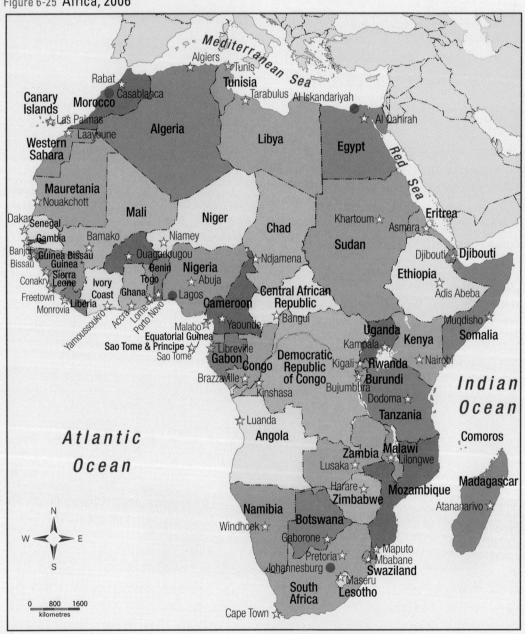

To what extent should contemporary society respond to the legacies of historical globalization? • MHR

2. Review the legacies of King Léopold of Belgium's rule in the Congo region. Think about how the region might have developed differently if it had remained independent. Consider the people, their government, and how the country's rich resources might have been used for their benefit.

   Present your predictions in the form of three separate headlines and subheads taken from imaginary Congolese and international newspapers. In a Canadian newspaper, for example, a headline and subhead might read

   ### DRC Rubber Co. launches new venture in Canada
   Plant for synthetic rubber likely to create hundreds of jobs

   If you wish, you may use computer presentation software to present your headlines.

3. As you learned in the Focus on Skills feature (pp. 142–143), cause-and-effect relationships may raise complex issues. The causes of one event may be the effects of an earlier event. Choose an event that you read about in this chapter and analyze these complex relationships. To help you do this, use a cause-and-effect organizer either like the one you developed earlier or like the one on this page.

4. Examine Canada's coat of arms on page 136. The symbols used clearly demonstrate the legacies of historical globalization. Research the meaning of the symbols, then write a general statement explaining three different legacies represented by these symbols.

   Canada has changed a great deal since the coat of arms was created in 1921. Explain why you do — or do not — think the coat of arms should be changed so it more closely represents the country today.

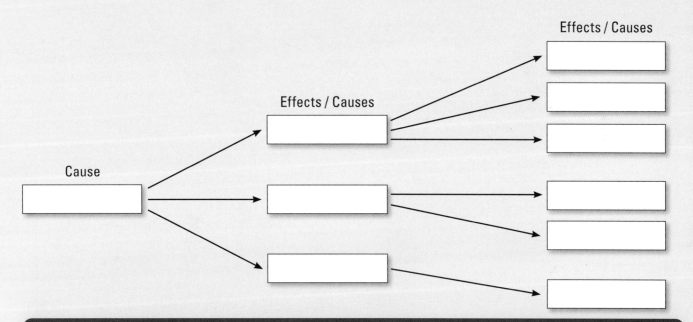

Think about Your Challenge

Return to the challenge for this related issue. It involves participating in a four-corners debate in which you will discuss, analyze, and evaluate responses to the related issue: To what extent should contemporary society respond to the legacies of historical globalization?

Review the material in this chapter and the activities you completed as you progressed through it. Make notes about ideas that could be useful in preparing for the debate. Continue developing the criteria and critical questions you will use to evaluate the material you are thinking of exploring as your contribution to the debate.

Chapter 7 Legacies of Historical Globalization in Canada

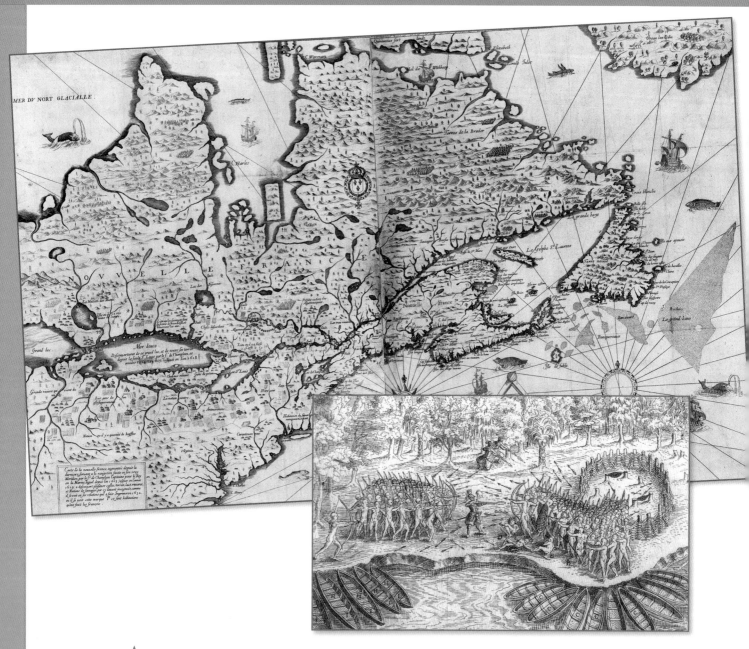

Figure 7-1 Like many Europeans who arrived in early Canada, Samuel de Champlain was a cartographer —
a mapmaker. He created this map of New France in 1632. It is based on his personal travels, as well as
information gained from other Europeans and First Nations peoples. Champlain also created the drawing,
which shows a 1609 battle in which he helped his Ouendat, or Huron, allies defeat a much larger force of
Haudenosaunee, or Iroquois.

SAMUEL DE CHAMPLAIN created detailed reports about his many voyages to New France, the name the French gave their possessions in Eastern Canada. But Champlain's explorations would not have been possible without the help of the Ouendat, or Huron, and Kichesiprini, or Algonquin, who lived north of the St. Lawrence River. With their help, he was able to travel to and map territory that was new to Europeans.

Champlain's alliance with the Ouendat and Kichesiprini also drew him into their traditional hostilities with the Haudenosaunee, or Iroquois. Although the Ouendat and the Haudenosaunee spoke Iroquoian languages and shared similar cultural traditions, the two groups were enemies.

Champlain's map and sketch provide insights into European attitudes toward North America and the peoples who lived there. Examine the map.

- What seem to be the most important places on the map?
- Why do you think Champlain might have drawn this map?
- What evidence of Eurocentrism does this map provide?

Now examine Champlain's sketch of the battle.

- Who appears to be most important in the sketch?
- How are First Nations people depicted?
- What message do you think Champlain hoped this drawing would convey?

Suppose these two artifacts were your only information about European attitudes toward First Nations people. How would you describe these attitudes? How do you think these attitudes contributed to the legacies of historical globalization?

KEY TERMS

Indian Act

status Indian

residential schools

cultural mosaic

multiculturalism

cultural pluralism

Quiet Revolution

LOOKING AHEAD

In this chapter, you will explore answers to the following questions:

- How did historical globalization affect Canada?
- What are some legacies of historical globalization in Canada?
- How has historical globalization affected Indigenous peoples in Canada?
- How do some legacies of historical globalization continue to affect Canada?

My Point of View on Globalization

Review the notes you have recorded so far to express your understandings of globalization, and think about what you have learned about historical globalization. Use words or images — or both — to show how your understandings of globalization have changed. Date your ideas and keep them in the notebook, learning log, portfolio, or computer file you are keeping as you progress through this course.

HOW DID HISTORICAL GLOBALIZATION AFFECT CANADA?

CHECKBACK

The foundations of historical globalization were introduced and discussed in Chapter 5.

FYI

During the 1500s, Catholicism was the dominant religion in Europe — and Catholics did not eat meat for 160 days of the year. This religious custom created a great demand for fish, and this demand fuelled European interest in the rich fishing grounds off Canada's Atlantic coast.

In 1497 Giovanni Caboto, or John Cabot, claimed the island of Newfoundland for Britain, and in 1535, Jacques Cartier sailed up the St. Lawrence and claimed the territory along this river for France. By this time, however, European colonies in the Caribbean and Central and South America were already thriving. For much of the 1500s, these prosperous southern colonies were the focus of the imperial competition between Britain, France, and other European powers.

At the time, Canada was considered little more than a remote northern outpost. Europeans had little interest in establishing permanent settlements there. For Europeans, the country's chief interest lay in the rich fishing grounds off its Atlantic coast. And some Europeans had not given up on the idea of discovering a new route for sailing to Asia. Finding this route, for example, inspired Cartier's exploratory trips up the St. Lawrence.

These factors meant that the effects of historical globalization were felt later in Canada than they were in more southerly colonies.

Early Contact

Although settlers did not start arriving in Newfoundland and New France until the early 1600s, some Europeans were already familiar with these areas. Throughout the 1500s, ships from Britain, France, Portugal, and other European countries had been sailing the waters off Canada's Atlantic coast in search of fish.

These European fishers often landed in coastal areas to stock up on food and water and to dry their catch so it would keep on the long trip home. When they did, they met the First Peoples of the area.

These early contacts were usually friendly and benefited both sides. First Nations were eager to obtain metal items, such as axes and cooking pots, and they traded food and animal pelts for them.

Compare the early relationship between Europeans and the First Peoples of present-day Canada with that between Europeans and the Indigenous peoples of the Caribbean and Central and South America. What might explain the differences?

Figure 7-2 The same forces that drove Europe's imperial powers to establish colonies in the Caribbean and Central and South America were at play in the European exploration of North America. But what factors might have explained the Europeans' relative lack of interest in colonizing Canada during the 1500s?

Imperialistic ambitions among European leaders motivated them to expand their areas of power and control. In part, this was to gain prestige in Europe.

The **growing consumer appetite for material goods**, particularly in European cities, stimulated trade and encouraged the imperial powers to explore new trading routes and form new trading partnerships, especially with Asian countries.

Forces Driving Colonization

Eurocentrism and ethnocentrism led Catholic Church leaders and European monarchs to believe that their mission was to spread Christianity and Western culture around the world.

Technological developments, such as better navigation tools and improved sails, enabled European explorers to venture farther than ever before — and return to tell the tale.

Establishing colonies in far-off lands enabled European imperial powers to gain **secure access to resources**, such as minerals and timber.

Colonization in Canada

In the second half of the 1500s, fashionable European men started wearing felt hats in various styles. Felt was made from beaver fur, and the demand for this fur was so great that by the early 1600s, European beavers had been hunted nearly to extinction.

In a search for new sources of beaver fur, European hatters turned to North America. As a result, the focus of exploration in New France shifted from finding a route to Asia to finding better ways of collecting furs. This marked the beginning of the fur trade — and historical globalization — in Canada.

First Peoples and the early fur trade

The First Nations of Eastern Canada helped the French make the fur trade work. They not only trapped the animals, but also transported the pelts to European outposts. Though this happened throughout northeastern North America, the area north of the Great Lakes produced furs that were especially desirable because they made high-quality felt.

This gave the Ouendat and Kichesiprini who lived in this region an advantage. Every spring, for example, the Ouendat of Huronia, a beaver-rich area south of Georgian Bay in present-day Ontario, would load up to 60 canoes with pelts. As many as 200 men would accompany these canoes to Québec.

The gruelling trip from Huronia to Québec and back took several months. Why might the Ouendat have gone to such lengths? How might this new trading venture have affected their culture and identity?

To exploit the fur resources of North America, France — and, later, Britain — set up companies similar to the East India Company. Investors were persuaded to provide the money needed to organize ships and sailors, and trade goods and traders, as well as to move large quantities of pelts. In return, they were promised high profits.

In 1627, for example, France granted a royal charter to the Company of New France, or the Hundred Associates. The charter gave the company a 15-year monopoly on the fur trade in all French territory in the Americas. In return, the company was required to attract 4000 settlers to New France and to encourage First Nations people to become Catholics. Later, the British chartered the Hudson's Bay Company.

List reasons the French government might have wanted to encourage settlement in New France, as well as Catholicism among First Peoples. Beside each reason, briefly note who would — and would not — benefit. Compare your list with that of a partner, then revise your list to incorporate new ideas that resulted from your discussion.

FYI

In 1974, the federal government declared the beaver, which appears on the back of Canadian nickels, a "symbol of the sovereignty of Canada." This declaration recognized the industrious rodent's importance to the historical identity of Canada.

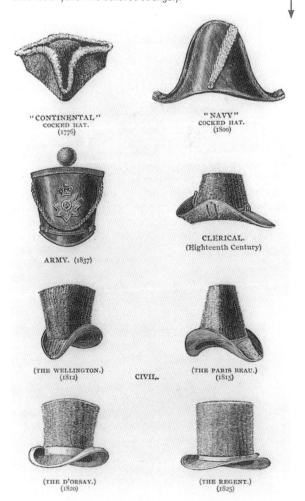

Figure 7-3 Hat making was hazardous. When the fur was scraped off beaver pelts, mercury helped the matting process, which allowed the felt to be compressed and moulded. But this process exposed hatters to mercury fumes. Mercury poisoning causes muscle spasms, interferes with speaking and thinking, and eventually causes death — and was so common among hatters that the expression "mad as a hatter" came to be used to describe anyone who behaved strangely.

"CONTINENTAL" COCKED HAT. (1776)

"NAVY" COCKED HAT. (1800)

ARMY. (1837)

CLERICAL. (Eighteenth Century)

(THE WELLINGTON.) (1812)

CIVIL.

(THE PARIS BEAU.) (1815)

(THE D'ORSAY.) (1820)

(THE REGENT.) (1825)

MODIFICATIONS OF THE BEAVER HAT.

First Peoples and European Settlers

The settlers who arrived in New France found the environment harsh and forbidding. They had to learn how to deal with long, cold winters and scarce resources — and First Peoples helped them do this.

The First Nations of Eastern Canada taught early settlers how to avoid scurvy, a disease that struck in winter when people did not get enough Vitamin C. They also taught settlers how to hunt and how to travel using canoes, snowshoes, and toboggans.

Clashing social values

Unlike Europeans, for whom social status was based on land ownership and wealth, the First Peoples of North America recognized few social or class distinctions. Status was defined by ability, and people shared equally in the bounty and scarcity of nature.

First Peoples believed that the Creator had placed them on the land at the beginning of time. They viewed themselves not as the owners of the land, but as its spiritual guardians and stewards. Land was a gift from the Creator, to be used for survival.

The European settlers, by contrast, came from societies in which land ownership was very important. It was a sign of security, social status, and wealth. As a result, the newcomers were eager to establish that they owned the land and the resources on and in it. How might these differing views of relationships with the land have led to conflict? How might these conflicts have been avoided?

Before contact with Europeans, First Peoples had used oral treaties to settle territorial disputes and other conflicts. The terms of these treaties were passed down by word of mouth. But European colonial governments were accustomed to written treaties.

Beginning in the early 1700s, the British began negotiating written treaties with First Nations in their North American colonies. For the British, the goal of these treaties was to prevent conflict with First Nations so that European settlers could live safely while establishing farms and settlements. At the same time, the colonial governments also made oral promises to First Nations. How might differing understandings of the value of oral promises lead to conflict? What kinds of situations today can be viewed as legacies of these differing understandings?

In your own words, rewrite the section of the treaty quoted in Figure 7-4. In the quoted section, which key phrases highlight the differences in the way First Peoples and Europeans understood land ownership? Explain why.

VOICES

We did not inherit the earth from our ancestors, we are borrowing it from our children.

— *A proverb from the Cree oral tradition*

Figure 7-4 This is part of a 1725 treaty between the British and First Nations of the Nova Scotia and Massachusetts area. It goes on to say that the First Nations who were part of the agreement could continue to fish and hunt on land that was sold to English settlers. Why might the language of treaties like this have led to problems for the First Nations who signed them?

> That His Majesties Subjects the English shall and may peaceable and Quietly Enter upon Improve & forever Enjoy all & Singular their rights of Land and former Settlements Properties & possessions within the Eastern parts of the said Province of the Massachusetts Bay Together with all Islands, Islets Shoars Beaches and Fishery within the same, without any Molestation or Claims by . . . Indians, and in no ways Molested Interupted, or disturbed therein.

The Destruction of the Beothuk

Although relations between Europeans and the First Nations of eastern North America were usually friendly, this was not always the case. On the island of Newfoundland, for example, the relationship turned hostile when European fishers set up their drying racks on the summer fishing sites of the First People of the region, the Beothuk.

When the Beothuk tried to drive away the newcomers by stealing or destroying their equipment, the Europeans began hunting and killing them. The Beothuk were driven inland, but even there, they were not safe. Without access to fish, their traditional summer food, they became undernourished and susceptible to European diseases. Those who were not murdered outright died of starvation or European illnesses.

By 1829, the only known Beothuk was Shawnadithit, a young woman who died that year of tuberculosis. Her death marked the complete destruction of the Beothuk people and culture.

What does the example of the Beothuk say about European attitudes toward the peoples they encountered? How did this attitude — a legacy of historical globalization — set the stage for some of the challenges facing First Nations today?

Europeans gain a foothold

In the early years of European settlement in North America, the newcomers were vastly outnumbered. First Peoples could easily have driven them out, but many factors combined to prevent this.

- The newcomers built fortified villages that they defended fiercely because they had nowhere to retreat.
- European muskets were superior to traditional weapons.
- Territorial conflicts among First Nations (e.g., between the Ouendat and Haudenosaunee) made taking united action difficult — and Europeans exploited these conflicts by forming alliances with some First Nations.
- European diseases weakened First Nations people both physically and socially.

Web Connection

To find out more about Shawnadithit and the Beothuk, go to this web site and follow the links.

www.ExploringGlobalization.ca

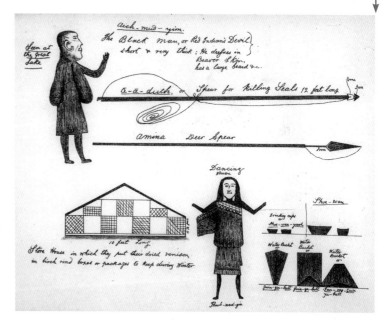

Figure 7-5 Almost nothing remains of Beothuk culture. What little is known of this people was learned, in part, from these drawings by Shawnadithit, a young Beothuk woman who died in 1829. Her pictures show Beothuk hunting spears, clothing, and a storage house.

REFLECT AND RESPOND

Suppose you are a First Nation leader at the time of contact. When deciding whether to establish peaceful relations with the newcomers, what are some pros and cons you would consider? Create a mind map showing the factors you would take into account.

With a partner or small group, brainstorm to create a list of words and phrases that describe the relationship between First Nations and mainstream Canadian society today. Link the words and phrases on this list to the factors on your mind map. Explain how each might be connected to a legacy of historical globalization.

THE GOVERNOR AND COMPANY OF ADVENTURERS OF ENGLAND TRADING INTO HUDSON'S BAY

With the French firmly in control of the fur trade in the St. Lawrence River valley, the British wanted to find a way of gaining a share of this highly profitable trade. An English explorer, Henry Hudson, had mapped the shores of Hudson Bay in 1610, but it was not until 1665 that the British started to realize its potential importance to the fur trade. In that year, two French traders, Pierre-Esprit Radisson and Médard Chouart Des Groseilliers, showed the British that Hudson Bay could provide direct access to the heart of the continent.

Figure 7-6 **Rupert's Land**

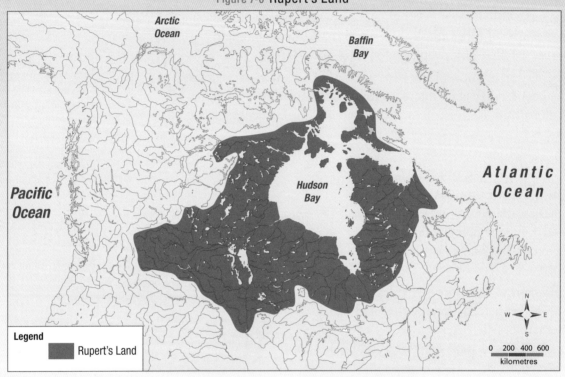

The Founding of the Hudson's Bay Company

In 1670, the British government granted a royal charter to the Governor and Company of Adventurers of England Trading into Hudson's Bay — the Hudson's Bay Company. The charter gave the company exclusive trading rights on all the lands whose rivers drained into Hudson Bay.

Though the British did not realize it at the time, this amounted to a huge area: seven million square kilometres. This area (see Figure 7-6) included much of present-day Manitoba, Saskatchewan, and Alberta, as well as parts of Nunavut, Ontario, and Québec. How might people react today if the government gave one company a monopoly on exploiting natural resources, such as Alberta's oil and gas reserves?

The vast region controlled by the HBC was named Rupert's Land, in honour of Prince Rupert, who had championed the creation of the company.

Cultural Change

The Hudson's Bay Company built forts along the shore of Hudson Bay. Every summer, the Cree would arrive at these posts in canoes loaded with pelts. Small boats carried the furs to waiting British ships, where they were exchanged for trade goods, such as guns, axes, textiles, blankets, and brandy. Because the company had a monopoly on trade, officials did not need to venture inland to buy the furs. This kept costs low — and ensured high profits.

This system changed the culture of the Cree and other First Nations in Western Canada. As trade flourished, the Cree became skilled go-betweens. They started exchanging trade goods, which were supplied by the company, for furs gathered from First Nations who lived farther inland. Gradually, the reach of the fur trade extended throughout Rupert's Land and beyond.

Figure 7-7 The Hudson's Bay Company, which was chartered in 1670, is the oldest incorporated joint-stock merchandising company in the English-speaking world. For many years, the Bay trading post was the only store in many northern communities.

Trade Rivalries

The monopoly in Rupert's Land was so profitable that merchants in Montréal — the centre of the fur trade in Eastern Canada — were jealous of the Hudson's Bay Company. They wanted to move into the West, but to do this, they needed to break the HBC monopoly. As a result, they established the North West Company in 1783.

To give their traders more incentive, the North West Company often made them partners. These men knew the trade routes, as well as how to survive on the land and the languages and cultures of the First Peoples. When NWC traders began bartering directly with First Nations trappers before their pelts could be shipped to HBC posts, the Hudson's Bay Company was forced to start sending representatives farther inland. How might this have affected the go-between role of the Cree?

The competition between the two companies meant that the First Nations trappers received better prices for their pelts. But higher prices led to overtrapping,

and beaver became more and more scarce. Higher costs and dwindling fur supplies sparked increasing violence between the traders for the two companies, as well as their First Nations allies. Finally, in 1821, the two companies merged. The HBC was once again the only player, and its territory became even larger. How has globalization made the HBC the subject of similar business mergers in more recent times?

Breaking the Monopoly

After the 1821 merger, independent Métis fur traders in present-day Manitoba refused to recognize the HBC's monopoly. Finally, in 1849, Pierre-Guillaume Sayer, a Métis trader, was arrested, tried, and convicted of illegal trading. But the jury recommended mercy because, they said, Sayer genuinely believed that the Métis were allowed to trade freely.

As a result, Sayer was set free, an action that effectively ended the HBC's monopoly in the southern part of Rupert's Land. Why do you think this court decision broke the HBC's monopoly in this area? How might breaking the monopoly have benefited all traders?

Explorations

1. Opinions on the Hudson's Bay Company's monopoly on the fur trade in Rupert's Land were divided. Write a paragraph that sets out a possible opinion of each of the following stakeholders:
   • an HBC official
   • a Cree go-between
   • a First Nations or Métis trapper
   • a North West Company partner

2. Choose the perspective or point of view you support and explain why you agree with it.

3. Think about the situation in Canada today. Create a mind map that shows some of the legacies that stem from the trading monopoly granted to the Hudson's Bay Company.

COMPARING SIMILARITIES AND DIFFERENCES IN HISTORICAL NARRATIVES

A narrative is a story. Narratives can be accounts of events or descriptions of things people have seen or done. Does your family, for example, have favourite stories about events or people? Do these narratives always relate events the way you remember them? Have these narratives changed over the years?

Historical narratives help people understand past events, connect the past to the present, provide insights into how different people perceive and remember events, and often indicate what is important to a culture. Narratives are always related from the point of view or perspective of the person or group telling the story. This means that narratives about the same event may be different, because no two people remember things in exactly the same way. As a result, it is always a good idea to consider the point of view or perspective of the writer or speaker.

The two narratives on the following page relate the stories of similar events. The following steps can help you compare these narratives — and others you will encounter as you progress through this course.

Steps to Comparing Similarities and Differences in Historical Narratives

Step 1: Ask powerful questions

When you compare narratives, it is important to be able to detect the narrator's point of view or perspective. Powerful questions like the following can help you do this:

- What is the narrator's goal (e.g., to tell the story of an event, to shape opinion about an event)?
- Does the narrator have the credentials (e.g., historical background, personal experience) to give the narrative weight and validity?
- How was the narrator affected by the events?
- Is the narrator speaking for a group or expressing an individual point of view?
- What biases does the narrative reveal?
- Who does the narrative benefit or harm?
- How does the narrative fit with what I already know?

Step 2: Read the narratives

Read the two narratives on the following page several times. Each describes conditions at a Hudson's Bay Company trading post in the 1800s. One focuses on the situation for First Nations and the other on the situation for company officials.

The first time you read, focus on understanding the narrative as a whole. The second time, jot point-form notes in response to your powerful questions. After doing this, read the narratives again to decide whether your understanding has changed as a result of thinking about the answers to the questions.

Step 3: Organize your comparison

To compare the narratives, create and fill in a chart like the one shown on the following page. This format enables you to see more clearly how each narrative answers your powerful questions. The chart includes an example of how you might set up your work.

Step 4: Practise the skill

Examine your chart and decide how the narratives are similar — and how they are different.

Asking yourself questions like the following can help you do this:

- Why were large groups of First Nations people camped around Fort McMurray?
- What had happened to their traditional ways of coping with food shortages?
- How is Narrative 2 an expression of Eurocentrism? Can the same be said of Narrative 1?

As a result of your comparison, what conclusions can you draw about the events described? For what purposes might these two narratives be useful? To gain a fuller understanding, what other perspectives or points of view should you investigate?

More than 50 years separate the two narratives. How do they reflect changes that occurred for Plains First Nations during that time?

With a partner, make up two inquiry questions that could help guide an exploration and comparison of the two narratives.

Narrative 1

This narrative is a letter written in 1842 by Letitia Hargrave to her father in England. Hargrave was the wife of the chief trader at Norway House, an HBC post north of Lake Winnipeg.

The rations at Norway House are all fish, while here each man has a lb. [a lb., or pound, is 453.6 grams] of flour a day, pease [a thick stew made of boiled peas], oatmeal, pork, pemmican, salt goose or plover, fresh partridges in winter or 9 months a year, besides ½ a pint of rum a week. If they wish anything but fish inland they have to buy it.

They have allowances for their wives and families but they seldom let their servants encumber them unless they are very useful men. Besides flour, pease and meal the rations are for a man one goose a day 3 ducks or 4 plovers or 4 partridges. I don't know the weight of fish but they always have them to breakfast.

They buy their own tea, sugar, butter, and fat, which is hard reindeer brought from Churchill. They take great quantities of tea, and drink it to dinner regularly.

Narrative 2

This narrative is from an 1897 book by J.W. Tyrell, an explorer and mapmaker in the Canadian north. It describes conditions at Fort McMurray, an HBC trading post in northern Alberta.

We soon found we were not the only ones waiting, and that anxiously, for the arrival of the scows [flat-bottomed boats used to carry freight] from the south. The entire population of Fort MacMurray was in a state of famine. Supplies to the post, having been insufficient for the demand, had become exhausted, and the Indians who had come to barter their furs were thus far unable to obtain food in exchange, and were obliged, with their families, to subsist upon the few rabbits that might be caught in the woods . . . At one Cree camp visited I witnessed a most pitiable sight. There was a whole family of seven or eight persons seated on the ground about their smoking camp-fire, but without one morsel of food, while children, three or four years old, were trying to satisfy their cravings at their mother's breast

Comparing Historical Narratives		
Powerful Question	Letitia Hargrave	J.W. Tyrell
What is the purpose of this narrative?	To show her father that food was plentiful.	To express concern over starvation at Fort McMurray.

VOCABULARY TIP

Compare means to find similarities and differences. **Contrast** means to find only differences.

Summing up

As you progress through this course, you will encounter many examples of narratives that relate stories of events from various points of view and perspectives. You can use a similar chart to compare these narratives and gain a fuller understanding of the events.

Both France and Britain generated great wealth by exploiting Canada's resources. But with these two imperial powers competing for trade and territory, it was only a matter of time before conflict erupted.

The Seven Years' War

The competition between France and Britain finally erupted in the Seven Years' War, which lasted from 1756 to 1763. This war drew in other European powers and spread to colonies in North America, West Africa, Cuba, the Philippines, and India. As a result, some historians say it was the first truly global war. How might the spread of this war be linked to historical globalization?

This war left legacies in all the countries that were involved. In North America, the British took over New France, as well as Cape Breton Island and Florida — making Britain the dominant colonial power in the region.

To define how Britain's new North American territories — one of which was renamed Québec — would be governed, King George III issued the Royal Proclamation of 1763. In an attempt to attract British settlers, the proclamation offered land grants to former British soldiers. Why would the British have wanted to encourage British subjects to settle in Québec?

An important element of the proclamation limited settlement in eastern North America by reserving a large part of the interior of the continent for First Nations, particularly the nations of the Six Nations Confederacy, and other nations that had traditionally inhabited that territory (see Figure 7-9). This vast inland reserve was intended to maintain peace with First Nations, who were being crowded out of coastal areas.

Settlers who had already crossed the Appalachian Mountains, which separated the coastal colonies from the interior of the continent, were ordered to leave, and individual settlers were forbidden to buy reserve land. Only the British government was allowed to buy land from First Nations.

Though the proclamation tried to limit European settlement, it failed. Settlers continued to trickle into the interior. At the same time, the official limit on settlement angered American colonists so much that, along with Britain's mercantilist policies, it is considered an important cause of the American Revolution.

Despite the proclamation's short-term failure, First Nations consider it groundbreaking because it recognized Aboriginal title. The French had never negotiated treaties with them, but the proclamation required the British to do so — and established a treaty-making process that remains in effect today.

Figure 7-8 **European Exploration of North America**

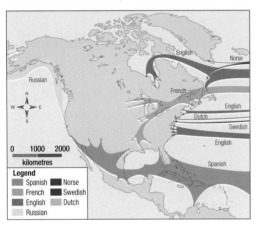

Figure 7-9 **North America after the Seven Years' War**

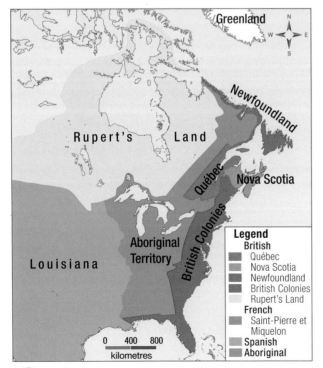

Some Legacies of Early French Rule

Both Britain and France left legacies that go well beyond the fur trade. They needed to create and adapt systems for managing trade, recruiting settlers, making laws, meeting people's religious needs, establishing peaceful relations with First Nations peoples they interacted with, and much more. Many of the systems and structures they created continue to exist in Canada today.

To strengthen French control of New France, the government wanted to attract settlers. As in some areas of France, the land was divided into large tracts, or seigneuries, which were given to people of noble birth — the seigneurs. The seigneurs were responsible for recruiting settlers, or habitants, who would clear and farm the land.

Because travelling by land was difficult, the habitants were given long, narrow lots — about 180 metres by 1800 metres — that extended inland from navigable waterways, such as the St. Lawrence River. How would this system have helped settlers? How was this system different from the pattern of settlement in Western Canada?

The long-lot system had one important weakness: the farms were difficult to defend. In 1644, the Haudenosaunee struck, using muskets they had bought from Dutch traders in what is now upper New York State. Ouendat villages and many French settlements were destroyed.

This conflict raged for more than 20 years, until France finally sent soldiers to protect the colony. By then, so many Ouendat had been killed that this once powerful First Nation had nearly disappeared. How might this loss have affected the French? The development of Canada?

Soon after the British took over Québec, the Québec Act of 1774 allowed French civil law to remain in force. Because one area of civil law deals with land ownership and property rights, this allowed the seigneurial system of tenant farming to continue — and it did, until the mid-1800s. Even today, the long-lot system remains visible in southern parts of Québec.

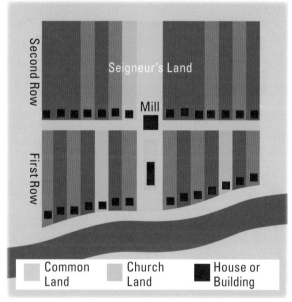

| Common Land | Church Land | House or Building |

Figure 7-10 Under the seigneurial system, early settlers were given the first row of farms, which fronted on rivers. The aerial photograph shows part of Québec today. Find the outlines of early long-lot farms.

Social changes

Over time, the Canadiens of New France developed a society that was different from that of France. Learning to survive in their new environment gave them a sense of independence and self-reliance. They became strongly attached to their new land and less willing to accept orders from France — or, later, Britain. Although the Catholic Church remained a strong, unifying force, it could not stop the changes in people's attitudes.

Think about Canada today. What is one important way that Canadiens helped shape this country?

Some Legacies of Early British Rule

At first, Hudson's Bay Company traders limited their activities to coastal areas and relied on First Nations, such as the Cree, to carry furs to them. But competition from the North West Company forced the company to change its tactics and set up trading posts and canoe routes at key inland locations. To help do this, traders such as David Thompson were sent deep into the interior of Rupert's Land.

The British were also involved in the Pacific maritime fur trade, transporting sea otter, marten, fox, and bear pelts to markets in China. By the time the HBC and the NWC merged in 1821, agents of both had travelled and mapped much of the Canadian West. What long-term implications might the global activities of these two companies have had for European settlers? For First Nations?

Figure 7-11 **David Thompson's Explorations, 1784–1850**

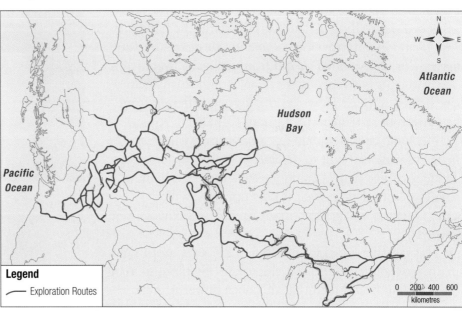

Clashing cultures

European settlement of Canada's West began with the Red River Colony. The idea for this farming settlement was proposed by Thomas Douglas, an HBC partner. In 1811, he persuaded the company to grant him 300 000 square kilometres in parts of what are now Manitoba, Minnesota, and North Dakota. Douglas believed that the colony would help solidify the company's control over the area and become a valuable source of food for its traders.

But Douglas's plans did not take into account the Métis who were already living in this region. This created tensions, and these tensions eventually led to the violent, divisive, and largely unsuccessful Métis uprisings of 1869–70 and 1885.

How might you and your neighbours respond if a foreign government gave its citizens the land your community stands on? The resistance of 1869–70 is called both the Red River Rebellion and the Red River Resistance; the resistance of 1885 is called both the North-West Rebellion and the North-West Resistance. How do these different names represent differing perspectives on these events?

Web Connection

The Red River and North-West resistances were led by Louis Riel, a charismatic and controversial figure in the history of the West. To find out more about Riel and the resistance, go to this web site and follow the links.

www.ExploringGlobalization.ca

CHECKBACK

You explored Métis culture in Chapter 2.

European immigration

Soon after the British took over, Canada became the destination for thousands of European immigrants, most from the British Isles. Many were fleeing widespread unemployment caused by industrialization. New machines in the textile industry, for example, had reduced by 80 per cent the number of workers needed to turn wool into yarn.

At the same time, many Scottish tenant farmers were being forced off their land. Demand for wool was rising, and landowners had discovered that it was more profitable to raise sheep than to rent land to tenant farmers.

Between 1790 and 1845, more than 750 000 immigrants arrived in Canada. What difference might this influx of British immigrants make to Francophones in Québec? To First Nations, Métis, and Inuit?

European exploration and settlement of Western Canada moved quickly during the early 1800s. How might this increase in immigration have stimulated the idea of a new country that would stretch from sea to sea? Discuss this question with a partner and record several points in response.

The legacy of mercantilism

Both France and Britain followed mercantilist policies in Canada. This meant that the country's natural resources were shipped to the home country, where they were used to manufacture finished products. Some of these products were then shipped back to the colony for sale.

During the period of French colonial rule, for example, it was illegal for Canadien entrepeneurs to establish hat factories in the colony. And when the British took over, laws required the use of British ships to carry raw materials and manufactured goods to and from Canada.

Some historians believe that mercantilism helped protect and foster Canada's early development. Others, such as the historian Harold Innis, argued that mercantilism stifled development by ensuring that the country's economy was limited to supplying raw materials.

Read Abraham Gesner's words in the Voices feature on this page. Do you think his vision of Canadians as "hewers of wood and drawers of water" showed that he was for or against mercantilism?

CHECKBACK

You read about industrialization and the textile industry in Chapter 5.

VOICES

It is vain to suppose that a free trade system will be beneficial to a new and struggling colony, which has nothing to export but raw materials; it is rather calculated to enrich an old commonwealth, whose people by their skill and labour make such raw materials valuable, and then return them for consumption. The result of the system . . . has been that suppliers of the raw material at last become hewers of wood and drawers of water to the manufacturers.

— *Abraham Gesner, Canadian scientist and inventor of kerosene, in* The Industrial Resources of Nova Scotia, 1849

REFLECT AND RESPOND

Create a comparison organizer to identify ways in which French and British legacies continue to be reflected in Canada. Include these topics on your organizer: settlement; culture; values; language; relations with First Nations, Métis, and Inuit; and economic activity.

To complete your organizer, combine your own knowledge with ideas you read about in this section of the chapter.

Compare your organizer with that of a partner. When you finish this discussion, you may wish to revise your organizer.

Choose two legacies of historical globalization in Canada and rate their effects on the country today. Use a scale of 1 to 10 (1 = very negative; 10 = very positive). Be prepared to defend your ratings.

HOW HAS HISTORICAL GLOBALIZATION AFFECTED INDIGENOUS PEOPLES IN CANADA?

When Europeans arrived in Canada, at least 500 000 Indigenous people occupied the continent. They usually lived in small bands that ranged over large territories. Their relationship to the land defined their cultural traditions and worldview.

The way of life and worldview of the European newcomers was different. In Europe, people tended to cluster in settlements, and owning land was an important status symbol. How is this worldview reflected in Canada today?

Both the French and British gradually took more and more land from the First Nations. In Eastern Canada, the British negotiated treaties to help them do this peacefully — and they continued this strategy in the West.

Figure 7-12 Estimated First Peoples Population of Canada, 1500–2001

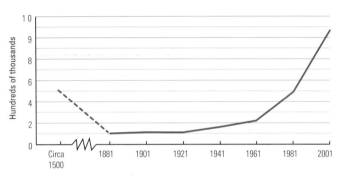

Source: Statistics Canada and Indian and Northern Affairs Canada

Note: The broken line (▬ ▬ ▬ ▬) indicates an unequal interval. Population figures are estimates because of differences in the way the government defined First Nations people and the way First Nations people defined themselves.

Depopulation of First Peoples

When Europeans settled an area, they took the best land for themselves — and pushed First Nations into unproductive spaces. When First Nations were driven from their familiar territories, their traditional relationship with the land and its resources was harmed.

Bands often migrated to areas occupied by other First Nations. Many Anishinabé, for example, originally lived north of Lake Superior. As Europeans moved into their territory, they began to migrate westward to lands occupied by Plains First Nations. These migrations sometimes created tension and conflict among First Peoples and upset the delicate balance between First Nations and the land.

In addition, European diseases often devastated First Nations. In 1870, for example, an outbreak of smallpox killed thousands of Cree and Blackfoot people (see Figure 7-13). How might these epidemics have affected the Plains First Nations' culture, way of life, and ability to assert their rights?

Examine Figure 7-12. What pattern does it show? If this pattern continues, do you think it will have a positive or negative effect on First Nations in the future?

Figure 7-13 First Peoples before European Contact

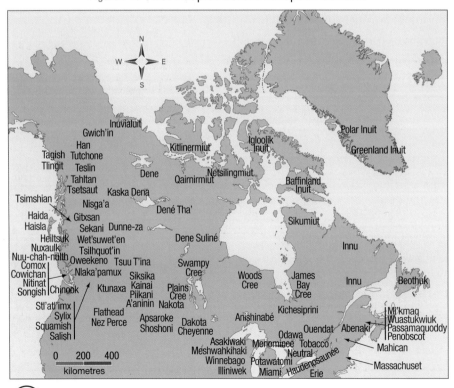

Assimilation

Two years after Confederation in 1867, control of Rupert's Land passed from the Hudson's Bay Company to the Canadian government. The government wanted to attract European settlers to the West. But to ensure the success of the settlement plan, the government needed to make sure that First Nations would give up their territory peacefully. To achieve this goal, government officials developed policies designed to encourage First Nations people to assimilate into mainstream Canadian society.

CHECKBACK

You read about the near extinction of the buffalo in Chapter 6.

The numbered treaties

By the 1870s, the buffalo population on the Prairies was declining, and fur-bearing animals were also becoming harder to find. In addition, many bands, such as the Blackfoot, had been depopulated by disease. These conditions helped encourage Plains First Nations to sign treaties with the Canadian government.

Between 1871 and 1877, seven treaties were signed. Four more were signed between 1899 and 1921. Each was given a number. These numbered treaties marked the beginning of a "cash for land" approach by the government.

In return for surrendering their territory and agreeing to live on reserves — defined areas that were "reserved" for First Peoples — First Nations were promised annual payments and other benefits, such as farm animals and tools. But the treaties usually placed the highly productive land in the hands of the government and confined the First Nations to smaller, less productive areas.

The treaties were negotiated according to the oral traditions of the First Nations. Then the government produced written documents. In many cases, promises that had been made orally by government negotiators were not included in the written versions of the treaties.

The First Nations and government negotiators also understood the treaties differently. First Nations viewed the money they received as a gift given in exchange for sharing their territory with settlers, not as payment for completely surrendering their land. Why might these differences in understanding have occurred? How do these misunderstandings remain a legacy in Canada today?

Should the First Nations have signed these treaties? Did they have any choice? What might have happened if they had refused to sign? Discuss responses to these questions with a partner.

VOICES

Now you see me stand before you all; what has been done here today has been done openly before the Great Spirit and before the Nation . . . and now in closing this council, I take off my glove, and in giving you my hand I deliver over my birthright and lands; and in taking your hand I hold fast all the promises you have made, and I hope they will last as long as the sun rises and water flows, as you have said.

— *Mawedopenais, chief spokesperson of the Anishinabé peoples, when Treaty 3, the Northwest Angle Treaty, was signed in 1873*

Figure 7-14 **Numbered Treaties in Canada**

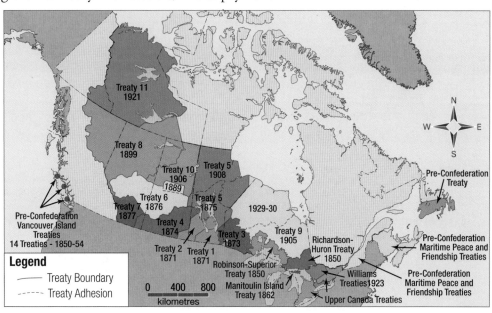

Legend
— Treaty Boundary
---- Treaty Adhesion

Treaty 11 1921
Treaty 8 1899
Treaty 10 1906 1889
Treaty 5 1908
Treaty 5 1875
Treaty 7 1877
Treaty 6 1876
Pre-Confederation Vancouver Island Treaties 14 Treaties - 1850-54
Treaty 4 1874
Treaty 2 1871
Treaty 1 1871
Treaty 3 1873
Treaty 9 1905
1929-30
Richardson-Huron Treaty 1850
Robinson-Superior Treaty 1850
Manitoulin Island Treaty 1862
Williams Treaties 1923
Upper Canada Treaties
Pre-Confederation Treaty
Pre-Confederation Maritime Peace and Friendship Treaties
Pre-Confederation Maritime Peace and Friendship Treaties

0 400 800
kilometres

Like the First Nations of North America, many cultures place a high value on oral tradition. Relating stories, myths, and legends helps explain the history of the culture to younger generations, validates the culture, and explains a people's place and role in the universe. But not everyone agrees that oral history is as important as written history. Here are the views of three people who have considered the value of oral history.

MBATHIO SALL, a consultant to the International Federation of Library Associations and Institutions, believes that societies that respect only written history can disregard an entire culture's oral history.

Indeed, according to Eurocentrists of the time, "the written act is the main support that operates in the fixing of realizations judged fundamental." Then, since the African societies are not characterized by writing, the existence of an African history becomes unlikely, the oral sources not being trustworthy enough . . .

What is to be kept in mind is that, in traditional Africa, the oral tradition was closely linked to the child's education. It was a real pedagogy [i.e., way of teaching].

ANDREI SIMIC, an anthropology professor at the University of Southern California in Los Angeles, warns against depending too heavily on oral tradition.

It is one thing to use folklore and oral tradition as a means of ascertaining or demonstrating what the members of an ethnic group believe (or once believed) about the world and their collective past. It is another thing entirely to use folklore and oral tradition as proof of the truth of what the group believes. As a general rule, folklore and oral tradition are not stable enough to be taken as inherently accurate witnesses from the remote past . . . Folklore and oral tradition are not fixed, immutable elements of an ethnic group's culture . . . Change can and often does occur with each new generation.

DEBORAH SCHWARTZ, of the Huron County Oral History Project, believes that written stories may be as flawed as oral histories.

There is no denying that oral testimony can be flawed and that human memory is not perfect. The flaws in oral testimony, however, have been exaggerated and to dismiss oral sources would be a mistake. Oral histories are no less valid than written ones; the historian must look at both with a critical eye. Documentation can have as many gaps as human memory and can contain just as many biases as oral sources. Documents too can be informed by the perceptions of those who wrote them and often only give what historian Gwyn Pris calls "history from above." Oral sources are valuable to the study of social history, as they are more than just the views of the elite.

Explorations

1. Examine the words of each speaker. For each, choose two or three phrases that represent his or her point of view.

2. What do you think might be the single most important consequence of ignoring oral histories? Explain your reasoning.

3. Deborah Schwartz quotes Gwyn Pris's phrase "history from above." What do you think this phrase means?

4. In small groups, use these three excerpts as the starting point of a brainstorming session to develop answers to this question: Can history that is transmitted orally be reliable?

The Indian Act

The **Indian Act**, which was first passed in 1876, was one tool the government used to encourage assimilation. This act remains in place today, although many of its provisions have changed. But in the 19th century and for much of the 20th century, it meant that the lives of First Nations people were strictly controlled by government officials.

One way the act controlled First Nations people was by defining who was — and was not — a status Indian. A **status Indian** is someone who is registered according to the provisions of the act and is therefore eligible to receive specific benefits.

The act also tried to suppress First Nations cultures by banning some traditional practices, such as the potlatch ceremony of Pacific Coast First Nations and the Sun Dance of Plains First Nations. In addition, only those who moved off reserves were allowed to vote in federal elections.

In 1927, the act made it illegal for First Nations to pursue land claims without the consent of the superintendent of Indian Affairs, who was an employee of the federal government. Where do you think the superintendent's loyalties would lie?

VOICES

Our object is to continue until there is not a single Indian in Canada that has not been absorbed into the body politic, and there is no Indian question and no Indian department.

— *Duncan Campbell Scott, poet and superintendent of Indian Affairs, 1920*

Ideas

Did European settlement have any positive outcomes?

The students responding to this question are Ling, who was born in Hong Kong but is now a Canadian living in Edmonton; Gord, a member of the Beaver First Nation near High Level; and Marie, a Francophone student from Medicine Hat.

The development of Canada shows that people can accomplish a lot if they put their minds to it. It took courage for the European explorers, fur traders, and settlers to go into areas that were unknown. I can see from a Eurocentric point of view that this shows that Canada was built by people who were prepared to solve problems and work hard for a better life — and this tells me that even if there are problems linked to globalization, we can overcome them.

Ling

European settlement in Canada had a tremendous impact on First Nations' cultures. By learning how people have worked to make it possible for me to continue to be who I am by correcting the injustices of treaties that have been either unfulfilled or violated, I have become interested in my history. My expanded understanding of history, the world, peoples, and cultures helps me protect my individual and collective identities.

Gord

Canada's official bilingualism has its roots in the exploration and settlement of the country. The Francophone presence and contributions have helped shape what the country has become. It has not always been easy for us Francophones to maintain our language and culture, especially in provinces where we are a minority. I admire those who persisted so that I could benefit from their legacy.

Marie

Your Turn

How would you respond to the question Ling, Gord, and Marie are answering? Which speaker most closely represents your point of view? What is one argument you might add to strengthen that speaker's position?

Residential schools

Figure 7-15 What words would you use to describe this scene of First Nations students in a residential school? In what ways does this situation reflect the Canadian government's attitude toward First Nations?

Residential schools — schools where First Nations children were gathered to live, work, and study — were another important tool in the government's assimilation policy. These schools were set up because the Indian Act made the federal government responsible for educating First Nations children. Starting in the 1880s, school-age children were taken from their families, sometimes by force, and placed in these schools. Responsibility for running the schools was shared between the government and Christian churches.

First Nations families were given no choice, no voice, and no options in the matter. Every August, children were taken from their family and shipped to school, where siblings were separated by age and by sex.

PROFILE

PHIL FONTAINE
DENOUNCING RESIDENTIAL SCHOOLS

Phil Fontaine was grand chief of the Assembly of Manitoba Chiefs when he became the first Aboriginal leader to speak out about the abuse he had endured at residential school. "In my Grade 3 class . . . if there were 20 boys, every single one of them . . . would have experienced what I experienced," he told CBC interviewer Barbara Frum.

That was in 1990, and Fontaine's revelations shocked the country. Since then, he and many other First Nations people have worked to promote healing and achieve compensation for residential school survivors.

Fontaine has dedicated his life to advancing the rights of First Nations people. His interest began in the 1970s, when he was a youth activist with the Canadian Indian Youth Council. After serving as chief of the Sagkeeng First Nation, he was elected grand chief in Manitoba, and in 1997, he was elected national chief of the Assembly of First Nations.

He ran for re-election in 2000 but was defeated by Matthew Coon Come. But Fontaine was not ready to give up, and in 2003, he ran again and succeeded. He was re-elected in 2006.

Fontaine is known for his diplomacy and his ability to negotiate solutions to the challenges facing Aboriginal peoples. He believes in Aboriginal self-government, and his goal is to build bridges among communities.

Figure 7-16 Phil Fontaine, a member of the Sagkeeng First Nation of Manitoba, is the national chief of the Assembly of First Nations. His first language is Ojibwa, and he holds a BA in political science, as well as several honorary degrees.

Legacies of residential schools

The schools were often far away from the children's home. Though some teachers were kind, many were poorly trained and cruel. Discipline was often harsh, and children were punished for speaking their own languages and forbidden to follow traditional ways. As a result, many children lost touch with their own history, language, and culture.

Though some residential schools were well run, many children suffered greatly. They were told that their own history and culture were not worth preserving. Abuse of all kinds was common, and many children emerged from the experience with deep emotional scars. When they finally did go home, they often felt like strangers because they had been cut off from their way of life for too long. They had not learned about love and nurturing from their parents, so they could not love and nurture their own children. This created a cycle of problems.

The residential school system reached its peak in the 1920s and 1930s, when about 80 of these schools existed across Canada. Under pressure from First Nations parents and activists, these schools began closing in the 1960s. The last one closed in 1996. By then, about 100 000 children had attended these institutions.

Read Rita Joe's poem, "I Lost My Talk," on this page. This poem is a cry to readers to let her find her own voice so she can tell them who she really is. If you could answer Joe's plea, what would you say?

FYI

Rita Joe, a Mi'kmaw from Nova Scotia, attended the Shubenacadie Residential School. Later, she wrote this poem to describe how she felt about what had happened to her there.

I Lost My Talk

I lost my talk
The talk you took away.
When I was a little girl
At Shubenacadie school.

You snatched it away:
I speak like you
I think like you
I create like you
The scrambled ballad,
  about my world.

Two ways I talk
Both ways I say,
Your way is more powerful.

So gently I offer my hand and ask,
Let me find my talk
So I can teach you about me.

REFLECT AND RESPOND

Review the information in this section of the chapter and create an event line that includes four major events and their effects on First Nations in Canada. To help complete this activity, you may also wish to consult other sources.

On your line, mark the event, action, or activity. Below this, list two or three points that describe its effects. If the first event on your event line were "First Contact," your line might start like this:

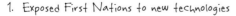

First Contact

1. Exposed First Nations to new technologies
2. Allowed Europeans to gain a foothold in Canada
3. Set in motion events that continue to create tensions today

HOW DO SOME LEGACIES OF HISTORICAL GLOBALIZATION CONTINUE TO AFFECT CANADA?

No matter what your heritage, and no matter how long your family has lived in Canada, you are affected by events that occurred during the period of historical globalization. Think, for example, about the language of this textbook. How can it be called a legacy of historical globalization? What is another legacy that affects your life today?

Immigration

Immigration is an important legacy of historical globalization in Canada. People from all over the world have migrated to Canada, giving this country an unparalleled diversity of cultures, languages, perspectives, and points of view.

Diversity has been a characteristic of Canadian society since Confederation, when both French and English were recognized as the languages of government and the courts.

But not all immigrants were always equally welcomed. In the early 20th century, for example, Canadian immigration policy was based on race. British immigrants were actively recruited, and those who did not come from Europe or the United States were discouraged. Still, attitudes were changing, and enough Canadians believed in respecting and accommodating differences that the foundations of a diverse society were laid.

By 1968, the country's immigration policy had become fairer. Immigrants were flowing from Asian, Caribbean, African, and Latin American countries. Since the 1970s, most immigrants to Canada have been members of visible minority groups. All added to the Canadian **cultural mosaic**, which was built on honouring people's ethnic and cultural roots. What are some ways this diversity is reflected in everyday life? How is it shown, for example, in Canadian radio and TV programs or in music?

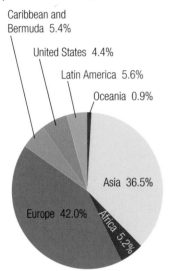

Figure 7-17 **Immigrant Population by Place of Birth, 2001**

Caribbean and Bermuda 5.4%
United States 4.4%
Latin America 5.6%
Oceania 0.9%
Asia 36.5%
Europe 42.0%
Africa 5.2%

On this map, the size of the circles is in proportion to the number of immigrants from those regions of the world. Which region of the world has been the largest source of immigrants to Canada? How does this pattern fit with the fact that 52 per cent of immigrants to Canada in 2002 came from Asia?

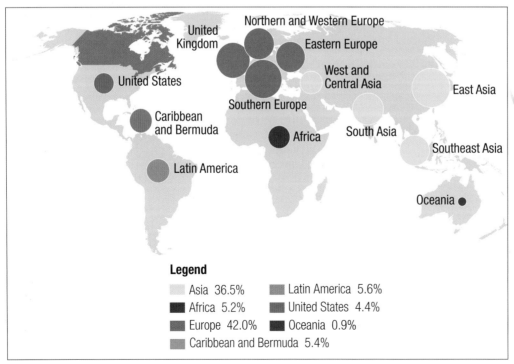

United Kingdom
Northern and Western Europe
Eastern Europe
West and Central Asia
East Asia
United States
Southern Europe
Caribbean and Bermuda
Africa
South Asia
Southeast Asia
Latin America
Oceania

Legend

Asia 36.5%	Latin America 5.6%
Africa 5.2%	United States 4.4%
Europe 42.0%	Oceania 0.9%
Caribbean and Bermuda 5.4%	

Multiculturalism

To deal with the changing makeup of the population, the Canadian government introduced a policy of **multiculturalism** in 1971. The term "multiculturalism" was coined in Canada, and this country was the first in the world to adopt this policy.

At the heart of official multiculturalism is the idea that Canadian society is made up of many culturally distinct groups. Multicultural societies reject assimilation and embrace **cultural pluralism** — the idea that people are free to retain their own cultural traditions. How do you think First Nations people, Métis, and Inuit might have greeted this policy?

Differing views on multiculturalism

When it was introduced, multiculturalism was controversial. Not all Canadians supported this policy. Some believed it would divide Canadians, while others feared that it would erode Canada's "British" heritage. In the West, John Diefenbaker, a former prime minister, viewed it as an attack on his vision of unhyphenated Canadianism. He believed that Canadians should be just that — Canadians — not "Ukrainian-Canadians" or "Chinese-Canadians."

Multiculturalism also encountered opposition in Québec, where some Québécois viewed it as a strategy to undermine Francophone culture. René Lévesque, a separatist politician who would go on to become premier of the province, said, "Multiculturalism, really, is folklore. It is a 'red herring.' The notion was devised to obscure 'the Québec business,' to give an impression that we are all ethnics and do not have to worry about special status for Québec."

Even today, not everyone supports multiculturalism. Novelist Neil Bissoondath, for example, immigrated to Canada from Trinidad in 1973. Twenty years later, he created a sensation when he wrote in *The Globe and Mail*: "[Multiculturalism] has highlighted our differences rather than diminished them, has heightened division rather than encouraged union. More than anything else, the policy has led to the institutionalization and enhancement of a ghetto mentality. And it is here that lies the multicultural problem as we experience it in Canada: a divisiveness so entrenched that we face a future of multiple solitudes with no central notion to bind us."

Despite the opposition, the idea of multiculturalism enjoys broad public support. A 2002 survey found that 74 per cent of respondents support this policy. Many have come to view diversity as a hallmark of Canadian identity. Is this your understanding of Canadian identity? Why or why not?

Figure 7-18 Pierre Trudeau (left), who was prime minister in 1971, was one of the chief architects of multiculturalism in Canada. This policy was opposed by René Lévesque (right), who was premier of Québec when this photograph was taken. Both Trudeau and Lévesque were Québécois, but they arrived at very different conclusions about multiculturalism.

Figure 7-19 When Yasmin Ratansi (left), Nina Grewal (middle), and Ruby Dhalla (right) were elected to the House of Commons in 2004, they became the first South Asian women to sit as members of Parliament. Do you think their election is something to be proud of — or something that took much too long to happen? Why?

Land Claims

CHECKFORWARD

In Chapter 8, you will read more about steps that have been taken to promote healing among First Nations, Métis, and Inuit.

Although treaties were signed with many First Nations, none were signed with First Peoples in northern Québec, Yukon, the Northwest Territories, or British Columbia. And even where treaties had been signed, many First Nations argued that the government had failed to honour its promises.

In the second half of the 20th century, First Peoples started to organize and press the government to recognize their rights. As a result, two broad classes of land claims — comprehensive and specific — were recognized in 1973. Comprehensive claims could be launched in areas where treaties had never been signed. Specific claims, which related to treaty conditions that had not been met, could be pressed in areas where treaties had been signed.

Despite this step forward, negotiating land claims proved to be a long, slow process. Over the next 20 years, only 15 comprehensive claims were settled, including the agreement that led to the creation of Nunavut. In 2007, about 70 comprehensive claims were still in process and more than 1000 specific claims remained unsettled.

MAKING CHOICES

TOM JACKSON
A LIFE-CHANGING CHOICE

As a teenager, Tom Jackson seemed to be headed for trouble. After dropping out of school, he lived on the streets of Winnipeg, then headed for Toronto to follow his dream of becoming a singer and actor.

In Toronto, Jackson carved out a career as a folksinger — and experienced a life-changing event. One day, he came upon a man who had fallen in the street and needed help. Passersby were stepping around him and hurrying on, but Jackson stopped to lend a hand. This incident marked the beginning of his determination to help others, and he often says that the man saved his life, not the other way around.

By the 1980s, Jackson — who was born to a Cree mother and an English father on the One Arrow Reserve near Batoche, Saskatchewan — had established himself as a singer and actor. In 1987, he organized the first Huron Carole concert. Until 2005, this concert was an annual event, and the money it raised helped support food banks.

In the meantime, Jackson's career was flourishing. In addition to appearing in films and TV shows and receiving two Gemini Award nominations, he recorded 14 albums and received two Juno Award nominations. Some of the money from album sales goes to the Canadian Association of Food Banks. Jackson's work was honoured in 2007, when he received the Humanitarian Award at the annual Juno Awards gala.

Figure 7-20 Tom Jackson has been the Canadian chair of UNICEF and has received a number of humanitarian awards, as well as the Order of Canada and the Queen's Jubilee Medal.

Explorations

1. Tom Jackson says that the man he helped actually saved his life, not the other way around. Explain what you think this statement means.

2. In what ways does Jackson's life reflect legacies of historical globalization?

The Quiet Revolution in Québec

The high levels of British immigration in the 19th and early 20th centuries caused Québécois to worry about assimilation. To resist being assimilated, thinkers such as Lionel Groulx, a Catholic priest and historian, said that Québécois must support Catholicism — the traditional religion of most Québec Francophones — as a way of maintaining their own language, culture, and values.

Globalization contributed to change in the 1960s, as people around the world — Indigenous peoples, women, blacks, and others — began to question and cast off traditional ways of thinking and demand equality. In Québec, this movement contributed to what has become known as the **Quiet Revolution.**

A changing society

During the Quiet Revolution, which took place from about 1960 to 1966, Québécois began rejecting some values that were based in traditional ways and conservative attitudes. The province entered a period of intense social, political, and economic change.

Changes in education were a key part of this change. Before the Quiet Revolution, the Catholic Church had controlled education, and the curriculum had lost touch with the modern world. A worrying indication of this was the fact that half of all students were leaving school by the time they were 15. As a result, the education system was reformed to reflect 20th-century needs and values. This included new colleges and universities.

Québécois also became more aware that Francophones were being discriminated against. Surveys showed, for example, that Québec Francophones earned much less than English-speaking workers.

The Quiet Revolution gave a voice to those calling for a renewal of Francophone language and culture in the province. Some influential Québécois, such as René Lévesque, came to believe that the only way to achieve their goals was to separate from Canada — and this sparked the formation of the Parti Québécois, a political party dedicated to achieving an independent Québec. How can this drive toward more rights and freedoms for individuals and groups be viewed as a response to the legacies of historical globalization?

Figure 7-21 René Lévesque was a young broadcaster who turned to politics during the Quiet Revolution in Québec. He was part of the provincial Liberal government that introduced sweeping reforms during the 1960s, then he helped found the Parti Québécois. For which of these roles in Canadian politics do you think Lévesque will be best remembered?

Web Connection

To find out more about the Quiet Revolution in Québec, go to this web site and follow the links.

www.ExploringGlobalization.ca

1. Examine this painting by Canadian artist Robert Harris. Its title is *Indian Woman and Child*, and it was painted in about 1886.

Describe the general feeling and mood of this painting. What techniques did Harris use to capture the feeling and mood? Why do you think he might have painted this image?

Write the description you would place beside this painting if you were in charge of displaying it in an art gallery. Your description should explain both Harris's intention in creating this painting and the emotions you think the First Nations woman is experiencing — and why.

2. Create a visual display or image, such as a Venn diagram, to show the interactions between Indigenous fur trappers and European fur traders. Your purpose is to capture the important components of the relationship between the two.

You may wish to introduce current knowledge and ideas into the visual to show how the events you are depicting have rippled down through time and become a legacy of historical globalization today. To your display or image, add labels or a caption that clearly communicates your message.

3. In a small group, create a roleplay involving officials of the Hudson's Bay Company and the North West Company. It is 1820, and the two companies have been experiencing increasing tension and violence. The purpose of the meeting is to find ways to reduce the violence and improve conditions so traders for both companies can safely take care of business.

Include factual material in your role play and ensure that it shows your understanding of the issues and conditions of the time. Think about the questions your classmates might ask when you finish your role play — and discuss how you might respond to them.

4. Historical empathy — the ability to imagine yourself as someone from the past — can help improve your understanding of historical events.

Work with a partner or small group to place yourself in the shoes of one of the characters on the list that follows. Think about how the character you choose might be influenced by historical events and the worldviews of other people.

Create a poster, a short video, or another visual presentation to tell the character's story. In your presentation, make it clear why your character holds particular opinions and beliefs. What, for example, helped shape your character's point of view?

Your purpose is to establish the basis of a story that can be passed down through the generations to keep this personal, historical point of view alive and vital.

a) a Ouendat boy, aged 13 to 15, watching the first meeting between his nation's Elders and French fur traders

b) a young woman, aged 17 to 20, arriving in New France with her family

c) a Cree trader presenting top-quality beaver pelts at an HBC trading post

d) a citizen in Britain or France reading or hearing about the "New World" and its "wonders"

e) someone else related to the legacies of historical globalization

Prepare notes to help you answer questions that you may be asked when you present your visual.

5. How successfully have other countries, such as Australia or New Zealand, responded to the legacies of historical globalization? Conduct research to analyze their responses to these legacies.

Prepare powerful questions to help guide your research, as well as criteria to use in assessing the information you gather. Show how the countries' responses are reflected today. Some topics you might consider investigating are

- current relationships between the mainstream culture and Indigenous peoples
- how resources were collected, allocated, and used, and how profits were shared
- effects of human activity on the physical environment since first contact
- settlement patterns
- a comparison of current social and cultural conditions of the Indigenous and mainstream populations
- relationship with the colonizing country or countries
- prospects for the future of Indigenous peoples

Present your findings in a way that clearly shows the legacies of historical globalization and how various groups have responded to these legacies. Include your assessment of the relative success or failure of these responses. In your presentation, include the powerful questions that guided your research and the criteria you used to assess your information, as well as a brief description of your research methods.

Think about Your Challenge

Think about the material in this chapter and the activities you completed as you progressed through it. Note ideas that could be useful as you prepare for the four-corners debate.

After reading this chapter, do you wish to add to the list of criteria and critical questions you are creating to help evaluate the data you are putting together? Do you wish to change any of your criteria or questions?

Chapter 8 Living with the Legacies of Historical Globalization

Figure 8-1 In 1994, a brutal civil war erupted in the African country of Rwanda. An estimated 800 000 to 1 million people were killed. Once the war was over, AVEGA Agahozo — l'Association des veuves du génocide, or the Widows of the Genocide — started helping widows and children rebuild their lives and their communities. This photograph shows some AVEGA members sorting coffee beans at a co-operative they formed.

MANY PEOPLE ARGUE that the 1994 civil war in Rwanda was a direct result of historical globalization. When this conflict ended, Rwandans began rebuilding their lives and their communities. Many organizations, including AVEGA Agahozo, are working on this rebuilding.

AVEGA supports the survivors of the conflict in many different ways. The governments, international agencies, and other organizations that are helping AVEGA include the International Committee of the Red Cross, the UN Development Fund for Women, the Canadian International Development Agency, UNICEF, Doctors without Borders, la Francophonie and an Alberta organization called Ubuntu Edmonton.

Examine the photograph on the previous page and respond to the following questions:

- What evidence can you see of individuals working together to rebuild their lives?
- What forces of ethnocentrism and Eurocentrism do you think the women and children of AVEGA must overcome?
- What legacies of historical globalization might have been factors in the civil war in Rwanda?
- Is it the responsibility of the global community to help Rwandans rebuild their lives?

KEY TERMS

genocide

gacaca courts

apartheid

enemy aliens

non-governmental organization

foreign aid

gross national income

LOOKING AHEAD

In this chapter, you will explore answers to the following questions:

- How effectively have people responded to the legacies of historical globalization?
- How effectively have governments responded to the legacies of historical globalization?
- How effectively have organizations responded to the legacies of historical globalization?
- How does historical globalization continue to affect the world?

My Point of View on Globalization

Review the notes you have been keeping on your understandings of globalization. Use words or images — or both — to express your current point of view on historical globalization. Date your ideas and add them to the notebook, learning log, portfolio, or computer file you are keeping as you progress through this course.

HOW EFFECTIVELY HAVE PEOPLE RESPONDED TO THE LEGACIES OF HISTORICAL GLOBALIZATION?

Around the world, people are still responding to the legacies that have been handed down from the time of historical globalization. Some of these responses, such as the 1994 civil war in Rwanda, are negative and cause great harm. Other responses, such as the founding of AVEGA Agohozo, as well as local and international efforts to rebuild communities in Rwanda, have been positive and give great hope.

One Response

AVEGA Agahozo is a national organization of 25 000 Rwandan women who survived the horrors of 1994 and who are trying to improve living conditions for themselves, their own children, and the estimated 95 000 children who were orphaned by the conflict. Esther Mujawayo, one of the founders of AVEGA, is a survivor whose mother, father, husband, and other relatives were killed. She has responded to her personal tragedy by appearing as a witness at the United Nations International Criminal Tribunal for Rwanda held in Arusha, Tanzania, and by becoming a psychotherapist at the Psychosocial Centre for Refugees in Düsseldorf, Germany. There, she works with people who have experienced the loss of their homeland and family members.

Around the world, global citizens try to find effective ways of responding to issues arising from the kinds of tragedies that Esther Mujawayo experienced.

The previous three chapters explored a number of legacies of historical globalization. Think about these legacies. Identify a current world issue or crisis that is rooted in these legacies. How is this issue or event a legacy of historical globalization? What social responsibility should a global citizen assume in situations like this? What is one thing a global citizen might do to help people rebuild their lives after suffering injustices such as these?

FYI

The official languages of Rwanda are French, English, and Rwanda, which is sometimes called Banyaruanda or Kinyarwanda. Rwanda is part of the Bantu language group. "Agahozo" is a Rwanda word meaning "to dry one's tears."

Web Connection

To find out more about the work of AVEGA Agahozo, go to this web site and follow the links.

www.ExploringGlobalization.ca

Figure 8-2 One legacy of historical globalization in Alberta is the diversity of people in the province. How do you, as a young Albertan, share in the legacies of historical globalization? How can you respond to those legacies?

Rwanda — A Response to Historical Globalization

Before the scramble for Africa in the late 1800s, the country that is now Rwanda was occupied by two main Indigenous groups: the Hutus and the Tutsis. Hutus made up about 85 per cent of the population and Tutsis about 15 per cent. Traditionally, the Tutsis held positions of power, while the Hutus were labourers whose social status was generally considered to be lower than that of the Tutsis — but the two groups usually coexisted peacefully.

In the scramble for Africa, the Rwanda region was claimed by Germany, and German colonial officials reinforced the traditional distinction between the two groups by appointing Tutsis to key positions in the colony. The Germans believed that the Tutsis were more like Europeans than the Hutus — and that this gave Tutsis the right to a higher status.

After Germany's defeat in World War I, the countries that negotiated the peace treaty gave this region to Belgium. The Belgians continued to give Tutsis key positions and fostered even greater divisions by requiring members of the two groups to carry cards identifying them as Hutus or Tutsis.

Consider this statement from the preceding paragraph: "the countries that negotiated the peace treaty gave this region to Belgium." What kind of thinking did this action represent? What effects might it have had on Rwanda, its peoples, and their sense of identity?

After World War II, most European colonies in Africa demanded independence. When the Belgians left Rwanda in 1962, civil conflict broke out between Hutus and Tutsis over who would have political power. When the majority Hutus formed a government, tension between the two groups became deadly. Many Tutsis fled the country.

In the late 1980s, economic problems made the Hutu government unpopular. In 1990, the Tutsi Rwandan Patriotic Front invaded Rwanda from refugee camps in Uganda. In response, the Rwandan government began a campaign against Tutsis, as well as Hutus who seemed to be sympathetic to the Tutsis. A peace agreement in 1993 ended the fighting, but not the hatred. The peace agreement required the government to share power with other political groups, including the RPF. This condition angered many Hutus.

Figure 8-3 During the civil wars that broke out after Rwanda achieved independence from Belgium in 1962 and during the genocide of 1994, hundreds of thousands of Rwandans — both Hutu and Tutsi — fled to neighbouring Uganda, Tanzania, Burundi, the Democratic Republic of Congo, and Zaire. How might this influx of refugees have strained the resources of these countries?

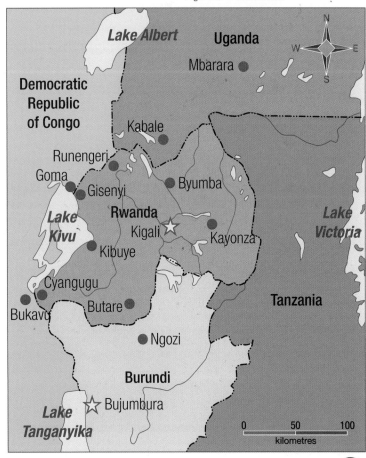

Figure 8-4 Rwanda

Genocide in Rwanda

On April 6, 1994, a plane carrying Rwandan president Juvénal Habyarimana was shot down. No one knew who was responsible, but the Rwandan government and Hutu militants blamed the Tutsis. Government and militia forces retaliated against Tutsis. Radio broadcasts encouraged Hutu civilians to take revenge. The militia favoured hacking their victims to death with machetes.

This began the Rwandan **genocide** — the mass killing of human beings, especially a targeted group of people. By July 19, 1994, an estimated 800 000 to 1 million Tutsis and moderate Hutus had been killed.

Discuss how the actions of the German and Belgian colonial occupiers of Rwanda encouraged a deadly degree of ethnocentrism. How did the colonizers' actions help encourage an environment of hate and mistrust in Rwanda?

FYI

UNICEF reported that during the genocide

- 99.9 per cent of Rwandan children witnessed violence
- 76.6 per cent of Rwandan children experienced death within their family
- 69.5 per cent of Rwandan children witnessed someone being killed
- 57.7 per cent of Rwandan children witnessed killings or injuries with machetes
- 31.4 per cent of Rwandan children witnessed rape or sexual assault

Tutsis and moderate Hutus tried to find shelter in churches or in United Nations buildings, but these people rarely survived. Other people crossed the border into neighbouring countries.

The genocide came to an end in mid-July after RPF forces captured Kigali, the capital city, and established a new multi-ethnic government. About two million Hutus then fled to neighbouring countries, fearing Tutsi revenge and creating a second wave of Rwandan refugees.

International response to the genocide

A small number of United Nations peacekeepers — under the command of Canadian lieutenant general Roméo Dallaire — had been stationed in Rwanda since the peace negotiations. In the weeks leading up to the genocide, Dallaire repeatedly warned UN officials of the rising tensions. But many UN member countries believed that the organization's role was to prevent conflict *between* countries — and to stay out of conflicts *within* countries.

As a result, UN officials refused to become involved in an "internal affair." They would not change the conditions of Dallaire's mission, and they ordered peacekeepers not to interfere and not to fire their weapons except in self-defence. They also told Dallaire not to try to protect civilians in case it looked as if the UN were taking sides. Peacekeeping activities were to focus on evacuating foreign nationals. Do you think the international community should be condemned for failing to stop the genocide?

Figure 8-5 Ntarama Church in Kigali Province, Rwanda, was the site of a massacre of nearly 5000 people who had fled to the Catholic church believing they would be safe there. The church is now a memorial to the people who died there.

Ten years after the Rwandan genocide, UN secretary-general Kofi Annan said that the killings had raised "fundamental questions about the authority of the Security Council, the effectiveness of United Nations peacekeeping, the reach of international justice, the roots of violence, and the responsibility of the international community to protect people threatened by genocide and other grave violations of human rights." Here is what three other people said as they looked back on the genocide.

BOUTROS BOUTROS-GHALI was secretary-general of the United Nations in 1994. The following excerpt is from a 2004 interview.

ROMÉO DALLAIRE commanded the United Nations force in Rwanda and said this in a 2004 interview.

For us, genocide was the gas chamber — what happened in Germany. We were not able to realize that with the machete you can create a genocide. Later, we understood this. But at the beginning, our definition of the genocide was what happened to Armenia in 1917 or 1919, it's what happened to the Jew in Europe, and we were not realizing . . . This was our perception — which was the wrong perception — [that] you need to have a sophisticated European machinery to do a real genocide . . . It is one of my greatest failures. I failed in Rwanda.

Rwanda will never ever leave me . . . Fifty to sixty thousand people walking in the rain and the mud to escape being killed, and seeing a person there beside the road dying. We saw lots of them dying. And lots of those eyes still haunt me, angry eyes or innocent eyes, no laughing eyes. But the worst eyes that haunt me are the eyes of those people who were totally bewildered . . . Those eyes dominated and they're absolutely right. How come I failed? How come my mission failed?

ESTHER MUJAWAYO survived the Rwandan genocide and co-founded AVEGA Agahozo. The following is from a 2004 international forum on preventing genocide.

Talking about [the genocide], even if the talking in itself is a big step, is not enough; there must be also actions, concrete actions. I give an example: What is the point of regretting, and commemorating 10 years later, when the orphans of the genocide who are living in atrocious conditions now are again forgotten? If we want to prevent genocide, if we want to use learned lessons, we must face the reality and agree that failing the survivors now, 10 years later, is another way of denying that this has happened and many have a responsibility in what happened.

Explorations

1. Reread each statement on this page. What common theme unites them? In two or three sentences, rewrite each statement to bring the common theme into sharper focus.

2. Consider the experiences of a survivor of the Rwandan genocide. What would be the most effective way of passing on the story of this tragedy to the next generation? Why did you make this choice?

Rebuilding Rwandan Society

Although Rwandans continue to face many social and economic challenges, they have set about trying to rebuild their society, heal the deep wounds in their communities, and reconcile with one another.

Justice and reconciliation

One of the greatest challenges facing Rwandans was to find justice for the victims of the genocide. In 1994, the United Nations Security Council created the International Criminal Tribunal for Rwanda to try high-ranking government and army officials accused of genocide, war crimes, and crimes against humanity. But by June 2006, the tribunal had come to only 22 judgments involving 28 people. At this rate, some people estimated that it would take 200 years to prosecute the 130 000 people who were in prison awaiting trial.

To speed up the process and encourage reconciliation, traditional Rwandan **gacaca courts** were set up in 2002. "Gacaca" means "justice on the grass," and these community courts were established to try low-level officials and other ordinary people accused of taking part in the genocide. The community, which elects the judges and is involved in the trials and the sentencing, seeks both justice and community reconciliation.

According to Human Rights Watch, an international organization, between 600 000 and 761 000 people accused of committing crimes during the genocide were to be tried in gacaca courts.

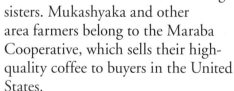

Figure 8-6 From 1996 to 1999, Louise Arbour, a Francophone lawyer and judge, was the chief prosecutor of the International Criminal Tribunal for Rwanda. Arbour was appointed to the Supreme Court of Canada in 1999, and in 2004, she became the United Nations High Commissioner for Human Rights.

Rebuilding the economy through coffee exports

Under Belgian colonial rule, coffee was such an important export that, in 1933, all Rwandan farmers were ordered to devote at least one-quarter of their farms to growing coffee. Even after Rwanda became independent in 1962, coffee remained a major export.

During the genocide, many coffee farms were destroyed. With the return of peace, some of these farms have been rebuilt with international help. In 2006, coffee sales accounted for 30 per cent of Rwandan exports.

Gemima Mukashyaka, who lost many family members during the genocide, now manages her family's coffee farm with her two surviving sisters. Mukashyaka and other area farmers belong to the Maraba Cooperative, which sells their high-quality coffee to buyers in the United States.

Members of the co-operative, both Hutus and Tutsis, receive a higher price for their crops than they did when they sold to private dealers. In 2006, Mukashyaka and her family made three times what they had earned five years earlier. Maraba members share 70 per cent of the profits and reinvest the other 30 per cent in running the co-operative.

Figure 8-7 The coffee industry employs 40 per cent of Rwandans. In coffee co-operatives, Tutsis and Hutus work side by side to rebuild the country's economy. The photograph on the left shows farm manager Gemima Makushyaka, and the photo on the right shows widow Belancila Nyirakamana picking ripe coffee beans.

To what extent should contemporary society respond to the legacies of historical globalization? • MHR

International support

In countries around the world, individuals and groups are helping Rwandans rebuild their lives. In many cases, this means helping Rwandan women, whose family members were killed in the genocide, who were raped and often infected with HIV/AIDS, and who struggle to support themselves and their children.

In Edmonton, Nicole Pageau, a Francophone, helped found Ubuntu Edmonton, an organization that supports the widows of the genocide and helps them build a strong future for their children. After hearing Esther Mujawayo speak, Pageau went to Rwanda. There, she is the project co-ordinator in Kimironko, a village near Kigali.

With Pageau's help, the women of Rwanda have set up co-operatives and won contracts to make school uniforms on sewing machines bought with a grant from the Rwandan government. As the women work together and share their traumatic experiences, they also end the isolation in which many of them have lived since the genocide.

Ubuntu Edmonton receives financial support from la Francophonie. During the time Rwanda was a Belgian colony, French was the language of the colonial rulers, and it remains one of the country's official languages.

Another organization active in Rwanda is Women for Women International, which provides financial and emotional support for women in conflict areas. The organization offers Rwandan women job skills and leadership training and helps them take control of their social, economic, and political lives. The group also helps women establish their own small businesses as individuals or in co-operatives.

In Rwanda, Women for Women helps Hutu and Tutsi women's co-operatives market their peace baskets, which have been a traditional art for a thousand years. The baskets tell stories of community celebrations and are traditionally given as gifts.

Figure 8-8 Nicole Pageau is Ubuntu Edmonton's project co-ordinator in Kimironko, a village of widows and orphans located near Kigali, the Rwandan capital.

FYI

So many men were killed in the Rwandan genocide that, in 2006, women made up 70 per cent of the country's population. Rwanda had the highest number of women parliamentarians — 49 per cent — in the world.

Figure 8-9 A group of Rwandan women use papyrus reeds and sisal fibres to weave traditional baskets. For generations, these baskets were a symbol of family values, for they were used as containers for gifts to newlyweds and new mothers. Now, they are exported for sale around the world.

REFLECT AND RESPOND

Create a timeline of the key events of the genocide in Rwanda. Think carefully about where your timeline will begin. Will it start, for example, before the country became a German colony? At each point on your timeline, add a point-form note explaining why you chose to include the event.

Choose one event from the timeline and explain how it was an effect of previous events — and a cause of events that followed. Explain how the outcome might have been different if international responses had been different. Conclude by suggesting actions the international community might take to ensure that a genocide like the one in Rwanda never happens again.

EXPRESSING AND DEFENDING AN INFORMED POSITION

Lieutenant General Roméo Dallaire witnessed the slaughter of hundreds of thousands of Rwandans and was unable to prevent their deaths. The experience left him shattered. As part of his personal journey toward peace and reconciliation, he wrote a book, *Shake Hands with the Devil*. Dallaire concluded his story by setting out what he believes must be done to avoid repeating the terrible slaughter in Rwanda.

> The only conclusion I can reach is that we are in desperate need of a transfusion of humanity. If we believe that all humans are humans, then how are we going to prove it? It can only be proven through our actions. Through the dollars we are prepared to expend to improve conditions in the Third World, through the time and energy we devote to solving devastating problems like AIDS, through the lives of our soldiers, which we are prepared to sacrifice for the sake of humanity.

People usually express and defend an informed position to persuade others, to change or initiate an action, or to make a clear statement about their stand on an issue. Suppose you were charged with the responsibility of expressing and defending Dallaire's position. The following steps can help you do this. You can use the same steps to express and defend an informed position on other issues you will encounter as you progress through this course.

Steps to Expressing and Defending an Informed Position

Step 1: Review the position

With a partner, review the material on Rwanda presented in the first part of this chapter. Then reread the excerpt from *Shake Hands with the Devil* at the top of this page and discuss answers to the following questions:

- The phrase "informed position" implies that you have enough background knowledge to understand and speak authoritatively on the issue. Do you need to check, recheck, or add to any of the information you have reviewed?

- When defending a position, it is important for the position to relate directly to the issue. What issue are you responding to? Express the issue clearly to yourself and your partner.

- The position you express should inform the audience about the issue. Is the nature of the issue you are responding to clearly evident in the position you are expressing? If not, discuss with your partner how you might revise the way you are expressing the issue.

- Your position should clearly state an action or actions that should be taken to resolve the issue. Does your position inform the audience about actions that could or should be taken?

Step 2: Identify the stakeholders

It is important to understand who has a stake in the issue so that you can express and defend a position that meets the needs of everyone involved.

Work with your partner to create a list of the stakeholders who will be affected by the position Dallaire expressed. Be sure to think beyond the immediate stakeholders (e.g., the people of Rwanda) to others who will be affected by your position (e.g., Canadian taxpayers). Note the interest of each stakeholder.

Step 3: Predict arguments for and against your position

For each stakeholder on your list, note a point he or she may make to support or oppose your position. Prepare some ideas that respond to the stakeholder's points. To do this, you may choose to use a chart like the one on the next page. An example has been partly filled in.

RESEARCH TIP

Review the Focus on Skills feature on pages 34 and 35 of Chapter 1 to refresh your ideas about how to develop an informed position.

FOCUS ON SKILLS

FOCUS ON SKILLS

FOCUS ON SKILLS

FOCUS ON SKILLS

FOCUS ON SKILLS

FOCUS ON SKILLS

FOCUS ON SKILLS

Step 4: Decide on the form of your presentation

With your partner, brainstorm to create a list of forms your presentation might take. You might, for example, decide to join other pairs in a round-table discussion. Or you might decide to use a computer presentation program to express and defend your position.

Step 5: Evaluate your presentation

As you prepare your presentation, present and explain sections of it to someone else, such as a classmate or your teacher. Revise your presentation based on their feedback. You and your partner may also assess yourselves by asking questions like these:

- Have we kept our position clearly in focus?
- Have we thought about the needs of the stakeholders?
- Is our position supported by evidence?
- Have we prepared responses to potential criticisms from stakeholders?

Action	Stakeholder	Arguments for and against the Action	Response
Must spend money	1. Canadian taxpayers — will cost money	Spend the money at home to help our own citizens first. Why can't other, richer countries pay the bills?	The outcomes of not spending the money are unthinkable. In a compassionate democracy, there must be money to do both: to help people at home and people in other countries. As humane beings, we cannot allow human disasters like the one in Rwanda to go unanswered or to be repeated.
	2. Charitable groups — need to raise money		

Summing up

As you progress through the course, you will encounter many situations in which you will need to express and defend an informed position. Following the steps set out in this activity will help you do this. It will also help you successfully complete the challenge for this related issue.

HOW EFFECTIVELY HAVE GOVERNMENTS RESPONDED TO THE LEGACIES OF HISTORICAL GLOBALIZATION?

The legacies of historical globalization are complex and long-lasting — and the responsibility for those legacies is often shared by different countries. Before Rwanda achieved independence, for example, the colonial rulers were Germany, then Belgium. In Canada, the colonial rulers were France, then Britain. Many governments today struggle to deal effectively with the legacies of historical globalization.

The United Nations and Indigenous Peoples

One organization that tries to persuade governments to work together is the United Nations. The goals of the UN are to keep peace, security, and friendly relations among the countries of the world; to promote human rights; to protect the environment; to fight poverty and disease; and to help refugees.

But what happens if your people are not represented at the United Nations? What if you are a member of an Indigenous group living in a country that was formed as a result of historical globalization and imperialism? What if the government of the country where you live does not speak for — or listen to — your people?

Consider the fact that First Peoples are trying to persuade Canadian governments to honour their rights. Canada is represented at the UN, but First Peoples are not. What conflicts might arise when First Peoples living in Canada try to gain an independent hearing at the UN?

Many of the 370 million Indigenous people in the world are not represented at the United Nations. As a result, their voices are not heard. To try to correct this situation, the United Nations established the Permanent Forum on Indigenous Issues in 2002. The forum discusses issues related to Indigenous economic and social development, culture, the environment, education, health, and human rights. Wilton Littlechild of the Ermineskin Cree Nation is the international chief of the Confederacy of Treaty 6 First Nations in Alberta. He has served two terms on the forum.

The forum is trying to persuade the United Nations General Assembly to pass the Declaration on the Rights of Indigenous Peoples, which Littlechild and other Indigenous leaders have been working on for 20 years.

CHECKBACK

You read about Wilton Littlechild and the Declaration on the Rights of Indigenous Peoples in Chapter 4.

Figure 8-10 To address the legacies of historical globalization faced by Indigenous peoples, the United Nations declared 2005 to 2015 the Second Decade of Indigenous Peoples. How does the fact that this is the *second* decade — the first decade was from 1995 to 2005 — show how difficult it is to address the consequences of imperialism?

INDIGENOUS PEOPLES: A DECADE FOR ACTION AND DIGNITY
PUEBLOS INDÍGENAS: UN DECENIO PARA LA ACCIÓN Y DIGNIDAD
PEUPLES AUTOCHTONES : UNE DÉCENNIE POUR L'ACTION ET DIGNITÉ
КОРЕННЫЕ НАРОДЫ: ДЕСЯТИЛЕТИЕ ДЕЙСТВИЙ И ДОСТОИНСТВА

South Africa — Redressing Inequities

Beginning in 1652, South Africa was colonized by the Dutch, Portuguese, French, and British. With each wave of colonization, the Indigenous peoples of the region lost more land and rights. The Eurocentric beliefs of the time ensured that both the Indigenous peoples of the region and immigrants from India were treated as second-class citizens.

Racism as government policy

In 1926, South Africa became an independent dominion within the British Empire. Because blacks outnumbered whites by more than 10 to one, the government passed laws to ensure that whites held onto political and economic control. Blacks, for example, were barred from voting.

After World War II, when Indigenous peoples across Africa demanded independence, the South African government introduced **apartheid** — laws that strictly segregated the population. All South Africans were classified as either white, Asian, coloured (of mixed ancestry), or black. The groups lived in separate areas, went to separate schools, and worked at racially designated jobs.

Throughout the 1970s and 1980s, many groups struggled to end apartheid, using non-violent and violent means. The government responded by banning protest organizations and locking up their leaders, including Nelson Mandela, who led the African National Congress.

Examine Figure 8-12. What conclusions can you draw about the effects of apartheid on various groups?

Student protest in Soweto

On June 16, 1976, between 15 000 and 20 000 black high school students in the South African township of Soweto demonstrated to demand better education. At the time, the government was spending 644 rands a year to educate every white student, but only 42 rands a year on each black student. In addition, the apartheid law said, "Natives must be taught from an early age that equality with Europeans is not for them."

Police officers opened fire on the students, who responded by throwing rocks and bottles and setting fire to buildings and vehicles. According to the government, 168 students were killed that day, but the people of Soweto said the number was closer to 350.

The killings made headlines around the world and caused a storm of protest against apartheid. Many historians believe that this tragedy marked the beginning of the end of apartheid.

Figure 8-11 Under South Africa's system of apartheid, it was illegal for whites and non-whites to mix in public places. Segregated beaches were one result of that policy.

Figure 8-12 **South African Inequality under Apartheid, 1984**

Racial Designation	Income per Person (In rands, South African currency)	Literacy Rate (Percentage of adults)	State Spending per Student on Education (In rands)
White	14 880	93	2 538
Asian	4 560	71	1 857
Coloured	3 000	62	1 286
Black	1 246	32	504

Note: In 2007, 1 rand = 16¢ Canadian or $1 Canadian = 6.25 rand.

Figure 8-13 In 2006, South African president Thabo Mbeki commemorated the death of 12-year-old Hector Pieterson, who was shot and killed by government forces during the 1976 Soweto demonstration. The photograph behind Mbeki shows the dying Hector being carried by another student. This picture helped spark worldwide condemnation of South Africa's apartheid regime.

We are deeply grateful to the
thousands of South Africans who
came to the Commission to tell us
their stories. They have won our
country the admiration of the world:
wherever one goes, South Africa's
peaceful transition to democracy,
culminating in the Truth and
Reconciliation process, is spoken
of almost in reverent tones, as a
phenomenon that is unique in the
annals of history.

— *Archbishop Desmond Tutu,
in the foreword to the* Truth and
Reconciliation Commission of South
Africa Report, *2003*

The Truth and Reconciliation Commission

Under pressure from both the international community and within the country, the South African government started dismantling apartheid in 1986. Over the next eight years, the country worked to gradually introduce fairness and equity.

In 1994, the country held the first elections in which all South Africans — regardless of colour — could vote, and Mandela was elected president. In 1995, Mandela established the Truth and Reconciliation Commission to help South Africans confront their country's violent past, to bring together the victims and those accused of crimes, and to try to reconcile peoples who had been in deadly conflict with each other for so long.

Archbishop Desmond Tutu was chosen to chair the commission's hearings. In a court-like setting, anyone who wished to be heard could speak. Those who were accused of human rights abuses could request amnesty — freedom from prosecution.

Although the commission found that the South African government, civil servants, and security forces were guilty of violating people's human rights, it also found that the African liberation movements had, on occasion, violated people's rights.

PROFILE

NELSON MANDELA
PRISONER AND PRESIDENT

As a young man, Nelson Mandela was one of many South Africans who took up the struggle to end apartheid. This was dangerous work under the apartheid regime, and like many South Africans, he was arrested, tried for sabotage and treason, and sentenced to life in prison. In prison, Mandela did not give up his work. He defended prisoners' rights and fought against abuse and injustice. As a result, he became a hero among black South Africans and among civil rights workers around the world.

Still, Mandela might have remained a prisoner if F.W. de Klerk had not become president of South Africa in 1989. De Klerk was committed to reform, and one of his first acts was to order the release of political prisoners such as Mandela. Once out of prison, Mandela and de Klerk worked together to continue the reform process.

In 1993, the two shared the Nobel Peace Prize for "their work for the peaceful termination of the apartheid regime, and for laying the foundations for a new democratic South Africa."

In his Nobel lecture, Mandela praised those who "had the nobility of spirit to stand in the path of tyranny and injustice" and who "recognized that an injury to one is an injury to all and therefore acted together in defence of justice and a common human decency."

Figure 8-14 Nelson Mandela comes from the Thembu people of the eastern Cape of South Africa. The first black lawyer in the country, he joined the African National Congress as a young man and helped organize protests against apartheid in the 1950s.

Legacies of Historical Globalization in Canada

Like many countries, Canada has attempted to deal with the consequences that imperialist policies and ethnocentric practices had on both Indigenous and non-Indigenous peoples.

The internment of German and Ukrainian Canadians

By the time World War I began in 1914, more than a million people from Germany and Austria-Hungary had immigrated in Canada. But Germany and Austria-Hungary were Canada's enemies in this war, and many Canadians feared that these immigrants were spies. People often feared those they considered outsiders.

As a result, people from Germany and Ukraine, which was part of Austria-Hungary at the time, were labelled **enemy aliens** and ordered to report regularly to the police. Although no evidence of disloyalty was ever found, their other rights were also restricted. Many, for example, lost the right to vote.

In addition, more than 8500 German and Ukrainian Canadians were interned — held in prison-like conditions. Some were forced to work in mines; others built roads in Banff and Jasper national parks.

Since then, Canadians of Ukrainian heritage have worked for redress. In 2002, Inky Mark, a federal member of Parliament, called on the government to "acknowledge that persons of Ukrainian origin were interned in Canada during the First World War and to provide for recognition of this event." Mark has tried to steer a bill recognizing this injustice through Parliament but so far has been unsuccessful.

Though the federal government has offered $2.5 million for memorials and education programs about the internment, Parliament has not apologized.

The internment of Japanese Canadians

During World War II, Canada was once again at war with Germany. Then, in December 1941, Japan entered the war on Germany's side. Japanese forces bombed the American base at Pearl Harbor, Hawaii, and attacked British and Canadian troops in Hong Kong.

In the late 19th and early 20th centuries, many Japanese people had immigrated to Canada. Most had settled in British Columbia, and just as people of German and Ukrainian descent had during World War I, they became the target of suspicion during World War II.

As a result, all Japanese Canadians were moved away from the Pacific coast to internment camps in the interior of British Columbia, or later, to the Prairies. They were allowed to take only what they could carry; everything else they owned was confiscated and later sold to pay for their internment. In the camps, as many as 10 families lived in cramped huts. Food was sometimes so scarce that the Red Cross had to supply emergency rations.

After the war, Japanese Canadians sought compensation for these injustices. Finally, in 1988, a settlement was reached. Each internee's survivor received $21 000. The government also apologized and established the Canadian Race Relations Foundation to help eliminate racism.

Figure 8-15 Armed guards and high wire fences ensured that none of the Germans and Ukrainians interned at Castle Mountain Internment Camp in Alberta escaped.

FYI

Nearly 21 000 people of Japanese descent were interned during World War II. Of these internees, 64 per cent had been born in Canada. At no point during the war was any person of Japanese descent charged with disloyalty or sabotage.

Figure 8-16 Japanese Canadians were shipped to camps in the interior of British Columbia for the rest of World War II. How were attitudes toward people of Japanese descent a legacy of historical globalization?

Legacies of the Indian Act

The Indian Act is a continuing and controversial legacy of imperialism in Canada. Although this act has been changed several times since it was introduced in 1876, First Nations say that it continues to embody legacies of colonialism.

Critics argue that the act

- ensures that First Nations peoples do not receive equal treatment
- limits First Nations' right to self-government and self-determination
- assumes that federal government officials are the best judges of the needs of First Nations peoples

For First Nations, Métis, and Inuit, the passing of the Constitution Act in 1982 — with its recognition of "existing aboriginal and treaty rights" — was a step forward because it opened the door to the settlement of land claims such as the one that established Nunavut.

But the Indian Act remains in place. In 2006, Sheila Fraser, who was Canada's auditor general at the time, pointed out that the federal government "has repeatedly acknowledged the need for meaningful change and a new relationship in order to correct long-standing problems" with First Nations. But, she added, the problems continue.

Think about what you know about the relationship between First Nations and the federal government. What key issue do you think must be settled if this relationship is to improve? Explain why you think your choice is the key issue.

The Royal Commission on Aboriginal Peoples

In 1991, the federal government established the Royal Commission on Aboriginal Peoples to investigate its relationship with First Nations, Métis, and Inuit. The commissioners were interested in answering one overriding question: What are the foundations of a fair and honourable relationship between the Aboriginal and non-Aboriginal people of Canada?

The commission held 178 days of public hearings in 96 communities and released its final report in 1996. According to the commissioners, the report tells the story

… of the relationship between Aboriginal and non-Aboriginal people that is a central facet of Canada's heritage

… of the distortion of that relationship over time

… of the terrible consequences of distortion for Aboriginal people – loss of lands, power and self-respect.

The commissioners concluded that "the main policy direction, pursued for more than 150 years, first by colonial then by Canadian governments, has been wrong."

CHECKBACK
You read about early uses of the Indian Act in Chapter 7.

VOICES

[The Indian Act] has . . . deprived us of our independence, our dignity, our self-respect and our responsibility.

— *Kaherine June Delisle, of the Kanien'kehaka First Nation, Québec, quoted in* People to People, Nation to Nation: The Royal Commission on Aboriginal Peoples, *1996*

FYI

Royal commissions are a legacy of British rule. They are established by the government to investigate matters of public concern. Commissioners listen to presentations by interested people, then produce a report that recommends actions. But a commission's recommendations are just that — the government is not required to follow the advice.

VOICES

Our relationships need to evolve [back] into a partnership . . . people-to-people, culture-to-culture, nation-to-nation. That is the direction we need to take.

— *Al Ducharme, Métis history teacher, La Ronge, Saskatchewan, quoted in* People to People, Nation to Nation: The Royal Commission on Aboriginal Peoples, *1996*

The statement of reconciliation

As a result of the findings of the Royal Commission on Aboriginal Peoples, the Canadian government issued a statement of reconciliation in 1998. This statement, which was widely interpreted as an apology, acknowledged the harm that had been done to First Nations, Métis, and Inuit. Here is some of what it said:

> Sadly, our history with respect to the treatment of Aboriginal people is not something in which we can take pride. Attitudes of racial and cultural superiority led to a suppression of Aboriginal culture and values. As a country, we are burdened by past actions that resulted in weakening the identity of Aboriginal peoples, suppressing their languages and cultures, and outlawing spiritual practices . . . We must acknowledge that the result of these actions was the erosion of the political, economic and social systems of Aboriginal people and nations.
>
> Against the backdrop of these historical legacies, it is a remarkable tribute to the strength and endurance of Aboriginal people that they have maintained their historic diversity and identity.

Figure 8-17 Phanuelie Palluq, an Inuit drum dancer, performs at a 1998 ceremony in Ottawa. During the ceremony, Jane Stewart, who was minister of Indian Affairs at the time, read a statement of reconciliation that acknowledged, among other things, the abuse many First Nations children had suffered at residential schools.

Changing the Indian Act

To try to deal with the shortcomings of the Indian Act, the Liberal government of Prime Minister Jean Chrétien introduced the First Nations governance bill in 2002. The purpose of the proposed legislation was to eliminate the harmful elements of the Indian Act while maintaining the government's financial and treaty obligations. The government said that the changes would give First Nations more power and help them become self-sustaining.

But many First Nations leaders disagreed. Critics, including the Canadian Bar Association and other non-Aboriginal groups, said that First Nations had been nearly shut out of the drafting process. The Assembly of First Nations boycotted the consultations held to create the proposed act because opportunities for First Nations people to participate were so limited.

In the face of this opposition, the government backed away from the bill — and the debate over what to do about the Indian Act continues.

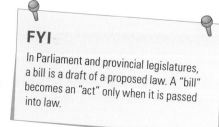

FYI

In Parliament and provincial legislatures, a bill is a draft of a proposed law. A "bill" becomes an "act" only when it is passed into law.

REFLECT AND RESPOND

Since contact, many First Nations, Métis, and Inuit have been denied basic rights. In 1914, many Canadians of German and Ukrainian descent were denied basic rights, and in 1942, the same thing happened to Canadians of Japanese descent.

Do you believe that circumstances could ever justify denying the basic rights of Canadian citizens? Explain your position with references to the legacies of historical globalization.

How effectively have organizations responded to the legacies of historical globalization?

Around the world, local and international organizations are working to help rebuild societies that have suffered the destructive legacies of historical globalization. An organization is a group of people who work together to achieve a specific goal. Members may have different tasks, but all their tasks are directed toward achieving the organization's goal. Churches, corporations, armies, schools, hospitals, clubs, and political parties are all organizations that are responding to the legacies of historical globalization.

Non-Governmental Organizations

AVEGA Agahozo, which is helping widows and children rebuild their communities after the 1994 genocide in Rwanda, is a **non-governmental organization**, or NGO.

There are tens of thousands of NGOs around the world. Though NGOs are not part of governments, some have influenced government policies at the national and international levels. NGOs have specific goals, and they try to raise public awareness and gain support in achieving those goals. Their goals may be local, provincial, national, regional, or international in scope. NGOs are not in the business of making money. They often depend on volunteer workers and charitable donations, but some also receive grants or contracts from governments and donations from corporations.

Some NGOs, such as Greenpeace International, focus on environmental issues. Members try to persuade governments to take action against climate change and environmental destruction and to protect the earth's forests and oceans.

Other NGOs, such as Human Rights Watch, advocate for human rights in countries around the world. Their members investigate and expose human rights violations and try to persuade the public and governments to end these violations.

Still other NGOs deliver services to people in need. They may, for example, provide food and housing to people who have been harmed by natural disasters or the devastation of war. Doctors without Borders is an example of an organization that provides emergency health care to people in areas of conflict.

Figure 8-18 In Papua New Guinea, which was a colony of Germany, Britain, and then Australia in the 19th and 20th centuries, Indigenous landowners invited the NGO Greenpeace to help them establish a community-run timber business.

NGOs' responses to legacies of historical globalization

NGOs help people rebuild communities in a variety of ways: by promoting environmental, arms control, and disarmament agreements; by strengthening Indigenous people's and women's rights; and by providing direct aid to people in countries that have been torn apart by conflict or natural disasters.

NGOs sometimes work together to pool their resources. In Malaysia, for example, where many communities need to be rebuilt, the Third World Network brings together NGOs by providing financial and development aid; by supporting health, trade, and Indigenous knowledge initiatives; and by protecting human rights.

Although NGOs do not have direct control over global decision making, they often influence government decisions. An example is the International Campaign to Ban Landmines, which was awarded the Nobel Peace Prize in 1997. More than 1400 NGOs in 90 countries united in this campaign because they recognized that landmines pose a threat to the work they all do. In support of this campaign, the Canadian government challenged other countries to sign an international treaty banning landmines. By 2007, 152 countries had signed the treaty.

Questioning the effectiveness of NGOs

Critics claim that some NGOs are sponsored by groups that want to undermine or overthrow governments. In 2006, for example, the government of Peru claimed that NGOs had funded a blockade of oil wells by Indigenous peoples in the Amazon region. As a result, NGOs operating in Peru were ordered to reveal their sponsors and how they planned to spend their money. And in 2003, the Indian government blacklisted 800 NGOs that it said were funding separatist rebels.

Other critics say that local grassroots organizations, such as AVEGA Agahozo, are harmed when international NGOs move in. These critics, such as Alejandro Bendana, who is quoted on this page, view international NGOs as a new form of imperialism. They question whether these organizations, whose headquarters are often in wealthy European and North American countries, can understand and respect the needs and wishes of people in local communities.

Still other critics say that the focus of NGOs is often too narrow to solve the complex problems that are the legacies of historical globalization.

Web Connection

To find out more about the International Campaign to Ban Landmines, go to this web site and follow the links.

www.ExploringGlobalization.ca

VOICES

Too often the NGO vision of global affairs is a narrow one that is shaped by being upper-level citizens of rich and historically colonizing countries . . . It is easy to respond to new and old progressive issues — such as environmental protection, debt relief, human rights, conflict resolution, and gender discrimination — while setting aside the structural links that bind together these and other issues.

— Alejandro Bendana, consultant for UNESCO Culture for Peace Program and founder of Centro de Estudios Internacionales in Managua, Nicaragua

REFLECT AND RESPOND

With a partner, choose one country and one negative legacy of historical globalization that continues to pose problems in that country. Describe an NGO you would create to help deal with the legacy you identified. In your description, outline the goals of your NGO, the kinds of volunteers it needs, and one action you would undertake to respond to the legacy of historical globalization you identified. Would you enlist the help of other NGOs? Which ones? How would you ensure that your NGO understands and respects the needs and wishes of people in the country you plan to help?

MUHAMMAD YUNUS
AND THE GRAMEEN BANK

IMPACT

When Pakistan gained independence in 1947, the country was made up of two regions — East Pakistan and West Pakistan — which were separated by 1600 kilometres of Indian territory. But East Pakistan, which is now Bangladesh, wanted independence. As a result, a series of wars erupted during the 1960s and early 1970s.

Bangladesh became a battlefield. Farms, roads, towns, and villages were destroyed. Hundreds of thousands of people were killed, and millions more became refugees. Finally, in 1971, Bangladesh won independence.

But this country, which has a population of about 147 million people, is in a region that suffers many natural disasters. Cyclones and floods have destroyed food resources, and this destruction has led to malnutrition and famine. During a long famine in 1973–74, for example, 1.5 million people died.

A Sense of Responsibility

In 1976, Muhammad Yunus was an economics professor at Chittagong University in Bangladesh. Seeing the poverty and devastation around him, he felt compelled to do something. With the help of his students and friends, he started the Grameen Bank — and 30 years later, he and this organization shared the Nobel Peace Prize.

"I wanted to do something immediate to help people around me, even if it was just one human being, to get through another day with a little more ease," Yunus said in his speech accepting the prize. "That brought me face to face with poor people's struggle to find the tiniest amounts of money to support their efforts to eke out a living."

Yunus believed that if people living in poverty were given very small loans — microloans — to help start a business, they could learn to support themselves. This idea, called microcredit, has worked successfully in many developing countries.

Yunus began by lending 42 people a total of $27 from his own pocket. Then he tried to persuade local banks to extend microloans, but the banks refused. When Yunus offered to guarantee to repay the loans himself, he got some money — but not enough. So he started the Grameen Bank.

As the bank grew, all its microloans were provided from money deposited by members. The Grameen Bank has been so successful in attracting new members that it has refused to take donations from aid organizations and continues to operate using only members' deposits.

By 2006, the Grameen Bank had lent an average of $8 (U.S.) to seven million poor people, 97 per cent of whom are women who live in 73 000 villages in Bangladesh. The repayment rate on the loans is 99 per cent. Though the loan amounts may seem very small to North Americans, the money can be enough to buy the raw materials to make handicrafts, a consumer item that can be sold in the street, or mosquito netting to protect against malaria.

Figure 8-19   Muhammad Yunus visits Grameen Bank loan holders in a village in Bangladesh.

Figure 8-20   **Growth of the Grameen Bank, 1976–2005**
(Dollar amounts are in millions U.S.)

Performance Indicator	1976	1987	1997	2005
All loans	$0.001	$83.04	$2062.96	$5025.61
Year-end outstanding amount	$0.001	$14.94	$233.01	$415.82
Housing loans during the year	0	$4.59	$15.69	$2.95
Number of houses built	0	23 408	402 747	627 058
Total deposits (balance)	0	$7.24	$132.27	$481.22
Number of members	10	339 156	2 272 503	5 579 399
Percentage of female members	20	81	95	96
Number of villages covered	1	7502	37 937	59 912

Notes: 1) 1976 figures show loans given through the Janata Bank. They do not include loans given personally by Muhammad Yunus. 2) Grameen Bank began operating as an independent in October1983. The housing loan program started in 1984.

Source: Grameen Bank

IMPACT IMPACT IMPACT IMPACT IMPACT IMPACT IMPACT

A Success Story

Some of the loans help women start small businesses. Asiran Begum, for example, knew that many women who lived in rural villages were reluctant to travel to bazaars to buy their saris. So she borrowed money from the Grameen Bank to start a business selling saris door-to-door in her own village and nearby villages. The first 10 saris sold quickly, so she bought more, which also sold quickly. Other women have borrowed from the bank to open small food shops or to buy sewing machines, which they use to make clothing.

Other loans are used to pay for children to attend school, which is a priority for many of the women who borrow from the bank. In 2006, the bank also awarded 30 000 scholarships to deserving students. Other loans are used for housing. Since 1984, housing loans have helped people — mainly women — build 640 000 homes in Bangladesh.

Among the people who have borrowed from the bank, 58 per cent have risen above the poverty line for the country.

Peace and Poverty

In his 2006 Nobel lecture, Yunus emphasized the connection between achieving world peace and alleviating poverty. In his view, terrorism can be defeated only if the lives of poor people around the world are improved.

"Peace is threatened by unjust economic, social and political order, absence of democracy, environmental degradation and absence of human rights," he said. "Poverty is the absence of all human rights."

Explorations

1. Muhammad Yunus and the Grameen Bank shared the Nobel Peace Prize. But the Nobel committee also awards a prize for economics. Imagine that you chair the committee that decided to award Yunus and the Grameen Bank the peace prize rather than the prize for economics. Write a brief explanation of your decision. Emphasize how making small, easy-to-repay loans to the very poor can contribute to world peace.

2. On a separate piece of paper, continue the flow chart started here. Add at least five more boxes in any direction. Explain how this chart shows that the actions of one person can make an important difference in the lives of many.

How a Grameen Bank Loan Works

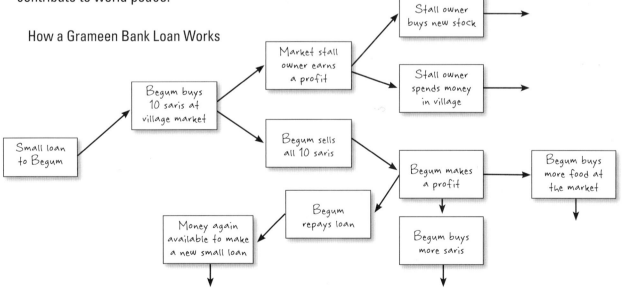

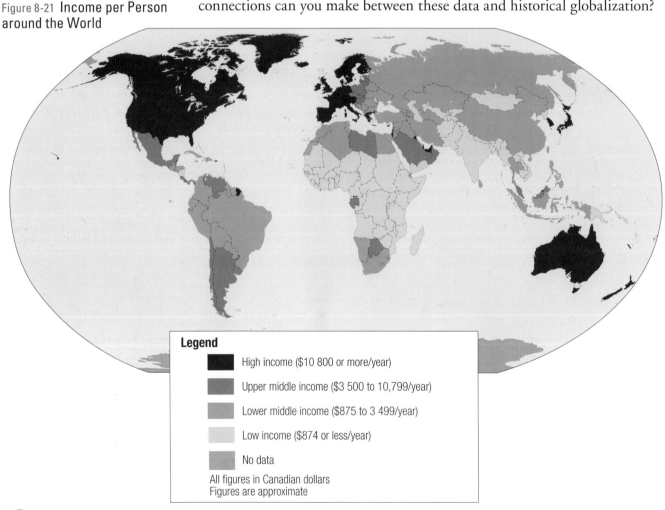
HOW DOES HISTORICAL GLOBALIZATION CONTINUE TO AFFECT THE WORLD?

One important legacy of historical globalization is the growing disparity in the well-being of people around the world. The increase in the speed, range, and depth of global trade has had an immense impact — both negative and positive — on the wealth of nations and individuals. The tremendous rise in the standard of living of most people in Europe and North America is a direct legacy of historical globalization. But most of the world's people have never had an opportunity to benefit from the positive aspects of global trade.

Global Income Inequality

The growing gap between the rich and poor of the world presents a growing challenge for everyone. Both governments and non-governmental organizations, such as Greenpeace and Doctors without Borders, have recognized the need to deal with this legacy of historical globalization and are responding to it in a variety of ways. These may include providing foreign aid, loans, professional and social assistance programs, and direct food distribution.

Examine the map on this page. List five countries with the lowest average per-person yearly income and five with the highest. What connections can you make between these data and historical globalization?

Figure 8-21 **Income per Person around the World**

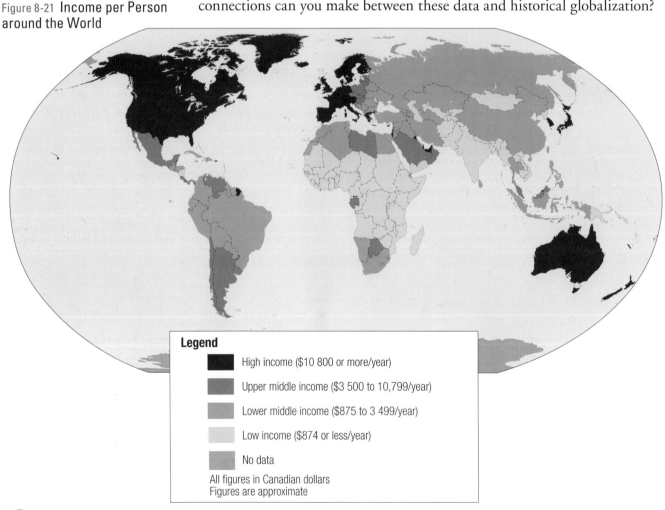

Legend

High income ($10 800 or more/year)

Upper middle income ($3 500 to 10,799/year)

Lower middle income ($875 to 3 499/year)

Low income ($874 or less/year)

No data

All figures in Canadian dollars
Figures are approximate

Foreign Aid

Foreign aid — the money, expertise, supplies, and other goods given by one country to another — is one response to the inequalities caused by historical globalization. The goals of foreign aid are to reduce poverty and encourage a more secure, equitable, and prosperous world.

The United Nations encourages developed countries to provide foreign aid to less developed countries and suggests that the amount be tied to a country's **gross national income**, or GNI. GNI is the amount of money earned by everyone in a country. The UN has set 0.07 per cent of GNI as an appropriate foreign-aid target — but no country has ever achieved this goal. Canada's foreign aid contributions, for example, rose above 0.05 per cent of GNI only once: in 1986.

Examine the cartoon on this page. What did the cartoonist intend to show? Why do you think Canada has never given 0.07 per cent of its GNI to foreign aid? Should the government use this money to help people at home? Should this response to historical globalization be an either–or decision?

.07% OF OUR BUDGET TO HELP SAVE AFRICA?

Figure 8-22 In 2005, Aislin, a cartoonist with the *Montréal Gazette*, made this comment on Canada's foreign-aid contribution. Do you think he was suggesting that Canada's contribution is too high or too low?

Ideas — How can I respond effectively to the legacies of historical globalization?

The students responding to this question are Tom, a fourth-generation Albertan who lives on a ranch near Okotoks; Ling, who was born in Hong Kong but is now a Canadian who lives in Edmonton; and Katerina, who lives in St. Albert and whose grandparents emigrated from Ukraine in 1948.

Governments are supposed to listen to the people and act when action is necessary — that's their job. They're the ones who are in a position to identify when the legacies of historical globalization are causing problems. Besides, governments are the ones with the resources, like time and money, to solve problems. I guess I need to become involved with politics so I can influence who is elected to run our governments. So I would say that I can respond to the legacies of historical globalization by becoming more politically active.

The most effective vehicles of change are people working together in NGOs. NGOs can focus on specific issues and bring together people who share similar viewpoints. These organizations are especially good at raising awareness of problems — and this can lead to the mobilization of resources to deal with specific situations. We need to get involved with NGOs, as members or as donors. These groups have the potential to respond effectively to the legacies of historical globalization.

When you get right down to it, individuals are the key to change. Nothing happens unless someone decides to make it happen. Governments and NGOs are only as good as the people who work for them. Individuals like me need to become more aware of the problems and issues and to react when people are being treated unfairly. When I see legacies of historical globalization that are creating problems, I must speak out, tell others, and get something done. Individuals have to take responsibility.

Tom

Ling

Katerina

Your Turn

How would you respond to the question Tom, Ling, and Katerina are answering? How can you personally respond to the legacies of historical globalization? In what ways have you already responded? Recall the idea of "glocal." What might be some ways that you could respond to these legacies in your own community — and in the wider world?

1. With a partner, conduct research into the genocide that occurred in Sudan, Africa, and prepare a presentation that identifies ways in which this genocide was a legacy of historical globalization.

   a) Create three to five questions to use as criteria for judging the information you collect. Your questions might deal with causes, effects, participants, international responses, the role of NGOs, and so on. (e.g., Was Sudan a colony at one time? Which country was the colonizer? How did Sudan become independent?)

   b) Decide where to look for information about the genocide. The Internet will be helpful, but remember that many web sites offer a one-sided view of issues. Try to find authoritative sources that take a balanced approach.

   c) Record answers to your research questions. As you organize the information, consider these questions:

      • What have we already learned about the legacies of historical globalization, and how can this learning be applied to this situation?

      • Do we have enough information to answer our questions?

      • Have we considered a variety of perspectives and points of view on the topic?

      • Have we taken into account the biases of the sources we are using?

   d) Use presentation software to prepare a report that summarizes your understandings of the topic. Ensure that your report identifies the extent to which the genocide in Sudan was a legacy of historical globalization. Think about questions you might be asked when you make your presentation (e.g., How effective were the responses to the genocide?) and prepare brief notes to help you answer these questions.

2. In his Nobel Peace Prize acceptance speech, Muhammad Yunus said,

   > The new millennium began with a great global dream. World leaders gathered at the United Nations in 2000 and adopted, among others, a historic goal to reduce poverty by half by 2015. Never in human history had such a bold goal been adopted by the entire world in one voice, one that specified time and size. But then came September 11 and the Iraq war, and suddenly the world became derailed from the pursuit of this dream, with the attention of world leaders shifting from the war on poverty to the war on terrorism. Till now over $530 billion has been spent on the war in Iraq by the USA alone.

   a) Which goal do you believe is more important: reducing world poverty or winning the "war on terror"? Or are the two linked? Explain your answer.

   b) If you were asked to explain the "war on terror" as a legacy of historical globalization, what would you say?

3. The legacies of historical globalization can take many forms. Examine the map on the following page. It shows the host cities of the modern Summer Olympic Games.

   a) Identify continents and countries where the games have never been held. Make a general statement that links the cities and historical globalization. In point form, indicate those countries you think should have hosted the games, their colonial past, and how the legacies of that past may have kept the games away from them.

   b) Report on another global event (e.g., in entertainment, sports, or politics, a disaster, or another field of your choosing) that displays a pattern that, like the one for the Summer Olympics, demonstrates the legacies of historical globalization.

Figure 8-23 **Location of Summer Olympic Games**

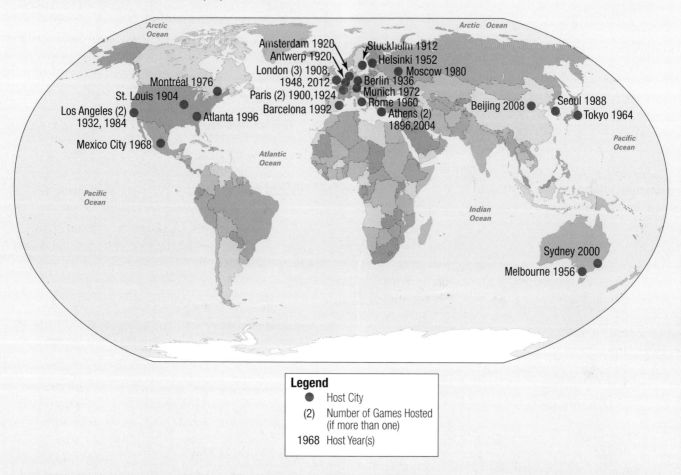

Legend
- Host City
- (2) Number of Games Hosted (if more than one)
- 1968 Host Year(s)

Think about Your Challenge

Look back at the challenge for this related issue. It asks you to prepare for a four-corners debate to express your position on this issue: To what extent should contemporary society respond to the legacies of historical globalization?

Review the material in this chapter and the activities you completed as you progressed through it. Add to the list of critical questions you will use to evaluate the data that you will explore and use in your statements during the debate. Prepare notes on why you have taken your position, as well as for questions you may wish to ask those who have taken different positions on the issue.

Key Issue
To what extent should we embrace globalization?

Related Issue 1
To what extent should globalization shape identity?

Related Issue 2
To what extent should contemporary society respond to the legacies of historical globalization?

Related Issue 3
To what extent does globalization contribute to sustainable prosperity for all people?

Related Issue 4
To what extent should I, as a citizen, respond to globalization?

Chapter 9
FOUNDATIONS OF ECONOMIC GLOBALIZATION

To what extent did world events shape contemporary economic globalization?

What does economic globalization mean?

How did 20th-century world events shape contemporary economic globalization?

What factors laid the foundations of contemporary global economics?

Chapter 10
EXPANDING GLOBALIZATION

To what extent do contemporary factors contribute to expanding globalization?

What factors contribute to expanding globalization?

How do international agreements and organizations contribute to expanding globalization?

How do transnational corporations contribute to expanding globalization?

How do communication technologies contribute to expanding globalization?

Chapter 11
GLOBALIZATION AND SUSTAINABILITY

To what extent does globalization affect sustainability?

What does sustainability mean?

How are globalization and sustainability related?

Have efforts to promote sustainability been successful?

Chapter 12
SUSTAINABLE PROSPERITY — CHALLENGES AND OPPORTUNITIES

To what extent can globalization bring sustainable prosperity to all people?

What is sustainable prosperity?

What political and economic challenges and opportunities are associated with globalization?

What choices are associated with sustainable prosperity?

Canada's Ecological Footprint

THE BIG PICTURE

You have explored the relationship between globalization and identity and the extent to which today's society should respond to the legacies of historical globalization. In this related issue, you will explore, analyze, and evaluate whether — and how — globalization contributes to sustainable prosperity for all people.

The question for this related issue raises issues of definition — What is prosperity? — and issues of fact — How should sustainability be measured? As you progress through the four chapters of this related issue, you will focus on exploring and evaluating answers to these questions and to the related-issue question: To what extent does globalization contribute to sustainable prosperity for all people? This exploration and evaluation will help you develop your response to the key question around which this course is structured.

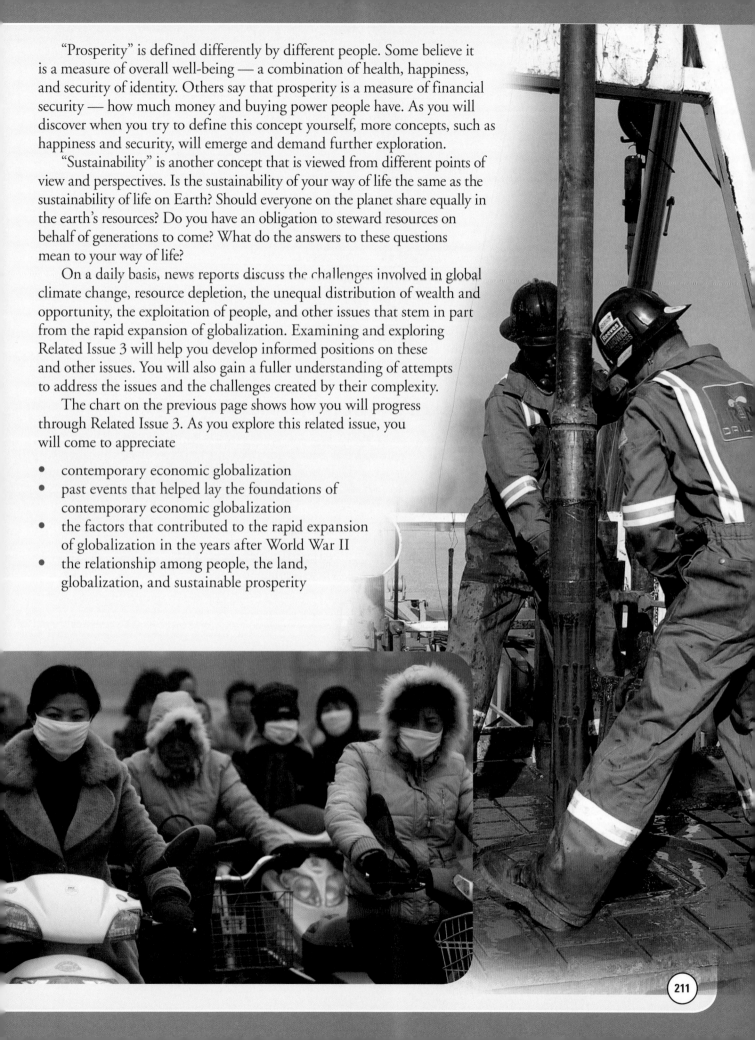

"Prosperity" is defined differently by different people. Some believe it is a measure of overall well-being — a combination of health, happiness, and security of identity. Others say that prosperity is a measure of financial security — how much money and buying power people have. As you will discover when you try to define this concept yourself, more concepts, such as happiness and security, will emerge and demand further exploration.

"Sustainability" is another concept that is viewed from different points of view and perspectives. Is the sustainability of your way of life the same as the sustainability of life on Earth? Should everyone on the planet share equally in the earth's resources? Do you have an obligation to steward resources on behalf of generations to come? What do the answers to these questions mean to your way of life?

On a daily basis, news reports discuss the challenges involved in global climate change, resource depletion, the unequal distribution of wealth and opportunity, the exploitation of people, and other issues that stem in part from the rapid expansion of globalization. Examining and exploring Related Issue 3 will help you develop informed positions on these and other issues. You will also gain a fuller understanding of attempts to address the issues and the challenges created by their complexity.

The chart on the previous page shows how you will progress through Related Issue 3. As you explore this related issue, you will come to appreciate

- contemporary economic globalization
- past events that helped lay the foundations of contemporary economic globalization
- the factors that contributed to the rapid expansion of globalization in the years after World War II
- the relationship among people, the land, globalization, and sustainable prosperity

Your Challenge

Prepare and present a persuasive essay in response to the question for this related issue:

To what extent does globalization contribute to sustainable prosperity for all people?

Checklist for Success

At the final editing stage, review your essay to make sure it includes all the elements necessary for success.

My Knowledge and Understanding of the Issue

My position on the issue is clearly stated.

Facts are clearly presented to support my position.

My conclusion is logical and based on strong evidence.

My Selection, Analysis, and Evaluation of Information

I have drawn information from a variety of reliable sources.

I have selected information that reflects diverse points of view and perspectives.

My inquiry questions clearly formed the basis of my research.

All sources and references are cited correctly and accurately.

My Essay

My message is clear and consistent.

My writing is interesting, grammatically correct, and suited to my audience and purpose.

Your Persuasive Essay

As you progress through this related issue, you will gather ideas, information, points of view, and perspectives to help you reach an informed position on how much globalization contributes to sustainable prosperity for all people. You may wish to review the Focus on Skills feature (p. 34), which outlines the steps to take in developing an informed position.

How You Will Develop Your Essay

A persuasive essay is one in which you present a position and lay out your reasons for reaching your conclusions. Your aim is to convince readers that your position is the logical one to take after exploring and analyzing the issue. An effective persuasive essay includes elements such as

- material in the form of quotations and references from informed and involved stakeholders
- clear examples that illustrate the ideas presented
- primary documents, where applicable
- references to many different sources, points of view, and perspectives

An index card you can use to organize information

State your inquiry question.

Main idea

Note points you can use in your essay.

Inquiry Questions

How is sustainability linked to globalization?

Point: Improved communication technologies have led to the rapid expansion of international trade

Source: Gardner, Robert, and Wayne Lavold. *Exploring Globalization*. Toronto: McGraw-Hill Ryerson, 2007. p. 47.

Point:

Source

Keep track of sources, including page references. Use the citation style set out by your teacher.

Steps to Writing a Persuasive Essay

Step 1

Develop four or five inquiry questions to help guide your research and reading. Inquiry questions focus on analysis rather than facts — and these questions form the basis of an effective persuasive essay.

Share your questions with a partner or your teacher. Based on the feedback you receive, revise or change your questions. Be prepared to revise or refine your questions again as you progress through Related Issue 3 and encounter information that inspires you to consider exploring in new directions.

Step 2

Once you have decided on your inquiry questions, you will be ready to gather and organize information. One way to organize this information is to record your inquiry question and notes on separate sheets of paper or index cards. You might also use a computer file. Be sure to include notes about your sources. An index card might look like the example on page 212.

Step 3

You can use a flow system like the one shown on this page to create an essay outline based on your notes. Share your outline and your inquiry questions with a partner or your teacher. If necessary, revise your outline based on their feedback.

Step 4

When you finish reading the four chapters in this related issue, prepare a first draft of your essay. Share this with a partner or your teacher and use his or her feedback to edit your essay. Then read your essay several times. Focus on a specific aspect each time.

State your position.
Outline how you will support it.

Subtopic 1
State and explain the first main point that supports your position.

Evidence: Include evidence that supports the point.

Relationship: Clearly indicate the connection between this subtopic and your position.

Subtopic 2
Evidence:

Relationship:

Tie your ideas together and show how they led to your position.

TIPS FOR DEVELOPING INQUIRY QUESTIONS

Effective inquiry questions inspire analysis and open new avenues of investigation and thought. Read the following questions and decide which is an inquiry question and which requires only a recitation of facts:

- When did the slave trade in Africa begin and end, and how many countries were involved?
- What effect did the slave trade have on African countries, and are its effects still being felt today?

The second question is an inquiry question because it requires you to establish criteria and make informed judgments.

Editing Your Essay

First Reading — Focus on the big picture. Ask yourself whether you have

- made your position clear throughout
- provided enough evidence to support your position
- presented your arguments in logical order

Second Reading — Focus on language. Ask yourself whether you have

- included logical transitions between paragraphs
- varied the length and structure of sentences
- used active verbs and vivid descriptions
- used language that is appropriate for your audience

Third Reading — Focus on grammar, spelling, usage, and other fine points. Ask yourself whether you have

- checked the spelling of words you are not sure about
- constructed sentences that are grammatically correct
- included an accurate and complete bibliography

Fourth Reading — Focus on reviewing the essay against the Checklist for Success.

Chapter 9 Foundations of Economic Globalization

Figure 9-1 At 8:15 a.m. on August 6, 1945, the United States dropped an atomic bomb on Hiroshima, levelling much of the city and killing about 140 000 people. This attack — and a second on the city of Nagasaki — was so devastating that the Japanese government surrendered and World War II ended. The picture at the top shows what Hiroshima looked like after the bomb was dropped. The picture at the bottom shows Hiroshima today. The Japanese people have rebuilt the city into an important industrial centre where 1.1 million people live and work.

BY THE TIME THE UNITED STATES dropped an atomic bomb on Hiroshima in 1945, World War II had involved 50 countries and had been going on since 1939 in Europe and since 1941 in Asia and the Pacific. The Hiroshima bomb was 2000 times more powerful than any previous bomb.

When the war ended, the Japanese, with help from people around the world, rebuilt their country's economy and their ruined cities. Today, Japan has one of the most powerful economies in the world. The people of Hiroshima, for example, manufacture and export automobiles, ships, electronic machinery, furniture, and textiles.

Examine the photographs on the previous page and consider answers to the following questions:

- How does war affect people?
- What happens to people's quality of life when they experience this kind of devastation?
- How do international conflicts arise from competition for economic power?
- How do people rebuild a country's economy after a catastrophe?
- How should the global community respond when a country experiences economic and natural catastrophes?

KEY TERMS

economic globalization

reparations

communism

economic depression

market economy

LOOKING AHEAD

In this chapter, you will explore answers to the following questions:

- What does economic globalization mean?
- How did 20th-century world events shape contemporary economic globalization?
- What factors laid the foundations of contemporary global economics?

My Point of View on Globalization

Look back at the notes you recorded as you progressed through Related Issues 1 and 2. What new ideas did you add to your understandings of globalization? Use words or images — or both — to answer this question. Date your ideas and add them to the notebook, learning log, portfolio, or computer file you are keeping as you progress through this course.

WHAT DOES ECONOMIC GLOBALIZATION MEAN?

Some people believe that globalization is all about economics. Those who hold this view believe that global trade, the global transportation and communication systems that increase prosperity for some people, the unequal distribution of wealth, and the conflicts between peoples and countries over natural resources are all rooted in economics.

Economic globalization includes the oil and gas pipelines and large tankers that carry oil products from Canada to markets around the world. Oil and gas exports have brought employment and prosperity to many Albertans. As an Albertan, you share in the opportunities and challenges that result from those exports. But these exports have also generated concerns about the climate change that results from the world's dependence on oil and other fossil fuels.

Economic globalization also affects the Canadian manufacturers who buy products and components from countries where workers are paid much less than Canadian workers. You may also benefit from this aspect of globalization when you save money on clothing, shoes, and other products made in another country. Or you may share in the downside when friends or family members lose their jobs because Canadian manufacturers can't compete in the global market as a result of the high wages they must pay Canadian employees.

Because international trade agreements between Canada and other countries keep tariffs low, you can buy fresh strawberries from Mexico in your local supermarket. But these low prices may also mean that the people who harvest the strawberries don't earn enough to support their families.

Figure 9-2 When you buy fresh produce in the middle of an Alberta winter, you are sharing in economic globalization. Where do the grapes and bananas that you enjoy in December come from? How did they get to your local store from the farms where they were grown?

Figure 9-3 How do these men, working on a drilling rig near High Level, share in a process that helps the Alberta government support the health and education programs in which you take part? In 2005 and 2006, money from exporting energy resources accounted for about one-third of the revenue collected by the Alberta government.

Figure 9-4 This young Albertan plans a career raising cattle on his family's ranch. But what if he can't sell his cattle on world markets? In 2003, cases of mad cow disease were discovered in Alberta. As a result, countries around the world banned imports of Canadian beef. When the borders reopened, Alberta cattle that had sold for $1300 each were selling for only $15.

Aspects of Economic Globalization

Some people see economic globalization as a force that creates healthy interdependence that will lead to prosperity for everyone. Others, such as economist William Tabb, acknowledge this global economic interdependence and say that it could be healthy — but they also say that it doesn't yet benefit all people.

Joseph Stiglitz, who won the Nobel Prize for Economics in 2001, believes that countries and peoples are more economically integrated today than ever before. He says that this interdependence has happened because communication and transportation costs have been greatly reduced and barriers to the flow of goods, services, capital, and knowledge have been taken down.

Naomi Klein, a Canadian author and journalist, agrees that economic globalization reaches into every aspect of life, but she believes that it builds fences between people. She says that globalization shuts some people out of schools, hospitals, workplaces, and even their own farms, homes, and communities. Because of globalizing trends, she says, people are unemployed and their basic needs are not being met. "These fences of social exclusion can discard an entire industry, and they can also write off an entire country."

VOICES

Globalization refers to the process of reducing barriers between countries and encouraging closer economic, political, and social interaction. Globalization could vastly increase the ability of people everywhere to improve their living standards by sharing knowledge and the fruits of human labor across those barriers. This, of course, does not happen.

— *William K. Tabb, economist*

Ideas   What does economic globalization mean in your life?

The students responding to this question are Tom, a fourth-generation Albertan who lives on a ranch near Okotoks; Gord, a member of the Beaver First Nation near High Level; and Ling, who was born in Hong Kong but is now a Canadian living in Edmonton.

My brother and I want to run this ranch someday. But now we worry about whether we could make a living selling Alberta beef around the world. We'd have so little control over something like mad cow disease. You could do everything right, follow all the Canadian and international rules about what to feed your cattle. But then something could happen to cause other countries to stop buying your stock and ruin your chances for any kind of prosperity.

Tom

Economic globalization means challenges in my life and the lives of many First Nations people in Canada and around the world. And those challenges have been around for a very long time. The problems that grew out of that oil discovery on Lubicon Cree land in northern Alberta were all about world demand for oil. Forests were destroyed. Water was polluted. Fish and animals are disappearing from the lands of my people. There are more job opportunities for people — but some are questioning the cost.

Gord

My grandmother was a teenager in Nanjing, China, when the Japanese took over during World War II. She told my father how terrible that time was. She said she was hungry most of the time — and frightened all the time. My father says the Japanese invasion was all about economic power. Japan took the oil and iron ore and rice to expand its empire. My grandmother never got over that experience.

Ling

Your Turn

How would you respond to the question that Tom, Gord, and Ling are answering? How does economic globalization affect your life? How does it affect the decisions you make every day?

CheckBack

You read about trade as a globalizing force in Chapter 2.

The relatively free movement of money, people, information, and goods across borders has helped increase the size and economic power of transnational corporations. Some multinationals have grown so big and powerful that they are wealthier than the government of some countries.

In his book *The Work of Nations*, Robert Reich, a former secretary of labour in the United States, wrote: "We are living through a transformation that will rearrange the politics and economics of the [21st century]. There will be no national products or technologies, no national corporations, no national industries. There will no longer be national economies, at least in the way we have come to understand that concept." If transnational corporations are already wealthier than some governments, how might this affect the decision-making power of citizens?

Computers, for example, often contain parts manufactured in many countries. These parts may be assembled in yet another country, and the finished computers may be sold in a dozen more countries. This means that the countries involved in this process, especially those with weaker economies, depend on the smooth operation of economic globalization.

Some people argue that this interdependence creates instability because a crisis in one country — whether it is caused by civil strife, an outbreak of mad cow disease, or a strike — can become a serious global economic problem that can lead to job losses, factory closures, and unemployment in many other countries. But many people argue that, at the same time, stability is increased because countries that trade with one another are unlikely to go to war.

In your notebook, write one more idea that could be added to each connection in the mind map in Figure 9-5.

FYI

Comparing corporate income with countries' gross national product — the value of all goods and services produced by the residents of a country, no matter where they perform their economic activity — shows that 51 of the world's top 100 economies are corporations. Wal-Mart, for example, is bigger than Indonesia, and General Motors is about the same size as Ireland, New Zealand, and Hungary combined.

Figure 9-5 **Factors That Affect the Global Economy**

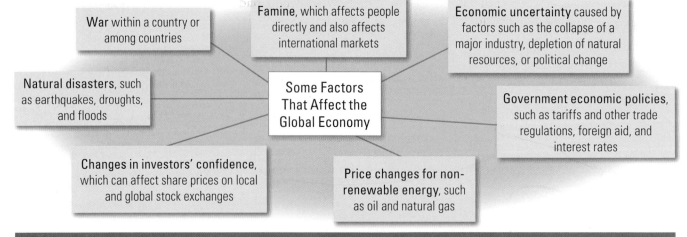

REFLECT AND RESPOND

In a speech on democracy and globalization, Canadian philosopher John Ralston Saul said,

> You'll hear it on a regular basis . . . as part of this argument that "people who trade with each other don't fight each other," and you've all heard this. It's a central argument of the last 25 years.
>
> And yet you look at the history of the British Empire and you discover that the whole core idea of the British Empire was you move in and start trading and then, when you're

not getting what you want in trade, you go in and beat the hell out of them. It's trade which led to the construction of the British and the French and the German and the Italian empires.

Think about the situation in the world today and about what you learned in earlier chapters about historical globalization. Do you agree with Ralston Saul, or do you believe that global trade reduces the likelihood of violence? Explain the reasons for your ideas.

HOW DID 20TH-CENTURY WORLD EVENTS SHAPE CONTEMPORARY ECONOMIC GLOBALIZATION?

In 1914, European empires controlled great wealth, vast territories, and the lives of millions of people around the world. Britain alone ruled about one-quarter of the world's population. The imperialists' trade arrangements with one another and with their colonies were complex and interdependent and had led to a massive increase in the production of goods.

The imperial powers wanted to protect — or expand — their colonies and trade. Colonies were still needed as a source of raw materials and a market for goods manufactured in the home country. Along with other factors, this competition led to World War I, which pitted Britain, France, and Russia against Germany and Austria-Hungary. Other countries, as well as the colonies of the imperial powers, were also drawn into the conflict.

Think about how important imperial trade arrangements were to countries like Canada in 1914. How would disturbing these arrangements affect the lives and prosperity of people in 1914? How might similar disturbances today affect your life and prosperity?

The Costs of World War I

About 15 million soldiers and civilians were killed during World War I. Canada, for example, lost more than 66 000 soldiers, many of them in their late teens and early 20s. Many more Canadian, French, Russian, British, Australian, German, South African, and Indian soldiers experienced horrors that scarred them for the rest of their lives. Early in the war, people had expected a quick victory. Instead, soldiers spent years in France — living in muddy, rat-infested trenches under the constant threat of bombardment, machine-gun fire, and poison gas.

The economic costs of the war were also high. European cities, towns, farms, roads, factories, ports, ships, and railways had been destroyed. Many European governments had borrowed heavily from the United States, and by 1918, they owed more than $7 billion (U.S.). Their economies were devastated.

In 1919, world production of manufactured goods was more than 25 per cent lower than it had been in 1913. In Russia, production had dropped by 80 per cent. After the war, many countries restricted international trade while they tried to rebuild.

Figure 9-6 **World Events, 1914–1945**

1914
World War I begins in Europe

1917
Revolution and civil war begin in Russia

1918
World War I ends

1922
Civil war ends in Russia with the Communist Party in control

1929
Great Depression begins when stock markets crash in major cities

1939
World War II begins in Europe

1939–1941
Great Depression ends in various countries

1941
World War II expands to Asia when Japanese forces bomb Pearl Harbor and capture Hong Kong

1945
World War II ends with the surrender of Germany and Japan

Figure 9-7 British artist John Singer Sargent painted this huge canvas titled *Gassed*. It shows lines of soldiers who have been blinded by poison gas being led to hospital tents and dressing stations. Lying on the ground are other soldiers waiting for treatment.

The costs of peace

The Treaty of Versailles, which was signed after World War I ended, was supposed to ensure peace and prevent another global war. But the negotiators at the peace conference imposed harsh conditions on Germany in the form of **reparations** — payments for war damages in Britain, France, Russia, and other countries.

American, Canadian, and other delegates warned that the reparations were too severe. John Maynard Keynes, a member of the British delegation, said that crippling Germany and Austria with war debts would starve the people and guarantee another major war.

The peace treaty also required Germany to give up its colonies. These were divided up among other European governments and Japan — without consulting the Indigenous people who lived in the colonies.

The effects of World War I on the Canadian economy

By 1918, World War I was costing the Canadian government more than $2.5 million a day and income taxes had been temporarily introduced to help pay the costs. After the war, interest payments on the country's war debt totalled $164 million a year and soldiers' pensions cost another $76 million a year. As a result, income tax became a permanent feature of Canadian life.

During the war, the need for soldiers, nurses, and farm and factory workers had led to a shortage of workers. This changed after the war as soldiers returned home and weapon manufacturing stopped. As a result, unemployment rose.

The Russian Revolution

In 1914, Russia was ruled by Czar Nicholas II. The Russian empire covered one-sixth of the earth's surface and included nearly 150 million people of more than 100 different nationalities. The czar was as an absolute monarch who completely controlled the country and its people.

Russian peasants lived difficult lives under an ancient economic system that allowed them little control over their labour or property. Industrialization in Russia lagged far behind that of Western Europe and North America, and workers struggled to survive.

When World War I started, Russian soldiers had poor weapons and leadership. They were defeated in battle after battle. Nearly four million Russian soldiers were killed, wounded, or taken prisoner in the first year of the war.

Figure 9-8 The three chief negotiators at the peace conference in France in 1919 were British prime minister David Lloyd George (left), French premier Georges Clemenceau (centre), and American president Woodrow Wilson (right).

Figure 9-9 The photograph on the left shows a Russian peasant village in 1891, while the picture on the right shows one of the palaces of the Russian czars, or rulers. Though many Russian peasants lived on the edge of starvation, Czar Nicholas II and his family lived in great luxury. How might this class distinction have contributed to the Russian people's demands for greater security and prosperity?

To what extent does globalization contribute to sustainable prosperity for all people? • *MHR*

Throughout Russia, food and fuel shortages became common. Workers rebelled, demanding better wages and working conditions. When peasants and deserting soldiers joined the rebellion, the Russian economy shut down. Nicholas II was forced to give up his throne in 1917 — and he and his family were murdered in 1918.

Russia was torn apart by civil war until 1922. Transportation systems broke down, and food could not be shipped to the cities. People starved. Between 1920 and 1922, a drought and famine killed at least five million people.

Communist Russia

In 1922, the Union of Soviet Socialist Republics emerged out of the former Russia. The USSR, or Soviet Union, was the world's first communist state. **Communism** was a new economic and political model that was supposed to get rid of class distinctions. From the beginning, communism opposed capitalism and capitalist countries such as the United States. In the USSR, land and other property were to belong to everyone. Everyone would work for the benefit of all and would receive help as he or she needed it.

The Soviet Union became a one-party state. The Communist Party controlled the government and the economy — farming, industry, and transportation. And by 1929, the people were again under the control of an absolute ruler. The dictator Joseph Stalin transformed the country's economy and made the Soviet Union into an industrial and military giant.

Stalin set production schedules for farms and industries. Hundreds of thousands of peasants were forced to work in factories or mines or on construction sites. Farmers were forced to grow grain on collective farms — farms that were operated by workers as a group — and to turn their grain over to the central government. By 1939, 95 per cent of farms in the USSR were collectives.

The government exported farm products to raise money for industrial and military spending. During the famine of 1932, for example, millions of people died, but the government still exported more than two million tonnes of grain.

Many historians believe that the people of the Soviet Union were worse off under Stalin than under the czars. Select the main evidence you think these historians would cite to support their position.

VOICES

The history of old Russia consisted, amongst other things, in her being beaten continually for her backwardness . . . We are 50 or a hundred years behind the advanced countries. We must make good this distance in 10 years. Either we do it, or we shall be crushed.

— *Joseph Stalin, Communist Party leader and president of the USSR, in* Pravda, *February 5, 1931*

Figure 9-10 **Soviet Union, 1922**

Lithuanian SSR
Finland
Poland
Estonian SSR
Latvian SSR
Belorussian SSR
☆ Moscow
Moldavian SSR
Ukraine SSR
Arctic Ocean
Pacific Ocean

Russian Soviet Federated Republic

Georgian SSR
Kazakhstan SSR
Azerbaijan SSR
China
Japan
Armenian SSR
Turkmen SSR
Uzbek SSR
Mongolia
Kirghiz SSR
Iran
Tajik SSR

Legend
☆ Capital
USSR in 1922
New Republics 1923–1940

0 500 1000 1500
kilometres

The Great Depression

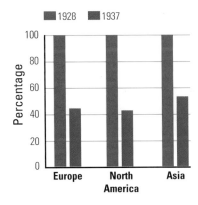

Figure 9-11 **Decline in Exports in Selected Areas**

During the late 1920s, many countries, including Canada, experienced an economic boom. Unemployment was low, and on stock exchanges — places where people buy and sell shares in publicly traded companies — the price of shares had been rising. Investors were confident. They believed that prices would continue going up and they would be able to sell their shares at a profit.

But on the New York Stock Exchange, share prices had started going down. And on Tuesday, October 29 — a day known as Black Tuesday — some worried investors started selling. This started a panic, and share prices plummeted. The downward slide turned into a crash.

The crash started a chain reaction. Many people who had lost money could no longer pay their bills. Those who had borrowed money could not repay loans — and those who were owed money could not collect.

This meant that many people had less money to spend on consumer goods — and this reduced demand. Many companies laid off workers, and some even closed their doors for good. Unemployment rose, reducing demand even more, causing even more production cuts and throwing even more people out of work. Gradually, the entire world moved into an **economic depression** — the Great Depression.

To try to protect their own industries, many countries threw up trade barriers, including tariffs on imports. As a result, international trade declined and even more people lost their jobs.

Examine the data on the bar graphs in Figures 9-11 and 9-12. Create a diagram that shows the chain reaction caused by the stock market crash.

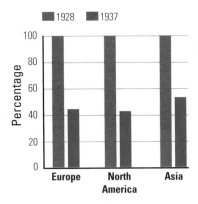

Figure 9-12 **Decline in Imports in Selected Areas**

The Great Depression in Canada

Between 1929 and 1933, Canadian exports fell by 50 per cent. By 1933, 26.6 per cent of Canadians were out of work — and the salaries of many of those who still had jobs had been cut.

Some Prairie communities suffered greatly. The price of grain fell steadily after 1929. In addition, a drought that had started in 1928 continued off and on until 1937. Topsoil blew away, and in some areas, grasshoppers flourished. These insects ate much of the little grain some farmers were able to grow.

Examine the bar graph in Figure 9-13. In Québec and Ontario, annual income per person dropped by about 45 per cent, but in Saskatchewan and Alberta, it dropped by more than 70 per cent. What do you think might explain this big difference?

Figure 9-13 **Decline in Average Annual Incomes in Canada, 1928–1933**

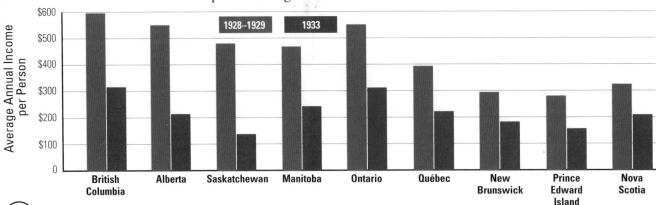

To what extent does globalization contribute to sustainable prosperity for all people? • MHR

World War II

The Great Depression hit especially hard in Germany, which was struggling to make reparation payments for World War I. Adolf Hitler and the Nazi Party promised to fix things, and in 1933, he was elected leader. He immediately dissolved the German parliament and declared himself führer, or absolute ruler.

Hitler was popular, and he convinced many Germans that they belonged to a master race that was entitled to rule other people. German forces took over the Rhineland, Austria, and Czechoslovakia — and on September 1, 1939, they invaded Poland. In response, Britain, France, Australia, New Zealand, and Canada declared war. The United States entered the war on the side of Britain and its allies when Japan attacked Pearl Harbor in 1941.

More than 50 countries and colonies were drawn into the war. More than 60 million people, both military and civilian, died. The countries that suffered the most were those where the war was actually fought. In Germany, 3.5 million people died; in China, estimates of the dead range between 1.3 million and 10 million; and in the USSR, an estimated 7 to 9 million died.

In the German death camps, the death toll is estimated to have been between 10 and 26 million people: Jews, Poles, Czechs, Greeks, Roma, Serbs, Ukrainians, and Russians, as well as homosexuals, people with mental and physical disabilities, trade unionists, prisoners of war, and Jehovah's Witnesses.

World War II in Canada

About 42 000 Canadians died in the fighting during World War II. Another 54 000 were wounded physically or psychologically. In one single disastrous raid on Dieppe, France, 882 Canadian soldiers were killed, 587 were wounded, and 1874 were taken prisoner.

The war had short- and long-term effects on the economic lives of Canadians. During the war, government spending increased and the manufacture of arms, airplanes, and ships rose. Farming became more mechanized. Unemployment fell, and more than a million women joined the workforce, many for the first time. From 1939 to 1941, employment in Canada's manufacturing sector rose by 50 per cent. By the end of the war, less than one per cent of Canadians were unemployed.

FYI

To try to pay its war reparations, the German government printed huge amounts of money. As a result, marks — German money — became almost worthless. In 1918, a loaf of bread cost two marks. By 1924, a loaf cost six million marks. People struggled to survive.

Figure 9-14 In the raid on Dieppe, France, 29-year-old Lieutenant Colonel Dollard Ménard of the Fusiliers Mont-Royal led 584 men onto the beach; 513 were killed. Ménard said of that day: "We had no cover. We couldn't dig in the pebbles — it was just like trying to make a hole in the water. You just can't do it. We were in a cross-fire from the two high sides of the beach and a frontal fire which covered the whole beach. We couldn't walk back, we couldn't get forward, we couldn't go on the sides. We were dead, really, before dying."

REFLECT AND RESPOND

Many events in the first half of the 20th century helped shape contemporary economic globalization. List three criteria you might use to judge which event had the most significant influence on contemporary globalization. Then choose the event that best meets your criteria and explain how it does this.

DECISION MAKING AND PROBLEM SOLVING FOCUS ON SKILLS

You make decisions every day. Some decisions deal with simple problems and have short-term effects. These decisions might include what to eat for lunch or how to spend an hour of free time. Other decisions deal with complex problems and have long-term effects — on your life and on the lives of people in your community.

At the end of World War II, people everywhere faced complex economic problems. In countries where fighting had taken place, governments had to find a way to rebuild ruined cities, railways, roads, homes, hospitals, shipyards, factories, and farms.

Although Canada did not need to rebuild destroyed cities, the federal government had gone into debt to support the war effort. For six years, Canadians had put up with shortages, and after the war, they wanted to return to normal life.

When the war was over, the government faced many new expenses, such as paying pensions to wounded soldiers. In addition, an unemployment insurance program had been established in 1941, and a family allowance program had been set up in 1944. The family allowance program guaranteed a monthly payment to all families with children.

Imagine that it is 1946 and the federal government has asked you, and all Canadians, to respond to this question: Should the government use taxpayers' money to help people in war-torn countries rebuild their ruined communities?

Steps to Decision Making and Problem Solving

Step 1: Consider the issues that underlie the question

Work with a partner to discuss answers to this question:

- What issues does the question raise?

Some countries, for example, do not have the money to rebuild cities and infrastructure, so this is an economic issue. And the Canadian government has only so much money to spend. If money goes to help people in Britain, Poland, or Japan, there might not be enough to help Canadians. This is a global citizenship issue.

Consider the issue from different angles (e.g., political, economic, social, and ethical). Make notes about these.

Step 2: Consider the complexities of the decision

Consider questions that you need answered before making a decision (e.g., How much financial aid is the government planning to give to other countries? What percentage of the annual budget might be used in this way? How can Canadians make sure that their money is spent appropriately?).

Use a graphic organizer like the one shown on the following page to summarize your arguments for and against. Some examples have been filled in for you. You can also add your questions. Do not try to reach a decision just yet.

Step 3: Consider possible consequences and make your decision

Before completing this step, you may wish to review the Focus on Skills feature in Chapter 4: Predicting Likely Outcomes. This will help you consider the possible consequences of your decision.

With your partner, join one or two other pairs. Discuss your arguments for and against offering help to war-torn countries. After this discussion, you may wish to add more arguments to your chart.

Once you have considered the consequences for Canadians and for people in the war-torn countries, come to a decision and explain why your decision will help resolve the problem facing the world. Be prepared to respond to the arguments of people who have come to a different decision.

Summing up

As you continue to explore issues that arise from economic globalization, you may wish to reconsider your decision or apply new ideas and new strategies to the decision-making process.

Decision-Making Graphic Organizer

Question: Should the government use taxpayers' money to help people in war-torn countries rebuild ruined communities?

Arguments for	Arguments against
If Canadians don't help, the ordinary people in the country will continue to suffer. That's not fair because they didn't start the war or hurt anyone. If Canadians don't help and the situation keeps getting worse, then someone like Hitler may come along and convince people in war-torn countries that he can help them. This could start another world war.	If the Canadian government gives money to help people in other countries, there may not be enough to take care of wounded Canadian soldiers who are coming home. (Question for the government: How will the government balance the financial needs of Canadians and the needs of the people in war-torn countries?) Canadians did without many things during the war. It's about time they had a chance to see some prosperity in their own country.

My Decision

Reasons for My Decision

WHAT FACTORS LAID THE FOUNDATIONS OF CONTEMPORARY GLOBAL ECONOMICS?

Even before the end of World War II, people knew they had to find a way of avoiding another similar global conflict. As a result, representatives of Britain, the United States, Canada, and other countries worked together to build an organization that would

- support people who wanted to choose their own government
- help countries co-operate on trade issues
- protect smaller countries against invasion by larger countries
- ensure that no single country controlled the world's oceans

The organization they built was the United Nations. The UN charter opens with these words: "We the peoples of the United Nations, determined to save succeeding generations from the scourge of war, which twice in our lifetime has brought untold sorrow to mankind . . . do hereby establish an international organization to be known as the United Nations."

In many countries around the world, people faced the task of rebuilding their lives and their prosperity. Stalingrad, Warsaw, Hamburg, Dresden, Hiroshima, Nagasaki, and other cities were in ruins. Refugees and survivors of the Nazi death camps were searching for safe homes. The war had cost more than $2 trillion. People wanted a chance to rebuild their lives on a secure economic basis.

Figure 9-15 During World War II, both sides bombed cities. Dresden, Germany (left), was destroyed by the British air force. Warsaw, Poland (right), was destroyed by the German air force. What would the consequences have been for the survivors of this destruction? How could people return to prosperity when their cities were in ruins?

The United Nations Monetary and Financial Conference at Bretton Woods

In July 1944, representatives of 44 countries met in the small New Hampshire town of Bretton Woods for a conference sponsored by the newly founded United Nations. World War II was not yet over — and would not end in Europe for another 10 months and in the Pacific for another 13 months. But conference delegates were already trying to figure out how they could prevent the kind of economic turmoil that could lead to another world war.

If you had been a young child during World War I, had grown to adulthood during the Great Depression, and had served in World War II, how important do you think security would be to you? If you had been asked in 1944 to try to set up a system that ensured prosperity and encouraged countries to co-operate with one another, what would you have suggested?

VOICES

There has never been such a far-reaching proposal on so great a scale to provide employment in the present and increase productivity in the future. And I doubt if the world understands how big a thing we are bringing to birth.

— *John Maynard Keynes, economist, speaking at the end of the Bretton Woods Conference, July 1944*

John Maynard Keynes and Government Involvement in the Economy

John Maynard Keynes, the British economist who had warned that the peace treaty that ended World War I was doomed to fail, led the British delegation at Bretton Woods.

Keynes believed that the unrestricted capitalism that had existed before World War I and between the two world wars had failed. He said that the collapse of global trade, the worldwide unemployment of the Great Depression, and the worst wars in history proved that the idea of the government's playing a very limited role in a country's economy was wrong.

Keynes believed, for example, that when a business laid off workers because there was no market for its goods or services — as had happened during the Great Depression — governments should set up programs to hire the unemployed. He said that ensuring that people had money to spend would generate demand. Businesses would then need to rehire laid-off workers to produce more goods and services.

Figure 9-16 John Maynard Keynes (left) and Friedrich Hayek became two of the most influential economists of the 20th century. Keynes's views influenced world economies after World War II. Hayek's influence came later, when British prime minister Margaret Thatcher and American president Ronald Regan adopted his approach in the 1980s.

Friedrich Hayek and Government Non-Involvement in the Economy

Friedrich Hayek disagreed with Keynes's views on the economic role of government. Hayek mistrusted government control, whether this was complete control, like that in the Soviet Union, or the partial control exercised by Western governments after World War II.

According to Hayek, a government should protect the market by ensuring that its rules and laws do not interfere with competition between businesses. He believed that competition and the market would keep an economy healthy, and that government should stay out of the way. How do you think Hayek's ideas might influence quality of life and prosperity?

The World Bank and the International Monetary Fund

The World Bank — also called the International Bank for Reconstruction and Development — and the International Monetary Fund, or IMF, were mapped out at the Bretton Woods meetings. These two organizations would be supported by the United Nations and would help expand international trade. Conference delegates hoped that persuading countries to agree on rules would not only get international trade working again, but also avoid the kind of conflict that might lead to another world war.

Both the World Bank and the International Monetary Fund maintain web sites for students. Why do you think these organizations dedicate sites to this target audience? What purpose do you think these web sites are intended to serve? After visiting these sites, do you think they achieve their goals?

Web Connection

To find out more about the World Bank, the International Monetary Fund, and contemporary economic globalization, go to this web site and follow the links.

www.ExploringGlobalization.ca

World Bank

Head of the bank is appointed by the U.S. government

Owned by the governments of its members, which provide its funds

Original Goals
- To lend money to help war-torn countries rebuild
- To speed up economic progress and industrialization in countries
- To help countries develop their natural resources
- To negotiate long-term loans to increase productivity in countries

Current Goals
- To increase growth and reduce poverty in developing countries
- To fund specific infrastructure projects

Both WB and IMF

- Headquartered in Washington, D.C.
- 29 member countries in 1945 and 185 member countries in 2006
- Established by international treaty to help countries in economic trouble
- Under the control of the UN

Purpose
- To help countries get back on a stable financial footing after World War II
- To agree on rules about how countries deal with monetary affairs
- To govern international trade and finance

International Monetary Fund

Head of IMF is nominated by the European Union; has a board of 24 executive directors

Funded by member countries, which pay a quota based on their wealth — countries that contribute more money have more votes

Original Goals
- To set dependable international exchange rates for world currencies
- To establish international economic stability and promote foreign trade

Current Goals
- To provide emergency short-term loans to countries
- To demand reforms in a country to promote good governance and get rid of corruption

Figure 9-17 **The World Bank and the International Monetary Fund: A Comparison**

Supporters of the World Bank and IMF say that these organizations have helped stabilize the global economy and brought prosperity to many countries. But critics say that they have become too influential and that their help, especially in developing countries, comes at too high a cost. When the IMF lends money to countries, for example, it may order the government to reduce spending.

General Agreement on Tariffs and Trade

At Bretton Woods, some countries agreed to work together to establish trade rules. This led to the General Agreement on Tariffs and Trade — GATT — which was signed in 1947. GATT members agreed to gradually eliminate tariffs and other trade barriers between themselves. Over the following decades, GATT representatives met many more times to lower tariffs and make trade freer.

The World Trade Organization emerged from the GATT in 1995. By 2007, the WTO was regulating trade in services, such as telecommunications and banking, as well as goods. It had also set rules to protect copyright and intellectual property, which refers to products of the mind or intellect, such as slogans, industrial designs, communication technologies, and patents on drugs.

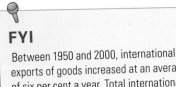

FYI

Between 1950 and 2000, international exports of goods increased at an average of six per cent a year. Total international trade in 2000 was 22 times higher than it was in 1950.

To what extent does globalization contribute to sustainable prosperity for all people? • *MHR*

The World Bank and IMF give structural-adjustment loans to developing countries on the condition that those countries carry out specified economic reforms. These reforms may include changing social policies, lowering trade barriers, and reducing government spending. Debate rages over the effectiveness of these conditions. Do they help decrease poverty and improve development? Or do they disrupt social programs and increase poverty? Here is how three people or organizations have responded to these questions.

JOSEPH STIGLITZ, a Nobel Prize–winning economist and former senior vice-president of the World Bank, told *The New York Times Magazine* that the structural-adjustment policy forces countries to take a back seat in decision making.

[The IMF] undermines the democratic process, because it dictates policies. When [South] Korea needed money, it was told, "Only if you open up your markets faster than had been agreed upon and only if you have a central bank independent and focused exclusively on inflation." In the United States, the Federal Reserve Board focuses on inflation, employment and growth. And yet the IMF gave Korea no choice. It's not only that I think it's bad economic policy, but I think those are the kinds of things that countries should decide for themselves.

DAVID D. DRISCOLL, works for the IMF and writes articles explaining its policies, as well as those of the World Bank.

The main objective of structural-adjustment lending is to restructure a developing country's economy as the best basis for sustained economic growth. Loans support programs that are intended to anticipate and avert economic crises through economic reforms and changes in investment priorities. By using so-called policy-based lending, the Bank stimulates economic growth in heavily indebted countries – particularly in Latin America and in sub-Saharan Africa – that are undertaking, often at much social pain, far-reaching programs of economic adjustment.

STEPHEN LEWIS, a Canadian and former NDP politician, was the United Nations special envoy for HIV/AIDS in Africa from 2001 to 2006.

There is a definite connection [between poverty and structural-adjustment programs] in the sense that structural-adjustment programs clearly impoverish countries and clearly have a devastating effect on the social sectors, particularly health, nutrition, education, water, and sanitation. So all of the elements of a society which expose poor people to risk – when you go to a school, you have to pay – all of it [was] imposed by the international financial institutions.

Explorations

1. With the comments you have just read in mind, explain what structural-adjustment loans might mean to people in a country where access to schools, health care, and employment is already limited. Should World Bank and IMF officials have the right to place conditions on these loans? Or should these loans be offered with no strings attached? Explain the reasons for your response.

2. Which speaker or writer do you think makes the most persuasive argument for his point of view? What criteria did you use to make this judgment?

3. Do the World Bank and IMF reduce poverty and improve economic development opportunities for people who are affected by these conditional loans? Explain the reasons for your answer.

Changing the Foundations of Economic Globalization

In the years after World War II, the United States and the Soviet Union became economic and military superpowers. The U.S. had a capitalist economic system and a democratic government. The Soviet Union had a communist economic system and a central government that was run as a dictatorship. These differences were a source of friction between the two — and the countries of the world lined up with one side or the other.

Although the superpowers battled for global influence and power, this conflict never erupted into open military warfare. As a result, this era became known as the Cold War.

The Cold War interfered with global trade. The IMF, the World Bank, and the GATT were unable to resolve the issues that divided communist and non-communist countries. But the Bretton Woods version of economic globalization needed open borders, free communication, and access to world markets.

During the 1980s, people in various communist countries struggled to throw off Soviet control, and in 1989, the Soviet Union began to collapse. The destruction of the Berlin Wall, which had separated capitalist, democratic West Berlin from communist East Berlin, became an enduring symbol of the fall of the Soviet Union and communist control in Eastern Europe.

When the Berlin Wall was torn down in 1989, East and West Berliners were united again in a single city. What role do you think globalization played in bringing down the Berlin Wall?

Figure 9-18 In November 1989, Berliners celebrated the destruction of the wall that had divided their city — and Germany — since the end of World War II. West Germany was an ally of the United States and East Germany was under the control of the Soviet Union. How do you think this might have affected the lives of Berliners before 1989?

FYI

In 1975, 8 per cent of the world's economies were capitalist and the value of foreign trade was $23 billion (U.S.). After the Cold War ended, 28 per cent of economies were capitalist and the value of foreign trade had grown to $644 billion (U.S.).

Figure 9-19 Today, Russians and international visitors can buy directly from sellers competing with one another in an open market. Outdoor markets, like this one in Moscow, sell everything from books and household items to souvenir chess sets, military hats, and religious icons. How are markets like this evidence of contemporary economic globalization?

Changing national economies

By the 1970s, some governments were spending so much on expanding their economy that they had built up huge debts. In addition, inflation was rising, and so was unemployment. But according to Keynes's theories, these things were not supposed to happen at the same time. In this new economic environment, the views of Hayek and his student and colleague Milton Friedman started to gain support. Some people began to embrace the idea that markets, not the government, should control a country's economy. By 1974, Hayek's ideas had become so popular that he shared the Nobel Prize in Economics. Friedman won the award two years later.

To what extent does globalization contribute to sustainable prosperity for all people? • MHR

Moving toward a market economy

Hayek and Friedman believed that less government intervention and freer markets would generate economic health and prosperity. Friedman's theories began to influence British prime minister Margaret Thatcher and U.S. president Ronald Reagan.

As a result, Britain and the U.S. began to move toward a **market economy** in which individuals were freer to make their own decisions with little intervention from the government — and where resources are the private property of individuals or companies. Others, however, were critical of Hayek's and Friedman's theories.

The debate between the two differing economic visions continues to reverberate in the world today. Canada, for example, has continued to maintain a mixed economy in which both the public and the private sectors play a significant role. Some resources are privately owned, but others are publicly owned. Many other countries follow a similar model.

FYI

The Index of Economic Freedom calculates a country's position on a list that measures business freedom, trade freedom, and freedom from government interference. According to the 2007 index, Hong Kong has the most economic freedom. Canada ranked 10th, after Switzerland. The country with the least economic freedom is North Korea.

PROFILE

MILTON FRIEDMAN — PROMOTING FREE MARKETS

PROFILE PROFILE PROFILE PROFILE

Supporters of Milton Friedman's views have called him the most influential economist of the second half of the 20th century. As a young man, Friedman supported the theories of John Maynard Keynes. But he changed his mind in the 1950s and eventually spearheaded the opposition to Keynes. Friedman became the chief spokesperson of a group of economists that became known as the Chicago School, after the University of Chicago, where he taught.

Friedman believed that everyone would experience greater prosperity, as well as more political and social freedom, if there was less government control and freer markets. He believed that communism and socialism represented the extreme of government control. At the other extreme, he said, people were free to make their own choices with a minimum of government control.

In Friedman's view, the system that would give people the greatest political and economic freedom — to buy from whomever they wanted, to sell to whomever they wanted, and to work for whomever they wanted — was the system that also provided the best chance of achieving prosperity.

In tough economic times, Friedman said, people should not expect to rely on government help. He believed that it was not the government's role to support people through hard times; rather, he said, people would be better off if they learned to adapt to changes in the market and in the demand for their goods and services.

Figure 9-20 The son of immigrants from Austria-Hungary, Milton Friedman was born in Brooklyn, New York, in 1912. While at university, he began his lifelong study of economics, and in 1976, he won the Nobel Prize in Economics.

ECONOMIC GLOBALIZATION IN THE PEOPLE'S REPUBLIC OF CHINA

In 1949, Mao Zedong and the Communist Party won a civil war that had engulfed China since the 1920s. This conflict had continued through World War II and the Japanese occupation of the country. When he took power, Mao announced to the Chinese people: "Fellow-countrymen, the founding of the People's Republic of China is proclaimed, and the Chinese people now have their own Central Government. In accordance with the Common Program, the government will exercise the people's democratic dictatorship over the length and breadth of China."

Figure 9-21 **China**

Dashed Hopes

For centuries, China's large peasant population had suffered under the harsh rule of warlords and landlords. As a result, many people enthusiastically supported Mao and his long struggle to take over the country.

Mao and the Chinese communists began the huge task of transforming China from an agricultural society into a modern industrial country. As Russian communists had done in the Soviet Union nearly 30 years earlier, Chinese communists nationalized businesses, established collective farms, and began to develop industries. They also established health care facilities and schools in rural areas.

For many reasons, most of these changes failed. The collective farms — poorly run and economically unsound — were a disaster. Tens of millions of people died of starvation. In addition, many of the industries either failed or were kept going only because the central government supported them.

Reforming the Economy

Mao died in 1976, and by 1978, a reform-minded leader, Deng Xiaoping, had won control of the government.

Deng brought in market-oriented economic changes and remained a major force in reforming China's economy during the 1980s and 1990s.

Though China continued to be a one-party state with a centrally planned economy, some private ownership of property and entrepreneurship were allowed. Farmers continued to turn over part of their earnings to the state, but they were also able to sell some produce privately and keep the profits. Collective farms were closed. Farm production increased, and many farm families became more prosperous.

China also became more open to foreign trade and investment. By the mid 1980s, more elements of a market economy were starting to appear, though the country was still under the control of the central government. Still, some businesses and industries were allowed to keep some of their profits, and others were set up to export products.

Deng dismissed complaints that China was moving away from its communist principles. He explained that a market economy did not have to be capitalist: "Socialism has markets too. Plans and markets are simply stepping stones . . . to universal prosperity and riches."

Taking Part in Global Trade

In the years right after the revolution, China remained largely closed to international trade. But by 2005, World Trade Organization statistics showed that China had become the third-largest importer and exporter in the world. Only the United States and the European Union imported and exported more. By 2006, China had the fastest-growing — and the second-largest — economy in the world.

According to Statistics Canada, China is the fourth-largest importer of Canadian goods in the world. Only the U.S. exports more to Canada than China does.

Figure 9-22 Canada–China Merchandise Trade, 2003–2006 (Billions of Canadian Dollars)

	2003	2004	2005	2006
Canadian Exports to China	$4.81	$6.77	$7.1	$7.66
Canadian Imports from China	$18.58	$24.1	$29.52	$34.47

Source: Statistics Canada, "Canada's Merchandise Exports and Imports, 2007"

Living in Industrial China

One effect of China's rush to develop its economy is severe air pollution. Coal is a major industrial energy source in China, which has 21 000 coal mines. The country is responsible for 90 per cent of the rise in world coal consumption in recent years. By 2009, China was expected to be the largest producer of greenhouse gases, which are a major contributor to global climate change.

Linfen, an industrial city in Shanxi Province, China's coal region, has been named one of the most polluted places on Earth. The people of Linfen suffer from respiratory illnesses caused by the coal smoke and dust from factory smokestacks.

In 2007, Geoffrey York, a Canadian journalist, wrote that pollution in Linfen is so bad that "cars turn on their headlamps in the daytime. Nobody wears a white shirt because it soon becomes grey. Half of the local drinking wells are polluted and unsafe. Elderly people stay indoors, afraid to breathe the air on the streets. Young children have grown up without ever seeing the stars at night because of the haze."

Yi Maosheng, a farmer in the region, said, "In the past, the wheat plants were very green. But now, they are covered in fine dust. The bees don't come to the flowers of the apple trees anymore."

Figure 9-23 When residents of Linfen, China, go to work in the morning, they wear masks to protect themselves from air that is polluted with coal smoke and dust.

Explorations

1. Examine the data in Figure 9-22. What do these data tell you about the balance of trade — the difference in value between imports and exports — between Canada and China? Do you think this balance of trade is healthy for Canada? For China? Explain the reasons for your answers.

2. As China's economy develops rapidly, its government believes that people must make some short-term sacrifices in the interests of economic growth. These include ignoring environmental and health concerns created by pollution.

In groups of three, discuss the problems of economic growth faced by expanding economies. Work together to suggest a balanced solution that takes into account economic growth, as well as environmental and health concerns. To help do this, you may wish to use the steps and the graphic organizer included in this chapter's Focus on Skills feature, which deals with decision making and problem solving.

1. You and two or three of your classmates are members of the cabinet of the government of Abstainia, a fictitious country that needs a large loan. Abstainia now imports food because farmers cannot produce enough to feed everyone. The loan will be used to develop new port facilities that can handle large container ships and to create a new power plant that will allow new factories to open and supply cheaper electricity to the people.

   The cabinet must decide whether to accept a structural-adjustment loan from the World Bank. The data in Figure 9-24 reflect Abstainia's current economic position.

   a) Using the steps set out in the Focus on Skills feature on pages 224 to 225, develop a decision-making process that will help you and your cabinet colleagues decide whether to accept the loan. If your group needs more information before making an informed decision, prepare and carry out a research plan. The World Bank funds some interesting cultural projects, and finding out more about these may add depth to your research. Go to this web site and follow the links: www.ExploringGlobalization.ca

Figure 9-24 **Abstainia: An Economic Snapshot**

Agricultural land available: 22%
Agricultural land in use: 9%
Population: 32 million
School-age children: 3 million
School-age children in school full-time: 1 million
Literacy: 60%
Languages: Arabic (official), English is widely spoken
Life expectancy: Male — 62; Female — 65
Annual average income: $3500 (Cdn)
Unemployment: 45%
Current government revenues: $1.8 billion (Cdn.)
Annual debt repayments if loan is taken: $0.75 billion (Cdn.)
Current expenditures including all social programs (schools, hospitals, doctors, etc.): $2.3 billion (Cdn.)

b) If you decide to accept the loan, decide on four conditions the World Bank must agree to if Abstainia is to make social and economic gains because of the loan.

c) If you decide to refuse the loan, decide on a plan to increase the number of children in school by at least 250 000 and to reduce unemployment by at least 10 per cent.

d) Whether you accept or refuse the loan, prepare a statement explaining your government's position to the World Bank.

2. With a partner, imagine that you are at the 1944 Bretton Woods conference. Think about what is going on in the world and what the delegates were trying to achieve. One of you will play the role of Friedrich Hayek or John Maynard Keynes. The other will play the role of a reporter at the conference. Then you will switch roles.

   a) Prepare one powerful question that you, as a reporter, can ask either Hayek or Keynes as he emerges from a conference session. Because you know what will happen in the decades after the conference, make your question as insightful and surprising and possible. Show your question to your partner so his or her character can prepare an answer.

   b) Prepare several follow-up questions that will enable your partner's character to delve more deeply into the issue you raise. Make notes about the answers so you can use them in the class discussion that will follow.

   c) Prepare your character's answer to your partner's questions.

      With the class, discuss the questions — and the answers. Conclude this discussion by deciding whether other questions should have been asked and why.

3. Ryokan, whose name means "good-large-heartedness" or "gentle tolerance," was a Buddhist monk and poet who lived in Japan from 1758 to 1831. In the poems on this page, Ryokan uses the begging bowl as a symbol of simplicity. He believed that owning less is the way to economic security and happiness.

Unlike Ryokan, many people today believe that expanding globalization creates a strong desire to own "things," which they believe will bring economic security and happiness.

Does your lifestyle reflect one of these positions? On a continuum like the one shown, locate your lifestyle. Is it possible to hold both views? Explain your reasoning.

Write a verse or a rap to illustrate your position. Share it with a partner, a small group, or the class.

The Way to Economic Security and Happiness

_____

Owning   Owning
less   more

Three Poems on My Begging Bowl

1
Picking violets
by the roadside
I've forgotten and left
my begging bowl –
that begging bowl of mine

2
I've forgotten
My begging bowl
But no one would steal it —
How sad for my
  begging bowl

3
In my begging bowl
Violets and
  dandelions
Jumbled together —
I offer them to the
Buddhas of the Three Worlds

Think about Your Challenge

Your challenge in this related issue is to write a persuasive essay on the extent to which globalization contributes to sustainable prosperity for all people.

You have developed criteria to use to evaluate the data you will include in your supporting paragraphs. Review these criteria in light of the ideas you explored in this chapter. On your inquiry-question cards or pages, review and complete the notes and source information that you have gathered so far. Have the ideas developed in this chapter caused you to rethink your criteria? Your position? If so, in what ways?

Chapter 10   Expanding Globalization

Figure 10-1 Cartoons can effectively focus attention on trends, people, or events. By limiting the information to a few details, the cartoonist can express a clear point of view. These cartoons are about the current trend of reducing costs by buying supplies and services in other countries.

THE POLITICAL CARTOONS on the previous page focus on one result of expanding globalization. Some businesses in developed countries have found that they can reduce costs by hiring people in less developed countries or less developed areas of their own country to do certain jobs. When you call technical support for help with new software, for example, you may end up talking to someone in India, the Philippines, or Moncton, New Brunswick. Some businesses find it cheaper to direct your call across the country or halfway around the world to people who work in places where wages are lower.

In a global economy, businesses can take advantage of cheaper suppliers in less developed parts of the world to remain competitive — sometimes at the cost of Canadian jobs.

Look again at the cartoons. What message is each cartoonist trying to send? Consider the following questions:

- Why do you suppose the cartoonist chose to draw the images in each cartoon?
- What element(s) of the issue has each cartoonist focused on?
- How do words help the visual elements deliver the message?
- How does each cartoon help you understand one point of view on expanding globalization?

Do these political cartoons add to your understanding of the effects of globalization? What would you change to make the cartoons more effective as comments on the issue of sending jobs to less developed parts of the world? What other information might you need to formulate an informed position on this issue?

KEY TERMS

outsourcing

containerization

trade liberalization

free trade

consensus

sanctions

LOOKING AHEAD

In this chapter, you will explore answers to the following questions:

- What factors contribute to expanding globalization?
- How do international agreements and organizations contribute to expanding globalization?
- How do transnational corporations contribute to expanding globalization?
- How do communication technologies contribute to expanding globalization?

My Point of View on Globalization

Review the notes you have recorded to express your understandings of globalization and think about what you have learned about whether globalization contributes to prosperity for everyone. Use words or images — or both — to express how your understandings of globalization have changed. Date your ideas and add them to the notebook, learning log, portfolio, or computer file you are keeping as you progress through this course.

WHAT FACTORS CONTRIBUTE TO EXPANDING GLOBALIZATION?

CheckBack

You learned about media convergence in Chapter 2.

Globalization creates changes in all aspects of people's lives — the kind of work they do, the food they eat, the clothes they wear, what they read, watch, and listen to, and even how they relate to the physical environment. **Outsourcing** — reducing costs by using suppliers of products and services in less developed parts of the world — is one of the changes that affects the work people do.

Communication Technologies

Innovations in communication technologies have changed the world. When the printing press, for example, was developed, it enabled people to share ideas and information much more easily. But this innovation spread across Europe relatively slowly — it took 20 years for the number of presses to reach 100. Today, communication technologies are changing so quickly that the rate of change has become far faster than ever before. Cellphones, television, radio, computers, and the Internet have come to affect nearly every aspect of people's lives.

Technological convergence is also increasing the rate of globalization. Cellphones, for example, take photographs, make short videos, store hundreds of recordings, function as personal organizers, capture updates on the latest sports scores via the Internet, send e-mails — and still allow you to make phone calls to others.

Convergence also brings together media companies. Today, a newspaper, a textbook publisher, a phone company, a TV network, and a movie production company may all be owned by a single transnational corporation.

Consider the communication technologies you use. Create a three-column chart. In the first column, list the technology (e.g., cellphone). In the second column, list ways the technology has changed over the past 5 to 10 years. In the third column, predict how you think the technology will change in the future and how it might contribute to expanding globalization. With a partner, discuss the similarities and differences in your predictions.

Figure 10-2 Telephones have changed a great deal since they first came into widespread use in the early 20th century. As recently as the 1960s and 1970s, many people, especially in rural areas, still used rotary-dial phones. Telephone technology in 2007 allows small, lightweight devices, such as the Apple iPhone, to combine products such as a mobile phone, an MP3 player with touch controls, and an Internet communication medium with e-mail, Web browsing, and Web searching.

Trade

Technology plays an important role in the expansion of global trade. Today, a typical consumer product is designed, developed, manufactured, and assembled by a host of companies, which may be located practically anywhere in the world. Cars and computers, for example, are often assembled only after they have been ordered by customers. Examine a piece of new technology, such as a cellphone or computer. Can you see where it was designed? Where its parts were made? Where it was assembled? Do you think that you, as a customer, should be entitled to know these things?

This expansion of trade has occurred because countries have opened their economies to outside influences. Governments have allowed foreign products and investment to enter their country. In exchange, businesses and industries in the country have opportunities to sell their goods in international markets.

Examine Figure 10-3 on this page. Some of the steps in this process are already under way. Who do you think will benefit from these changes? What might be some of the benefits? Who will not benefit from these changes? What might be some of the drawbacks? Do you think the benefits outweigh the drawbacks — or vice versa?

Web Connection

To learn more about how the government of Canada is promoting world trade and helping businesses make connections, go to this web site and following the links.

www.ExploringGlobalization.ca

Figure 10-3 **The Future of Auto Making**

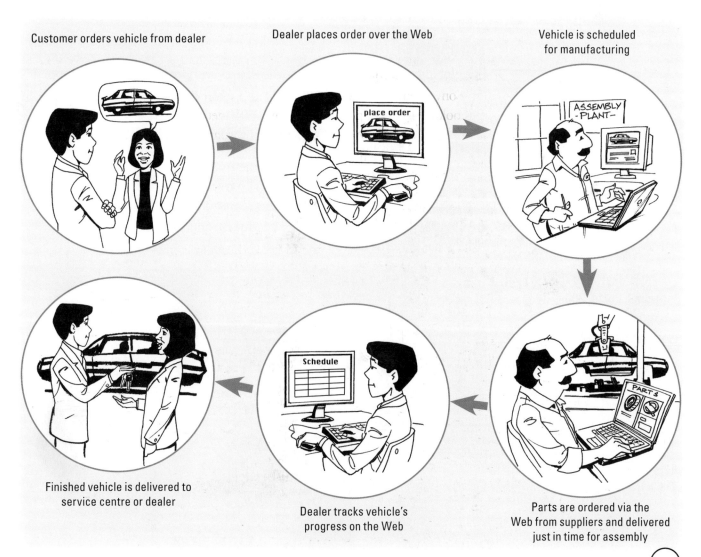

Customer orders vehicle from dealer

Dealer places order over the Web

Vehicle is scheduled for manufacturing

Finished vehicle is delivered to service centre or dealer

Dealer tracks vehicle's progress on the Web

Parts are ordered via the Web from suppliers and delivered just in time for assembly

Figure 10-4 Flow of Global Trade

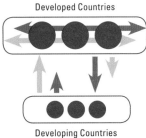

Before 1970

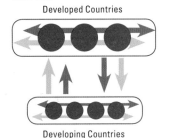

After 1970

Industrial pole | Flow of merchandise | Flow of raw materials

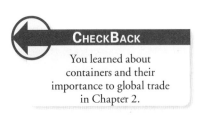

FYI

By weight, 96 per cent of world trade products is carried on ships. A large share of this trade is carried in containers.

Reshaping trade patterns

The globalization of trade has been reshaping international trade patterns since 1970. Until then, most goods and services moved between developed countries in North America, Europe, and the Asia–Pacific region, especially Japan. Developing countries supplied raw materials and bought some manufactured goods.

Today, goods and services are flowing more frequently between developing countries, particularly those that are developing quickly, such as South Korea, China, Malaysia, India, and Mexico. And more manufactured goods are also flowing out of developing countries to more developed — and wealthier — countries.

Still, exports from developed countries now make up about 75 per cent of the world's total exports. About 83 per cent of these exports are manufactured goods. Developing countries produce 25 per cent of the world's exports, with manufactured goods making up more than 56 per cent of this total. But this balance is starting to shift. The balance of trade between China and the United States, for example, has been in China's favour for several years.

Examine Figure 10-4. This diagram suggests that increased global trade has benefited developing countries. What factors do you think have encouraged this pattern?

Transportation

For globalization to operate smoothly, parts and products must be shipped cheaply and in a timely manner. The key to shipping goods more cheaply and efficiently has been **containerization** — the transporting of goods in standard-sized shipping containers. Containers of goods are shipped along clearly defined routes to large transshipment terminals at strategic locations around the world. Figure 10-5 shows the importance of ports like Hong Kong, Singapore, and New York to the movement of containers.

The unit called TEU in Figure 10-5 stands for "20-foot equivalent unit" — a container that is 6.1 metres long. But most containers today are twice this size. What patterns do you see on the map?

Figure 10-5 **Traffic at the Largest Container Ports, 2004**

CHECKBACK

You learned about containers and their importance to global trade in Chapter 2.

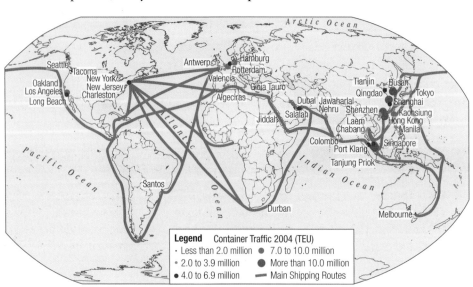

Just-in-time delivery systems

The just-in-time delivery and inventory system used today by many manufacturers means that parts are ordered and scheduled to arrive at the factory at the moment they are needed. They are shipped, unloaded from containers, and moved directly onto the factory floor. This saves handling and storage costs because parts no longer need to be kept in warehouses until they are required. How might this system enable businesses to compete more successfully?

The Media

Though the media and communication technologies are closely connected, the media play a distinct role in expanding globalization.

One way the media contribute to expanding globalization is by running commercials that encourage consumers to buy products. This expands the market for goods and services. The effect of the media becomes even stronger when celebrities — whose influence is boosted by media coverage — lend their names to product lines. Think about how you decided which brand to choose last time you went shopping. How much did ads you heard on the radio, read in magazines, or saw on TV influence your buying decisions?

A desire for these products and services also encourages consumers to support government efforts to make it easier for foreign products and services to enter a country.

Media convergence has also resulted in the commercialization of news. Former CNN correspondent Charles Bierbauer, for example, said that a war is going on in newsrooms — and it is "newsrooms versus entertainment." He said that the quest for higher ratings often dictates decisions about which news stories are covered.

Meanwhile, technological convergence has enabled people to connect in a number of ways. Cellphones, for example, allow people to learn about events and other people's ideas and thoughts, often before the mainstream media deliver the story. And if you have a cellphone, it can even make you part of the media. With devices that take pictures and record videos that can be sent to news programs or posted on social networking sites, you can contribute to local and global newsmaking.

Figure 10-6 A new line of clothing by pop star Madonna for Swedish cheap-chic retailer H&M sold out in minutes after going on sale in March 2007 — and the buying frenzy was fed by media coverage. Do you think that events like this are newsworthy and should be covered as news stories?

REFLECT AND RESPOND

Create a mind map to show how the four topics discussed in this section of the chapter contribute to expanding globalization. In the centre of the map, place this term: "Factors Contributing to Expanding Globalization." Extending outward from the centre, draw and label four branches: "Communication Technologies," "Trade," "Transportation," and "The Media." Add point-form comments at the end of each branch, then look for connections among them.

Stretching the length of the border between the United States and Mexico is a 210-kilometre strip of land known as the maquila or maquiladora zone. Maquilas, or maquiladoras, are foreign-owned factories. In Mexico, where 40 per cent of people live below the poverty line, maquiladoras provide jobs for more than a million people. But these jobs come at a cost that some people say is too high. The labourers, many of them women, work very long hours for low wages in conditions that are often difficult.

"The job is a terror," one woman told an interviewer. "The noise. The monotony. The constant danger of the machine . . . Sometimes I have a nightmare in which the machine swallows me whole. In the factory, the [assembly] line is the worst. It crushes your fingers and, in the end, your mind as well."

Pros and Cons of Maquiladoras

More than 3000 maquiladoras employ about 17 per cent of the Mexican workforce. This makes maquiladoras Mexico's second-largest source of jobs. This sector accounts for 25 per cent of the country's gross domestic product and 45 per cent of its exports.

Because of the low wages and harsh working conditions, maquiladoras are controversial. Some people defend them, saying they provide a way for Mexicans to get ahead. But others say that when companies move their operations to Mexico to take advantage of lower labour costs and looser environmental rules, they are exploiting Mexican workers and taking high-paying jobs away from workers in developed countries.

How Maquiladoras Began

The term "maquiladora" is a Latin-American Spanish word that has come to mean foreign-owned plants where goods are assembled for export to the United States.

The maquiladoras were set up under a special government program that started in 1965 and offered tax breaks to companies that located in the maquiladora zone.

In 1972, the program was expanded to include all of Mexico. Now, every Mexican state has at least one maquila. But most plants remain in the maquiladora zone to take advantage of lower transportation costs to the U.S.

About 87 per cent of maquiladoras are either directly owned branch plants of American corporations or subsidiaries of U.S. companies. Transnationals that operate maquiladoras include BMW, Volkswagen, Fisher Price, Ford, General Motors, Honda, Nissan, IBM, and Mattel.

In the past, most maquila jobs were low-wage assembly-line positions that required few skills. Low taxes and low wages meant higher profits for manufacturers. But today, new plants are being built and more jobs involve automated manufacturing, research, design, and development. And working conditions in many maquiladoras are improving.

Figure 10-7 The Maquiladora Zone

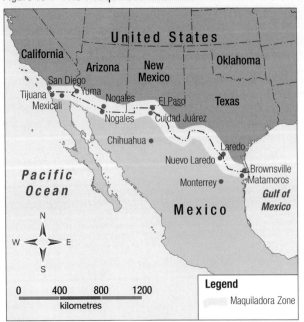

Figure 10-8 Advantages of Maquiladoras for Foreign-Owned Companies

Working Conditions and Costs	Advantages
Wages	Wages for assembly-line workers are much lower than in developed countries.
Work Week	The standard work week in Mexico is 48 hours, compared to 40 hours — or less — in the United States and Canada.
Costs	Government programs keep start-up costs and the overall costs of making goods lower than in developed countries.
Transportation	Being close to markets in the U.S. keeps transportation costs low and allows goods to be moved by rail or road.

Concerns about Workers

Most maquiladora workers are young girls and women. Employers prefer to hire women because women in developing countries generally receive lower wages. In addition, companies find that women will often tolerate worse working conditions than men. This has led critics of maquiladoras to charge that the sector exploits women.

But employers argue that maquiladora workers earn more than female workers in other parts of Mexico. They are also acquiring new skills. And the balance of the labour force is shifting — in 1980, 80 per cent of maquiladora employees were female, but this figure is now about 60 per cent.

Low wages are the key to attracting foreign companies to Mexico, so there is pressure to keep pay rates down. This means that for many workers, salaries are not high enough to meet basic needs. Estimates have suggested that some labourers must work more than four hours to earn enough money to buy four litres of milk. And most workers live in hastily built and inadequate shantytowns, often far from their home and family.

In addition, forced overtime is common, conditions are often unsafe, and some workers are younger than the minimum working age, which is 14 in Mexico.

Employment stability is also a problem. Employee turnover in some maquiladoras reaches 80 per cent because of poor working conditions. In addition, the maquiladoras act as shock absorbers for the foreign corporations that own them. When these companies face hard times, they lay off Mexican workers or close plants. Currency exchange rates can also make Mexican wages more expensive than wages in Malaysia or China, for example, and this can trigger a shifting of work out of Mexico.

Concerns about the Environment

Many maquiladoras use toxic chemicals in their operations, and these may be harmful to workers. In addition, international agreements require companies to transport their hazardous waste into the United States for disposal. But to save money, many companies simply dump it — illegally — in Mexico. Because these companies pay little in taxes and can threaten to move if their costs become too high, local governments can do little to protect the environment.

Figure 10-9 These workers at a maquiladora in Reynosa, Mexico, are packaging seat-belt components for export to the United States.

Explorations

1. Explain why maquiladoras have become an important part of expanding globalization. What do foreign companies gain? What do consumers gain?

2. Examine Figure 10-8. Based on the information it contains, what do you think Mexican workers gain from maquiladoras? Do you think the benefits of maquiladoras outweigh the costs — or vice versa? Locate your position on a continuum like the one shown. Explain the criteria for your judgment.

3. As globalization continues, what do think will happen to maquiladoras? Will this sector expand or become smaller? What will be the major forces behind this change? Explain your thinking to a classmate and work together to write a brief summary of your ideas.

Too costly _____ Highly beneficial

How do international agreements and organizations contribute to expanding globalization?

A key element in expanding globalization is reducing trade barriers so that goods and services can move around the world easily. This process is called **trade liberalization**.

To achieve this goal, countries must get rid of measures — such as tariffs, quotas, regulations, and standards — that protect and regulate businesses and industries within their borders. When two countries agree to eliminate all tariffs and taxes on goods and services traded between them, the result is **free trade.** In theory, free trade is reciprocal. Businesses and industries in both countries benefit because they can sell their goods or services in the other country. Local companies can expand into new markets. This creates jobs, uses resources, and reduces the cost of consumer goods.

Examine Figures 10-10 and 10-11, which show how liberalizing trade in clothing affected Canada and other countries. Who do you think benefited and who was harmed by this action?

FYI

Some countries have taken free trade farther by joining one another in a free-trade organization. The North American Free Trade Agreement, for example, links Canada, Mexico, and the United States in a free-trade relationship. In 1994, countries in North, Central, and South America started negotiations to extend NAFTA by uniting 34 democracies, including Canada, in a Free Trade Area of the Americas. Though efforts so far have failed, the idea remains alive.

The World Trade Organization

The World Trade Organization was established in 1995 to increase international trade by lowering trade barriers and making trade more predictable. The WTO ensures that the terms of trade agreements are followed, settles trade disputes between governments, and conducts trade negotiations. Decisions made by the WTO are binding — member countries must abide by its rulings.

The WTO officially has a one-country, one-vote system, but in practice, decisions are made by coming to a **consensus** — a general agreement. All members must support a consensus decision. Why might the WTO's members have chosen this method of making decisions? Why might a yes-or-no vote not work as well at the WTO?

Building consensus often means that it takes a long time to reach a decision, and in an effort to satisfy the concerns of everyone involved, final agreements sometimes end up using language that is open to interpretation.

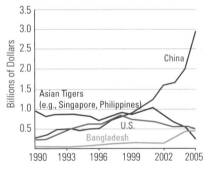

Figure 10-10 Clothing Imports to Canada, 1990–2005

Figure 10-11 Effects of Trade Liberalization on the Canadian Clothing Industry

Period	Trade Conditions	Effects
1989–1995	Canada–United States Free Trade Agreement eliminated tariffs on clothing imports and exports between the two countries.	Canadian clothing exports to the U.S. grew, as did imports from the U.S. into Canada.
1995–2002	Canada eliminated quotas on some clothing products from developing countries.	Clothing imports from developing countries grew; imports from the U.S. dropped.
2002–2005	All trade restrictions were removed from clothing imported to Canada from developing countries.	Imports from China and Bangladesh more than tripled, while imports from other developing countries and the U.S. dropped. Domestic production fell. Clothing prices in Canada declined by 5.8 per cent.

Resolving disputes at the WTO

When one member country says another member country is treating it unfairly in a trade matter, the WTO must settle the dispute. A panel of three WTO officials hears the arguments of both sides and makes a decision. The panel's decision may force one of the countries to change its laws or make a payment. The WTO has the power to use **sanctions** — economic actions, such as a trade boycott — to enforce its decisions.

In 2002, for example, Canada asked the WTO to rule on a longstanding dispute with the United States over softwood lumber. In 2006, the WTO finally ruled in Canada's favour. The decision removed American tariffs on Canadian lumber and required the U.S. to repay about 80 per cent of the more than $5 billion it had collected in tariffs on lumber imports from Canada.

Perspectives on the WTO

Those who oppose the trade liberalization that fosters globalization have targeted the WTO for criticism. They have said

- The WTO has too much power. It can force countries to change their laws and regulations to make them fit WTO rules.
- The WTO is not democratically accountable. Hearings on trade disputes are closed to the public and the media.
- The WTO does not care enough about the problems of developing countries. It has not forced rich countries to fully open their markets to products from developing countries.
- The WTO has not done enough about the environment, child labour, workers' rights, or health care.

Those who support the WTO point out that its rules were written by member states, many of which are democracies. They also say that trade improvements brought about by the WTO have raised — and will continue to raise — living standards around the world.

Do you support the work of the WTO, or do you think the criticisms of this organization are valid? Explain your answer. How could you find out more about the WTO so that your position can be better informed? With a partner, create a five-step plan that could guide an investigation of the strengths and weaknesses of the WTO.

Web Connection

The United Nations gathers statistics on all the countries of the world so that planners in organizations like the WTO can use the data to make informed decisions. To read the UN's 2005 human development report, including the chapter on trade, go to this web site and follow the links.

www.ExploringGlobalization.ca

Figure 10-12 WTO meetings attract protesters. In 2000, these people marched in Seattle, Washington, to commemorate the first anniversary of a huge protest that took place when WTO representatives met there in 1999.

Voting is a quick way of making decisions, but the result may leave those in the minority feeling left out of the decision-making process. As a result, some organizations and groups use a different process. Indigenous peoples such as the Haudenosaunee Confederacy, for example, often make decisions based on consensus, or general agreement. Consensus building is also known as collaborative problem solving.

Coming to a consensus is a group process that involves exchanging ideas, listening carefully to others, and negotiating and compromising to find a solution that everyone can live with. Achieving consensus can take longer than voting because everyone plays a role in the process and everyone's voice is heard.

Suppose your class was asked to write a collective letter to the editor of your community newspaper or add to a collective blog expressing support for, or opposition to, the WTO. Which position would you take? As a class, follow these steps to reach a consensus on the group's position.

Steps to Building Consensus

Step 1: Brainstorm

Choose someone to guide the discussion and someone to record ideas. If you are working in a small group, the discussion guide and recorder might be the same person.

Begin by brainstorming to create a list of ideas or options that should be included in the decision to support or oppose the WTO. Be sure that everyone has a chance to contribute ideas, and remember that all ideas are welcome. Do not judge the ideas at this stage — even ideas that seem silly or unrelated can inspire other helpful ideas. Set a time limit for this part of the process or stop after no new ideas have been added for a minute or two.

When you finish brainstorming, narrow down the options on your list. As a group, combine those that are similar and remove those that do not seem to fit.

Step 2: Discuss pros and cons

Think about and discuss the advantages and disadvantages of each option. Make sure everyone has an opportunity to contribute opinions and ask questions. The recorder should note areas of agreement and disagreement. A chart that organizes these points would be useful at this stage.

Step 3: Compromise and negotiate

Identify points on which there seems to be agreement. Then identify the points on which there is disagreement. Consider the reasons for the disagreements and try to resolve these differences by exploring answers to the following questions:

- Can an option be changed slightly to make it acceptable to more group members?
- Can options be combined to satisfy more group members?
- Would a new, different option satisfy all group members?

Step 4: Call for consensus

When one option seems right for the group, the discussion guide should ask whether anyone still has concerns. Pause long enough to give group members a chance to express their thoughts. If no one raises concerns, the discussion guide can declare that a consensus has been reached.

If members of the group express concerns, go through the steps again. It is important for all group members to feel that their voices have been heard.

VOCABULARY TIP

Consensus means general agreement, but this does not mean that everyone in a group necessarily supports the decision with the same enthusiasm. The first choice of some group members might have been different — but they may be willing to live with the group's decision for the sake of reaching agreement. In other words, consensus can mean a lack of disagreement rather than enthusiastic agreement.

A **general consensus** usually suggests that most, and perhaps even all, members of a group agree with a decision — to a greater or lesser extent. A **rough consensus** suggests that many people in a group agree, but others still have doubts.

Tips for Making Consensus Building Work

Trust one another. Building consensus is not a competition. All members of the group must be comfortable about expressing their ideas and opinions.

Make sure everyone understands. Check often to ensure that all group members are listening carefully to — and understanding — one another.

Make sure everyone has a chance to contribute. Consensus building works best when all group members feel that their voices have been heard and everyone plays a role in reaching the group's decision.

Stay on track. Building consensus can be a long process. It sometimes helps to appoint a group member to remind people to stay focused on the topic.

Be prepared to compromise. Be flexible and willing to give up something to reach an agreement.

Keep the issue separate from personalities. Consider your own reactions and make sure that you are not agreeing or disagreeing because you like or do not like someone.

Be patient. Building consensus takes time, and rushing may result in a decision that may not be the best in the long run.

When consensus cannot be reached

Sometimes, group members cannot reach a consensus. When this happens, they may decide to take a vote. But this does not always mean that the majority wins and the minority loses. Even voting can be set up so that it represents a rough consensus.

Here is one way of doing this.

1. Count the number of options on the list and divide by three. The quotient is the number of votes assigned to each group member. If the list includes 12 options, for example, each group member can vote four times (12 ÷ 3 = 4).

2. In this example, each group member votes for her or his four top choices. This may be done by a show of hands or by giving each group member four stickers to place beside his or her choices.

3. Count the total number of votes for each option. The option with the highest number of votes is the one chosen.

Summing up

As you progress through this course, you will encounter other occasions when you may wish to reach a decision by building consensus. You can use similar steps to help you do this.

The North American Free Trade Agreement

The Free Trade Agreement between Canada and the United States went into effect in 1989. On January 1, 1994, this agreement was expanded to include Mexico — and the North American Free Trade Agreement, the largest free-trade area in the world, was the result. NAFTA, which was the world's largest free trade zone at the time, immediately eliminated half the trade barriers between the three countries. The remaining barriers were to be phased out over the next 15 years.

The negotiations that led to NAFTA sparked bitter debate. People for and against the agreement expressed strong views about the effects of the agreement. These differences of opinion arose because this was the first free-trade agreement between countries with such different levels of development. What groups do you suppose supported NAFTA? What groups were likely to oppose it?

In the years since Canada joined NAFTA, the country's economic relations have changed.

- Canadian exports to Mexico increased fourfold between 1993 and 2005.
- Canadian exports to the U.S. rose to $359 billion in 2000 from $183 billion in 1994.
- Canadian investment in Mexico rose 200 per cent between 1990 and 2006.
- Canadian investment in the U.S. tripled between 1990 and 2003. At the same time, U.S. investment in Canada rose by 150 per cent.
- Since NAFTA came into effect, the Canadian economy has grown an average of 3.4 per cent a year and 2.5 million new jobs have been created.

During the same period, more than 7000 manufacturing jobs shifted out of Canada to Mexico. And wages in manufacturing have remained the same or declined since NAFTA came into effect.

In 2005, Ipsos Reid, a Canadian polling company, studied pubic opinion in Canada, Mexico, and the U.S. to find out whether people believed that they had won or lost as a result of NAFTA. The results are shown in Figure 10-13.

Examine the data in Figure 10-13. What patterns do you see? How do the opinions of people in the three countries compare with one another? Why might there be differences in the perception of winners and losers from one country to another? How does your opinion of NAFTA compare with the opinions shown on the graph? Compare your answers with those of a partner, then work together to draft a brief description of your attitudes toward NAFTA.

Figure 10-13 **Perceived Winners and Losers under NAFTA**

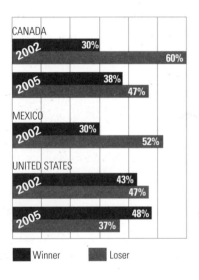

CANADA
2002 — 30% / 60%
2005 — 38% / 47%

MEXICO
2002 — 30% / 52%

UNITED STATES
2002 — 43% / 47%
2005 — 48% / 37%

■ Winner   ■ Loser

Source: Ipsos Reid

Figure 10-14 **Differing Views on NAFTA**

NAFTA Supporters	NAFTA Opponents
Supporters believed that NAFTA	Opponents believed that NAFTA
• would create thousands of high-paying jobs • would raise living standards in Canada, Mexico, and the U.S. • would improve environmental and employment standards • would transform Mexico from a developing country to a developed country	• would cause thousands of jobs to leave Canada and the U.S. for Mexico • would create a "race to the bottom" for wages in all three countries • would undermine health, environmental, and safety standards • would undermine the ability of member states to make their own decisions

To what extent does globalization contribute to sustainable prosperity for all people? • *MHR*

The European Union

The European Union, or EU, has created a liberalized trading area in Europe. As a result, goods, services, money, and people can move easily from one country to another — an effect some people describe as a regional variation on globalization.

The EU has tied member countries more closely together, integrating their economies and even replacing separate national currencies with the euro. How might using a common currency tie countries together? How might this encourage globalization?

The EU came into effect in 1991 after more than 40 years of negotiations. Today, most obstacles to cross-border trade among EU member countries have been eliminated. By acting as one large market, the EU enables members to take advantage of the opportunities created by economic globalization. At the same time, it protects members against some of the challenges created by globalization. These challenges may include pressure to reduce spending on social programs to keep a country's economy competitive. What advantages might EU membership offer to Europeans?

If you were a business leader in a developing African or Asian country, would you view the European Union as a threat or an opportunity? Explain the reasons for your judgment.

More than a trade agreement

The EU goes farther than other free-trade agreements. Though member countries have their own national governments, a European parliament makes decisions on issues that affect the region as a whole. An important focus for this parliament is to ensure that social progress is linked to economic progress. Recent initiatives have included taking action to end discrimination and to protect workers' rights. These programs have been guided by a belief that investment in social resources is necessary if Europe is to remain competitive in a globalizing world.

Figure 10-15 **The European Union and NAFTA**

Category	European Union	NAFTA
Area	4 324 782 sq. km	21 588 638 sq. km
Population (2006 est.)	486 642 000	438 992 672
Members	27	3
GDP (2006)	$12.82 trillion (U.S.)	$15.279 trillion (U.S.)
GDP per Person (2006)	$29 400 (U.S.)	$34 805 (U.S.)

Figure 10-16 Holding EU and Romanian flags, this man celebrates Romania's entry into the EU on January 1, 2007. The circle of 12 stars on the EU flag represents solidarity and harmony among the peoples of Europe. The number 12 is a traditional symbol of perfection, completeness, and unity — and the flag can remain the same as the EU expands. If you were creating a flag for NAFTA, what symbol(s) would you include? Why?

REFLECT AND RESPOND

Recall what you learned in Chapter 9 about the ideas of economists John Maynard Keynes, Friedrich Hayek, and Milton Friedman. Then think about what you have learned about trade liberalization and the roles of the WTO, NAFTA, and the EU. Whose ideas do you believe were most influential in the creation of these organizations? How are these ideas shaping contemporary economic globalization? Explain the reasons for your judgment.

HOW DO TRANSNATIONAL CORPORATIONS CONTRIBUTE TO EXPANDING GLOBALIZATION?

Transnational corporations reduce costs and increase profits by building factories, service centres, and retail outlets in various countries. They do this to ensure that they have

- the resources and parts needed to manufacture their products
- a steady, reliable source of labour
- markets where they can sell their goods and services

The increased trade liberalization of globalized economies has led to a sharp increase in the number of transnational corporations. In 1990, about 35 000 transnationals operated around the world. By 2002, this number had grown by about 86 per cent to more than 65 000.

Transnationals have also been growing larger as they increase sales and buy other companies. About 70 per cent of global trade transactions involve transnationals, but more than half these corporations are based in just five countries: the United States, Japan, France, Germany, and Britain. Why do you suppose transnationals are so closely connected to such a small group of countries?

Figure 10-17 Top 25 Transnational Corporations, 2005

Rank	Company	Revenues (millions of $ U.S.)
1	Wal-Mart	287 989
2	BP	285 059
3	Exxon Mobil	270 772
4	Royal Dutch/ Shell Group	268 690
5	General Motors	193 517
6	Daimler Chrysler	176 687
7	Toyota	172 616
8	Ford	172 233
9	General Electric	152 866
10	Total	152 609
11	Chevron Texaco	147 967
12	ConocoPhillips	121 663
13	AXA	121 606
14	Allianz	118 937
15	Volkswagen	110 649
16	Citigroup	108 276
17	ING Group	105 886
18	Nippon Telegraph & Telephone	100 545
19	American International Group	97 987
20	IBM	96 293
21	Siemens	91 493
22	Carrefour	90 382
23	Hitachi	83 994
24	Assicurazioni Generali	83 268
25	Matsushita	81 078

Source: *Forbes* magazine

The Influence of Transnational Corporations

Transnational corporations dominate some key parts of the world economy. They control most of the world's energy and extract most of its mineral resources. They manufacture a huge share of the world's chemicals, medicines, cars, aircraft, communication satellites, and home and office electronics. An estimated 85 per cent of the world's grain supply, for example, is controlled by six companies: Cargill, Continental Grain, Louis Dreyfus, Bunge, Andre/Garnac, and Mitsui/Cook. In what ways might this control by transnationals affect you and other Canadian consumers?

The ability of transnationals to move their operations around the world means that governments must compete to attract their business. And the threat that a transnational might leave a community forces governments to make concessions. To attract and keep transnationals in their community, some governments have used strategies like reducing taxes, selling natural resources at bargain prices, and adopting policies that transnationals will find helpful. This makes transnationals very powerful and, in some senses, reduces the decision-making power of governments. Do you think people should be concerned about this trend?

Examine Figure 10-17. How many of the transnationals on this list are familiar to you? What are some of the goods and services they produce? On a scale of 1 to 10 (1 = highly negative; 10 = highly positive), rank the effects of the growth in the number of transnationals. Explain the reasons for your judgment.

Transnational Corporations and Poverty Reduction

Many economists believe that one way to reduce poverty in developing countries is to invest in businesses and infrastructure, such as power grids and transportation facilities. In the past, most money for investments like these came through foreign aid from the governments of wealthy countries. In 1990, for example, foreign aid accounted for 75 per cent of the investment in developing countries.

The shift toward liberalized trade has moved the focus from governments to private companies. Today, 75 per cent of investment in developing companies comes from the private sector, especially transnational corporations. By 2000, private investment in developing countries had exceeded $250 billion (U.S.). How do you think the goals of government investment and private sector investment are different? The same?

Some countries have benefited from private sector investment. Poverty rates in countries such as South Korea, Malaysia, and India have been reduced because these countries have large markets and liberalized trade policies. For most countries, however, private foreign investment has made little or no difference. Smaller countries have a hard time attracting investors. Competition among developing countries for investment dollars has the negative effect of pushing wages down while reducing social spending. In the end, even if countries can attract investment, poverty remains a persistent problem.

Imagine a world in which transnational corporations have replaced national governments as the most powerful forces. How might this affect the lives of people in both developing and developed countries? Do you think that the growing power of transnational corporations will eventually encourage or discourage prosperity for all? Explain your answer.

Talisman Energy — A Canadian Transnational

Once a Canadian subsidiary of British Petroleum, Talisman Energy became an independent company in 1992. With headquarters in Calgary, Talisman is one of Canada's largest oil and gas producers. This transnational corporation has interests in crude oil, natural gas, and liquid natural gas around the world. The company's activities include exploration, development of energy resources, production, and marketing.

Talisman has focused its efforts in Western Canada and the North Sea, which account for about 77 per cent of production. But activities in other parts of the world help Talisman reduce its risks and take advantage of other opportunities.

VOICES

The costs and benefits of trade have been unevenly distributed across and within countries, perpetuating a pattern of globalization that builds prosperity for some amid mass poverty and deepening inequality for others.

— *United Nations,* Human Development Report 2005

FYI

Wages are usually lower in developing countries. The minimum wage in Alberta, for example, was $7 an hour in 2006. In Indonesia or Bangladesh, factory workers might be paid $1 or $2 a day. Lower wages help transnational corporations remain competitive and meet profit targets.

Figure 10-18 In 1999, villagers in Heglig, Sudan, celebrated the inauguration of an oil pipeline. Canadian flags were waved because of Talisman Energy's heavy involvement in this project, which later sparked heated controversy. Why do you think these Sudanese people were excited by this project?

Talisman and corporate responsibility

Talisman was linked to a controversial operation in Sudan, where the company had developed an oil field while the country was involved in a brutal civil war. Critics accused Talisman of supporting a government that was committing genocide against civilians in rebel-held territories. Pressure from church groups and non-governmental organizations was so strong that Talisman sold its Sudan operations in 2003. Do you think Talisman's sale of its Sudan operations demonstrated corporate social responsibility? Explain your response.

In 2006, Talisman and Scottish and Southern Energy won approval to lead a consortium — an association of large companies — to test a deepwater wind-farm project in the North Sea. If the pilot project is successful, a wind farm will be built about 19 kilometres offshore. When complete, the project is expected to produce enough energy to supply about one-fifth of Scotland's energy needs.

List some Talisman Energy activities that are typical of transnational corporations. Why do you think the company pursues these activities? Which is more important: a transnational corporation's obligations to its shareholders or its obligation to operate in a socially responsible manner?

Figure 10-19 In August 2006, the first of two huge wind turbines developed by Talisman Energy and a consortium of other companies was transported to a location in the North Sea. The blades of the turbine are 63 metres long, and the structures will tower 170 metres above sea level.

Figure 10-20 When Talisman Energy held its 2002 annual general meeting, demonstrators gathered in Calgary to protest the company's involvement in Sudan.

REFLECT AND RESPOND

Using some of the vocabulary you have learned so far (e.g., trade liberalization, tariffs, and outsourcing), write three sentences that describe the conditions that provide the most significant benefits for transnational corporations.

Then write a three-paragraph opinion piece that describes the extent to which transnational corporations contribute to expanding globalization.

What are some of the challenges and opportunities that go along with expanding globalization? Here are three people's thoughts on this question.

ED BROADBENT is a former member of Parliament, former leader of the New Democratic Party of Canada, and founding president of the International Center for Human Rights and Democratic Development. He made these remarks in a 2003 speech.

The cliché is true: We are no longer citizens of our cities, provinces and countries. We Canadians are now citizens of the world whose daily life is being shaped by the new trade rules of globalization . . . As global citizens, we must make sure that the governments we elect and the corporations we buy from live up to basic democratic requirements . . . Until this happens, there can be no global democracy.

MAUDE BARLOW is an author; the national chairperson of the Council of Canadians, a citizens' group; and a director of the International Forum on Globalization, an organization that monitors the effects of globalization. She made these comments in a 1999 message titled "Who's in Charge of the Global Economy?"

The dominant development model of our time is economic globalization . . . Everything is for sale, even those areas of life once considered sacred. Increasingly, these services and resources are controlled by a handful of transnational corporations who shape national and international law to suit their interests. At the heart of this transformation is an all-out assault on virtually every public sphere of life, including the democratic underpinning of our legal system.

KOFI ANNAN was secretary-general of the United Nations from 1997 to 2006. These remarks were part of his address to the World Economic Forum in 2001.

My friends, the simple fact of the matter is this: if we cannot make globalization work for all, in the end it will work for none. The unequal distribution of benefits, and the imbalances in global rule-making, which characterize globalization today, inevitably will produce backlash and protectionism. And that, in turn, threatens to undermine and ultimately to unravel the open world economy that has been so painstakingly constructed over the course of the past half-century.

Explorations

1. In one sentence for each speaker, summarize the key point made by each. On a scale of 1 to 5 (1 = most optimistic; 5 = most pessimistic), assess each speaker's level of optimism about the effects of expanding globalization. Explain your ranking.

2. If you had an opportunity to ask each speaker two questions, what would you want to know? Record your questions in writing. Beside each, explain why you would ask the question.

3. In small groups, use the three quotations as the starting point of a brainstorming session to develop responses to this question: To what extent should we embrace globalization? Try to reach a consensus within the group.

HOW DO COMMUNICATION TECHNOLOGIES CONTRIBUTE TO EXPANDING GLOBALIZATION?

CHECKBACK

You learned about the digital divide in Chapter 3.

Figure 10-21 Canadian Jeffrey Skoll was the first employee and founding president of eBay, one of the world's most successful dot-com companies. Though it started as a small online business in 1995, eBay has become one of the most successful online companies — and Skoll is a multi-billionaire.

Figure 10-22 Conservative MP Steven Fletcher was the first person with quadriplegia — partial or complete paralysis of the arms and legs — to be elected to Parliament. Computer technology helps Fletcher operate a special chair that allows him to ask questions from an upright position in the House of Commons.

Information and communication technologies have made globalization possible. But access to these technologies is not equal everywhere in the world, or even across Canada. Differences in financial status, education and skills, age, and geographic location can widen the digital divide.

People and societies that cannot make effective use of contemporary information and communication technologies may have a hard time competing in the global economy and may find themselves at a disadvantage. What disadvantages might people experience as a result of lack of access to these technologies?

E-Commerce

Electronic commerce — or e-commerce — is an area that has been stimulated by communication technologies. Businesses like Amazon and Canadian Tire operate online stores where people can buy what they want, 24 hours a day, and have their purchases shipped to their homes. An online site like eBay connects buyers and sellers and enables them to buy or sell nearly anything. Enhanced Internet security measures have also promoted online credit card sales. Many major retailers and small businesses now earn substantial revenues from e-commerce.

In 2005, online consumer spending by Canadians amounted to $7.9 billion. Nearly 7 million Canadians placed more than 50 million orders. The average order totalled $160. Travel services such as hotel reservations and car rentals were the most common purchase, followed closely by books, magazines, and digital products.

Have you or members of your family shopped online? If you have, what goods or services did you buy? What factors inspired you to shop online? If you have not shopped online, what has kept you from using this source of goods and services? How are online shopping and expanding globalization linked?

Figure 10-23 In 2007, an $8.7-million (U.S.) government-supported pilot project in downtown Tokyo, Japan, embedded computer chips in lampposts, subway station ceilings, and road cement. The chips beam maps, information about history, and store guides to portable computers connected to earphones.

E-commerce and prosperity

The prosperity generated by e-commerce is largely restricted to people who live in developed countries. Why do you think this would be so?

People in many developing countries do not yet have access to the information and communication technologies that would enable them to share in the benefits of this technology. In most developing countries, the technology infrastructure is either inadequate or non-existent, though new generations of wireless communication technologies may help improve this situation. Distribution and delivery chains may also be inadequate.

In addition, creating a climate of trust in cultures that have traditionally placed great importance on personal contact may create a challenge for the development of e-commerce. And some governments and communication systems are not Internet-friendly. In much of Europe, for example, people must pay for every telephone call and connection, whether it is local or long-distance.

> Examine Figure 10-24. Based on the data you see, what prediction would you make about business use of the Internet over the next 10 years in Canada?

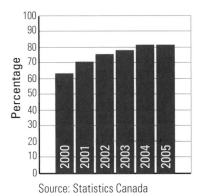
Figure 10-24 **Percentage of Canadian Businesses Using the Internet**

Source: Statistics Canada

Ideas

How do my personal communication systems make me part of expanding globalization?

The students responding to this question are Tom, a fourth-generation Albertan who lives on a ranch near Okotoks; Ling, who was born in Hong Kong but is now a Canadian who lives in Edmonton; and Deven, who was born in India but is now a Canadian who lives in Calgary.

> I enjoy finding out about people and places around the world. With just a few keystrokes, I can find out about new ideas, watch important events as they happen, or just watch people in other places. People have never had such immediate access to so much information. Sometimes the ideas overwhelm me, but I feel fortunate to have digital communications in my life.

Tom

> I like having my cellphone and using my computer, but I'm concerned that these are advantages that other young people don't have. What will happen to people in other parts of the world if we keep moving forward and the digital divide gets even wider? If the inequalities are too great, at some point global systems won't be able to operate. We should be thinking about making the world a fairer place for everyone.

Ling

> My communication systems make my life good. I can keep in touch with the people who are important to me. I especially like to use my computer for entertainment, like playing games and watching movies. Right now, my parents pay for all this — but in a few years, I'll have to start doing this myself. So I worry about the high costs of staying connected. I don't know how I would manage without my cellphone or my high-speed Internet access.

Deven

Your Turn

How would you respond to the question Tom, Ling, and Deven are answering? What are some positive ways that personal communication systems connect you to expanding globalization? What communication challenges might you face over the next few years as a result of expanding globalization? Explain the reasons for your answers.

1. Imagine that you are a 15-year-old living in a small city in the African country of Kenya. Conduct research to identify some aspects of expanding globalization and how they might affect your life. List aspects that affect you directly, as well as those that affect you indirectly. You might organize your ideas on a chart like the following. To help you get started, one section has been filled in.

Globalization Forces Affecting a Teenager in Kenya	
Direct Effects	Indirect Effects
A transnational company has built a manufacturing plant in our city. I might be able to get an assembly-line job there.	The government has reduced spending on environmental protection. Instead, it is building an airport to encourage foreign investment.

Then think about your own life in Alberta — and how expanding globalization affects you directly and indirectly.

Write a paragraph comparing the effects of expanding globalization on your life with its effects on the life of a Kenyan teenager. Be sure to include comments on the reasons for the similarities and differences.

2. Read the following excerpt from the United Nations *Human Development Report 2005*:

> The rules of the game are at the heart of the problem. Developed country governments seldom waste an opportunity to emphasize the virtues of open markets, level playing fields and free trade, especially in their prescriptions for poor countries. Yet the same governments maintain a formidable array of protectionist barriers against developing countries . . . Such policies skew the benefits of globalization in favour of rich countries, while denying millions of people in developing countries a chance to share in the benefits of trade. Hypocrisy and double standards are not strong foundations for a rules-based multilateral system geared towards human development.

How would you rate the validity of this document as a source of information? Why? What problem does this report identify? How would you change "the rules of the game" to give everyone a fair chance of achieving prosperity? With a partner, brainstorm to create a list of ways in which trade rules could be made fairer for developing countries.

Present your suggestions to the class and work with the class to achieve consensus on one way of changing global trade rules to make them fairer.

3. With a partner or small group, brainstorm to create a list of some possible environmental effects of trade liberalization. Create a T-chart like the one shown. In the first column, list possible positive effects, and list possible negative effects in the other. Think about factors such as extracting natural resources, disposing of industrial and household waste, using energy efficiently, and funding environmental protection programs. To help you get started, some examples have been filled in.

Possible Environmental Effects of Trade Liberalization	
Positive	Negative
Countries can pass similar laws to protect the environment.	Transnational corporations might dump waste illegally.

Use the ideas in your chart to create five questions you could use to guide an exploration of the environmental effects of trade liberalization. Conduct research in the library or on the Internet to find answers to your questions. Present your findings in a two-minute audio report, which will be broadcast on the WTO's online youth forum. Be sure to include references to the sources you used when gathering your information.

4. A deep-seated challenge of expanding globalization is that many developing countries enjoy few of the benefits of trade liberalization. Their economies are not strong enough to keep pace with the economic growth of developed countries.

Suppose you are a reporter for a news service. You have been handed the assignment of covering a meeting of delegates from the world's least developed countries. On the agenda is a discussion of strategies for achieving some of the benefits of trade liberalization and globalization. To prepare for the meeting, you must conduct research so you can ask the delegates informed questions.

a) Make point-form notes on
   • barriers that stand in the way of developing countries' achieving economic benefits
   • opportunities that could be explored
   • strategies that might be tried
b) List five questions you would like to ask the key participants. Make sure that your questions show that you are informed about the topics covered in your questions.

5. The economic growth that has resulted from the North American Free Trade Agreement has encouraged governments and advocates of free trade to consider how the idea could be expanded. Several large conferences have been held to talk about turning the Americas into one large free-trade area.

But not everyone is in favour of this proposal, and the meetings have attracted large protests. Figure 10-25 shows a 2001 demonstration at Gazebo Park in Edmonton. The marchers were lending support to protesters who had gathered in Québec City, where the Summit of the Americas was held.

Conduct research to find out more about the proposed Free Trade Area of the Americas. When your research is complete, you should be able to answer these questions:

• What are the goals of advocates of the FTAA?
• What arguments are raised by those who oppose the idea of the FTAA?
• What is the Canadian government's position on this issue?
• What progress has been made on this idea so far?

Present your findings. You may choose to do this in the form of a written report or an oral presentation. Or you may decide to use computer presentation software. Conclude your report or presentation by stating your own position on the creation of the FTAA and identifying the arguments you found most persuasive in helping you arrive at this position.

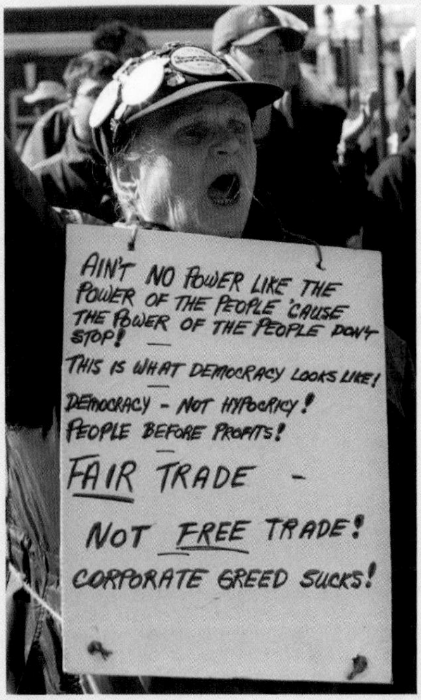

AIN'T NO POWER LIKE THE POWER OF THE PEOPLE 'CAUSE THE POWER OF THE PEOPLE DON'T STOP! —
THIS IS WHAT DEMOCRACY LOOKS LIKE!
DEMOCRACY - NOT HYPOCRISY!
PEOPLE BEFORE PROFITS!
FAIR TRADE -
NOT FREE TRADE!
CORPORATE GREED SUCKS!

Figure 10-25

Think about Your Challenge

Your challenge for this related issue is to write a persuasive essay on the extent to which globalization contributes to sustainable prosperity for all people. Review the notes you have been keeping in preparation for writing your essay's support paragraphs. Share what you have done so far with a partner or your teacher. If necessary, revise your inquiry questions to reflect the feedback you received.

Chapter 11   Globalization and Sustainability

Figure 11-1 This photograph by Canadian Edward Burtynsky is titled *Shipbreaking No. 4*. When ships become too old to be useful, they are sold to recyclers. Shipbreaking is big business in Bangladesh, India, China, Pakistan, and Turkey, where ships are run up onto beaches and dismantled. The steel and other materials are recycled and used in new products. But shipbreaking can have severe effects on the environment and on the health of the workers involved.

SHIPS ARE VITAL TO GLOBALIZATION, but the lifespan of an average ship is 25 to 30 years. After that, it is cheaper to build a new ship than to try to keep an old one in service. But ships contain many materials — especially steel — that can be recycled.

Because recycling is labour-intensive, it is expensive in developed countries. Globalization has given shipowners an alternative. Obsolete ships are sold to shipbreakers in developing countries, such as India, Bangladesh, and China. Workers there are paid a few dollars a day to dismantle old ships, and the recyclable materials are sold to local companies for reuse.

In 2000, Edward Burtynsky completed a photo essay on shipbreaking in Bangladesh. Visually stunning, his photographs document this activity in a way that words alone cannot. Examine Burtynsky's photograph on the previous page and consider answers to these questions:

- What is the physical setting of this activity?
- What are the workers doing?
- What is happening to the ships?

Sometimes is it as important to think about what photographs do not show as it is to examine what they do show.

- What tools or technologies are the workers using?
- What conclusions can you draw about the safety of the workers?
- What environmental protection measures can you see?
- Why do you think shipbreaking is taking place at this location?

KEY TERMS

ecological footprint

sustain

sustainability

stewardship

flag of convenience

LOOKING AHEAD

In this chapter, you will explore answers to the following questions:

- What does sustainability mean?
- How are globalization and sustainability related?
- Have efforts to promote sustainability been successful?

My Point of View on Globalization

Based on your current understanding, use words or images — or both — to express your current point of view on globalization. Date your ideas and keep them in the notebook, learning log, portfolio, or computer file you are keeping as you progress through this course.

WHAT DOES SUSTAINABILITY MEAN?

Figure 11-2 **Components of Canada's Ecological Footprint**

7.25 Hectares per Person

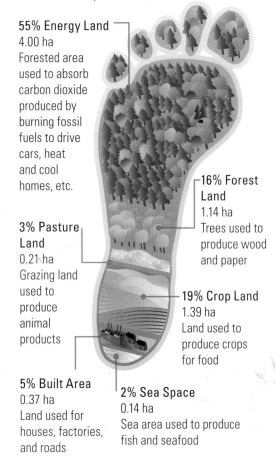

55% Energy Land
4.00 ha
Forested area used to absorb carbon dioxide produced by burning fossil fuels to drive cars, heat and cool homes, etc.

16% Forest Land
1.14 ha
Trees used to produce wood and paper

3% Pasture Land
0.21 ha
Grazing land used to produce animal products

19% Crop Land
1.39 ha
Land used to produce crops for food

5% Built Area
0.37 ha
Land used for houses, factories, and roads

2% Sea Space
0.14 ha
Sea area used to produce fish and seafood

People cannot live without having some effect on the environment. Everyone needs

- materials to make homes, clothing, tools, and so on
- fuel for heat and transportation, and to provide electricity
- food to stay healthy
- water for drinking, cooking, cleanliness, and health

Scientists use the term **ecological footprint** to describe the load people impose on nature. Your ecological footprint represents the area of the earth's surface necessary to sustain the level of resources you use and the waste you create.

The ecological footprint of an individual or group is a measure of how much biologically productive land and water resources are needed to keep them alive. Dividing the bioproductive area of Earth by the total population reveals that 1.89 hectares of productive area are available for each person.

Canada's Ecological Footprint

Earth's resources are not shared equally. Canadians, for example, have a much larger ecological footprint — 7.25 hectares per person — than people in most other countries. How does this compare with the amount of bioproductive land available to each person on Earth?

Examine Figures 11-2, 11-3, and 11-4. If everyone consumed as much as Canadians, four more planets like Earth would be needed to meet their needs. Consider the lifestyles of Canadians, taking into account factors such as the climate and how farming and manufacturing are carried out. What are some reasons Canadians have such big ecological feet?

Figure 11-3 **Some Factors That Affect Ecological Footprint**

Household or Individual Footprint	Town, City, or Region Footprint
• Amount of consumer goods bought • Amount of packaging used • Amount and type of food eaten • Extent of recycling and waste reduction • Size of house or apartment • Amount of electricity used • Fuel efficiency of vehicles • Distance travelled by car, transit, bike, and foot	• Waste management and recycling efforts • Population densities • Average household size • Consumer spending patterns • Average energy use • Transportation options • Land-use patterns

Figure 11-4 **Ecological Footprint of Canada and Selected Cities**

Source: Anielski Management Inc.

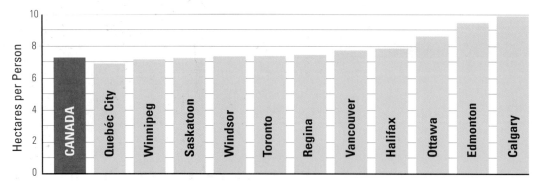

Bangladesh's Ecological Footprint

While Canada has one of the biggest ecological footprints in the world, Bangladesh has one of the smallest: 0.6 hectares for each person. In large part, this is because Bangladesh is one of the world's least developed countries. Bangladeshis have little money to spend on consumer goods, large houses, and expensive vehicles. Only 33 per cent of people, for example, have access to electricity. As a result, their consumption of resources is far lower than that of Canadians. And because Bangladeshis consume less, they produce less waste.

Examine the charts and photographs on this page. Compare these with what you learned about the ecological footprint of the average Canadian. What factors might contribute to the difference in the average footprint of a Bangladeshi and a Canadian?

Figure 11-5 **Bangladesh and Canada: A Comparison**

Statistic	Bangladesh	Canada
Population (2006)	147 300 000	33 100 000
Population Density	1023 persons per sq. km	3.3 persons per sq. km
Population Growth Rate	2.09%	0.88%
GDP per Person	$2 200 (U.S.)	$35 200 (U.S.)
Life Expectancy	62 years	80 years

Source: *CIA World Factbook*

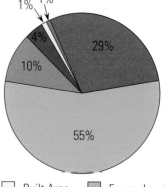

Figure 11-6 **Components of Bangladesh's Ecological Footprint**

1% 1%
4%
29%
10%
55%

- ☐ Built Area
- ☐ Pasture Land
- ☐ Sea Space
- ☐ Energy Land
- ☐ Crop Land
- ☐ Forest Land

Source: Globalis

Figure 11-7 The photograph on the left shows a farmer in Bangladesh, while the one on the right shows a street in Dhaka, the country's capital. Identify aspects of life in Bangladesh that affect the country's ecological footprint.

Global Perspectives on Ecological Footprints

The ecological footprint of 70 per cent of the world's people is smaller than the 1.89 hectares available for each person. But the remaining 30 per cent of people take much more than their share — in fact, this remaining 30 per cent consume about 90 per cent of the world's ecological capacity.

Figure 11-8 **Average Ecological Footprint by Region**

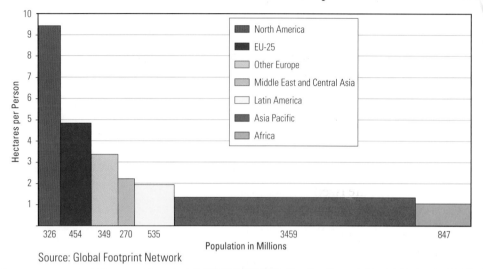

Source: Global Footprint Network

Examine Figure 11-8. The bars show the average ecological footprint by region. The width of each bar is in proportion to the size of the population of each region. Why do you suppose the ecological footprint of North America is so large? What do you suppose would happen if the ecological footprint of the Asia Pacific region were as big as that of North America?

MAKING CHOICES

THE KOGI — AT THE HEART OF THE WORLD

The Kogi, who live in the mountains of northern Colombia, believe they are responsible for looking after this area, which they call the "heart of the world." Their society has remained largely unchanged for the past 500 years because they have stayed completely separate from the outside world. They allow no outsiders on their land, which they view as sacred. Calling themselves the "Elder Brother," they refer to the people of the developed world as "Younger Brother."

The Kogi have been cultivating their fields continuously for more than a thousand years. They believe that their mission is to care for the planet, and their culture is inseparable from the rainforest where they live. Agricultural rituals that are respectful of the natural world play an important part in their religious practices. Crops, for example, are planted according to a timetable determined by astronomical calculations.

Spiritual leaders, called Mamas, control Kogi society and help them make important decisions. The Mamas spend years learning about astronomy, meteorology, and ecology so that they can preserve the delicate balance between humans and nature. This knowledge is passed down orally.

The ecological footprint of the Kogi is very small. In the 1980s, the Kogi began noticing that less snow was falling and that their rivers were no longer as full. In 1988, believing that the world was in trouble, they allowed the British Broadcasting Corporation to film a documentary about the region. The film, *From the Heart of the World: The Elder Brothers' Warning*, begins with the Kogis' main message: "We Mamas see you are killing [the world] by what you do. We can no longer repair the world. You must."

Figure 11-9 A Kogi harvests food.

Explorations

1. In what ways would the ecological footprint of the Kogi be different from that of the average Canadian?

2. Explain why a detailed knowledge of the natural world is important to the Kogi.

3. Suppose you are a documentary filmmaker whom the Kogi have allowed to make a film about their way of life. List five topics you would like to investigate in your film. Explain why you chose these topics.

The resource gap

The gap between the resources the earth can reasonably supply — 1.89 hectares per person — and what the people of the world now consume — 2.8 hectares per person — presents a challenge. To meet this deficit, people are using up resources that could be left for future generations. Think about what would happen to a family that spends more money than it earns and borrows to make up the difference. At some point in the future, this debt must be repaid. The same thing is happening with the environment. Most environmentalists agree that people cannot continue to borrow against the future. At some point, the earth will not be able to **sustain** — provide the basic necessities needed to support life — actions like this. The debt will have to be repaid.

Population growth

Over the next four or five decades, the world's population is expected to grow by two to five billion. The earth's resources are fixed, but an ever-increasing number of people will need to share them. How do you think this situation might affect smaller, less developed countries with limited access to natural resources? How do you think North Americans will respond to this challenge?

Examine Figure 11-10. The three population projections shown on this graph are based on different assumptions about the future. What assumptions do you think underlie the high forecast? The low forecast?

Consumption of resources

Many of the world's people are striving to improve their material well-being by consuming more goods and services. The more they consume, the larger their ecological footprint grows. At the same time, individuals and groups, such as the United Nations, are warning that this will affect **sustainability** — the ability of the earth to provide the resources necessary to meet people's needs. These individuals and groups are promoting the idea of environmental **stewardship**, which involves accepting responsibility for ensuring that the earth's resources remain sustainable. What would happen if all the world's people were to achieve the same consumption levels as Canadians?

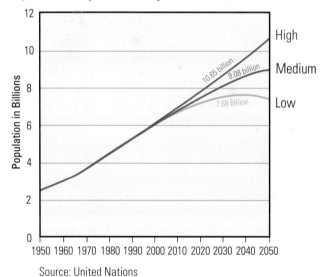

Figure 11-10 **Population Projections, 1950–2050**

Population in Billions

10.65 billion
9.08 billion
7.68 billion

High
Medium
Low

Source: United Nations

REFLECT AND RESPOND

Most Canadians are familiar with the three Rs: reduce, reuse, and recycle. But some believe that a fourth R — refuse — must be added to this list to reduce the size of people's ecological footprint and to move toward the sustainability of the earth's resources. They believe that to steward the earth's resources, people should refuse to buy things they do not need or that are enclosed in excessive packaging.

With a partner, list "refuse" actions you could take. Explain how each action on your list would contribute to sustainability.

ANALYZING RELATIONSHIPS IN GEOGRAPHY

To understand sustainability, people must be able to make connections between their actions and the health of the natural environment. The study of geography uses tools that focus on these relationships and connections.

Suppose you were asked to investigate answers to this question: Which wood-harvesting method — clear-cutting or selective cutting — is more sustainable?

To answer this question, you will need to investigate the relationship between cutting methods and sustainability. The following steps will help you do this. As you progress through this course, you can use similar steps to respond to other questions.

Steps to Analyzing Relationships in Geography

Step 1: Ask powerful research questions

Asking powerful questions is a crucial first step in any investigation because your questions determine the directions your investigation will take. Your questions may have a variety of purposes that include

- determining cause and effect — understanding causal relationships and finding out about consequences
- comparing — understanding similarities and differences
- predicting — suggesting likely outcomes

Review the purpose of your investigation into wood-harvesting methods and prepare at least three questions to help guide your inquiry. Then choose one or two and make them the focus for your research.

Step 2: Acquire geographic information

To answer your research questions, you need to gather information from a variety of sources. Start by listing the information you need, as well as potential sources. Gathering information may require you to

- identify useful sources, which may include maps, photographs, satellite images, GPS systems, and computer graphics
- locate information
- interpret maps and other graphic representations
- conduct field investigations or interview key people
- record your information

You may wish to include the photographs and illustration on the following page in the information you gather.

Step 3: Organize geographic information

Raw information needs to be organized and filtered to show the relationships that will answer your research questions. Various kinds of information should be separated and classified, perhaps by using headings to create categories. Using a table or chart is often an effective way to structure data. You may wish, for example, to use a chart like this.

Wood-Havesting Methods		
Type	Advantages	Problems
Clear-cutting	— most economical —	— environmental damage —

Step 4: Analyze information

Analyze the data you have collected by focusing on relationships and connections. As you do this, you will

- look for patterns
- find similarities and differences
- note connections among items
- make inferences based on maps, graphs, diagrams, tables, and so on
- identify biases in your sources.

To help analyze your data, you may be able to use GIS — geographic information systems — technology.

Step 5: Answer geographic questions

Use your analysis to answer the questions you posed when you began your investigation. Be prepared to consider new issues and new ways of viewing the situation. Decide on an effective way of communicating the results of your investigation, using technologies that are appropriate to the task.

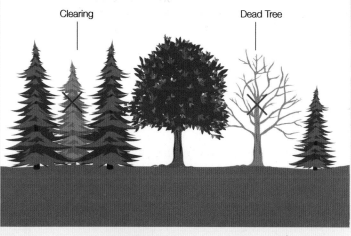

Figure 11-12 A Clear-Cut Area at Ground Level

Figure 11-11 A Clear-Cut Area from the Air

Figure 11-13 A Selectively Cut Area at Ground Level

Clearing   Dead Tree

Figure 11-14 How Selective Cutting Works

Summing up

How sustainable are clear-cutting and selective cutting of forests? What is the relationship between cutting methods and sustainability? Suppose you were asked to complete this analysis. What do you think your conclusion might be? Explain your ideas.

CHECKBACK

You read about shipping and containerization in Chapters 2 and 10.

FYI

In recent years, Chinese shipbuilding has increased by more than 40 per cent a year. China now boasts 861 shipbuilding centres. Germany, Singapore, Hong Kong, Australia, and Britain are important markets for Chinese-built ships

HOW ARE GLOBALIZATION AND SUSTAINABILITY RELATED?

Transportation is an important globalizing force — and shipping is an important element of the globalized transportation systems that move goods and materials between suppliers, manufacturers, and buyers. Following the life cycle of a typical ship reveals one aspect of the relationship between globalization and sustainability.

Where Ships Are Built

In recent years, shipbuilders have been struggling to keep up with the demand for more ships. From 2000 to 2005, shipbuilding grew an average of 8.3 per cent a year, and shipbuilders had a three- to four-year backlog of orders. The rise in global trade, as well as the need to replace older vessels, is driving this demand.

In the 1970s, the shipbuilding industry was dominated by Europe and the United States. But shipbuilding is labour-intensive, and this industry has shifted to Asia, where labour costs are lower. As Figure 11-15 shows, South Korea and Japan now dominate shipbuilding, although Japan's share is slipping rapidly as China — with its low wage rates — emerges as a key player in this industry. How do you think this change will affect environmental sustainability?

Examine Figure 11-15. Why do you suppose shipbuilding is dominated by so few countries? Identify some possible economic, social, political, and environmental effects of the shift in shipbuilding from developed to developing countries. Create a four-column chart with the headings "Economic Effects," "Social Effects," "Political Effects," and "Environmental Effects," and brainstorm with a partner to fill in the chart.

Environmental impact of shipbuilding

Hyundai Heavy Industries' Ulsan shipyard in South Korea is currently the largest in the world, covering an area of 720 hectares. The large area needed by shipyards increases their potential for pollution. Hazardous materials such as lead are routinely used in the coatings and paints needed to withstand saltwater conditions, and anti-fouling paints, which are designed to inhibit the growth of barnacles and algae, also contain toxic chemicals. Overall, shipyards make heavy demands on electricity and water supplies and generate large amounts of solid and toxic waste. How would you describe the ecological footprint of shipyards?

Figure 11-15 Shipbuilding Market Share, 1995–2005

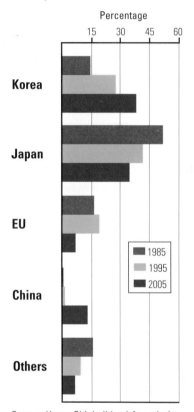

Percentage

Legend: 1985, 1995, 2005

Korea, Japan, EU, China, Others

Source: Korea Shipbuilders' Association

Figure 11-16 This shipbuilding yard in Shanghai, China, shows the size of the site needed to build a ship. Identify some environmental impacts of large shipbuilding facilities.

Ships and the Environment

Ocean-going vessels use just 3 per cent of the fossil fuels consumed globally, but they emit about 15 per cent of the world's nitrogen and sulfur dioxide. This is because ships use bunker fuel, which is cheap and dirty. A single container ship creates as much pollution as 2000 diesel trucks.

In addition, ships carry millions of litres of seawater in their hulls as ballast. This water is pumped around to keep the ship balanced correctly in changing sea conditions. It is also pumped out as ships are loaded and pumped in as they are unloaded.

One study found that ballast water pumped out of ships in Canadian ports contained as many as 12 392 marine creatures per cubic metre. These are sometimes invasive species that cause problems when they are introduced to new environments. Scientists believe, for example, that zebra mussels, a non-native species that has created problems in the Great Lakes, arrived in the ballast water of ships from Europe.

Flags of convenience

Many merchant ships operate under a **flag of convenience**, a practice that is often called flagging out. It occurs when a ship is registered in a country other than that of its owner. Canada Steamship Lines, for example, is a Canadian-owned company, but up to 50 per cent of its ships are registered in — and fly the flag of — countries such as those shown in Figure 11-17.

In 2004, about 64 per cent of the total tonnage of ocean-going ships was flagged out. The advantages of flagging out include

- lower costs — Registration fees and other charges are much lower. The savings can total millions of dollars a year for every vessel.
- ease of registration — Little paperwork is required. In some cases, ships can be registered by fax.
- weak environmental and labour laws — Ships must obey the laws of the country in which they are registered. Environmental laws in countries that offer flags of convenience are often less strict than rules in Europe and North America. Labour laws are also less strict. Working conditions are rarely monitored, and international maritime conventions are seldom enforced.

Who benefits — and who is harmed — by the practice of flagging out? Explain how.

Figure 11-17 **Some Countries Offering Flags of Convenience**

Country	Ships Owned	Ships Registered
Antigua and Barbuda	57	980
Bahamas	186	1119
Belize	153	295
Bermuda	6	108
Cambodia	286	479
Cyprus	127	972
Liberia	73	1465
Malta	63	1140
Netherlands Antilles	10	168
Panama	617	5005

Source: International Transportation Workers' Federation

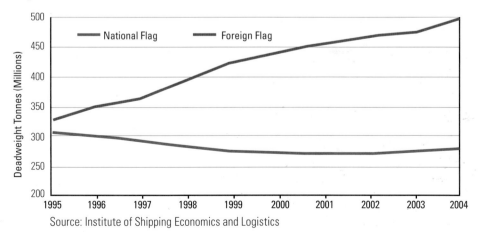

Source: Institute of Shipping Economics and Logistics

Figure 11-18 **World Merchant Fleet by National and Foreign Flag, 1995–2004**

Disposing of Old Ships

Once ships are 25 to 30 years old, they become too expensive to maintain and are scrapped. Every year, about 600 to 700 ships end up on the beaches of Asia, including Bangladesh. There, workers earning $1.50 to $2.50 (U.S.) a day break them down so the metals and other materials can be sold as scrap to recyclers.

Death of a ship

When ships are broken apart, hazardous materials are released into the environment. Ballast water, for example, is simply discharged onto the beach. Insulating materials such as asbestos, as well as fuels and lubricants, escape, as do residues from final cargoes. Machinery, scrap metal, and discarded barrels end up littering beaches. As a result, fishing and farming near shipbreaking beaches become impossible.

Shipbreaking is one of the most dangerous jobs in the world. A lack of safety standards means that workers face great risks. Workers' cutting torches frequently ignite trapped gases and cause life-threatening explosions; grinding tools send toxic, cancer-causing particles such as asbestos into the air that is breathed by workers; and workers are sometimes crushed to death by falling steel beams and plates.

An average of one death occurs in shipbreaking yards every day, and an estimated one in four shipbreaking workers will die of cancer caused by workplace exposure. Why do you think workers would take jobs in shipbreaking yards? What conditions might persuade you to work at a job that you knew was dangerous?

Figure 11-19 This shipbreaking yard is on a beach in Alang, India. Recently, various individuals and groups have focused attention on the environmental and labour practices of some of these yards — and conditions have improved somewhat. Identify some of the problems you see.

The shipbreaking industry raises the issue of whether people in developed countries have a responsibility – or even a right – to demand that industries in developing countries observe the same environmental and labour rules as they do. Here is how three people have responded to this issue.

RUNE LARSEN is a Norwegian photographer who was born into a family of shipbuilders and whalers. His interest in ships led him to visit 15 shipbreaking yards in Chittagong, Bangladesh. The following is an excerpt from his commentary on his photographs.

No effort should be spared in improving the conditions surrounding the shipbreaking industry in Bangladesh. At the same time, the workers relying on the industry for a livelihood must be given a chance to continue making a living. In the long term, minimum standards on environmental and labor conditions in the shipbreaking industry will hopefully be enforced through the United Nations' maritime organization, [the International Maritime Organization]. But who will pay for the cost of improved labor conditions and the environmental effort? Who is responsible? Is it the ship breakers, the shipbuilders, the ship owners or the government?

PAUL BAILEY is a shipbreaking expert with the International Labour Organization. The following remarks were published in *ILO Online*, the organization's electronic publication.

Before shipbreaking, Bangladesh, for example, imported all of its scrap steel. Today the wrecked ships satisfy 80 per cent of its needs. But scrap steel is not the only value imported from the gaping holds of these ships. Lining the streets close to the shipbreaking yards are various shops selling anything from bathtubs and toilets to boilers and generators removed from the ships after they are beached. The shipyard owners estimate around 200,000 Bangladeshis benefit indirectly from this business conducted on their shores. In India, the biggest shipbreaking nation, the figure is half a million.

MARCELLO MALENTACCHI is the general secretary of the International Metalworkers' Federation. He made the following remarks during a 2006 news conference about his organization's concerns about shipbreaking.

In many countries the state of shipbreaking is an open scandal. The answer is not to shut it down – to call for that is to ignore that it is a vital industry for tens of thousands of people for whom no alternative employment exists. The solution is to reform, train and support.

Negotiations are under way at the [International Maritime Organization] to develop internationally agreed regulations on the recycling of ships. However, adoption of the regulations is not expected until 2009, and proper implementation by 2015 at best, if at all.

Explorations

1. In one sentence for each speaker, summarize the point he is making.

2. How would you answer the questions Rune Larsen asked at the end of his statement? Who do you think should bear the costs of improving conditions for shipbreakers in developing countries? Explain who would be affected if your ideas were adopted.

3. Join two or three other students in a small group and use the three excerpts as the starting point of a brainstorming session to achieve consensus on answers to this question: What two key conditions must be met to make shipping an environmentally sustainable industry?

Proposals to Improve the Sustainability of Shipbreaking

The costs of shipbreaking can be high, for both the environment and workers. In some parts of the world, such as North America, laws govern

how shipbreaking is carried out. This is why shipbreaking companies now operate in a handful of developing countries, where the rules are less strict.

Figure 11-20 These workers are doing their jobs at a shipbreaking yard in Bangladesh. What evidence tells you that they are not well protected?

Ideas

Should all industries and governments be encouraged to adopt stricter environmental protection laws?

The students responding to this question are Ling, who was born in Hong Kong but is now a Canadian who lives in Edmonton; Marie, a Francophone student from Medicine Hat; and Tom, a fourth-generation Albertan who lives on a ranch near Okotoks.

We can't impose our values and standards on people in other countries. We have our own ways of doing things, and our laws are based on these traditions. People in other countries have their own ways that are different from ours. Take Bangladeshi shipbreakers, for example. If we imposed environmental laws on them, workers would lose their jobs. For Bangladesh, shipbreaking, with all its problems, is an important industry. In a way, the steel that they get from the ships is like the metals we get from our mines. It's their raw material.

Ling

The rest of the world should be helping developing countries deal with some of their problems. An environmental problem in one part of the world really affects us all. Developing countries don't have the resources to solve all their environmental and resource problems. It's going to take global co-operation to set standards and find solutions. Developing countries shouldn't have to solve what really are global problems all by themselves.

Marie

It isn't necessary for all countries to have the same conditions. The world needs to have differences. And really, a lot of the good things in our lives come about because people earn less in developing countries. If we made them follow tough environmental and labour laws, the cost of the goods and services we want would rise. These countries should have the same chance to improve conditions in their own time and in their own way as we in the developed world did. They can learn from developed countries, but they should be free to make their own decisions.

Tom

Your Turn

How would you respond to the question Ling, Marie, and Tom are answering? Do you believe that all countries should contribute to a sustainable future by following the same environmental standards? Do you think that requiring sustainable practices would help or hinder the expansion of globalization? Explain your ideas.

At the same time, organizations such as Greenpeace, the International Maritime Organization, and the International Labour Organization are pressing for more comprehensive international rules and tighter enforcement to persuade the shipbreaking industry to become more sustainable. As Figure 11-21 shows, some regulations now exist, but they are neither comprehensive nor well enforced.

Identify some barriers to creating international laws to control the shipbreaking industry. Who might oppose these laws? What groups are likely to support these laws? Explain to a partner your estimate of the likelihood that these laws will be developed and enforced within the next few years.

Figure 11-21 **Some Existing Controls on Shipbreaking**

Existing International Laws and Regulations	Problems with Enforcement
Movement of hazardous waste across international borders	Owners are required to notify shipbreaking yards when ships are carrying hazardous materials across international borders. But little effort is taken to ensure that notification has occurred, and this regulation is often ignored by shipbreaking countries.
Discharges of waste from ships	Waste is supposed to be discharged in approved facilities so that it is contained. The person in charge of the ship is responsible for reporting leaks or improper discharges. In shipbreaking yards, leaks and discharges go unreported.
Human rights obligations	Under the Universal Declaration of Human Rights, the dumping of hazardous materials that might affect people nearby is prohibited. A UN report clearly identifies shipbreaking as an important source of pollution.
Safety of workers	The International Labour Organization sets out standards for the safety and health of workers, including shipbreakers. But these recommendations are not legally binding and do not override national laws.
Guidelines that cover normal shipping operations	The International Maritime Organization has drafted guidelines for shipbreaking and shipbreaking countries. But these are voluntary, and a number of important issues are not covered.

REFLECT AND RESPOND

Transportation by ship is crucial to the globalization process, but is the shipping industry sustainable? Create a two-column chart like the one shown to record evidence for and against the sustainability of shipping. Then review what you have read in this chapter so far. You may also wish to consult other sources.

When you finish, share your ideas with one or two classmates and discuss the similarities and differences in your ideas. Based on this discussion, you may wish to add ideas to your chart.

Is the shipping industry sustainable?	
Evidence for Sustainability	Evidence against Sustainability

Last year, 2006, was a lost year for the federal government in contributing to the fight to stop global warming and meeting Canada's international obligations under the Kyoto Protocol. Federal programs were slashed and the importance of the issue downplayed. The lost year followed a decade of procrastination, half-measures and delays by the previous government . . . Canada remains an international laggard in reducing greenhouse gas emissions.

— Sierra Club of Canada, "Kyoto Report Card 2007"

FYI

Over the past 100 years, the world has warmed by 0.6° C, while Canada's average temperature has increased by 1° C.

Figure 11-22 Most Canadians support taking decisive action to reduce the greenhouse gas emissions that lead to climate change. These demonstrators gathered outside a 2005 UN-sponsored climate change conference in Montréal.

HAVE EFFORTS TO PROMOTE SUSTAINABILITY BEEN SUCCESSFUL?

The sustainability of economic activities is a growing concern worldwide. Environmentalists, governments, industries, and individuals are making efforts to improve the sustainability of many economic activities. The success of these efforts can be evaluated by examining examples in three areas: the Kyoto Protocol, the Alberta tar sands, and alternative energy sources.

The Kyoto Protocol

Problem Around the world, increased output of greenhouse gases is contributing to a rise in average global temperatures. A further increase of between 1° C and 5° C is predicted — enough to damage physical systems and cause economic losses of up to $5 trillion. Developing countries will suffer more than developed countries.

Proposed Solution At a 1997 conference in Kyoto, Japan, 141 countries, including Canada, signed an agreement that became known as the Kyoto Protocol.

Goals The Kyoto Protocol called on countries to reduce greenhouse-gas emissions to 5.2 per cent below 1990 levels by 2012. Canada set a target of 6 per cent.

Actions Countries were free to develop their own plans to meet the targets. In Canada, plans focused on reducing fossil-fuel use. Initiatives included requiring large factories and power plants to cut emissions, federal government partnerships with provinces and municipalities to make infrastructure improvements, support for energy alternatives, and encouraging industries, such as automakers, to take voluntary actions.

Successes A 2006 poll by McAllister Opinion Research found that 77 per cent of respondents believed that Canada should meet or exceed its Kyoto targets. The federal and some provincial governments have adopted strategies to reduce greenhouse-gas emissions; some municipalities have also developed plans; and some industries have taken action. But in 2004, Canada's emissions were 27 per cent higher than 1990 levels.

Barriers Canada has made no progress toward achieving its Kyoto targets. Opposition to Kyoto is strong in some provinces, such as Alberta, and in some industrial sectors, such as the oil industry. Some people say that meeting the targets will mean huge job losses. By early 2007, the federal government had taken no decisive action.

With a partner, find out how the situation in Canada has changed since early 2007. What action(s) do you think Canada should take to slow the process of climate change?

Alberta Tar Sands

Problem Though the Alberta tar sands contain an estimated 180 billion barrels of heavy oil, separating the oil from the sand requires a great deal of energy. It now takes one barrel of oil to extract three barrels of usable crude. This energy-intensive process means that the tar sands project is a huge source of greenhouse gases. These problems will increase as the project moves from its current extraction rate of one million barrels a day to a projected five million barrels a day by 2030.

Goals To lower the energy needed to extract oil from the tar sands, to save on production costs, and to reduce greenhouse-gas emissions.

Actions New, more efficient methods of extracting deeper oil are being tried. These include using steam to loosen the oil and allow producers to draw it upward to the surface, and blasting out the oil using compressed air. One initiative works to extract carbon dioxide emissions from exhaust flues.

Successes More than 80 per cent of the tar sands are owned by the Alberta government and are leased to producers. Government agencies oversee the various projects and monitor environmental conditions. Royalties from the tar sands are invested in projects and programs that benefit all Albertans.

Barriers Though Alberta is considered a business-friendly province with minimum regulations, some investors remain suspicious of the tar sands project because of its high costs and unresolved environmental problems. At the same time, the world's supply of accessible light crude oil is running out, and energy companies are turning to dirtier sources such as the tar sands, which have the potential to meet a substantial portion of Canada's energy needs in the coming decades.

Conduct research to find out how an oil company is trying to increase the sustainability of its tar-sands operations. Rate these efforts on a scale of 1 to 5 (1 = more effort needed; 5 = excellent effort).

Web Connection

To find out more about how oil is extracted from the tar sands, go to this web site and follow the links.

www.ExploringGlobalization.ca

Figure 11-23 A conveyer-belt system is used to extract oil at Syncrude's operation in Fort McMurray. What are some environmental issues suggested by this photograph?

Companies working [in Alberta] say they are making considerable strides in protecting the environment. They are eager to discuss their efforts to reduce air pollution and water use and boast of their post-mining restorations, including one where rolling hills support bison herds … But critics say the environmental work done so far has been highly experimental and that there is no definitive answer as to the long-term harm tar sands production is doing to northern Alberta.

— *Mary O'Driscoll, reporter,* Environment and Energy Daily, *2005*

Figure 11-24 Cattle graze near wind turbines at the McBride Lake East wind farm near Fort Macleod. Creating energy from wind turbines like these is an expanding business in Canada. Identify some pros and cons of wind energy.

Alternative Energy Sources

Problems Alternative energy sources, such as solar and wind power, have fewer environmental impacts and are more sustainable because they do not use up non-renewable resources, such as oil and gas. But alternatives to fossil fuels are developing slowly.

Goals To replace a substantial portion of the fossil fuels that currently dominate Canadian energy supplies with a mix of alternative energy sources. Along with this shift in energy sources would be a focus on reducing energy consumption through conservation measures.

Actions Many organizations and businesses are exploring ways of using alternative energy resources. These strategies include retrofitting existing buildings to use "green" energy resources and developing new buildings with a mix of energy sources. Some governments are calling for greater energy efficiency standards for vehicles. In general, alternative energy initiatives are at the preliminary or experimental stage.

Successes Several wind farms in Alberta have shown that wind energy has potential as a source of clean energy. In addition, the cost of producing solar energy using photovoltaic cells is steadily dropping, making these units more affordable and increasing their potential as an alternative energy source. And several newly developed small-scale hydroelectric plants in Alberta show that hydroelectricity also has potential as a renewable energy source.

Barriers Prices for energy from alternative sources are generally higher than for conventional sources of power. Existing tax structures favour conventional sources, such as fossil fuels, over alternative sources. Solar and wind power do not provide a continuous supply of power and require the development of ways to store energy or to mix energy sources that can be used as needed.

Some observers suggest that people are investing in "green" energy because they are hoping that governments will change their policies. How might government policies affect the development of alternative energy sources? What role do governments play in maintaining the world's long-term dependence on fossil fuels? In what ways do government policies affect the sustainability of globalization? Use examples to illustrate your ideas.

Individual Initiatives

In many cases, people are not waiting for governments to do something about improving sustainability. Like students in Cochrane, Alberta, who raised the money to install a combined solar and wind project at their school, people are taking steps of their own. Many investors, for example, are directing their money to companies that are developing "green" energy technologies. What purposes might investments like these serve?

Donald McInnes, president of Plutonic Power Corp., noted this trend when he said, "It's no secret that increasing concerns about the high price of fossil fuels and greenhouse-gas emissions has sparked new life into the alternative energy sector. Investment is pouring into the industry as hopes for new, improved 'green' energy technologies are translating into government policy at the local, regional and national level. Clean energy–related investment in North America soared to $2.1 billion in 2006, almost triple the $739 million invested in the energy category in 2005."

Web Connection

Students at Cochrane High School in Cochrane, Alberta, have earned international acclaim for their efforts to improve their school's sustainability. To find out more about the initiatives they have taken, go to this web site and follow the links.

www.ExploringGlobalization.ca

PROFILE

WANGARI MAATHAI AND THE GREEN BELT MOVEMENT

In Kenya, concern for sustainability is a central issue on the political agenda, thanks in large part to Wangari Maathai. Maathai is the founder of the Green Belt Movement. This internationally acclaimed tree-planting organization works to offset the destruction of African forests and the loss of natural resources. More than 30 million trees have been planted since the movement was founded in 1977.

The campaign has mobilized many people, especially women, to fight unsustainable practices that lead to deforestation, soil erosion, and environmental degradation. The Green Belt Movement operates in more than 600 communities across Kenya, and in 1986, the Pan-African Green Belt Network was established. This network has spread tree-planting programs to several other African countries, including Tanzania, Uganda, Malawi, Lesotho, Ethiopia, and Zimbabwe.

A firm believer in the power of one, Maathai was awarded the 2004 Nobel Peace Prize for her efforts. "The core of the Green Belt Movement is really about empowering people to take charge of the environment," she has said. "Tree planting is the action, is the symbol, is the focus. But the actual transformation is in the individual."

Figure 11-25 Kenyan Wangari Maathai, the first African woman to win the Nobel Peace Prize, was born into a farming family in the highlands of Mount Kenya. She earned a doctorate from the University of Nairobi, where she taught veterinary anatomy.

1. Are ships — or can ships be — a sustainable form of transportation? Apply what you have learned about the process of analyzing relationships in geography to this issue by following the steps set out in the Focus on Skills feature on pages 264 to 265. Decide on an appropriate way of communicating your new understandings to others.

2. In October 2006, several workers from the shipbreaking beaches of India were invited to speak to a meeting of the International Maritime Organization in London, England.

   Vidyadhar Rane, one of the workers, explained that "people here don't have goggles, they don't have helmets, masks or safety boots — many don't have any kind of boots. There should be work, but there should be no compromise on safe work. I am appealing to the developed countries who send their ships to Asia to take some responsibility and save lives."

   Write reports about this meeting from the points of view of two reporters.

   a) The first reporter writes for a business magazine that caters to the shipping industry and counts among its advertisers many shipping companies and ship builders.

   b) The second reporter writes for a social issues magazine that focuses on human rights and improving working conditions.

   Your reports should include facts and ideas from this chapter and other sources, as well as several points of view and perspectives on sustainability and its relationship to globalization. Be sure to acknowledge the sources you used.

3. How have governments, businesses, industries, organizations, individuals and others in your community tried to improve sustainability? Using Internet sources, information from municipal and government agencies, and information drawn from family members and friends, list three actions or programs that have been undertaken in your community. Some areas you might investigate are

   • water supplies
   • sewage treatment
   • disposal of solid wastes
   • energy sources
   • energy conservation in public facilities
   • industrial initiatives
   • transportation

   Record your findings in a chart like the one shown on this page. An example is filled in to help get you started.

Program or Initiative	Goals	Effects So Far
To improve recycling of metals and plastics in the community	Reduce by 50% the amount of solid waste that is being buried in landfill sites within five years	Recycling rates have improved somewhat; more efforts needed to reach target

4. Read this excerpt from a newspaper opinion piece by Don Lenihan, Tim Barber, Graham Fox, and John Milloy, who are the authors of *Progressive Governance for Canadians: What You Need to Know.* In their newspaper article, the writers considered the role of government in achieving sustainability.

> From a public policy viewpoint, global warming is the mother of all issues. Not just because our fate hangs in the balance, but because it calls for a response that would shake modern government to its foundations.
>
> Rebuilding our society around the goal of sustainable development would force governments to overhaul and align virtually every policy field, from industry to education, transportation to labour, agriculture to health. It would take co-ordination, co-operation and collaboration on a scale we have not yet seen.
>
> If there is a silver lining in this cloud, it is that our governments desperately need this kind of overhaul. They were designed for the 19th century and function as if the world had hardly changed. As a result, they are increasingly ineffective — and risk becoming simply irrelevant

a) Suppose you are a politician in Canada. How would you respond to this criticism of governments? Do you think that the criticisms are valid? Explain the reasons for your judgment.

b) Identify and explain three actions that governments might take to improve the sustainability of Canadian energy supplies.

5. Reread the material on Wangari Maathai and the Green Belt Movement on page 275. Explain why you think Maathai was awarded the Nobel Peace Prize for her environmental work.

6. With a partner, compose a letter to the president of a shipping company. Explain your position on flagging out.

Figure 11-26 A large oil tanker. What impact does a vessel like this have on the sustainability of globalization?

Think about Your Challenge

Review the challenge for this related issue. Your assignment is to write a persuasive essay on the extent to which globalization contributes to sustainable prosperity for all people. Review the notes you have been assembling. Prepare an outline for your first draft. You may wish to use the model shown on page 213. Share your outline with a partner or your teacher. Based on the feedback you receive, revise your outline and begin writing the essay.

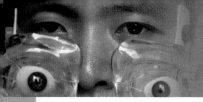

Chapter 12 Sustainable Prosperity— Challenges and Opportunities

Figure 12-1 The young people in these photographs are about the same age. In the bottom photograph, young Sambura women carry water from a communal well to their homes in northern Kenya, Africa. In the top photograph, Canadian students eat lunch in a café. Their water is easily obtained.

THE YOUNG PEOPLE IN THE two photographs on the previous page live very different lives. Their prosperity and sense of safety, comfort, security, and health — the factors that contribute to quality of life — are affected by the communities and countries in which they live.

In the dry northern part of Kenya, young women spend hours every day carrying water from wells and rivers to their family homes. Because they are helping to keep their families alive, they do not have time to go to school. The water they collect is often polluted, and this contributes to Kenya's high death rate from water-borne diseases.

In North America, young people spend hours every day at school, where they prepare themselves for the future. They can go to a fountain for a drink of clean water and to a cafeteria to eat lunches they have either brought from home or bought at school.

As you examine the photographs on the previous page, consider the following questions:

- What does "prosperity" mean to the young people in these photographs?
- How do the photographs reflect their quality of life? Their prosperity?
- How will the daily activities of the young people in the two groups affect their future prosperity?
- How are the needs of the young people in these photographs the same? How are they different?

KEY TERMS

sustainable prosperity

sustainable development

knowledge economy

privatization

global climate change

LOOKING AHEAD

In this chapter, you will explore answers to the following questions:

- What is sustainable prosperity?
- What political and economic challenges and opportunities are associated with globalization?
- What choices are associated with sustainable prosperity?

My Point of View on Globalization

Use words or images — or both — to express your current view on economic globalization. Compare this with the points of view you have already recorded in your notebook, learning log, portfolio, or computer file. Is your point of view changing? If so, how? Date your ideas and record them so that you can continue to return to them as you progress through this course.

WHAT IS SUSTAINABLE PROSPERITY?

Like the word "globalization," the term "**sustainable prosperity**" is defined differently depending on a person's point of view and reason for using the term in a particular context. For some, sustainable prosperity means practising stewardship of the environment and resources for future generations. Their goal is to balance environmental, social, and economic factors. What do you think it means to have prosperity that is sustainable? How can people sustain this prosperity in a globalized world?

Global sustainable prosperity is connected to global economic prosperity. But as Benjamin William Mkapa says in the Voices feature on this page and as the photographs on the opening page of this chapter show, "prosperity" can mean different things to people who live in developed and developing countries.

In March 2007, the Nova Scotia government proposed legislation called the Environmental Goals and Sustainable Prosperity Act, which said that the "health of the economy, the health of the environment and the health of the people of the Province are interconnected." Among other things, the bill aims to reduce greenhouse-gas emissions, as well as the amount of garbage going to landfills, and to encourage people to produce electricity from renewable sources.

For other people, sustainable prosperity is more closely tied to freer trade among all countries, including developing countries. In this view, resolving international trade issues will lead to sustainable prosperity that is shared by all people around the world. Prosperity will be sustained if the world is integrated economically and if every country increases its productivity, eases trade restrictions, and reduces government intervention in the economy. Peter Ellyard says that sustainable prosperity will be achieved only when it extends beyond economics and trade to include all the needs of society and of the environment.

The United Nations and other organizations use the term **sustainable development** instead of "sustainable prosperity." According to the UN 1987 World Commission on Environment and Development, development is sustainable when it meets the needs of the present without compromising the ability of future generations to meet their needs.

As this chapter progresses, you will encounter many views about how people can achieve sustainable prosperity. Write a one-sentence explanation of the concept of sustainable prosperity as you now understand it.

Figure 12-2 A technician checks out a giant windmill at the Horns Rev wind farm in Denmark, where wind generates about 20 per cent of all electricity for the country. Globally, wind supplies less than 1 per cent of electric power, but it is a fast-growing source. How might this kind of technology contribute to sustainable prosperity and development?

Sustainable prosperity and global interdependence

Balancing economic and social prosperity can be a challenge, especially when economic and social goals clash. In Salaberry-de-Valleyfield, Québec, for example, two manufacturing plants closed for similar reasons. Gildan Activewear, one of the world's largest T-shirt manufacturers, closed in October 2006. Over the previous 10 years, this Canadian-owned company had gradually moved its operations to countries where workers are paid less. By 2007, Gildan employed 15 000 people, most in Honduras, Nicaragua, Haiti, and the Dominican Republic. Gildan officials explained that they moved so they could continue to compete with Asian companies.

In January 2007, about 800 people lost their jobs when the Goodyear Tire and Rubber Co., an American company, also closed its Salaberry-de-Valleyfield plant. The company president explained that the closing was because of "today's intensely competitive and increasingly global business environment."

What economic and social goals clashed in Salaberry-de-Valleyfield? Create a cause-and-effect diagram that illustrates the chain of events that led to the plant closings. Be sure to include an assessment of what you think happened after the plants closed.

Figure 12-3 This is the main street of Salaberry-de-Valleyfield, Québec. How do you think the closing of Gildan Activewear and the Goodyear Tire and Rubber plants affected the retailers on this street? How might the effects on retailers affect other people in the town?

Ideas

What things must change if all people are to enjoy sustainable prosperity?

The students responding to this question are Katerina, who lives in St. Albert and whose grandparents emigrated from Ukraine in 1948; Ling, who was born in Hong Kong but is now a Canadian living in Edmonton; and Deven, who was born in India but is now a Canadian who lives in Calgary.

> People have to realize that sustainable prosperity is everyone's responsibility — not just the people who run governments and big companies. My uncle lives in Leaf Rapids, Manitoba. His town banned plastic bags in grocery stores. The town gives shoppers reusable cloth bags. So everyone who changes over to cloth bags is doing a little bit to make sure that the environment will be sustainable.

Katerina

> Living in Alberta means that we really do have to figure out what to do about sustainable prosperity. After all, our own prosperity depends on the sale of fossil fuels — and they're a non-renewable resource. My mom and dad work in the oil industry. The province gets billions of dollars in royalties every year. But every step of the process, from getting the oil out of the ground to the way it's used as fuel in homes and vehicles, has some effect on people, animals, plants, soil, air, and water.

Ling

> We have to change the way we think about prosperity for everybody on the planet. That's the real challenge. I keep thinking about those girls in Kenya who have to spend hours every day collecting water for their families. All I have to do to get clean water is turn on the tap. If we're really going to make the world safe for those girls in Kenya — and for ourselves — we'd better all start learning more about what we can do to promote sustainable prosperity for all people.

Deven

Your Turn

How would you respond to the question Katerina, Ling, and Deven are answering? What changes do you think must be made to ensure that sustainable prosperity extends to all people in Canada and around the world?

CHECKBACK

You read about GDP in Chapter 6 when you learned about how the economic legacies of historical globalization continue to affect people in former colonies.

Measures of Prosperity

Groups and organizations use various measures to try to develop an accurate picture of how countries are sharing in sustainable prosperity and of how the sustainable prosperity of a country has changed over time. Some of these measurements are based on the standard of living: how well the people in a community or a country live and the number and quality of goods and services they enjoy. The more money a country has, the higher its standard of living is.

Gross domestic product as a measure of prosperity

Gross domestic product is a widely used measure of the health of a country's economy and the prosperity of its people. Comparing the GDP per person of a number of countries, such as those in Figure 12-4, provides an idea of differences in living standards in various countries.

Changes in GDP can be used to track the health of a country's economy. Agencies like Statistics Canada monitor and record these changes. Statistics Canada, for example, reported that Alberta's GDP growth between 2002 and 2005 was 43 per cent, the highest ever recorded by any province.

The income and standard of living of the people in a country are closely tied to the GDP. To measure how much money individuals in a country have to live on, GDP is averaged over the number of people in the country.

One of the drawbacks of this method of measuring prosperity is that it is an average — and averages can be deceiving. When GDP per person is calculated, for example, everyone is counted, including children. But children rarely work. If children were removed from the calculation, would the GDP per person be higher or lower?

In February 2007, *The Globe and Mail* reported that the chief executives of some companies in Canada earn up to 400 times more than the average worker. If a company has 100 workers who earn $35 000 a year and a president who earns 200 times as much, what would be the total earnings of the workers and the president? What happens when you average the earnings of these 101 people? How accurately does this number reflect the real prosperity of the workers? Of the company president?

Figure 12-4 **GDP per Person in Selected Countries, 2006**

Country	GDP per Person (U.S. Dollars)
United States	39 676
Norway	38 454
Canada	31 263
South Africa	11 192
China	5896
Ecuador	3963
India	3139
Honduras	2876
Kenya	1140

FYI

In 2005, the top 300 000 income earners in the United States earned nearly as much as the bottom 150 million income earners combined — and the top 1 per cent of the U.S. population earned 21.8 per cent of all reported income.

Web Connection

To learn more about the human development index and to examine current figures, go to this web site and follow the links.

www.ExploringGlobalization.ca

The human development index as a measure of prosperity

The human development index was created by the United Nations Development Program to measure quality of life in UN member countries. The HDI is used to classify countries as developed, developing, or underdeveloped and to measure how economic policies affect the quality of life of a country's people.

HDI calculations are based on three main categories:

- longevity, which is measured by life expectancy at birth
- knowledge, which is measured by school enrolment and adult literacy
- standard of living, which is measured by GDP per person

Examine the data in Figure 12-5 on page 283. Norway ranks first on the HDI, and Canada ranks sixth. Which countries do you think ranked second, third, fourth, and fifth? Explain why you made each prediction, then check the accuracy of your predictions by following the links in the Web Connection on this page. What factors affected the accuracy of your predictions?

Figure 12-5 Some HDI Scores, 2006

Country	HDI Ranking	GDP per Person (U.S. Dollars)	Life Expectancy at Birth (Years)	Adult Literacy Rate (Percentage)
Norway	1	38 454	79.6	99
Canada	6	31 263	80.2	99
U.S.	8	39 676	77.5	99
China	81	5896	71.9	91
Ecuador	83	3963	74.5	91
Honduras	117	2876	68.1	80
South Africa	121	11 192	47.0	82
India	126	3139	63.6	61
Bhutan	135	1970	63.4	42
Kenya	152	1140	47.5	47

The HDI was created to draw the attention of governments, the media, and NGOs to indicators that go beyond GDP and to reveal information that is not reflected in GDP statistics. Kuwait, for example, has a very high GDP but a low level of education attainment. And Canada, which ranks high on the HDI, has been criticized for the sharp differences between the level of quality-of-life indicators for the general population and for Aboriginal people.

Figure 12-6 The HDI Gap: All Canadians and Registered Indians, 1980–2001

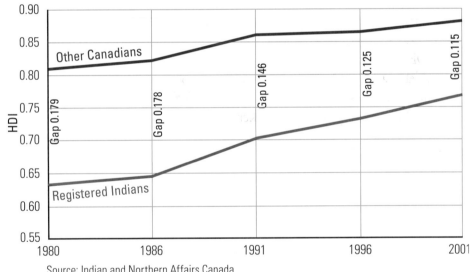

Source: Indian and Northern Affairs Canada

VOICES

Registered Indians living on reserves are ranked approximately 68th [on the HDI], somewhere between Bosnia and Venezuela, while off-reserve Indians are ranked 36th. These are contested statistics, but they do give some indication of the inequality of life between Canada's Aboriginal and non-Aboriginal communities.

— *Scott Fogden, program co-ordinator, Cultural Diversity Institute, University of Calgary, in "Native Social Issues in Canada," 2003*

Human development and access to clean water

The United Nations Development Program and other international organizations track global sustainable prosperity over time, focusing on issues that need particular attention. In 2006, for example, the *Human Development Report* focused on access to clean water and on the ability of societies to use water as a productive resource. The young women pictured on the opening page of this chapter may be among the 1 billion people in the world who do not have access to clean water. Currently, about 1.8 million children die every year of diseases caused by unclean water and poor sanitation.

In the past, few countries have considered water and sanitation to be political or social priorities. According to the UN, some of the world's poorest people are paying some of the world's highest prices for water.

Water may be something that many people in Canada take for granted, but in other countries — and in some parts of Canada — water availability and quality are important concerns. The following shows how three people have responded to these concerns.

JEFF PARKER is an award-winning editorial cartoonist whose work appears in *Newsweek*, *Time*, the *Washington Post*, and *Florida Today*.

PHIL FONTAINE, chief of the Assembly of First Nations, spoke out about the need for government and First Nations leaders to find a solution to the problem after a 2003 government report found that 30 per cent of First Nations' water systems were at "high risk" of contamination and were a danger to health.

If these conditions were being experienced by the general population, there would be a national outcry and an immediate response . . . Canada is not a poor country and these conditions should not be allowed to fester in our communities. There are moral, political, and legal reasons that compel the government to work with First Nations on a new approach to safe drinking water.

MARQ DE VILLIERS is a Canadian journalist and writer. This except is from his book *Water: The Fate of Our Most Precious Resource*.

The trouble with water — and there is trouble with water — is that they're not making any more of it. They're not making any less, mind, but no more either. There is the same amount of water in the planet now as there was in prehistoric times . . . Humans can live for a month without food but will die in less than a week without water. Humans consume water, discard it, poison it, waste it, and restlessly change the hydrological cycles, indifferent to the consequences: too many people, too little water, water in the wrong places and in the wrong amounts.

Explorations

1. Return to the ideas about sustainable prosperity you recorded earlier. After examining Jeff Parker's cartoon and reading Phil Fontaine's and Marq de Villiers's comments on the earth's water supply, rewrite your explanation to reflect changes in your thinking.

2. Can the difference between access to clean water for Aboriginal people in Canada and the general Canadian population be attributed in some ways to historical globalization? Explain your answer.

Other measures of prosperity

Some people believe that measures such as gross domestic product and even the human development index leave out important elements of prosperity.

King Jigme Singye Wangchuk of Bhutan, for example, created the gross national happiness index in 1972. The king says that the GNH index is based on Buddhist spiritual values rather than economic growth. The focus is on the inner happiness and the well-being of the people in a country — their spiritual and material development.

The purpose of the GNH index is to

- promote sustainable and equitable social and economic development
- preserve and promote cultural values
- conserve the natural environment
- establish good governance

The king is determined to help Bhutan keep its own cultural identity despite outside pressures, including the influence of television and the Internet. The government strictly controls trade, tourism, and foreign investment. In a globalizing world, some people think that the GNH index should be a guiding force in economic and political decisions.

The genuine progress index is another new index being developed to measure sustainability, well-being, and quality of life. Advocates of the GPI say that GDP does not measure growth accurately because it does not take people's real prosperity into account. GDP, for example, does not reflect the toll of economic growth on the environment, nor does it measure the inequality of income among the people in a country.

According to those who are developing the GPI, this system will more accurately measure economic progress. It will include environmental and social assets, such as volunteer work and time spent raising children. Measurements like these are not included in GDP calculations.

VOICES

Gross national happiness is more important than gross national product. Happiness takes precedence over economic prosperity in our national development process.

— *King Jigme Singye Wangchuk of Bhutan, 2002*

Figure 12-7 **Bhutan**

Figure 12-8 These children are riding a water taxi on a river in Bhutan. The country's infant mortality rate is 98.41 deaths per 1000 live births. By comparison, Canada's rate is 4.69 deaths per 1000 live births. What do statistics like these reveal about human prosperity and happiness?

REFLECT AND RESPOND

Think about the various measures of prosperity you have read about. Some try to include intangible items, while others focus mainly on economics. List five factors you would use to measure the overall well-being of the people in a country. For each factor, write a brief explanation of why you chose it. Provide a short introduction to set the stage for your new measure. Give a name to your measure of well-being.

WHAT POLITICAL AND ECONOMIC CHALLENGES AND OPPORTUNITIES ARE ASSOCIATED WITH GLOBALIZATION?

CHECKBACK

You read about the theories of Friedrich Hayek and Milton Friedman in Chapter 9.

VOICES

[The globalization] process can broadly be categorized as follows: growth and expansion in the few leading or fully participating countries; moderate and fluctuating growth in some countries attempting to fit into the globalization/ liberalization framework; and marginalization or deterioration experienced by many countries unable to get out of the acute problems such as low commodity prices and debt, unable to cope with problems of liberalization and unable to benefit from export opportunities.

— *Martin Khor, director of the Third World Network and author of* Rethinking Globalization, *2001*

Governments, businesses, communities, and individuals in countries around the world face both challenges and opportunities as a result of rapidly expanding economic globalization. Because of the speed of electronic connections, changes in a country's economy can happen very quickly and can deeply affect people and institutions. A natural or human-made disaster in Asia, for example, can present immediate problems for that country's trading partners and investors in other countries.

In recent years, Friedrich Hayek's and Milton Friedman's ideas of ensuring freedom and prosperity by promoting a market economy that is free of government interference have taken hold among many government leaders, especially in North America and Europe. According to this view, governments serve their people best by getting out of the way and letting their economies expand. Even China, a communist state, is determined to expand its economy through global trade.

Economic Growth and Sustainable Prosperity

Economic growth depends on businesses to produce more goods and services faster, more efficiently, and at a lower cost than the competition. According to many economists, continuous economic growth leads to greater prosperity for everyone in a country. But because so many countries are trying to achieve the same goals, competition is fierce.

Economic growth is measured by the rate at which a country's overall income grows. One way of measuring this growth is by tracking changes in GDP from year to year.

Though economic globalization has contributed to an increase in GDP in some countries, it is harder to tell how much it has contributed to sustainable prosperity. As Martin Khor points out in the Voices feature on this page, not everyone benefits from rapid economic growth.

Economic growth and the living standards of a country's people depend on the success of a country's businesses. Governments are affected by changes in economic growth because most of their revenue comes from the taxes paid by individuals and businesses. Businesses in Canada, for example, pay between 25 and 40 per cent of their profits in taxes to the federal, provincial, and municipal governments.

Business owners are also affected by changes in economic growth. These owners, who take the financial risks of running businesses, provide jobs for people in their communities. The employees and the business owners earn money that they use to buy the goods and services that are provided by businesses.

Figure 12-9 **The Fuel That Powers Economic Growth**

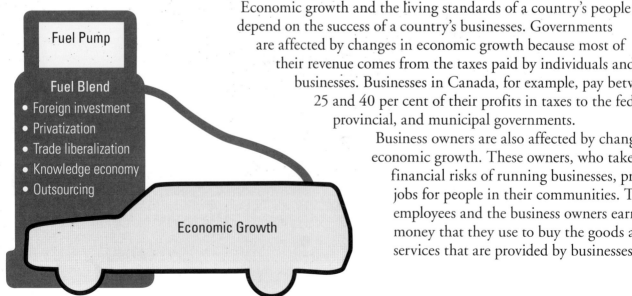

Fuel Pump

Fuel Blend
- Foreign investment
- Privatization
- Trade liberalization
- Knowledge economy
- Outsourcing

Economic Growth

Trade Liberalization and Sustainable Prosperity

Some people believe that the economic growth inspired by trade liberalization is the best way to ensure prosperity for all people. Horst Köhler, who heads the International Monetary Fund, has said, "Trade liberalization is the most important element to promote sustained growth for industrialized countries and for low-income countries."

But other people, such as environmentalist David Suzuki, are not convinced of the truth of this idea. In 2001, for example, St. Lucia's prime minister, Kenny Anthony, told delegates at the Summit of the Americas in Québec City: "Until the hemisphere as a whole can enjoy the fruits of trade liberalization, we cannot proclaim its glories. Until all the peoples of the Americas are free from hunger and free from the fear of unemployment, we cannot celebrate the benefits of trade liberalization. True, trade liberalization may bring new prosperity for some, but we must be honest and admit that it will destroy the lives of others."

VOICES

Economics and a reliance on science and technology to solve our problems has led to an unsustainable situation where continued growth in consumption is required for governments and business to be considered successful. This is a form of insanity. Economics is at the heart of our destructive ways and our faith in it has blinded us.

— *David Suzuki, Canadian scientist, environmentalist, and broadcaster, 2002*

Subsidizing farmers

Though governments around the world have cut tariffs on many goods and services, they have had trouble cutting farm subsidies — government grants that keep food prices low because farmers do not need to pass on all their production costs to consumers. Who do you think does — and does not — benefit from farm subsidies?

Through the early years of the 21st century, the members of the World Trade Organization tried to agree on how to liberalize trade in agricultural products. But as of February 2007, the problem remained unresolved.

Some people say that liberalizing trade in agricultural products would help the economies of developing countries because they would no longer need to spend money to support agriculture. They also accuse developed countries, such as Canada and the United States, of subsidizing their farmers so much that farmers in developing countries cannot compete.

In late 2005, the World Bank predicted that if all tariffs, subsidies, and other supports for agriculture were abolished, the global economy could grow by nearly $200 billion over the next 10 years.

What challenges do governments face when trying to negotiate international trade rules for farm products? What might happen to the sustainable prosperity of a country if farmers could not make a living — or if food prices went way up because the government stopped subsidizing agriculture? Revisit your explanation of sustainable prosperity. Revise this in light of your understandings of farm subsidies.

Figure 12-10 These farms are located in Ireland (left), Alberta (right), and Uganda (bottom). What similarities and differences can you see?

WRITING FOR DIFFERENT PURPOSES AND AUDIENCES

Whenever people write something — a text message, a to-do list, a telephone message, a letter, or an essay — they write with a specific purpose and audience in mind.

The purpose and audience determine the kind of writing needed. You might, for example, write a text or e-mail message to a friend one way — and a letter applying for a job another way. In each case, your purpose and audience are different. Focusing on your purpose and audience helps you decide on the most effective way of presenting your views so that they will be accepted by others.

The following steps will help you focus on a purpose and audience for your writing. You can use these steps to help you prepare the persuasive essay you are writing as the challenge for this related issue. You can use the same steps to prepare other persuasive essays and position papers as you progress through this course and others.

Steps to Writing for Different Purposes and Audiences

Step 1: Think about one purpose and audience

Imagine that you are representing a developing country's farmers at a World Trade Organization summit on agricultural subsidies. You are presenting a position paper with the goal of persuading developed countries, such as Canada and the United States, to consider reducing their farm subsidies so that farmers in your country can export produce that competes with Canadian- and American-grown produce.

Think about what you want to achieve and how you will inform at the same time as you persuade. In addition, consider the effect you want to create. The following chart sums up the purpose and audience for your position paper.

My Position Paper	
Purpose	To persuade Western countries to reduce farm subsidies
Audience	Delegates from Western countries Media from my country and the West

Step 2: Think about different audiences

When you are presenting your position on an issue, you need to think about the people you are trying to convince of the validity of your ideas. You need to anticipate what they are likely to think and be ready to respond to alternative ideas.

With a partner, discuss responses to the following questions:

- What are your audience's views on this issue likely to be? How will their experiences and viewpoints shape their reaction to your point of view?

- What will your audience know about the issue? What experiences related to this issue do you and your audience likely share? Will they need background information? Will some concepts need to be explained?

- What kind of supporting evidence will you need to assemble to persuade people to consider your point of view when they try to resolve this issue?

- What are the areas of common concern that you think all delegates agree on? How can you present your ideas so they can be heard and understood through the filter of these areas of common concern?

On a sheet of paper, copy the chart on the following page. With your partner, fill in the chart to show how your position paper might change when you are writing for different audiences. An example is partially filled in for you.

Audience	Purpose	How would the position paper change to suit the audience? How would the position paper stay the same?
Canadian senior citizens living on fixed incomes	To convince audience that higher food prices may be offset by other advantages	Would need to provide lots of background about what farm subsidies are and their effects Would include acknowledgement of concerns about possibility that food prices in Canada will go up Would need to provide suggestions for coping with higher food prices Would need to list advantages of increased competition
A group of Canadian consumers		
Canadian politicians		
Farmers in your own country		
Politicians in your own country		

Step 3: Think about different purposes

With your partner, talk about how your position paper would change

- if its purpose were to persuade conference delegates to agree not to reduce farm subsidies
- if its purpose were to persuade people to join a demonstration against farm subsidies

  Present your ideas to a small group, and listen as other group members present their ideas.

Summing up

When the group discussion concludes, revise your chart to reflect ideas gathered during this discussion. Then think about the persuasive essay you are working on in response to the challenge for this related issue. Preparing a similar purpose-and-audience chart will help focus your thinking as you work on the essay.

The Knowledge Economy

The **knowledge economy** is another term whose meaning changes depending on who is using it and why. In general, the knowledge economy includes businesses and individuals who use research, education, new ideas, and information technologies for practical purposes. Knowledge-based industries include those that create high-tech products for businesses: microsystem technologies, computer software, robotics, and biotechnology. Biotechnology innovators, for example, have developed new forms of antibiotics, as well as genetically engineered insulin, which can be produced more quickly and cheaply than older forms of this drug.

The knowledge economy offers both challenges and opportunities for sustainable prosperity. Because this branch of the global economy often offers high-income jobs, developed and developing countries try to create education systems that will help students land these jobs in the future.

The knowledge economy contributes to the evolution of technologies and increased global trade and competition. To remain competitive, knowledge workers must constantly upgrade their skills. On the one hand, people can now work in global networks to solve problems and create new ideas for products. On the other hand, keeping up to date can be difficult.

New technologies

Robots were once characters in science fiction novels, like those written by Isaac Asimov. Today, inventors create robots that have many practical and innovative uses. Car manufacturers such as General Motors have been using robots to build cars since the 1980s. When robots took over the assembly line, the people who were replaced had to find new careers. But robots can also be used for tasks that are dangerous for people, such as inspecting the exterior of buildings for flaws or detecting landmines.

Robotics in the field of medicine have improved human health. Robots are used, for example, to dispense medicines in hospitals to cut down on human error. And scientists are developing mini-robots that can be used in delicate surgery, as well as robotic eyes for people who have lost an eye because of illnesses.

The knowledge economy has also provided technologies that improve people's everyday lives. The wide use of cellphones, for example, means that many more people are able to communicate over distances than ever before. In some countries where the infrastructure for telephone land lines is still being developed, cellphones are used instead. In South Africa, for example, nearly 80 million people have cellphones, more than twice the number who have land lines.

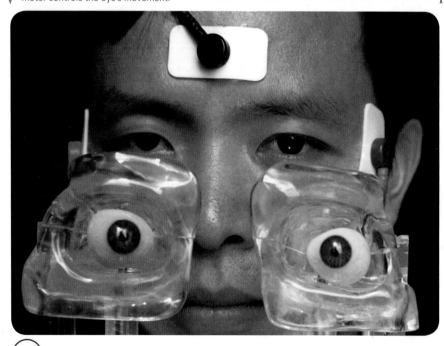

Figure 12-11 Jason Gu was a PhD student at the University of Alberta in 2000, when he and a team of scientists, engineers, and doctors from Misericordia Hospital began to develop an artificial eye that can move. When the robotic eye is perfected, people who have lost an eye because of cancer can have the device implanted. A tiny motor controls the eye's movement.

Privatization

Providing public services such as postal services can be costly. To eliminate the cost of operating these services and to raise cash, some governments are choosing **privatization**. Privatization involves selling a public service to a private company, so that the service is no longer owned by the government. Around the world, governments have privatized services such as electric utility companies, health care, highway repair and upkeep, and even water supply.

Figure 12-12 The president of Japan Post is shown with models wearing the uniforms that were to be be worn by employees when the company was privatized.

In 2007, for example, Japan privatized its government-owned post office. Many Japanese people use the post office not only to send mail, but also as a savings and investment bank. The Japanese post office is the world's largest savings bank, with 500 million accounts and 4000 branches. The new post office was divided into four separate companies: a bank, an insurance company, a courier service, and a post office.

Privatization advocates believe that it is an important trade liberalization reform. They say that

- privatization lowers taxes because the service is no longer paid for by taxpayers
- the competition that results from privatization improves the quality of service and leads to lower prices

Those who oppose privatization say that it makes services more expensive because private companies must make a profit, and the company's profit is calculated into the cost of the service. They maintain that governments can provide the service more cheaply because they do not need to make a profit. And they add that govenment-run services meet the needs of all citizens, not just those who can afford to pay for them.

Privatization doesn't always work. In 1989, the New Zealand government sold Air New Zealand to an international group that included Qantas and American Airlines. But in 2001, Air New Zealand ran into severe financial problems, and in 2002, the government took back control. The government rescued the company because the airline is essential to New Zealand's economy.

Sometimes privatization is controversial. According to the business magazine *Fortune*, the control of water resources is "one of the world's great business opportunities. It promises to be to the 21st century what oil was to the 20th." In 56 countries, the water supply is controlled by large transnational corporations that profit from providing people with water. In some cases, this has resulted in improved service, but it can also result in higher costs for the people who need the water.

Find out which services (e.g., telephone, electricity, garbage collection, public transit) in your community are publicly owned and which are privately owned. Record two arguments you would use to persuade people to support continuing public ownership and two you would use to support private ownership.

Web Connection

To find out more about the issues involved in water privatization, go to this web site and follow the links

www.ExploringGlobalization.ca

VOICES

Everything about global capital markets seems to be breaking records these days . . . Of course, it has long been possible to trade goods, but being able to move billions of dollars around the world with a touch of a button is new. Technology has revolutionized capital markets more dramatically than almost any other part of the economy.

— *John Micklethwait and Adrian Wooldridge, in* A Future Perfect: The Challenge and Hidden Promise of Globalization, *2000*

Figure 12-13 **Canadian Foreign Investment, 1990–2005**

Year	Canadian Investment in Other Countries (Millions of Dollars)	Foreign Direct Investment in Canada (Millions of Dollars)
1990	98 402	130 932
1995	161 237	168 167
2000	356 506	319 116
2005	464 058	415 561

Source: Department of Foreign Affairs and International Trade Canada

Privatizing water

In some developing countries where the World Bank has made structural-adjustment loans, governments are encouraged to privatize water utilities. This can result in high costs and affect the sustainable prosperity of the very people who can least afford to pay for water. Do you think that supplying water should be a public or private service?

In its 2006 report called *Beyond Scarcity: Power, Poverty and the Global Water Crisis*, the United Nations Human Development Program comments that the debate over water privatization often overlooks "the fact that the vast majority of the poor are already purchasing their water in private markets," which sometimes charge high prices for water. But the Human Development Program also warns that privatizing water may result in a monopoly, which is then free to charge high prices for water. In addition, some governments do not regulate the private providers to make sure that the water is safely and efficiently delivered to everyone in a country.

Foreign Investment

Foreign investment is the purchase of assets in one country by individuals, institutions, or governments in another country. Foreign investors can buy shares in existing businesses, set up new businesses, or invest money in the currency of another country.

Those who favour Canadian foreign investment see it as an opportunity to keep Canada competitive in an interconnected and fast-moving global economy. In this view, foreign investment strengthens the sustainable prosperity of Canadian companies, consumers, and workers. It also strengthens ties among Canada's trading partners. The Canadian government says that "Canada has a clear interest in providing for stability, transparency, predictability, non-discrimination, and protection for Canadian companies and individuals that invest abroad, as well as for foreign investors wishing to invest in Canada."

Risks of foreign investment

At the same time, some people are concerned that foreign investment can cause sudden and dangerous risks to a country's economy. By the early 1990s, for example, South Korea boasted the world's 11th largest economy and was growing rapidly. This growth attracted foreign investment that helped stimulate the economy, increase employment, and raise the living standards of many South Koreans.

But in 1997, something went very wrong. The value of a number of East Asian currencies — including South Korea's — fell. Investors around the world lost confidence in the South Korean economy and started to pull their money out. This happened very quickly, thanks to the electronic interconnections in money markets around the world. The South Korean economy shrank, the government had to borrow $58 billion from the International Monetary Fund, some of the country's largest companies closed down, and many South Koreans were thrown out of work. The standard of living they had enjoyed disappeared, and investors lost billions of dollars.

Foreign investment and Kurdistan

Kurdistan is in the northern region of Iraq and, compared with some other areas of the country, was relatively peaceful in 2007. The Kurdish people suffered under Iraqi dictator Saddam Hussein. More than 100 000 Kurds were killed by Saddam's forces during the late 1980s. Thousands more fled to neighbouring countries. Their farms, villages, and economic base were destroyed.

When Saddam was overthrown, Kurdistan became an autonomous region under the new Iraqi constitution. People who had fled began to return home, where the unemployment rate stood at about 30 per cent.

To help correct this situation and stimulate the economy of the region, Kurdistan government officials are trying to attract foreign investment. Money is needed to rebuild homes, roads, hospitals, schools, hotels, and shopping areas that were destroyed in the conflicts of the past decades. They are also looking for foreign investment in agriculture, mining, tourism — and oil. Kurdistan is thought to be rich in oil reserves, and this has attracted the attention of foreign oil companies, which are investing in exploration in the region.

Figure 12-14 **Kurdistan**

Canadian companies in Kurdistan

Among foreign oil companies investing in the region is WesternZagros, which is a wholly owned subsidiary of Western Oil Sands of Calgary. Western Oil Sands was formed in 1999 to participate in the development of the Alberta tar sands. The company will explore a 2120-square-kilometre region of Kurdistan for oil.

Heritage Oil Corp., also of Calgary, which has exploration projects in Uganda and the Democratic Republic of Congo, is also "pursuing opportunities" in Kurdistan.

Figure 12-15 Kurds were persecuted by Iraqi dictator Saddam Hussein. Many people lived in exile for decades but are now starting to return home. Awat Najat is one. She stands in front of her makeshift home in Kirkuk.

REFLECT AND RESPOND

Create a chart like the one shown. On your chart, identify five groups for whom globalization presents a challenge or opportunity. For each, jot a note explaining why globalization presents a challenge or an opportunity — or both. An example has been filled in.

Compare your chart with that of a partner. With your partner, choose one group identified on one of your charts and decide on three points you would mention if members of the group were the audience for a presentation you are making on the challenges — or opportunities — of globalization.

| Challenges and Opportunities of Globalization ||
Group	Challenge, Opportunity, or Both
Knowledge workers	Challenge — Must keep upgrading skills to stay competitive Opportunity — Access to higher-paying jobs

Figure 12-16 Proportion of People Living on Less Than $1 a Day, 1990 and 2002

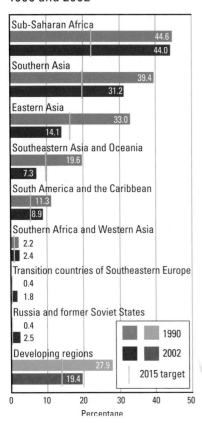

Figure 12-16 Proportion of People Living on Less Than $1 a Day, 1990 and 2002

Sub-Saharan Africa — 44.6 / 44.0
Southern Asia — 39.4 / 31.2
Eastern Asia — 33.0 / 14.1
Southeastern Asia and Oceania — 19.6 / 7.3
South America and the Caribbean — 11.3 / 8.9
Southern Africa and Western Asia — 2.2 / 2.4
Transition countries of Southeastern Europe — 0.4 / 1.8
Russia and former Soviet States — 0.4 / 2.5
Developing regions — 27.9 / 19.4

■ 1990   ■ 2002   2015 target

Percentage: 0 10 20 30 40 50

Figure 12-17 Millennium Development Goals

 1 Eradicate Extreme Hunger and Poverty

 2 Achieve Universal Primary Education

 3 Promote Gender Equality and Empower Women

 4 Reduce Child Mortality

 5 Improve Maternal Health

 6 Combat HIV/AIDS, Malaria, and Other Diseases

 7 Ensure Environmental Sustainability

 8 Develop a Global Partnership for Development

WHAT CHOICES ARE ASSOCIATED WITH SUSTAINABLE PROSPERITY?

Economic globalization offers complex challenges and opportunities. Governments, non-governmental organizations, communities, and individuals around the world face the challenges of ensuring that people have opportunities to achieve sustainable prosperity. But there is debate over how to achieve this goal most effectively.

Millennium Development Goals

In 2000, the United Nations and leaders of more than 150 countries held an assembly at which they agreed to work toward a world in which everyone had an opportunity to achieve sustainable prosperity and development. The eight millennium goals are listed in Figure 12-17.

Since then, the UN has monitored the world's progress toward achieving these goals. One goal, for example, calls for the eradication of extreme hunger and poverty. To help achieve this, the UN set a target of cutting in half, by 2015, the proportion of the world's people whose income is less than $1 a day. Although the gap between rich and poor remains wide — both among countries and within countries — the proportion of people who live on less than $1 a day has been reduced.

Think about your spending over the past three days. List everything you buy and what it cost, then calculate the total. Divide this total by 3 to arrive at your average daily spending. Then add to your list everything you used but did not pay for (e.g., shelter, food, clothing, telephone, and computer). Estimate their costs and recalculate your average daily spending. How difficult would it be for you to live on $1 a day?

Jeffrey D. Sachs helped the United Nations prepare the millennium development goals. In his book *The End of Poverty: Economic Possibilities for Our Time,* he outlined a plan for managing some of the challenges faced by people trying to reduce poverty in their country.

- **Decentralization** — The people who live in the affected communities must be the ones who decide what should be done and how money should be spent.
- **Training** — People need to be trained to run poverty-reduction programs. This training should be carried out at the national, district, and village level.
- **Information technologies** — The people involved in poverty-reduction programs need to have access to computers, e-mail, and mobile phones so that they can communicate quickly with one another.
- **Measurable benchmarks** — A benchmark is a standard. People must have specific goals that are designed to suit their national conditions, needs, and availability of data.
- **Audits** — No country should receive funding unless spending can be audited.
- **Monitoring and evaluation** — Budgets and plans for monitoring programs should be part of all poverty-reduction programs.

Which millennium goal do you think you might be able to influence most directly? Explain why.

Climate Change and Sustainable Prosperity

Ensuring sustainable prosperity for all people on Earth is a challenge, one that many governments, businesses, scientists, and environmentalists are joining forces to meet. The interdependence and constant shifting of political, economic, and environmental factors make this challenge highly complex.

Global climate change

People around the world have been burning more and more fossil fuels — coal, oil, and natural gas — to create the energy needed to heat and cool homes, power cars, and run factories. The burning process releases carbon dioxide and other greenhouse gases that had been trapped in these fuels.

Greenhouse gases form a barrier in the atmosphere. This barrier absorbs heat from the earth's surface and radiates it back to Earth instead of allowing it to pass into space. This phenomenon is called the greenhouse effect, and many scientists say that it contributes to **global climate change** — small but steady changes in average temperatures around the world.

Many scientists believe that greenhouse gases already in the atmosphere will cause global temperatures to increase by an average of 0.5° C every year until at least 2025. This warming increases the risk of drought and evaporation of water from lakes and rivers. According to Gordon McBean, who heads the Canadian Foundation for Climate and Atmospheric Sciences, "Our climate is changing and it will continue to change for decades. Canadians need to think about what that means to them." But scientists also believe that actions taken now can slow the rate after 2025.

In April 2007, the Intergovernmental Panel on Climate Change issued a report on the effects of climate change. The IPCC is made up of scientists and government representatives from 100 countries. Susan Solomon, one of the lead authors of the report, said, "We can be very confident (i.e., with 90 per cent certainty) that the net effect of human activity since 1750 has been one of warming."

The IPCC report said that unless people around the world unite to stop the progress of climate change, the poorest people in the world will suffer the most as climate change affects animals, plants, and water supplies. The hardest-hit regions will be the Arctic, sub-Saharan Africa, small islands, and large deltas in Asia.

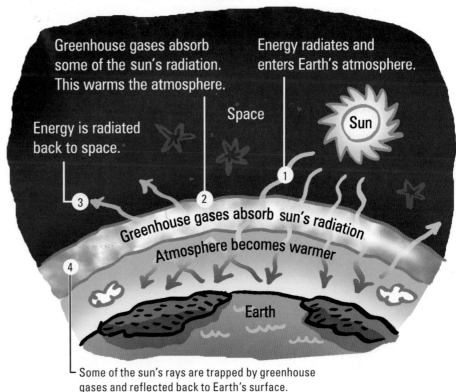

Figure 12-18 **The Greenhouse Effect**

Greenhouse gases absorb some of the sun's radiation. This warms the atmosphere.

Energy radiates and enters Earth's atmosphere.

Energy is radiated back to space.

Space

Sun

Greenhouse gases absorb sun's radiation

Atmosphere becomes warmer

Earth

Some of the sun's rays are trapped by greenhouse gases and reflected back to Earth's surface.

Country	Total CO$_2$ Emissions (Millions of Tonnes)	CO$_2$ Emissions per Person (Tonnes)	GDP per Person (U.S. Dollars)
Norway	35.21	7.9	38 454
Canada	521.40	16.9	31 263
U.S.	5762.10	20.2	39 676
China	3473.00	2.7	5896
Ecuador	20.70	1.7	3963
Honduras	5.00	0.8	2876
South Africa	344.60	7.8	11 192
India	1008.00	1.0	3139
Kenya	10.20	0.3	1140

Figure 12-19 **Carbon Dioxide Emissions in Selected Countries, 2005**

The writing of the report was controversial. Some scientists, for example, wanted to say that they had "very high confidence" (more than 90 per cent) in their findings. But representatives of some governments — the United States, Saudi Arabia, China, and India — wanted to reduce this estimate. The final report says that the confidence level was "high" (more than 80 per cent). Why do you think countries might have had different agendas?

Examine the data in Figure 12-19. What relationships do you observe? What factors do you think account for the large difference between the carbon dioxide emissions of Canada and the United States?

Changing Government Policies

The Intergovernmental Panel on Climate Change is an example of joint governmental efforts to meet the challenge of dealing with climate change. In Canada and other countries, local, provincial, and national governments — and individual citizens — are also trying to do their part.

Bolivia

The Bolivian government is very concerned about the speed at which the glaciers in the Tuni Condoriri mountains are melting. These glaciers supply 80 per cent of the water for residents of La Paz, the country's administrative capital. Water from the runoff is captured in a reservoir.

From 1983 to 2006, the glaciers shrank by more than a third. Oscar Paz, the head of the Bolivian national climate change program, says, "These glaciers are our water stores. One of our great concerns is the future of our drinking water supplies." What would loss of their water supply mean to the people of this city? How would this challenge affect people in a country where the GDP per person is only $3000?

Norway

The Norwegian government and the Global Crop Diversity Trust Foundation have co-funded the Svalbard Global Seed Vault, which is located far above the Arctic Circle on one of Norway's most northerly islands. The project is designed to save Earth's diverse seed sources in the event of a global catastrophe or plant epidemic. One goal is to prevent the kind of loss that has occurred in the United States, where 6800 of the 7100 varieties of apples once grown no longer exist.

Although there are 1400 seed banks around the world — including an Agriculture Canada bank in Saskatoon — the Svalbard vault will include seeds from both developed and developing countries around the world. Why do you think maintaining seeds in vaults is important?

Figure 12-20 The Svalbard Global Seed Vault will be built deep inside a mountain. Scientists believe that the thick rock and permafrost will ensure than millions of seed samples from around the world will remain frozen. This drawing shows what the entrance to the vault was to look like.

To what extent does globalization contribute to sustainable prosperity for all people? • MHR

Alberta

In April 2007, the Alberta government asked Albertans to help shape the province's climate change action plan and policies by responding to an online questionnaire. Alberta's greenhouse-gas emissions are the highest in Canada, even though the province has about one-quarter the population of Ontario and less than half the population of Québec. In responding to the questions, Albertans were asked to think about how their decisions might affect the province's economy, society, environment, communities, and future generations.

Albertans were asked to respond to questions like the following:

1. What goals do you want to set?
2. What important steps need to be taken?
3. What actions should Albertans take?
4. What role can individuals play?

Web Connection

To find out more about climate change and what the Alberta government plans to do about it, go to this web site and follow the links.

www.ExploringGlobalization.ca

PROFILE

WILLIAM MCDONOUGH
PROMOTING ZERO POLLUTION AND TOTAL RECYCLING

William McDonough is an architect and community designer who is dedicated to changing the design of the world to increase sustainability. He promotes "zero pollution and total recycling" and believes that buildings and products should be designed so that they contribute to a "diverse, safe, healthy and just world with clean air, water, soil and power."

McDonough designed Nike's energy-efficient and environmentally friendly European headquarters in Hilversum, Netherlands. The roof of this building collects rainwater that is used to irrigate the gardens. The heating and cooling system includes a large reservoir of water. In summer, the heat from the water is stored. In winter, this stored heat is used to help warm the buildings.

In his design for the Guantang Chuagye Park New Town Concept in Liuzhou, China, McDonough says the main energy systems will be solar energy. He foresees a day when "China will be the largest solar manufacturer in the world."

Figure 12-21 William McDonough designed the huge roof of the Ford Rouge Center truck factory in Dearborn, Michigan. It has been planted with a drought-resistant groundcover called sedum. The sedum grows in a four-layer mat of vegetation that collects and filters stormwater runoff (right). The roof helps cool the atmosphere in the surrounding community, absorbs carbon dioxide, and creates oxygen.

1. Review the description of sustainable prosperity you developed as you progressed through this chapter.

   a) Expand your description by adding an explanation of how you reached your understanding of this concept.

   b) Create an illustration that sends a clear message about your understanding of the concept of sustainable prosperity. The intended audience is your class. Match the form of your illustration to your message. You may choose, for example, to create

      • a political cartoon that points out the steps you and your classmates must take to help achieve sustainable prosperity
      • a poster that highlights an action your community has taken to promote sustainable prosperity
      • a magazine advertisement urging students to take steps to help your community achieve sustainable prosperity

   c) Prepare a short description of your visual explaining the various elements, what they represent, and why you chose them.

2. a) Return to the Points of View feature on page 284. Write your own quotation to add to the views included on this page. Ensure that your quotation reflects your understanding of sustainable prosperity.

   b) Review the data in Figure 12-19 (Carbon Dioxide Emissions in Selected Countries, 2005) on page 296 of this chapter. Select two countries from the list. Prepare a quotation from a farmer in one country and a politician in the other. The quotations should reflect what you think the views of these two people would be — on the basis of the data included on the chart. Before writing the quotations, you may wish to conduct further research into conditions in the country.

3. Return to the questions (p. 279) you responded to when this chapter began, and think about the answers you gave.

   a) The first question asks, What does "prosperity" mean to the young people in these photographs?
      Assume the character of one of the Kenyan teenagers. In character, write a short paragraph that sets out her response to the question. Then assume the character of one of the Canadians. Write a second short paragraph setting out her response.

   b) Compare the needs of the Kenyan and Canadian teenagers by creating a chart like the one shown. One row has been filled in as an example. Identify four more items under "Similar Need" and four items under "Different Need." Examine your chart and comment on what it shows.

Similar Need	How easily can the need be met?
Water	Most Canadians can get it easily anytime. Some Kenyans must spend most of their day collecting it.
Different Need	Why is the need different?

   c) How might one of the Kenyan girls define sustainable prosperity? Is this definition different from the one you developed in response to Question 1? Explain why this is so.

4. With a partner or small group, prepare a checklist that you can use to conduct an audit of your school and its efforts to achieve sustainable prosperity (e.g., How is waste paper handled? Is it recycled? Reused?).

When you complete your audit, create a report card for your school. Grade its efforts to
- reduce
- reuse
- recycle
- refuse

Work with your partner or group to recommend ways your school could improve its efforts to achieve sustainable prosperity. Create an action plan describing how you could persuade other students and school officials to put your recommendations into effect.

5. Read "Watershed Rap" on this page.
   a) Summarize its essential message in a couple of sentences.
   b) With a partner, add two or more verses that expand the rap's message and include mention of sustainable prosperity.
   c) With your partner, perform your verses for the class.

Watershed Rap

Adapted by Peter Donaldson
from the original by the Washington Department of Ecology

Interesting fact, whatever it's worth
70 per cent of big old Earth
Covered by a fabulous fluid force
H two O, life at its source

In all us people, truth to tell
There be a miraculous parallel
The part of humans that water claims
70 per cent, exactly the same

Open your eyes, it be everywhere
Down in the ground, up in the air
Fog, mist, dew drop diamond
Cloudburst sun, rainbow shinin'

Make you to think in a whole new way
How we do water every — every day
For drinking and swimming and boat transportation
Showers and flowers and crop irrigation

Pump it from rivers, industrial use
Spin turbines for electrical juice
Citizens want it, turn on the faucet
Flush it all down yo water closet

This be the dirt, crystal clear
Ain't so easy with water you hear
Cars and factories pollute up the air
Ssst — acid rain drizzle down everywhere

Ain't one source, ain't one clear solution
Here come the nightmare non-point pollution
And this be the clincher to make you queasy
All them problems from just one species

Get it together, man, on the double
Old water cycle really — really in trouble
Best thing to do is help spread the word
Takin' water for granted be way absurd

Step to the front, get out of the bleacher
Become the sermon and the preacher
Do the science, be the seeker
Protect yourself and every creature

Think about Your Challenge

Your challenge for this related issue is to prepare and write a persuasive essay. As you revise and edit your essay, revisit the editing steps on page 213 and revisit the Checklist for Success on page 212. Ask a partner to read and comment on your essay. Make final revisions based on the feedback you receive.

Key Issue
To what extent should we embrace globalization?

Related Issue 1
To what extent should globalization shape identity?

Related Issue 2
To what extent should contemporary society respond to the legacies of historical globalization?

Related Issue 3
To what extent does globalization contribute to sustainable prosperity for all people?

Related Issue 4
To what extent should I, as a citizen, respond to globalization?

Chapter 13
HUMAN RIGHTS, DEMOCRACY, AND GLOBALIZATION

To what extent have democracy and human rights shaped — and been shaped by — globalization?

What are human rights?

How are ideas about human rights and democracy related?

How are globalization, human rights, and democracy related?

Chapter 14
GLOBAL AWARENESS

To what extent does global awareness affect quality of life?

How has globalization affected awareness of issues?

How has global awareness affected gender issues?

How has global awareness affected labour and employment issues?

How are global awareness and quality of life related?

Chapter 15
GLOBAL CONNECTIONS

To what extent do global connections affect people?

How does globalization change communities?

How does the global need for resources affect people?

How does globalization affect people's health?

How have people responded to global issues?

Chapter 16
THE GLOBAL CITIZEN

To what extent should I embrace global citizenship?

What does global citizenship mean?

What does a global citizen do?

What is my role in the globalizing world?

THE BIG PICTURE

To what extent should we embrace globalization? This question presents the key issue of the course and has guided your inquiries as you have progressed through *Exploring Globalization*. In the four chapters of Related Issue 4, you will pull together the strands of the many ideas you have explored, analyzed, and evaluated in the previous three related issues as you considered your personal responses to globalization.

The question for this related issue — To what extent should I, as a citizen, respond to globalization? — encompasses many complex ideas. Does the concept of "I" mean you alone? Or is it necessary to consider the larger community when coming to understandings of the role of "I"? And does "respond" refer to an action, a set of ideas or ideals, a frame of mind, or a list of responsibilities? To help you respond effectively to the key course issue, you will explore and analyze ideas about quality of life, human rights, and democracy — and their interrelationship with the forces of globalization — as you progress through this final related issue.

Citizenship of a country is a relatively easy concept to grasp because it is a legal status. Either you are, or you are not, a citizen of Canada. But global citizenship is less well defined. Who decides what global citizenship means? Can you say no and opt out of global citizenship? And if you are a global citizen, what are your responsibilities? Many scholars argue that once change, such as that brought about by globalization, begins, it cannot be stopped. How, then, will you fit into a globalizing world?

In a globalizing world, you will be called upon to think beyond boundaries — both tangible and intangible — to connect with people and cultures with differing worldviews. The globalizing world has come to your country, to your community, to your front door. Many people believe that you are already involved in globalization, so that the only question that remains is how to respond to it most effectively.

In the fifth century BCE, the Greek philosopher Socrates said, "I am a citizen, not of Athens, or of Greece, but of the world." The concept Socrates was expressing continues to face people today. As you explore the ideas and issues in Related Issue 4, you will be challenged to develop understandings of the relationship between human rights, democracy, and the forces of globalization. The positions you develop will help inform your response to the key course issue.

The chart on the previous page shows how you will progress through Related Issue 4. As you explore this related issue, you will come to appreciate

- the idea of human rights

- the relationship between human rights, democracy, and globalization

- how global awareness has changed the way issues are viewed

- the concept of global citizenship

Your Challenge

Keep a journal or blog that concludes with your informed position in response to the question for this related issue:

To what extent should I, as a citizen, respond to globalization?

Then work with the class to build a consensus in response to the key course question:

To what extent should we embrace globalization?

Checklist for Success

As you keep your journal or blog and participate in the consensus-building activity, refer to this checklist.

My Knowledge and Understanding of the Issue

My position clearly shows my understanding of globalization.

My position shows the many opportunities and challenges that globalization presents.

My position is clearly expressed and supported by strong evidence.

The answers I prepared for questions from my classmates demonstrate my understandings of the issues.

My Selection, Analysis, and Evaluation of Information

My criteria for arriving at my informed position are clearly expressed.

My position shows that I considered diverse points of view and perspectives on the issues.

I correctly and accurately cited all sources and references.

My Contribution to the Consensus-Building Process

I effectively expressed and defended my position.

I participated respectfully as others expressed and defended their positions.

I showed a willingness to consider new ideas and other points of view and perspectives.

Preparing to Meet the Challenge

This challenge includes two elements.

1) Keep a journal or blog that you can draw on to develop and express your informed position on the related-issue question: To what extent should I, as a citizen, respond to globalization?

2) Use your informed position on the related-issue question as the basis of your contribution to the process of building a class consensus on the key course question: To what extent should we embrace globalization?

Your journal or blog

As you progress through this related issue, you will keep a journal or online blog that focuses on responding to the related-issue question: To what extent should I, as a citizen, respond to globalization? You will use your journal or blog to monitor and track your evolving responses to the ideas, information, points of view, and perspectives you encounter. As you do this, you will develop criteria to use to help you arrive at an informed judgment on the issue.

At the end of each lesson, you will have an opportunity to update your journal or blog — and to respond to the journal or blog entries of your classmates. When you reach the end of this related issue, you will draw on the ideas you expressed in your journal or blog to develop an informed position on the extent to which you, as a citizen, should respond to globalization.

Your contribution to building a class consensus

You will express your informed position on the extent to which you, as a citizen, should respond to globalization. This will be your starting position as the class engages in building consensus on a response to the overall key course question: To what extent should we embrace globalization?

Steps to Completing This Challenge

Jeremy's Globalization Blog
To what extent should I, as a citizen, respond to globalization?

Links

If you decide to keep a blog, your first page might look similar to this.

Day 1

Links

You may include as many entries as necessary.

My Informed Position

Links

Your final informed position on the related-issue question.

Step 1

If you decide to keep a journal, organize your pages so that there is room for your classmates to jot comments and provide feedback about your entries. If you decide to keep a blog, you may wish to examine some online blogs to see how they are organized so that people can respond.

Whether you are keeping a journal or blog, you may wish to review the material in the notebook, learning log, portfolio, or computer file you have been updating at the beginning of each chapter as your understandings of globalization evolved. On the basis of this material, as well as the ideas you will explore, analyze, and evaluate in this related issue and other research you may complete, you will develop criteria that you will use to make an informed judgment in response to the question for this related issue.

As you develop criteria and prepare an informed position on the issue, thoroughly analyze and interpret the elements of the issue question. How, for example, will you interpret the word "citizen"? Does it mean a citizen of Canada — or a citizen of the world? What responsibilities does this word imply? Include this analysis in your first journal or blog entry.

Step 2

Your classmates will have opportunities to respond to your journal or blog entries — and you will have opportunities to respond to theirs. As you progress through this related issue and expand your ideas in response to your reading and your classmates' comments, you may find that your analysis and interpretations change. Note these changes in your journal or blog.

Step 3

When you reach the end of this related issue, review the ideas and understandings you included in your journal or blog. Think about the criteria you used to make your judgments and draw from these to develop the criteria you will use to develop your final informed position on the related-issue question. Express this judgment in the final entry of your journal or blog and specify how it developed from your earlier entries and the criteria you used. Be sure to cite all sources you drew evidence from when developing your position.

Think about questions your classmates might ask when you present your position, and prepare possible responses to their questions.

Step 4

Present your informed position to the class — and respond to classmates' questions. Listen carefully as your classmates present their positions. Then contribute to the class consensus-building activity, which involves developing a response to the overall course question: To what extent should we embrace globalization?

To help you do this, you may wish to review "Focus on Skills — Building Consensus" (pp. 246–247). You may also wish to practise some of the effective listening and leadership tips set out in "Focus on Skills — Demonstrating Leadership during Discussions" (pp. 312–313).

Chapter 13 Human Rights, Democracy, and Globalization

Figure 13-1 The protesters in these photographs are expressing their beliefs about controversial issues. Think about the label "protesters." What connotations does this label suggest? Would another label be more appropriate? Explain the reasons for your response.

THE PHOTOGRAPHS ON THE previous page show people protesting actions taken by governments and corporations. Knowing that the media might report their protest to audiences around the world, what do you think the goals of the protesters in each photograph might be?

Examine the photographs and respond to the following questions:

- Do you think the photographs were taken in democratic countries? What evidence in the photographs supports your answer?
- What rights are the protesters exercising?
- What do you think the protesters in each photograph are demanding? What evidence in the photographs supports your answer?
- These photographs were published in various media (e.g., in newspapers and on the Internet). What effect do you think the pictures might have had on audiences around the world?
- What evidence of globalization can you see in these photographs?

Some images may be more effective at achieving the protesters' goals than others. With a partner, rank the photographs on the previous page from most to least effective at raising awareness about an issue.

KEY TERMS

basic needs

inalienable

human trafficking

LOOKING AHEAD

In this chapter, you will explore answers to the following questions:

- What are human rights?
- How are ideas about human rights and democracy related?
- How are globalization, human rights, and democracy related?

My Point of View on Globalization

Based on your current understanding, use words or images — or both — to express your current point of view on globalization. Date your ideas and keep them in a notebook, learning log, portfolio, or computer file so that you can return to them as you progress through this unit.

WHAT ARE HUMAN RIGHTS?

The photographs on the opening page of this chapter show that many people believe that having their basic needs met is a fundamental human right. But what does the fact that people believe that they must stage a protest to ensure that a need is met or a right is acknowledged say about the level of agreement on this issue?

The issue of basic needs and human rights raises a number of questions: What are people's **basic needs**? Is having one's basic needs met a fundamental human right? Who should be responsible for meeting these needs?

With a partner, brainstorm to create a list of everything you need in your life. To get started, you may wish to refer to the photographs on this page. Sort the items into categories (e.g., physical needs, social needs, and emotional needs). Once you have created categories, assign each need on your list to a category and rate each on scale of 1 to 4 (1 = It's nice to have, but if necessary, I could do without it; 4 = I absolutely cannot live without it). Which list includes the most number 4 rankings? What would happen if these things were not available to you? Where would you turn for help?

Figure 13-2 This man in Allahabad, India, is drinking polluted water from the Ganges River. The Ganges has great religious significance for Hindus, but the World Wide Fund for Nature has identified this river as one of 10 that are most at risk of being destroyed by pollution. Is clean drinking water a human right? Who should be responsible for ensuring that water supplies are clean?

Views on Human Rights

People have many different points of view and perspectives on human rights. In 1948, the United Nations created the Universal Declaration of Human Rights. The title of this document reflects the belief that human rights are universal — and that everyone in the world has the same rights because they are human beings. These rights include freedom of speech, the right to an education, and freedom to practise one's religion. People who share this perspective believe that making exceptions because of a failure to agree that human rights are universal opens the door for countries to abuse people's rights.

Figure 13-3 These Indonesians are taking shelter in a makeshift tent after their homes were destroyed by an earthquake in 2007. Do these people have a right to a better home than this? Who should be responsible for ensuring that their home is rebuilt?

Figure 13-4 Refugees from Hurricane Katrina, which devastated New Orleans in 2005, are lined up in a Denver, Colorado, shelter to pick out clothing. Do people have a right to clothing? Who should be responsible for ensuring that they have clothing?

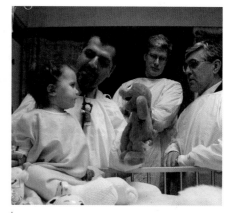

Figure 13-5 This one-year-old Edmonton girl is receiving medical treatment at the University of Alberta Hospital. Is medical care a human right? Who should be responsible for providing medical care?

Not everyone agrees with this perspective. Those who disagree argue that different cultures have different beliefs and traditions that must be taken into consideration. Shashi Tharoor, the UN's under-secretary-general for communications and public information, believes that human rights are universal, but he has summarized the opposing view by asking these questions: "Can the values of the consumer society be applied to societies that have nothing to consume? Isn't talking about universal rights rather like saying that the rich and the poor both have the same right to fly first class and to sleep under bridges? Don't human rights as laid out in the international covenants ignore the traditions, the religions, and the socio-cultural patterns of what used to be called the Third World?"

Others point out that the focus on individual freedoms in North American and European countries undermines important collective rights and values emphasized by other countries and Indigenous peoples. Those who take this view might, for example, argue that focusing on individual freedom of action can limit people's ability to protect the environment, which is a basic need.

Web Connection

To find out how the United Nations defines human rights, go to this web site and follow the links.

www.ExploringGlobalization.ca

Ideas

Do all human beings have the same rights?
Do you ever expect to be treated differently from others?

The students responding to these questions are Katerina, who lives in St. Albert and whose grandparents emigrated from Ukraine in 1948; Gord, a member of the Beaver First Nation near High Level; and Marie, a Francophone student from Medicine Hat.

I think all people should have the same rights. During World War I, the rights of Canadians of Ukrainian descent were taken away in Canada. They were moved away from their homes and families and sent to internment camps. When citizens of a country are scared or angry, they might be tempted to restrict the rights of immigrants. That's unfair. Everyone should have equal rights in Canada.

I've heard lots of people complain that First Nations have special rights and privileges in Canada. Some people, for example, believe that people living on reserves don't pay the same taxes as other people in Canada. But they don't understand Canada's history and the agreements that the Canadian government signed with First Nations. Shouldn't the government live up to the promises it makes to people? Wouldn't anyone want that?

I sometimes feel as if Canadians forget that there are Francophones who live outside Québec. Francophones all over Canada should have the right to protect their language and culture.

Katerina

Gord

Marie

Your Turn

How would you respond to the questions Katerina, Gord, and Marie are answering? Does being treated fairly mean being treated the same as everyone else? If your needs are different from other people's, should you have different rights? Explain the reasons for your answer.

The Evolution of Ideas about Human Rights

Figure 13-6 How Western Ideas about Human Rights Evolved

1700s
Increasing focus on individual freedom and rejection of idea of authoritarian rulers

Late 1800s and early 1900s
Increasing focus on rights of religious and ethnic minorities, prisoners of war, working conditions, right to vote

Later 1900s
Increasing focus on fundamental freedoms and expansion of rights to include political, social, and economic rights; focus on eliminating discrimination and abuse of women, children, people with disabilities, and so on

Late 1900s and early 2000s
Increasing focus on rights of citizens, Aboriginal peoples, and consumer rights in the face of increasing power of transnational corporations

Throughout history, various societies have held values and passed laws that reflect respect for human rights. But ideas about which rights are **inalienable** — cannot be taken away or transferred — have varied widely.

Contemporary Western ideas about human rights coincided with the development of a large European middle class that believed in individual independence and freedom. By the 18th century, during a period that became known as the Enlightenment, European philosophers such as John Locke and Adam Smith were arguing that governments should exercise only limited control over citizens. These philosophers believed that people are fundamentally free and that rulers have a responsibility to protect their freedom.

Other philosophers picked up on these ideas and began to focus on individual rights. As these ideas spread, they changed the political structure of many countries in Europe. They also spread to North America, influencing Britain's American colonies to fight a war of independence and win freedom from British rule. At the same time, however, many other colonies remained under the rule of imperial powers. The principles of freedom and liberty were not yet applied equally to all people.

A number of factors contributed to the spread of ideas about rights. The invention of the printing press meant that books, pamphlets, and newspapers could be printed and distributed more cheaply and quickly. Other technological changes meant that people could travel farther, faster, and more often than before. The same factors that had made slavery a global phenomenon, for example, also helped spread the ideas that would lead to its abolition.

REFLECT AND RESPOND

With a partner, compile a list of rights and freedoms that you know are protected in Canada, or examine the rights covered in the United Nations Universal Declaration of Human Rights. From the list, choose five rights that Canadians may take for granted. These might be rights or freedoms that Canadians are so used to having that they cannot imagine living without them.

With your partner, choose three rights or freedoms that you believe are sometimes limited in Canada. Provide an example of a situation in which a particular right has been limited or taken away. Do you believe that limiting this right is ever justified? Record your ideas on a chart like the one shown. To help you get started, an example is provided.

A right that is sometimes limited or restricted	An example of when this right is limited or restricted	Is the restriction of this right justified in this circumstance?	Reasons for my judgment
Freedom of speech	When someone is spreading hate toward a particular group in society	Yes	Individual rights should never be used to harm others

HOW ARE IDEAS ABOUT HUMAN RIGHTS AND DEMOCRACY RELATED?

"Democracy" and "human rights" seem to be expressions that go hand in hand. But some people question the assumption that human rights are always protected in democracies. And others say that people should not assume that those who live in democracies are the only ones who care about human rights.

Early Ideas about Human Rights

A number of ancient societies, such as those that follow, developed law codes for citizens to follow. How might putting laws in place ensure at least a degree of equality?

- **Ancient Persia** — Cyrus, the king of Persia in the sixth century BCE, is said to have instituted many reforms. When he conquered Babylon, which is part of present-day Iraq, he is said to have ruled with religious tolerance. He even restored the temples of the people he conquered.

    Archeologists believe that Cyrus ordered his promises recorded on the Cyrus Cylinder (see Figure 13-7), which describes his conquest, and then the just and tolerant way people would be treated. Some historians call this cylinder an early version of a charter of rights.
- **Ancient Greece** — In the sixth century BCE, any male citizen of Athens could vote and participate in democratic debate.
- **Ancient Rome** — In the first century CE, the Roman emperor Claudius passed laws protecting slaves who were sick. He also decreed that conquered peoples could become Roman citizens and even members of the Senate.
- **Ancient India** — The Laws of Manu are said to have been written down in about the first or second century CE, but they grew out of traditions that had existed long before that. The laws include statements about how women, children, and various members of different castes — social classes defined by the Hindu religion — should be treated and how they should behave.

Create a three-column chart that examines each example on this page. In the first column, identify the society. In the second, identify an action that seems to indicate a concern for human rights. In the third column, outline evidence that human rights in today's sense were not a priority for that society. If the human rights initiatives of these societies were judged according to current Western standards, how would they rate? If they are judged according to what was normal or common at the time, would they seem progressive? Explain your responses.

Figure 13-7 In ancient Babylonian civilization, important information was sometimes inscribed onto a clay cylinder. This small cylinder (23 by 8 cm), which was inscribed at the order of King Cyrus of Persia, was unearthed in 1879 and is called the Cyrus Cylinder. What might a primary source like this reveal about the period in which it was created? How readily do you think what was engraved on this cylinder should be accepted as fact? How could you find out whether this is a credible account of what happened?

Milestones in the Evolution of Democracy and Human Rights

Oral constitutions, such as the Great Law of Peace, and written documents, such as the American Constitution, the Universal Declaration of Human Rights, and Canada's Charter of Rights and Freedoms, are often considered milestones in the evolution of ideas about human rights.

The Great Law of Peace

The Great Law of Peace was created by the Haudenosaunee, who lived near the lower Great Lakes. Before the arrival of Europeans, five Haudenosaunee nations had formed the Iroquois Confederacy. The Great Law of Peace set out a decision-making process in which elected representatives of each nation met to make decisions on issues that concerned the confederacy.

> All the business of the Five Nations Confederate Council shall be conducted by the combined bodies of the Confederate statesmen. First the question shall be passed upon by the Mohawk and Seneca, then it shall be discussed and passed by the Oneida and Cayuga.
>
> The procedure must be as follows: when the Mohawk and Seneca Chiefs have unanimously agreed upon a question, they shall report their decision to the Cayuga and Oneida Chiefs who shall deliberate upon the question and report a unanimous decision to the Mohawk Chiefs. The Mohawk Chiefs will then report the standing of the case to the Firekeepers, who shall render a decision . . . in case of a disagreement by the two bodies, or confirm the decisions of the two bodies if they are identical. The Fire Keepers shall then report their decision to the Mohawk Chiefs who shall announce it to the open council.

The American Constitution

The Constitution was created in 1787 by representatives of the 13 colonies that had formed the United States. This document established the Congress, which consists of the Senate and the House of Representatives, and set out a decision-making process.

> We the People of the United States, in Order to form a more perfect Union, establish Justice, insure domestic Tranquility, provide for the common defense, promote the general Welfare, and secure the Blessings of Liberty to ourselves and our Posterity, do ordain and establish this Constitution for the United States of America . . .
>
> All legislative Powers herein granted shall be vested in a Congress of the United States, which shall consist of a Senate and House of Representatives . . .
>
> Every Bill which shall have passed the House of Representatives and the Senate, shall, before it become a Law, be presented to the President . . . If he approve he shall sign it, but if not he shall return it, with his Objections to that House in which it shall have originated, who shall . . . proceed to reconsider it. If after such Reconsideration two thirds of that House shall agree to pass the Bill, it shall be sent, together with the Objections, to the other House, by which it shall likewise be reconsidered, and if approved by two thirds of that House, it shall become a Law.

Review the excerpts from the Great Law of Peace and the American Constitution. What similarities link the spirit of these two documents? What do these similarities reveal about the effect of globalization on democracy and human rights?

Web Connection

To find out more about the Great Law of Peace, go to this web site and follow the links.

www.ExploringGlobalization.ca

FYI

In his book *Forgotten Founders*, Bruce E. Johansen noted that, in the 18th century, Benjamin Franklin was one of the official printers of the colony of Pennsylvania. Before playing an active role in developing the American Constitution, Franklin became familiar with the Great Law of Peace when he printed the minutes of meetings of the Iroquois Confederacy and sat in on treaty council meetings. The ideas he encountered influenced his views on the way the government of the new American republic should work.

The Universal Declaration of Human Rights

To try to prevent a recurrence of the atrocities of World War II, the United Nations adopted the Universal Declaration of Human Rights in 1948. This document declares that all "human beings are born free and equal in dignity and rights" and sets out individual rights in six areas:

- political rights (e.g., right to vote and to participate in government)
- civil rights (e.g., right to freedom of opinion and expression)
- equality rights (e.g., right to be free from discrimination)
- economic rights (e.g., right to fair wages and safe working conditions)
- social rights (e.g., right to education and adequate health care)
- cultural rights (e.g., right to speak one's home language)

The preamble to the declaration says that the UN General Assembly

proclaims this [declaration] as a common standard of achievement for all peoples and all nations, to the end that every individual and every organ of society, keeping this Declaration constantly in mind, shall strive by teaching and education to promote respect for these rights and freedoms and by progressive measures, national and international, to secure their universal and effective recognition and observance.

Since its adoption, the declaration has served as a model for similar documents, such as the Canadian Charter of Rights and Freedoms.

The Canadian Charter of Rights and Freedoms

The Canadian Charter of Rights and Freedoms was adopted in 1982 as part of the Constitution Act. It evolved from a growing commitment to human rights and protects the following rights and freedoms:

- fundamental freedoms (e.g., right to freedom of conscience and religion)
- democratic rights (e.g., right to vote)
- mobility rights (e.g., right to move from place to place within Canada)
- legal rights (e.g., right to life, liberty, and security of the person)
- equality rights (e.g., right to protection of the law without discrimination based on race, national or ethnic origin, colour, religion, sex, age, or physical disability)
- language rights (e.g., the equality of the French and English languages in particular situations)
- minority-language education rights (e.g., provincial governments must provide certain language rights to English or French minorities, where numbers warrant)

But the Charter also includes a limiting clause that specifies that its guarantees are subject to "such reasonable limits prescribed by law as can be demonstrably justified in a free and democratic society."

The graphs in Figure 13-8 show the results of opinion polls taken on the 20th anniversary of the creation of the Charter. For each graph, write a sentence that summarizes what it shows. How would you respond to each question? Explain your reasons.

FYI

New Brunswick-born John Peters Humphrey was a lawyer who was appointed the first director of the UN's Human Rights Division in 1946. In 1947, Humphrey wrote the first draft of the Universal Declaration of Human Rights. After retiring from the UN in 1966, he continued his work toward achieving human rights for all.

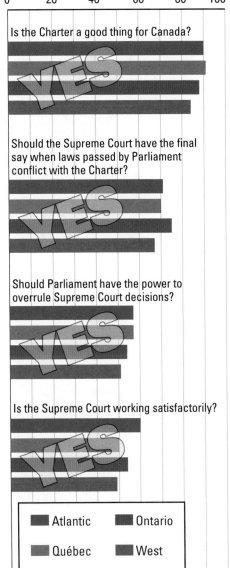

Figure 13-8 **Canadian Opinion on the Charter, Parliament, and the Courts, 2002**

Source: The Centre for Research and Information

DEMONSTRATING LEADERSHIP DURING DISCUSSIONS

The Great Law of Peace, the American Constitution, the Universal Declaration of Human Rights, and the Canadian Charter of Rights and Freedoms were developed by groups of people who worked together. These groups met, discussed their views, communicated a variety of informed positions, and arrived at a consensus. In each group, leaders played an essential role.

Ken Kesey, an American author, observed, "You don't lead by pointing and telling people some place to go. You lead by going to that place and making a case." Effective leaders build positive relationships with those around them, and people respond to them because they trust and respect them.

Leadership skills can be learned, practised, and used to enhance your ability to lead group discussions. Suppose you were asked to work with a group to create a charter of rights and responsibilities for your social studies classroom. Your real purpose in completing this assignment is to demonstrate leadership skills during the group discussion. The following steps will help you do this.

Steps to Demonstrating Leadership during Discussions

Step 1: Brainstorm to create a list of class goals

When creating a charter of rights and responsibilities, your first step might be to develop a list of goals that class members want to achieve. Once these goals are clarified, your charter can become an important tool in helping all class members achieve their goals.

With a small group, brainstorm to create a list of possible goals. Your group may, for example, wish to include goals like completing the course successfully and developing social skills, such as consideration for others.

When groups brainstorm, one or two people sometimes dominate the discussion. Others might not feel comfortable about jumping into a discussion or interrupting others to express their view. Before starting the brainstorming session, you might suggest ways of ensuring that everyone has an opportunity to be heard. When leading a discussion, you might

- suggest that the group member whose ideas seem to be gaining support take over leadership of that part of the discussion.
- transfer the role of discussion leader from group member to group member at regular intervals. The role of the original leader is to ensure that the discussion remains on topic and progresses toward the group's goals. At each leadership change, she or he is also responsible for bringing the ideas and issues back into focus.

LISTENING EFFECTIVELY

Members of your group may have differing ideas about the classroom environment that is necessary to achieve your goals. Practise your leadership skills by listening carefully to the point of view of all group members and encouraging everyone else in the group to do the same. You may hear ideas you had not considered or powerful arguments that change your mind.

Be respectful.
- Encourage the expression of differing points of view and perspectives.
- Establish an atmosphere that invites people to feel safe about sharing ideas.
- Remind group members to comment on the ideas, not the speaker.
- Listen to many ideas before bringing the discussion to a close.

Be critically aware.
- Listen actively and attentively — keep your mind alert.
- Take notes on what you are hearing and the ideas that flow from what is said.
- Engage with the speaker — ask questions, add ideas, and invite discussion.
- Make connections between new ideas and the group's goals.
- Paraphrase the ideas of others so they know they have been heard and understood. Give people an opportunity to correct misunderstandings.

Be aware of your biases.
- Understand your own biases on the subject.
- Control your biases as you listen.
- Be prepared to change.
- Allow new ideas that you may not agree with to enter the discussion.
- Listen for bias in the comments or questions of other group members.

Step 2: Imagine the ideal learning environment

Work with your group to describe the classroom environment that will help achieve the goals you listed in Step 1. The group may decide, for example, that it's important for the classroom to be safe and free of unnecessary distractions.

Step 3: Reflect on class members' differing needs

With your group, create a web diagram that identifies the needs of those who gather in your social studies classroom. One branch might, for example, represent the needs of students for whom English is a second language. Another branch might represent the needs of your teacher. An example has been started for you.

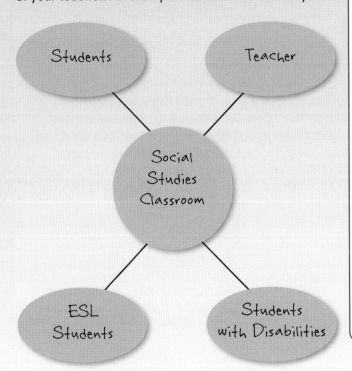

Step 4: Conclude the discussion

Work with your group to draw together the threads of your discussion.

- Keep your goals clearly in mind as the discussion moves forward.
- Set reasonable time limits on the discussion.
- Ensure that all group members have had an opportunity to participate and make themselves heard.
- Using your notes, summarize the discussion and your conclusions.
- Work with the group to decide on the next steps.

SETTING AN EXAMPLE

When talking about the needs of groups and individuals, it is important to create an inclusive environment that encourages people to participate. As leader, you can foster an atmosphere of openness and respect that will inspire group members to participate enthusiastically.

You can foster an atmosphere of respect by
- listening politely
- asking questions
- looking at the speaker
- taking notes
- waiting your turn to speak

You can foster openness by
- acknowledging and accepting differing points of view
- exploring various points of view
- expressing your own opinions tactfully and honestly
- accepting change
- recognizing new ways of viewing issues

Summing up

The leadership skills you have practised as you completed this activity will be useful in many other group situations, both in and outside school.

Human Rights and Colonization

At the same time as people in Europe and the United States were becoming more and more focused on individual rights and freedoms, they were also building empires. Imperialism continued to be an important force well into the 20th century — and was an important factor in causing both World War I and World War II. Is it possible for a country to be an imperial power and still support individual rights and freedoms? Is imperialism acceptable if the colonizers believe they are helping the colonized?

As early as the 16th century, Bartolomé de Las Casas, who had witnessed the atrocities committed against the Indigenous peoples of the Caribbean, wrote in *Brief Account of the Devastation of the Indies*,

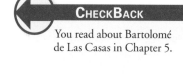
CHECKBACK
You read about Bartolomé de Las Casas in Chapter 5.

> [The peoples of the Caribbean] are the most guileless, the most devoid of wickedness and duplicity, the most obedient and faithful to their native masters and to the Spanish Christians whom they serve . . . Yet into this sheepfold . . . there came some Spaniards who immediately behaved like ravening wild beasts, wolves, tigers, or lions that had been starved for many days . . . Their reason for killing and destroying such an infinite number of souls is that the Christians have an ultimate aim, which is to acquire gold . . . [T]heir insatiable greed and ambition . . . is the cause of their villainies.

In a 1907 lecture at Columbia University, Woodrow Wilson, who later became president of the United States, said,

> Since trade ignores national boundaries and the manufacturer insists on having the world as a market, the flag of his nation must follow him, and the doors of the nations which are closed against him must be battered down. Concessions obtained by financiers must be safeguarded by ministers of state, even if the sovereignty of unwilling nations be outraged in the process. Colonies must be obtained or planted, in order that no useful corner of the world may be overlooked or left unused.

John Gray, a professor at the London School of Economics, believes that "the age of globalisation will be remembered as another turn in the history of human servitude." In *False Dawn: The Delusions of Global Capitalism*, Gray wrote,

> The thinkers of the Enlightenment, such as Thomas Jefferson, Tom Paine, John Stuart Mill, and Karl Marx never doubted that the future for every nation in the world was to accept some version of western institutions and values. A diversity of cultures was not a permanent condition of human life. It was a stage on the way to a universal civilization, in which the varied traditions and culture of the past were superseded by a new, universal community founded on reason.

Figure 13-9 How do you think the artist who created this contemporary cartoon would view the American presence in Iraq or Canada's presence in Afghanistan?

With a partner, review the three quotations on this page and examine Figure 13-9. Create a mind map showing how these four items are linked.

"SPREADING DEMOCRACY IS HELL!"

Human Rights in Former Colonies

During the 19th and 20th centuries, many colonies of European imperial powers gained independence. The imperialist powers either granted them independence or lost control when the colonies fought for — and won — the right to govern themselves.

Canada for example, won the right to self-government in 1867. Many African countries, such as Ghana, Nigeria, the Democratic Republic of Congo, and Kenya, did not gain this right until the 1950s and 1960s. Why do you think there was a difference of about 100 years?

For many former colonies, independence did not bring peace and stability. The legacies of imperialism presented enormous challenges that often led to violence and human rights abuses.

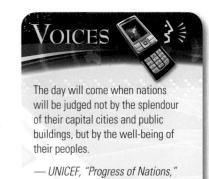

Some Legacies of Imperialism		
Cause	Effect	Example
Imperial power destroyed traditional political and social systems and left colonies with few resources to meet the people's needs.	Newly independent countries sometimes faced discontent and political unrest and turned to authoritarian leaders.	Kenya — Like many other former African colonies that gained independence in the 1960s, Kenya turned to authoritarian one-party rule to try to solve social and economic problems.
Imperial power relied on colonized people to become educated in the imperial power's language and customs and to help govern.	Colonized people who benefited from education often helped run the government when the colony gained independence.	India — Indians educated in the British-style system and trained in governing were able to rise to positions of power.
Imperial power either split up or joined communities and groups that had not traditionally been organized in this way.	Created ethnic conflict or national rivalry leading to human rights abuses.	Rwanda — Ethnic rivalries created by Germany and reinforced by Belgium exploded into genocide.
Imperial power changed traditional political structures and economic practices.	Led to greater ability to integrate into world markets *or* undermined ability to self-govern or to be self-sufficient.	Canada — Aboriginal peoples continue to advocate for and promote their right to political and economic self-determination.

REFLECT AND RESPOND

With a partner, create a list of important words and phrases related to democracy and human rights. As well as terms, your list might include titles of documents, people's names, and other relevant words, such as names of places. Use this list to create a concept map that explores connections between democracy and human rights.

CHECKFORWARD ➡

Alternatives to Daniel Griswold's view will be explored in Chapters 14 and 16.

HOW ARE GLOBALIZATION, HUMAN RIGHTS, AND DEMOCRACY RELATED?

The debate over whether the forces of globalization help spread human rights and democracy continues. Daniel Griswold, a trade specialist with the Cato Institute, an American think tank that promotes free trade and limited government, believes the answer is yes.

In 2006, Griswold wrote: "For the past three decades, globalization, human rights, and democracy have been marching forward together, haltingly, not always and everywhere in step, but in a way that unmistakably shows they are interconnected."

As proof, Griswold and others often cite the annual reports of Freedom House, an American organization that monitors the state of freedom around the world. This group has recorded substantial increases in the percentage of the world's population enjoying full political rights and civil liberties.

Freedom House rates political rights and civil liberties in individual countries on a scale of 1 to 7 and classifies countries as free, partly free, or not free. In 2006, Canada, for example, was classified as free and rated number 1 in both political rights and civil liberties. Libya, by contrast, was classified as not free and drew the lowest rating — 7 — in both political rights and civil liberties.

PROFILE

NGUGI WA THIONG'O RESPONDING TO IMPERIALISM

Soon after Kenya gained independence from Britain in 1963, this African country became a dictatorship. People who dared to criticize the government were arrested and imprisoned.

This is what happened to Ngugi wa Thiong'o, a Kenyan writer of Gikuyu descent. His works were openly critical of the government. When he was released from prison, wa Thiong'o fled to England, where he continued writing and teaching.

During the 1980s, he published *Matigari ma Njuruungi* in Gikuyu. Matigari, the main character in the novel, asks questions about truth and justice — and Kenyan authorities felt so threatened by this that they seized all copies of the work. When the book was later translated into English, wa Thiong'o told CBC interviewer Eleanor Wachtel, "There was a time when Matigari existed only through English translation in London."

Wa Thiong'o is keenly aware of the irony of this situation, for he believes that using English, the language of Britain, prolongs the effects of imperialism. Like many other African writers, wa Thiong'o started his career writing in English — but he now writes in Gikuyu and urges other African writers to publish in their own language.

In his 1986 book, *Decolonising the Mind*, he explained the importance of language: "Language carries culture, and culture carries, particularly through orature and literature, the entire body of values by which we perceive ourselves and our place in the world ... Language is thus inseparable from ourselves as a community of human beings with a specific form and character, a specific history, a specific relationship to the world."

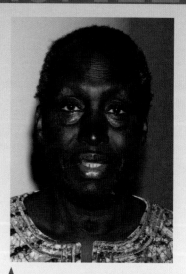

Figure 13-10 When writer and teacher Ngugi wa Thiong'o was born in 1938, he was named James Ngugi — a reflection of the British colonial influence in Kenya. In 1977, he changed his name to symbolize his belief in the importance of affirming and promoting the Gikuyu language.

Trade and Transnational Corporations

Economic globalization presents both challenges and opportunities. For transnational corporations, economic globalization is about securing their right to move people and goods freely across borders so they can maximize profits for shareholders. Many transnationals move factories to countries or regions where labour costs are lower and environmental regulations are less strict. This practice has led to human rights violations and a growing grassroots movement protesting the practices of some transnationals.

Economic globalization has also placed pressure on governments to reduce spending — and lower taxes — by decreasing the money earmarked for providing services such as health care, education, electricity generation, and water. This pressure sometimes comes from international economic organizations like the World Bank, which may require a country to meet specific conditions in exchange for a structural-adjustment loan.

Human rights activists argue that cutbacks in government spending increase inequality. They say that when governments stop providing basic services, such as health care, private corporations step in — and the price of these services often rises. This is what happened when the World Bank pressured Bolivia, for example, to privatize its public water systems. Bechtel, an American company, took over, and water prices increased by about 50 per cent. The poorest Bolivians could not afford to buy clean drinking water. Do you believe that access to clean drinking water is a basic human right?

At the same time, trade can be a powerful force in stopping human rights violations. During the apartheid era in South Africa, many countries, including Canada, boycotted South African products and refused to trade with the South African government. Economic sanctions like these are sometimes an effective tool in persuading a government to stop violating people's human rights. How might trade sanctions place pressure on a government?

But trade sanctions do not always work — and can sometimes make a bad situation even worse. In 1990, for example, the United Nations imposed economic sanctions on Iraq after President Saddam Hussein ordered troops to invade Kuwait. As a result of the sanctions, Iraqi citizens suffered tremendously because they were deprived of basic necessities, such as food and medicine. But they were also living in a repressive dictatorship and were powerless to persuade Saddam to change his ways.

Trade creates the habits of freedom, [and the habits of freedom] begin to create the expectations of democracy and demands for better democratic institutions. Societies that are open to commerce across their borders are more open to democracy within their borders.

— *George W. Bush, president of the United States, 2002*

Today's real borders are not between nations, but between powerful and powerless, free and fettered, privileged and humiliated. Today, no walls can separate humanitarian or human rights crises in one part of the world from national security crises in the other.

— *Kofi Annan, secretary-general of the United Nations, in his Nobel Peace Prize acceptance speech, 2001*

FYI

Latin American leaders such as Venezuelan president Hugo Chavez and Bolivian president Evo Morales have blamed the lending policies of the World Bank and the International Monetary Fund for the continuing poverty in their countries. These leaders have suggested creating their own international lender, which may be called the Bank of the South.

Figure 13-11 A man sits outside a Starbucks coffee house in Shanghai, China. Starbucks is an American-owned transnational corporation. How does this photograph illustrate economic globalization?

Transportation and the Movement of People

Globalization has led to the freer movement of goods — and people. In some ways, this has made life easier for millions of people who immigrate to new countries in search of better lives for themselves and their families.

But many migrants do not leave their homeland voluntarily. They are trying to escape economic hardship, political violence, and human rights abuses. People who fear persecution can flee to another country and apply for refugee status.

But many situations, such as economic hardship, do not allow people to qualify for refugee status. In these cases, some people migrate illegally, and their status as illegal migrants sometimes leads to human rights abuses in their new home.

People who are legitimately trying to move to another country in search of employment are sometimes fooled by criminal organizations. A company or individual, for example, may recruit young Asian women with the promise of jobs as domestic servants in Canada or the United States. But when these young women arrive in North America, they find themselves forced into prostitution. This is called **human trafficking** and is one of the tragedies of globalization.

Both illegal immigrants and victims of human trafficking are often exploited because they are not protected by their home country or their newly adopted country. They generally do not have access to health care in their new country either.

Figure 13-12 When the military took over the government of Myanmar in 1988, the Padaung people were forced off their traditional land. Some were abused and tortured. Many, like the woman in this photograph, fled to neighbouring Thailand, where they are not allowed to work.

Figure 13-13 Because of the violence in their own country, thousands of Iraqis like these, who were gathered outside the office of a UN refugee agency in Syria, have fled to neighbouring countries. Syria has complained that it cannot cope with the high number of Iraqi refugees. What challenges might large numbers of refugees present to a country like Syria? Who should be responsible for helping refugees resettle?

The Media

The media can be a powerful force in the fight for human rights. But access to contemporary media can also fundamentally change a culture and contribute to the destruction of traditional values.

India is an example. The world's most populous democracy, this country is home to people of many different religions and cultures. India is changing rapidly, and the media have played a large role in this.

American television shows and films started appearing on Indian screens in the 1990s. In a country where it was considered improper for girls to wear shorts, the introduction of the popular American television show *Baywatch* created a sensation and began to change ideas about beauty.

Women with round figures were once considered ideal; now, urban girls and women are striving to fit into size 0 jeans. Indian parents complain that their children are becoming too "Westernized," but young people argue that Western-style fashions, music, and habits are the new norms.

Some scholars have called what is happening in India a form of cultural imperialism. How is cultural imperialism different from historical imperialism? How is it the same?

FYI

More than 1795 daily newspapers are published in India — the largest number of any country in the world. Nearly 50 per cent are in Hindi, about 8 per cent are in English, and the rest are in various languages and dialects.

MAKING CHOICES

MAKING CHOICES   MAKING CHOICES   MAKING CHOICES

TANK MAN — STANDING UP FOR HUMAN RIGHTS

In 1989, as communism was collapsing in the Soviet Union and Eastern Europe, a protest movement was also growing in China. By mid-May that year, 1.2 million people were occupying Tiananmen Square in Beijing to protest the government's control of the media, limits on freedom of speech, and human rights abuses.

But the government decided to crack down and sent in tanks and troops to stop the protests and clear the square. Some people say that thousands were killed and wounded as the troops opened fire.

Then, as tanks rolled toward the square, a single, unknown man walked up and stood in front of them. Would they keep rolling forward or stop? In the end, they stopped, and the man climbed up on the lead tank and spoke briefly to the driver before being pulled away by others lining the street.

North American and European photographers and videographers caught the incident on camera and broadcast it around the world. Because the man was never identified, he was nicknamed "Tank Man" or the "Unknown Rebel." To this day, no one knows who he was, what motivated his action, or what happened to him afterwards. But the image of his courageous act became one of the most famous pictures of the 20th century.

Figure 13-14 This famous photograph of Tank Man made headlines in newspapers around the world and was the lead story on countless news broadcasts. In 1998, *Time* magazine named the Unknown Rebel one of the 100 most influential people of the 20th century.

Explorations

1. On a continuum like the one shown, locate your assessment of Tank Man's action. Discuss your assessment with a partner, then join another pair and add their opinions to your continuum.

   Foolish, ineffective, insignificant ——————— Courageous, effective, highly significant

2. Consider this event from a variety of points of view and perspectives (e.g., Tank Man, tank driver, onlookers, Chinese government, audiences in democratic countries, audiences in communist countries). What emotions do you think they felt? How might this incident shape their future decisions.

Web Connection

How are organizations using the Internet to run global campaigns against transnational corporations? To find out more, go to this web site and follow the links.

www.ExploringGlobalization.ca

Communication Technologies

Activists around the world have been successfully using the Internet to launch global campaigns against corporations. It has also been a powerful tool for human rights organizations. As a result, the Internet has been called a source of "information democracy" or "media democracy." Not only can anyone access information, but anyone can also post information on the Internet. Activists can create large coalitions of people and organizations that otherwise would probably never have come together. They can target transnational corporations and inform a worldwide audience about protests through mass e-mails, blogs, e-zines, eye-witness accounts, and online petitions.

When Bolivians, for example, protested the increased water prices that occurred when Bechtel took over the country's water systems, the government eventually cancelled the contract. As a result, Bechtel sued the Bolivian government for millions of dollars in lost profits.

Bechtel planned to take its suit to the World Bank's trade court, the International Center for Settlement of Investment Disputes, where it would be heard in secret. Neither the media nor the public would be allowed to attend.

But protesters around the world joined forces to try to persuade Bechtel to drop the suit. The Internet played an important role as people sent thousands of e-mail messages to the heads of the corporation. In San Francisco, protesters gathered at the company's headquarters. More than 300 organizations in 43 countries circulated petitions, and world media picked up the story. Bechtel dropped the case in 2006.

Despite stories like these, the Internet has limitations. One problem with "media democracy" is that information is not always accurate. Another problem is the digital divide, which refers to some people's limited access to online information. And some people are skeptical of the Internet's significance when they compare the small number of sites devoted to activism and public debate with the large number of commercial web sites.

Figure 13-15 Amnesty International is an example of a human rights organization that uses the Internet to inform people about current issues, organize online petitions and letter-writing campaigns, and co-ordinate protests worldwide. These photographs show people in Madrid (left), Berlin, and Paris (right) holding a co-ordinated day of protest against the American government's detention of "terrorists" at Guantanamo Bay.

Have democracies done a good job of protecting human rights in the 20th century? Here are two people's points of view on the relationship between democracy and human rights.

AMARTYA SEN won the 1998 Nobel Prize for Economics. The following is an excerpt from an essay titled "Democracy as a Universal Value." It is based on a speech he gave at a 1999 conference on building a worldwide movement for democracy.

In the terrible history of famines in the world, no substantial famine has ever occurred in any independent and democratic country with a relatively free press. We cannot find exceptions to this rule, no matter where we look: the recent famines of Ethiopia, Somalia, or other dictatorial regimes; famines in the Soviet Union in the 1930s; China's 1958–61 famine with the failure of the Great Leap Forward; or earlier still, the famines in Ireland or India under alien rule. China, although it was in many ways doing much better economically than India, still managed (unlike India) to have a famine, indeed the largest recorded famine in world history: nearly 30 million people died in the famine of 1958–61, while faulty governmental policies remained uncorrected for three full years.

The policies went uncriticized because there were no opposition parties in parliament, no free press, and no multi-party elections. Indeed, it is precisely this lack of challenge that allowed the deeply defective policies to continue even though they were killing millions each year. The same can be said about the world's two contemporary famines, occurring right now in North Korea and Sudan.

Famines are easy to prevent if there is a serious effort to do so, and a democratic government, facing elections and criticisms from opposition parties and independent newspapers, cannot help but make such an effort. Not surprisingly, while India continued to have famines under British rule right up to independence (the last famine, which I witnessed as a child, was in 1943, four years before independence), they disappeared suddenly with the establishment of a multi-party democracy and a free press.

• • • • •

FAREED ZAKARIA is the editor of *Newsweek International* and the author of *The Future of Freedom: Illiberal Democracy at Home and Abroad*. The following is an excerpt from a 2003 interview.

If we look at Russia after the fall of communism, it's a very interesting and somewhat tragic tale. There was an enormous emphasis put on elections, on political freedom, and what happens is Boris Yeltsin, and Putin after him, winning free and fair elections, begin to severely undermine the independence of the courts, severely undermine the local autonomy of government, they fire regional governors they don't like, appoint super-governors, sacked people of the upper house of Parliament, of the Duma, and intimidate a once free Russian media into being entirely cowards and almost totally silent and subservient to the state. So what you've seen in Russia is the flourishing of democracy, but the withering of liberty. And that process, that dynamic, is true in Venezuela, it's true in Iran, it's true in Russia, it's true in most of central Asia. Forty-two of forty-eight African countries have held elections, but I don't think any of us would really call what has happened there democracy.

Explorations

1. Both Amartya Sen and Fareed Zakaria refer to the crucial importance of freedom of the press in guaranteeing that a democracy protects individual freedoms. With a partner, create a flow chart or mind map that shows the connections these authors make between democracy, freedom of the press, and human rights.

2. Summarize the arguments of Sen and Zakaria. Include the terms "democracy" and "human rights."

3. Extend one of the arguments. How might the speaker view globalization? Do you think he believes that globalization helps ensure that democracies protect human rights? What evidence from the excerpt supports your answer?

1. In his poem "The Rose Garden," the 13th-century Iranian poet Saadi of Shiraz said that "those who are indifferent to the suffering of others are traitors to that which is truly human."

   a) Rewrite this idea in your own words, explaining both its surface and deeper meanings.

   b) Keeping in mind the idea behind the poet's words, develop five statements about human behaviour, human rights, and personal involvement. Note the word "indifferent" in Saadi's phrase. Be sure at least one of your statements reflects this term. If you wish, you may write your statements in the form of a poem or rap.

2. With a partner, join two other pairs and imagine you can reach back in time. Choose three societies discussed in this chapter — and one character who might have lived in each society. Each pair will choose one of the characters as the focus of an interview.

   a) In the group of six, develop two or three questions about human rights to ask all three characters. Your questions for all three characters will be the same. To help your group work effectively, review the leadership skills discussed on page 312–313.

   b) Return to your original pairs. Decide which partner will play the character and which will play the interviewer. To prepare for the interview, the partner playing the character should conduct research into conditions at the time.

   c) Conduct the interview. The interviewer will ask the questions and make notes on the answers.

   d) Return to the group of six and compare the answers each interviewer received. Prepare a short statement summarizing the information gathered during the interviews.

   e) The interviewer should meet with interviewers from other groups to compare summary statements and develop a consensus report to present to the class. During this presentation, the partners who played the character can support, add to, or disagree with the consensus report.

3. In countries like Canada, most people take clean water for granted. Think about water in your life — how you use it, where it comes from, and where it ends up.

   a) Track your water use for three days. A chart like the one shown on this page can help you do this. If you are not sure of the amount you used, estimate as accurately as possible.

      At the end of the three days, analyze your water use and decide on categories (e.g., eating and drinking, hygiene, general cleaning). Calculate the amount of water used in each category.

My Water Use		
Day and Time	Use	Amount
Monday, 7 a.m.	Shower	95 litres
Monday, 8 a.m.	Glass of water	200 ml
	Cup of coffee	200 ml
	Brush teeth	200 ml

   b) Prepare a plan to show how you might reduce your water use by at least 20 per cent. Which elements of your plan affect others in your family? Which elements are completely within your control? Explain your plan to a partner. Encourage your partner to ask questions that will test the soundness of your plan (e.g., Do you really think you can cut the length of your shower by two minutes?)

   c) Using one of the categories you established for analyzing your water use, create a cause-and-effect diagram to indicate what would happen if your family were forced to survive on 10 litres of water a day. Your diagram might start like the one at the top of the following page.

   d) With your partner, conduct research to find out about the availability of clean water to people in two countries. One country should be a developing country, and the other should be a developed country.

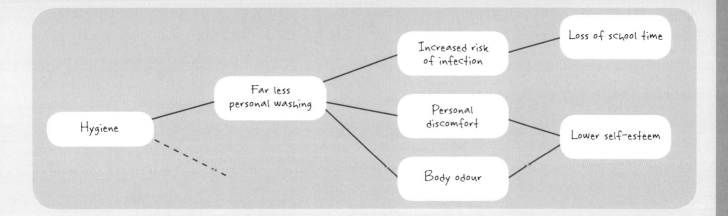

4. The following phrases describe what people can do to become global citizens:

- develop cross-border relationships
- learn to imagine the different
- foster co-operation

a) Add three more similar phrases to the list.

b) Keeping in mind that the purpose of each phrase is to encourage people to practise global citizenship, briefly explain the meaning of each.

c) For each phrase, including the three you added, list a specific action you could take to show that you are becoming a global citizen.

5. This course has focused on helping you respond to a single key question: To what extent should we embrace globalization? The challenge for this related issue is also based on developing answers to this question.

   In a group of three or four, imagine that you are responsible for preparing a four-week course of study on globalization for a group of students from several countries, including Canada. These students will represent diverse cultures, backgrounds, points of view, and perspectives. To help your group work together, review the Focus on Skills features on building consensus (pp. 246–247) and demonstrating leadership during discussions (pp. 312–313).

a) Develop a key issue for the course and express it in the form of an issue question. This question should be broad enough to act as a foundation for the four-week course, but focused enough that the students will be able to develop responses by the end of the course. Your group may find it useful to begin by developing criteria for judging the effectiveness of your key question.

b) Present your key-issue question to the class, along with a description of the methods you used to develop it. This presentation should include a summary of your criteria, working plan, and the methods you used to reach agreement.

c) As a class, develop a single key-issue question. Compare it with the key-issue question for this course. Discuss the differences between them and why you think these differences arose.

Think about Your Challenge

By now, you have recorded several entries in the journal or blog you are keeping in response to the related-issue question: To what extent should I, as a citizen, respond to globalization?

Think about the criteria you used when making your comments — and start developing a list of criteria that you think you may use when reaching the judgment that will become your final informed position on this issue. Include this list in your journal or blog.

Examine the journals or blogs of some of your classmates, and comment on whether you agree with what they have said so far and with the criteria they have used to make their judgments.

Chapter 14 Global Awareness

Figure 14-1 The glamour and style of the fashion industry (left) contrasts with the reality for many workers in the clothing industry. The photograph at the top right shows sweatshop workers in a clothing factory in Guangzhou, China. They work long, hard days to turn out apparel for consumers in developed countries. A few successful campaigns against sweatshops have helped make consumers aware of sweatshop conditions. But all clothing factories are not sweatshops. The workers in the bottom photograph are employed by American Apparel in Los Angeles. This company says it can make money without overworking and underpaying employees.

MOST PEOPLE IN DEVELOPED countries, including Canada, enjoy the benefits of globalization, such as cheaper clothing, vehicles, and electronics. More people in these countries can afford to buy items that were once considered luxuries. But if some people have benefited from globalization, others have not.

Examine the photographs on the previous page and respond to the following questions:

- What similarities do you see between the workers in Guangzhou and the workers in Los Angeles? What differences do you see?
- Which group of workers do you think has benefited more from global awareness?
- If you were planning to buy a T-shirt, would being aware that it was manufactured in a sweatshop affect your purchasing decision?
- If you decided not to buy a T-shirt because it was made in a sweatshop, how might your decision affect the sweatshop workers?
- Do you think these photographs fairly represent the fashion industry in a globalizing world?

KEY TERMS

ingenuity gap

gender gap

labour standards

LOOKING AHEAD

In this chapter, you will explore answers to the following questions:

- How has globalization affected awareness of issues?
- How has global awareness affected gender issues?
- How has global awareness affected labour and employment issues?
- How are global awareness and quality of life related?

My Point of View on Globalization

At the beginning of Related Issue 3, you recorded your views on whether the effects of globalization have been largely positive, largely negative, or somewhere in between. Has your view changed since then? Use words or images — or both — to show whether your view has changed or stayed the same. Record your ideas in your notebook, learning log, portfolio, or computer file. Date your ideas and record them so that you can continue to return to them as you progress through this final related issue.

HOW HAS GLOBALIZATION AFFECTED AWARENESS OF ISSUES?

CHECKBACK

The role of the Internet in expanding globalization by improving communication technology was introduced in Chapter 2.

Thomas Friedman, an editorial writer for the *New York Times*, delivers a mixed verdict on the Internet, a tool that many Canadians rely on to understand the world. Friedman argued that "at its best, the Internet can educate more people faster than any other media tool we ever had. At its worst, it can make people dumber faster than any other media tool we ever had." He goes on to point out that uninformed people "don't realize the Internet at its ugliest is an open sewer: an electronic conduit for untreated, unfiltered information."

Some Ripple Effects of Globalization

Without question, the Internet — an important tool in the globalizing process — has provided many people with opportunities to make global connections. Users can tap into vast quantities of information and opinion. The popularity of blogs and social networking sites shows that Internet users welcome this opportunity. Individuals and organizations can present their understandings of the world to any who will listen.

But for critics like Thomas Friedman, these opportunities to present information also represent opportunities to reinforce ignorance. Information drawn from the Internet often lacks context and may be unreliable. On any controversial topic, a search will locate a range of points of view and perspectives. It is sometimes hard to judge which points of view are thoughtful, unbiased, and based on sound research and logic. And though the media and the Internet connect people around the world and provide access to a huge reservoir of knowledge and opinion, these communication technologies also link people to less pleasant aspects of human life, such as terrorism, poverty, human trafficking, and environmental degradation.

Think of a current controversial issue. What might be some unreliable sources of information on this topic? Where might you locate reliable information that you can use to develop an informed position?

Opportunities to expand one's understanding of issues is one ripple effect of globalization. But there are also other ripple effects. Global commerce, for example, now takes place 24 hours a day. As a result, the number of hours Canadians work has increased. Between 1998 and 2005, the average workweek of Canadians rose to 46.3 hours from 44.6 hours.

In addition, to stay connected and competitive, people must constantly update their technological know-how and equipment. In some respects, technology ties people down by requiring greater and greater investments of time and money.

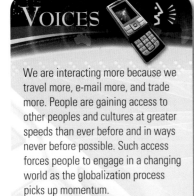

VOICES

We are interacting more because we travel more, e-mail more, and trade more. People are gaining access to other peoples and cultures at greater speeds than ever before and in ways never before possible. Such access forces people to engage in a changing world as the globalization process picks up momentum.

— *Duane Bajema, professor at Dordt College, Sioux Center, Iowa, 2006*

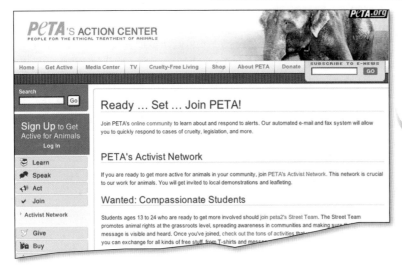

Figure 14-2 This is a page from the web site of People for the Ethical Treatment of Animals, one of many organizations that exist to share ideas about animal welfare and rights. What are some criteria you could use to judge the validity of the information found on web sites such as this?

Darin Barney, the author of *Prometheus Wired: The Hope for Democracy in the Age of Network Technology* and a McGill University professor who specializes in studying the relationship between technology and citizenship, told an interviewer: "Technological mythology leads us to believe that technologies arise, as if by magic, to address pre-existing needs and to provide solutions to pre-existing problems. In reality, technologies tend to create more needs than they address . . . Was the ability to engage in phone conversation while riding the bus really a pressing social need prior to the arrival of the cellular phone, or did our perception of that as a need arise after this technology became widely available?"

Based on your own experience, identify one unexpected consequence of globalization for individuals or society in general. Discuss your ideas with a partner or small group.

Web Connection

To hear Darin Barney's provocative views on people's relationship with technology, go to this Web site and follow the links

www.ExploringGlobalization.ca

Ideas — Can people be too globally connected?

The students responding to this question are Katerina, who lives in St. Albert and whose grandparents emigrated from Ukraine in 1948; Gord, a member of the Beaver First Nation near High Level; and Tom, a fourth-generation Albertan who lives on a ranch near Okotoks

> Sometimes I feel that there is just too much information to handle. I look around and I see all kinds of problems and issues, and I don't know what to make of them. Should I do something? Ignore the problem? Join a group? I just don't know how to figure out which problems are important — and which aren't. I don't know how to decide on priorities. I need some way of filtering information so that I can focus on what's important and where I can actually make a difference. I know that globalization is affecting me directly, but I'm at a loss about what I should do.

Katerina

> It's important to be connected so that we know what's going on and so we have a forum where our voices can be heard. Look at the situation for First Nations. If we talk about issues that concern us, there are so many voices out there that our voices can barely be heard. But if we join other Indigenous peoples from around the world who share our concerns, we have a much louder voice together. Being globally connected is just the first step. After that, people and groups need to use the connections to achieve their goals.

Gord

> What I try to do is be careful about how I connect to the rest of world. I filter the information I get by connecting to people and places that I think will help me reach my goals. I have my favourite web sites, magazines, and TV programs, and I don't get upset about what I'm missing. After all, I can only handle one problem at a time. Maybe I don't know about everything that's going on, but I know about the things that are important to me.

Tom

Your Turn

How would you respond to the question Katerina, Gord, and Tom are answering? How can you find a balance between too much information and not enough? How might too much — or too little — information affect your life? Do you think you need to filter and organize the information you receive? Explain your ideas.

MHR • To what extent does global awareness affect quality of life?

The Ingenuity Gap

Canadian political scientist Thomas Homer-Dixon uses the term **ingenuity gap** to refer to the gap between people's *need* for new and innovative solutions to problems and their *ability* to supply those solutions. He says that people often rely on scientists or entrepreneurs to come up with innovations that will solve the problems faced by societies. After all, globalization has provided a world full of resources and people with great ideas. In the past, this ingenuity has helped raise productivity and solve problems. But what happens if the problems remain unsolved? This "gap" is dangerous to a society, says Homer-Dixon, especially if it goes on for a long time. Over time, the problems tend to become more complex and urgent.

Homer-Dixon suggests that four factors can become hurdles that prevent problem solving.

- Market failure — The market does not provide opportunities for businesses to make money, perhaps because the necessary resources are not available.
- Shortage of capital — Financial and human resources are not available to solve the problems.
- Science cannot operate — Scientific research cannot be conducted for reasons such as lack of funding or the controversial nature of the topic being explored.
- Social conflict — In times of turmoil, groups take action to protect their own interests rather than the interests of society as a whole.

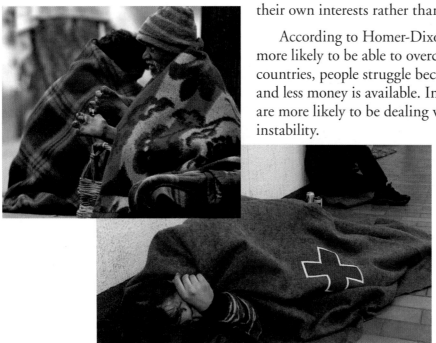

Figure 14-3 Poverty is a problem that often forces people to live on the streets. The photograph on the left shows homeless men in Jammu, India, suffering through a month-long cold spell that killed 1600 people in 2003. The photograph on the right shows homeless people in Edmonton sleeping in public transit stations. How do these photographs illustrate the ingenuity gap?

According to Homer-Dixon, people in developed countries are more likely to be able to overcome these hurdles. In developing countries, people struggle because market forces are often weaker and less money is available. In addition, developing countries are more likely to be dealing with internal conflicts that create instability.

In a globalizing world, people have the opportunity to observe the ingenuity gap in other places and to become aware of the problems various societies are trying to solve. But many observers are pessimistic about the outcome. They believe that the world is too fast-paced, too complex — and too dangerously close to spinning out of control.

REFLECT AND RESPOND

With a partner, brainstorm to create a list of ways you use to develop your awareness of other places, people, and events. On your list, note specific sources, such as web sites, blogs, TV programs, radio stations, newspapers, books, and magazines.

Then organize the items on your list into categories, such as culture, recreation, entertainment, and hard news. Analyze your results to provide a snapshot of your connections to the wider world. Write a statement that assesses your level of global awareness.

How has global awareness affected gender issues?

Over the past several decades, awareness of gender roles has steadily increased. Many countries have taken steps to reduce the **gender gap**, the social, economic, and political differences that separate men and women. Actions have included guaranteeing human rights for females, increasing access to education for girls, and improving health care for girls and women. The importance of this trend was noted in 1984 when the United Nations set up the Development Fund for Women to promote gender equality and empowerment initiatives for women. Yet many analysts agree that progress toward gender equality has been slow and inconsistent.

A 2005 study by the World Economic Forum measured the extent to which women in 58 countries had achieved equality with men in terms of economics, politics, education, and health care. Selected results are shown in Figure 14-4. Countries were scored on a scale of 1 to 7, with 7 representing full gender equality. Why do you think Canada didn't rank higher?

What geographic patterns do the data in Figure 14-4 reveal? Describe and explain these patterns. What did you find most surprising about the rankings? Explain why. The highest-ranked country on the list scored only 5.53. What do you think this means?

Gender Issues and Communication Technologies

Many of the improvements in gender equality have come about because women's organizations have used communication technologies to share ideas, information, and documents. Access to reliable information is an important factor in developing effective programs and raising awareness among target populations. Communication technologies also enable people to participate in making decisions about issues that affect them. Even in areas where computer networks are not available, organizations have been able to use other communication methods, such as faxes and radio.

Figure 14-4 **The Gender Gap in Selected Countries**

Country	Rank	Gender Gap Score
Sweden	1	5.53
Norway	2	5.39
Iceland	3	5.32
Denmark	4	5.27
Finland	5	5.19
New Zealand	6	4.89
Canada	7	4.87
United Kingdom	8	4.75
Germany	9	4.61
Australia	10	4.61
United States	17	4.40
Costa Rica	18	4.36
Colombia	30	4.06
South Africa	36	3.95
Japan	38	3.75
Zimbabwe	42	3.66
Italy	45	3.50
Mexico	52	3.28
India	53	3.27

Source: World Economic Forum

Figure 14-5 Women march in São Paulo, Brazil, to mark International Women's Day, 2006. Women's organizations often deal with broad issues, including peace and security. Why do you think women link peace and security to gender equality issues?

MHR • To what extent does global awareness affect quality of life? **329**

The communication gap

One difficulty faced by women's organizations is that some of their members, as well as many of the people they are trying to reach, do not have access to contemporary communication technologies. This is especially true in developing countries and among groups that are at the margins of society. When members of these groups try to use technologies, they face barriers such as social and cultural expectations, language difficulties, and lack of education and money. As a result, women tend to have less access to communication technologies than men, and less ability to use these technologies in a way that meets their needs. Does this conclusion seem to apply to females you know? Why or why not?

A variety of programs have been initiated to try to close the gap for women. In Uganda, for example, the Women of Uganda Network set up a computer-training centre for rural women. Among their difficulties is the lack of telephone land-lines in the area. How might money and modern technologies overcome the lack of land-lines?

PROFILE

JIN TING ZHAO — CONNECTED TO THE WORLD

While in junior high school, Jin Ting Zhao sang "O Holy Night" for a local radio contest. Her performance caught the attention of an Edmonton music producer who had connections in Taiwan, and the Edmonton teenager was soon recording — in Mandarin — songs that became hits halfway around the world.

Jin Ting didn't need to live in Taiwan to record her CDs. Because of advances in communication technologies, she was able to write and record the basic tracks in Edmonton with lyrics that were written in Taiwan. Instrumentation was added in recording studios in Calgary and Los Angeles. MP3 files of the songs were then sent over the Internet to Taiwan for final mixing in Taipei. Jin Ting's first CD, titled "Lying Tears," came out in 2002. She now has two CDs to her credit, as well as videos, and even a public service message for the government.

Jin Ting said, "Learning to adapt Western-style songs to Chinese is a bit hard, and when I went to do concerts and videos, I had to learn a lot about Taiwanese culture. People there have very different ideas about pop music and celebrities than we do here in Canada."

Figure 14-7 Jin Ting Zhao was born in Shanghai, China, in 1985 and immigrated to Canada with her family when she was three years old. While living in Canada, she has used the opportunities provided by global communication technologies to develop a career as a singer in Taiwan.

Women in Government

One goal of groups that focus on gender equality is to encourage women to play a greater role in politics. The first woman to sit in a national legislature was elected to the Finnish parliament in 1907. In Canada, the first woman to sit in the House of Commons was elected in 1921.

Since then, more women have entered politics, but by 2007, no national legislature included 50 per cent women — even though women make up roughly half the population of most countries. Rwanda had the highest proportion of women parliamentarians: 48.8 per cent. If women form roughly 50 per cent of the population, why do you suppose they do not hold half the elected positions in governments?

Examine the information in Figure 14-9. If this graph were your only source of information about the status of women in Canada, what conclusion(s) might you reach? What information would you need to develop a more complete picture of the status of women in this country?

Women and Employment

Employment equity in Canada and other countries continues to be a concern. In 1967, Canadian women who worked full-time outside the home earned only 58.4 per cent as much as men. Since then, the gap has been reduced by campaigns to correct this inequity and laws requiring women to receive equal pay for work of equal value. But a gap continues to exist. In 2003, women earned 71.2 per cent as much as men, a figure that had remained largely unchanged since 1990.

Women are also striving to rise to leadership positions. In 2006, only 5.4 per cent of the top earners at Canada's 500 top corporations were women, and only 15.1 per cent of top corporate positions were filled by women. "Overall, women remain largely excluded from the key jobs that signal corporate power and influence, despite comprising nearly half of the Canadian labour force and more than one-third of all management roles," said Deborah Gillis, executive director of Catalyst Canada, the research organization that studied the situation.

The need to balance paid and unpaid work has contributed to women's struggle to achieve economic equality. Statistics suggest that women in Canada spend an average of 4.3 hours a day doing unpaid work, such as housework and caring for children, compared to 2.8 hours spent by men. How might this unpaid work affect women's earnings and their ability to forge a career?

Figure 14-8 **First Women Parliamentarians in Selected Countries**

Year	Country
1907	Finland
1911	Norway
1917	United States, Sweden
1921	Canada
1945	France
1946	Japan
1952	Mexico, India
1957	Egypt
1973	Bangladesh
1993	Russia

Figure 14-9 **Percentage of Women in National Parliaments in Selected Countries, 2007**

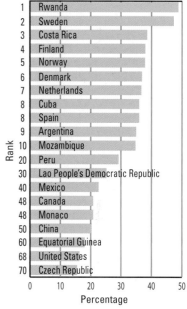

REFLECT AND RESPOND

Examine the cartoon. What is the cartoonist's message? What techniques has the cartoonist used to communicate this message? Suggest a change that would make the message more powerful.

Create a cartoon commenting on the fact that women hold only 20.8 per cent of the seats in Canada's House of Commons, even though they make up 51 per cent of the population.

INITIATING CONFLICT RESOLUTION STRATEGIES FOCUS ON SKILLS

In February 2007, Asmahan Mansour, an 11-year-old soccer player from Ottawa, was given a choice — remove her hijab or forfeit her chance to play in a tournament in Laval, Québec. Mansour is Muslim and, in keeping with religious tradition, wears a hijab to cover her hair. The referee said that the hijab violated a no-headgear rule that was in place to ensure players' safety. The Québec Soccer Federation supported him. Mansour's team, and three others from the Ottawa area, quit the tournament in protest.

This incident sparked a lively debate in Québec and the rest of Canada about what "reasonable accommodations" should be made for ethnic, cultural, and religious minorities. Québec soccer officials held firm to their decision, citing international rules that prohibit jewelry and articles of clothing that may be a safety hazard. Meanwhile, Ontario soccer officials said that they allow players to wear a hijab as long as it is safely tucked in and secured.

This incident shows that when people hold strong views on an issue, conflicts can arise. When this happens, it helps to be aware of strategies that can be used to resolve differences. The goal is to help all sides understand the views of the others and to work toward making accommodations that will allow everyone to get along peacefully.

Form a group and select an issue that students at your school feel strongly about (e.g., a rule banning cellphone use during school hours). Divide the group in half. One half will argue one position, and the other will argue another. Follow these steps to arrive at a peaceful resolution. The same steps can help you resolve conflicts in other situations.

Steps to Initiating Conflict Resolution Strategies

Step 1: Clarify each person's position on the issue

Begin by giving the members of each group an opportunity to clearly set out their position on the issue. This should include a description of how the conflict has affected them.

As you explain your position, practise positive speaking.

- Make no accusations.
- Assign no blame.
- Use no degrading or abusive language.

As you listen to the other party's position, practise positive listening.

- Listen actively.
- Allow all voices to be heard.
- Ask questions when you need clarification.

Step 2: Check understanding

Listening does not always ensure hearing. Avoid misunderstanding by

- echoing or repeating what you think you heard said
- rewording your position until the other parties are satisfied that they have understood (use different language rather than merely repeating what wasn't understood)

Step 3: Identify points of agreement

Select one person to record ideas as they are presented. Allow everyone opportunities to suggest changes to what is recorded. Then brainstorm to find a middle ground or consensus. Part of this step might involve trying to identify other positions that people may have on the conflict. The goal is to find a course of action that will accommodate to a reasonable extent the differences in positions on the conflict. But realistically, people may not find an accommodation they can support. In this case, the resolution may be that the parties agree to disagree.

Step 4: Share responsibilities

On the basis of the ideas that emerge and are accepted in Step 3, all parties to the conflict identify some actions that they could take to help resolve the conflict or solve the problem. These actions should be realistic and show a clear willingness to settle the dispute. A timeline for carrying out the actions should be discussed, and if necessary, a written agreement might be drafted and signed. The agreement might include statements about how future disagreements will be handled.

PRINCIPLES OF CONFLICT RESOLUTION

Listen actively

You must hear what the other parties in a conflict are saying before you can understand their position. Listening actively helps you pay attention to what they are saying, both through their words and body language.

Think, then react

Reacting quickly to what others are saying often makes matters worse. Think about what is said, then consider the most effective response.

Attack the problem, not the person

Conflict brings out strong emotions. People often respond by focusing on the people on the other side of the conflict, rather than on what is causing the conflict.

Accept responsibility

Blaming others rarely helps resolve conflicts. Instead, it creates anger and resentment. Every conflict has many facets, and all parties must accept their share of the responsibility for the conflict.

Communicate directly

Use "I" messages to express your thoughts and concerns. Avoid "you" messages that blame or criticize the other person. It is more helpful to say, "I need more information," than "You don't give me enough information."

Work to understand

Try to understand what is important to all sides, and what outcomes will work for everyone.

Focus on the future, learn from the past

For the conflict to be resolved, the problems that created it must be addressed. All sides must consider what must be changed to eliminate the problems. The future must be different from the past, or the conflict will continue.

Summing up

Suppose you were asked to develop a conflict resolution process to help those involved in the situation with Asmahan Mansour. Draft a plan of action that includes a list of those you would invite to the conflict resolution session, how you might help them express their positions on the issue, and how you might proceed if the sides agreed to disagree. What do you think would be an appropriate resolution to the situation?

CHECKBACK

In Chapter 2 , you explored the banana trade and how it illustrates the forces of globalization.

Web Connection

To find out more about the goals of the International Trade Union Confederation, go to this web site and follow the links.

www.ExploringGlobalization.ca

Figure 14-10 Demonstrators representing the Québec Federation of Labour and the province's teachers blocked access to the port in Québec City in 2003. They were protesting against forthcoming provincial legislation that they believed would limit their collective-bargaining power.

HOW HAS GLOBAL AWARENESS AFFECTED LABOUR AND EMPLOYMENT ISSUES?

Canadians enjoy cheap bananas because of trade connections between this country and banana-producing countries such as Ecuador. But the bananas that arrive in Canadian supermarkets are often produced at a high cost to workers in many banana-producing countries. More and more people are becoming aware of intricate connections and relationships like these — and some are uncomfortable with what they reveal.

Unions and Collective Bargaining

In the era of globalization, unions have often been under attack. In many countries, the power of unions has been undermined by the perceived need for national economies to be lean and competitive. Unions are viewed as contributing to rising manufacturing costs and promoting "special interests" — those of their members — over the interests of consumers, corporations, and some governments.

Around the world, union membership has fallen sharply over the past several decades. In many countries, less than 20 per cent of workers are union members. In 2006, for example, only 12 per cent of American workers belonged to unions, down from 35 per cent in the 1950s. In Canada, the rate of union membership is higher, but it has also been declining. Nearly 36 per cent of the workforce — excluding agricultural workers — was unionized in 1990. By 2006, this figure stood at about 30 per cent.

In large measure, this loss of union jobs can be linked to outsourcing, the shifting of low-skill, low-paying jobs out of developed countries to developing countries. Despite their reduced membership, unions continue to exert power and influence at the national and international levels.

International initiatives

Although unions at the international level remain fragmented and have yet to gain real power, efforts are focused on changing this situation. Some unions are moving to create super-unions that cut across national borders and include larger populations. In 2006, for example, unions around the world united to form the International Trade Union Confederation to ensure that globalization does not erode workers' rights — and more.

In an effort to define a vision of society that is different from that now experienced by many workers, international unions are beginning to focus on campaigns geared toward safeguarding basic human rights and eradicating poverty. As long as major differences exist in wages and quality of life, unions say that all workers are vulnerable to the forces of globalization.

In what way does globalization present both challenges and opportunities for unions? How might the goals of international unions be different from those of the shareholders of transnational corporations? How might they be the same?

Labour standards

Just about every meeting of the World Bank, the International Monetary Fund, or the G8 over the past decade has been accompanied by noisy and sometimes violent demonstrations. The protesters dislike globalization, but are particularly angry about how globalization threatens **labour standards**. Labour standards are measures that protect workers and the environment. Protesters say that international bodies such as the World Bank have done a great deal to protect investors but little to protect workers.

The protesters represent non-governmental organizations, activists, and unions. They have no policy-making authority — but their efforts to raise public awareness of labour issues have led to changes. They have pressured organizations to place labour standards on their agendas.

The IMF, for example, has made eradicating poverty one of its main goals, and transnational corporations have begun to develop codes of conduct to guide their actions. For its part, the International Labour Organization identified four "fundamental principles and rights at work," which every country is expected to respect and promote. These principles and rights include

- freedom from forced labour
- freedom from discrimination in the workplace
- a ban on child labour
- the right to organize and bargain collectively

Despite these developments, the battle over labour standards continues, especially in developing countries. Governments and corporations continue to argue that setting high labour standards will reduce a country's competitiveness. They believe that encouraging trade and investment will naturally lead to economic growth, which will be accompanied by improvements in working conditions.

Opponents of globalization counter by arguing that without labour standards, the "race to the bottom" increases inequality and suffering. They continue to demand that measures to encourage labour standards be tied to trade agreements and enforced with the same rigour as standards of commercial conduct.

VOICES

While activists are commonly labeled anti-trade or anti-globalization, the vast majority actually protest current rules and practices. Rather than being anti-globalization, their movements are themselves global. Most seek a kinder, gentler globalization, one that spreads economic benefits to more people and protects the environment.

— *J. Michael Adams and Angelo Carfagna, in* Coming of Age in a Globalized World, *2006*

Figure 14-11 This banner on a Shell station in Managua, Nicaragua says, "Trademark seized by the law on behalf of 4200 banana plantation workers . . . victims of Nemagon." A Nicaraguan court had ordered Shell to pay $550 million (U.S.) to banana workers who were harmed in the 1970s by Nemagon, an insecticide manufactured by Shell and other companies. When Shell ignored the court order, a judge ordered the transnational's Nicaraguan trademark seized as punishment. How is pesticide use connected to labour standards? Who — or what — else would be affected by this use of a toxic pesticide?

THE FAIR-TRADE MOVEMENT

When you pay $1.50 for a medium coffee at your local coffee shop, many people share in the proceeds. The retailer takes a substantial portion, the coffee importer gets something, a share goes to transportation companies, and the grower is also paid a small amount. But the market is set up so that very little of your money — only about 15 cents — ends up in the pockets of the growers or producers.

This situation is now changing. A rapidly growing movement is trying to create a fair price system so that farmers and producers will receive a return that reflects the value they add. Under fair trade, coffee producers are paid 28 cents of every dollar, and less money goes to the people who handle the product between the farm and the store. With this additional share of the revenues, producers can afford to live and work in a sustainable manner and invest in their businesses and communities. Many consumers have welcomed this development, and globally, purchases of fair-trade products are growing by about 20 per cent a year.

Started in 1964, the fair-trade movement has focused on raising consumer awareness of their relationship with producers. This movement has expanded to 20 developed countries and now includes more than 20 products, with coffee generating the largest sales. Products that meet fair trade standards carry a label like the one shown here. It identifies them as fair-trade-certified.

Figure 14-12 Fair Trade by the Numbers

Number of certified producer organizations	548
Number of countries with producer organizations	51
Number of registered traders	464
Number of companies licensed to sell fair trade products	550
Number of families benefiting from fair trade	1 000 000+

Source: Fair Trade Labelling Organizations International

FAIR-TRADE PRINCIPLES AND PRACTICES

Figure 14-13 In 2006, Rica Lewis, a French clothing manufacturer, introduced fair-trade jeans. The jeans are made from cotton bought from African growers at prices well above current market prices. Would you be willing to pay more for your jeans because of fair-trade agreements? What criteria would you consider when making this decision?

The fair trade movement is based on the following ideas:

- **Fair price** — Member producers are paid a guaranteed minimum price and can receive credit based on harvest returns.

- **Fair working conditions** — Forced and child labour are prohibited and safe working conditions are promoted.

- **Democratic decision making** — Producers and workers democratically decide how to invest their fair-trade revenues.

- **Community development** — Producers and workers are encouraged to invest in community development projects, such as scholarships and training programs.

- **Direct trade** — Producers trade directly with importers as much as possible, reducing the number of handlers who take a share of the profits.

- **Safe environment practices** — Producers are encouraged to use environmentally sustainable methods that protect natural systems.

A Growing Movement

For years, coffee was the main product sold through fair-trade organizations, and its share of the market remained small. Canadians, for example, drink about 40 million cups of coffee a day, or about 2.6 cups for every coffee drinker. But only about 2 per cent of coffee sold in Canada is fair-trade-certified. Still, as Figure 14-16 shows, this is changing as Canadians become increasingly aware of fair-trade products and make an effort to buy them. Have you purchased fair-trade coffee or other fair-trade products?

Ellen L. Lutz, executive director of Cultural Survival, an NGO focused on Indigenous peoples, said, "Of all the purposes of fair trade, perhaps the most important is educating consumers who have stopped asking questions. Free-market capitalism may be the dominant economic model in today's world, but that does not guarantee that it is the only model, or even the best model."

The range of fair-trade products available in Canada is growing, as are their sales. And the number of companies licensed to use the fair-trade logo on their products is also growing. Some of the country's large coffee chains are among the companies that are fair-trade-certified. They offer fair-trade coffee as an option for customers.

Figure 14-15 **Number of Fair-Trade-Licensed Companies in Canada**

Year	Number	Year	Number
1997	5	2002	97
1998	13	2003	110
1999	30	2004	124
2000	65	2005	155
2001	77	2006	185

Source: Transfair Canada

Figure 14-14 **Estimated Retail Sales of Fair-Trade Products in Canada (Thousands of Dollars)**

Product	2000	2001	2002	2003	2004	2005	2006 (Est.)
Cocoa products			485	1558	2175	3131	6557
Roasted coffee	4762	8320	12 750	19 913	28 164	41 046	66 000
Sugar		5	98	152	363	513	1520
Tea		192	431	590	909	1364	1700
Fresh fruit					419	568	NA
Sport balls					37	68	88
Cereals (rice, etc.)						93	160
Cut flowers						33	796
Total	4762	8517	13764	22 213	32 067	46 816	76 821

Source: Transfair Canada

Figure 14-16 **Awareness of Fair-Trade Coffee in Canada, 2001–2005**

Year	2001	2003	2005
Aware of fair-trade coffee	11%	17%	27%
Purchased fair-trade coffee	4%	8%	16%
Purchased organic coffee	7%	8%	Unknown

Source: Coffee Association of Canada

Explorations

1. Analyze the statistical data in Figure 14-14. Identify and describe three trends. Predict the figures for the year 2015.

2. List three new items you think could become products bought and sold under fair-trade agreements. Indicate how this would affect your purchasing power — the amount of a commodity you can buy for each dollar you spend.

3. To what extent should you, as a consumer, be concerned about the way a product reaches the marketplace? Explain your position.

4. Create a mind map showing the direct and indirect connections between the fair-trade movement and the globalization of the marketplace.

The Knowledge Economy

The shift in the world's workforce as a result of globalization has created a division between workers who can use knowledge to generate ideas and those who cannot. The knowledge economy needs workers who can come up with innovative ideas and transform them into commercial products and services that consumers want. Traditional methods of organizing industries and businesses made manufacturing very effective, but often discouraged innovation. In today's globalizing world, there is a growing gap between societies that have knowledge and entrepreneurial attitudes and skills and those that are tied to older methods.

Some observers predict that workers who possess the skills and attitudes demanded by the knowledge economy will experience the greatest success in the coming years. They say that jobs in the knowledge economy will be closely tied to information technologies, and most new growth opportunities will take place in service sectors, such as health care and education. These are sectors that emphasize the application of technologies.

But in many parts of the world, workers have few opportunities to acquire or apply these skills and attitudes.

In a short paragraph, respond to this statement: "Instead of money, developed countries should be sending teachers and entrepreneurs to underdeveloped countries."

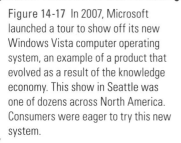

Figure 14-17 In 2007, Microsoft launched a tour to show off its new Windows Vista computer operating system, an example of a product that evolved as a result of the knowledge economy. This show in Seattle was one of dozens across North America. Consumers were eager to try this new system.

Figure 14-18 **Comparing the Old Industrial Economy and the New Knowledge Economy**

Element	Old Industrial Economy	New Knowledge Economy
Economic progress	Steady, predictable	Volatile, unpredictable
Key economic drivers	Large industrial firms	Entrepreneurial, knowledge-based firms
Life cycle of products and technologies	Long, investments returned over years	Short, investments returned over days or months
Competitive situation	Size is important (the big beat the small)	Speed is important (the fast beat the slow)
Decision making	Vertical, top-down	Distributed, based on knowledge
Organizational structures	Hierarchical, bureaucratic	Flexible, networked
Valued skills	Fit to expectations	Flexible, change expectations
Educational requirements	Skill or degree	Continuous learning
Attitude toward employees	A necessary expense	An investment in the future

REFLECT AND RESPOND

Research a current example of a labour or employment issue in Canada. It may be a strike that is escalating, a demand to raise the minimum wage, a member of a First Nation spotlighting inequities in the education system, a protest against outsourcing, or another issue you find interesting.

Identify the stakeholders involved and note their points of view and perspectives. Think about how the issue is connected to expanding globalization. Develop a conflict resolution strategy that the parties could follow to resolve the issue and arrive at a reasonable outcome.

HOW ARE GLOBAL AWARENESS AND QUALITY OF LIFE RELATED?

What kind of shoes are you wearing? You and many of your classmates may be wearing name-brand sports shoes, and you — or your parents — may have paid up to $200 for those shoes, which are made in developing countries, using cheap labour.

Stephon Marbury, a point guard for the New York Knicks of the National Basketball Association, wears $15 shoes. This NBA star is making a statement: people do not need to spend a lot of money to be cool. In 2007, he launched his Starbury line of basketball shoes that don't carry big price tags. When Marbury was young, his parents could not afford to buy him the top labels, and he remembers the pressure he felt to fit in by wearing what was popular. Now, he wants to help change attitudes and reduce the pressure on young people to become consumers of expensive products.

Figure 14-19 Basketball star Stephon Marbury is marketing a line of basketball shoes that cost $15 a pair. Marbury plans to donate a pair to every high school basketball player in New York.

Becoming aware of unfair or inequitable conditions is the first step on the path toward change. Canadians are becoming aware of some of the challenges of globalization and its effects on quality of life, and many people are working to change conditions. What do you do to try to change conditions that you think are unfair?

Social Clauses

Being aware of inequities created by global trade has led some organizations to push to include a "social clause" in all trade agreements. A social clause would require countries to take measures to stop the most extreme forms of labour exploitation, such as forced labour, very low wages, and child labour. If countries fail to abide by this rule, other parties to the agreement could impose trade sanctions. Advocates of this strategy view social clauses as a way of establishing minimum labour standards on a global scale.

Effective Governance

When people are governed effectively, their quality of life improves. Effective governance includes

- respect for human rights
- efficient and effective institutions, such as courts, that protect citizens
- police forces that do not use their powers for their own benefit
- parliaments that reflect the goals and aspirations of the citizens of a country

Many international organizations and NGOs promote effective governance by exposing corrupt and unfair practices and by offering to help governments improve their standards. Amnesty International, for example, runs campaigns to make the public aware of governments that abuse human rights.

Figure 14-20 To help improve governance in Haiti, a country torn apart by poverty, corruption, and internal conflict, RCMP help train local police. In this photograph, a Canadian staff sergeant offers advice to a Haitian officer. What might be the biggest challenge facing a Haitian police officer who wants to effect change?

Foreign Debt

CHECKBACK

You explored structural-adjustment loans in Chapter 9.

Foreign debt can dramatically reduce the quality of life in a country. Foreign debt builds up when a country borrows from other countries or international lending agencies, such as the World Bank, to fund projects or make up budget shortfalls.

In some cases, the money was borrowed for questionable reasons, such as to build lavish government buildings. In other cases, the money was wasted through corruption. But in many cases, the money was used to try to make the country more competitive on a global scale by, for example, improving transportation facilities or developing power grids. Many developing countries have found repaying these debts more difficult than expected, and the debts have limited the country's economic and social development.

On a personal level, how might being burdened with a large debt narrow the range of choices available to you? What similar problems might occur when a country incurs a high debt?

International funding agencies

The World Bank and the International Monetary Fund are key players in the debt situation. When countries borrow money from these bodies, both require them to make structural adjustments to improve their ability to repay the loan. Structural adjustments focus on reducing government spending and improving earnings — and strategies for achieving these goals often include eliminating government subsidies on food, reducing spending on health care and education, and removing investment barriers, such as strict labour and environmental standards.

As a result, many developing countries have found that structural-adjustment programs have reduced people's quality of life. Lower spending on social programs means less access to health care and education. Ending food subsidies results in more hunger. And because efforts to increase foreign investment often rely on offering very low wages, poverty increases. In addition, high debt payments have undermined the ability of many developing countries to modernize.

Figure 14-21 Foreign Debt in Selected Countries, 2005

Country	Total Debt (Billions of U.S. Dollars)	Per-Person Debt (U.S. Dollars)
Brazil	214.9	1154
China	197.8	151
Mexico	159.8	1568
India	101.7	94
Philippines	58.0	660
Chile	43.1	2700
Pakistan	33.5	206
Egypt	30.0	391
Bangladesh	18.1	125
Ecuador	15.7	1174

Source: *CIA World Factbook*

As churches and NGOs have become aware of the situation, they have begun pressing developed countries to forgive these loans. These groups argue that the generation that is suffering to repay the debt did not incur it, that innocent citizens should not be required to repay debts incurred by corrupt leaders, and that the lenders should bear some responsibility for the situation.

In 2006, Canada's national debt stood at about $481 billion, or about $16 000 a person. What is one important reason this huge debt has not negatively affected the quality of life of Canadians?

How does globalization affect quality of life? Here is how three writers have tried to answer this question.

INDUR GOKLANY is an American writer and researcher and the author of *The Improving State of the World*. This is an excerpt from a 1999 article titled "The Future of the Industrial State."

Despite the massive increase in human numbers during this millennium, the state of humanity — as measured by broad aggregate indicators of quality of life — has never been better. The average person is better fed, healthier and lives longer. He is better educated and wealthier. She is freer to choose her rulers and express her views . . . Not only is work less physically demanding, he works fewer hours, and has more leisure time and money to devote to optional pursuits. The majority of these improvements have occurred over the last two centuries, coinciding with global industrialization and the tremendous increases in global population and energy usage.

NAOMI KLEIN is a Canadian activist and journalist. This is an excerpt from her book *Fences and Windows*, a critical examination of globalization.

Globalization is now on trial because on the other side of all these virtual fences are real people, shut out of schools, hospitals, workplaces, their own farms, homes and communities. Mass privatization and deregulation have bred armies of locked-out people, whose services are no longer needed, whose lifestyles are written off as "backward," whose basic needs go unmet. These fences of social exclusion can discard an entire industry, and they can also write off an entire country, as has happened to Argentina. In the case of Africa, essentially an entire continent can find itself exiled to the global shadow world, off the map and off the news, appearing only during wartime when its citizens are looked on with suspicion as potential militia members, would-be terrorists or anti-American fanatics.

PAUL HELLYER is a former Canadian cabinet minister and author of *The Evil Empire: Globalization's Darker Side*. This quotation is from a 1999 speech.

I can give you a fairly accurate picture of what globalization is accomplishing. Universal access to health care is being cut back in Canada and around the world. I don't think there is a single exception. Universal access to education is being cut back in Canada and all around the world. Concern for the environment is being cut back in Canada and all around the world. Unemployment has been high in Canada . . . It's absolutely, totally immoral and it's the same all around the world — 350 million people are employed and a total of about one billion people are either unemployed or underemployed. It's a genuine tragedy.

Explorations

1. Write a short summary of the message of each writer. Share your summary with a partner. Discuss the similarities and differences in your interpretations. Did your understandings change as a result of your discussion? Explain why or why not.

2. In a small group, use the three excerpts as the starting point of a brainstorming session to develop ideas connected to this question: To what extent does global awareness affect quality of life?

2. Based on the ideas generated in response to Question 2, write one sentence stating your current position on whether globalization is a positive or negative force on the quality of life of most people on Earth.

1. Draw on your expanded awareness and understanding of globalization to identify three points you would make to support or oppose the statements people are making in the following situations:

   a) A young woman who is just starting out in business says, "Women have no reason to be concerned about equality with men. The women's movement has improved conditions for women around the world."

   b) A senior executive of a transnational corporation says, "Workers in developing countries shouldn't complain about low wages. After all, North American spending on imported goods means that they have jobs. Now they can work hard and make good careers for themselves."

   c) A Grade 10 student in Canada says, "The quality of life that people in developing countries have is not connected to me here in Canada. People make their own quality of life by using their resources and talents. If they have bad governments or poor economies, it's not my fault."

2. In *Coming of Age in a Globalized World*, J. Michael Adams and Angelo Carfagna wrote:

   > Consider what globalization has done. Only a century ago, the vast and overwhelming majority of the planet's citizens were born and died in the same local region, without (or rarely) making contact with those from different areas. Technology now rapidly carries us across the planet and enables us to communicate regularly with those halfway around the world. Our family, friends, and colleagues, no matter where they live, can be reached in seconds.
   >
   > Our increasing contact with others sometimes confronts us with serious challenges, but it also leads to tremendous satisfaction, widespread benefits, and new ways of thinking. It also starkly reveals our common interests and shared fates. Often, technology and that realization can combine to form a greater, global form of civil society.

   In this passage, the authors state that increasing contact among people and countries reveal "our common interests and shared fates."

   a) In your own words, explain the meaning of "our common interest and shared fates."

   b) Choose a global issue that could become a shared fate. Explain your choice.

   c) List three things that you think are common interests across cultures and nations. Explain your choices.

3. In a small group, decide on one serious challenge you face because of globalization. Explain how this challenge could escalate into a major disagreement or conflict.

   With your group, develop a plan of action that will head off the problem before it escalates. State the actions required by all parties. Create a flow chart to indicate the connections between the people and issues involved and to show how your plan defuses the issue.

4. You are a member of a group that has just finished a fundraising campaign that has raised a substantial amount of money to help AIDS orphans in Africa. About half of the members propose donating the money to a religious organization that is already running an orphanage in Africa. Most of the rest want the money to go to an organization, such as UNICEF or the Red Cross, that is not linked to a specific religion.

   The discussion becomes quite heated. You decide that you are in a position to help the club resolve the disagreement by initiating a conflict resolution process.

   a) Describe the process you would use to help group members through a conflict resolution session.

   b) Identify several outcomes that you think would be appropriate. In your opinion, which would resolve the issue most effectively?

   c) Think about the conflict resolution approach you practised earlier in this chapter. Identify a major strength and how this might help lead to a successful resolution. Identify a major stumbling block that could stand in the way of success. In each case, explain the reasons for your response.

5. Donella Meadows, an environmental scientist, estimated that if the world were a village of 1000 people, it would be made up of

- 584 Asians
- 123 Africans
- 95 Europeans
- 84 Latin Americans
- 55 Soviets (based on the old Soviet Union)
- 52 North Americans
- 6 Australians and New Zealanders

a) What implications for Canada do these data reveal?

b) On the basis of the data, suggest two required subjects that should be added to the curriculum in your school system. Explain your reasons.

c) Choose one country from each region on Meadows's list. Conduct research to find out

- the average annual income
- the GDP
- the literacy rate
- the life expectancy at birth
- a major issue that could become global in nature

d) Based on the information gathered from your research, suggest one country that Canada should help. Recommend the kind of assistance and how it should be delivered. Prepare to answer this question: Why should Canadians be helping there and not spending the money at home?

6. Predicting the future is not an exact science. The Scottish mathematician William Thomson Kelvin once said that radio had no future. When computers were first being developed, the president of IBM assured an audience that the world would never need nor want more than two or three computers. A record-company executive refused to sign the Beatles because he predicted that guitar groups were nothing but a passing fad.

a) Think about technologies, events, and ideas that are emerging today. Select one new technology, event, or idea that you believe will either change the way people view the world or change the quality of life of a significant number of people. Explain the reasons behind your selection and how the changes will come about.

b) Prepare a flow chart or mind map to illustrate your explanation.

c) On a scale of 1 to 5 (1 = very negative; 5 = very positive), rate the effect on the world of the item you selected. Explain your rating.

7. On an outline map of the world, locate each major event you hear or see reported over the next week.

a) Near each event, add a symbol that indicates your assessment of its significance. Add a legend that explains the symbols and provide the criteria you used to make your assessment.

b) At the end of the week, tabulate the number of times each event was reported on, the level of significance of the reports, and the potential effects on Canada.

c) To what extent is this kind of awareness of global events valuable to you?

Think about Your Challenge

Review your journal or blog entries so far, as well as the criteria you have developed and the comments your classmates or teacher may have added in response to what you have written. If necessary, revise your criteria, and note these revisions — and your reasons for making them — in an entry.

In your journal or blog, predict which criteria will be most important when the time comes to take a final position on the related-issue question: To what extent should I, as a citizen, respond to globalization? In addition, predict whether the positions you have taken so far are likely to change as you progress through the final two chapters of this related issue. Explain the reasons for your predictions.

Chapter 15 Global Connections

Figure 15-1 One of the signs of a globalizing world is the need to communicate clearly in various languages. The photograph at the top shows a sign in China. The middle photograph shows road signs in Israel, and the bottom photograph shows signs in Iceland. In addition, various organizations have developed symbols to convey basic information, no matter what language people speak.

The people of the world are connected in myriad ways — socially, politically, and economically. These connections affect everyone. In some cases, the connections are obvious: through the foods that are available in supermarkets, the makes of vehicles on the streets, the languages on signs. But in other cases, the connections are more subtle. The subtle effects of a globalizing world may have more to do with what people think and do in specific situations. Because these influences occur over long periods, they seem natural and normal, and people may not even realize that they are changing. This chapter will focus on the ways that global connections affect people.

Examine the photographs and symbols on the previous page and respond to these questions:

- Why do you suppose the signs in China, Israel, and Iceland include English translations even though English is not an official language of any of these countries?
- What conclusions can you draw on the basis of the signs in these photographs?
- What might bilingual signs say about the people who live in a place?
- If you were visiting one of these places, how might these bilingual signs affect you?
- What does each of the international symbols mean?
- The international symbols were developed only in the last half of the 20th century. Why do you suppose they were not developed before that?
- Examine the international symbols carefully. What evidence identifies their origin?
- What statement(s) do the bilingual signs and international symbols make about a globalizing world?

KEY TERMS

virtual communities

pandemic

<u>**LOOKING AHEAD**</u>

In this chapter, you will explore answers to the following questions:

- How does globalization change communities?
- How does the global need for resources affect people?
- How does globalization affect people's health?
- How have people responded to global issues?

My Point of View on Globalization

Review your notes and think about the changes that have occurred in your understandings of globalization. Predict ideas that you might encounter in these final chapters and think about how they may change your point of view again. Use words or images — or both — to record your predictions. Date your ideas and keep them in the notebook, learning log, portfolio, or computer file you have been using.

HOW DOES GLOBALIZATION CHANGE COMMUNITIES?

CHECKBACK

You learned about individual and collective identity in Chapter 1.

VOICES

Although [online] networks are still in their infancy, experts think they're already creating new forms of social behavior that blur the distinctions between online and real-world interactions . . . Increasingly, America's middle- and upper-class youth use social networks as virtual community centers, a place to go and sit for a while (sometimes hours).

— BusinessWeek *magazine, December 2005*

A community is made up of people who identify with others through shared connections. The connection may be shared religious beliefs and traditions or a common language — or it may be less formal. Wearing the colours of a particular sports team, for example, and cheering on that team at games identifies fans as members of a particular community. The connection people share may be geographic — living in a village, town, or big-city neighbourhood. Belonging to communities is important to people's identity and helps define who they are. To what communities do you belong?

Globalization has affected the communities people identify with. Contemporary communication technologies and the speed of transportation mean that people can identify with others from all over the world. The Asian tsunami that killed hundreds of thousands of people in December 2004 reminded many people of their shared connections. As the rest of the world heard about the disaster, people rushed to donate emergency supplies and money because they believed that part of their global community needed help and support. Globalization has made the term "global community" more meaningful than ever.

New Communities

Globalization is expanding people's ideas about "community." Internet users, for example, might say that their communities include people they have never met in person. They spend time together in chat rooms, blogs, instant messaging buddy lists, and social networking sites. These interactions create a sense of community, and these **virtual communities** may be as important as traditional communities in shaping people's identity.

Membership in these virtual communities is often fluid. People come and go as their interests move them. Combined with the huge range of topics available to online users, this makes virtual communities less demanding than traditional communities. Users have the ability to move about freely, interacting with others around the world.

At the same time, virtual communities have become hunting grounds for online criminals, including identity thieves and sexual predators — and users must be constantly on guard. Observers have also expressed concerns that virtual communities are undermining some people's ability to maintain real-world relationships.

What virtual communities do you belong to or know about? What interests link the people in each community? What do you think is the main advantage and disadvantage of belonging to a virtual community?

Figure 15-2 When a tsunami hit parts of Asia in December 2004, Canadians responded by donating money and supplies — and offering basic medical help. In this photograph, a Sri Lankan father and his sons ride past a Canadian convoy in Colombo. The tsunami occurred on December 26, 2004. This photograph was snapped on January 9, 2005. How does it illustrate the effects of globalization?

Transnational Corporations and Communities

People have widely differing views on the effects of globalization on communities, especially towns and cities. On the one hand, supporters of globalization point out that the economic activity stimulated by expanded global trade has strengthened towns and cities. In many places, transnational corporations are the driving force behind economic expansion. They build factories where none existed, and shops and services spring up to meet the needs of people attracted to the area by the new employment opportunities. In addition to greater access to jobs, community residents also gain access to services and opportunities that did not previously exist.

On the other hand, critics argue that globalization has created more challenges and problems than opportunities. The low wages often paid by transnational corporations mean that poverty is widespread, and this is often made worse by the migrants who flood into an area in search of a job. In addition, the natural environment may deteriorate if environmental standards are lowered to attract transnationals and keep them in a community.

Figure 15-3 These shoppers are outside a Wal-Mart store in Shanghai, China. Why might Chinese shoppers welcome new Wal-Mart stores? Why might these stores create concerns? What does the store's sign say about globalization?

Wal-Mart and communities

Wal-Mart, the world's biggest retailer and one of the world's most successful transnationals, has long been a target of critics of globalization. When this American-based company establishes a big-box store in a community, critics argue that the disadvantages outweigh the advantages. They say that

- high-paying jobs are replaced by low-paying jobs.
- Wal-Mart offers few benefits, such as health care, to workers.
- small, locally owned retailers are undercut by Wal-Mart's low prices. When local businesses are forced to close, shopping and job options are reduced.
- Wal-Mart stores are typically located on the outskirts of communities. This contributes to the decline of downtown shopping areas.
- locating stores on the outskirts of communities encourages car-based shopping patterns, which contribute to high greenhouse-gas emissions and fewer pedestrian-oriented shopping districts.

Despite these criticisms, Wal-Mart continues to build stores, and people continue to shop at them. Supporters of the chain point out that new stores often stimulate economic activity in the surrounding area, filling nearby shopping malls with new stores. And many people in smaller communities welcome Wal-Mart because the store helps people save money and provides products that may not previously have been available.

For its part, Wal-Mart maintains that its stores support communities in many ways. The chain allows non-profit groups to hold fundraisers on its property and encourages employees to participate in community events. In the United States, Wal-Mart has created a community grant program that donated more than $61 million to community organizations in 2006. What is your view on the presence of Wal-Mart stores in communities?

Figure 15-4 What argument is this cartoonist making about Wal-Mart?

Wal-Mart put my store out of business so I had to get a job at Wal-Mart. Thanks to Wal-Mart, I can now only afford to shop at Wal-Mart. Enjoy shopping at Wal-Mart.

GREETER GONE WILD

The Effects of Immigration on Communities

Immigration has long been an important force in Canada. In recent years, immigration has kept Canada's population growth rate higher than that of any other developed country. In 2006, immigration made up more than two-thirds of the increase in Canada's population. Canada's birth rate is falling and the population is aging. As a result, economists and statisticians predict that, within a few decades, immigration will account for all population growth. Why might economists believe that population growth is essential for a healthy economy?

Canada introduced official multiculturalism in the 1970s, and this sparked a remarkable shift in the source of immigrants. Before the 1970s, most immigrants arrived from Europe. Today, Asia is the biggest source.

FYI

In 2005, the top four countries of origin for immigrants to Canada were China, India, the Philippines, and Pakistan. Together, these countries contributed more than 40 per cent of the 262 236 immigrants who arrived in Canada that year.

Ideas   What are the boundaries of your community?

The students responding to this question are Gord, a member of the Beaver First Nation near High Level; Ling, who was born in Hong Kong but is now a Canadian who lives in Edmonton; and Deven, who was born in India but is now a Canadian who lives in Calgary

> What I consider to be part of my community has really grown. It's much more than geography. I've realized that other people in the world share my views about what's important, and the Internet helps me connect with these people. We talk about things like Indigenous people, respect for the environment, human rights, and so on. So my community — and by "community," I mean people whose interests are similar to mine — is worldwide. I might not be able to see them, but I can communicate with them and share ideas. And that's a good thing. Global communication has allowed me to expand my community.

Gord

> When I was a child, before I came to Canada, my community was made up totally of Chinese people. But here in Canada, I came into contact with people from many cultures. I see people who have different roots in my school, in my neighbourhood, on Canadian television shows — basically, all around me. I no longer see my community as people who share my culture, but as people who share my interests. My community is a lot bigger than it used to be!

Ling

> I'm not sure how to answer the question. What I identify as my community keeps changing. When I was younger, my community was focused on my family and on friends who lived nearby. But as I've grown, my community has come to include friends who live farther away, people who share my culture, and people who like the same things as I do — like playing soccer. I'm sure in the future, after high school, what I view as my community will change again. It will expand as I experience more of the world.

Deven

Your Turn

How would you respond to the question Gord, Ling, and Deven are answering? What do you see as the boundaries of your community? In what ways has your definition of community changed over the years? In what ways is it likely to continue changing?

Most immigrants to Canada head for the largest cities in the country. Toronto alone welcomes more than 40 per cent of immigrants. Other large cities, such as Vancouver, Montréal, Calgary, and Edmonton, are destinations for most other newcomers. Only a small number of immigrants settle in smaller communities. How might this trend affect Canada?

The pie chart on this page shows the destination of the immigrants who arrived in Canada in 2005. Nearly three-quarters of these new arrivals settled in just three census metropolitan areas. A census metropolitan area is a large city and surrounding communities.

Newly arrived immigrants consider a number of factors when deciding where to settle. They often want to be

- close to family and friends who are already in Canada
- close to where other members of their cultural group have already established businesses, places of worship, cultural centres, and so on
- where jobs and economic activities are most plentiful
- where services like education and health care are most accessible

Large cities are more likely than smaller communities to meet the needs of immigrants. Why do you think each of the considerations listed would be important to immigrants?

Analyze the data in Figure 15-6. To do this, look for

- patterns, such as numbers that are consistent
- inconsistencies, such as a percentage for one census metropolitan area that is markedly different from others

Suggest reasons for the patterns, inconsistencies, and regional trends you identified.

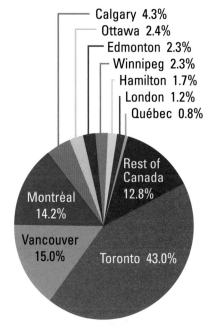

Figure 15-5 Top 10 Census Metropolitan Area Destinations for Immigrants, 2005

- Calgary 4.3%
- Ottawa 2.4%
- Edmonton 2.3%
- Winnipeg 2.3%
- Hamilton 1.7%
- London 1.2%
- Québec 0.8%

Rest of Canada 12.8%

Montréal 14.2%

Vancouver 15.0%

Toronto 43.0%

Source: Citizenship and Immigration Canada

Region of Birth	Census Metropolitan Area (Percentage of Immigrants)				
	Toronto	Vancouver	Montréal	Calgary	Edmonton
United States	1.9	3.1	2.4	5.2	4.4
Central and South America	6.7	2.8	7.6	4.5	4.7
Caribbean and Bermuda	8.2	0.8	10.6	2.2	2.4
Britain	7.0	9.4	2.3	12.9	11.7
Other Northern and Western Europe	3.7	6.1	9.2	8.7	11.3
Eastern Europe	9.0	4.9	8.0	8.7	11.0
Southern Europe	15.5	4.9	19.1	6.4	7.3
Africa	4.9	3.3	11.8	6.3	5.1
Middle East	5.5	3.7	10.1	4.6	4.1
Eastern Asia	14.7	35.6	5.2	15.6	12.7
Southeast Asia	8.7	12.0	7.6	14.4	15.3
Southern Asia	13.7	10.3	5.6	8.9	7.9
Oceania and other	0.4	3.0	0.2	1.6	1.9
Total Immigrants	2 032 960	738 550	621 885	197 410	165 235

Figure 15-6 Immigrant Population by Place of Birth for Selected Census Metropolitan Areas, 2001*

Source: Statistics Canada

* This chart shows all immigrants living in the identified census metropolitan areas, regardless of when they arrived in Canada.

REFLECT AND RESPOND

With a partner, interview someone (e.g., a parent or other relative, a neighbour, or a teacher) who has lived in your community for at least 10 years. As an alternative, you may wish to invite this person to visit your classroom to talk about how the community has changed.

Before the interview, prepare a list of questions that focus on change in areas such as housing, business, industry, transportation, entertainment, and services. Record the interview subject's responses, then discuss whether — and how — each change is linked to globalization. Rate each change on a scale of 1 to 5 (1 = very weak link; 5 = very strong link).

Figure 15-7 Battleground Iraq, 1908–2003

1908
Oil is discovered in the Middle East.

1914
During World War I, Britain attacks the Ottoman Empire and occupies what is now part of Iraq.

1919
British control over Iraq is established at the Paris Peace Conference that ends World War I.

1922
British and American interests gain control of the oil industry in the area.

1932
Britain grants "independence" to Iraq but continues to rule indirectly.

1941
Britain reoccupies Iraq to secure the oil industry; leaves Iraq at the end of World War II.

1958
A coup overthrows the British-supported monarchy and establishes a republic.

1972
The oil industry in Iraq is nationalized.

1979
Saddam Hussein becomes president.

1980
Iran-Iraq war begins when Iraq invades Iran.

1988
Iran-Iraq war ends in a stalemate.

1990
Iraq invades Kuwait.

1991
A coalition of 32 countries led by the U.S. defeats Iraq and frees Kuwait; sanctions are imposed on Iraq.

2003
The U.S. and a coalition that includes Britain invade Iraq; an appointed government is installed.

HOW DOES THE GLOBAL NEED FOR RESOURCES AFFECT PEOPLE?

In a globalized world, the need for resources is great. Some resources, such as oil and water, are so valuable that some governments are willing to use force to secure their supply. Though the study of historical globalization reveals that using force to secure resources is not a new strategy, it has taken new forms in the 21st century. What is one past example of resources being seized by force?

Oil in Africa

Blood oil is a new term that refers to oil obtained through violence and bloodshed. In the first decade of the 21st century, blood oil flowed out of several countries, including Nigeria and Sudan in Africa.

In Nigeria, several transnational corporations, including Shell, Chevron, and Total, have been developing oil fields in the delta of the Niger River. The people who live in the area say that the activities of these companies have damaged the environment — and that they were persecuted when they tried to protest. The Nigerian government, which was controlled by the military at the time, co-operated with the oil companies by brutally suppressing opposition.

In 1995, the government executed nine Ogoni activists who had been fighting to preserve their people's homeland, which was in the area slated for oil development. Among those killed was author and environmentalist Ken Saro-Wiwa, whose death provoked worldwide outrage. Since then, a civilian government has come to power, and the oil companies have changed some of their practices — but many people continue to oppose the development.

Since the 1990s, a deadly civil war has raged in Sudan so that the government could push unco-operative local groups out of an oil-rich area. Millions of Sudanese were displaced and reports of genocide were rampant. Critics said that revenue from the sale of the oil was used to buy military equipment to expand the civil war and give the government even more power.

Iraq, Oil, and War

Iraq has huge oil reserves. By 2007, only 15 of its 74 oil fields had been developed. Known reserves total 112 billion barrels, but estimates say that potential reserves could top 300 billion barrels, amounting to about one-quarter of the world's oil. Conservative estimates place the value of Iraq's oil at more than $3 trillion. In addition, the country has enough natural gas to supply the United States for 10 years.

Until the early 20th century, Iraq was largely ignored by the imperial powers. But this changed when oil was discovered there. The invention of the automobile and the use of fossil fuels to power vehicles and heat homes and businesses meant that Iraq's oil reserves were suddenly highly desirable — and the country became the focus of many conflicts.

The United States leads an invasion of Iraq

Many people have argued that the 2003 American-led invasion of Iraq was a thinly veiled attempt to solidify Western control of the country's massive oil resources. Western access to the oil had been uncertain since Saddam Hussein took control of Iraq in 1979.

Saddam's refusal to submit to American demands in the years after the 1991 Gulf War made him even more of a threat. As long as Saddam controlled Iraq, the global supply of oil was at risk. Although American president George W. Bush justified the 2003 invasion by accusing Saddam of developing weapons of mass destruction, evidence of these weapons was never found. By then, however, Iraq was in the hands of the U.S. and its allies, and Western oil companies controlled the country's oil fields.

> Review the information in Figure 15 7 on page 350. What additional research would you want to conduct before making a judgment about the connection between Iraq's oil reserves and the conflicts that have taken place there?

Figure 15-8 An American soldier helps guard an oil field in Kirkuk, Iraq. Thousands of American military personnel and hundreds of thousands of Iraqis were killed during and after the U.S.-led invasion. What aspect(s) of globalization does this photograph illustrate?

Alberta and Oil

Though blood oil is a disturbing aspect of resource exploitation, much of the world's energy resources have developed in socially acceptable ways. The oil and gas industry in Alberta is one example.

In the early 20th century, neither the Canadian government nor Canadian investors were willing to play a leading role in developing Alberta's oil. As a result, international companies came to dominate the province's petroleum industry. Until 1969, Canadian representatives of transnational corporations — mostly American-based — dominated the industry. The "big four" were Shell, Imperial, Gulf, and Texaco.

By 1969, foreign ownership was sparking fears that Canada was losing control of its energy future, and the Liberal government of Pierre Trudeau began trying to Canadianize the industry. The Trudeau government introduced the controversial National Energy Program, which was designed to increase Canadian control, and created Petro-Canada to ensure a Canadian presence in the global development of energy resources.

The Free Trade Agreement between Canada and the United States and, later, the North American Free Trade Agreement reduced restrictions on foreign ownership in the energy sector and spurred development of Alberta energy projects, including the tar sands.

> Is it important for Canadians to own a large share of Alberta's oil and gas industry? How would you find out how much of oil industry profits remain in Canada?

Figure 15-9 The pumpjack has become an enduring symbol of Alberta's energy industry. How has the province's oil and gas industry affected you?

FORT MCMURRAY — COPING WITH GLOBALIZATION

IMPACT

Fort McMurray, the focus of the oil sands development in northern Alberta, is booming. The city has been growing by leaps and bounds — and municipal officials have been struggling to keep up with the demands created by the world's need for oil.

In 1995, Fort McMurray amalgamated with the surrounding district to form the Regional Municipality of Wood Buffalo. The entire regional municipality is under a single government, and Fort McMurray is the seat of this government. Between 1999 and 2006, the community's population grew an average of 8.5 per cent a year.

Early Development

The explorer Alexander Mackenzie recorded the first description of the tar sands in 1788. He wrote: "At about 24 miles [38.6 km] from the fork [of the Athabasca and Clearwater rivers] are some bituminous fountains into which a pole of 20 feet [6.1 m] long may be inserted without the least resistance."

By 1870, the community of "Fort Mac" was a Hudson's Bay Company post. The first efforts to extract oil from the tar sands were made in 1925, but progress was slow, and by the early 1960s, Fort McMurray's population was only about 2000. But when an oil-sands plant opened in 1967, the population took off, reaching more than 30 000 by 1981. During the 1980s, low oil prices slowed development, but improvements in mining and extraction technologies during the 1990s stimulated a new wave of construction. The population of the area is expected to reach 100 000 by 2012.

Paying the Price of Growth

The flood of workers into the Fort McMurray area has placed a tremendous strain on municipal services. In 2006, Wood Buffalo municipal officials estimated that 3000 more homes were needed. The municipality also needed a new water treatment plant, a police station, a fire hall, a recreation centre, and two more schools. To pay for this infrastructure and services, municipal taxes increased frequently.

Although the oil business has fuelled the population explosion, the key companies involved in developing the oil sands have been reluctant to help the municipality fund services and build infrastructure. Darcie Park, spokesperson for Suncor, one of the largest companies working in the area, told Canadian Press: "Industry should do what industry does best, which is to work to responsibly develop the resource. Governments should do what they do best, which is to identify needs for public funding and provide the funding."

Figure 15-10 **Alberta Oil Sands**

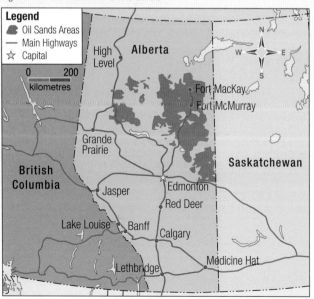

Figure 15-11 **Population Growth in Fort McMurray, 2001–2006**

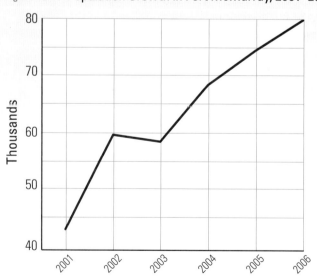

Source: Official Population List, Alberta Municipal Affairs

Figure 15-12 This sign reflects the desperate labour shortage among businesses in Fort McMurray. Why do you suppose they have such difficulty finding workers?

The population explosion has also created a demand for service industries, such as restaurants, shops, and hotels. But even though they offer improved benefits and higher wages than businesses elsewhere in the province, they are having trouble finding enough employees to meet the demand.

Environmental Concerns

Fort McMurray is located in the **boreal forest**, an environmentally sensitive sub-Arctic region that consists mostly of coniferous trees such as spruce, fir, and pine. The rapid expansion of oil sands development is raising concerns about the sustainability of the area's environment.

Each barrel of oil extracted from the tar sands requires the mining of two to five tonnes of earth and uses enough natural gas to heat a home for one to

five days. The process creates such large emissions that Alberta produces more greenhouse gases than any other province. Oil companies are conducting research into more efficient processes, and when they finish mining an area, they are required to restore the land to a self-sustaining, productive state. But environmentalists and First Nations people worry that the development is too huge and happening too quickly for the forest to be restored.

In addition, say First Nations people, the development has destroyed their way of life. "The environmental cost has been great," Jim Boucher, chief of the Fort McKay First Nation told the *Washington Post*. "Hunting, trapping, fishing is gone."

Figure 15-13 Huge trucks and machines extract earth from an open pit mine near Fort McMurray. Hot water is then used to separate the oil from the sand.

Explorations

1. Create a timeline showing the development of Fort McMurray. For each event on the timeline, write a phrase that identifies its effect on the community.

2. Think about your understandings of the globalization process. Explain how the growth of Fort McMurray is tied to globalization. Which aspect of globalization do you think is most important in driving the growth of Fort McMurray? Explain your ideas.

3. Suppose you are an observer at a meeting between the Wood Buffalo municipal council and officials of the oil companies in the area. The two groups have met to discuss the rapid population growth of the area and some of the challenges that have resulted. Identify two main points that each group might make, as well as the evidence each would use to support its position. Who else do you think should have a voice at this meeting? Explain why.

Sustainability

CHECKBACK

Sustainability and globalization were considered in Chapter 11.

Environmental sustainability is a concern in the Fort McMurray area — and around the world. The destruction of rainforests, the collapse of important fish stocks, and the loss of genetic diversity are just some of the environmental challenges that profoundly affect people. What are some ways environmental challenges might affect your life?

Many economists and environmentalists have begun to recognize that economic growth is essential, but they also agree that it must not be achieved at the expense of future generations. It must be sustainable. To ensure sustainability, they believe that decisions about development must stem from assessing and balancing three factors: economic growth, social progress, and environmental stewardship. Figure 15-14 shows how these factors are interrelated.

Figure 15-14 **Three Components of Sustainability**

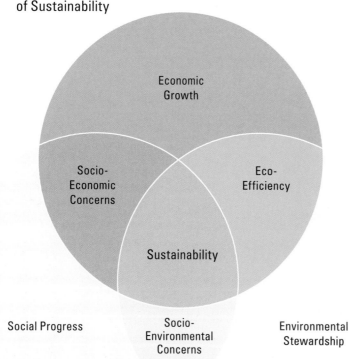

The goals of economic growth are to

- ensure a sustainable economy
- encourage innovation and productivity
- maintain high levels of employment

The goals of environmental stewardship are to

- protect and enhance natural systems
- make efficient use of natural resources
- make efficient use of energy supplies

The goals of social progress are to

- ensure justice for all citizens
- encourage social inclusion
- achieve personal well-being
- create sustainable communities

REFLECT AND RESPOND

Globally, people feel the effects of any disruption to the oil supply. With a partner, create a flow chart that shows how an interruption in oil supplies might affect you and your community. Consider factors such as price, affordability, availability of electricity for homes and industry, changes in transportation, and just-in-time production.

Recall ways you and your community are connected to the global economy and identify how the effects you have identified will affect your way of life (e.g., the supply of fresh fruit and vegetables in winter, clothing prices, and jobs).

Compare your flow chart with those of others in your class. How would you summarize your predictions?

HOW DOES GLOBALIZATION AFFECT PEOPLE'S HEALTH?

A **pandemic** is an epidemic that spreads around the world. Medical experts today are concerned that pandemics pose a more serious threat than ever because of people's ability to travel farther and faster than ever before. But pandemics are nothing new, as the Black Death and the Spanish flu show.

The Black Death

In the 14th century, an epidemic of bubonic plague that became known as the Black Death started in Asia and spread across Europe. By the time it had run its course, 75 million people had died, including up to two-thirds of the population of Europe. How might such a large number of deaths have changed social and economic conditions on the continent?

Many experts believe that the Black Death was carried by rats but spread through human contact. The plague was carried to Europe by traders using the Silk Road. It struck at a time when Europe was already vulnerable. Wars had disrupted farming and trading, creating widespread famine in Northern Europe. In addition, weather conditions had been colder than usual — this period was called the Little Ice Age — and food supplies were limited. On top of everything else, a pestilence, possibly anthrax, was killing sheep and cattle. Economies were in tatters and social conditions were deteriorating, so people could do little to limit the spread of the disease. Less severe outbreaks of the same disease occurred almost every generation until the 1700s.

Examine Figure 15-15. It took more than four years for the Black Death to spread across Europe. What evidence suggests that the disease originated in Asia? What factors would have contributed to its slow spread? Suggest reasons the area around Warsaw experienced only a minor outbreak.

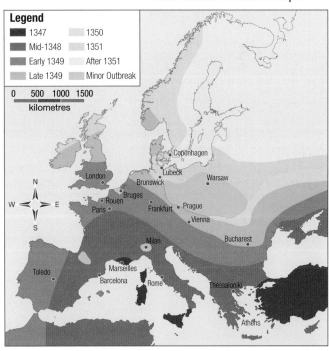

Figure 15-15 **The Spread of the Black Death across Europe**

Legend
- 1347
- Mid-1348
- Early 1349
- Late 1349
- 1350
- 1351
- After 1351
- Minor Outbreak

0   500   1000   1500
kilometres

The Spanish Flu

The most deadly pandemic of the modern era occurred just after World War I, between 1918 and 1920. Called the Spanish flu, it killed an estimated 100 million people, a death toll that was many times higher than that of the war. An unusual aspect of the disease was that it killed healthy young adults, rather than the very young, the very old, and those who were already ill — the usual victims of influenza outbreaks.

World War I did not cause the Spanish flu, but concentrations of soldiers helped spread the disease. The soldiers' movements from one area to another ensured that the disease moved quickly over a large geographical area.

Web Connection

To find out more about the Black Death and the Spanish flu, go to this web site and follow the links.

www.ExploringGlobalization.ca

Pandemics Today

Severe acute respiratory syndrome — SARS — was a recent pandemic that resulted in 774 deaths worldwide. The first case was discovered in rural China when a farmer died of an unidentified disease in November 2002. But the Chinese government did not report the incident to the World Health Organization, the United Nations agency that monitors global health security.

As a result, news of the disease did not become public until February 2003, when an American man travelling to Singapore from China fell ill. The plane stopped in Vietnam, where the man died. Several people who treated him developed the same disease. On March 12, the WHO issued a global alert, but the disease had already spread. By the time the outbreak ended in July 2003, SARS cases had been identified in 26 countries, including Canada.

SARS could have become a deadly pandemic, but it was held in check by the quick action of the WHO and national health agencies. Quarantines halted its spread, as people who might have come into contact with an infected person were isolated in their homes for 10 days. No contact with others was allowed.

Although SARS was successfully contained, the global response to AIDS — acquired immune deficiency syndrome — has been less successful. Every year, about 3 million people, including about 500 000 children, die of AIDS. Another 4 million people contract the disease. As of January 2006, an estimated 39.5 million people were living with AIDS, which had killed another 25 million. There is no cure for AIDS, although expensive drug therapies help prolong victims' lives.

The social stigma associated with AIDS has worked to limit effective prevention programs. In the beginning, AIDS was considered a disease of homosexual men. Health officials now recognize that anyone can contract AIDS, but its association with sexual activity remains. Many people who might be infected do not get tested for fear of testing positive. Those who do admit they are positive are often ostracized.

Many governments in Africa were very slow to develop prevention and treatment programs because they did not want to admit that AIDS was a problem in their societies. Now, two-thirds of all AIDS cases are found in sub-Saharan African countries.

List three ways in which globalization has established conditions that encourage diseases to spread. How are these conditions similar to the ways globalization encourages the spread of ideas and products?

FYI

AIDS was first identified in 1981 when doctors in the United States, France, Haiti, and Zaire began to notice patients dying of minor infections. Canada recorded its first case of AIDS in 1982.

Figure 15-16 SARS Cases in 10 Hardest-Hit Countries, November 1, 2002–July 31, 2003

Country or Region	Cases	Deaths	Fatality Rate (Percentage)
China	5327	349	7
Hong Kong	1755	299	17
Taiwan	346*	37	11
Canada	251	43	17
Singapore	238	33	14
Vietnam	63	5	8
United States	27	0	0
Philippines	14	2	14
Germany	9	0	0
Mongolia	9	0	0

Source: World Health Organization

*Since 2003, 325 cases have been "discarded" as laboratory evidence was incomplete.

The United Nations recognizes that AIDS presents a special challenge in Africa. But why is this so? The following are the responses of three people to some of the difficulties and dilemmas related to AIDS in Africa.

STEPHEN LEWIS is a Canadian AIDS activist who served as the UN special envoy for HIV/AIDS in Africa. The following is an excerpt from a 2005 speech in which he compared efforts in Western countries and Africa to prevent babies from contracting the disease from their infected mothers during childbirth.

Why do we tolerate one regimen for Africa (second-rate) and another for the rich nations (first-rate)? Why do we tolerate the carnage of African children, and save the life of every Western child? Is it possible to do full therapy in Africa rather than single-dose nevirapine [a drug used to reduce the risk of transmitting AIDS]? Of course it is...

It leaves the mind reeling to think of the millions of children who should be alive and aren't alive, simply because the world imposes such an obscene division between rich and poor. That's about to change, but why does it always come after an horrific toll is taken?

LOUISE BINDER is a Canadian AIDS survivor and activist. She made these comments in a 2006 newspaper interview.

The rates [of HIV/AIDS] are climbing, disproportionately, among women everywhere. Most of these women live in Sub-Saharan Africa. These are women in the prime of their lives. They leave behind orphans — millions of them, in fact — and deprive communities of food producers, caregivers, teachers, and of course, mothers, daughters, and sisters. Many are very young, just girls really. Their deaths are the loss of an entire generation in some parts of the world.

For most of these women, the greatest risk of HIV infection is being married . . . Marriage and women's own fidelity are no protection . . . Women have no power to negotiate safer sex practices with their partners and married men often have multiple sexual partners with whom they practise unsafe sex.

Radio
Diaries

THEMBI NGUBANE is a young South African woman who kept an audio diary for a year after she found out she had AIDS. In 2006, she explained to an interviewer why she kept the diary.

I wanted to reach other young people who are also infected with HIV, who are hiding, who are afraid to come out and disclose their status. I thought that I would be affecting someone's life, helping some person who maybe has not disclosed his status or some person who has not been tested.

By the time I got sick, my community members suspected, so every time I went to the clinic, they all started to stare and started to point and started to give names. So I just thought to myself, "What the hell," because I am hiding and they can see it. I don't think anyone can hide the sickness.

Explorations

1. Write a short summary of each speaker's message. Share your summary with a partner. Compare your interpretations. What role does globalization play in your interpretations? Did your own responses change as a result of your discussion? Explain why or why not.

2. Examine each message and complete a chart like the one shown. In the final column, note how the situation in your community is similar to or different from the situation described by each speaker.

Speaker	Reason for Speaking Out about AIDS	Point of View on Why AIDS Is Under-Treated	Situation in My Community
Stephen Lewis			
Louise Binder			
Thembi Ngubane			

Web Connection

HEALTHmap is a global disease alert map that is constantly updated to show the geographic distribution of disease outbreaks. To chart and follow global health information, go to this web site and follow the links.

www.ExploringGlobalization.ca

Figure 15-17 Infectious Disease Deaths as a Proportion of All Deaths, 2001

Percentage

	0	10	20	30	40	50	60	70
Africa								
Eastern Mediterranean								
Southeast Asia								
Western Pacific								
Americas								
Europe								

Responses to Health Crises

The World Health Organization is at the centre of the global response to health crises. This organization systematically gathers reports about suspected outbreaks of diseases. Formal reports come from ministries of health in various countries, academic institutions, WHO regional offices, non-governmental organizations, laboratories, and other agencies. But to get a complete picture, the WHO also monitors informal sources of information. Health Canada worked with the WHO to develop the Global Public Health Intelligence Network. This early-warning tool continuously scans web sites and newswires to pick up information about disease outbreaks. In more than 60 per cent of disease crises, the first clues come to WHO through informal channels.

Centers for Disease Control

Though the WHO co-ordinates disease control measures at the international level, most of the monitoring, reporting, and responding to disease outbreaks take place at a national level. The Centers for Disease Control and Prevention in the United States is one of the best-known national agencies. Monitoring and responding to pandemics is just a small part of this agency's day-to-day activities. It also deals with healthy living, emergency preparedness, environmental health, violence and safety, workplace safety, and travellers' health.

Figure 15-18 An outbreak of a mysterious disease causing pneumonia occurred in Guangzhou, China, in 2003. Residents took precautions while the WHO and local authorities tried to figure out the nature of the illness.

REFLECT AND RESPOND

Analyze the pattern shown in the graph in Figure 15-17. What inequities do you see? What factors do you think contribute to these inequities? What aspects of this pattern may cause concerns for public health officials preparing for and responding to pandemics? On the basis of this pattern, suggest two measures you think would help prevent or reduce the impact of pandemics.

How have people responded to global issues?

The worldwide connections that exist through globalization mean that people today can be informed of harmful or unfair situations in other places in greater detail and more quickly than ever before. When people are informed, many are moved to take action. People can respond in a variety of ways — as individuals, as part of a larger society, as part of a corporation, and through their government.

Consumers

Consumers can choose where to spend their money — and groups have formed to inform consumers about abuses and questionable practices by manufacturers and retailers. Organizations in many Western countries, including Canada, may encourage consumers to press their local supermarkets to carry fair trade products. Other consumer action programs have targeted name-brand clothing companies and retail clothing chains. Activists want these companies to introduce a code of conduct to ensure that suppliers' products are not produced in sweatshops. The goal is to provide consumers with information so they can make informed decisions about where and how they spend their money. Would you and your family be prepared to pay more for consumer goods to guarantee equality in the workplace?

One form of consumer action is a boycott, which involves refusing to buy a company's products. A boycott is a form of direct action in which activists try to achieve their goals by targeting corporations, rather than working through the government. One current high-profile boycott urges consumers not to buy Nestlé products. This company has been accused of providing free or low-cost infant formula to new mothers in developing countries so that the women would choose formula over breastfeeding. Once the mothers were using the formula, the price increased. The activists charged that some babies became undernourished because the mothers could no longer afford to buy formula and watered it down so it would last longer.

Nurturing a Civil Society

In the past, two sectors of society — governments and business — were thought to exert the most power and influence in making decisions and setting policy. But in recent years, a third sector has begun to make its voice heard. This sector is made up of many groups — community groups, non-governmental organizations, faith-based groups, universities, and so on — and has become known as **civil society**. Civil society has become more visible and stronger, as the rapid growth in the number of NGOs demonstrates.

The growing importance of civil society may be a response to the rising strength of corporations and the apparent decline in the power of governments. Name some organizations that you think would be elements of civil society.

VOICES

Citizens can influence governments, shape market realities, and help to determine global labor and environmental standards. They can not only shine a global spotlight on miscreants who seek to circumvent such standards, but help to adopt new standards and expectations. That is the power of globalization.

— *J. Michael Adams and Angelo Carfagna, in* Coming of Age in a Globalized World, *2006*

Web Connection

To find out more about the Nestlé boycott and others, go to this web site and follow the links.

www.ExploringGlobalization.ca

Figure 15-19 Protests against Canada's seal hunt have tried to convince consumers that the hunt is brutal. At this 2005 protest on Parliament Hill, an Inuk offers an alternative view: that the hunt is part of the culture and livelihood of the Inuit. How does this photograph illustrate that civil society groups do not always speak with one voice?

Initiatives such as protecting the environment, stopping potential pandemics, and creating sustainable societies are complex and challenging. Achieving results often requires people to work in collaboration with one another.

Collaboration means working co-operatively and productively with other members of a team to accomplish tasks and achieve goals. Studies have shown that collaboration is an effective way to handle tough tasks because team members

- encourage and support one another, so they feel positive about their work
- understand the task and their roles because they explain, summarize, and defend their ideas to others as they work on a task
- learn from the skills and experiences of others in the group

When working collaboratively, group members must take on a variety of roles like those set out on this page. Some roles may be assigned, but others will be shared or accepted when a specific job must be done. Group members must be prepared to step up and take on specific roles as needed.

Suppose you and a group of classmates are asked to work collaboratively to draft a social responsibility statement for your school. Following these steps can help you achieve this goal. You can use similar steps whenever you work in collaborative groups.

Steps to Collaborating in Groups

Step 1: Clarify the problem or question

With group members, identify and discuss the group's task to make sure everyone understands the assignment. Each group member should work to clarify what she or he means and to understand what other members are saying.

The goal of this initial discussion is to reach agreement on what the final product or outcome should be, what it should look like, and how it will be presented. Write a statement that names the challenge and spells out these details.

Step 2: Assign roles and define responsibilities

Assign roles to help ensure that the task is accomplished. You may wish to select roles from those shown in the box on this page.

Some roles, such as recording or timekeeping, may be played by the same person for the duration of the group session. Other roles may be played by different group members as needed. It may be a good idea, for example, to rotate the roles of taskmaster and leader. Depending on the size of the group, some roles may overlap or be shared, or one group member may play more than one role. The cheerleader and encourager, for example, may be the same person.

TYPICAL ROLES IN COLLABORATIVE GROUPS

Group leader — Is responsible for organizing the group and leading discussions (see Building Consensus, p. 246, and Demonstrating Leadership during Discussions, p. 312).

Recorder — Keeps notes, logs, or journals for the group.

Materials handler — Obtains, distributes, and keeps materials needed by the group.

Reporter — Tracks group's progress toward goal and at appropriate times, presents an oral summary of the group's progress or product.

Cheerleader — Keeps group members motivated and focused on the task.

Encourager — Makes sure all members are working in a positive, supportive manner.

Taskmaster — Reminds group members when they stray from the task or are wasting time.

Timekeeper — Reminds the group of time limitations and when the process must be concluded.

Step 3: Complete the task

Work together to complete the task outlined in Step 1. The length of time this takes will depend on the task. It may be necessary to set up a series of meetings or work sessions. During long tasks, it is important for cheerleaders and encouragers to keep morale high and people feeling good about the task and the group.

You might ask one group member to observe the group at work, noting helpful behaviour and strategies. To do this, a chart like the following may be helpful.

Our Group at Work		
Group Member	Assigned Role	Positive Behaviour
Aparna	Cheerleader Timekeeper	Encouraged others to give their opinion. Thanked a group member for staying on task.

Step 4: Reflect on what you achieved — and how

At the end of each session and when you complete the task, take a few minutes to reflect as a group on how effectively you worked together and achieved your goals. This is a time for group members to solidify working relationships. During these sessions, focus on the positive so that group members feel good about the roles they played.

You may also wish to note areas where the group as a whole could improve its performance. If the group task involves more than one session, you may wish to review these notes at the beginning of the next session.

To help you complete this step, you may wish to respond to questions like the following:

- What goals did we set for our group today?
- What goal(s) did our group achieve today?
- What information and ideas did each group member contribute to the discussion? How?
- How effectively did we complete our tasks?
- Did we listen respectfully when others were talking?
- Did we encourage everyone to participate? How?
- What could we do differently to achieve more?
- What goals might we set for the next session?

In addition, each group member may wish to assess his or her contribution to the group session by asking questions like the following:

- How would I describe my contribution to the discussion?
- How well did I complete my assigned task?
- Did I encourage others to participate fully?
- In what areas could I improve my performance?
- What goals might I set for myself to achieve during the next session?

Summing up

With the class, share ideas about the strategies that helped your group achieve its goal. What challenges did you face? How did you overcome these challenges? How might you work together more effectively in the next group session?

The role of civil society

Civil society plays an important role in shaping globalization and may help counterbalance the strength of business forces in influencing government policy making. Those involved in civil society groups have often developed expertise in specific areas and can offer advice and evidence that help shape policies. The United Nations, for example, routinely draws on the expertise of civil society organizations in areas such as health care and population policies. The Internet is used for online consultation, a strategy that gives the UN the broadest access to ideas and evidence.

One challenge faced by civil society groups is that they do not always share the same points of view and perspectives. Do you think this lack of agreement strengthens or weakens democracy? Explain why.

List two important ways that civil society may influence the globalization process. Provide examples to illustrate your ideas. Share your list with a partner. Discuss why you developed different lists. Are both lists valid?

Figure 15-20 **How Business, Government, and Civil Society Shape Globalization**

Civil Society — Government — Business — Direction of Globalization

---

PROFILE

SAMANTHA NUTT
CARING FOR THE CHILDREN OF WAR

Samantha Nutt, a doctor, is the founder and driving force behind War Child Canada. This international non-governmental organization provides rehabilitation programs for children affected by war and raises awareness of children's rights everywhere in the world. To do this, the group tried to connect with Canadian young people, informing them of the intolerable situations for children in developing countries. War Child Canada is linked to War Child groups in other countries.

Nutt has spent more than 10 years working with children in war zones. Some of her projects have taken her to Afghanistan, Iraq, the Democratic Republic of Congo, Somalia, Sierra Leone, Liberia, and other troubled places. As a specialist in maternal and child health, she sees first-hand how violent conflicts affect women and children. Malnutrition, infectious diseases, poor maternal health, and violence against women — these are the issues that compel her to continue her work.

Recently, advocating for women and children has taken more of her time. When asked about this shift in direction, she said, "It's the opportunity to tell the stories of people who haven't yet had the chance to be heard . . . the opportunity to give the issues a voice — whether it's me, the young people we work with or the music artists saying it. Eventually someone is going to listen, and that's what keeps me coming to work."

Figure 15-21 Samantha Nutt has said that she would like to be remembered for "having the courage to do things differently and for being too stubborn to know when to give up (this has served me well)."

Corporate Citizenship

Transnational corporations, whose operations span national boundaries, are in key positions to find solutions to important global challenges. They often have the expertise and financial resources to make a difference. Many businesses, for example, have developed corporate citizenship statements that mention a commitment to promoting sustainable development, human rights, and community involvement.

These corporations understand that these actions not only help build public goodwill and investor confidence, but also create a working environment that is rewarding for employees.

Web Connection

The Dow Jones world sustainability indexes use social, environmental, and economic data to calculate the environmental and social responsibility of the world's largest 2500 corporations. To find out more about these indexes and where corporations rank, go to this web site and follow the links.

www.ExploringGlobalization.ca

ISO standards

Many corporations are showing their commitment to corporate citizenship by voluntarily adopting standards set by the International Organization for Standardization, or ISO. This NGO is a network of national standards institutes that work to develop technical standards for industries and services. These standards are designed to make the manufacturing and supply of goods and services more efficient,

Figure 15-22 Sarah Ferguson, duchess of York, joins an official of the Ronald McDonald House Charities at a ribbon-cutting ceremony in Warsaw, Poland. McDonald's donated a mobile care unit to help diagnose cancer in Polish children. How do actions like this influence your opinion of transnationals?

safe, and environmentally sustainable. They also protect consumers and workers. One example is the use of common health and safety symbols that can be understood in any language. Companies that have met ISO requirements often promote this in their advertising. Do you think this is an effective marketing tool?

Government Responses

Governments at various levels are also in influential positions to work to achieve fairness and equity. In Canada, for example, federal laws have established the Canadian Human Rights Commission to administer the Canadian Human Rights Act and ensure that the Employment Equity Act is followed in areas under federal jurisdiction. Federal jurisdiction applies to businesses such as banking, airlines, and television stations. Provincial agencies, such as the Alberta Human Rights and Citizenship Commission, are responsible for areas, such as education, employment, and housing, that are under the control of provincial governments.

Are you aware of examples of government programs or actions that try to resolve problems of fairness and equity? If you are, briefly describe one such action. If not, work with a partner to discover one.

Figure 15-23 Teenagers Amy (left) and Jesse Pasternak took their case to the Manitoba Human Rights Commission when the province's high school athletic association barred them from playing hockey on their high school's boys' team. The commission ruled that the Pasternaks had suffered sex discrimination.

1. Create a visual to show how global connections affect individuals and communities. Your visual could be a sketch or drawing, a photograph that you have altered using computer software, a display board, or even a three-dimensional object, such as a mobile.

   Here are some questions to think about as you plan your visual. Incorporate some of these ideas into your work.

   - What community are you describing?
   - Who are the people in the community?
   - How might those people be affected by global connections? What are some positive and negative effects?
   - How might I, as part of this community, be directly affected?
   - What response should I recommend the community make to the global connections?

2. Predict what you think will happen in the oil-producing Middle East over the next five years. Review the information on pages 350–351 of this chapter, then conduct an Internet search to find out what has happened since 2003. Give reasons for your predictions (e.g., point to past events that may influence future conditions).

3. In a small group, participate in a round-table discussion of this statement: Global connections make us aware of unfair conditions around the world. Once we know about these conditions, we are obliged to help improve them.

   Before the discussion begins, develop two or three criteria to use when formulating a response to these questions and prepare a brief statement setting out your point of view. Present your statement during the group discussion, and be ready to respond to questions about it and the criteria you used when developing it.

   When the discussion ends, work with the group to prepare a consensus statement that reflects the group's collective perspective on the issue. Share this with other groups in the class. Formulate one overarching statement that reflects a class consensus.

4. As you have progressed through this textbook, you have read many quotations by a variety of people. Now, make up some quotations that might have been included in this chapter.

   Your goal is to summarize as concisely as possible an important idea or relationship on the topic of how global connections affect people. Complete a chart like the following by making up, for each person on the chart, a quotation about one of the five topics listed for each person on the chart. An example has been started.

   a) The growing importance of virtual communities
   b) The presence of Wal-Mart stores in small towns
   c) The importance of immigration to Canada
   d) The success of the United States in building a stable Iraq
   e) Rapid population growth in Fort McMurray
   f) The success of efforts to achieve sustainable development in Canada
   g) Solutions to the AIDS crisis in Africa
   h) The role of global connections in developing civil society

Person	Topic	Quotation
High school student	c.	Immigration is a —
Orphaned child in Africa		
Newspaper columnist in your community		
Premier of Alberta		
Consumer activist		
President of a transnational corporation		
Person of your choice		

5. Most people would agree that blood oil presents a problem for the world community. Oil is a valuable natural resource that is in great demand. But does allowing violence and killing to play a role in the development of this resource send a message that exploiting natural resources is more important than people's lives?

In a small group, work collaboratively to develop a plan of action that could help the global community identify "blood" resources and bring this practice to an end. Follow the steps set out in "Focus on Skills — Collaborating in Groups" (pp. 360–361).

When your plan is in place, work together to evaluate how effectively your group functioned.

6. Examine and analyze the cartoon on this page.

- What message is the cartoonist conveying?
- What global connections does this cartoon suggest?

In light of this cartoon's message, reflect on some of the ideas in this chapter. How do you think the cartoonist might reply to this question: How does globalization affect individuals and communities?

Figure 15-24

Think about Your Challenge

The first part of your challenge for this issue is to keep a journal or blog to help you develop an informed position on the related-issue question: To what extent should I, as a citizen, respond to globalization? Review the predictions you made at the end of Chapter 14. Did your position change as you progressed through this chapter? If so, note in your journal or blog the evidence that persuaded you to change your mind. If not, note the evidence that persuaded you to stay on the same track.

Chapter 16   The Global Citizen

Figure 16-1 This photograph of the earth from space was taken by a NASA — National Aeronautics and Space Administration — astronaut in 1972. Early photographs like this enabled people to see their planet from a different point of view, as a single undivided sphere "floating" in space.

WHEN ASTRONAUTS TOOK the first photographs of Earth from space, people everywhere were astounded. Buckminster Fuller, the noted American philosopher, inventor, and architect, coined the phrase "Spaceship Earth." Boundaries that divided countries were not evident in the photographs, and people saw Earth as one unified object. The photographs made it easier to understand how what happened in one place in the world could affect other places, regardless of political boundaries.

People could also see that there were obvious limits to "Spaceship Earth." The expression "We're all in the same boat" took on real — and in some ways frightening — meaning. Viewing Earth from space helped people see how interdependent they really were.

Examine the photograph on the previous page and consider these questions:

- How might seeing Earth in this way affect your point of view on globalization?
- How might thinking about Earth as a unified whole affect your point of view on the meaning of global citizenship?
- What does the term "Spaceship Earth" reveal about the need for stewardship?
- Would you identify yourself as a crew member or a passenger — or both — aboard Spaceship Earth?

KEY TERMS

cross-cultural communication

LOOKING AHEAD

In this chapter, you will explore answers to the following questions:

- What does global citizenship mean?
- What does a global citizen do?
- What is my role in the globalizing world?

My Point of View on Globalization

Over the past 15 chapters, you have formulated and reformulated your point of view on globalization. This is the last chapter of this book. As you complete it, develop an informed point of view on globalization. At the end of the chapter, you are asked to develop a definition of globalization. The notes and ideas you have collected as you progressed through the course will help you do this. They will also help you complete the challenge for this related issue.

WHAT DOES GLOBAL CITIZENSHIP MEAN?

You and most of your classmates are probably Canadian citizens. But what does Canadian citizenship mean? It could mean you were born in Canada or born somewhere else to Canadian parents. It could also mean that you have immigrated to Canada and become a citizen through the naturalization process.

Your citizenship represents a legal status that is officially designated by a variety of documents. You may have a Canadian passport, a Canadian birth certificate, or a statement of citizenship from the courts. Your citizenship status can be defined and checked. With this legal recognition of citizenship come specific rights and responsibilities.

Examine the text boxes on this page and develop a statement that encompasses what the rights and responsibilities of Canadian citizenship entail. Share your statement with a partner and work together to create a statement that you both agree on.

Deciding to Be a Global Citizen

If you were born in Canada, you are a Canadian citizen. But you were also born on Earth, so are you automatically a global citizen? If this is the case, where would you apply for a global passport?

Being a world citizen is a way of thinking and acting. Global citizens are self-defining; that is, someone who acts and thinks like a global citizen *is* a global citizen. But what does being a global citizen actually mean?

Figure 16-2 Corneille Nyungura is shown in Québec City on November 5, 2004, the day he became a Canadian citizen. With him is his adoptive aunt, Louise Sauvageau. Nyungura, who is a Francophone songwriter and musician, survived the 1994 genocide in Rwanda, but his family was killed. In 2005, he campaigned for the Canadian Red Cross on behalf of child soldiers, and he is an ambassador for UNICEF's campaign against AIDS.

SOME RESPONSIBILITIES OF CANADIAN CITIZENS

The responsibility to
- understand and obey Canadian laws
- participate in Canada's democratic political system
- vote in elections
- allow other Canadians to enjoy their rights and freedoms
- appreciate and help preserve Canada's multicultural heritage

SOME RIGHTS OF CANADIAN CITIZENS

The right to
- equal treatment before and under the law without discrimination
- participate in political activities
- be presumed innocent until proven guilty
- enter and leave Canada
- use either English or French to communicate with Canada's federal government and certain provincial governments

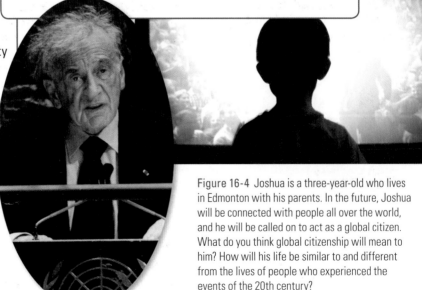

Figure 16-3 During World War II, Elie Wiesel, who is Jewish, was imprisoned in Nazi concentration camps. All his life, he has fought for justice for people around the world. In 1986, he was awarded the Nobel Peace Prize. Wiesel is shown here speaking to the UN General Assembly on the 60th anniversary of the liberation of Nazi concentration camps. How has Wiesel embodied global citizenship during his life?

Figure 16-4 Joshua is a three-year-old who lives in Edmonton with his parents. In the future, Joshua will be connected with people all over the world, and he will be called on to act as a global citizen. What do you think global citizenship will mean to him? How will his life be similar to and different from the lives of people who experienced the events of the 20th century?

Taking action

People show their status as global citizens in different ways. Aysha Wills, for example, was only 10 years old when she decided to help victims of the tsunami in Southeast Asia. Maude Barlow, a director of the International Forum on Globalization, decided to become a social activist and warn people about the dangers of some aspects of economic globalization. Wilton Littlechild of the Ermineskine Cree Nation decided to involve himself in Indigenous people's fight for rights in Canada and at the United Nations.

Can someone simply say, "I do not wish to be a global citizen?" Considering the ideas you have explored during this course, what do you think? Given the economic, political, environmental, and moral interconnections of the globalized world, is it practical or logical to withdraw from global citizenship?

Ideas — What does global citizenship mean to you?

The students responding to this question are Gord, a member of the Beaver First Nation near High Level; Ling, who was born in Hong Kong but is now a Canadian living in Edmonton, and Katerina, who lives in St. Albert and whose grandparents emigrated from Ukraine in 1948.

> It's fine for me, safe here in Canada, to talk about global citizenship, but what about the tens of millions of people who don't even have enough to eat each day? Talking about global citizenship in a real way is more than just about fancy electronics and big malls; people must take personal responsibility and speak out against the inequities in the world. I believe there can be global citizenship, but it's a personal decision and responsibility.

Gord

> I've lived in several different countries. I was born in Hong Kong and now I'm Canadian. In China, they're just starting down the path to development as we know it here in Canada. I'm not sure what I'm supposed to do or say to the Chinese as they struggle to feed all their citizens. Do I tell them that, as global citizens, they have a responsibility to slow down their economic development because it's polluting my world? Is it fair or right that I protest their actions at the same time as I buy the products they make? What am I, a Canadian of Chinese heritage, supposed to do? I'm quite bewildered by the whole notion of global citizenship.

Ling

> This course has shown me that one of the main traits of global citizenship is recognizing, understanding, and accepting differences. Then, as an individual, I can get involved as a global citizen. Everything has to start somewhere, and if I can make a start, no matter how small it seems, at accommodating diversity, then I believe I'm acting as a responsible global citizen.

Katerina

Your Turn

How would you respond to the question Gord, Ling, and Katerina are answering? Do you think that the concept of global citizenship is a reality? Can you become a responsible global citizen — and what does this mean?

Identifying the Global Citizen

Though you are automatically a citizen of the country in which you were born, you must still apply for a passport. This means that you agree to the terms and conditions your country has established for citizenship.

Oxfam, an international non-governmental organization working to eradicate poverty, has described a global citizen as someone who

- is aware of the wider world
- respects and values diversity
- is willing to act to help others
- accepts responsibility for his or her own actions

Do you agree with this description? What traits would you add to this list?

For most of history, the concept of citizenship focused on those who belonged and those who did not — us and them. Women, for example, have struggled for centuries to become part of the political "us." In many countries today, it remains difficult, if not impossible, for minorities, the poor, and people who are different in some way to exercise the full rights of citizenship. Global citizenship transcends the idea of insiders and outsiders. Anyone, anywhere, can decide to be a global citizen. In what ways might the concept of global citizenship increase international co-operation? The well-being of humankind?

Recognizing and welcoming an identity that includes nationality, race, gender, family, job, and social milieu is necessary to understanding and accepting global citizenship. This enlarged vision of oneself is reflected in the words of Canadian philosopher Mark Kingwell, who says that citizenship is "a way of meeting one of our deepest needs, the need to belong . . . the need to be part of something larger than ourselves."

With a partner, create a list of ideas about how defining yourself as a global citizen can expand your self-image and your identity.

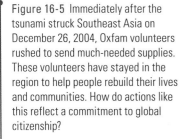

Figure 16-5 Immediately after the tsunami struck Southeast Asia on December 26, 2004, Oxfam volunteers rushed to send much-needed supplies. These volunteers have stayed in the region to help people rebuild their lives and communities. How do actions like this reflect a commitment to global citizenship?

REFLECT AND RESPOND

With a group, brainstorm a list of ideas about what it means to be a global citizen. Draw a mind map that illustrates your connections to others around the world. Start the mind map with the word "Me" in the centre. It might include categories such as music, sports, and clothes.

Examine current media reports and record examples of events occurring far from your community. Select one. State how it might affect you. Then describe one action you and your classmates might take, as global citizens, to respond to and influence the event.

WHAT DOES A GLOBAL CITIZEN DO?

More than 6.5 billion people live on Earth — and this number is growing. With a population this size, are conflicts over interests, beliefs, cultures, and needs inevitable? Think about the situation with your own family, friends, clubs, or classmates. Even when the number of people involved is relatively small, tensions and conflicts can arise.

Acting like a Global Citizen

Global citizens assume responsibility for making globalization work in a way that benefits as many people, in as many situations, as possible. This idea may seem overwhelming until it is examined in light of individuals, such as Wangari Maathai, who are doing things — on a small and large scale — in a globally responsible manner.

Recall the habits of mind you read about in the prologue (p. 7). With a partner or small group, use them as a basis for developing a list of the habits of mind of a global citizen.

Global citizens work collaboratively to respond to global events. They recognize that a need in one part of the world requires both an individual and a collective response from people in the rest of the world. The interconnectedness of globalization implies that in the global village, everyone is a neighbour.

Global citizens act locally and think globally. Wangari Maathai, for example, started the Green Belt Movement in Kenya. Before that, she had completed her global education, earning university degrees in the United States, Germany, and Kenya. Maathai has inspired women in 21 countries to fight deforestation and improve sustainable development by planting trees. As a global citizen, she also supports the drive to help HIV/AIDS victims, helps revitalize Indigenous cultures, and campaigns for the rights of women.

Figure 16-6 What key global change would be necessary to turn the message of this cartoon from one that is apparently negative to one that is apparently positive?

Figure 16-7 Nobel Peace Prize winner Wangari Maathai, who founded the Green Belt Movement, waters a tree she planted to mark the opening of the 2004 UN conference on Women and the Environment in Nairobi, Kenya. By planting trees, Maathai is contributing to sustainability for the generations of Kenyans who will come after her.

Correcting injustices

Global citizens see beyond the immediate. They envision a different world, in which injustices are corrected and solutions to global problems are found. Like an artist, a global citizen reinvents the immediate and explores new possibilities.

Slavery, for example, was an entrenched social practice in the late 18th and early 19th centuries. Many European economies relied on the cheap, disposable labour provided by slaves, and many Europeans believed that slavery was acceptable. But in Britain, for example, William Wilberforce and others began to imagine a world without slavery — and through their efforts, this practice was brought to an end in the British Empire.

DEVELOPING CROSS-CULTURAL UNDERSTANDING

FOCUS ON SKILLS

Globalization breaks down borders, brings together people from many places and cultures, and creates a need to communicate effectively across languages and cultures.

In the globalizing world, **cross-cultural communication** is an essential skill. Communication relies heavily on cultural expectations, customs, and body language. When communicating with someone from a different culture — in which the expectations, customs, and body language may be different — you may not receive the signals you expect.

A key aspect of cross-cultural communication is realizing that accepting and understanding another's point of view does not mean that you must change yours. Hearing and understanding are the starting points of communication. They are opportunities for everyone involved to expand their identity and are key elements in overcoming cross-cultural miscommunication.

With a partner, practise cross-cultural communication. Each of you will assume the identity of someone from another culture. One of you may become Chinese or American; the other may become Mexican or French. One of you will play the role of a representative of an NGO that is interested in environmental sustainability. The other will play the role of a farmer. The goal of the NGO is to negotiate an agreement allowing it to conduct an environmental assessment of the farm.

With this scenario in mind, you can follow these steps to gain an understanding of cross-cultural communication. You can use similar strategies to help you communicate with people from other cultures.

Steps to Successful Cross-Cultural Communication

Step 1: Learn about the culture

Before beginning your roleplay, find out about the culture of the characters whose identity you will assume. Discover, for example, what people might wear, watch on TV, and listen to on the radio. What is their likely educational background? What customs are important? Did colonialism play a role in the culture's history? Do conflicts play a role today? What customs are considered polite when people from the culture communicate with one another?

Use magazines, newspapers, and the Internet to develop a sense of the culture and how you, as a member, might respond to the "other," including body language, facial expressions, and personal space.

DOS AND DON'TS OF SUCCESSFUL CROSS-CULTURAL COMMUNICATION

DOS	DON'TS
Respect others Honour their point of view by listening respectfully. Acknowledging that you have heard another's point of view is a deep statement of respect.	**Don't use stereotypes as your model** All Canadians do not share the same point of view on any topic — nor do all Britons, Mexicans, or Americans. Communicate with the individual, not the stereotype.
Learn about their history Understand that the past carries weight. You and the others at the negotiating table bring a collective cultural history to the discussion. Past events can colour communication in the present.	**Don't assume that there is only one way of doing things** Many cultures have solved similar problems in different ways. Perhaps a combination of processes and ideas would be most effective.
Recognize that your point of view may not be universal Others have a different and equally valid way of looking at the world. Like you, people from other cultures have experienced success using their points of view and cultural perspectives to solve problems. It is unreasonable to expect those at the table to abandon their belief system.	**Don't assume that a breakdown in communication has occurred because "they" don't get it** Resolve to question your own ability to communicate ideas effectively. Be sure you are responding to the question that was asked. Try to understand the other person's meaning.

Step 2: Recognize potential problems

Before meeting your partner to begin negotiations, list four or five areas in which you may disagree. For each, note the reason you believe a disagreement might arise. Then add another note indicating how you will respond.

Cross-cultural miscommunication often stems from

- **cultural blind spots** — People view the world through the lens of their own culture, and culturally imposed behaviour is so familiar that people often fail to recognize it. In Canadian supermarkets, for example, people pay the price marked on the item. Bargaining is not part of the process. But in other cultures, bargaining is not only acceptable, but also expected. To communicate successfully with people from other cultures, it is important to understand your own cultural filters.

- **jumping to conclusions** — Assuming immediately that you understand a person from another culture may be the beginning of a problem. A person may, for example, smile and nod at what you are proposing. You might assume that this behaviour implies acceptance of your point of view. But the person from the other culture may have smiled and nodded out of politeness and to show that she or he hears you.

- **lack of patience** — The pace, rhythm, and structure of the other person's speech may be very different from yours. In many cultures, for example, it is considered rude to begin talking business as soon as you meet. As you begin your discussion, take your cues from the other person.

Step 3: Be an active listener

Active listening is a key to hearing what the other person means. Some strategies of an active listener include

- **repeating the message** — Say back to the person what you believe has just been said. In this way, both of you can be sure that you are sending and receiving the same message.

- **watching body language** — People communicate with more than words. Facial expressions, body gestures, and stances have different meanings in different cultures. Be aware that the other person is signalling through his or her culture, not yours.

Step 4: Complete your negotiation

When you and your partner feel prepared, assign the two roles. During your roleplaying session, make notes about the kinds of problems that arose and how you handled them. Write a short report outlining the process. In your report, include explanations of

- the roles you played
- the research you conducted
- the problems that arose
- whether solutions were found
- your conclusions, including tips for the next set of negotiators

Summing up

Like all effective communication, cross-cultural communication begins by accepting that the views of the "other" are valid. Accepting this may be difficult, because people are trained from the beginning of their lives to conduct themselves in ways that are considered acceptable in their culture. During cross-cultural communication — or any difficult communication — self-examination helps streamline the process.

Civil Society

Civil society includes non-governmental organizations such as the Red Cross, environmental movements such as Greenpeace, and Indigenous peoples' associations such as the Assembly of First Nations, as well as religious groups, citizen advocacy organizations, and trade unions. Civil society contains elements of public-spiritedness, social trust, non-violence, and tolerance.

Aims of civil society

Civil society raises awareness of highly focused and specific ideas, concerns, and programs that a group is advocating and working to have implemented. Greenpeace, for example, is working around the world to bring an end to the hunting of whales. This environmental organization has organized demonstrations in Japan, Nicaragua, China, and other countries that continue to support whaling.

Contemporary communication technologies, such as the Internet, have enabled groups like Greenpeace to organize on a very large scale. In March 2007, for example, more than 12 million people marched in countries around the world to protest the war in Iraq.

Figure 16-8 Thousands of demonstrators holding torches formed a giant peace sign in Heroes' Square in Budapest, Hungary, on March 17, 2007. How might peaceful demonstrations like this influence government policy? How might they influence the points of view of people in other countries?

MAKING CHOICES

IRSHAD MANJI — SPEAKING OUT FOR HER FAITH

Irshad Manji calls herself a "Muslim refusenik." This does not mean that Manji renounces her faith; rather, it means that she wants to reform it.

As a teenager in Vancouver, the Ugandan-born Canadian feminist, author, journalist, and activist attended both a public school and an Islamic religious school, known as a *madrassa*. Manji excelled at the public school, but by her own account, she was expelled from the religious school for asking too many questions.

A devout Muslim, Manji spent the next 20 years studying Islam. She strongly supports the ideal of *ijtihad*, which she describes as Islam's lost tradition of independent critical thinking. She believes that the economic empowerment of women in the Muslim world is the key to reviving and democratizing the spirit of *ijtihad*. She also argues that Muslims in the West are best positioned to rediscover *ijtihad* because "it is here that we have the precious freedoms to think, express, challenge, and be challenged on matters of religion, without fear of government reprisal."

In 2003, Manji published a controversial book titled *The Trouble with Islam Today: A Muslim's Call for Reform in Her Faith*. When the book was banned in several Muslim countries, Manji used the power of the Internet to publish online translations in Arabic, Urdu, and Persian. At the same time, the book has drawn praise from many Muslims. Indonesia, for example, is the world's most populous Muslim country. There, the *Jakarta Post* named Manji one of three Muslim women who are creating positive change in Islam.

Figure 16-9 With her family, Irshad Manji fled the Uganda of dictator Idi Amin when she was four years old. She has recently launched Project Ijtihad, with the goal of developing the first leadership network for reform-minded Muslims.

Explorations

1. Explain why you think Irshad Manji is — or is not — displaying the qualities of global citizenship. Support your answer by citing evidence from this feature.

2. Why would the concept of universal *ijtihad* be so controversial? Explain the reasons for your response.

Views of civil society

Some critics of civil society say that the aims of groups involved in this sector are too narrow and too focused on single issues. Critics say that the groups ignore the complexity of the issues involved.

In the 1990s, for example, civil society groups waged a successful campaign against Nike for using sweatshops to manufacture their products. As a result, Nike stopped manufacturing goods in Indonesian and Cambodian sweatshops. But when the company moved elsewhere, thousands of people were thrown out of work — and the families of the newly unemployed workers suffered great hardship.

Other critics believe that strong societies will be built only when individuals and organizations work in partnership with governments. Speaking before the United Nations Human Rights Council in 2006, Wangari Maathai said that civil society must rise to the challenge of working with government leaders to maintain the rule of law and to foster human rights for all people. She and the Green Belt Movement are advising the African Union — an organization made up of the governments of 53 African countries — on how to manage African affairs more justly and responsibly.

▶ With a partner, consider who is likely to achieve goals more quickly and efficiently: governments empowered to act in the interests of all citizens or civil society groups acting for a specific purpose? Must it be an either–or situation? Explain your response.

Figure 16-10 Hundreds of protestors from Global Exchange, a San Francisco advocacy group, lined the entrance to NikeTown at the store's grand opening in 1997. Global Exchange members were protesting the use of sweatshop labour, claiming that Indonesian workers who created Nike shoes and apparel were paid a mere 29 cents an hour.

REFLECT AND RESPOND

The Carnegie UK Trust explores civil society for educators. The trust has said, "We may never share a common vision about what a 'good' society might look like and how it might be achieved, but we can be committed to a process that allows people of all ages and backgrounds to share in defining how the different visions are reconciled." Explain this statement in your own words.

Differences exist among civil society groups and the sectors of society they target. In addition, each group operates in its own culture. List what you think are the five key factors that must be considered when reconciling cross-cultural differences. Prepare a flow chart that illustrates some of the effects of each of your choices. In addition, indicate some of the interconnections among them. An example of what part of your chart might look like is shown.

Factor 2

Factor 1
Knowledge of the other culture

Factor 3

Knowledge supports and is supported by . . .

↓
Better understanding
↓
Greater tolerance

Factor 4

Factor 5

The way you respond to the forces of globalization will reflect how — and whether — you accept the responsibilities of global citizenship. Here are the ideas of three people who have thought about this concept.

MICHAEL COLLINS was an astronaut on the Apollo 11 mission. In his book *Carrying the Fire: An Astronaut's Journey*, he recounted his experience of viewing his home planet from space and explained how he came to believe that people are global citizens whether they recognize this fact or not.

I really believe that if political leaders of the world could see their planet from a distance of 100 000 miles [161 000 km], their outlook would fundamentally change. That all-important border would be invisible, that noisy argument suddenly silenced.

STEVEN PINKER, a Canadian-born psychology professor at Harvard University, suggests that becoming an active global citizen could enhance the process of humanizing globalization. This excerpt is from his book *The Blank Slate: The Modern Denial of Human Nature*.

While conflict is a human universal, so is conflict resolution. Customs that were common throughout history and prehistory — slavery, punishment by mutilation, execution by torture ... the legal ownership of women — have all vanished from large parts of the world . . . For all its selfishness, the human mind is equipped with a moral sense, whose circle of application has expanded steadily and might continue to expand as the world becomes interdependent.

RICK SALUTIN, a playwright, author, and columnist with *The Globe and Mail*, contends that globalization is being forced on the world by business and financial interests. He believes that people should resist globalization and think more about individual fulfilment.

"Demain, c'est la mort." [Loosely translated, this French phrase means "Tomorrow is death."] That could mean various things, like: Globalization is destroying the world. But I choose to think it means, You only have one life, so live it as something worthy rather than as a cog in a stifling, commercial system, don't let yourself be globalized to death. Something like that. It's a thought that seems to come most often from the young, although it's actually even more apt for the old.

Explorations

1. In a two-column chart like the one shown, list each writer, then summarize the arguments he presents to support or oppose fully embracing globalization and global citizenship. Use the Internet, library, newspapers, or other sources of quotations to find two more points of view on each side of the discussion. Add these to your chart.

Points of View on Globalization	
Writer	Arguments

WHAT IS MY ROLE IN THE GLOBALIZING WORLD?

The Canadian philosopher John Ralston Saul said, "Democracy is the only system capable of reflecting the humanist premise of equilibrium or balance. The key to its secret is the involvement of the citizen." Do you think this statement also applies to global citizens?

Some argue that the problems of the world are just too big and overwhelming for individuals to make a difference. But Mother Theresa, a Catholic nun who dedicated her life to helping people living in deep poverty, disagreed. She said, "We ourselves feel that what we are doing is just a drop in the ocean. But if that drop was not in the ocean, I think the ocean would be less because of that missing drop."

Active Citizens

Mother Theresa believed that the actions of a single person can bring about change. George Manuel, of the Secwepemc Nation of British Columbia, for example, believed that only through working together in "mind, body and spirit" can Aboriginal people shape their own destiny.

Manuel started at the local level, then broadened the scope of his activities. In the 1970s, he helped found the World Council of Indigenous Peoples and served as the organization's first president from 1975 to 1981. Manuel travelled the world to promote Indigenous people's interests, and in 1977, he helped write the UN Draft Universal Declaration on the Rights of Indigenous Peoples, then lobbied the United Nations to adopt its principles. In what ways did Manuel embody the concept of global citizenship?

Active Students

Like George Manuel and many others, high school students have responded actively to the challenges of globalization at the local, national, and international levels. At Harry Ainlay High School in Edmonton, for example, students organized the Breaking Borders Club in 2006. The club's motto — Breaking borders . . . one stereotype at a time — reflected the students' desire to build worldwide understanding of cultures, traditions, and religions.

Club projects have included a letter-writing campaign urging the government to help disarm child soldiers in Africa and inviting speakers to talk to students about issues such as helping refugees in Africa.

Muhammed Al-Nuaimi, the student who led the club in 2007, said that club members hope to "build a foundation for groups to reach out to each other. Gaps of the unknown or confusion will be filled with understanding and the new connections will break down barriers between peoples."

Figure 16-11 George Manuel, one of the founders and leaders of the World Council of Indigenous Peoples, shakes hands with Prime Minister Pierre Trudeau in 1972. At the time, Manuel was president of the National Indian Brotherhood, the forerunner of the Assembly of First Nations.

VOICES

The United Nations and countries like Canada recognize differences, but we wanted to celebrate and express our backgrounds and find similarities more than differences. We're all part of the same world.

— *Jocelyn Nand, a founding member of Breaking Borders*

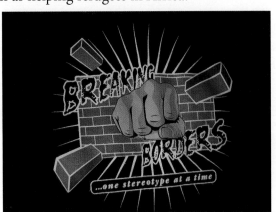

Figure 16-12 The student-designed logo for the Breaking Borders Club is used on T-shirts, posters, and other material they send out. Do you think this logo effectively expresses the group's aims?

Figure 16-13 Heather Mills McCartney leads a PETA celebration outside a Los Angeles J. Crew store. In 2005, the retailer agreed to stop selling furs after the animal rights organization led a successful consumer boycott of its stores.

Figure 16-14 The Body Shop actively promotes fair trade and global citizenship through displays like this. Some of the profits from the sales of this product are donated to support the global activities to combat the spread of HIV/AIDS.

Active Consumers

Companies are in business to make a profit, and consumer activists have learned that they can influence corporate policies by affecting their profit margin. In many instances, consumer activism has successfully persuaded companies to change the way they do business.

- Boycotts protesting the use of animals in the testing of cosmetics led Avon (1989), L'Oréal (1994), and Gillette (1997) to abandon this practice.
- In 2001, a "No Sweat" campaign by university students, such as those at the University of Alberta, successfully persuaded many North American universities to stop buying clothing, such as T-shirts, from companies that produce the goods in sweatshops. The campaign persuaded many apparel companies to adopt policies to improve working conditions in their factories around the world.
- After a public campaign highlighted some of the unsustainable practices used by suppliers of Staples and Office Depot, both companies pledged to become more environmentally responsible in 2003.
- Continuing protests against wearing fur by People for the Ethical Treatment of Animals have succeeded in changing the fashion industry's attitude toward selling furs.

Active Corporations

Many corporations recognize that it is good business to act as good global citizens. Yves Chouinard, owner of Patagonia, a sports clothing company, believes that "there are no profits to be made on a dead planet." Other companies such as the Body Shop and Mountain Equipment Co-op support this philosophy and have moved away from focusing on profit as their sole motivation. These companies recognize that ignoring the environment and human rights will hurt everyone in the long run.

The Body Shop, founded by Anita Roddick, is often cited as an example of a corporation that operates according to principles of social responsibility. Activist Naomi Klein, for example, has said that the Body Shop "may well be the most progressive multinational on the planet." Roddick argues that "today's corporations have global responsibilities because their decisions affect world problems concerning economics, poverty, security, and the environment."

Active You

Awareness of the opportunities and challenges offered by globalization is probably the single most important aspect of global citizenship. In their book *Coming of Age in a Globalized World*, J. Michael Adams and Angelo Carfagna write: "A global education enables us to understand our roles in a global community and teaches us how our actions affect people across the world. It also demonstrates how events around the world affect us as individuals, and therefore cannot be ignored."

Think about this course in light of Adams and Carfagna's statement. Has this course helped expand your understanding of the need for a global education? Express your answer in a single sentence.

Buckminster Fuller, the American inventor, philosopher, and architect, said, "Whether humanity is to continue and comprehensively prosper on Spaceship Earth depends entirely on the integrity of the human individuals and not on the political and economic systems." What do you suppose he meant?

Jeffery Sachs, an American economist, echoed Fuller's words when he said, "In the end, it comes back to us, as individuals. Individuals, working in unison, form and shape societies. Social commitments are commitments of individuals. Great social forces . . . are the mere accumulation of individual actions."

To what extent should we embrace globalization? This is the question you have focused on as you progressed through the course and this textbook. Would you have chosen a different question to pursue? Explain your thoughts.

Figure 16-15 People such as astronaut Michael Collins believe that those who act globally are automatically global citizens. If you were asked to identify one trait that connects the people pictured here, what would it be?

1. In the prologue, you read about several different ways of interpreting and defining globalization. Then, as you began each chapter, you kept notes on your changing understanding of this concept.

   a) Use the information from these and other sources to arrive at your own definition of globalization.

   b) Analyze your definition by identifying each of the concepts you included and explaining why you chose them and how they relate to globalization. A definition of "house," for example, might say, "A place where living things dwell in security." When analyzing this definition, you might explain what "place" means, why you chose "living things," and what "living things" implies (e.g., animals as well as humans), as well as why you chose to include "security" in your definition.

   c) Share your definition with a partner. Note comments made by your partner. If necessary, revise your definition and the notes on your analysis.

   d) Present your definition for a small group or the class to consider and comment on. Be prepared to defend your position.

   e) With a small group or the class, develop a definition that is supported by a consensus.

2. Work with a small group to create a global citizenship report card for an organization.

   a) Select a broad area to examine (e.g., the environment), then choose a specific organization that is involved in this area (e.g., an NGO such as Greenpeace, a corporation such as Dole). Then develop three or four criteria to use to judge the performance of the organization.

   b) Conduct research using various sources (e.g., the Internet, *Exploring Globalization*, newspapers, and magazines) to discover the aims of the organization and how it is working to achieve its goals. Corporations often have web sites that describe their corporate goals and the actions they have taken to reach them. Civil society groups also operate web sites.

   d) After conducting the research, review your criteria. If necessary, revise your criteria to reflect changes in your thinking. Then use your criteria to prepare a report card that rates the organization's performance as a global citizen.

3. Imagine that the want ad shown on the computer screen on this page appeared on a job-search web site.

   Work with a small group of four to six. Divide the group in half. One half will play the role of members of the GCI hiring committee; the other half will play the role of job applicants.

Hiring Committee

a) Prepare three to five criteria you will use to evaluate the applicants' letters.

b) Prepare questions to ask the candidates during a job interview.

Applicants

a) Prepare and submit the one-page letter as specified in the ad.

b) Prepare notes to guide your responses during the job interview.

Roleplay a brief interview with each candidate. Afterwards, meet as a whole group to discuss the process, your thoughts, and what you would do differently next time.

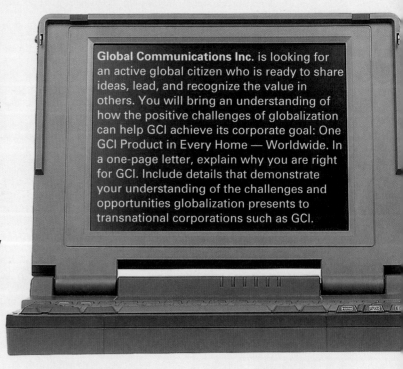

Global Communications Inc. is looking for an active global citizen who is ready to share ideas, lead, and recognize the value in others. You will bring an understanding of how the positive challenges of globalization can help GCI achieve its corporate goal: One GCI Product in Every Home — Worldwide. In a one-page letter, explain why you are right for GCI. Include details that demonstrate your understanding of the challenges and opportunities globalization presents to transnational corporations such as GCI.

4. On this page are three maps that present the world from three different points of view.

a) Write a brief, one-sentence description of each map.

b) Which view represents the most appropriate way of looking at the world? Explain your answer.

c) Most maps — even those created in Australia, South America, and China — are oriented so that north is at the top. To what extent do you think this convention is a result of historical globalization? What other factors might have influenced this convention? Explain your answers.

d) Find examples of maps that show different views of the world. Why might you use an Atlantic Ocean-centred map like Map 2, or the view you found.

e) If maps usually showed South America at the top, do you think this would have affected your point of view on Central and South America? World politics? Why?

f) If Canada were an imperial power and you were a government official, which view would you recommend using in school textbooks? Explain your choice.

g) Consider your understanding of the importance of global citizenship and make a recommendation to the ministry of education about the use of maps in Alberta classrooms. Provide at least three reasons for your recommendation.

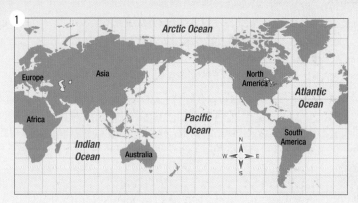

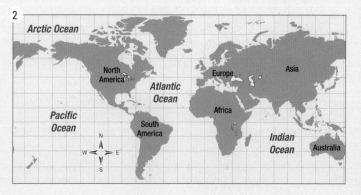

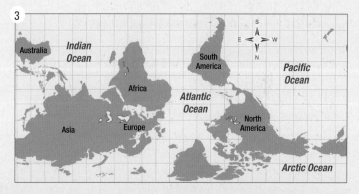

Think about Your Challenge

Complete your blog or journal and finalize your informed position on this related issue: To what extent should I, as a citizen, respond to globalization? In preparation for completing the second part of the challenge — building a class consensus on the key issue — prepare a statement of your own response to this question. Review the material on group leadership (pp. 312–313) and consensus building (pp. 246–247) in preparation for the class activity.

Glossary

A

accommodation A process that occurs when people from different cultures come into contact and accept and create space for one another. The customs, traditions, technologies, beliefs and languages of both cultures may be affected.

acculturation The cultural changes that occur when two cultures accommodate, or adapt to, each other's worldviews.

apartheid An Afrikaans word that refers to a policy of segregating and discriminating against non-whites in South Africa.

assimilation A process that occurs when the culture of a minority group is absorbed by another culture. The cultural identity of the minority group disappears as its members take on the identity of the other culture.

B

basic needs People's basic physical needs include food, clothing, shelter, and water, but they also have social needs, such as family and friends, and emotional needs, such as a sense of belonging and being loved.

biodiversity Variety in plant and animal species.

blood oil Oil that is obtained through violence and bloodshed.

boreal forest An environmentally sensitive sub-Arctic region that consists of mostly coniferous trees, such as spruce, fir, and pine.

C

capitalism An economic system that advocates free trade, competition, and choice as a means of achieving prosperity.

civil society A sector of society made up of non-government and non-business groups. Civil society includes community groups, non-governmental organizations, faith-based groups, and universities.

collective A group to which a person belongs and identifies with.

communism An economic and political system whose purpose is to eliminate class distinctions. Everyone would work for the benefit of all and would receive help as he or she needs it.

compare To find similarities and differences.

connotation The emotional associations people attach to a word or phrase.

consensus General agreement.

containerization The transporting of goods in standard-sized shipping containers.

context Circumstances or surroundings.

contrast To find differences between or among things or ideas.

cross-cultural communication Communication that occurs among people of different cultures.

cultural content laws Laws passed by a government to prevents a group's cultural identity — including its artists, performers, songs, movies, and literature — from being overwhelmed by the media of a more dominant culture.

cultural diversity Variety in cultures and identities.

cultural mosaic A society that is made up of many distinct cultural groups.

cultural pluralism The idea that a variety of peoples are free to affirm and promote their customs, traditions, beliefs, and language within a society.

cultural revitalization The process of affirming and promoting people's individual and collective cultural identity.

D

deindustrialization The reduction in or loss of industries.

denotation The dictionary meaning of a word or phrase.

depopulation A reduction in population caused by natural or human-made forces.

digital divide The gap that separates people who do — and do not — have access to up-to-date digital technology.

E

ecological footprint The area of the earth's surface necessary to sustain the level of resources a person uses and the waste she or he creates.

economic depression A period of low economic activity accompanied by high levels of unemployment.

economic globalization The spread of trade, transportation, and communication systems around the world in the interests or promoting worldwide commerce.

economies of scale Savings that are achieved by producing, using, and buying things in large quantities.

effect A noun meaning "result" or a verb meaning "brought about" or "caused."

enemy alien A label assigned during World War I and World War II to people from countries that were at war with Canada. The rights of enemy aliens were sometimes restricted, and some were even interned in camps.

ethnocentrism A word that combines "ethnic" and "centre." It refers to a way of thinking that centres on one's own race and culture. Ethnocentric people believe that their worldview is the only valid one.

Eurocentrism A form of ethnocentrism that uses European ethnic, national, religious, and linguistic criteria to judge other peoples and their cultures.

F

flag of convenience A flag flown by ships when they are registered in a country that is not the country of their owner.

foreign aid Money, supplies, and other goods, as well as expertise, given by one country to another.

free trade The trade that occurs when two or more countries eliminate tariffs and taxes on the goods and services they trade with one another.

G

gacaca courts Community courts established in Rwanda to try low-level officials and ordinary people accused of taking part in the Rwandan genocide. The purpose of these courts was to speed up the process of bringing to justice those who had participated in the genocide and to encourage reconciliation.

gender gap The social, economic, and political differences that separate men and women.

general consensus Agreement that occurs when most, or even all, members of a group agree.

genocide The mass killing of human beings, especially a targeted group of people.

genuine progress index (GPI) A system that measures the sustainability, well-being, and quality of life of a country and its people.

global climate change Small but steady changes in average temperatures around the world.

grand exchange A trading process that began when Christopher Columbus brought seeds, fruit trees, and livestock to the Americas, where they were cultivated and became staples. In return, native North American species were exported to Europe. This exchange expanded to include different countries and products around the world.

gross domestic product (GDP) The value of all the goods and services a country produces in a year. GDP is often used to measure the strength of a country's economy.

gross national income (GNI) The amount of money earned by everyone in a country.

H

historical globalization A period that is often identified as beginning in 1492, when Christopher Columbus made his first voyage to the Caribbean, and ending after World War II, when the United States and the Soviet Union emerged as superpowers.

homogenization The erasing of differences. When this term is applied to people, it often refers to the erasing of cultural differences so that peoples become more and more similar.

human trafficking A crime that occurs when people seeking a better life in a new country are preyed on by criminal organizations that help them immigrate illegally, then force them to work in substandard conditions or in criminal activities.

hybridization The combining of elements of two or more different things to create something new.

I

imperialism One country's domination over another country's economic, political, and cultural institutions.

inalienable Referring to rights that cannot be taken away or transferred.

Indian Act First passed by the Canadian Parliament in 1876 and amended several times since then, this act continues to define who is — and is not — a status Indian. Early versions of the act banned some traditional practices of First Nations cultures and allowed only those who renounced Indian status to vote in federal elections.

Industrial Revolution The period between about 1750 and 1850, when work became mechanized and began to occur in factories. The Industrial Revolution brought about dramatic economic, social, and cultural change.

ingenuity gap The gap between people's need for new and innovative solutions to problems and their ability to supply those solutions.

K

knowledge economy Businesses and individuals who use research, education, new ideas, and information technologies for practical purposes.

L

labour standards Measures that protect workers.

legacy Something that has been passed on by those who lived in the past.

M

market economy An economy in which government regulations are reduced to a minimum and businesses are free to make their own decisions.

media concentration The gathering of ownership of newspapers and other media in the hands of a few large corporations.

media convergence The use of electronic technology to integrate media such as newspapers, books, TV, and the Internet.

mercantilism A policy followed by European imperial powers from the 16th to the 19th century. In colonies, trade was strictly controlled to benefit the economy of the imperial power.

multiculturalism An official Canadian government policy founded on the idea that Canadian society is pluralistic — made of many culturally distinct groups who are free to affirm and promote their own cultural identity.

N

non-governmental organization (NGO) An organization established by groups of people to work toward specific goals and to gain public support in achieving these goals. NGOs depend on volunteer workers and donations, but they may also receive grants or contracts from governments. They may influence government policies at national and international levels.

O

outsourcing A business strategy that involves reducing costs by using suppliers of products and services in countries where labour is cheaper and government regulation may be less strict.

overgeneralizing Drawing a conclusion based on too little information.

P

pandemic An epidemic that spreads around the world and poses a serious threat because of people's ability to travel farther and faster than ever before.

pop culture A short form for "popular culture," which is the culture of the people. This term often refers to current cultural trends that are spread by commercial mass media.

privatization The selling of a public service, such as electricity delivery or health care, to a private company so that the service is no longer owned by the government.

propaganda Ideas and information spread for the purpose of achieving a specific goal.

Q

Quiet Revolution A period of intense social, political, and economic change in Québec. During this period, which lasted from about 1960 to 1966, Québécois began to assert their rights and affirm and promote their language and culture.

R

reparations The act of making amends for wrongdoing. Reparations may include payments made by a defeated enemy to countries whose territory was damaged during a war.

residential schools Boarding schools where First Nations children were gathered to live, work, and study. These schools were operated or subsidized by the Canadian government as an important element of the government's assimilation policy. The last residential school closed in 1996.

role model Someone to whom others look as an example to emulate.

rough consensus An agreement that involves most people in a group.

S

sanction A penalty. Often an economic penalty, such as a trade boycott, taken to pressure a government to agree to carry out certain actions or follow certain rules.

status Indian A First Nations person who is registered according to the provisions of the Indian Act and is therefore eligible to receive specific benefits.

stereotyping Placing people in categories according to preconceived beliefs about how members of a particular group think or behave.

stewardship Accepting responsibility for ensuring that the earth's resources remain sustainable.

sustain To provide the basic necessities needed to support life.

sustainability The degree to which Earth is able to provide the resources necessary to meet people's needs.

sustainable development Development that meets people's needs in the present without compromising the ability of future generations to meet their needs.

sustainable prosperity Practising stewardship of the environment and resources so that future generations are able to achieve prosperity.

T

trade liberalization A process that involves countries in reducing or removing trade barriers, such as tariffs and quotas, so goods and services can move around the world more freely.

transnational corporation A company that is based in one country while developing and manufacturing its products, or delivering its goods and services, in more than one country. Also called a multinational corporation.

U

universalization The spread of culture, trends, customs, and practices around the world.

V

virtual community A community made up of people who may never have met in person but who interact via the Internet in chat rooms and blogs, through instant messaging, or through social networking sites.

Index

Photo Credits

Prologue, **p1** CP/Wong Maye-E; **p4** CP/Ryan Remiorz; **p5** CP Images

Related Issue 1

p14 CP/Jason DeCrow; **p15** *left* CP/Deddeda Stemler, CP/Kevin Frayer;

Ch 1 Opener, **p18** and **19** Photos courtesy of the artist Joane Cardinal; **p20** upper left clockwise David Austen/Stock Boston/PictureQuest, Rob Van Petten/Digital Vision World Family, CP/Jacques Boissinot, CP/Deddeda Stemler; **p21** CP/Jonathan Hayward; **p23** *top* CP/Fred Chartrand, CP/J.P. Moczulski; **p25** *top* Christine Osborne Pictures/Photo Researchers, CP/Alan Klein; **p26** *left* Hisham F. Ibrahim/PhotoDisc, CP/Kevin Frayer; **p28** *left* CP/Ryan Remiorz, CP/J.P. Moczulski, CP/REX/Francis Dean; **p29** Dan www.CartoonStock.com; **p30** *left* CP/Tim Krochak, Val Wilkinson/Valan Photos; **p31** James Schaffer/PhotoEdit Inc.; **p37** *top* CP/Riccardo Gaggale, Photo courtesy of Aysha Wills; **p38** CP/Jacques Boissinot; **p39** *top left clockwise*, Photo courtesy of Satya Das, CP/Charlie Riedel, Photo courtesy of Long Litt Woon; **p41** *My Village in Nunavik* ©1999 National Film Board of Canada;

Ch 2 Opener, **p42** *top left clockwise*, Bill Ivy, Photo courtesy of Bombardier, Photo courtesy of Maersk Lines, Al-Jazeera–www.aljazeera. net, CP/Richard Drew; **p44** *top*, Bird Creature by Kiawak Ashoona NGC/35529, NAC C-035376; **p45** David Tanaka; **p46** Photo courtesy of Maersk Lines; **p47** CP/Sam Morris; **p50** CP/Don Denton; **p52** CP/Kent Gilbert; **p53** Photo courtesy of NRK/Brennpunkt; **p55** CP/Kent Gilbert; **p57** *top* Photo courtesy of The Council of Canadians, CP/David Boily; **p58** *top* AP/Anthony Mitchell, CP/*Winnipeg Free Press*; **p60** *top* CP/Shaun Best, Reproduced courtesy of the Nunatsiaq News; **p61** CP/*Edmonton Sun/* Robert Taylor; **p62** *top left*, Reproduced courtesy of the Metis National Council and the Metis Nation of Alberta, David Tanaka; **p63** AFP/Getty Images

Ch 3 Opener, **p66** Nerilicon/caglecartoons.com; **p68** CORBIS; **p69** Photo courtesy of Laptopical.com; **p70** *top* Photo courtesy of Telesat Canada, CP Photo; **p71** Photos courtesy of the Aboriginal People's Television Network; **p73** Steve Greenberg; **p74** Photo courtesy of TakingITGlobal Canada; **p75** Keefe/caglecartoons.com; **p76** *top left clockwise* CP/Everett, CP Photo, CP/Amy Sancetta; **p79** Used by permission CNN; **p80** *top* CP/Rex Features, CP/Jason DeCrow; **p81** Chappatte in "NZZ am Sonntag" (Zurich), www.globecartoon.com; **p82** *top* CP/AL Engel/INFGoff.com, CP/Dennis Van Tine/ABACAUSA. COM, CP/Tom Gannam; **p83** Joe McNally Photography; **p84** *top* Claro Cortes IV/Reuters/CORBIS, David Tanaka; **p85** REUTERS/Ho New;

Ch 4 Opener, **p88** *top left clockwise* CP/Adrian Wyld, Photo courtesy of the Stampede Parade, CP/Larry MacDougal; **p90** CP/Kevin Frayer; **p92** Chappatte in *International Herald Tribune* - www.globecartoon. com ; **p93** Photo courtesy of Mitali Perkins; **p97** Photos courtesy of Douglas Cardinal Architect Inc.; **p99** David Samuel Robbins/CORBIS; **p100** CP/Lethbridge Herald/Ian Martens; **p101** Photos courtesy of the Governor General; **p102** Photos courtesy of the Department of Canadian Heritage. Reproduced with the permission of the Minister of Public Works and Government Services Canada, 2007; **p103** *top* Photo courtesy of Taqramiut Nipingat Inc.; *My Village in Nunavik* ©1999 National Film Board of Canada; **p104** Yannick Jooris; **p105** Photos courtesy of the Department of Canadian Heritage. Reproduced with the permission of the Minister of Public Works and Government Services Canada, 2007; **p106** *top* CP/Frank Franklin11, Reproduced by permission of the Assembly of First Nations; **p107** Reproduced by permission of UNESCO;

Related Issue 2

p110 Jeremy Bright/Robert Harding World Imagery/Getty Images; **p111** *left* Glenbow Archives NA-1406-21, Melanie Stetson Freeman/*Christian Science Monitor*/Getty Images

Ch 5 Opener, **p114** First Image; **p117** *top* Rosmi Duaso/Time & Life Pictures/Getty Images, Franz-Marc Frei/CORBIS; **p120** *top* Bettman/CORBIS, The Granger Collection; **p121** An English Sloop and a Frigate in a Light Breeze (oil on canvas) by Swaine, Francis (1730-1782) ©Yale Center for British Art, Paul Mellon Collection, USA/ The Bridgeman Art Library; **p126** *top* National Archives of Canada-c007300m, The Spanish State Council in 1518. Brother Juan de Quevedo (d.1519) and Bartolome de Las Casas (1474-1566) defending the cause of the Indians before Charles V (1500-58) (coloured engraving) by Spanish School, (19th century) Private Collection/ Index/ The Bridgeman Art Library; **p127** Hulton Archive/Getty Images; **p129** The Brickyards of England, Children carrying the clay, 1871 (engraving) (b/w photo) by English School, (19th century) Bibliothèque des Arts Décoratifs, Paris, France/Archives Charmet/The Bridgeman Art Library; **p130** Louie Psihoyos/CORBIS; **p131** Bettman/CORBIS; **p132** *top* The Workshop of a Weaver, 1656 (oil on canvas) by Rombouts, Gillis (1630-78) Frans Hals Museum, Haarlem, The Netherlands/ Index/The Bridgeman Art Library, CORBIS; **p133** *top clockwise* Bettman/CORBIS, Used by permission of West End Press, Photo courtesy of Tunde Obadina;

Ch 6 Opener **p136** *left clockwise* Mary Evans Picture Library, Private Collection/ Photo Crane Kalman Gallery, London, UK/The Bridgeman Art Library, Bill Ivy; **p138** Ian Waldie/Getty Image News; **p140** CP Photo; **p141** CP/Mary Evans Picture Library; **p145** *top clockwise* Alinari Archives/ The Image Works, CP/Aijaz Rahi, CP/George Osodi; **p146** *top clockwise* Krzysztof Dydynski/Lonely Planet Images/Getty Images, Ram Shergill/ Stone/Getty Images, Panoramic Images/Getty Images; **p147** REUTERS/ Ralph Orlowski; **p148** New York Public Library/Art Resource; **p150** Bennett Dean/Eye Ubiquitous/CORBIS; **p151** Adam Woolfitt/ CORBIS; **p152** Margaret Bourke-White/Time Life Pictures/Getty Images; **p153** Panoramic Images/Getty Images; **p155** CP/David Longstreath; **p156** Gavin Hellier/JAI/Corbis; **p157** Jeremy Bright/Robert Harding World Imagery/Getty Images, Esquivel/caglecartoons.com;

Ch 7 Opener **p160** NAC NMC-51970, inset NAC/C-005750; **p163** *top* IVY IMAGES, NAC/C-017338; **p165** NAC/C-028544; **p167** *left* Provincial Archives of Manitoba/Hudsons's Bay Archives/ 1987/363/V-100, Glenbow Archives NA-1406-21, Bill Ivy; **p171** Canada Centre for Remote Sensing; **p178** *top* NAC-a023095, CP/Fred Chartrand; **p179** CP Photo; **p181** *top clockwise* CP/Drew Gragg, Photo courtesy of Ruby Dhalla, CP/Fred Chartrand, Photo courtesy of Yasmin Ratansi; **p182** Photo by Bill Borgwardt; **p183** CP/Montréal Gazette; **p184** NGC-15234;

Ch 8 Opener **p186** REUTERS/Finbarr O'Reilly; **p188** Sarah Ivy/IVY IMAGES; **p189** CP/Ryan Remiorz; **p190** George Kourounis; **p191** *left* CP/Jonathan Hayward, CP/Simon Hayter; **p152** *top clockwise* CP/Binod Joshi, Melanie Stetson Freeman/Christian Science Monitor/ Getty Images, Photo courtesy of Union Coffee Roasters; **p193** *top* Canadian Broadcasting Corporation. Used by permission of Nicole Pageau, AP Photo/Rodrique Ngowi; **p196** Poster by Carlos Jacanamijoy (www.carlosjacanamijoy.com); **p197** *top* UN Photo-151906C, REUTERS/Siphiwe Sibeko; **p198** CP/Themba Hadebe; **p199** *top* Glenbow Archives NA-1870-6, NAC\Tak Toyota C-046350; **p201** CP/ Fred Chartrand; **p202** Natalie Behring; **p204** Karen Kasmauski/CORBIS; **p207** Aislin;

Related Issue 3

p211 *left* Natalie Behring, CP/Larry MacDougal;

Ch 9 Opener **p214** *top* Bettman/CORBIS, Blaine Harrington III/ CORBIS; **p216** *left* Alexander Walker/Taxi/Getty Images, CP/Larry MacDougal, CP/Jeff McIntosh; **p219** *Gassed*, an oil study, 1918-19 (oil on canvas) by John Singer Sargent (1856-1925) Private Collection/ Photo Christie's Images/The Bridgeman Art Library; **p220** *top clockwise* Bettman/CORBIS, Jerry Kobalenko/Photographer's Choice/Getty Images, David King Collection; **p223** NAC C-014160; **p226** Bettman/CORBIS; **p227** Hulton Archive/Getty Images, **p229** *top* Aizar Raldes/AFP/Getty Images, CP/Nathan Denette; **p230** *top* CP/Lionel Cironneau, Jonathan Smith/Lonely Planet Images/Getty Images; **p231** CP/Eddie Adams; **p233** Natalie Behring

Ch 10 Opener **p236** *top clockwise* Wright/caglecartoons.com, Chappatte in *International Herald Tribune* - www.globecartoon.com; **p238** *left* Bill Ivy, CP/Rex Features; **p241** Yui Mok/AP Images; **p243** CP/L.M.Otero; **p245** CP/Elaine Thompson; **p249** CP/Vadim Ghirda; **p251** CP/RAOUF; **p252** *left* CP/Rex Features, CP/Adrian Wyld; **p253** *top clockwise* CP/Fred

Chartrand, Photo courtesy of the Council of Canadians, CP/Charlie Riedel; **p254** *top* clockwise CP/*Toronto Star*/Keith Beaty, CP/Katsumi Kasahara, CP/Fred Chartrand; **p257** CP/*Edmonton Sun*/Jack Dagley;

Ch 11 Opener **p258** Image courtesy of Nicholas Metivier Gallery, Toronto; **p261** *left* REUTERS/Jayanta Shaw, CP/John Moore; **p262** Tairona Heritage Trust; **p265** *left* clockwise O.Bierwagon/IVY IMAGES, CP/Rex Features, Bill Ivy/IVY IMAGES; **p266** REUTERS/ Claro Cortes; **p268** REUTERS/Anuruddha Lokuhapuarachchi; **p269** Photos courtesy of Paul Bailey and Marcello Malentacchi; **p270** Ruben Dao/Greenpeace; **p272** CP/Ian Barrett; **p273** John DeVisser/IVY IMAGES; **p274** CP/Adrian Wyld; **p275** AP Photo/Charlie Neibergall; **p277** T. Meyers/IVY IMAGES;

Ch 12 Opener **p278** *top* Ryuichi Sato/Taxi Japan/Getty Images, Hugh Sitton/Photographer's Choice/Getty Images; **p280** Sara Leen/ National Geographic; **p281** Winston Fraser/IVY IMAGES; **p284** *top clockwise* Photo courtesy of Jeff Parker, CP/Fred Chartrand, Photo by Paul Orenstein and used by permission of Marq de Villiers; Parker/ caglecartoons.com; **p285** CP/Steve White; **p287** *left* clockwise Tim Thompson/Stone/Getty Images, Daryl Benson/The Image Bank/Getty Images, Matthew Septimus/The Image Bank/Getty Images; **p290** CP/*Edmonton Sun*/Christine Vanzella; **p291** CP/Shuji Kajiyama; **p293** CP/Lauren Frayer; **p296** Photo courtesy of Global Crop Diversity Trust, A Foundation for Good Security; **p297** Photos courtesy of Ford Motor Company;

Related Issue 4
P300 CP/Jeff Widener; **p301** *top* CP/Greg Baker, CP/Larry MacDougal;

Chapter 13 Opener **p304** *left* clockwise CP/*Winnipeg Sun*/Jon Schledewitz, CP/Melissa Engle/Ecumenical Advocacy Alliance, CP/PA Photos Limited, CP/Jay Thornton/INFGoff.com; **p306** *top* CP/Rajesh Kumar Singh, *left* CP/Achmad Ibrahim, CP/Ed Andrieski, CP/Ian Jackson; **p309** HIP/Art Resource, NY; **p314** www.cartoonstock.com; **p316** Tammie Arroyo/ AP Images; **p317** Eugene Hoshiko/AP Images; **p318** *left* CP/Richard Crampton/Rex Features, CP/Bassem Tellawi; **p319** Jeff Widener/AP Images; **p320** *left* CP/Daniel Ochoa de Olza, CP/Michel Euler; **p321** *top*

CP/Manish Swarup, Jason DeCrow/AP Images;

Chapter 14 Opener **p324** *left* clockwise CP/Gregorio Binuya/ ABACAUSA.COM, CP/Richard Jones/Rex Features, CP/Ric Francis; **p326** Reproduced by permission of PETA; **p328** *left* CP/Channi Anand; CP/*Edmonton Sun*-Robert Taylor; **p329** CP/Andre Penner; **p330** *top* CP/Gurinder Osan, Photo courtesy of Jin Ting Zhao; **p331** cartoonstock. com; **p334** CP/Jacques Boissinot; **p335** CP/Ariel Leon; **p336** *top* David Tanaka, CP/Lionel Cironneau; **p338** CP/Ted S.Warren; **p339** *top* CP/ Mary Altaffer, CP/Paul Chiasson; **p341** *top clockwise* Photo courtesy of Cato Institute, CP/Peter Bregg/Macleans, CP/Moe Doiron;

Chapter 15 Opener **p344** *top* Bill Lowry/IVY IMAGES, REUTERS/ Jim Hollander, REUTERS/Bob Strong, Symbols from International Commission on Technology and Accessibility; **p346** CP/Adrian Wyld; **p347** *top* CP/Eugene Hoshiko, Bizarro. June 8, 2006. Dan Piraro, used by permission Dan Piraro; **p351** *top* CP/Kevin Frayer, Mike Sturk; **p353** *left* CP/Larry MacDougal, CP/Larry MacDougal; **p357** *top* CP/ Nathan Denette, Photo courtesy of Louise Binder, Photo by Melikhaya Mpumela. Used by permission of www.radiodiaries.org; **p358** CP/Greg Baker; **p359** CP/Tom Hanson; **p362** War Child Canada; **p363** *top* CP/Alik Keplicz, CP/Winnipeg Sun/Marcel Cretain; **p365** Cam/caglecartoons.com;

Chapter 16 Opener **p366** NASA/Getty Images; **p368** *left* CP/Jacques Boissinot, CP/Richard Drew, Wayne Lavold; **p370** CP/David Jones/ PA; **p371** *top* Chicago Tribune, CP/Karel Prinsloo; **p374** *top* CP/Bela Szandelszky, CP/Religion News Service Photo courtesy of Renna Communications; **p375** CP/Ben Margot; **p376** *top clockwise* CP Photo, Photo courtesy of Steven Pinker, Deborah Baic/*The Globe and Mail*; **p377** Breaking Borders Club, Harry Ainlay High School, Edmonton; **p378** *top* CP/Lionel Hahn/Abacausa.com, CP/PA Photos Limited; **p379** *top row left* CP/Jonathan Hayward, Photo courtesy of APTN, CP/Frank Franklin11, *middle row* REUTERS/Ralph Orlowski, CP/Tim Krochak, Photo courtesy of Mitali Perkins, *bottom row* CP/Kevin Frayer, CP/Aijaz Rahi

Text Credits

p2 Excerpt from *Coming of Age in a Globalized World: The Next Generation* by J. Michael Adams and Angelo Carfagna, Kumarian Press, 2006, p.3; **p8** "Pyramid of Powerful Questions," from *The Art and Architecture of Powerful Questions*, by Eric E. Vogt, www.javeriana.edu. co; **p34** Excerpts from *Last Stand of the Lubicon Cree*, by John Goddard, Douglas & McIntyre, 1991, pp xi and 6; **p57** Excerpt from Maude Barlow speech from *Alternatives to Economics Globalization: How Do We Want to Live?* used by permission; Excerpt from Pascal Lamy speech www.globalpolicy.org; Excerpt from debate between Benjamin Barber and Tyler Cowen, www.cato.org Used by permission; **p74** Tamoy, Richa Mathur and Frederick Bernas stories excerpted with permission of TakingITGlobal; **p87** "Another Day and Counting" used by permission of Zara Houshmand; **p93** "Magic Carpet" story by Mitali Perkins, used by permission; **p109** "The Thread" by Tom Wayman, used by permission; **p133** Excerpts from "Columbus Day" by Jimmie Durham, ©1993 by Jimmie Durham, published in *Columbus Day*, West End Press, 1993 (West End Press, P.O. Box 27334, Albuquerque, NM 87125); **p135** Excerpt from *Coming of Age in a Globalized World: The Next Generation* by J. Michael Adams and Angelo Carfagna, Kumarian Press, 2006, p. 164-165; **p140** Excerpt from *King Leopold's Ghost* by Muhunzo Kioko, pp15-16 ©Adam Hochschild, First Mariner Books, Houghton Mifflin Company, New York, NY; **p147** Excerpt from *Things Fall Apart* by Chinua Achebe, first published in 1958, expanded edition Oxford: Heinemann Educational, 1996; **p176** Mbathio Sall from his paper at the

65th International Federation of Library Associations and Institutions Council and General Conference, Bangkok, Thailand, August 1999; Andrei Simic, used by permission of Professor Andrei Simic; Deborah Swartz, Huron Oral History Project of the Library of the University of Guelph; **p179** "I Lost my Talk" by Rita Joe; **p241** Jean-Paul Rodrigue, "Transportation and Globalization" in *Encyclopedia of Globalization*, R. Robertson and J.A. Sholte, (eds), London: Routledge; **p251** Jeremy Brecher in *Transnational Corporations: The New World Order* by Douglas Gnazzo, www.financialsense.com; **p271** "Existing Controls on Shipbreaking," www.greenpeace.org; **p277** Excerpt from "Overhauling Canada's Government," *Toronto Star*, March 20, 2007, page A23 by Don Lenihan, Tim Barber, Graham Fox and John Milloy; **p294** Adapted from *The End of Poverty: Economic Possibilities for Our Time* by Jeffrey Sachs, Penguin Books, 2005, pp 278-279; **p295** Used by permission of Rachel Qitsualik; pp 278-279; **p299** "Watershed Rap" used by permission of Peter Donaldson, www.peterdonaldson.net; **p335** Excerpt from *Coming of Age in a Globalized World: The Next Generation* by J. Michael Adams and Angelo Carfagna, Kumarian Press, 2006, p.64; **p342** Excerpt from *Coming of Age in a Globalized World: The Next Generation* by J. Michael Adams and Angelo Carfagna, Kumarian Press, 2006, p. 40; **p359** Excerpt from *Coming of Age in a Globalized World: The Next Generation* by J. Michael Adams and Angelo Carfagna, Kumarian Press, 2006, p. 83; **p379** Excerpt from *Coming of Age in a Globalized World: The Next Generation* by J. Michael Adams and Angelo Carfagna, Kumarian Press, 2006, p.159.